RELIGION IN MODERN INDIA

RELIGION IN MODERN INDIA

Edited by

ROBERT D. BAIRD

(Second Revised Edition)

SOUTH ASIA PUBLICATIONS

ISBN 0-945921-03-9

© Robert D. Baird

First Published 1981
Second revised edition 1989

Published in the United States of America
by South Asia Publications, Box 502,
Columbia, Mo 65205 by arrangement with
Manohar Publications, 1 Ansari Road,
Daryaganj, New Delhi-110002.

Printed in India

PREFACE TO THE SECOND EDITION

In 1913, J.N. Farquhar, Literary Secretary of the Y.M.C.A. in India, gave eight lectures at Hartfort Seminary on "Modern Religious Movements in India." This became the title of an expanded version of the lectures published in 1915. The book was wide ranging, and was based on personal visits, correspondence, and interviews. At that time little else was available on many of the movements on which Farquhar wrote. Thanks to a long residency in India, and, beginning in 1912, the freedom to write such a work was possible.

Farquhar was not only knowledgeable, but operated with an overarching system of interpretation. "The old religions are the soil from which the modern movements spring; while it will be found that the seed has, in the main, been sown by Missions" (p.l.). Though marked by profound sympathy for the faiths that he studied and about which he wrote, Farquhar was finally a missionary, and the significance of what he studied for the propagation of the Christian faith is found in all of his works.

For years Farquhar's *Modern Religious Movements in India* has served as a basic introduction to religion in modern India, even when its readers have not shared or appreciated his missionary thrust. The reign of Farquhar can be attributed to the level of his scholarship and to the fact that religion in modern India has received limited attention since his time. This was surely true in 1981 when the first edition of the present work was published.

With the growing interest in Indian studies and the growing number of historians of religions who have developed competency in Sanskrit, it was the ancient and classical periods which first received attention. Many modern thinkers were considered weak reflections of classical systems and the view has been widely held that if one's time is limited it would be preferable to spend it with intellectual and spiritual giants, of which the modern period has few. When thinkers such as Radhakrishnan and Aurobindo were studied, they were frequently seen as interpreters of an ancient tradition, with little attention to the modifications and/

or systematizations of those ancient traditions that their thought embodied. Classicists who studied the Indian traditions seldom applied their critical abilities to the modern period.

Those who did deign to study the modern period (1800 on) were frequently anthropologists who studied the "little traditions" and who were more interested in the context than the text. Without minimizing the importance of classical studies or village studies, it was felt that after some sixty-five years those who studied religion in modern India were entitled to a new introduction to their area.

Since a modern Farquhar had not appeared on the academic horizon, a number of us took it upon ourselves to produce a composite work. We included some material not found in Farquhar, and at the same time, some of the movements and topics found in Farquhar are not dealt with in this collection. Although the first edition approximated five hundred pages, it was still necessary to echo the frustration of Farquhar, who in 1914 wrote in the preface to his work, "I have felt cramped for want of space. To deal with the whole subject adequately would have required two volumes instead of one." This judgment is equally true for this second edition. Nevertheless, we are confident that we have provided an introduction to some of the important movements and thinkers in the study of religion in *modern* India. Much more remains to be done for *contemporary* India. Guru cults continue to be inadequately represented, and cult has been virtually ignored.

Since this is a composite work, it lacks the overarching interpretative framework that is found in Farquhar's work. Nevertheless, all contributors have addressed their topics with the issues of religious change and continuity in mind. Although our work was not done primarily on the basis of interviews and conversations, as was Farquhar's, most of the contributors have done field work in India and their experience has found its way into their work.

This volume is neither theological nor missionary in intent. It embodies religious studies in that it deals with ultimate goals and values of the movements and thinkers studied. It is historical in that it attempts a descriptive analysis of the human past. Some contributors have explicitly dealt with ultimate values, while others have been more content to embody a descriptive analysis of the human past. But all of the contributors have attempted a sympathetic analysis of their data, for we are academics who have in most cases committed overselves to the study of things Indian. There is, however, a difference between sympathetic study and advocacy. Advocacy goes beyond history and has been excluded from this volume.

No bibliography has been included because of the extensive notes, which will supply the reader with sufficient bibliographical information to probe more deeply into the movements and thinkers we have considered.

Planning for this work began in the fall of 1978. Ten of the chapters of the first edition were presented at a conference on "Religion in Modern India" held at the University of Iowa in April of 1980. In this second edition, Arvind Sharma's chapter on Dayananda Sarasvati has been rewritten. New chapters have been included by N. Gerald Barrier on the Sikhs, Eric J. Sharpe on Christians, and John R. Hinnells on the Parsis.

Part III of the first edition, "Religion and National Goals," was a distinctive part of the original work. But, with the additional new chapters, inclusion of Part III would have made it impossible to publish the work in one volume. For this reason it has been dropped. The chapter by Kenneth W. Jones on the Hindu Mahasabha has been retained under religious movements. The editor intends to incorporate his two articles on " 'Secular State' and the Indian Constitution" and "Uniform Civil Code and the Secularization of Law" into a subsequent independent volume.

Since 1981 there has been renewed interest in religion in modern India. We will continue to be satisfied if we are able to stimulate fresh thought and continued research on such topics.

The editor would be remiss if he did not express his appreciation to N. Gerald Barrier of South Asia Books and to Ramesh Jain of Manohar Publications for their support in continuing the publication of this work in a second edition.

2 October 1988

Robert D. Baird
New College
Sarasota, Florida

CONTENTS

CONTRIBUTORS

ROBERT D. BAIRD
Leonard S. Florsheim, Sr. Eminent Scholars Chair in the Liberal Arts and Sciences, New College of the University of South Florida

N. GERALD BARRIER
Professor of History at the University of Missouri

JOHN R. HINNELLS
Professor of Comparative Religion, Manchester University

KENNETH W. JONES
Professor of South Asian History at Kansas State University

SPENCER LAVAN
Dean, Meadville Theological Seminary

SHEILA McDONOUGH
Professor of Religion ot Concordia University, Montreal

DAVID M. MILLER
Professor of Religion at Concordia University, Montreal

ROBERT N. MINOR
Professor of Religion and Chair of the Department of Religion at the University of Kansas

RONALD W, NEUFELDT
Professor of Religion and Chair of the Department of Religion at the University of Calgary

JAMES N. PANKRATZ
Professor of Religion at Mennonite Brethren College of Arts in Winnipeg

ARVIND SHARMA
Professor of Religion at McGill University

ERIC J. SHARPE
Professor of Religious Studies at the University of Sydney

DONALD R. TUCK
Professor of Religion at Western Kentucky University

GEORGE M. WILLIAMS
Professor of Religious Studies at California State University, Chico

BOYD H. WILSON
Associate Professor of Religion at Hope College

PART I

RELIGIOUS MOVEMENTS

1

THE BRAHMO SAMAJ:
INDIA'S FIRST MODERN MOVEMENT
FOR RELIGIOUS REFORM

Spencer Lavan

Charismatic leadership appears clearly to be a hallmark of modern religious reform movements in India. The focus of renewal around one person—Dayananda Saraswati in the Arya Samaj, Sri Ramakrishna in the Ramakrishna movement, Mirza Ghulam Ahmad in the Ahmadiyah Islamic reform movement—who stands over and above both the leading disciples and the later organizational expertise, seems to be the rule. The Brahmo Samaj may be the exception among the reform movements under study in this volume, for the Brahmo Samaj may be said to have had two founders and at least four major figures dominating its organization during the nineteenth century.[1]

More than the other three reform movements, the Brahmo Samaj spoke in its most effective day to an educated generation of young Bengalis seeking a way, as educated Hindus, to respond religiously to the world in which they were living. In a real sense the Brahmo Samaj was the first modern religious movement in India responding to events precipitated by the presence of the British East India Company and, after 1813, by the increasing activity of evangelical Christian missionaries.

The period of Mughal rule in India from 1560 to the death of Aurangzeb in 1707, during which an Islamic presence was felt throughout the subcontinent, was a period of sharp decline for

Hinduism. The Rajput princes in western India, and especially the militant Shivaji, attempted to reassert Hindu devotional values in face of Islamic political supremacy. Reformers such as Kabir, Ramananda, and Guru Nanak attempted assimilations of what they believed to be the best in Hindu and Muslim teaching. Nanak's piety and reform led to the creation of the Sikh movement, whose members' bitter experiences in the struggle against the Mughal emperors turned them away from the broad reforming ideas of Nanak toward a self-consciously organized new religious movement.

A new day of Hindu self-awareness, neither militant nor assimilationist, began during the period 1797-1805, when the Marquis Wellesley, a conservative English aristocrat, was sent to India as governor-general. Fearing French expansion into India under Napoleon, and believing many of the company's civil servants to be unprepared for their duties, Wellesley proclaimed in 1800 the formation of Fort William College, whose purpose it would be "to fix and establish sound and correct principles of religion and government in their minds at an early period of life . . . which could . . . provide for the stability of British power in India."[2] Wellesley envisaged a college modelled on Oxford or Cambridge, with a staff of professors teaching Arabic, Persian (the language of government at the waning Mughal court), Urdu and Sanskrit, as well as courses on Muslim and Hindu law, English jurisprudence, and traditional European studies such as the classics.

An interest in and revival of "Oriental studies" had started several decades earlier with a loosely established Asiatic Society of Bengal. Following the founding of Fort William College, the two institutions came closer together, especially after the death of Sir William Jones, founder of the Asiatic Society. Many of the translation projects of Hindu scripture he began were continued by groups of scholars at the college. Two kinds of problems began to emerge from the work being done at Fort William: those developed by scholarly interest in India's antiquity and those which would help the East India Company civil servants govern more effectively.

One particular group of Christian missionaries, those at Serampore, first a Danish and then a British territory, combined an interest in Oriental studies and a renewal of ancient Hindu culture through the study of texts. At the same time they sought to convert Hindu Bengalis to Christianity. The reason for discussing Fort William College, the Asiatic Society, and the Serampore missionaries is that all three were sources providing an impact on increasing numbers of young Hindu intellectuals learning English and undertaking academic studies. This was the generation of Bengalis who also served as tutors of the indigenous Indian languages to the English civil servants at Fort William College. The educational encounter did not provide a sudden enlightenment leading to a repudiation of Hinduism or conversion to Christian orthodoxy. It represented instead a developing realization by a new generation of Hindus of the benefits of English education as well as a renewed awareness of the potential value of long-forgotten Hindu roots. The intersection of these forces has been described as the "Bengal Renaissance." It was from this renaissance that Rammohun Roy, "Father of Modern India" and founder of the Brahmo Samaj, emerged.

It is significant at this point to note in some detail the impact of Western education and Rammohun's involvement with Christian missionaries as a prelude to discussing the Brahmo Samaj. That Rammohun died in England and was buried in 1833 in a Unitarian churchyard in Bristol, eulogized by the Rev. Lant Carpenter, was no accident. He came to England in 1830, shortly after he had established the Brahmo Sabha or Brahmo Society, a trust deed for which was signed on January 23 of that year.

The events leading up to that signing begin with Rammohun's diverse and complex education and his early exercises reinterpreting the Upaniṣads. Rammohun's focus on monotheistic vedantic Hinduism had already been noticed in Western publications before his controversy with Dr. Marshman, the Christian missionary, began in 1820.[3] Before beginning his *Precepts of Jesus,* Rammohun had been acquainted with Christians in Calcutta for at least four years. He may have learned some Greek and Hebrew. Thus far he was reforming Hinduism on an academic level. It, therefore, seemed appropriate to him that he should study other religions. Out of a deep concern for ethics and morality, Rammohun began a study of the Gospels in order to separate the ethical teachings of Jesus from the "accretions" the missionaries were teaching as Christianity.

"The simple code of religion, and morality," he wrote, "is so admirably calculated to elevate men's ideas to high and liberal notions of one God, who has equally subjected all living creatures, without distinction of caste, rank or wealth, to change, disappointment, pain and death, and has equally admitted all to be partakers of the bountiful mercies which he has lavished over nature, and is also so well fitted to regulate the conduct of the human race in discharge of their various duties to God, to themselves, and to society, that I cannot but hope the best effects from its promulgation in the present form.[4]"

From his writings about Christianity, it is clear that Rammohun was an Arian, or Unitarian. His writings emphasize the ethical teachings of Jesus extracted from the theology and Christology of Christianity. For his unusual efforts Rammohun received criticism rather than praise from missionary Joshua Marshman. This led to a continuing debate between the two men and the publication by Rammohun of three additional "Appeals" to *The Precepts* to strengthen his case for an "enlightened" Christianity.

While one might think that such a controversy would have intimidated Rammohun, it actually led him to establish a close relation with two other Baptist missionaries, the Revs. William Yates and William Adam. Together, the three undertook a translation of the New Testament into Bengali, with Yates and Adam rendering the Greek text into English, and then, with Rammohun's assistance, into Bengali. The work of the translation went well until the three men reached the third verse of the first chapter of the Gospel of John. There a new controversy arose over the Greek preposition *dia* and whether it should be rendered "by" and "through" in the phrase "All things were made through Him." Fearing the tinge of Arianism if "through" rather than "by" were used, and that the position of Christ in the Trinity would thereby be compromised, Yates withdrew from the project.[5]

As outcasts, Adam and Rammohun Roy became close friends. Both decided while finishing the translation that there was indeed no proof of the Trinity to be found in the New Testament. The impact of Adam's decision to publicize his change in theological orientation was his expulsion from the Baptist church mission. For their outspokenly liberal positions, Rammohun and Adam were now opposed both by the *brahmins* and the Christians in Calcutta.

Together they decided to establish a Unitarian church. This

decision coincided, by striking chance, with the founding of organized Unitarian movements in Boston and London. Journalists in both countries had already reported to Unitarians Rammohun's controversial stand with Hindus and Christians. Adam had received sermons by the Rev. William Ellery Channing, father of American Unitarianism. By 1823, a correspondence between the two Calcutta men and both the American and British Unitarian organizations had begun.[6]

The excitement of this new relationship was shortlived. Calcutta's requests for money to support a mission took months to cross the ocean. The financial responses were too small to allow for any significant development in Calcutta. By far the largest financial support came from Rammohun himself and from Dwarkanath Tagore, a wealthy merchant, father of Debendranath Tagore, the next major Brahmo leader, and grandfather of Rabindranath Tagore, the poet. The other pervasive problem in the Calcutta-England-American axis was the Unitarian desire to describe Rammohun as a "Christian." This suggested a level of paternalism at work in the relationship. Unitarian services, while they were held under Adam's leadership, were conducted in English rather than Bengali.

By 1828, Rammohun and his closest friends felt that a reform within Hinduism would be a far better approach than that of attempting to establish a Unitarian church where Hindus would never play a leadership role equal to that of British members. While William Adam was disappointed not to have them as part of his struggling Unitarian community, he takes credit in letters written to Boston in the winter of 1828 for having urged the *brahmin* leadership of the Unitarian movement to go in the direction of an indigenous reform movement.[7]

Adam also provides us with the earliest description of Brahmo worship in a letter he wrote to the Rev. Joseph Tuckerman of Boston in 1829. The service illustrates how the Brahmo Samaj in its earliest days helped upper-caste intellectual Hindus to reform their tradition without closing off religious, cultural, or caste identity.

The service begins with two or three of the Pandits singing, or rather, chanting in the cathedral style, some of the spiritual portions of the Ved, which are next explained in the vernacular

dialect to the people by another Bengali...and the whole is concluded by hymns both in Sanskrit and Bengali, sung with and
accompanied by instrumental music, which is also occasionally
interposed between other parts of the service. The audience generally consists of from fifty to sixty individuals, several Pandits, a
good many Brahmins and all decent and attentive in their
demeanour.[8]

Finding a sense of religious identity which could speak to the
needs of a more educated, intellectual, *brahmin*-born elite seems
clearly to have been the earliest motivaton for establishing the
Brahmo Samaj. Disappointed but understanding of what had
happened, William Adam wrote again to Tuckerman,

Rammohun Roy, I am persuaded, supports this institution [the
Brahmo Samaj] not because he believes in the divine authority of
the Ved, but solely as an instrument for overthrowing idolatry.
To be candid, however, I must add that . . . in my mind . . . he
employs Unitarian Christianity in the same way, as an instrument
for spreading pure and just notions of God, without believing in
the divine authority of the Gospel.[9]

Thus it was that the Brahmo Samaj had its origins. Rammohun
Roy combined in his personality and intellect a depth of spirit that
saw new light from the two traditions essentially conflicting in
Calcutta. On the one hand, Vaiṣṇava sectarianism with its practices such as *sati* (widow burning) and highly emotional bhakti seemed
to offer nothing to speak to the needs of the early nineteenth-
century educated urban Hindu. On the other hand, the British
East India Company presence, with its new educational institutions
and, after 1813, a Christian missionary participation, evangelical
in its orientation, also did not speak to the needs of men such as
Rammohun.

From Brahmo Sabha to Samaj:
Debendranath Tagore

Although a detailed discussion of Brahmo institutional development and the forces at work in it would require a study of the depth

of that undertaken recently by David Kopf, it is here important to cite at least Akkhoy Kumar Dutt (1820-66) as one contemporary of Debendranath Tagore who brought a different perspective to the liberal religious movement. A product of both Hindu and Christian education, Dutt also attended Calcutta Medical College shortly after it opened in 1835. His philosophical orientation was centered in rationalism, deism, and scientism.[10] Although he was accused of being an atheist and can certainly be labelled a secularist, Dutt's conception of the divine rested not on a Christian doctrine of prayer or a vedantist experience of union with *brahman*, but rather on an understanding of science and the natural laws which revealed the harmoniousness and interrelatedness of the universe. Dutt represents one extreme to which the combined presence of Western and Hindu education could lead a keen mind.

The Charter of 1833, which put an end to all restrictions on Christian missionary activity, led to new kinds of responses among the Calcutta intelligentsia. Renewal movements such as the Brahmo Sabha (Samaj) organized to include a broader base of the educated young Bengali generation meant that Dutt, who did not come from a wealthy family background and who held rather radical views, could find a place in the movement. The new freedom of Christian missionaries led also to a considerable amount of antimissionary propaganda by the vernacular press, as well as rising opposition in the Hindu community to any attempts to teach Christianity in either government or missionary schools.

By 1839, Dutt had discovered Debendranath Tagore and had joined his Tattvabodhini Sabha, a reform movement roughly parallel to the Brahmo Sabha but more clearly dedicated to opposing the Christian expansion into Bengal. That Tagore, who was very much more a mystic and theist, should welcome the more theologically radical Dutt is a sign that Hindu religious liberalism was willing, at this stage, to be accepting and expansive. By the mid 1840s, Dutt was a teacher in Tagore's school and editor of the Brahmo Samaj newspaper, the *Tattvabodhini Sabha*.[11]

Debendranath Tagore stands out as a figure markedly different from others of his generation. This is because he was already a second generation "Brahmo," the product of a wealthy landowning family steeped in Western liberalism and eclectic in its life-style. Dutt, by contrast, was the first in his family—as were so many other young men of the 1840s—to experience a break with conservative caste-dominated Hindu culture. Western education, the sciences, openness in examining the meaning of life, were new to him.

Tagore married early in the traditional Hindu style, but was exposed to non-Hindu practices of meat eating and wine drinking at an early age. The death of his grandmother in 1835 seems to have been a traumatic experience for him. His autobiography also reports that Debendranath turned to religious concerns during a deep depression and after accidentally finding a passage from the Upaniṣads that spoke almost mystically to him.[12]

This direct experience of God turned Tagore away from the luxurious and sensuous ways of his father. He gave up meat and wine, and rebelled directly against his father Dwarkanath in other ways. For a period he studied traditional Hindu scriptures and theology, becoming deeply aware that in his father's house traditional idols continued to be present, in direct contradiction of Brahmo values repudiating polytheism. The yearly celebration of Durga Puja in the home, and the fact that after dining with European members of the household purified themselves by washing in the Ganges, were both sources of distress to Tagore.[13]

Because of his father's close ties to Rammohun Roy and the founding of the Brahmo Sabha, Debendranath stood back for a time to assess what was happening in Calcutta. During the period of his first spiritual crisis in 1835 at age eighteen, Thomas Babington Macauley and Governor-General Lord William Bentinck were advocating secularized Western education as a salvation for India over against the Orientalist tradition, which had for several decades been attempting the restoration of traditional cultural values. After 1830, Alexander Duff, a Presbyterian from Scotland, also played a major role in combining the power of Christian missions with a rationalist and modernist outlook. Duff turned out to be a major opponent of *brahmin* Hindu intellectuals during the 1840s.

It is in this context that one needs to see why Debendranath Tagore established the Tattvabodhini Sabha before joining forces with the Brahmo Sabha and changing its name to the Brahmo Samaj. The explicit purpose of the organization newly established in October 1839, was to stem the rapid growth of Christianity while familiarizing the Hindu population with its own scriptural tradition through extensive publications. Even when Debendranath joined the Brahmo Sabha in 1843, he kept his other organization alive. The Tattvabodhini Sabha continued its work and grew in membership up to 1859, when it merged with the Brahmo Samaj. Tagore's main tools against the missionaries were a school he founded in 1840 to oppose the values of Duff's missionary school, where all teaching was in Bengali rather than in English, and the *Tattvabodhini Patrika,* an outspoken newspaper.

The new association held weekly meetings to discuss religious and theological matters. This provided members with a chance to clarify questions and to come to some consensus about their beliefs. Debendranath wanted to use the organization to allow him to defend Hindu cultural values over against those of Christianity, while at the same time allowing the rational faith of Brahmoism to catch hold among the young Bengali intelligentsia. It was in such an atmosphere that Tagore and Dutt, coming from different orientations and backgrounds, could still work together.[14]

On December 21, 1843, Tagore and twenty others took an oath binding them to the tenets of the Brahmo Sabha. This action opened the way for the Tattvabodhini and Brahmo Sabhas to connect officially. Because the organizing by-laws of the Brahmo Sabha did not contain strong statements of ideology, Tagore's act of affirmation with the Sabha seems clearly to have been a turning point for both Tagore and the organization which Rammohun had begun in 1828. Because the Brahmo Sabha was relatively inactive between 1833 and 1843, some scholars date the real establishment of the Brahmo Samaj from the date Debendranath Tagore took his oath.

Tagore quickly developed a new statement of faith for the Samaj, expressing clearly the theological position of the renewed organization.

1. God is a personal being with sublime attributes.
2. God has never become incarnate.
3. God hears and answers prayers.
4. God is to be worshipped only in spiritual ways. Hindu asceticism, temples, and fixed forms of worship are unnecessary . . . all castes and races may worship God acceptably.
5. Repentance and cessation from sin are the only ways to forgiveness and salvation.
6. Nature and intuition are sources for the knowledge of God. No book is.[15]

Debendranath's great strength seems to have been as an organizer of the rejuvenated organization. In the year 1845-46, the membership rose sharply from 145 to 500. Many college students joined. Clearly Tagore's two reform movements were the most significant such organizations in Bengal until well into the 1860s.

By 1850, Debendranath prepared a codification of Brahmo teachings, emphasizing both ethics and theology, entitled *Brahmo Dharma*. Shortly before this, Debendranath had decided to remove "the Vedantic element of Shankara" from the Brahmo Covenant.[16] Brahmos with a more rationalist bent than Debendranath were overjoyed on learning that their leader, finding no way for the Vedas or traditional Vedanta to make sense for modern Hindus, had decided to remove those teachings. The theological part of the *Brahmo Dharma* was drawn almost entirely from the Upaniṣads. While texts from traditions other than Hinduism were not included, there was no diatribe directly against Christianity. A sense of universalism pervaded the introduction. Here Tagore wrote that "to be a theist or a professor of theism, it is not necessary to belong to a particular country, age or nationality. The theists of all countries have the right to teach about God."[17]

In the ethical portion of the book, evidence of the Brahmo "Puritan" ethic appears. While one might get the impression that the influence of John Calvin had worked upon Debendranath in this section, it appears that as a Hindu modernist he was rewriting the Code of Manu to meet the needs of the times. Debendranath's moral precepts include carefully explained duties of husbands, wives, and children, one to the others. The rules are not stated for their own sake, but are rationalized, offering the basis for family harmony. Writing that social good was derived from such qualities as "sincerity, devotion, purity, forgiveness and gentleness,"[18] one might almost see the influence of Confucius at work in Debendranath's writings. As well, he developed sections from Manu on the nature of work reminiscent of Benjamin Franklin: "Acquire knowledge, religion and the habit on industry early in life" or "Do not be enchanted with earthly things in forgetfulness of the transitory character of life."[19] Such Puritan ethics were soon to become the basis for the Brahmo doctrine of Keshub Chunder Sen.

Keshub Chunder Sen: Prophet of Harmony

Where some have declared Rammohun Roy to be founder of the Brahmo Samaj and others held Debendranath Tagore to be the moving organizational force for the movement, still other scholars and observers would insist that it was Keshub Chunder Sen who truly turned the Samaj to a national religious reform. Born in 1838 to a Vaiṣṇava family, Keshub was educated at Hindu College and exposed at an early age to the pervasive influences of British and Christian culture in Bengal. Already religious, and even bordering on the ascetic as a young man, he lived in two worlds, exposing himself to Western missionaries and also maintaining his traditional Hindu ties. Although married in 1856 at the age of eighteen, it appears that by 1857 Keshub had made a conscious decision "not to be overly fond of wife or world."[20] During his period of university studies, in his interactions with such missionaries as the social activist Reverend James Long and the Unitarian Charles Dall, and during his involvement in public organizations such as the Goodwill Fraternity, Keshub had begun a search for religious meaning through devotionalism and a moderately ascetic life.

Keshub's conversion to Brahmoism took place after he read a pamphlet, "What Is Brahmoism?" written by Raj Narain Bose, a close colleague of Tagore and Dutt. About that time Keshub and his cousin, Protap Chunder Mazumdar (the fourth major figure in the movement) saw Debendranath Tagore for the first time. Sen was impressed. "He was tall, princely, in the full glory of his health and manhood; he came attended by liveried servants, and surrounded by massive stalwart Brahmos, who wore long gold chains and impenetrable countenances. We who were very young men . . . were highly elated and encouraged by such company, and it was an inducement to follow with zeal our religious career."[21]

After reading the Bose tract, Keshub wrote, "I found that it corresponded exactly with the inner conviction of my heart, the voice of God in the soul. I always felt that every outward book must be subordinated to the teachings of the inner Spirit,—that where God speaks through the Spirit in man all earthly teachers must be silent, and every man must bow down and accept in reverence what God thus revealed in the soul. I at once determined that I would join the Brahmo Samaj, or Indian Theistic Church."[22]

The basis of Keshub's rise to leadership in the Brahmo movement

was above all religious. Yet, as early as 1860 in his speech
to "Young Bengal," the fraternal organization of secularized Hindu
students, there were overtones suggesting that social and political
reform would also be needed to regenerate India. Keshub's ideas
were not highly original. Many views he espoused had been in
the air since the time of Rammohun Roy. Many were similar to
those views opposing the Christian mission movement. Many among
the Young Bengal group saw the need for a religious faith, freed
from the fetters of traditional vaiṣṇava Hinduism, which would
raise the Hindu personality out of the social and religious predicament in which it found itself. Keshub's skill seems to have been
as the reshaper of ideas already in the air. It was not long before
he discovered that, through his speaking and vigorous organizational skills, he could make a significant impact on the Bangali Hindu
community.

His biographer has written that "from the moment he had
entered the Brahmo Samaj, he had taken the vow of finding in it
'a Religion of Life'; as opposed to a religion of theories. Every
principle that he developed, every reform that he undertook, was
the result of that vow."[23]

Within a few years after the time the young Keshub had joined
the Samaj in the shadow of the awesome Debendranath Tagore, he
was lecturing and leading a dynamic new missionary thrust for the
movement well beyond the borders of Bengal. Social concerns
were first and foremost on his mind in the early years. In an 1863
lecture, "Social Transformation in India," he asserted that once all
people came under one church and one God, all caste distinctions
would "naturally perish in the uncongenial atmosphere of religious
brotherhood."[24] It was this kind of idea, drawn from both
Brahmo and Western ideas of social reform, that was the basis of
the Goodwill Fraternity, an organization whose members, in 1861,
voted to end caste distinctions within that group while pledging to
educate their wives and to abstain from the alcohol already taking
its toll among the younger secular generation. Keshub was part of
this movement. Throughout the 1860s, young Brahmos, under the
influence of Keshub's personality and his teachings on social and
religious reform, began publication of *The Indian Mirror*, the earliest
English language newspaper published by Indians. They convened
as well public meetings to draw government attention to the need
for educational reform and programs to alleviate poverty.

What was unusual about Keshub's religious leadership was the model he offered Young Bengal. It was not one normally to be expected in Calcutta. Keshub's exemplar was Jesus, the center of Christian salvation. Keshub's Jesus, however, was adapted to an Asiatic context, the reformer who was "meek" like an Indian and not "rough, stern, impulsive and fiery as Europeans were."[25] Jesus, the Asiatic, was the force of creative civilization West and East. It was not the English, but the spirit of Christ ultimately at the root of English rule, that was responsible for the progressive changes that had occurred in India. Jesus' life was the ultimate symbol of selflessness which, when considered in the Indian context, meant an end to caste distinctions and willingness to work for the greater good of all mankind.[26]

But for Keshub, Brahmoism was to be sharply differentiated from Christian sectarianism. His position sounded much like that of late nineteenth-century British and American Unitarianism, despite the fact that Keshub claimed that even Unitarian Christianity was not "absolute religion." The essence of Brahmoism, as Keshub articulated it in his 1860 essay "Religion of Love," was "Love God as thy Father and man as thy brother."[27] Keshub seems clearly to have been fully motivated by the concept of Christ, revering him above all prophets and teachers, even above so major a figure to Bengalis as Chaitanya. But for Keshub, Jesus, like Chaitanya, could not be a mediator between God and man, for Brahmoism out of its vedantic tradition was a faith based on belief in God as *brahman*, the One without a second. "Christianity," Keshub argued in a 1863 lecture, "has prepared the world for the Brahmo Samaj, but has not given birth to Brahmoism," for God, not the Bible, was the source and inspiration of Brahmo ideas.[28]

Throughout the 1860s, Keshub and the other Brahmos engaged in polemics and controversy with Christian missionaries. Keshub directly answered charges when attacked by the Reverend Dyson of Krishnagar, by the native preacher Lal Behari Day, and also by a Scottish Christian merchant who had deliberately insulted the Indian character. The impact of Keshub's work was far-reaching. In 1862, ten per cent of the entering class of the University of Calcutta declared themselves "Universalists, Brahmos, pantheists, deists or atheists." While Keshub would not have agreed with those in the latter category, he was certainly pleased to see young Bengali students moving away from declared anti-Hindu secularism to more sophisticated theological positions.

The attacks on or rebuttals against the missionaries were but one stage in Keshub's quest to articulate a sense of identity for young liberal religious Hindus. A sense of patriotism comes through in the words spoken in 1860 when Keshub was only twenty-two years old:

> Rest assured, my friend, that if in our country intellectual progress went hand in hand with religious development, if our educated countrymen had initiated themselves in the living truths of religion, patriotism would not have been a mere matter of oration and essay, but a reality in practice; and native society would have grown in health and prosperity . . . and effectually surmounted many of those difficulties in the way of social reforms which are not constituted insuperable.[29]

In "Jesus Christ: Europe and Asia," Keshub exhorted the new generation of Indians to reject the selfishness he believed to be the principal negative characteristic of Indians, so long a "subject race." "We have too long been under foreign sway to be able to feel anything like independence in our hearts. Socially and religiously we are little better than slaves. From infancy up we have been trained to believe that we are Hindoos only as far as we offer slavish obedience to the authority of the Shasters and the priests, and that any want of disobedience would be so much a want of our nationality."[30]

Although Debendranath Tagore had defended the Brahmo movement against the incursions of Christianity, Keshub's words and call for a new religious and national identity were far louder and clearer. Perhaps the time was now more ripe for such a call. In 1866, Keshub Chunder Sen stood at the turning point of his career. He had taken a stand for Christ, but for Christ in a universal sense; he had called out for needed social reform, which also implied political reform. All this would require a major change in attitude and a religious revolution among the Hindus. It would not be enough to speak of reform; significant action was required.

Keshub's stance against caste was especially controversial. Debendranath Tagore was not prepared to give up the sacred thread of brahminism in favor of a true democracy for Brahmoism. In 1865, Keshub and his supporters had taken control of the Brahmo newspaper, *The Indian Mirror*, while also beginning a far more dynamic program of missionary expansion for the Brahmo Samaj.[31] More than anything else, it was Keshub's two strongly articulated lectures, "Jesus Christ: Europe and Asia," and "Great Men," in which he quoted from Christian history almost directly, that demonstrated his sharp refutation of the ahistorical stance of most Hinduism.

The time was ripe. Keshub led a split in the Samaj in November 1866, establishing the Brahmo Samaj of India. Debendranath's faction was now to be known as the 'Adi or Original Brahmo Samaj. The split between the two groups also had its roots in Keshub's 1864 decision to carry out a major missionary journey throughout India. By this time, the Brahmo Samaj and its opposition to the efforts of Christian missionaries was well enough known for him to want to pursue a more broadly based religious reform movement beyond the borders of Bengal. Well received in Madras, Bombay, and Poona, it was only a matter of time before active chapters would exist there. Debendranath, while concerned with social service in needy areas of India, did not have a vision through which the Samaj would be carried into non-Bengali areas. Neither could he accept the kind of social reform which would mean strong advocacy of legal status for Brahmos to conduct their own interreligious marriages, widow remarriage, and intercaste marriage. Perhaps the greatest difference and that which eventually split the two men was Keshub's "Christian training" and his desire to integrate the best of Christ into the Brahmo religious movement.

Although Keshub's lecture "Jesus Christ: Europe and Asia" had as its fundamental statement the concept that Chirst was an Asiatic and not a European, his second major 1866 lecture, "Great Men," had the basic purpose of using Christ as one example of how God sends great men to serve and save humanity. Here Keshub's familiarity with biblical literature and teaching stands out. In the lectures "Regenerating Faith" (1868), "The Future Church" (1869), and "The Kingdom of Heaven" (1874) Keshub was utilizing Christ's concept of an ideal religious situation to set an ideal before his Indian audience.[32] He was describing "an invisible reality which must be sought in the domain of the spirit, and not in the world of matter."[33]

The contrast between Keshub's approach to Christ and Rammohun's approach to Jesus is clear. Where the latter came to

Jesus because of a sense of the inadequacy of the Hindu spiritual life of his time (the 1820s), the former came to Christ (not the human Jesus) for the opposite reasons: to spiritualize a generation of young Bengal which had fallen from faith, albeit a corrupted Vaiṣṇavism.

In reaching out to a new audience, Keshub tried to synthesize aspects of Hindu devotionalism and festivals in an attempt to formulate a non-western but also antitraditional, anticaste religious community. Debendranath Tagore had turned Rammohun Roy's ideals around by limiting the Samaj to *brahmin* membership. By contrast, Keshub believed his Brahmoism was not just a variation or reformation of Hinduism, but a "catholic" religion, a religion in which all the various sects and peoples of India could be reconciled to each other and live in peace.

In 1870, Keshub's impact reached beyond India's shores. He travelled to England, where he met and spoke before Unitarian and social reform organizations. In meetings with figures such as Lord Lawrence, Sir Charles Trevellyan, the Dean of Westminster, and Oxford scholar F. Max Müller, Keshub was well received. His ability to communicate with Westerners was quickly evident from the text of his first sermon in a Unitarian chapel. He chose the passage from Acts 17, "In Him, we live and move and have our being," a text appropriate enough for a Christian, a Unitarian, or a vedantic Hindu.[34]

In his English speeches, Keshub did not hesitate to speak out for reforms in India, nor did he hesitate to criticize failures of Christian culture. He made it clear that he was not in England to study Christian doctrine as much as he was there to observe "the truly Christian life as displayed and illustrated."[35] While impressing his hosts with kindness towards them, Keshub in later speeches attacked Christians who beat Hindus and enslaved them, sharply criticizing the English propagation of liquor and opium in India. He called for much more significant roles for educated Indians in government, and improved education and life-styles for Indian women.[36]

In his lecture of May 18, 1870, Keshub spoke as a Hindu theist about the significance of Christ for his life and why he did not become a Christian. He explained his Christology: "I studied Christ ethically, nay spiritually—and I studied the Bible also in that spirit and must tonight acknowledge candidly and sincerely that

I owe a great deal to Christ and to the Gospel of Christ"[37] ; "Jesus is not a proposition to be believed, nor an outward figure to be seen and adored but simply a spirit to be loved, a spirit of obedience to God that must be incorporated into our spiritual being.[38]

If there is significance in discussing Keshub in England and his vibrant impression upon liberal Christians there, it is to demonstrate that in the liberal wing of the Brahmo Samaj there was a sense of mission beyond that which Keshub had already carried from Bengal to outer India. Keshub believed fervently that the Brahmo Samaj had a mission for the Western world as well. Until Svami Dayananda of the Arya Samaj and Svami Vivekananda carried the concept of mission outreach much further in their own movements, what Keshub was doing was truly radical within Hinduism—an apologetic and new dimension of eclecticism for his faith.

A New Dispensation

The Brahmo Samaj reform program that developed during the late 1860s and the 1870s under Kesub's leadership was impressive. The Brahmo Marriage Act passed in 1872 after four years of education and lobbying. In spite of opposition from the 'Adi Brahmos the Act reformed the practice of child marriage and allowed Brahmos to ignore the old practices of caste associated with marriage. The liberalization and simplification of other life-oriented ceremonies accompanied the marriage reforms in the Samaj. Keshub and his followers were also instrumental in founding the Indian Reform Association, a normal school for girls, and a campaign for temperance.[39]

By 1876 and 1877, Keshub Chunder Sen had taken the Brahmo Samaj in a new direction. He felt an increasing pull towards *bhakti* or traditional Hindu devotionalism. At the same time, he drew his closest followers into an increasingly ascetic community which developed meditative disciplines over and above those usually practiced in the Samaj. But a new crisis arose for the movement in 1878 when Keshub announced that he had arranged for his daughter, very much underage, to marry the youthful Maharajah of Kuch Behar. Loud criticism arose immediately on three counts: (1) that this was a breach of the Brahmo Marriage Act in regard to age, (2) that the marriage could not be performed

without idolatrous ceremonies taking place, and (3) Keshub had
arranged the marriage because of the material benefits that would
come to his family. Keshub, on the other hand, justified the
decision with claims that God had revealed to him the fact that he
was in the right. While Protap Chunder Mazumdar, Keshub's
cousin, and Gour Govind Roy wrote to defend Keshub's actions,
opposition continued adamant. Many of Keshub's early followers
withdrew to establish the Sadharan Brahmo Samaj, the Samaj
branch active to the present day. Keshub himself continued as
leader of the Brahmo Samaj of India. By 1881, however, his group
called itself the Navavidhan or Church of the New Dispensation.

The attitude of British and American Unitarians towards Keshub
changed markedly after these events. His claims in lectures justi-
fying the Kuch Behar marriage and his increasingly devotional
theology flew in the face of the clear-headed, rational reformer they
had seen in Keshub in England a decade earlier. A survey of
articles in the Western church press indicates clearly complete
opposition to Keshub because of what he had done.[40]

In February 1880, Keshub's reassociation with Vaiṣṇṇavism became
clear. He and his followers conducted a major procession through
Calcutta. Stopping at one point, Keshub called on his followers
for a religious revival of *bhakti*. The procession was filled with
flags, musical instruments, and Brahmos, some of whom had come
from as far away as Bombay and Sind. This event seems to have
been one of the first clearly identified with the New Dispensation.
Its emotional and revivalist character seems to have fused Salvation
Army and traditional Vaiṣṇava appeal. Some 5,000 Hindus are
reported to have prostrated themselves before Keshub, chanting a
kīrtan especially written for the occasion.

The same year Keshub also began a process of seminars on the
teachings of the world's great prophets such as Socrates, Moses,
and Muhammad. It was more than an academic experience for
those who joined in it. It was very much of a pilgrimage in which
the participants would hold a dialogue with a speaker representative of the prophet under study. Much in the spirit of Ramakrishna,
who was emerging about the same time, Keshub was drawing his
followers together, with strands from many differing faiths, toward
a universal world faith.

While many would argue that Keshub's preoccupation with
devotional matters in the 1880s foreclosed his involvement in social

reform, other supporters claim that his concern was to provide
moral transformation of individuals before attempting new major
social changes. For all this he came under severe criticism from
Sadharan Brahmos who wanted to follow his earlier reform and
missionary path for a rational Hinduism to speak to the needs of the
modern age. Four essays Keshub wrote in his new periodical, *The
New Dispensation*, might have led his readers to the conclusion
that he was an honest mystic, or else that he had gone mad. In
these he spoke of his own "madness," of being haunted by the Holy
Ghost, or hearing speakers everywhere that had no tongue. Serious
physical illness was coming upon him. His death came quickly in
January 1884.[41]

Although the leadership of Keshub Sen spiralled the Brahmo
Samaj to new prominence, it had also created a three-way split in
the movement. One might think that such a split would cause the
movement to lose its effectiveness. In one sense, the Brahmo Samaj
of the post-1880s gave way to new movements whose first-genera-
tion enthusiasms stirred Indian minds and hearts in more dynamic
and emotional ways. On the other hand, one more figure emerged
in the movement, making an especially strong impact for the Samaj
in England and America—Protap Chunder Mazumdar, Keshub's
cousin and associate throughout his career.

Two years younger than Keshub, Protap remained in the
shadow of his cousin during Keshub's lifetime. An heir apparent,
he failed to take over the leadership of the Samaj in 1884 on his
return from a trip around the world because of the predominance
of Keshub's neo-Vaiṣṇava and *bhakti*-oriented followers who did
not want the Westernized, well-travelled, urbane Mazumdar to
become their leader. A second factor involved was the meteoric
rise of Svami Vivekananda, once a Brahmo himself, who caught
the public eye despite Mazumdar's presence as the official representative of Hinduism to the World Parliament of Religions in
Chicago in 1893.

Some of Keshub's followers, such as Bijoy Krishna Goswami,
wanted to propagate Brahmoism among rural and less well-educated peoples, while Protap Mazumdar, himself educated, Wes-
tern-oriented, and deeply influenced by Christian Unitarianism
(this is evident from his numerous writings), preferred to travel
throughout India by train, joining Keshub on his missionary journeys to Madras, Punjab, and elsewhere. While the Brahmo Samaj

might be spread in the Bengali language in the environs of Calcutta or Dacca, English, rather than Tamil, Urdu, or Marathi could be used in other areas.[42] Throughout his travels in India, Mazumdar appears to have been a major factor in organizing chapters, keeping them alive, and moving them towards political and social reform.

In many respects, Protap Mazumdar is best known by his writings. His first book, *The Faith and Progress of the Brahmo Samaj*, was an 1882 defense of Keshub's "spiritual universalism" published in Calcutta. This volume was dedicated to Rammohun Roy, however, described as "one who first cast on the wild waters of Hindu society, the bread, which, in the writer and others, has been returned a hundredfold."[43] The image was biblical if the reference to Rammohun was not.

Mazumdar's letters to Oxford Professor F. Max Müller indicate as early as 1881 the extent to which Protap Mazumdar was disturbed by Keshub's move away from Unitarian-oriented Brahmoism. Impressed by Müller's comparative method in the study of religion, Protap wanted to see it applied to faith and devotion in the context of the Brahmo Samaj. "The fatherhood of God is a meaningless abstraction unless the unity of truth in all lands and all nations is admitted. And the brotherhood of man is impossible if there is no recognition of the services which the great people of the earth have rendered unto each other."[44]

Protap's book *The Oriental Christ* helped make him a favorite of American Unitarians. Here he developed in a different way the Keshubite doctrine of Christ the Asiatic. He was careful not to present Christ in an uncritically universalist manner, writing that he had come to Jesus out of a secular vacuum. He had been awakened, he said, to "a sense of deep inner unworthiness" and "a strong sense of sin."[45] Keshub and the general Indian environment of the times, rather than a direct association with Christianity, were the source of his commitment to Christ. His experience seems to have combined views of Rammohun and those of Keshub. Protap's encounter was with both the human Jesus and Christ as an ideal.

Protap drew his specific theology from two of Keshub's lectures. Denying that either he or the Brahmos were pantheists, he nevertheless appeared as something of a vedantist when he wrote of the experience of *samādhi*. This was a direct experience of Christ rather than the understanding of Christ one would receive from the European dogmatic tradition. In his 1893 work, *The Spirit of God,* Mazumdar set forth a comparative evolutionary principle between Hinduism and Christianity. Here he compared the Vedas to the Old Testament, the Purāṇas to the Gospels, the Upaniṣads to the letters of Paul, asserting that Christianity clearly offered a dispensation of the Father and the Son but very little of the Spirit. The Brahmo Samaj was the one worshipping community in which one could see that the Spirit of God was drawing all religions together. "Socrates is for the Greeks, Moses is for the Hebrews, Confucius for the Chinese, Krishna for the Hindus. But there is a need for a central figure, a universal model, one who includes in himself, all these various embodiments of God's self manifestations."[46] Christ was this figure.

Although Protap Mazumdar's voyages to England and America in 1874 and 1884 were major events in his career, his presence at the Chicago World Parliament of Religions in 1893 was surely a highpoint for him personally as well as for Brahmo outreach to a new generation. The Parliament, organized as a humanistic adjunct to the technology of the fair, was conceived of by American religious liberals. One hundred seventy-two addresses by representatives of dozens of religious groups were heard. It was surely the first time in human history when representatives. of all the world's religions were gathered to hear one another, even if Christians predominated.

Protap's two speeches, "The Brahmo Samaj" and "The World's Religious Debt to Asia"[47] were both profound, intellectual, and intelligible. The speech on the Brahmos emphasized both history and social reform, while the second and longer lecture stressed the sense of immanence, mysticism, and spiritualism, so much a part of the Asiatic traditions. Protap made clear his broad knowledge of Asian religiousness, presenting something of universalism but little of nationalism in his talks.

That Protap made such a strong impression on his American Unitarian listeners was evident from the invitations he received. These included the four Lowell Lectures in Cambridge, Massachusetts, in the fall of 1893, and the raising of a pension, which provided Protap with an annual stipend until his death in 1905. Although the traditional historical record makes Svami Vivekananda out to be the Hindu hero of the World's Parliament, Protap Mazumdar's impact was far-reaching in a more subtle way. His role has only recently been uncovered.

Whatever impression Protap Mazumdar made on his American audiences, he was never able to become the leader of the Brahmo movement in India that Rammohun, Debendranath, or Keshub had been. Most likely his defense of Keshub and his affiliation with the New Dispensation movement had worked against him in the eyes of those in the 'Adi and Sadharan Samaj groups. At the same time, his Western ways did not endear him to the neo-Vaiṣṇavas who had been attracted to Keshub's later devotionalism.

Sivanath Sastri and Ananada Mohun Bose were prime movers in the Sadharan Brahmo Samaj, which consisted of those who remained behind from Keshub's original split with Debendranath but who did not join the Church of the New Dispensation. The Sadharan Samaj maintained the traditional Brahmo practices of faith in a personal God, belief in practising congregational prayer, and condemnation of "mysticism and sentimentalism" which diverted religious enthusiasm away from "channels of practical usefulness." The Sadharan group also emphasized brotherhood, opposed caste distinctions, urged freedom of conscience, and lastly, urged members to use their "moral energy" to promote the spiritual regeneration of the race."[48] These were precepts very much in the spirit of the early Keshub. They remain the backbone of the existing Samaj to the present day. Where the emotionalism of Keshub's Navavidhan could not survive organizationally, the well-ordered program of the Sadharan did. The Sadharan, of course, did not speak to the political issues of the twentieth century as Rammohun and the young Keshub had spoken to the social and religious issues of the nineteenth.

The meaning of the Brahmo Samaj and its significance for religious trends in modern India is several-fold. First, charismatic leadership in at least four major and several minor figures demonstrated that the old Hindu tradition of the guru could be transplanted to a setting in which modern social reform was called for. Second, the Brahmo Samaj demonstrated that theological reform in response to Hindu decline could be indigenous and at the same time draw on the best of what foreign, in this case Christian, culture had to offer. Third, the example set by Christian missionaries was first picked up and effectively used as a counterfoil to the missionaries themselves. What the Brahmo Samaj proved it could do successfully was soon to be imitated by the Arya Samaj, the

Ramakrishna movement, and the Ahmadiyah movement in Islam. But for a Hindu religious organization to seek to convert, and to welcome to its membership those of varied castes, was to break significant new ground. Finally, the Brahmo movement built its membership on those who had fallen away from traditional Vaiṣṇava *bhakti* and *brahmin* caste practices, and who felt a religious vacuum in their lives.

The threads of the Brahmo Samaj story are far more complex than have been hinted at here. The chronology of events as we have traced them should suffice as an introduction to both the intellectual and organizational development of this first modern Indian challenge to foreign domination, Christianity, and internal religious disintegration. For its time it was an answer to those who could find their identity with the movement. The Brahmo impact reached far beyond its numbers but in the end failed to speak to the needs of India's masses. Likewise, the third and fourth generations of Brahmos, without having to fight the fight of first generation Brahmos, lived comfortably in religious liberalism, unable to respond critically to the crisis of the 1906 partition of Bengal or to the massacre at Amritsar. Whatever indictment one may make of the Brahmo Samaj in the context of twentieth-century political events, the movement's contribution to the new age of the nineteenth century is without parallel.

Notes

1. The definitive work on the Brahmo Samaj is, without doubt, David Kopf's monographs, *The Brahmo Samaj and the Shaping of the Modern Indian Mind* (Princeton: Princeton University Press, 1979). I wish to express my appreciation to David Kopf for the inspiration his work as a historian has provided me in all my studies of the Brahmo Samaj and its interactions with American and English Unitarianism. For the perspective offered on the interaction see Spencer Lavan, *Unitarians and India: A Study in Encounter and Response* (Boston: Beacon Press, 1977). Both Kopf and Lavan contain notes and bibliography indicating primary sources for a complete study of the movement.
2. David Kopf, *British Orientalism and the Bengal Renaissance* (Berkeley: University of California Press, 1969), p. 47.
3. Spencer Lavan, *Unitarians and India*, p. 36.
4. K. Nag and D. Burman, *The English Works of Rammohun Roy*, Part 5 (Calcutta: Sadharan Brahmo Samaj, 1948), p. 4 of the "Introduction" to the Precepts of Jesus.

5. Lavan, *Unitarians and India,* pp. 41-42,

6. William Adam and Rammohun Roy, *Correspondence* (with the Rev. Henry Ware) *Relative to the Prospects of Christianity and the Means of Promoting its Reception in India* (Cambridge, 1824).

7. Sophie Dobson Collet, *Raja Rammohun Roy,* eds. D.K. Baswas and P.C. Ganguli, 3rd ed. rev. (Calcutta: Sadharan Brahmo Samaj, 1962), p. 227.

8. Ibid., p. 226.

9. Ibid., p. 227.

10. Kopf, *Brahmo Samaj,* p. 49.

11. Ibid.

12. Debendranath Tagore's autobiography was translated by S.N. Tagore and I. Devi (London: Macmillan, 1914).

13. Kopf, *Brahmo Samaj,* p. 190.

14. Ibid., p. 162.

15. M.M. Ali, *The Bengali Reaction to Christian Missionary Activities (1833-1857)* (Chittagong: Mehrub, 1965), p. 21. The statement appeared in Debendranath's *Autobiography* and was republished in the article by J.N. Farquhar in the *Encyclopaedia of Religion and Ethics* (Edinburgh: T. & T. Clark, 1909), p. 815.

16. Ali, *The Bengali Reaction to Christian Missionary Activities,* p. 33.

17. Kopf, *Brahmo Samaj,* p. 106.

18. Ibid., p. 107.

19. Ibid.

20. Protap Chunder Mozoomdar, *The Life and Teachings of Keshub Chunder Sen* (Calcutta: Navavidhan Publications, 1931), p. 332.

21. Ibid., p. 68.

22. Ibid., p. 69.

23. Ibid., p. 270.

24. Prem Chunder Basu, ed., *Life and Works of Brahmananda Keshav* (Calcutta: Navavidhan Publishing Co., 1940).

25. Keshub Chunder Sen, "Jesus Christ: Europe and Asia" in *Lectures in India* (Calcutta: Navavidhan Publication Committee, 1954).

26. Ibid., pp. 35-36.

27. Keshub Chunder Sen, "The Religion of Love," in *Essays: Theological and Ethical,* 5th ed., (Calcutta, 1916), p. 26.

28. P.C. Basu, *Life and Works of Brahmananda Keshav,* p. 75.

29. Keshub Chunder Sen, "Young Bengal: This is for You," in *Essays,* P. 6.

30. Sen, "Jesus Christ: Europe and Asia," p. 30.

31. Sivinath Sastri, *History of the Brahmo Samaj,* 2d ed. (Calcutta: Sadharan Brahmo Samaj, 1974), pp. 163ff.

32. All these lectures are included in Sen, *Lectures in India.*

33. "The Kingdom of Heaven," in Sen, *Lectures in India.*

34. Keshub Chunder Sen, "Diary in England," in *Keshub Chunder Sen in England,* 3rd ed. rev. and enlarged (Calcutta, 1938), p. 37; see sermon text, pp. 61-70.

35. Ibid., pp. 100-101.

36. See his addresses in *Keshub Chunder Sen in England*: "England's Duties Towards India," pp. 300-307; "Indian Reforms," pp. 307-315; and "The Duties of Christian Missionaries in India," pp. 315-329.
37. "Christ and Christianity," in Sen, *Keshub Chunder Sen in England*, p. 229.
38. Ibid., p. 234.
39. For details, see S.D. Collet, ed., *Brahmo Yearbook*, 1879, pp. 43-52.
40. Spencer Lavan, "Liberal Religion in India: The Keshub Chunder Sen Controversy," in *Alone Together: Studies in the History of Liberal Religions*, eds. Peter Iver Kaufman and Spencer Lavan (Boston: Beacon Press, 1979), pp. 77-87. This essay details the attitude of Unitarians towards Keshub during his varied career.
41. Kopf, *Brahmo Samaj*, pp. 278-79.
42. See Keshub Chunder Sen, "Diary in Madras," in *Essays*, for details of Protap's journeys.
43. Protap C. Mozoomdar, *The Faith and Progress of the Brahmo Samaj* (Calcutta, 1882).
44. Friedrich Max Müller, "The Letters of Protap Chunder Mozoomdar to Max Mueller" (August 20, 1881), in *Biographical Essays* (New York: Charles Scribner and Sons, 1884), p. 146.
45. P.C. Mozoomdar, *The Oriental Christ* (Calcutta: Navavidhan Publication Committee, 1933).
46. P.C. Mozoomdar, *The Spirit of God* (Boston: George H. Ellis, 1894), p. 239.
47. P.C. Mozoomdar, "The Brahmo Samaj" and "The World's Religious Debt to Asia," in *Lectures in America and Other Papers* (Calcutta: Navavidhan Publication Committee, 1955), pp. 4-29.
48. David Kopf, *Brahmo Samaj*, p. 143.

2

THE ARYA SAMAJ IN BRITISH INDIA, 1875-1947

Kenneth W. Jones

Scholars have long agreed that the Arya Samaj became a significant force in British India, yet the last overall account of this movement appeared as a chapter in *Modern Religious Movements in India* by J.N. Farquhar, published in 1919. Since then general accounts have appeared in Hindi and specialized studies in English,[1] but no general assessment of the Arya Samaj exists in English. This chapter will attempt to fill this gap with a sketch of the Arya Samaj from its founding in 1875 to the creation of India and Pakistan in 1947. A detailed examination of the Samaj remains beyond the scope of this study, but we can provide an outline of its founding and growth through this period, the complex of institutions and programs created by the Samaj, and the major historical forces which acted to shape the history of this movement. Among all the socio-religious movements which were founded in nineteenth-century colonial India, the Arya Samaj created the most extensive institutional structure, stretching over much of north and central India and beyond into the world of emigrant Indian settlements in Africa, Southeast Asia, the South Pacific, and the Caribbean. Beginning as a small sect the Samaj grew to resemble denominations as we know them in the West. It created its own Arya Jagat, or Aryan world, and it is this world we hope to delineate in the next few pages.

Founder and Founding

The origins of the Arya Samaj are embedded in the personality of its founder, Svami Dayananda Saraswati. Born in 1824 in the small town of Tankara located in the Kathiawar Peninsula,[2] Dayananda was raised as an orthodox Shaivite *brahman*. The young Dayananda demonstrated a strong involvement in religion, but he began to raise numerous questions about the rituals and beliefs accepted by his parents. Unwilling to be married and accept the normal duties of a householder, Dayananda fled his home at the age of twenty-two. He became a wandering *sannyāsi*, joined the Saraswati order with the name of Dayananda, and focused his attention on a personal pursuit for salvation. After searching for an acceptable guru Dayananda met Svami Virajanand in November 1860. He studied with the blind Virajanand for three years at Mathura and left him in 1863 to continue his ascetic existence. There was, however, a crucial change in Dayananda for he no longer sought a personal goal. After leaving Virajanand, Dayananda turned increasingly toward reforming contemporary Hinduism, which he felt was corrupted with superstition and error. The basic technique needed to comprehend this reform was the study of grammar. Dayananda believed that all truth lay in the Vedas and could be perceived only through a proper reading of these texts. To do so one must know the works of the grammarians Panini and Patanjali. Then the Vedas could be read correctly and truth revealed. For Dayananda the Vedas were *ārsha*, i.e., derived from the *ṛṣis*, inspired sages of antiquity. The Vedas contained all truth and were the ultimate authority against which other texts were to be compared. Those works which did not agree with the Vedas were considered '*unārsh*', that is, false, illegitimate, and filled with error.[3]

Dayananda's vision of vedic Hinduism rejected most of the major elements of the Hindu religion: idolatry, polytheism, the Purāṇas, priestly privilege, popular rituals, and deities. Dayananda's religion was monotheistic, open to all, rationalistic, and compatible with modern science. It was, as well, the one true faith. Not only did he reject popular Hinduism but also all other religions, Buddhism, Christianity, Islam, Zoroastrianism, for these too were false beliefs, since only vedic Hinduism contained the truth. In his basic ideological treatise, the *Satyārth Prakāsh*, first published in 1875, Dayananda laid out his beliefs and his criticisms of other religions. He also provided in his writings an explanation of the present degenerate state of Hinduism. He declared that the Mahabharata, that great war of antiquity, had led to a loss of correct vedic knowledge, which in turn began a lengthy process of decline among the Hindus. Without proper knowledge the Hindus were defeated first by the Muslims and later the Christian English. They became, as Dayananda saw them, a defeated people steeped in error and superstition.

After leaving Virajanand, Dayananda began to preach his own vision of Hinduism. He entered into debates with orthodox pundits, visited religious fairs, and traveled extensively throughout northern India. He spoke in Sanskrit and primarily addressed members of the brahmanical community. In 1872 Dayananda visited Calcutta and met with leaders of the Brahmo Samaj. This encounter led him to change his tactics for reforming Hinduism. He began to speak in Hindi and to address the literate middle classes of the Hindu community. He found the educated elite far more responsive to his message than the priestly groups. With their support Dayananda founded schools and published periodicals to express his ideals. He also wrote extensively, publishing two versions of the *Satyārth Prakāsh*, one in 1875 and a second re-written edition in 1883, plus numerous other books and pamphlets.[4] In 1875 he founded the first successful Arya Samaj in Bombay. This new organization prepared a list of principles and regulations which expressed Dayananda's ideas as well as his program for the reform of Hindu society. Although the Bombay Arya Samaj continued to exist, it was in north India that Dayananda found the greatest acceptance of his message.

In 1877 Dayananda traveled to Delhi for the Durbar in honor of Queen Victoria. Here he met with Hindu leaders from the Punjab, who invited him to visit that province. Dayananda journeyed north from Delhi, reaching Lahore on April 19, 1877. He stayed in the Punjab until July 11, 1878. Yet in these few months Dayananda either directly or indirectly established the Arya Samaj in eleven different cities. Many Punjabi Hindus responded to his ideas with enthusiasm and religious fervor, especially among the young college-educated men of Lahore. Hindus of the Lahore group rewrote and condensed the lengthy statement produced by the Bombay Arya Samaj into ten short, easily grasped principles which became the basic ideological statement of the Samaj. These principles were adopted by the Lahore Arya Samaj when it held its first meeting on July 24, 1877. The principles then became the standard statement for all Arya Samajes, and the Lahore Samaj became the organizational center of the new movement. When Dayananda left the Punjab, behind him were a growing collection of Samajes throughout the province. The newly founded Arya Samajes created an air of religious controversy by their militant ideology.[5] Aryas clashed openly with orthodox Hindus, other Hindu reform groups, and Christian missionaries.

After his visit to the Punjab Dayananda toured the United Provinces, giving speeches, holding debates, and founding branches of the Arya Samaj. In spite of two extensive trips throughout this area he had only succeeded in adding six more Arya branches by 1880.[6] Some of these were founded while he was still present in a particular town, others before or after his arrival. The response he met in the United Provinces proved less enthusiastic than that of the Punjab, yet in time this would be the province with the largest number of Aryas in it. Numerically the Arya Samaj had its core in the western districts of the United Provinces and throughout the Punjab. Its leadership, however, was heavily Punjabi and would remain so, although as long as Dayananda lived, he was the spiritual and to a degree practical head of the movement. Yet Dayananda soon turned his attention elsewhere. In May 1881, he arrived in Rajasthan, where he spent the last year and a half of his life. Dayananda had long been fascinated with the ruling Hindu princes and hoped to persuade them to accept his concepts of a reformed Hindu state and thus open the way back to previous Hindu greatness. During this period in Rajasthan Dayananda remained in contact with numerous Arya Samajes, but did not provide direction for the young movement. As a result each of the Samajes tended to act on its own initiative and according to its own interpretation of Dayananda's ideas. Meanwhile, Dayananda toured Rajasthan, preached to the ruling princes, and in October 1883, after visiting the state of Jodhpur, fell seriously ill. After returning to Ajmer he died on October 30, 1883.[7]

The death of its founder, rather than restricting the progress of the Arya Samaj, acted as a catalyst. The common reaction to Dayananda's death was that the Aryas should create a memorial to him, preferably a school or college which would teach vedic

Hinduism along with the regular English-oriented curriculum.[8] The Lahore Arya Samaj provided the leadership for this educational movement. In January 1886, after raising funds for the proposed school, they established the Dayanand Anglo-Vedic Trust and Management Society and approved an educational scheme drafted under the leadership of Lala Lal Chand. The Dayanand Anglo-Vedic High School opened in Lahore on June 1, 1886. Lala Hans Raj, a brilliant young graduate, became the principal of this institution on the basis of his agreement to serve in this position without pay and for life. The school quickly proved a success, enrolling 550 students by the end of the month. By 1889 it became a college and was recognized as such by the Punjab University.[9] For many Aryas this was their first and foremost "cause." For it they raised funds and recruited students with great diligence. The Lahore school provided a model for local Arya Samajes, who soon founded elementary and middle schools upon the lines of the Dayanand Anglo-Vedic College. By the end of the century this single school became the foundation stone for a system of schools throughout the Punjab, the United Provinces, and adjacent areas. The Arya Samaj not only won converts and established new branch Samajes but it also began the process of institution building.

The success of the Lahore college stimulated increasing ideological strain within the new movement. Each Samaj and each individual Arya could develop his or her own concepts of what it meant to be an Arya and of the historic role of its founder. Two differing schools of thought began to emerge. One group, "the moderates," saw Dayananda as a great reformer, a teacher and a guide to religious and social practice. They were heavily involved in the Dayanand Anglo-Vedic College and would, in fact, be called the "College Party." Opposed to them were the "militants" who believed Dayananda was a *ṛṣi* or divinely inspired teacher, whose words were infallible. For the militants the Arya Samaj represented a new religion that demanded a total commitment from its followers. The differences between these two groups surfaced first over the nature of the education provided through the new school. The moderates wanted and got a school curriculum that was essentially the same as the government and missionary schools, with the addition of Arya Samaj principles. The militants wanted a dramatically different education, one which would be taught

primarily in Hindi and Sanskrit with considerable time devoted to
the study of scriptures, Arya writings, and the correct methods
needed to interpret vedic texts.[10]

Debates over the nature of an Arya education soon fused with
other issues that divided members of the movement. The militants
maintained that all Aryas should be strict vegetarians, while the
moderates claimed that diet was a personal matter and not a part
of the Arya code. This issue of vegetarianism came to symbolize
each party. By the 1890s open struggles for control had erupted,
first in the Dayanand Anglo-Vedic Trust and Management Society
and secondly in the Arya Pratinidhi Sabha, Punjab. The Pratinidhi Sabha was founded in October 1886, as a provincial representative body for the Punjab. Similar provincial sabhas were created
to provide some central point of coordination for the expanding
Arya world. By 1893 the Punjabi Aryas were bitterly divided. The
moderates retained control over the schools through the Dayanand
Anglo-Vedic Management Society, while the militants took over
the Pratinidhi Sabha and a majority of the local Arya Samaj branches. This created a crisis for both groups. Supporting the Lahore
college and its associated schools had been the major task for all
Aryas. Now those in charge of the schools retained their "cause"
but had lost most of the organizational structure needed to sustain
it. Conversely the militants retained the structure and resources
but needed new forms of activity to utilize them.[11]

The moderates succeeded in maintaining their schools and
began to establish their own branch Arya Samajes, with the result
that in many Punjabi towns there were two Arya Samajes, each allied
with a different faction. In 1903 the moderates founded the Arya
Pradeshik Pratinidhi Sabha, a provincial body parallel to the older
Arya Pratinidhi Sabha.[12] Power and leadership among the moderates remained, however, centered in the Dayanand Anglo-Vedic
Trust and Management Society. It contained representatives from
all the Samajes allied to the moderate party, controlled a system
of schools and the funds raised to support these schools. The
moderates, however, did not limit themselves to educational work.
As a group they tended to see Hindus as members of a community, a
group of individuals sharing a similar religious heritage. As a result
the moderates turned to various forms of community service, to
famine relief, care for orphans, and in time to politics. Leading
moderates, such as Lala Lal Chand and Lala Lajpat Rai, would

have a deep involvement in both nationalist politics of the Indian National Congress and later the openly Hindu politics of the Punjab Hindu Conference and the Hindu Mahasabha.[13]

Support for the Indian National Congress during the 1880s and 1890s fluctuated from enthusiasm to apathy, depending largely on whether the Congress and Punjabi Hindus shared similar goals. In 1900 Aryas flocked to the Congress meeting in Lahore, but shortly afterwards turned away from politics in general and the Congress in particular. The partition of Bengal in 1905 brought another wave of enthusiasm for the Congress, a wave which merged with the Punjabi political unrest of 1907. At this time Lala Lajpat Rai and a number of moderate Aryas became politically active, condemning the British government openly and with considerable passion. The arrest and deportation of Lajpat Rai, followed by the jailing of other prominent Aryas, opened a period of government suspicion of and hostility to the Samaj.[14] It was seen by them as a seditious organization which must be guarded against and, if necessary, suppressed. The government was particularly hostile to the moderate party with its schools and supply of activist students. As a result Lala Hans´ Raj and other leaders of the Dayanand schools took a position against political activity by the Samaj. They feared that the schools might be closed and sought above all else to maintain these institutions to which they had dedicated their lives. The last major political shock prior to World War I came in 1909-10, when the Sikh state of Patiala arrested numerous Aryas and closed down the local Samajes. Gradually the era of politics and government suppression eased, especially for the militants, as the government made clear its approval of religiously-oriented Aryas.[15]

One major development of these years came with the first meeting of the Punjab Hindu Conference. Hindu fears reached a climax in the years 1908-9, as they increasingly saw themselves faced with a de facto alliance between the British government and the Muslim community. Lala Lal Chand expressed these concerns in a series of letters to the *Punjabee*, entitled "Self-Abnegation in Politics." His vision of gloom became one of doom in a series of letters to the *Bengalee* written by Lt. Col. U.N. Mukerji under the title "A Dying Race." Mukerji focused on the decline in numbers of Bengali Hindus and the eventual possibility of extinction which faced the Hindus of that state. Lala Chand turned his attention to the uselessness of the Congress, calling for the establishment of a new organization which would be openly Hindu in its politics. The Punjab Hindu Conference, which met for the first time on October 21-22, 1909, in Lahore, became just such an organization. It met annually and was transformed in time into the Akhil Bharat Hindu Mahasabha.[16] The evolution of the Mahasabha received Arya support and leadership, but it also moved beyond the limits of the Samaj, which remained divided in its political attitudes. Many Aryas were firm advocates of the Indian National Congress, others of the Mahasabha, while some remained relatively apolitical.

The militants, with their vision of the Arya Samaj as a religious movement and a religious experience, turned to a concern for *vēd prachār*, preaching the Vedas. They developed a system of paid missionaries, *updēshaks*, which aimed to transform popular Hinduism into the "purer" vedic form of that religion. The militants also extended and utilized the institution of *śuddhi*. Dayananda had used *śuddhi* to reconvert individuals who had joined either Islam or Christianity. The use of *śuddhi* to reconvert Hindus from either Christianity or Islam increased throughout the 1880s and 1890s. A Śuddhi Sabha was established and conducted by Aryas and Sikhs, since both groups faced the same religious challenges.[17] By 1896 the Aryas began to perform *śuddhi* with groups of people and by 1900 had extended *śuddhi* to a new area, the uplift of untouchables who were transformed into "pure caste" Hindus. On June 3, 1900, militant Aryas purified a group of Rahtias, Sikh untouchables, much to the horror of the Sikh community.[18] This opened the door to both winning back those lost to Hinduism as well as ending untouchability.

Concern for untouchability stemmed in part from the realization that this segment of society was the most likely to convert to another religion. The success of Christian missionaries among untouchable Hindus and Muslims had demonstrated this possibility, as had Islamic conversion prior to the arrival of the British. In the years before World War I *śuddhi* campaigns were conducted among various untouchable groups in the northwest: Odes, Meghs, Doms, Rajputs, and the Sheikhs of Larkhana in Sind. On June 23, 1911, the All India (Bhārat) Śuddhi Sabha was founded by Ram Bhaj Datta. The Arya Samaj had developed *śuddhi* as a weapon of defense from the conversion threat posed by both Christianity and Islam.[19]   Anxiety over the future of the Hindu community and Aryan ideology merged to produce radical attacks against caste privilege as well as militant efforts at proselytization, conversion, and reconversion. The aggressive stance of the Arya Samaj heightened religious competition as they engaged in a multisided struggle with orthodox Hinduism, reform organizations, and militant groups from other religious communities. Certain Aryas, such as Pandit Lekh Ram, specialized in criticism of a particular religion, in his case against Islam. In speeches, tracts, and newspapers he condemned Islam as a religion founded on greed, violence, and ignorance. In 1897 the bitter rivalry between Aryas and Muslims peaked in Punjab with the murder of Pandit Lekh Ram.   The resulting religious conflict was a preview of the more extensive violence of partition.[20]

The militant Aryas, determined to create the new world of Aryanism as envisioned by Dayananda, engaged in radical social reform. To do so they performed new vedic life-cycle rituals of birth, marriage, and death. They entered the field of education for women by founding the Kanya Mahavidyalaya of Jullundur on June 14, 1896. The Kanya Mahavidyalaya was girls' high school which would in time add college classes as well. Aryas preached widow remarriage and began to practice this within their own families. In addition they sponsored education for widows and built homes for them. In order to create a new Hindu, an individual who would not be tainted by contemporary corruption, the militants, led by Lala Munshi Ram (later Svami Shraddhanand), moved to create a dramatically different educational system. In 1902 they opened the Gurukula Kangri, just outside of the city of Hardwar. This was a resident educational institution, teaching students from the elementary through the college level. As at the ancient Hindu institutions, students remained at the Gurukula under the direction of religious teachers and separate from their families and from society. Instruction was in Hindi and Sanskrit, with a heavy emphasis on religious training, although much of the standard curriculum was retained. This institution sought to mold the entire personality of its students into the patterns of life and thought demanded by Arya ideology. Its graduates would be the first truly reformed vedic Aryas.[21]   With the creation of the Gurukula Kangri the militants completed their own institutional structure as a rough parallel with the moderates, although both groups would continue to add new institutions for specific purposes.

The division between two groups remained a specifically Punjabi phenomenon. Only in Punjab were there two provincial sabhas with rival branches allied to each. All other provinces had a single representative organization. Whatever differences of interpretation existed did so within individuals, and were not institutionalized. Also, it must be remembered that rivalry between the two parties contained elements of personal struggle between two entrenched organizations, as well as opposing interpretations of the Samaj. These differences, however, did not mean that either party was prohibited from joining with members of the opposing group to support similar causes, or that either group did not take up independently similar work being carried out by the other. Both would engage in preaching, missionary work, *śuddhi*, and various programs of social reconstruction. Also, the growth of the Arya Samaj tended to make this division less crucial than it had been during the nineteenth century, even though the separate institutional structures within the Samaj continued to exist and still do today.

Expansion of the Arya Samaj

During the first twenty-five years of its existence the Arya Samaj grew steadily. In 1891 the census report recorded a total of 39,952 Aryas, and ten years later the total had jumped to 92,419, an increase of 131 per cent. This indicated primarily an intensification of the Samaj in two provinces, the Punjab with 25,000 Aryas and the new center of the movement in the United Provinces with 65,268.[22] The Samaj also began to move outward in all directions. This expansion led to the establishment of new provincial (*pratinidhi*) sabhas in the United Provinces, 1886; Rajasthan, 1888; Bengal/Bihar in 1889, a joint Madhya Pradesh/Vidarbha Sabha, also in 1889, and the Bombay provincial sabha in 1902.[23] Continued growth of the Samaj created the need for a central coordinating body, even as expansion at the provincial level had made the founding of *pratinidhi* sabhas a necessity. Dayananda did leave behind one central organization, the Paropkarini Sabha. He established this society on August 16, 1880, with the writing of his will.[24] The Paropkarini Sabha was to act, and did so act, as the executor of his estate, particularly in regard to his written works. While it could have provided overall leadership for the Arya Samaj, it failed to do so, largely due to the appointive nature of its membership, who did not necessarily speak for major constituencies of Aryas. Instead there was a growing consensus that the Samaj needed to found a new coordinating organization which would be able to act on behalf of all Aryas.

A number of Aryas who attended the Bharat Dharam Maha-mandal meeting in Delhi during 1900 began seriously discussing the need for such an organization. Nothing concrete was done, how-ever, until 1908, when at the anniversary celebration of the Gurukula Kangri a subcommittee was chosen to draft the regula-tions and structure of the proposed Sarvadeshik (All-India) Sabha. On September 15, 1908, a full committee met in Agra with repre-sentatives of the various provincial sabhas and on August 31, 1909, the Sarvadeshik Arya Pratinidhi Sabha convened its first meeting in Delhi. Twenty-seven delegates were elected to the Sarvadeshik Sabha from six provincial *pratinidhi* sabhas. All provincial societies were represented save one, the Arya Pradeshik Pratinidhi Sabha of Punjab, which had been created by the moderate party in that province. The organizers of the Sarvadeshik Sabha asked the Punjabi moderates to send representatives to the new organization, but were told they would do so only if the Pradeshik Sabha would be the sole representative body of Punjabi Aryas. This was un-acceptable to the organizers and so the Arya Pradeshik Pratinidhi Sabha, Punjab, remained the only provincial group outside the newly instituted Sarvadeshik Sabha.[25] Over the years efforts were made to incorporate this group into the overall representative body, but without success. In spite of their formal separation, the Punjabi moderates did cooperate with the Sarvadeshik Sabha on numerous occasions.[26]

The new Sarvadeshik Sabha presided over a steadily expanding movement as the Arya Samaj gradually extended beyond those areas in which it was originally located. It also added members within those areas. The Samaj had penetrated into the Muslim state of Hyderabad during the late nineteenth century, but signi-ficant movement south would wait until historic forces brought the Samaj there in the 1920s.[27] In the meantime the Arya Samaj began to follow the flow of Indian immigrants abroad. In 1896 the *Satyārth Prakāsh* was carried to Mauritius by members of the Bengal Infantry.[28] Within the next two decades Arya Samaj branches

were founded there in what became the first major center of the
Samaj outside of British India. In 1911 two Arya leaders, Dr.
Maniklal and Dr. Chiranjiv Bhardwaj, succeeded in publishing the
Mauritius Patrika, an Arya Samaj newspaper.[29] The Samaj traveled
further west in 1904, when Pandit Purnanandji went to Nairobi.
He was followed in the next year by Bhai Parmanand, who reached
Durban and then went on an extensive tour of South Africa. South
and East Africa became centers of successful Samaj missionary
activities, as branch Samajes were opened throughout the area and
were supported by the local Indian communities.[30] By the 1920s
the Samaj had also reached the Fiji Islands, and by 1921 had
become sufficiently settled there to open a girls' school.[31] Diffusion
abroad moved in a pattern of waves as the Samaj penetrated new
areas settled by Indian immigrants.

In 1933 another period of overseas expansion began with the
departure of Pandit Ayodhya Prasad Ji for the World Fellowship
of Faith Conference held that year in Chicago. The pandit visited
this conference and then spent a year preaching in the United
States. The next wave of Arya expansion began, however, when
he left the United States. Pandit Ayodhya Prasad first visited
Trinidad, where he preached and performed *śuddhi* ceremonies to
reclaim Hindus who had converted to Islam and Christianity.[32]
The pandit next traveled to Dutch Guyana and British Guyana.
Arya Samajes were founded in all these areas and grew steadily
through local efforts, as well as through continual visits of Arya
missionaries. During the 1920s and '30s overseas Aryas organized
their own provincial sabhas which became affiliated with the Sarvadeshik Pratinidhi Sabha: British East Africa, 1922; South Africa,
1927; Fiji, 1928; Mauritius, 1930; and Dutch Guyana, 1937.[33]
Continued growth within India brought additional provincial sabhas
into the central organization. Bihar joined as a separate body in
1930 and in 1935 a provincial sabha was established for the Muslim-
dominated state of Hyderabad.[34]

Continued growth of the Arya Samaj was recorded by the
decennial census reports in British India. Even without the figures
for the widely spread Arya movement outside of India, there still
was an impressive growth. By 1911 the total given for the Samaj
was 243,000, an increase of over 163 per cent from 1901. A decade
later the Aryas had again doubled to 467,578 and in 1931 reached
the total of 990,233.[35] The census of 1941 and all censuses

afterward no longer carried figures for the Arya Samaj, but it is safe to assume that growth did not end. In 1947 the Samaj must have been somewhere between one and a half to two million' members, both inside British India and throughout the world. This growth in numbers carried with it the addition of provincial and local Samajes. The *Arya Directory* of 1941 indicates over 2,000 Arya Samajes affiliated with the provincial sabhas.[36] The creation of new local Samajes led to a continual development of specialized organizations, particularly in education.

The Dayanand Anglo-Vedic movement began with a single school in Lahore and then grew rapidly as elementary, middle, and high schools were founded throughout the province. The picture of educational institutions, however, is complex. A number of schools were controlled by the Dayanand Anglo-Vedic Trust and Management Society, but many also were under the administration of local Arya Samajes or various provincial sabhas. It was a fluid situation with schools being opened, occasionally closed, and at times taken over by other groups when it appeared that they might not survive. By the 1940s the educational world of the Samaj stretched throughout India, as far south as Sholapur in Maharashtra and the state of Hyderabad. By then there were 179 schools and 10 colleges in India and Burma. These included regular art schools, industrial training institutions, girls' schools, Sanskrit Pathshalas, and religious training centers.[37] In addition the Gurukula Kangri had become the basis for an alternate system of education. Schools patterned after the Gurukula Kangri were founded at all levels. Some of these were affiliated with the Arya Pratinidhi Sabha, Punjab, and others were administered locally. In 1921 the original Gurukula became a university and by the 1940s there were seven other major institutions in the Gurukula system. The *Arya Directory* listed a total of thirty-three establishments labelled as "Gurukulas."[38] One of these was a women's college, the Kanya Gurukula, located in Dehra Dun, founded in 1923. Like the Gurukula Kangri this was a national school, drawing students from throughout India.[39] As with the Lahore high school, the Gurukula Kangri became the basis of an entire educational system.

By the creation of an independent India and Pakistan in 1947 the Arya Samaj had grown into a complex world, an Arya Jagat, of associations at the local, provincial, and central level. These

associations in turn managed and maintained numerous institutions—schools, orphanages, student hostels, widows' homes, reading rooms, libraries, tract societies, newspapers, journals, missionary societies, and various organizations dedicated to social reform, particularly among the untouchables. Clearly the most
fundamental task of the Samaj lay in administering and financially
supporting these organizations. A complex of programs in differing socio-religious areas was maintained by the Samaj, providing
an organizational impact that is difficult to examine but should
not be underestimated. The original message of Svami Dayananda
Saraswati was magnified and molded by the establishment of the
Arya Samaj and its growth over the decades prior to independence.
The original dynamics of Dayananda's ideology were modified by
historical forces, particularly during the 1920s and '30s.

The Arya Samaj from World War I to Independence

The outbreak of World War I had little direct effect on the
Arya Samaj, but the intensification of the nationalist fervor at the
close of the war and just afterward drew many Arya Samaj leaders
into active involvement with the Indian National Congress. Svami
Shraddhanand, for example, became a major figure in the campaign
against the Rowlatt Bills. He and others then went on to support
Mahatma Gandhi's first non-cooperation campaign.[40] At the height
of this movement, in August 1921, a group of Muslims, the
Moplahs of Kerala, rose against the British and their Hindu
neighbors. The Aryas were shocked and horrified since the
Moplahs not only attacked Hindu property and person, but also
conducted a number of forced conversions to Islam. Lala Hans
Raj heard the news and at a meeting the next day of the Arya
Pradeshik Pratinidhi Sabha in Lahore sponsored a resolution to
send help to the Hindus of Kerala. This they did, as Pandit
Rishi Ram, Sriyut Khushal Chand, and Pandit Mastan Chand
were dispatched to Kerala. Others would follow. The prime
service the Aryas could and did provide was the institution of
śuddhi, which they used to bring converted Hindus back into the
fold of their religion and society. In doing so the Aryas won
considerable acceptance of *śuddhi* by orthodox Hindus. Originally

leaders of Hindu orthodoxy had strongly opposed the use of *śuddhi*, but at this time it was the only effective weapon Hindus possessed to counter forced conversion. Also Aryas provided financial aid and assisted in rebuilding damaged Hindu temples. The Moplah affair marked a major step in the introduction into south India of ideas and institutions developed in the northern areas of acute religious conflict. On this occasion northern attitudes of communal defense flowed into an area already the center of religious competition.[41]

Following the cessation of the non-cooperation campaign in February 1922, north India sank into a morass of religious conflict and violence. Major riots erupted in many cities: Multan and Saharanpur in 1922, Delhi in 1924 and 1926, Kohat in 1924. In fact, no city was without its share of religious strife as such incidents became endemic in even small towns and villages.[42] Although many conflicts arose spontaneously, emerging from inherent points of conflict between Islam and Hinduism, each community grew increasingly aggressive about its rights, particularly in regard to proselytization, conversion, and reconversion. A community of Muslims, the Malkana Rajputs, had sought ready mission into Hinduism. This group, living in the area where three provinces meet, United Provinces, Rajasthan, and Madhya Pradesh, had been converted to Islam but still retained much of their Hindu culture. The All-India Kshatriya Mahasabha at its annual meeting in Agra on December 31, 1922, agreed to accept the Malkanas back into the fold of Rajput society. On February 13, 1923, a meeting of approximately eighty representatives of caste sabhas and various Hindu groups—Aryas, Sanatanists, Sikhs, and Jains—was held in Agra to plan this proposed reconversion campaign. Svami Shraddhanand attended and at his suggestion they organized the Bharatiya Hindu Śuddhi Sabha. Shraddhanand became president and Lala Hans Raj first vice-president.[43] The Śuddhi Sabha raised funds, supported missionaries, and began an extensive campaign to win back the Malkanas. Although this was a broader movement than the Arya Samaj, its leadership was Arya and included individuals from both wings of the movement. For this type of issue transcended divisions within the Hindu community.

The Śuddhi Sabha and its work heightened communal competition between Hindus and Muslims. Almost immediately Muslim groups in north India formed counter-movements to send missionaries to persuade the Malkanas and others to remain within the

Islamic community. Among Hindus the twin slogans of *śuddhi*
(conversion) and *sangathan* (unity) expressed their heightened
religious aggressiveness. Muslims reacted with parallel movements
for *tanzīm* and *tablīgh*. The Arya Samaj with its institutional base,
resources of money, and manpower became deeply involved in
this religious competition. In turn, the Samaj was affected in its
own program by the demands of communal defense. Perhaps no
issue better typifies this period of history and its atmosphere of
strife than does the case of Mahasaya Rajpal, a bookseller and
devout Arya Samajist. In 1924 he published an Urdu tract entitled
Rangīla Rasūl, the *Merry Prophet*. This was a vicious attack on
the Prophet Muhammad which offended many Muslims throughout
the north. They tried to have it banned by the government and
failed, but in the process Rajpal became a bitter symbol of all
aggressive Hinduism.[44] As a result Rajpal was attacked by a
Muslim in September 1927, and finally killed on April 3, 1931.[45]
The Rajpal affair illustrates the tensions and underlying violence
of this period. During these years the Arya Samaj reacted to such
events which stimulated Samaj programs, particularly on the issue
of continued caste prejudices within the movement. At the 1922
anniversary celebration of the Lahore Arya Samaj, Bhai Parmanand
presented a vigorous condemnation of the caste system, particularly
its persistence among members of the Samaj. Shortly afterward
came the establishment of the Jat Pat Todak Mandal dedicated
to the removal of all caste distinctions. The Mandal decided to
work first among Aryas since it was necessary to remove caste
distinctions within the Arya Samaj in order to facilitate the incor-
poration of new members brought in through *śuddhi*.[46] Concern
for an end to caste distinctions, *śuddhi*, and communal defense
were linked and reinforced each other.

Within the context of communal tensions a new Samaj institution
began to evolve. In September 1920, at a meeting of scholars
and *sannyāsis* held in Delhi, it was decided to hold a centenary
celebration of Dayananda's birth at Mathura. A managing committee was established and the celebration scheduled for February
15-21, 1925. Among the eighty-six members of this committee
were representatives from the Sarvadeshik Sabha, both Pratinidhi
Sabhas of the Punjab, the Paropkarini Sabha, and various other
groups.[47] The two wings of the Samaj which had cooperated in
the Moplah and Malkana *śuddhi* campaigns once again worked

together, as the longstanding division within the Samaj tended to close under the pressures of communal conflict. When this centenary celebration met, Aryas came from all sections of the Samaj. They stayed and worked in Arya Nagar, a tent city with fourteen camps, five bazaars, one huge mandal, and four smaller ones. A procession was held, hymns sung, and rituals conducted, along with speeches and the passing of resolutions.[48] This meeting had two purposes, first, the celebration of Dayananda's birth with all the pomp that could be mustered, and, secondly, the passing of resolutions which provided direction and goals for the movement. Such a grand meeting offered a new method for gathering opinions of leading Aryas and expressing them in a series of statements. For while such a gathering could and did advocate various steps for the Samaj to take, it had no machinery to carry out a particular program. That would have to be left to others, such as the Sarvadeshik Sabha.

The centenary celebration contained more than one meeting. The planning committee had established a Dharm Parishad (religious council) and an Arya Vidvat Parishad (a learned council), which met continuously in the smaller mandals. In addition, there were a number of conferences on different religions, a gathering of individuals who had met Dayananda, and a poetry conference. Following the centenary celebrations various Arya groups held their own sessions. These included the Arya Swarajya Sammelan, the Arya Kumar Sammelan, the Dalitoddhar Sammelan, the Jat-Pat Todak Sammelan, the Pradeshak Sammelan, a Gau Conference, a Kshatriya Conference, and Brahman Conference.[49] Among the various resolutions passed, the Arya Vidvat Parishad recommended that a Dharmarya Sabha be established. This group would act to decide religious issues and remove doubts within the Samaj.[50] The executive committee of the Sarvadeshik Sabha, at a meeting on January 27, 1928, decided to establish such a sabha and thus carry out the resolution passed in 1925. The Dharmarya Sabha functioned extensively for the next twenty-five years.[51] The centenary conference also decided to hold a second celebration at Tankara, Dayananda's birth place. Arya Samajists gathered at Tankara on February 12, 1926, conducted a grand *nagar kīrtan* and visited the home of Dayananda as well as other historic sites in the area.[52] This was solely a meeting in honor of Dayananda; no working sessions were held nor resolutions passed. The 1925 gathering had managed to set a precedent which would be followed in 1927, although this next conference would be stimulated by a different set of causes.

Religious violence grew bitter in 1926 and 1927 with the Arya Samaj as a major target of the Islamic Community. At least that was how the Aryas saw events of this period. The murder of Svami Shraddhanand at the close of 1926 was followed in early 1927 by riots in the Bareilly area on the occasion of Muharram. Arya Samaj individuals and buildings were attacked, allegedly with the assistance of the local police. The Sarvadeshik Sabha met on July 24, 1927, and called for a series of meetings to take place in north India on August 7, 1927. At these meetings, Hindus, Sikhs, Parsis, and Jains, as well as the Aryas, were asked to pass resolutions expressing their anger at the apparent police hostility toward Hindus and at the violence which resulted. They were then requested to send copies of these resolutions to all levels of the government. In September a managing committee was established to organize the first Arya Mahasammelan, or great conference, to take place early in November in Delhi.[53] Unlike the centenary conference this gathering was called specifically to deal with the question of religious violence and of the Hindu community's reaction to it. The Delhi Mahasammelan became the first of four such conferences to be held prior to independence.

The Delhi Mahasammelan followed in organization and function the model of the 1925 centenary celebration. Once again all factions of the Samaj participated. The president of the meetings, Lala Hans Raj, was joined by leading members of the moderate and militant Aryas. This conference passed a series of eighteen resolutions, beginning with a tribute to Svami Shraddhanand in which the Aryas stated their general view that they recognized the hatred and anger of the Muslims of these provinces which their leaders have toward the Hindus in general and the Arya Samaj in particular.[54] They then went on to pass the remaining resolutions which accused the government of failing to protect the Hindu community, condemned Muslim violence, called for more extensive suddhi campaigns, continued work among the depressed castes, and asked for an end to caste distinctions among all Aryas. All these resolutions centered on communal defense and solidarity, on suddhi and sangathan. Two new institutions were created, the Arya Raksha (Defense) Committee, and the Arya Vir Dal.[55]

Branches of the Vir Dal were founded throughout the Samaj, funds raised, and volunteers recruited. This militant arm of the Samaj served on a variety of occasions, from the *satyāgraha* struggle in Hyderabad to the upheavals of partition in Punjab.[56] The Delhi Mahasammelan clearly grew out of and focused on the issue of religious violence, while the normal functioning of the Samaj's institutions and programs drew little attention. A similar set of circumstances lay behind the Bareilly Mahasammelan of 1931.

One of the byproducts of the religious tensions during the 1920s was a number of restrictions on religious demonstrations at both the local and provincial levels. The Arya Samajists found it necessary to take out licenses from the local police before they could hold processions or march singing through the streets of a particular town. Occasionally permission was not granted and the annual anniversary ceremonies could not be held in the traditional manner. Both Hindus and Muslims had become increasingly aggressive in demanding their traditional rights as they saw them and in objecting to those rituals employed by the opposing community when they seemed to interfere with their own religious practices. Hindu processions complete with hymn singing were offensive to Muslims, especially when they passed a mosque at prayer time. From the standpoint of the Aryas all attempts to limit, let alone ban, their normal rituals were seen as elements of oppression by the government with its de facto allies, the Muslims. By 1929 the Arya Pratinidhi Sabha of the United Provinces was engaged in a lengthy quarrel over such limits in that state. Similar difficulties arose in Punjab, as it seemed to the Samaj that all governments were acting to curb their activities.[57] In response to this rising frustration the Sarvadeshik Sabha decided to hold a second Mahasammelan on February 1931, in Bareilly. They had already concluded that Mahasammelans would be called whenever a major problem faced the samaj.

The Bareilly Mahasammelan considered a wide range of issues centering on the need of the community for self-protection. The Arya Vir Dal was praised and all Aryas urged to support it, to found local branches, and to raise both funds and recruits for the Dal. The main task of the Dal was to protect Aryan culture, assist the oppressed, and provide social services.[58] Educational developments, the system of Arya preachers, and internal social reform among members drew attention and resolutions. Two

areas, though, are of special interest. Now that the Samaj saw
satyāgraha as an important tool for itself and others, it had become
concerned over the rights of Hindu prisoners, particularly Arya
prisoners. Consequently they passed a resolution demanding that
jail regulations be changed to allow Aryas to practice their own
religious rituals while interned. The Mahasammelan also turned
its attention to restrictions on various Arya Samaj activities in the
major Muslim states, specifically Hyderabad, Bhopal, Bahawalpur,
and Rampur.[59] This last concern would grow rapidly during the
1930s and finally culminate in the Arya Samaj's first *satyāgraha*
campaign.

Unlike the Delhi and Bareilly Mahasammelans the third one
was centered on the fiftieth anniversary of Svami Dayananda's death.
The idea of holding such a meeting may have been discussed at the
Mathura conference, but the first concrete plan came from the
Paropkarini Sabha at the instigation of Sriman Nahar Singh. The
Sarvadeshik Sabha agreed to assist in this Mahasammelan which
was planned for October 14-20, 1933, and held in Ajmer.[60] The
lack of a major overriding problem behind the conference meant
that resolutions, nine in all, tended to be relatively general, covering major themes of the movement.[61] By contrast the significance
of the celebration stemmed from the wide variety of Arya institutions and organizations which participated. Special conferences
and programs were presented from throughout the Samaj. An Arya
Mahila Sammelan (Ladies Conference) met with representatives of
women's groups, especially the Kanya Gurukulas, to pass twenty-
three resolutions on issues particularly important to women.[62] A
special conference was held of those who had met Dayananda, and
another group presented a demonstration of physical exercises and
training.[63] A wide variety of organizations held their own meetings, such as the Arya Vir Dal and the Arya Kumar Sabha. Special
conferences focused on Hindi, Sanskrit, poetry, *sannyāsis*, overseas
Indians, untouchability, and widow remarriage.[64] This was to be
the last Mahasammelan for eleven years. There were no centen-
aries to celebrate during the next decade and the intensity of religious conflict in the north had abated somewhat. Instead Arya
Samaj attention began to be increasingly focused on the Muslim-
dominated state of Hyderabad.

The Arya Samaj had been in the Hyderabad state since the
nineteenth century, but only in the late 1920s and early 1930s had

there been an active expansion of its role. New Samajes were founded and Arya missionaries from outside of Hyderabad began aggressive campaigns of preaching. By 1932 the first of a series of clashes between the Samaj and the government of Hyderabad took place. An Arya missionary, Pandit Chandra Bhanu, was charged with being a political agitator, and the Samaj as being a political organization. The Samaj attempted to answer these charges both to the Nizam's government and the British Indian government but did not succeed in doing so.[65] Over the next few years incident after incident took place as relations between the Arya Samaj and the Hyderabad government steadily deteriorated. Also tensions became severely strained between the Hindu majority and the Islamic minority in this state.[66] In 1935 the Arya Pratinidhi Sabha of Hyderabad was organized as the number of Samaj branches and institutions continued to increase. The Nizam's government grew steadily more suspicious of the Samaj. As they saw it, "The Arya Samaj has been working in the Dominions of his Exalted Highness for several years. It has eighteen organizations in the Capital City while its central organization, known as the Arya Pratinidhi Sabha, Nizam Rajya, is located in Udaigir with branches in different parts. . . . Ostensibly, its principal functions are to hold periodical congregations, organize processions, establish akhadas (gymnasiums) and employ missionaries for Shuddhi and Sangathan work. Outside preachers are often invited to deliver lectures and enroll fresh converts."[67] Tensions between the government and the Samaj accelerated until 1938, when they resulted in open conflict.

The Arya Samaj had been particularly active in the Marathi-speaking areas of Hyderabad, and it was here that frustrated Aryas began to engage in *satyāgraha* against the government.[68] These were local affairs with some support from Arya Samajes across the border in Bombay Province. The Sarvadeshik Sabha, in response to requests from the Hyderabad Aryas for support, decided to hold an Arya Conference at Sholapur just beyond the borders of Hyderabad. It met on December 24-26, 1938. By this time the Samaj had begun to gather its support for the coming struggle and had also received offers of aid from other Hindu organizations, especially the Hindu Mahasabha. The Sholapur Conference aired Arya grievances, particularly those against the Nizam's police. "Our chief complaint of very, very long standing is that the unscrupulous Police of the Nizam's Government fabricates unfounded lies

against the Arya Samajists, sheer out of bigotry."[69] By this time
the Nizam's government published its own view of the Samaj and
Samaj activities.

> Audiences have been exhorted to rise, fight the Muslims, kill
> them and overthrow them as the country belonged to the Hindus
> and not the Muslims. In certain areas, they have gone so far as
> to exhort the ryots not to pay land tax and to boycott Govern-
> ment official and Muslims. Every act and intention of the
> Government is deliberately misinterpreted in order to bolster up
> complaints that they and the Hindu community generally are
> being "oppressed." . . . In addition to written and spoken pro-
> paganda, definite acts of lawlessness on the part of Arya Samaji-
> sts have now become common. Instances are the taking out of
> Arya Samaj processions in defiance of the orders issued by the
> local authorities in the interest of public peace, the processionists
> being armed with deadly weapons, shouting offensive slogans,
> singing provocative songs and firing guns in crowded localities.[70]

Both sides feared and distrusted each other and both saw the other
as motivated primarily by religious fanaticism. As in the north the
Aryas felt that their traditional rights and privileges were being
taken from them by the Nizam's government, which in this case
was an expression of the Muslim community. A struggle proved
inevitable.

A *satyāgraha* campaign against the government manned by
Arya Samajists within the state had started in October, well before
the Sholapur Conference. The Aryas found allies in the newly-
formed and almost immediately-banned Hyderabad State Congress. The Sholapur Conference declared January 22, 1939, as
Hyderabad Day in order to popularize the movement and bring
support throughout the country. On January 31, 1939, the Arya
Samaj began its *satyāgraha*.[71] With the backing of the Sarvadeshik
Sabha other Arya groups, such as the Arya Vir Dal, joined this
campaign, as did students from the Gurukulas as well as Arya
leaders throughout British India. The Hindu Mahasabha also sent
in parties of its followers to perform *satyāgraha*. This campaign
continued through spring and into early summer and ended when
the Nizam's government announced a set of political reforms on
July 17, 1939. By this time approximately 8,000 Hindus had been

jailed.[72] On August 17, all political prisoners were released and the *satyāgraha* campaign was discontinued by the Arya Samaj and the Hindu Mahasabha.[73] This marked the first successful *satyāgraha* campaign for both organizations. It also was another instance, as in the case of the Moplah uprising, of Arya Samaj penetration into an area of the South already caught up in Hindu-Muslim conflict. Only in such an area did the Arya Samaj find an acceptance of their ideology and techniques; in the rest of South India barriers of language and culture made it extremely difficult for the Samaj to gain adherents.

Following the Hyderabad *satyāgraha* the Arya Samaj became once more involved in Hindu-Muslim conflicts in the north. The constitutional reforms of 1935 opened the way for parliamentary government in the provinces. With the outbreak of World War II the Indian National Congress resigned its elective positions, but the Muslim League did not. Muslim-dominated provincial governments established themselves in those provinces with a Muslim majority, one of which was Sind. As in the Muslim princely states tensions developed between a Muslim-dominated government and the Arya Samaj. In the case of Sind, however, the majority of the population was also Muslim. The Hindus of this area were a small minority located primarily in the cities and towns. By 1943 the Sind provincial government found itself under pressure by various Muslim groups to ban the *Satyārth Prakāsh* of Svami Dayananda Saraswati. Muslims objected in particular to chapter 14, in which Dayananda attacked Islam at considerable length, attempting to show that it was a false religion based on ignorance and greed. On June 25, 1943, the *Hindustan Times* claimed that the Sind government was considering just such a ban. This both shocked and angered the Arya Samaj, since it was to them another example of Muslim intolerance. The Sarvadeshik Sabha telegrammed its answer to the Sind government: "Shocked learning your ministry's contemplated move proscribing *Satyarth Prakash,* Aryas' indispensable religious book. If materialised, all Aryas will accept challenge. Ready sacrificing all for religious liberty as in Hyderabad State. Please give up unwisest proposed step avoiding bitter struggle."[74] The Sind government responded that it would not take such a step. But there was increasing pressure from Muslim groups, particularly the Muslim League.

On August 13, 1943, the League passed a resolution urging all

Muslim governments and the government of India to ban the
Satyārth Prakāsh. It reiterated this demand at its annual session
held in Karachi during that December.[75] The Arya Samaj objected
and stepped up its pressure by calling a Mahasammelan. It met in
Delhi on February 20-22, the fourth and last such gathering before
independence. The Delhi Mahasammelan had as its president
Dr. Shyama Prasad Mukerjee, a non-Arya, but prominent leader of
the Hindu community. Three thousand delegates came and according to Arya estimates, fifty thousand men and women attended.
Numerous resolutions were passed but the center of focus remained
the issues in Sind and relations between Hindus, Muslims, and the
British regime. The Delhi Mahasammelan brought together Aryas
and also members of the Sanatan Dharm Sabhas, who saw this as a
struggle between the two religious communities.[76]   Other units
within the Samaj held meetings during the spring and summer. The
Sind government vacillated but finally on October 26, 1944,
announced that "The Government of Sind is pleased to direct that
no copies of the book entitled 'Satyarth Prakash' written by Swami
Dayananda Saraswati shall be printed or published unless Chapter
XIV (Chapter fourteen) thereof is omitted."[77]

The Arya Samaj continued its campaign against this ban and in
August 1945, the Sind government announced a modification of its
ruling.[78] This was, however, unacceptable to the Samaj, but since
the ban had not been effectively enforced and was due to lapse in
September 1946, they waited to see what would happen next.
Within ten days of its lapse, the Sind government restored the
ban.[79] This was the last straw, and on January 1, 1947, the All-
India Satyarth Defense Committee led by Mahatma Narayan
Svami announced that

the Sind Provincial elections are now over. People of Sind
cannot now legitimately ask for further postponement of Satyagraha on the issue of ban on the Satyarth Prakash in Sind.

I, accompanied by Rajguru Pandit Dhurendra Shastri and
Lala Khushal Chand Annand, am reaching Karachi on 3rd
January 1947. Satyagraha will be launched in consultation
with the workers of the Sind Provincial Arya Pratinidhi Sabha.

I call upon the Aryas, Arya Samajes and Provincial Arya
Pratinidhi Sabhas to send to me the names of the persons who
may reach Karachi to offer Satyagraha on a week's notice.[80]

The *satyāgraha* campaign began on January 14, 1947, and was over by the 20th. The Sind government simply ignored the *satyā-grahis* and refused to arrest them even when they publicly defied the ban. The Aryas interpreted this as a capitulation by the Sind government and so terminated their campaign as another successful struggle for the protection of their rights. Following the Sind campaign the Arya Samaj was soon engulfed by the chaos and confusion of partition and independence. The Samaj lost property and valuable institutions, such as the Lahore Dayanand Anglo-Vedic College in the area of the newly-created state of Pakistan, and thousands of its members became refugees. In the 1950s and 1960s the Samaj went through a period of reestablishing lost institutions and reorganizing itself.

We have seen here only a brief outline of the Arya Samaj, yet that outline is impressive because of the scope and variety of Samaj achievements. The personal vision of Svami Dayananda Saraswati was transformed into an ideology and a movement. This ideology was sufficiently persuasive to attract individuals who, in many cases, made a lifetime commitment to the Arya Samaj. These ideas provided for numerous individuals a coherent explanation of the past and present as well as a method for the creation of a reformed Hinduism and a return to ancient greatness. Converts to Arya ideology gave to this movement their personal abilities and resources, which in turn were used to create, manage, and sustain a large number of organisations and institutions. The Samaj launched programs in the areas of education, proselytization, communal defense, social uplift, and social service. As they struggled to defend their own ideology and give substance to Dayananda's vision, they also contributed to the heightening of religious tensions, first in the north and then into south India. The Arya Samaj also was able to continue to draw new members into the movements and to expand its institutional structure within and beyond India. As a result the Samaj played an important role in nineteenth- and twentieth-century India. Its impact can only be crudely estimated at this time, since extensive research would be needed before we could compile a detailed and verified account of its history and of the areas of its influence. Scholars have been correct in seeing the Arya Samaj as historically significant, but we must await the future before this significance can be clearly delineated. In the meantime this article can act as a starting point for students of the Arya Samaj and its place in recent history.

Notes

1. J.N. Farquhar, *Modern Religious Movements in India* (New York: Macmillan, 1919), pp. 102-29; and Lala Lajpat Rai, *The Arya Samaj* (London: Longmans, Green, 1915) are both generalized in their approach. In Hindi the best general history of the Samaj is the two-volume work by Indra Vidyavachaspati, *Ārya Samāj kā Itihās* (Delhi: Sarvadeshik Arya Pratinidhi Sabha, 1957). For a study of the Samaj in the Punjab, see Kenneth W. Jones, *Arya Dharm: Hindu Consciousness in 19th-Century Punjab* (Berkeley: University of California Press, 1976) and his article, "Social Change and Religious Movements in Nineteenth-Century Punjab," in *Social Movement in India*, ed. M.S.A. Rao (Delhi: Manohar, 1979), 2:1-16. For additional bibliographic references, see Kenneth W. Jones, "Sources for Arya Samaj History," in W. Eric Gustafson and Kenneth W. Jones, eds., *Sources on Punjab History* (Delhi: Manohar, 1975), pp. 130-70.

2. Numerous biographies of Dayananda have been written, but the most authoritative and scholarly is by J.F. Jordens, *Dayānanda Saraswatī, His Life and Times* (Delhi: Oxford University Press, 1978). A useful, older biography was done by Har Bilas Sarda, *Life of Dayanand Saraswati, World Teacher* (Ajmer: Vedic Yantralaya, 1946).

3. For a discussion of Dayananda's basic ideology, see Jordens, *Dayānanda Saraswatī*, pp. 99-126, 245-95; and Jones, *Arya Dharm*, pp. 30-36.

4. Sarda, *Life of Dayanand*, pp. 405-12, and Yudhishthir Mīmānsak, *Rishi Dayānanda kē Granthōn kā Itihās* (Ajmer: Prachyavidhya-Pratishthan, 1949), pp. 16-46.

5. Jones, *Arya Dharm*, pp. 36-50.

6. Sarda, *Life of Dayanand*, has lengthy lists of those places visited by Dayananda with the dates of each visit, see pages 337-47.

7. Jones, *Arya Dharm*, pp. 243-44, and Sarda, *Life of Dayanand*, pp. 324-36.

8. Jones, *Arya Dharm*, pp. 67-77.

9. Ibid., p. 85.

10. Ibid., pp. 88-90.

11. Ibid., pp. 90-93.

12. Ibid., pp. 230-31; also see Vidyavachaspati, *Ārya Samāj kā Itihās*, 2:212-13.

13. Jones, *Arya Dharm*, pp. 235-41.

14. Ibid., pp. 241-79: also see N.G. Barrier, "The Arya Samaj and Congress Politics in the Punjab, 1894-1908," *Journal of Asian Studies* 26, no. 3 (May 1967), and by the same author, "The Punjab Government and Communal Politics, 1870-1908," *Journal of Asian Studies* 27, no. 3 (May 1968).

15. Jones, *Araya Dharm*, pp. 299-303.

16. Ibid., pp. 280-99.

17. Kenneth W. Jones, "Ham Hindū Nahīn: Arya-Sikh Relations, 1877-1905," *Journal of Asian Studies* 32, no. 3 (May 1973):463.

18. Ibid., p. 471.

19. Jones, *Arya Dharm*, pp. 303-12; for a study of the aftermath of Arya Samaj uplift work among untouchables, see James M. Sebring, "The Formation of New Castes: A Probable Case from North India," *American Anthropologist* 74, no. 3 (June 1972):487-600.

20. Ibid., pp. 193-202.

21. Ibid., pp. 215-23.

22. *Census of India, 1901 General Report*, Subsidiary Table No. 1, pp. 289, 395.

23. Radhuvir Singh Shastri, *Sarvadeshik Arya Pratinidhi Sabha ka Sankshipt Itihas* (New Delhi: Sarvadeshik Arya Pratinidhi Sabha, vikrami samvat 2018), p. 1.

24. Jordens, *Dayananda Saraswati*, p. 215.

25. Radhuvir Singh Shastri, *Sarvadeshik*, pp. 1-6.

26. Ibid., p. 8.

27. Carolyn M. Elliot, "Decline of a Patrimonial Regime: The Telengana Rebellion in India, 1946-51," *Journal of Asian Studies* 34, no. 1 (November 1974):56.

28. Vidyavachaspati, *Arya Samaj ka Itihas*, 2:47.

29. Ibid., p. 48.

30. Ibid., pp. 41, 47.

31. Ibid., p. 48.

32. Ibid., p. 186.

33. Radhuvir Singh Shastri, *Sarvadeshik*, p. 5.

34. Ibid., p. 5; also see Vidyavachaspati, *Arya Samaj ka Itihas*, 2:183. Apparently a provincial sabha was organized for Burma in the late 1930s.

35. *Census of India, General Reports* for 1911, 1921, and 1931.

36. These figures are approximate and may be on the low side. As with much of the information concerning the Arya Samaj, extensive research would needed to establish accurate data. See *Arya Dairektari arthat Samvat 1997 Vikrami ki Arya Jagat ki Pragatiyon ka Vivaran* (Delhi: Sarvadeshik Arya Pratinidhi Sabha, vikrami samvat 1978), pp. 43-81.

37. *Arya Dairebtari*, pp. 120-33.

38. Ibid., pp. 86-119. No definition was given as to exactly which institutions were classed as Gurukulas and why.

39. Gurukula Kangri Vishwavidyalaya, *An Introduction* (Hardwar: Gurukul Kangri Vishwavidyalaya, 1962) p. 25.

40. Svami Shraddhanand, *Inside Congress* (Bombay: Phoenix Publications, 1946), pp. 46-123.

41. Vidyavachaspati. *Arya Samaj ka Itihas*, 2:130-31; G.R. Thursby, *Hindu-Muslim Relations in British India* (Leiden: E.J. Brill, 1975), pp. 137-45.

42. Thursby, *Hindu-Muslim Relations*, p. 161.

43. Ibid., pp. 150-51; also see *Bharatiya Hindu Shuddhi Sabha ki Pratham Varshik Report* (Agra: Shanti Press, vikrami samvat 1980) and other annual reports through 1927.

44. N. Gerald Barrier, *Banned: Controversial Literature and Political Control in British India, 1907-1947* (Columbia: University of Missouri Press, 1974), p. 99.

45. Vidyavachaspati, *Arya Samaj ka Itihas*, 2:167.

46. James Reid Graham, "The Arya Samaj as a Reformation in Hinduism with Special Reference to Caste" (Ph.D. dissertation, Yale University, 1942), pp. 537, 563-69.

47. Radhuvir Singh Shastri, *Sarvādeshik*, p. 18.

48. Ibid.

49. Vidyavachaspati, *Ārya Samāj kā Itihās*, 2:136-41.

50. Radhuvir Singh Shastri, *Sarvadēshik*, p. 19.

51. Ibid., p. 141.

52. Ibid., p. 25.

53. Vidyavachaspati, *Ārya Samāj kā Itihās*, 2:157.

54. Ibid., p. 158.

55. Ibid., pp. 158-64.

56. Radhuvir Singh Shastri, *Sarvadēshik* p. 99; Thursby, *Hindu-Muslim Relations*, p. 92; and Vidyavachaspati, *Ārya Samāj kā Itihās*, 2:162-63. Considerable competition and some animosity developed between the Arya Vir Dal and the Rashtriya Swayam Sevak Sangh. See *Sarvadēshik Ārya Pratinidhi Sabhā kē Nirnay* (Delhi: Sarvadeshik Arya Pratinidhi Sabha, vikrami samvat 2018), pp. 15-17.

57. Vidyavachaspati, *Ārya Samāj kā Itihās*, 2:169.

58. Ibid., p. 172.

59. Ibid., pp. 168-71.

60. Radhuvir Singh Shastri, *Sarvadeshik*, p. 25.

61. Vidyavachaspati, *Ārya Samāj kā Itihās*, 2:175.

62. Ibid., p. 176.

63. Ibid., pp. 176-77.

64. Ibid., p. 180.

65. Radhuvir Singh Shastri, *Sarvadeshik*, p. 45.

66. Elliot, "Decline of a Patrimonial Regime," pp. 30-35.

67. *The Arya Samaj in Hyderabad* (Published by order of His Exalted Highness the Nizam's Government, n.d.), p. 1.

68. Elliot, "Decline of a Patrimonial Regime," pp. 35-36.

69. *The Arya Samaj in Hyderabad*, p. 2.

70. *Nizam Defence Examined and Exposed, A Rejoinder to the Pamphlet "The Arya Samaj in Hyderabad"* (Delhi: International Aryan League, n.d.), p. 5.

71. Vidyavachaspati, *Ārya Samāj kā Itihās*, vol. 2.

72. Elliot, "Decline of a Patrimonial Regime," p. 36.

73. Vidyavachaspati, *Ārya Samāj kā Itihās*, 2:209-10.

74. S. Chandra, *The Case of the Satyarth Prakash (Light of Truth) in Sind* (Delhi: International Aryan League, 1947), p. 20.

75. Ibid., pp. 20, 27.

76. Vidyavachaspati, *Ārya Samāj kā Itihās*, 2:142-43.

77. Chandra, *The Case of the Satyarth Prakash*, pp. 60-61.

78. Ibid., p. 71.

79. Ibid., p. 82.

80. Ibid., p. 94.

3

THE RAMAKRISHNA MOVEMENT: A STUDY IN RELIGIOUS CHANGE

George M. Williams

The pattern of ultimate concern of an organization or movement can be more complex to portray than that of an individual. Such is indeed the case with the Ramakrishna movement. This movement has been credited with championing the cultural revival or renaissance of modern India, defending the total religious heritage of the Hindu tradition when others were in retreat, and purifying Hindu monasticism so that its members have become exemplars of Indian spirituality.

This study will focus on the religious ideals of this movement, seeking to articulate what has been of ultimate concern.[1] Initially, nine descriptors of the pattern of ultimacy of the Ramakrishna movement will be presented. Then, the second portion of this study will offer a diachronic examination of this general pattern of ultimacy, which has led to three findings: (1) There are variations diachronically in the relative emphases given different elements of the pattern of ultimacy. As in cooking, all the ingredients may be the same, but different portions yield cake, bread, or saltine crackers. For a *māyāvādi*, in this case a historian of religions, the difference in taste is worth noting.[2] (2) There are inner tensions within the major elements of the pattern of ultimacy. None of the central ideals of the movement are without an internal dynamism which prohibits later followers of the realization of Sri Ramakrishna from emphasizing an aspect of a central ideal. (3) Six periods of relative emphasis of various ideals emerge over the century of existence (1880-1980) of the Ramakrishna movement. Because of the limits of this study, a full discussion of each period cannot be attempted; rather, a selective discussion will be undertaken to emphasize salient religious changes within the movement. The reader will need mentally to relist general ideals which do not change in each period.

I

The General Descriptors of the Ramakrishna Movement

During the history of the Ramakrishna movement, nine descriptors have been used repeatedly by members and others to describe it. It has been portrayed as monistic, monastic, universal, tolerant, nonsectarian, liberal, humanitarian, progressive, and scientific. These descriptors are linguistically rooted in the religious ferment of nineteenth-century Indian religion. Yet, all of them continue to be used to describe the Ramakrishna movement today. The descriptors have a general linguistic history but also serve the special function of carriers of truth claims for the movement's teachings. It is this latter function of the terms which will be briefly presented in this section. These descriptors reveal the invisible "convictional worldview" of Ramakrishna Vedanta. What follows is a general overview of the nine descriptors:

Monistic. The Ramakrishna movement found in the Vedanta a central truth: that truth is one. Unity of life, of mankind, of religion, of the self, of God, is an unequivocal one. The Personal God and the Impersonal are the same.

Monastic. True spirituality requires renunciation of the fruits of one's actions. The monastic life promotes spiritual growth through actual renunciation.

Universal. The Ramakrishna movement, its organizational super-structure of the Ramakrishna Math and Mission, or its message of the *sanātana dharma* (the eternal principles) are not a religion. Its teachings are the universal foundation of all religion or, more properly, of spirituality itself.

Tolerant. The Vedanta of the Ramakrishna movement proclaims that all religions are true. It teaches humanity the basis for universal tolerance, which is "unity in diversity." Ramakrishna Vedanta teaches that all faiths—Hindu, Muslim, Christian, Buddhist —lead to the Godhead.

Nonsectarian. The Ramakrishna movement is not a sect within Hinduism, but a defender of the entire Hindu tradition. It demonstrates that each of the paths *(jñāna-mārga, bhakti-mārga,* and *karma-mārga)* and any sect (whether Vaiṣṇava, Śaiva, or Śakta) is true. All spiritual tendencies lead to the goal of unity.

Liberal. The movement is dedicated to the social uplift of mankind through the goals of liberty, justice, equality. According to the principles of the *sanātana dharma,* religion and society throughout the world can be reformed.

Humanitarian. The Ramakrishna movement is dedicated to the service of all creatures. Its programs of relief in famine and flood are renowned throughout India. Service to the suffering is service to the Godhead.

Progressive. Education aids the progress of humanity. The Ramakrishna movement has emphasized the need for mass education, especially for the lower and underprivileged classes. That education has as its central purpose to raise the masses to the level at which they may realize the eternal principles.

Scientific. As truth is one, so also is true science and true spirituality. Western science and the eternal principles can be taught and practiced together. Both will awaken mankind.

This delineation of these nine descriptors of the Ramakrishna movement is necessarily stark. If we now proceed diachronically to study these descriptors, we will see how they are valued within the pattern of ultimacy which the movement perceives as unified, as unified as the *sanātana dharma* itself.

II

The Historical Periods of the Ramakrishna Movement

Our interest in the various periods of the ideals of the Ramakrishna movement leads us to suspend judgment concerning the validity of its central truth claim (i.e., that the teachings of Sri Ramakrishna are the eternal principles of spirituality). Instead, we will look at each period to see how the descriptors function as elements in the pattern of ultimate concern in each period.

Period One.   Sri Ramakrishna Paramahamsa (c. 1880-86): Birth

By 1880 a small movement had begun to form around the person of a Kālī priest at the Dakshineswar Temple outside Calcutta.   They were drawn to a priest of an endowed temple who had deviated significantly from his expected role as *pūjāri* or *brahman* ritualist.   Sri Ramakrishna behaved as a *sannyāsi*; even though he was married to Saradamani Devi, the marriage was never consummated.   Years of practice of various *sādhanās* (spiritual disciplines) led him to teach that all religions were essentially true.   He taught that the God of each, whether Vaiṣṇava, Śakta, Christian, or Muslim, was the same and could be worshipped according to one's inherent preference for the type of religious practice.   He demonstrated exceptional spiritual powers (*siddhis*), being able to go into prolonged trance states such as *nirvikalpa samādhi* or induce altered states of consciousness in others.

The message of Sri Ramakrishna centered on God-realization and renunciation of "women and gold."   Professor C.T.K. Chari correctly observed a unique feature of Ramakrishna Vedanta: the denial of the law of the excluded middle.[3]   His mystical experience of *neti, neti* and the devotional experience of Śakti's grace form a "mystical unity of opposites" transcending the laws of identity, non-contradiction, and the excluded middle.   *Brahman*, the impersonal absolute, and Śakti, the personal Godhead, were the same. *Jñāna* and *bhakti* led to the goal.   Ramakrishna realized that even the philosophies of *advaita*, *viśiṣṭādvaita*, and *dvaita* (monism, qualified monism, and dualism) were different only because of the varying spiritual tendencies within the individual, but that they ultimately resolved themselves as different ways of expressing the same truth.   Ramakrishna taught that he could know this because he was an *iśvarakoti*, one who could merge with the Absolute and return.   By implication, he taught that he was an *avatāra*, for he was not different than Kṛṣṇa or Rāma.

Sri Ramakrishna appears to have instructed his disciples in two ways regarding renunciation.   For householders he taught the mental renunciation "of the *Gita*," but for those who had never touched women, he taught that they also renounce "in actuality." His requirement to renounce "gold" set them against the world of material goods and left only mendicancy.

The monastic order which bears his name did not solely come from his message or his practice. He initiated no one as a *sannyāsi* in his lifetime. He entitled no one svami nor set a rule for them. He did ask his favorite disciple, Narendranath Datta, the future Vivekananda, to keep his "boys together" and to "teach them."

The differences between the teachings and practice of Sri Ramakrishna as noted from direct evidence, and the message (*sanātana dharma*) of the Order (the Ramakrishna Math and Mission) which followed him can be demonstrated by briefly reviewing the nine descriptors. Ramakrishna's monism dissolved *advaita, viśiṣṭādvaita*, and *dvaita* into the experience of truth's unity. Ramakrishna's monasticism was as a *brāhman pūjāri* in a Śakta temple, not a monastery. It entailed total abstinence from sexual contact and the touching of money. Ramakrishna's universalism was total; at the highest level, there were no distinctions. Liberal religion in the 1880s taught that religion based on reason could rid the world of superstition, idolatry, and the social ills which weighted down the men and women. However, Ramakrishna was not interested in any of these issues, and therefore, cannot be judged a religious liberal. Nonsectarianism was addressed by Sri Ramakrishna when he stated that he did not want to start any sect. This may well have been the reason he initiated no one and taught that all Hindu sects—Vaiṣṇava, Śaiva, Śakta, Tantra—were equally true. He himself did not affiliate with any of the existing monastic orders in India. Yet, he affirmed their worth as equally capable of bringing one to God-realization. He practiced Śakti-pūjā (worship of the Mother Goddess Kālī) and taught that the best path (*mārga*) in this evil age was *bhakti* (devotionalism).

The descriptor of tolerant, as used by the Ramakrishna movement to stress non-conversion to another faith, because all faiths are true—does not fit Sri Ramakrishna. He did believe in reconversion of Indians to Hindu sects. Sri Ramakrishna used all his spiritual powers to bring Narendra to do *pūjā* to Kālī in her manifestation at the Dakshineswar Temple as a basalt image. In so doing, Narendra was "converted" from his faith and practice as a Brahmo Samaji.[4] Ramakrishna's humanitarianism was traditionally Hindu. He taught service to all beings (the five *dānas*) and taught nothing of work (*karma-yoga*) or its dignity for *sannyāsis*. Ramakrishna was not the source of the Ramakrishna movement's teaching about being progressive, in the way in which the term acquires meaning in the Hindu renaissance. He was anti- or non-intellectual. He did not believe that education aided spiritual growth. In fact, he often stated that too much study was not helpful. Finally, Ramakrishna was not scientific. He did teach the oneness of truth, but was not scientific, even in the peculiar sense of the Indian renaissance.

Sri Ramakrishna's extraordinary achievements were in the area of the human spirit, not in the intellectual realm, for he was almost illiterate. His humility, humanity, and purity are a monument to the heights that few reach, even the most saintly. But Ramakrishna was not the single source of the Ramakrishna movement's teachings and practice.

Period Two. Svami Vivekananda's 'Militant Hinduism' (1886-1902): Infancy

The death of Sri Ramakrishna in August 1886, left a nascent movement with an appointed leader and the single instruction of "staying together." Yet, the four final years of their master's life had left "his boys" with the resolve to continue his central concerns of God-realization and renunciation of "women and gold." Some began to exhibit spiritual powers such as those so amply demonstrated by Ramakrishna himself, but Narendra discouraged the acquisition of these powers. They all practiced severe disciplines (*sādhanās*) in order "to see God." Visions occurred but certainty about God did not, at least for Narendra.

The main spiritual routine during their master's lifetime had been *bhakti*. Ramakrishna-pūjā was now added to Kālī-pūjā. The movement had become a traditional localized ascetic group of *bhaktas*, dedicated to devotion for their guru and Kālī. When Narendra left the group in 1890, he condemned their practices.[5] He intended never to have contact with them again, due to his frustration with their excessive devotionalism. Yet, he contacted them from America in 1893, after years of silence, and tried to win them to his mission. When he returned triumphantly to India in 1897, he soon encountered almost total resistance to his plan from his former fellow disciples.[6] Only through the dominance of his will were these *śakta-sannyāsis* moved from their central focus on God-realization through renunciation and *pūjā* to trying "his plan" and "the Mission," which involved work in the world.

Vivekananda actually used all nine descriptors which are representative of the elements in the Ramakrishna movement's pattern of ultimacy. He joined the realizations of Sri Ramakrishna with the liberal ideals of the Brahmo Samaj.[7]

Monism. Advaita Vedānta was the rational articulation of the Absolute and the principles of oneness. The *māyāvāda* doctrine of Sankara was accepted as definitive. But in the realm of multiplicity, *viśiṣṭādvaita* validated one's involvement in the world. Ramakrishna's radical destruction of the epistemological differences of *advaita*, *viśiṣṭādvaita*, and *dvaita* in his experiential harmony of all approaches can be portrayed by the model of the wheel with three spokes coming to the oneness of truth at the center. Vivekananda's solution to the same problem used the model of the ladder and postulated, as Professor Nalini Devdas correctly observed, "a reasoned system in which *Dvaita* and *Viśiṣṭādvaita* are the stages and *Advaita* is the goal."[8]

The thirst for the realization of God as *brahman* or *śakti* or *Kālī* or even in Ramakrishna as the *avatāra* of the *satya yuga* was relegated by Vivekananda to a subordinate role for intermittent periods of time after 1890. What became more important than realizing God and attaining *mukti* was his "God the poor and the miserable." But as a *viśiṣṭādvaitan* the poor and God were the same, only perceived from different levels of reality. For the poor he would forego his own liberation—the traditional reason for the total renunciation of the *sannyāsi*. Nor did it matter much experientially whether or not Sri Ramakrishna was really God. Epistemologically, Ramakrishna's *avatāra* nature vouchsafed the unity of *brahman* and *śakti*, for only an *avatāra* could return from merger in the oneness of the Godhead and know its identity with the God of form. Yet Vivekananda's ladder model placed *advaita* at the top as the truest philosophical expression and relegated *avatāras* to the relatively real of *vivārta* (appearance).

Monasticism. Narendra became Svami Vivekananda at the suggestion of the Raja of Khetri. When Vivekananda went to America, he claimed to be a monk of the oldest order of *sannyāsis* in India, that of Sankaracharya.[9] He allowed himself to be known as a *brahmin*, he identified himself as being from Bombay or even Madras, and was credentialed to speak before the World Parliament of Religions on the basis of these verbal claims. After his remarks in defense of Hinduism and often at the expense of other Indian religious groups (the Brahmo Samaj and Theosophy, in particular), some attacked him as a liar. These attacks almost aborted his work in America, but he managed to get resolutions of support from the Raja of Khetri and from lay disciples in Madras proving that he represented pure Hinduism. His former *gurubhāis* did not provide him with the needed credentials.

When Vivekananda returned to India in 1897 and asserted his leadership over the circle of Ramakrishna monks, he accommodated more to their monasticism than they did to his. (This will be treated in the next period.) When they accused him of being Western and said that his teachings were not compatible with those of Sri Ramakrishna, Vivekananda responded "with great fervour": "How do you know that these are not in keeping with his ideas? Do you want to shut Sri Ramakrishna, the embodiment of infinite ideas, within your own limits? I shall break these limits and scatter his ideas broadcast all over the world. He never enjoined me to introduce his worship and the like. The methods of spiritual practice, concentration and meditation and other high ideals of religion that he taught—those we must realise and teach mankind. Infinite are the ideas and infinite are the paths that lead to the Goal. I was not born to create a new sect in this world, too full of sects already."[10]

Vivekananda's monasticism would lead the movement away from total renunciation of gold to its use for mankind. His was an "in-the-world" asceticism which was not practiced by their master, Sri Ramakrishna.

Universalism. The nineteenth-century quest for the foundations of universal religion which proved the unity of all religions was founded by Svami Vivekananda in Vedanta. He equated the principles of Vedanta and *sanātana dharma*. These were the principles of spirituality with its realization of the One. This was the pure Hinduism.

Toleration. Sri Ramakrishna had realized all religions as true. This was experiential and grounded in the special nature of his experiments with Islam, Christianity, and the Hindu sects (such as Tantra, Śakta, Vaiṣṇava, Śaiva). Neither Svami Vivekananda, nor any other monk known to the author, ever carried out his own experiments. They all accepted the truth of all religions on the basis of their master's work. Svami Vivekananda tried to lead in some comparative studies—reminiscent of those at the Brahmo Samaj. But no one actually went into the practice of Islam or

Taoism. The Ramakrishna movement's outer form would be Hindu.

Vivekananda's message asserted that Hinduism is the most tolerant of all religions in the world. It accepted all as true. Unity was the basis of tolerance. But as the defender of Hinduism at a time when cultural inferiority was a bitter reality, Svami Vivekananda often lapsed into what Sister Nivedita (Margaret Noble, a British disciple) termed his "militant Hinduism." Taken out of this historical context, many of his remarks about Christianity, Judaism, Buddhism, and Islam appear hypercritical and do little to further this ideal of tolerance. But these critical remarks were often cherished more by his countrymen desiring some area of superiority than the mild statements of unity and tolerance.

Nonsectarian. Vivekananda applied the doctrine of universality to the Hindu tradition and sought to lessen any divisiveness among its sects. He wanted to lead all Indians to a purified Hinduism, diverse enough for all. Following Sri Ramakrishna's realizations about difference resting on the variety of spiritual paths (*mārgas*), Vivekananda taught that there were four tendencies through which mankind sought God. Hinduism was the only religion that recognized that the religious capacities of persons vary according to their inner tendencies (*saṁskāras*).[11] These capacities must be channeled into a proper method or path (yoga), and only Hinduism taught the four yogas (*jñāna, bhakti, karma,* and *rāja*).[12] Each of these paths had the same goal, oneness with *brahman*. (He did not seem to notice that *jñāna* yoga and *rāja* yoga covered much of the same spiritual territory—the non-rational or intuitional knowledge of the Absolute.[13]) Vivekananda insisted that *karma* yoga was the best path for the present and even *sannyāsis* should forsake other paths and work for the awakening of all.

Liberalism. Liberal religion in the nineteenth century was founded on beliefs in universal reason, in progress, and in the potential of the masses—democracy or socialism. Justice, liberty, and equality were liberal religion's principles. These taught that the lack of food and clothing was unjust and a social rather than a personal ill. Therefore, liberal religion sought social reform through legal redress and educational uplift for the underprivileged and downtrodden. These ideas came to Vivekananda as part of his education in Scottish Church College in Calcutta and through his involvement as a member of the Brahmo Samaj (1878-85). These ideas were not primary concerns of Sri Ramakrishna—not in these ways. When Svami Vivekananda acted as a liberal, he called for the end of puranic superstitions and for a reform of the religion of "don't touchism" (a reference to untouchability and defilement by touch) and the religion of the kitchen (a reference to the restrictions on intercaste dining). At times he even predicted an end to the caste system itself because the principle of *sanātana dharma*, and consequently purified Hinduism, was oneness—even of caste. In the *satya yuga*, which was coming into being through the preaching of "fiery mantras" to the masses, all would become *brāhmins*. Svami Vivekananda was especially critical of priestcraft. He predicted it would lose its business. He was hurt deeply when his *gurubhāis* resembled puranic priests instead of *advaita sannyāsis*. He attacked their devotions on many occasions before he finally lapsed into silence:

> You think you understand Shri Ramakrishna better than my-self? You think Jnana is dry knowledge to be attained by a desert path, killing out the tenderest faculties of the heart. Your Bhakti is sentimental nonsense which makes one impotent. You want to preach Ramakrishna as you have understood him which is mighty little. Hands off! Who cares for your Rama-krishna? Who cares for your Bhakti and Mukti? Who cares what the scriptures say? I will go to hell cheerfully a thousand times, if I can rouse my countrymen, immersed in Tamas, and make them stand on their own feet and be Men, inspired with the spirit of Karma-Yoga. I am not a follower of Ramakrishna or any one, I am a follower of him only who carries out my plans! I am not a servant of Ramakrishna or any one, but of him only who serves and helps others, wit caring for his own Mukti.[14]

Vivekananda demanded that his *gurubhāis* be "in-the-world" ascetics. He demanded that these *sannyāsis* who had renounced the world to gain *mukti* must become servants of the poor and underprivileged. He called it karma yoga, but as Professor A.L. Basham has observed, this respect for physical work is a purely Western idea.[15] Vivekananda's genius was to establish the connection between the *Bhagavadgītā's* call to action with India's modern awakening, ignoring its demand that all action be given to Kṛṣṇa as *pūjā*. This awakening linked social reform in India to liberal, progressive education of the masses. In the nineteenth century liberal religionists believed that this was the formula for world reform. It would end in a brotherhood of mankind and a commonwealth of nations.

Humanitarianism. Svami Vivekananda's liberal principles for social reform were supported by humanitarian commitments. His "Practical Vedanta" taught karma yoga as service to all creatures (*seva dharma*). He formulated "the Plan" for dedicated *sannyāsis* to teach the masses industrial and agricultural technology, develop them intellectually, and then raise them to their true nature through the highest principles of Advaita Vedanta. He differed with Sri Ramakrishna in that he believed that even householders could be taught the principles of unity with the Absolute, the relative reality of the university (*māyāvāda*), and renunciation while remaining in the world of duty and toil. He believed that even *sannyāsis* should give up their selfish goal of *mukti* and work to feed, educate, and lift the masses to their true greatness, in full knowledge of the Divine within.

Progressive. Nineteenth-century liberal religion linked social reform, humanitarianism, and progressive education. Education was the key to awakening the masses of the world from the darkness of ignorance. Progressive education was universal in principle and democratic in philosophy. Vivekananda believed that proper study would help the paralyzing ills of poverty and superstition. The basic content of these studies would be the Vedanta, to learn the principles of true spirituality, and Western science, to utilize the discoveries which would better material existence. First one must eat; then one can explore spirituality's heights.

Scientific. As just mentioned, Svami Vivekananda sought to bring the science of the West to India. He believed that Vedanta was the only scientific religion. Since its principles were grounded in the Absolute, there could be no incompatibility with science.[16]

Period Three. Svami Brahmananda and the Young Order (1902-22): Adolescence

When Svami Vivekananda returned to Calcutta after seven years' absence, he asserted his right to lead his former *gurubhāis*, who were then staying in their Math in Alambazar. Svami Vivekananda called a meeting on May 1, 1897, at a layman's home in Calcutta and founded the Ramakrishna Mission. Through funds

from his Western disciples Vivekananda purchased property for
Belur Math and brought the monks together there. He appointed
their implicit spiritual leader, Svami Brahmananda, as head of the
Math. The monks called Brahmananda "the son of Ramakrishna,"
because of his high devotional qualities, and *maharaj*, because they
recognized him as their spiritual leader. Brahmananda was later
appointed head of the Ramakrishna Mission, six months before
Vivekananda died (1902). The official histories of the Order note
that Svami Vivekananda had lost interest in these organizations
several years after founding them.[17]

Svami Brahmananda placed spirituality above humanitarian
service. He placed total control of the Mission under monks. He
organized the monastic life and slowly incorporated Vivekananda's
"plan" of action to feed, education, and spiritualize the "poor and
miserable" of India.

The nine descriptors of the Ramakrishna movement's pattern of
ultimacy received a different emphasis during this period. The
process of harmonizing may again be observed. The realization of
Sri Ramakrishna and the teachings of Svami Vivekananda were
joined as one:

Monism. Svami Brahmananda did not share Vivekananda's
periodic rejections of *bhakti*. He made it a central part of the
Ramakrishna Math and Mission's activities. Birthdays of Ramakrishna, Vivekananda, Sarada Devi were celebrated with *puja* along
with the major Hindu festivals and the birth of Christ.[18] He
brought into the cultus a wide variety of orthodox Hindu ceremonies
such as Rama-, Radha-, and Siva-*samkIrtanas*.[19]

Vivekananda's ladder model with Advaita Vedanta at the top
was established as the unquestioned interpretation of the stages of
philosophical development. Realization of God at the highest level
was the impersonal absolute (*brahman*), but in the world of manifestations worship of one's own favorite expression of God or of godly
men was not only helpful but often necessary.

Monasticism. Svami Brahmananda established the process of a
long tenure before initiation as a *sannyasi*. Eight or more years of
training were necessary before *sannyasa* might be awarded.[20]
Although the Order had few rules, the process of a long inspection
period allowed the instrumental nature of the spiritual practices
(*sadhanas*) to have their result. This extremely long period of
spiritual infancy under the guidance of senior monks allowed the

mature monk to be sent out in relative freedom, carrying the un-written monastic rule within.

Brahmananda believed that the ratio of spiritual training to humanitarian service was three parts to one. He would teach: "The only purpose of life is to know God. Attain knowledge and devotion; then serve God in mankind. Work is not the end of life. Disinterested work is a means of attaining devotions. Keep at least three-fourths of your mind in God. It is enough if you give one-fourth to service."21

Universality and *tolerance* were easily harmonized and fixed in the pattern of ultimacy of the Ramakrishna Order. Any strident tones of spiritual militancy were softened. Complaints by Vaiṣṇavas and Theosophists about Svami Vivekananda's tendency to condemn their religious ideas and practices would cease. No longer would one hear: "We implore the Svami (Vivekananda) to spare us such sweeping denunciations and judgments of men and things, as usually adorn his lips in every meeting now."22

The spiritual quest was divorced from politics. Brahmananda, and succeeding leaders of the Order, would remember Vivekananda's words: "No amount of politics would be of any avail until the masses of India are well educated, well fed and well cared for." Even "the national ideals of India are religion and service,"23 Vivekananda had counseled.

The ideals of a *nonsectarian* Hindu order were quickly harmon-ized. The four yogas began to be a guide for the completion of the monk's training. Karma yoga was subordinated for monks to fourth place. The internal struggles over *bhakti* were silenced with a clear vision of its rightful place as one of the four spiritual tendencies which each monk would develop. Leaders of the Order would never again doubt the Ramakrishna movement's use of *bhakti* or repeat Svami Vivekananda's fear: "What I am most afraid of is the worship room. It is not bad in itself but there is a tendency to make this all in all and set up that old-fashioned non-sense over again—that is what makes me nervous. I know why they busy themselves with these old, effect ceremonials. Their spirit craves for work, but having no outlet they waste their energy in ringing bells and all that."24 More importantly, outsiders would cease to draw attention to differences between its two great leaders, as this Vaiṣṇava journal's obituary notice did in 1902: "Though a disciple of the Paramhangsa, Vivekananda chalked out a path for himself. The Paramhangsa was a bhakta, but Vivekananda preached yoga, and there is a wide divergence between the two cults. Vivekananda also preached the Avatarship of his Guru, the Paramhangsa, and this led Swami Abhayananda (Madam Marie Louise), whom he had initiated and who is now in our midst delighting the Calcutta public by her sweet discourses on the religion of the Lord Gauranga to secede from him."[25]

Humanitarianism. When Svami Vivekananda got ochre-robed monks to do relief work for the first time in 1900, the results could not be measured in physical terms. The Indian press found new heroes, servants of the suffering who were neither Christian missionaries nor foreigners. Despite whatever doubts the *gurubhāis* may have had about a *sannyāsi* laboring for social change, once they were recognized as archetypes of a new spirituality, or an ancient spirituality recovered, there was no turning back. By practicing this ideal, they had adopted it.[26]

Progressive. The dedication of the Order to progressive education was firmly established in this period. As the monks prepared themselves to teach and preach the *sanātana dharma*, studies of the glory of Hindu spirituality emerged. Translations and commentaries on the "most spiritual" scriptures of the Hindu tradition were made available in English and the regional languages of India. These translations often required a more formal study of Sanskrit, English, and at least one regional language other than their own. Mass education meant the founding of schools and colleges and the beginning of journal and magazine publications. The *Brahmavadin* had been started even before the *gurubhāis* of Ramakrishna had begun to work on Vivekananda's "Plan"—and that by lay Madrasi disciples in 1895.[27]

The descriptor of *scientific* was harmonized into the pattern of ultimacy of the Order. By working with this ideal in the speeches of Svami Vivekananda, editors were taught the place of science alongside the *sanātana dharma*. Monks no longer had to have direct exposure to Western educational institutions; they had Vivekananda's canonical statements.

Period Four. A General Convention (1926): Young Adulthood

During the third presidency, that of Svami Sivananda, there occurred an event that would suggest that the Ramakrishna movement had reached a new period in its development. This was the first General Convention in 1926.[28] Svami Saradananda, in giving the Chairman's Address of Welcome, pointed out that the movement had passed through "two stages of opposition and indifference" and had now entered a stage of acceptance.[29] Warning that this might bring "a relaxation of spirits and energy," he called upon the Order to "keep close to their purity and singleness of purpose, their sacrifice and self-surrender."[30]

Svami Sivananda told the Convention: "What we after all know is that Sri Ramakrishna was the mainspring of all that the Swamiji (Vivekananda) spoke and did. It was the Master's message that Swamiji carried from door to door, elucidating it to all in the light of what leading he had from the Master himself."[31] From the point of view of the Order there could be no doubt about the harmony between the teachings of Ramakrishna and Vivekananda.

The Order's monism was so well established that no time was wasted defending its relation to worship. Their collective mind seemed to move between the levels of the real and relative reality when shifting from oneness with *brahman* to *pūjā* before images of Kālī or Ramakrishna. These aids meant nothing on the higher level (Vivekananda's model of the ladder); but the warmth of *bhakti* was as legitimate as any other form of worship (Ramakrishna's model of the spoked wheel with all leading to God-realization equally).

This period in the life of the movement had three major emphases: a repetition of the central principles, a justification of its stand against political involvement, and an administrative concern about the significant growth of humanitarian and educational operations.

Svami Saradananda's summary of the realizations of Sri Ramakrishna at the convention indicates that the descriptors of *monism, universality, tolerance,* and *nonsectarianism* had been routinized. They would be expressed more or less elegantly throughout the succeeding decades, but their meaning was set. One should note in Saradananda's summary that spiritual practices were again producing the *siddhi* of "religion transmitted by touch." This sevenfold summary emphasized the spiritual rather than the humanitarian aspects of the movement,[32] even as they became increasingly involved in the latter:

(1) Every sincere devotee of any religion whatsoever will have

to pass through the three stages of dualism, qualified monism and ultimately monism.

(2) As all jackals howl in the same pitch, so all devotees of any religion whatsoever have declared in the past and will continue to do so in future, their oneness with the Deity on realising the heights of monism.

(3) That there need not be any quarrel between dualism, qualified monism and monism, for each comes in turn to every devotee in accordance with the growth and development of his spiritual life.

(4) The positive part of every religion, in which are found the way and the method of procedure through that, as well as the goal which its sincere follower would reach in the end—is true. But the negative, which speaks of punishment and damnation, eternal or otherwise, for the straggler, is not so, being added to the former for keeping the members of the community from deserting and straying to other folds.

(5) That religion can be transmitted to others by will and touch by the great teachers.

(6) In the Sanatana Dharma of the Vedanta are to be found the eternal principles and laws that govern every single manifestation of religion in a particular time, place and environment.

(7) Stick to your own religion, and think that the followers of other religions are coming to the same goal through different paths.

—Svami Saradananda (1926)[33]

Ramakrishna's concern for humanitarian service was portrayed to the convention by Svami Sivananda in a retelling of Sri Ramakrishna's denial of Narendra's request to be initiated. The lack of the master's initiation was to be interpreted as having a spiritual end. (A more novel interpretation within the Order is the notion of a valid initiation "by touch.")

The Admonition of his Master to forego the selfish enjoyment of Samadhi and dedicate his life to the welfare of the many, seeing Him alone immanent in the Universe, haunted him day and night ever since that memorable day when Sri Ramakrishna in a mood of inward absorption handed over to his illustrious disciple the precious fruits of his own realisations reaped in the course of the crowded period of his Sadhana and made him the happy conduit for the flow of the elixir of spirituality that the world needed at a great psychological period of its history.

—Svami Sivananda (1926)[34]

The inner tension between spiritual liberation (*mukti*) and social service (*seva*) was resolved organizationally rather than philosophically. Svami Sivananda stated that "Any attempt to make a cleavage between the existing Math and Mission works is distinctly against the ideal of Swamiji and therefore stands self-condemned."[35] It was further "unholy and dangerous."[36] "This Math represents the physical body of Sri Ramakrishna. He is always present in this institution. The injunction of the whole Math is the injunction of Sri Ramakrishna. One who worships it, worships him as well. And one who disregards it, disregards our Lord."[37]

Institutionalization had occurred, though in a youthful form. The institution could now speak as a body. *Sannyāsis*, free and renunciate to the world, now worked and spoke as a body. They were now svamis—bound by the will of an Order.

The movement would reaffirm its non-involvement in politics. Even when asked by the Gandhi movement for support, the Ramakrishna Mission and Math stayed out of the political struggle against the British. National leaders seemed to understand, however aloof the Ramakrishna movement remained, that this movement was functioning as "the soul of the nation."[38] The movement might resist politicization, but many of Svami Vivekananda's one million recorded words awakened more than quiet spirituality.

The third concern of humanitarianism and progress was celebrated at the convention with calls for renewed effort, without losing sight of spiritual goals. The Order's relief and educational work set it apart as the exemplar of spirituality in an awakening India.

Period Five.   Indian Independence and the Order: Mature Adulthood

When independence was won in 1947, even though the Order had not taken an active role politically, it had become the archetype of spiritual service. Praised even by Prime Minister Nehru, who otherwise characterized all *sādhus* as parasites, the movement responded to nation-building with differing emphases in its thoroughly routinized pattern of ultimacy. Svami Tejasananda pointed to four

ideals of the Ramakrishna movement in this report from 1954; they
were:

(1) to conduct the activities of the movement for the establishment of fellowship among the followers of different religions,
knowing them all to be so many forms of one Eternal Religion;

(2) to train men so as to make them competent to teach such
knowledge or sciences as were conducive to the material or
spiritual welfare of the masses;

(3) to promote and encourage arts and industries; and

(4) to introduce and spread among the people in general Vedantic
and other religious ideals in the light of the life and teaching of
Sri Ramakrishna.[39]

The descriptors are implicitly there. They seem to have become
so commonplace that the spiritual elements need not be stressed,
while humanitarian concerns head the list. Within the same report
Tejasananda recited an impressive listing of ten concerns which
were being engaged in by the Ramakrishna movement: "liquidation
of illiteracy, rural reconstruction, work among laboring and back-
ward classes, economic and social uplift, removal of untouchability,
female education, relief works in times of natural calamities,
preservation of indigenous culture, dissemination of the accumulated spiritual wisdom of the race, and evolution of a cultural synthesis."[40] The movement had grown from the five Maths and centers
in the lifetime of Svami Vivekananda to 84 Maths and missions in
India alone.[41]

Its educational work in the year 1949-50 was comprised of two
full degree colleges, 17 high schools, 121 lower grade and other
schools, and 50 student houses, with a total enrollment of 27,000
students. Its work for women involved 3,000 students. Its medical
work included 10 general hospitals, one maternity hospital, 65 dispensaries, and reached 13,000 "indoor patients" and two million
"outdoor patients."[42]

While never more than seven hundred monks and a few nuns
served in the Order, their prodigious literary production increased
with more translations, monographs, and series, lectures, cultural
activities, and regular classes. These activities were manifestations
of the vitality of the spiritual quest of the Order.

Professor Gerald Cooke, in a study sponsored by the Christian

Institute for the Study of Religion and Society in Bangalore, reported on the everyday activities of a Ramakrishna Math in south
India in the mid-sixties. Since his study focused on historical and
sociological questions, it is even more impressive that he had such
high words of praise for the movement: "It is not difficult to acknowledge the blessings which the Ramakrishna Math and Mission
brings to India. Indeed it would be humanly and religiously
insensitive not to rejoice in the constructive efforts and results of
this movement."[43]

Yet Cooke noticed that the ideals of universalism and nonsectarianism were working out somewhat differently in history than the
ideal. "For all its stress on a universal, super-sectarian outlook,
the Ramakrishna-Vivekananda movement is rooted in Hindu traditions and in actuality serves primarily Hindus."[44] He noted that
monasticism was not a role of highest prestige "even of young
people who maintain constant contact with the Ramakrishna movement."[45] This observation is reinforced by the field work of Professor David Miller in Bhubaneswar during 1964.[46] Miller noted
another sectarian feature: "In 1964, the trend seemed to be toward
making the deity's presence more immediate to the laity through
the worship of gurus."[47] John Yale and Christopher Isherwood
both speak of the cult of Sri Ramakrishna and its increasing importance during this period.

Period Six. The Call for a Second General Convention: Old Age

By the end of the seventies, with a sensitivity rare for organizational leaders, Svami Gambhirananda, president of the Ramakrishna Math and Mission, had begun to talk about calling a
second General Convention of the movement. On the one hand,
statisticians would be comparing the reports on the activities of the
movement in the seventies with any very successful business:
increased centers, libraries, hospitals, patients, colleges, schools,
students, and all other indices of growth, save one. The number
of svamis remained about seven hundred. On the other hand,
there were definite signs that a new stage in the life of the movement had been entered.

The last of the disciples trained by the direct disciples of Sri
Ramakrishna are reaching their eighties. A totally different generation of leaders will soon take over the movement. Yet to an outsider their spirituality is remarkable in its own right. But the sure

signs of old age are admitted when the body cannot cope with all its demands. The very success of the movement in physical terms (maths, centers, publishing houses, journals, schools, colleges, hospitals, and dispensaries) has overtaxed the Order. It has begun to show signs of not coping fully with life's demands. This pattern of ultimacy does not vary significantly in the articulation (the ideal level) from the previous period. Yet old age almost invariably demands a comparison of the ideals one has lived by with actual achievement. There have been questionings in the author's presence by leading svamis of the movement. The thesis of this study is that the Ramakrishna movement has now entered old age because of the dynamics of its own pattern of ultimacy. It shows signs of not coping with the demands of its own ideals.

This is a historical point of view. The historical actuality does not address the idealist vision. As Cooke observed in his study of the movement, "It is characteristic of Hindu thought and belief to regard historical actuality as less decisive for human life than inner private experience."[48] That ideals will both influence and be influenced by historical contingencies is an unstated assumption in Western thought—an assumption capable of being examined and falsified. Yet, following Cooke's argument, "This devaluation of the objective stuff of history may encourage the view that ideas and exhortations and right inner convictions . . . are enough to constitute" the ideal.[49] The *advaita* view that the realized ideal is real and the *viśiṣṭādvaita* and *dvaita* demand that truth manifest itself in the world reasserts itself. Despite its ways of harmonizing this problem, the movement slights history and reform or revolution.

The Ramakrishna movement is being attacked in Bengal by Communists who actually share the last three ideals of the movement (e.g., reform of society, a belief in progress, and a belief in science). There are increasing incidents of students and lay faculty attacking the curriculum of the movement's schools as superstitious. They find the offerings too narrow to facilitate progress. They find the movement's commitment to reform of the caste system hypocritical.[50] When the Bengali government began "modernizing" the movement's schools, a lawsuit regained control by arguing that the Ramakrishna Mission was literally a minority religion and subject to the constitutional rights of article 25-1.[51] Sadly, in order to retain its schools, the movement no longer claimed to be universal and nonsectarian.

Another line of attack has come from India's new rationalists, who are going back to the very foundations of the descriptors to which the Ramakrishna movement has been able to claim sole ownership for the last eighty of its hundred-year history.[52] The rationalists show other ways of actualizing many of the same ideals. For instance, the liberal commitment to social reform is not hampered by an idealist commitment to the caste system. The new rationalists are joining the Indian Communists in demanding action to alleviate inequality. Sanskrit scholars have argued other ideals within Indian scriptures than monasticism. And it is not unusual to hear Indian scientists charging that the Ramakrishna movement is antiscientific in that the method (falsifiability) and scope (every facet of life being examined critically) have not been utilized in Ramakrishna Vedanta.

What does this have to do with the way the Ramakrishna movement currently emphasizes the various descriptors of its vision of ultimacy? At the beginning of the eighties in India there is pronounced unrest. Whereas it could once be assumed that the Ramakrishna movement articulated the spiritual aspirations of the Indian renaissance (and that was the positive conclusion of Bharati's essay),[53] these very ideals are calling the movement into question. Of the nine descriptors of the movement only the ideal of monasticism is rejected by some as irrelevant for modern India. The other eight have survived into the eighties but function now to judge the Ramakrishna movement's commitment to actualizing them in history.

In December 1978, the author conducted twenty-five interviews with svamis of the Ramakrishna Order in India. Among the svamis were Gambhirananda, Lokeswarananda, and Ananyananda. The conclusions of these interviews regarding the movement's pattern of ultimate concern are (1) that the radical commitment to social reform inherited from the Brahmo Samaj and Svami Vivekananda has been lost, (2) that Vivekananda's criticisms about puranic superstitions and ignorant priestcraft are thought by the members of the movement to apply in no way to the Ramakrishna Math and Mission, (3) that Vivekananda's call to lead worshippers from lower *bhakti* characterized by fear and greed does not apply to any of the worship in the movement's institutions, (4) that reform and spiritual growth are extremely slow processes requiring many lifetimes and the movement should be judged by the progress

made by the few who are totally engaged in those endeavors, (5)
that eternal principles realized by Sri Ramakrishna and Svami
Vivekananda can only reach a small portion of the world's population through Ramakrishna education institutions and publications,
and (6) that monasticism is necessary for God-realization.

Period Seven. The Ramakrishna Movement and the the Future:
Death or Rebirth?

The sixth stage of life can be extended for some time into and
possibly beyond the 1980s. What can be said about the Ramakrishna movement's future? The extraordinary caliber of monks
and nuns who have been attracted to and trained by the Ramakrishna Math will no longer : eet the needs of the movement. The
administration of the publishing, medical, relief, and education
operations will begin to buckle under the strain of its dependence
on monastics as top decision-makers. Much as Roman Catholic-
ism has already begun to experience, the Ramakrishna Mission
will face an ever decreasing supply of monastic leadership. But
whereas the former has a large cadre of lay workers to rely on,
the Ramakrishna Mission does not. Early on, it concluded that
its laymen were not sufficiently interested in its mission nor sufficiently spiritual to be given real leadership. There are no age
statistics available to document what must be stated as a general
observation: the Order is aging faster than it is currently filling
its ranks. How will the Order respond to the deaths which will
strike drastically at its ascetics who are now over sixty? Without
dramatic rejuvenation the Order will enter a marked decline in the
number of svamis available to run its operations. It will face a
dilemma: either allow lay volunteers or hired workers governance
of many activities, or cease their operation. The latter alternative
would mark a certain decline, while the former may not preserve
the Order's hallmark: the incorruptibility of its spiritual leaders.

But its greatest crisis appears to be similar to that of the
Brahmo Samaj when merely speaking great ideals was not enough.
The movement has served the poor and given relief to many
millions in times of acute need, but now other movements who
stress immediate action and the urgency of changing the social
system are addressing reform and revolution in India. For the
Ramakrishna movement to be reborn, it will need to reexperience and
re-vision these nine descriptors in less narrow and parochial terms.

Notes

1. The Ramakrishna movement designates this religious movement in its entirety. Its monastic order is known as the Ramakrishna Math, while its humanitarian concerns are administered by the Ramakrishna Mission.

2. Of the hundreds of works concerned with the Ramakrishna movement and its leaders, only a few deserve special mention. Only one history has emerged, Svami Gambhirananda's *History of the Ramakrishna Math and Mission* (Calcutta: Advaita Ashrama, 1957), which often lacks objectivity. Many svamis have studied the lives and teachings of Ramakrishna and his direct disciples. The bibliographies in Christopher Isherwood's or John Yale's books provide an adequate listing of these in-house works. Although her study centers on the work of Svami Vivekananda in America, Marie Louise Burke's contributions are noteworthy: *Swami Vivekananda in America: New Discoveries* (Calcutta: Advaita Ashrama, 1958), and *Swami Vivekananda: His Second Visit to the West: New Discoveries* (Calcutta: Advaita Ashrama, 1978). Harold W. French's *The Swan's Wide Waters* (Port Washington, NY: Kennikat Press, 1974) deals with the Ramakrishna movement in the West. Svami Nirvedananda's essay, "Sri Ramakrishna and Spiritual Renaissance," appears in the four-volume *The Cultural Heritage of India*, ed. Haridas Bhattacharyya, rev. ed. (Ramakrishna Mission Institute of Culture, 1956). Minor assessments of its own work have been published in its journals, *Prabuddha Bharata*, and *Vedanta Kesari*.

    Two other studies should be cited: Leo Schneiderman's "Ramakrishna: Personality and Social Factors in the Growth of a Religious Movement," *Journal for the Scientific Study of Religion* (Spring 1969); and the *Swami Vivekananda Centenary Memorial Volume*, ed. R.C. Majumdar (Calcutta: Swami Vivekananda Centenary, 1963), which contains several interesting essays on the movement.

3. Nalini Devdas, *Svāmī Vivekānanda* (Bangalore, India. Christian Institute for the Study of Religion and Society, 1968), p. 6.

4. Cf. George M. Williams, "Svami Vivekananda: Archetypal Hero or Doubting Saint?" in this volume, and *The Quest for Meaning of Svāmī Vivekānanda* (Chico, CA: New Horizons Press, 1974), pp. 22-37.

5. At first he was content to wander with Svami Akhandananda, but then he even needed total solitude. By late 1890 had severed all connections with his brother monks (cf. Williams, *Svāmī Vivekānanda*, pp. 54f). Before he left for America several accidental meetings occurred and each time he restated his separation from them. *The Life of Swami Vivekananda by His Eastern and Western Disciples*, 4th ed. (Calcutta: Advaita Ashrama, 1965), pp, 191, 205, 282 (hereafter *LVK*).

6. For the struggle prior to his return read his letters in Swami Vivekananda, *The Complete Works of Swami Vivekananda*, 6th ed. (Calcutta: Advaita Ashrama, 1964) (hereafter *CW*), 6 : 250, 6 : 263, 5 : 33, 5 : 42, 6 : 278, 6 : 287, 6 : 289, 7 : 475, 7 : 480, 7 : 483, 6 : 296, 6 : 304, 6 : 310, 6 : 314, 6 : 321,

6 : 326, 6 : 350, 6 : 362, 6 : 369, 7 : 488, 5 : 111, 6 : 503; *LVK*, 504-9; French, *The Swan's Wide Waters*, pp. 81ff.

7. The documentation is so extensive in the chapter on Svami Vivekananda in this volume that one is referred there for citings of his usage of the descriptors in *CW*.

8. Devdas, *Svāmī Vivekānanda*, p. 32.

9. There are a number of histories of the World's Parliament of Religions: Walter R. Hougton, ed., *Neely's History of the Parliament of Religions and Religious Congresses at the World's Columbian Exposition* (Chicago: F.T. Neely, 1893); John Henry Barrows, ed., *The World's Parliament of Religions*, 2 vols. (Chicago: Parliament Publishing Co., 1893); J.W. Hanson, ed., *The World's Congress of Religions* (Chicago: International Publishing Co., 1894). Marie Louise Burke in *Swamī Vivekananda in America: New Discoveries*, 2nd rev. ed. (Calcutta: Advaita Ashrama, 1966) details some of the times he identified himself as a "Brahmin monk" and defends it as being "due to expediency" and thus "a careless but forgivable error" (p. 69). "Later, however, Swamiji's enemies made capital out of these casual and typically American errors, imputing to him a deliberate misrepresentation of his status" (p. 70).

10. *LVK*, p. 504.

11. *CW*, 7:98.

12. *CW*, 5:12, 292, 455; 8:152.

13. *Raja-Yoga* (*CW*, 1 : 119ff.) taught methods of "psychic control" for "the liberation of the soul through perfection" (124, 122). Its textual basis was Patanjali's *Yoga Sūtras*. This comprised his major exposition of the mystical path. In *Jnana-Yoga* (*CW* 2:55ff.) Vivekananda defined the way of philosophy (knowledge). Yet both of these paths utilized as the highest *Pramāṇa* direct realization.

14. *LVK*, p. 507.

15. Agehananda Bharati, *Journal of Asian Studies*, (February 1970):207.

16. One should note that Vivekananda's reconciliation of both science and humanitarian work required an epistemological shift from *advaita's* posture toward science which would assign it to *vivārta* while *viśiṣṭādvaita* would find science and knowledge about God compatible.

17. Swami Satprakashananda, *Swami Vivekananda's Contribution to the Present Age* (St. Louis: Vedanta Society of St. Louis, 1978), p. 132; French, *The Swan's Wide Waters*, pp. 162, 211.

18. Satprakashananda, *Swami Vivekananda*, pp. 178ff.

19. Ibid., pp. 181-82.

20. This training period still exists today. Gerald B. Cooke in *A Neo-Hindu Ashrama in South India* (Bangalore: Christian Institute for the Study of Religion ad Society, 1966) describes this in some detail (pp. 1-5).

21. Christopher Isherwood, *Ramakrishna and His Disciples* (New York: Simons and Schuster, 1965), p. 328.

22. Quoted from French, *The Swan's Wide Waters*, p. 94.

23. *Swami Vivekananda Centenary Memorial Volume*, p. 457.

24. Svami Vivekananda, *Letters of Swami Vivekananda* (Calcutta: Advaita Ashrama, 1960), p. 117.

25. *Amrita Bazar Patrika*, July 7, 1902, quoted in *Vivekananda in Indian News-papers, 1893-1902*, eds. Sankari Prasad Basu and Sumil Bihari Ghosh (Calcutta: Basu Bhattacharyya and Co., 1969), pp. 324-25.
26. *Swami Vivekananda Centenary Memorial Volume*, Svami Lokeswarananda's "Ramakrishna Order of Monks: New Orientation of Monasticism," pp. 439ff., and C.P. Ramaswami Aiyar's "New Type of Monasticism by Swami Vivekananda," pp. 453ff.
27. Satprakashananda, *Swami Vivekananda*, p. 128.
28. *The Ramakrishna Math and Mission Convention—1926* (Belur: The Math, 1926). Hereafter, *RMMC*.
29. Ibid., pp. 7f.
30. Ibid., pp. 19-20.
31. Ibid., p. 46.
32. Ibid., p. 95.
33. Ibid.
34. Ibid., p. 23.
35. Ibid., p. 34.
36. Ibid.
37. Ibid., p. 31.
38. This metaphor refers to the work of Sidney Mead.
39. Swami Tejasananda, *The Ramakrishna Movement: Its Ideal and Activities*, 2nd ed. (Belur: Belur Math, 1956), pp. 12-13.
40. Ibid.
41. Ibid.
42. Ibid.
43. Cooke, *A Neo-Hindu Ashrama in South India*, p. 42.
44. Ibid., p. 45.
45. Ibid., p. 46.
46. David M. Miller and Dorothy C. Wertz, *Hindu Monastic Life: The Monks and Monasteries of Bhubaneswar* (Montreal: McGill-Queen's University Press, 1976).
47. Ibid., p. 136.
48. Cooke, *A Neo-Hindu Ashrama in South India*, p. 52.
49. Ibid.
50. Interviews by author in India, December 1979 through February 1980.
51. French, *The Swan's Wide Waters*, p. 155.
52. An example is Nirenjan Dhar's *Vedanta and Bengal Renaissance* (Calcutta: Minerva, 1977).
53. Bharati, *Journal of Asian Studies* (February 1970): 207.

4

THE DIVINE LIFE SOCIETY MOVEMENT

David M. Miller

If one were to read many of the books and the articles written by Western scholars who deal with modern India, one might conclude that the Hindu renaissance ends with the death of Aurobindo or Radhakrishnan, who were most certainly the intellectual giants of the post-independence period. But a visit to India provides the intelligent observer with a different picture. Even the uninformed tourist, who does no more than browse through the excellent bookstores in the major hotels, becomes immediately aware that *new* gurus have taken the places of those who have died, and that the Hindu revival continues in full bloom, perhaps flowering anew with the recent North American interest in the gurus of India. Writers Aubrey Menon and Khushwant Singh, and former General Sujan Singh Uban have provided popular accounts of a host of living gurus, most of whom engage in the rhetoric of the Hindu apologetic and, hence, would be considered "modernists" by Bharati's definition.[1] Khushwant Singh sums up such accounts as he says, "The number of saintly men and women are beyond enumeration. Every district has its quota of living saints to whom people turn for advice on spiritual and worldly matters. . . . And everyone will come for their *darshan*. Of the living saints the most famous is Anandamayee Ma. Prime Minister, Indira Gandhi, has visited her on many occasions."[2] Each writer has his own preference; Aubrey Menon favors Svami Chinmayananda, of Bombay, while General

Uban mentions the Bengali *sādhu*, Baba Sita Ram Das Omkarnath, more often than others.

The point that I wish to make here is that the Hindu, in all ages, swears his allegiance to a *living* guru whom he has chosen, and at the death of that guru, he probably will turn to another one in order to fulfil the spiritual bond that he has lost. The quest for the living, charismatic guru is an unending one that the Hindu usually undertakes alone, as indeed he does many other spiritual things. The guru, therefore, represents the immediacy or the indwellingness of the divine within the human sphere, and the gurus are those persons of "genius" whom W.C. Smith characterizes as the ones who "have conspicuously modified and ramified and enriched...the cumulative tradition in its developing course."[3] In studying Svami Sivananda and the movement that he began we shall study the most recent phase of this development.

But before entering upon a historical description of Svami Sivananda and the Sivananda movement, I must make a few notes about the structure of Hindu monasticism. I have said elsewhere that "Hindu monastic orders are organized around the concept of a teaching tradition *(sampradāya)* related to a famous teacher *(ācārya)* who first enunciated the philosophical religious system of the order."[4] Although Hindu monastic orders are found as early as upanisadic times, the best-known orders were begun by: Sankara (788-820); Ramanuja (ca. 1017); Nimbarka (ca. 1162); Madhva (1199-1278); and Vallabha (ca. 1500). The history of Hindu monastic orders, however, is much more complex than it might appear if one were to read G.S. Ghurye's *Indian Sadhus*.[5] Although an initiate into a particular teaching tradition or *sampradāya* traces back his spiritual lineage *(guruparamparā)* to one of the great *ācāryas*, such as Sankara, the links are, at best, weak. Furthermore, a monastic who becomes recognized as a famous guru begins, in every way, a new *sampradāya*. The almost limitless flexibility of the Hindu understanding of *sampradāya* as a concept and as religious institution allows for a claim to tradition, while at the same time ever adapting to new situations and times.

If we were to look closer at the structural elements of a *sampradāya*, we would discern a pattern of ever and ever larger circles moving outward from the center, much as heat waves emanate from a blazing fire. Yet, at the same time the "pull" or movement is toward the center. The guru is at the center of the *sampradāya* and those nearest to him are his closest disciples, most often asce- tics who have taken initiation into *sannyāsa* or *brahmacarya*. Equally close are lay disciples who live at the monastery and who share in its life. Other lay disciples live outside the monastic center and visit it occasionally; but they play important roles as patrons by providing financial and material support for the monas- tic center. Often they will establish lay organizations in their local- ities that promote and advance the goals of the monastic center.[6]

The further one is from the center and from the guru, the less one feels the intimacy and warmth of the guru; thus, there exists a continual "pull," as it were, toward the center, toward the living guru, who, for a brief moment in time, fulfils that closeness to the divine that the Hindu seeks. But just as a fire will die out if not rekindled, so also a monastic movement will die with the death of the guru unless a charismatic disciple is able to pull his fellow disciples back toward the center. The study of Svami Sivananda and the Sivananda movement helps us understand the centrality of and the dynamic character of the *sampradāya* within Hindu tradition.

I do not wish to imply that the Sivananda movement has created the impact within India and elsewhere that was caused by the Ramakrishna movement; far from it. Rather, the Siva- nanda movement is important because it is typical of many other modernist movements centered around a living guru, movements that are dynamic factors in the difficult process of religious, social, and cultural change that is taking place in India today.[7] Let us now look closer at Svami Sivananda and the Sivananda movement, which is known as the Divine Life Society.

Svami Sivananda (1887-1963) : The Man and the Legend

The historian faces particular difficulty when he attempts to understand the early years in the life history of a guru who has taken the vows of *sannyāsa*. If the guru in question has been a serious renunciant, he would have cut himself free from his past prior to his renunciation; symbolically, he would have been dead to that past and reborn into another life history at his initiation into ascetic orders. Much more so-called "historical fact" might be known about the guru's later life as he gathered disciples about him who wrote about their experiences with him.   Yet, in time, often while the guru is alive, a legend is constructed about those earlier years by his disciples, who borrow patterns from legendary or mythological figures such as Kṛṣṇa, Rāma, or Caitanya, to tell their story.   Svami Sivananda's life history is an excellent example of this process.   Although a skeletal life history prefaces most of his written works, it was not until 1958, five years before his death, that Svami Sivananda wrote his autobiography. Much to the frustration of his closest disciples, Sivananda's autobiography adds little to what was known before.

In his foreword to *The Autobiography of Swami Sivananda,* Svami Sadananda Saraswati wrote: "When I received the manuscripts bearing the title: *The Autobiography of Swami Sivananda,* I jumped with joy because I expected . . . that there was a chance to know many of the details of Master's life, which in spite of my fairly long stay with him (running into many years) I was unable to learn either from him or from anyone else.   But how great was my surprise—not to say disappointment when I found that I could not obtain even a glimpse of what my mind was curious to know. . . . He [Svami Sivananda] considers it wasteful to write about such incidents in his life as are not directly beneficial for spiritual progress of the reader."[8]

Two years after Sivananda wrote his autobiography, Svami Venkatesananda, another close disciple, wrote a monumental volume entitled *Gurudev Sivananda,* which has become the standard history of the life of Svami Sivananda.   Venkatesananda beautifully paints in the details of Sivananda's early life, using the brush of a true *bhakta* who holds his guru to be the descent or *avatāra* of the Divine announced in *Bhagavadgītā* IV. 7-8.   Yet, Venkatesananda's words also echo the Hindu apologetic as he says:

Gurudev's place in the history of the world is that of a Buddha or a Jesus.   Historians will regard him as not only the greatest among modern religious leaders but also as an incarnate Divine Power that was able to work a miracle in the Heart of Man. Buddha Himself was a King; so, his religion soon earned royal patronage.   Lord Jesus and His immediate followers won mass adherence to His religion by spectacular martyrdom.   The twentieth century is an era of democracy.   Gurudev's religion has to appeal to the heart of every individual, not merely the king, in order to spread far and wide. ... Moreover, the twentieth century is an age of science, and people would not subscribe to a doctrine just because someone gave up his life for it—they have to be convinced that it is the Truth, that it is useful and that it is practical. ... It is this superhuman factor that ranks Gurudev, in the devout mind of a seeker after Truth, with great Incarnations of the Lord Himself, like Rama and Krishna.[9]

Venkatesananda's words, however, are in opposition to Sivananda's intended self-image. In his autobiography Sivananda forcefully put down any attempt to identify him with an *avatāra*. "I am not pleased when people call me 'Sat Guru' or 'avatar.' I am dead against Gurudom. That is a great obstacle and has caused the downfall of great men in the spiritual path. Gurudom is a menace to society. ... In 1933 the publishers in Madras wrote articles on my life and mentioned me as an 'avatar.' Immediately I gave a reply which explains the attitude I have always maintained: 'Kindly remove all "Krishna Avatar" and "Bhagawan" business.'"[10] Keeping in mind the tension between the "facts" of Sivananda's life, as recorded in his autobiography, and the retelling of that story by his disciples, I shall bring the two sources together in an attempt to describe a man and a movement that are typical of Hindu modernity and that have many parallels in the life histories and movements of other contemporary Hindu gurus.

Svami Sivananda was born to high caste *brāhmin* parents, Parvati Ammul and P.S. Vengu Iyer, as their third son, on Thursday, September 8, 1887, "at the time of sunrise, when the star, Bharani was in ascendence." His father was a *taksildar* for the raja of a large estate near Pattamadai, Madras (Tamil Nadu), at the southern tip of India. He was named Kuppuswamy.

Sivananda discloses very little about his parents, but we are told that his father was a kind and generous man who was loved by all who knew him. He was a devotee of Śiva and a descendant of the family of Appaya Dikshitar, a sixteenth-century Sanskrit scholar whom Sivananda describes as "peerless not only among his contemporaries but even among scholars of several decades before and after him."[11] In fact, Sivananda writes considerably more about Appaya Dikshitar than he does about his father. Sivananda tells us almost nothing of importance about his childhood; in 1901 at the age of fourteen he was selected to give the welcoming address to the governor of Madras upon his visit to Pattamadai, and two years later he passed his high school matriculation examinations, ranking first in his class.

If, however, one were to read Venkatesananda's account of Sivananda's childhood a wholly different picture is revealed. The birth of Sivananda was a miraculous birth:

The day of great rejoicing drew near. A divine delight filled the hearts of a pious and Godly couple in Pattamadai. . . . They had supernatural experiences and visions. . . . For, to them had been allotted the good fortune of fathering and mothering a son who was soon to prove that he was an incarnation of God Himself with a prophetic mission. . . . Everyone rejoiced when the Lord was born. A learned neighbour well versed in the Shastras read the almanac. "Bharani", he explained, "He who is born in Bharani will rule the world". . . . Many were the auspicious sights that foretold of the greatness of what to them was but a most charming child. Nature was in her best form and glory.[12]

In his early childhood, according to Venkatesananda, Sivananda was mischievous, like Kṛṣṇa or Caitanya, playing boyish pranks upon his patient and loving mother. As he grew, he became extremely religious and enjoyed chanting bhajans and performing kīrtans. He was kind-hearted and served all who came to Pattamadai. "His special attention, even as a boy was bestowed upon Sannyasins and wandering monks. He took the greatest delight in entertaining them. Beggars and decrepits too enjoyed special privileges at his hands."[13] His high degree of intelligence astounded his parents, and once, like Jesus, he resolved a point of intellectual debate that had divided the temple priests of his village. In high school he excelled in Tamil literature and always stood first in his examinations. Furthermore, he was "a good athlete and a first-rate gymnast: handsome and tall, his was a robust, healthy and strong constitution."[14] Sivananda, then, as an incarnation of God, was the wonder child for the modern age.

One story that Venkatesananda tells us is important for our understanding of Sivananda, the man, and indeed, we are asked to

believe that the story was told to Venkatesananda by Sivananda as
it is written in the first person singular. That story follows:

> I learnt fencing from a teacher who belonged to a low caste; he
> was a Harijan. I could go to him only for a few days before I
> was made to understand that it was unbecoming of a caste
> Brahmin to play student to an untouchable. I thought deeply
> over the matter. One moment I felt that the God whom we all
> worshipped in the image in my father's Puja room had jumped
> over to the heart of this untouchable. He was (my) guru all
> right. . . . I placed flowers at his feet and prostrated myself
> before him. Thus did God come into my life to remove the veil
> of caste distinctions. How very valuable this step was I could
> realize very soon after this: for, I was to enter the medical profes-
> sion and serve all, and the persistence of caste distinctions would
> have made that service a mockery.[15]

Let me now return to *The Autobiography of Swami Sivananda*.
In 1903 after he graduated from high school, Kuppuswamy Iyer
attended S.P.C. College at Trichinopoly. Again, Sivananda tells us
little about his life as a student, except that he excelled in his
subjects, and in 1905, he played the part of Helena in a dramatiza-
tion of Shakespeare's *Midsummer Night's Dream*. Later in 1905,
upon graduation from college, Kuppuswamy entered Tanjore
Medical Institute, about which he writes:

> I was a tremendously industrious boy in school. During my
> studies at the Tanjore Medical Institute, I never used to go home
> in holidays. I would spend the entire period in the hospital. I
> had free admission into the operation theatre. I would run about
> here and there and acquire knowledge of surgery—which only a
> senior student would possess. . . . I was first in all subjects. . . .
> With all humility I may mention that I possessed greater knowledge
> than many doctors with covetable degrees. In the first year of my
> study in the Medical School I could answer papers which the
> final year student could not.[16]

But something happened that interrupted Kuppuswamy's study
of medicine. He does tell us that: "My mother and brothers would
persuade me to take up some work in some other line."[17] Since

Sivananda does not mention his father, nor does he refer to him again after this time, the implication is that his father died or that, at least, he was no longer present in the family. And indeed, if Sivananda had completed medical school and had received a MBBS degree (as some scholars believe), certainly he would have written about it, as he remained totally committed to the study and practice of medicine. Venkatesananda, who elsewhere exalts Sivananda as the best in whatever he might undertake, does not mention the degree. The silence upon these matters is unsettling for the historian.

The next event that Sivananda records in his autobiography occurs in 1909, when he was twenty-two. With financial aid from his mother, Kuppuswamy began a medical journal entitled *Ambrosia*, for which he served as editor and principal contributor. Most of the articles were written in English, and he published the journal with limited success from 1909 until 1913. Sometime during the latter part of this period, Kuppuswamy took a job as an assistant in Dr. Heller's Pharmacy in Madras City. "Here I had to manage the accounts, dispense medicines and attend to patients," Sivananda later said.

In Madras City, for reasons that are not made explicit by either Sivananda or Venkatesananda, Kuppuswamy suddenly decided to leave India and to move to Malaya in order to practice medicine. His decision met with the opposition of his mother and two brothers who protested that the Shastras forbade a high-caste *brāhmin* from "crossing the seas." Venkatesananda comments that not all traditional rules apply to the present day world and that in search of a field of service Kuppuswamy was right to ignore conventional codes of conduct; after all, was not the call of the sick, the call of the Lord Himself? Kuppuswamy traveled by boat to Malaya, and within a few days of landing he secured a job as medical practitioner for a large rubber plantation, near Seremban and managed by A.G. Robins. Kuppuswamy was now twenty-six years old and his starting salary was $150 per month.

Kuppuswamy served as medical practitioner at the rubber estate from 1913 until 1920; from 1920 until 1923 he took a position at Jahore Medical Office, located near Singapore, as an assistant to Doctors Parsons and Green. In his autobiography Sivananda briefly notes: "I spent all my energy and time relieving human suffering by serving the poor and the sick, day and night, with a

sympathetic heart.   This kind of selfless service gave me purification of heart and mind and led me to the spiritual path. . . . I had
a special gift from God for the miraculous cure effected in the
patients and [they] acclaimed me as a very kind and sympathetic
doctor with a charming and majestic personality. . . . There was
not a single available English medical book at the time that I had
not read and digested."[18]

The picture that Sivananda sketches for us of this period is
given greater detail by Venkatesananda.   Kuppuswamy constantly
treated the sick and served the poor, giving food and money to
whomever needed it.   He was a hard-working, seriously committed young man of action and compassion.   At Jahore, Kuppuswamy employed Narasimha Dikshitar as his cook.   Venkatesananda makes Kuppuswamy speak, as it were, through the mouth
of Narasimha Dikshitar, who, twenty-four years later, rejoined
Sivananda as a *sannyāsin*-disciple at Rishikesh.   Kuppuswamy is
said to have spoken thus to Narasimha during their days together
in Jahore:

What is the difference between you and me?   You earn
a little less and I earn a little more; that is all.   Both of us take
the same food. . . .   Why then should you wait for me to take
food?   Are you not feeling hungry at the same time? . . .   Why
should you go about in dirty clothes?   You have as much self-
respect as I have, and the same principles of health and hygiene
apply to both of us.   Those are foolish ideas of superiority and
inferiority entertained by some arrogant rich men.   I know their
habits.   They will reserve spoilt food and stale plantain for their
servants.   I loathe even the thought.   You shall be one of the
members of my family.[19]

Again, Sivananda is pictured as one who early in his life broke
caste rules and sought equality with his fellow man. But Sivananda
presents another side to his personality and life as a Malayan
physician, one which is all but ignored by Venkatesananda, who
sought to present his guru as the divinely inspired and divinely
directed Doctor. Sivananda writes: "I got rapid promotions
and with that my salary and private practice increased by leaps
and bounds. . . .   In my youth I had a great liking for high class
dress, collections of curious and fancy articles of gold, silver and

sandalwood. Sometimes I used to purchase various kinds of gold, rings and necklaces and wear them all at a time. When I entered shops I never used to waste any time in selection. I gathered all that I saw. I did not like haggling and bargaining. I paid the shop-keepers' bills without scrutiny. . . . I had many hats, but never wore them."[20]

Here we are introduced to a man of the world, a man of affluence who enjoyed material things that gave him status. Yet toward the end of his stay at Jahore, Kuppuswamy began to have other thoughts. Sivananda reflects upon his change in attitude toward worldly life as he writes, "The doctor's profession gave me ample evidence of the sufferings of the world. For a Vairagi who has a sympathetic heart, the world is full of pain. True and lasting happiness cannot be found merely in gathering wealth. With the purification of heart through selfless service, I had a new vision. I was deeply convinced that there must be a place—a sweet home of pristine glory and purity and divine splendour—where absolute security, perfect peace and lasting happiness can be had through self-realization."[21]

We are not told more about the events that led to this change in attitude, but we do know that Kuppuswamy had begun to study the Upaniṣads and the *Bhagavadgītā* during his last years in Malaya. Kuppuswamy left Malaya as suddenly as he had come. In 1923, at the age of thirty-six, Kuppuswamy sailed from Singapore, leaving behind him all of his earthly possessions. Upon his re-entry into India, he became like "a wandering mendicant" and journeyed to Banaras, where he took refuge in the Visanatha Temple dedicated to Śiva. Venkatesananda provides the following interpretation of Kuppuswamy's renunciation of worldly life: "That is what we find in these two heroes: Lord Buddha and our Gurudev. They lodged themselves on the brink of the ocean of Samsara, smelt its captivating though deluding ozone, understood its deceptive essence and took to wings, thus mocking the very Maya and defeating her at her own game. . . . Such was the pleasure-palace that Maya had built for Him in Malaya, even as the King had built for Prince Siddhartha to prevent Him from renouncing the world."[22]

From Banaras, Kuppuswamy wandered along the Ganges River northward to Rishikesh, where he received initiation into *sannyāsa* from Paramahansa Viswananda Saraswati, about whom we learn nothing from Sivananda, who writes: "From the sacred hands

of Paramahansa Viswananda Saraswati, I received Holy initiation
on the banks of the Ganges on 1st June 1924. The religious rite of
Varag Homa was done for me by Acharya Guru Sri Swami
Vishnudevananda Maharaj at Kailas Ashram."[23] We know from the
title "Saraswati" that the *sādhu* who performed the initiation ceremony was a member of the Dashanami Sannyasin suborder Saraswati, which, according to tradition, was founded by Sankara.[24]
But we know nothing more. We do not know whether Viswananda
Saraswati was a monastic, resident at Rishikesh, or whether he was
one of the thousands of wandering ascetics who frequently pass
through Rishikesh on their way to other pilgrimage sites. We know
nothing of the philosophical position that Viswananda held. And
to make matters worse, Sivananda does not mention him again.
The Kailas Ashram, however, remains today as one of the largest
ashrams within Rishikesh, but it served simply as the background
for the rite of *homa*. Venkatesananda's description of the same
event indicates that the two met at Charan Das Dharmasala, a
place of temporary lodging for wandering ascetics. Venkatesananda's account does provide, however, a depth of feeling that is
lacking in Sivananda's simple statement:

> His face was aglow with the Fire of Knowledge. It captivated
> Gurudev's heart, the moment he had the old Sannyasin's Darshan
> early in the morning. Gurudev fell at his feet and bathed them
> with his tears. Fondly, the saint Swami Viswanandaji raised
> him and embraced him with all love and affection. "My dear
> child! I see something on your forehead which tells me that you
> are going to be the fittest instrument in the hands of God for
> conveying His Message to the world. . . . Am I right in assum-
> ing that you have renounced the world and desire to lead the
> life of a monk?" "Most Holy Sire! Yes, you are right. Oh,
> how fortunate I am to have the Darshan of a divine sage. . . .
> Shower your grace on this poor humble seeker. For, it is only
> through thee can I attain my goal."
> "Well said, my child! I should myself feel it the greatest
> privilege to initiate you into Sannyasa."[25]

Viswananda Saraswati, of course, gave Kuppuswamy Iyer the name
Sivananda Saraswati, thus continuing the tradition of the Dashanami
suborder, but his relationship to Sivananda was more like that of

John the Baptist to Jesus than the typical Hindu relationship of guru-disciple. In any case, Viswananda is not mentioned again. We assume, then, that Sivananda is in the category of "self-realized" gurus.

For the remainder of 1924 Sivananda lived along the banks of the Ganges River near Rishikesh, first at Lakhmanjhula (about two miles north and across the river from Rishikesh), and then at the Swargashram (directly across the river from Rishikesh). We are not told under whom Sivananda studied, if indeed, anyone, but he does mention that he read the Upàniṣads, Tulsidas' *Rāmāyana*, and a work entitled "Yoga Vasishtha," upon which Sivananda later wrote a commentary. He also opened a small, free dispensary at Lakhmanjhula and continued to treat and serve the sick and the poor. This period, however, was one of inner-reflection and solitude in which he remained within his small room at Swargashram for most of the day, rising at 3:30 to bathe in the Ganges. He became well known to travelers passing through Rishikesh, and in the manner of an efficient doctor placed a sign on his door which read: "Interviews between 4 and 5 p.m.—only 5 minutes at a time." He obviously wanted to be alone.

Sometime in 1925 Sivananda began a period of wanderings that continued at irregular intervals until 1938, but Rishikesh always remained his base of operations. On his first pilgrimage in 1925 he traveled south, visiting all the sacred sites along the way. He arrived at the ashram of Ramana Maharishi at the time of great Tamil guru's birthday on December 30, but Sivananda says only, "I did Bhajan and Kirtan in the big Hall before Sri Bhagavan Ramana and the devotees and perambulated the Arunachala Hill and worshipped the Tejas Linga."[26]

Venkatesananda's account is equally sparse. Yet, Ramana must have greatly influenced Sivananda, as Sivananda often refers to him in later writings.

At this point, *The Autobiography of Swami Sivananda* becomes little more than a listing of pilgrimage places that Sivananda visited from 1925 until 1931. In 1931 he and three other ascetics made the long and difficult trip from Almore to Mt. Kailas and return—a trek that totalled 460 miles and took two months. Such journies are characteristic of many men (and women) after they have received the vows of *sannyāsa,* and the accounts of Sivananda's travels tell us only that he was following the traditional path of the

great gurus such as Sankara, Ramanuja, and Madhva, who began
their ascetic lives in that way.

By 1933 Sivananda began to attract a large number of listeners
wherever he spoke. In a letter written shortly after 1933 he notes,
"My time is spent in delivering thrilling lectures during the day and
Kirtans at night. I pump joy and power in the devotees. I roar
like a lion. People do not leave me even a second. . . . I had a
Virat Kirtan with 3000 people. . . . I will have Kirtans with Harijans
today."[27]

In 1929, according to Venkatesananda, Sivananda published
The Practice of Yoga, volume 1, the first of 340 books and pamphlets that were to follow over the next thirty-four years. His publisher
was R.K. Vinavagam of Madras, and between 1933 and 1936
Sivananda published (at least) eight more books and pamphlets,
all of which dealt with Yogic and ascetic disciplines. He wrote in
English in order to reach a wider, pan-Indian audience. I should
note that Bharati has criticized contemporary Hindu gurus for using
English as their language of communication.[28] But they had no
other choice if, indeed, they were to appeal to educated moderns,
most of whom did not know Sanskrit.

Sivananda's public lectures and widely distributed publications
began to draw disciples to him at Rishikesh. One of his first ascetic-
disciples was Svami Paramananda, a former employee of the South-
eastern Railroad, who had taken *sannyāsa* into the Ramakrishna
order of monks. Paramananda joined Sivananda in 1932. The
first disciple to be initiated into *sannyāsa* by Sivananda was Svami
Atmananda, who had been a former disciple of Mataji Omkaresh-
war. And gradually the number grew. Sivananda tells us about
those first disciples:

> With a view to training a band of right lives, I permitted some
> aspirants to live in the adjacent Kutirs. I arranged for their
> meals . . . and gave them initiation. . . . I encouraged them and
> infused Vairagya in them. I took special care of their health. I
> frequently enquired about their Sadhana and gave useful hints
> for the removal of their difficulties and obstacles in their medita-
> tion. When they offered their services to me, I asked them to go
> from Kutir to Kutir and find out the old and sick Mahatmas
> and serve them. . . . I asked some educated students to take
> copies of my short articles and send them to magazines and

newspapers for publication. . . . Instead of studying the ancient
sacred scriptures for decades, the students spent a few minutes
daily in making copies of my articles and thereby learnt Yoga
and philosophy easily in a short period.[29]

In January 1934, Sivananda and four disciples left Swargashram
and moved across the river to an area one mile north of Rishikesh.
Sivananda took lodging in two small rented rooms owned by the
Ram Ashram and located on the bathing *ghāt* leading down to the
Ganges. These two small rooms served as his living quarters until
his death in 1963, although, in time, a complex of larger, better
equipped buildings were constructed near his kutir. Later that
year, in reply to Sivananda's formal request for land, the Maharaja
of Tehri Garhwal donated several acres of land, up the hillside
from the river, for the site of the Sivananda Ashram. A building,
which became known as Ananda Kutir, was included in the dona-
tion of land, and Sivananda's disciples used part of the building for
their quarters; another room became the main office, and Sivananda
established and ran a free dispensary out of a small room on the
lower level.

The organization around Sivananda was formally named the
Divine Life Society, and in 1936 the Trust of the society was officially registered with the government of Uttar Pradesh, marking the
beginning of the Sivananda movement.

Svami Sivananda and the Divine Life Society Movement: Institutional Structure

I shall now depart from a strict sequential historical development and group together for discussion the institutional forms or
means that Svami Sivananda created in order to accomplish the
aims and goals of the Divine Life Society as stated in the Deed of
Trust.[30]

Publications

As I noted earlier, Sivananda is credited with writing an astonish-
ing 340 books and pamphlets, in English, from 1929 until his
death in 1963. Most of these were published in the 1950s. From
1930 until 1939 he published twenty-two books detailing the major

yogic systems. In 1939 he finished an exhaustive translation of and commentary on the *Bhagavadgītā*, an 816-page tome, which established him in the line of vedantic commentators who trace their beginnings back to the great *ācāryas*, Sankara and Ramanuja. Sivananda, like other modernists or neo-vedantins, such as Vivekananda, sought to bring together philosophical or religious teachings of the early founders, at least as he understood them.

From 1940 until 1949 he published seventy-four books covering a wide range of subjects, from household medicine to Hindu philosophical and religious topics. In 1946 he wrote *Mind: Its Mysteries and Control*, which I regard as one of the best presentations of Sivananda's neo-vedantic system. In 1949, he completed his monumental philosophical commentary on the *Brahma Sutra*, which initially appeared as a two-volume work totalling 981 pages. Thus, by 1949, Svami Sivananda had established himself as one of India's most significant interpreters of the Hindu cumulative tradition. His name and his writings had become known to thousands of readers throughout India.

Sivananda wrote and published most of the remaining 344 materials between 1950 and 1963; a few volumes were published after his death. The range of subjects of his works published in this period is too vast for commentary here; he did, however, write several small treatises on other religions, most importantly on Christianity and Buddhism, and one senses a shift from Hindu philosophical systems to more universal philosophical and religious concerns involving a dialogue among the world religions.

I have used the word "published" in most cases because, although publishing dates are easily taken from the title page of the work, it is nearly impossible to know when and where Sivananda wrote or spoke the words that appear in the published text. Almost every word that Sivananda delivered to a gathering of his disciples or others was copied down and, in later times, taped. Then someone, like Svami Venkatesananda, edited and published the speech or lecture. In this way Svami Sivananda produced 340 works, of which less than one-third are in print today.

The monthly journal of the movement, entitled the *Divine Life Society Magazine*, was first published in September of 1938. Each month articles by Sivananda and a host of other ascetic and lay disciples would appear, and many of these articles were later published in book form. The journals are in themselves a gold-

mine of information, and each year, often in July, the Divine Life
Society published its annual report in the society magazine. In
1978 an annual subscription cost Rs. 12, and the magazine was sent
to over 5,000 individuals and societies in India and throughout the
world.

All publications are printed, bound, and distributed from the
Sivananda Ashram at Rishikesh, and many ashramites participate
in the process, thus acting upon their guru's injunction to engage in
karma yoga. The amount of printed material sent out each year
by the Sivananda Publications League (which was founded in 1939)
is enormous, more than fulfilling Sivananda's goal of disseminating
spiritual knowledge through "publication of books, pamphlets and
magazines dealing with ancient, oriental and occidental philosophy,
religion and medicine in the modern scientific manner."[31]

Conferences

Svami Sivananda was as good at organizing religious conferences
and religious fellowships as he was at writing and publishing books,
pamphlets, and magazines. In 1945 he founded the All-World
Religious Federation at Rishikesh, "to establish the much-needed
unity of religions and to re-establish faith in unchanging ancient
truths and to preserve ancient traditions in so far as they are not
incompatible with modern conditions of life."[32] Although the opening of the All-World Religious Federation attracted little attention
outside of Rishikesh, in 1956 Sivananda organized and sponsored a
World Parliament of Religions that was well attended. Seventy-
five delegates, most of whom were monastics, presented papers on
the world's great religious traditions. Among the delegates were:
N.C. Chatterjee, president of the Hindu Maha Sabha; B.L. Atreya,
provost of Banares Hindu University; Major-General A.H. Sharma,
a retired army doctor; H. J. Hablutzel, of the Self-Realization
Fellowship, California; and Reverend John E. St. Catchpool, of
the Friends International Center, Delhi.

Sivananda's speech to the delegates and to the others in an
audience of about 1,000 people illustrates his concern for creating
an ideal community of religions:

The word community as used here means a unity with variety,
namely, a world-wide association of co-operating religions whose
members at once share certain common basic interests and yet

endeavor to demonstrate particular values which they especially esteem. Such an association would be bipolar in operation; it would encourage both a measure of unity through universal principles and multitude of variety through adventurous experimentation. The advantages of such a community are suggested by a Bahai metaphor: "A garden displaying a richly ordered variety of plants is far more enjoyable than a garden consisting of one type of flower."33

The publication of books, pamphlets, and journals combined with religious conferences and festivals began to attract large numbers of lay disciples, who, although drawn to Sivananda, remained within their own localities where they founded branches of the Divine Life Society. At the local level Sivananda organized and promoted annual conferences that brought together all of the Divine Life Societies within a particular geographical area. These annual conferences, which drew thousands of listeners, served as an effective means for communicating the message of Svami Sivananda and of the Divine Life Society to all parts of India and to all levels of society, as the organizers and participants spoke in vernacular languages as well as English. I attended the 1978 All-Orissa Conference of Divine Life Societies, which was opened by the governor and the chief minister of the state of Orissa and which was presided over by Svami Chidananda, the spiritual heir of Sivananda. The conference drew 30,000 Oriyas who listened attentively to speeches in Oriya, Hindi, and English for three 8-hour days. The 30,000 people were housed and fed by the local committee, who numbered about ten people.

Medical and Educational Institutions

Since Sivananda began his professional life as a medical practitioner, it was only natural that he would continue his interest in medicine and in treating the sick and the ailing after he established himself in Rishikesh. I have already mentioned the free dispensary that Sivananda set up in 1934. The demand for medical treatment increased over the years, and donations from lay patrons enabled Sivananda to expand the ashram medical facilities. In 1950 a two-story building was constructed to house the Sivananda General Hospital, and Dr. K.C. Roy, MBBS, and Major-General A.H. Sharma, MBBS, joined the staff. In that year Dr. Sivananda

Adhvaryoo, MBBS, of Gujarat, held the first of yearly "eye-camps" at which patients underwent surgery and treatment for cataracts. In 1958 the hospital treated 16,768 patients, who, although the hospital had ten beds, were mostly out-patients. Although Sivananda began a leprosy relief program, it wasn't until after his death that the program became operative. Under the leadership of Svami Chidananda, who sits on the U.P. Leprosy Relief Committee, the Sivananda Ashram sponsors and administrates three "model" villages for lepers, who are taught to weave cloth for buyers in Europe and North America.

In 1948 Sivananda founded the College of Yoga and Vedanta, which was renamed ten years later the Yoga-Vedanta Forest Academy. Sivananda describes the "ideal" students who would attend the Academy:

> This is not a university like the others in the world. People are not trained here to become clerks, advocates and scientists. . . . They will be initiated in all the processes of self-realization by a combination of the teaching and practice of all schools of Yoga and Vedanta. After training they will become the most potent instruments for good wherever they go. They will carry with them the spiritual power and revitalize society. . . . It is the aim of the college to make its trainees competent to establish similar spiritual centers in different parts of the world so that the teaching received from the parent institution may permeate everywhere.[34]

The faculty who taught the courses were the senior ascetic disciples who had been with Svami Sivananda since the middle forties. From time to time distinguished visiting scholars, such as Edwin Burtt, Graham Howe, and Maryse Chaisy, participated in the instruction. And after 1957 ascetic disciples, trained at the Yoga-Vedanta Forest Academy, went to North America, Europe, and South Africa to establish "sister" organizations. I shall comment on them later.

The Academy was divided into three "branches" or departments: 1) śastra-jñāna, or theoretical studies; 2) sādhanā, or practical studies; and 3) abhyasā yoga, or research studies. The curriculum was further subdivided to include theory, practice, and research in the following subjects: 1) Vedanta and Shankhya;

2) karma, bhakti, haṭha, rāja, and jñāna yogas; 3) comparative religions; 4) Buddhism; and 5) mysticism.

Sivananda also encouraged the Indian branches of the Divine Life Society to establish educational institutions. Although an adequate discussion of the Indian branches would take us beyond our present task, let me note that the Delhi chapter founded a vocational training center for lower-caste women who were taught how to operate electric sewing machines, so that, with this new vocation, they might be able to better their lives.

Much more might be written about the institutional forms or means that Sivananda created in order to act upon the stated goals of the Divine Life Society Deed of Trust. I hope, however, that I have given the reader a sense of the dynamic growth of the movement. I turn now to a description of the ascetic and lay disciples who gathered about Svami Sivananda and who represent the inner core of the Divine Life Society movement.

Svami Sivananda and the Divine Life Society Movement: Ascetic and Lay Disciples

Sridhar Rao (later known as Svami Chidananda) was born on September 24, 1916, to high-caste, wealthy brāhmin parents who lived near Mangalore, Karnataka. In 1938, Sridhar graduated with honors from Loyola College, Madras City, where he had supplemented Christian subjects by reading the Upaniṣads, the Bhagavad-gītā in translations, and the writings of Vivekananda. He first learned of Sivananda through articles on yoga that Sivananda had written in the 1930s for "My Magazine of India," which was published weekly in Madras City. In The Practice of Yoga (1929) Sivananda had listed names and addresses of gurus whom his readers might contact to further their study and practice of yoga. Sridhar made contact with sannyāsins at the Ramakrishna Math, Madras City but in 1943, at the age of twenty-seven, he wrote Sivananda and requested permission to live at the ashram in Rishikesh. Sivananda replied, "Yes, you can come and remain here. As 24 hours meditation alone cannot be done in the beginning, I will also give you some work. You will have to do Karma Yoga, here, any sort of service, along with your study and meditation."[35]

One year after he had taken up residence at the Sivananda Ashram, Sridhar wrote Light Fountain (1994), a delightful bhakta's portrait of his guru, which remains today as his most popular book.

In 1948 Sivananda appointed Sridhar, who was then a *brahmacārin,* as vice-chancellor and professor of rāja yoga at the Yoga Vedanta Forest Academy that Sivananda founded in that year. In the same year the Board of Trustees, at the recommendation of Sivananda, appointed Sridhar as secretary-general of the Divine Life Society, the highest administrative position in the Sivananda organization. In 1949, on Guru Purnima, Sivananda initiated Sridhar into *sannyāsa* and gave him the name of Chidananda Saraswati. Ten years later, Sivananda sent Svami Chidananda on a world tour, to North and South America and Europe. He returned in 1962, and traveled through south India, arriving back at the Sivananda Ashram ten days before the death (*mahāsamādhi*) of his guru. After the death of Svami Sivananda on July 14, 1963, the Board of Trustees elected Svami Chidananda as president of the Divine Life Society, affirming Chidananda as the spiritual heir of Sivananda. He has continued as president of the Divine Life Society since that time and spends many months each year lecturing in the West.

Subbaraya Puthuraya (later known as Svami Krishnananda) was born on April 25, 1922, to highly orthodox *brāhmin* parents in the village of Kemminji, Kerala. For generations, males on both sides of his family had served as temple priests, and Subbaraya learned Sanskrit from early childhood. Later, he referred to Sanskrit as "his second mother tongue." His formal education, however, ended with completion of high school, although he was a brilliant student. In 1943, at the age of twenty-one, Subbaraya left a position in the state government and went to Banaras, where he continued his studies in Sanskrit. In 1944, he was in Rishikesh where he met Sivananda while the latter was taking his evening bath in the Ganges River; without knowing who Sivananda was, Subbaraya became attracted to him and asked to become his disciple.

Sivananda assigned Subbaraya, as a *brahmacārin,* to work in the charitable dispensary, and in 1946 he took initiation into *sannyāsa* under Svami Sivananda, who renamed him Svami Krishnananda Saraswati. In 1948, with the establishment of the Yoga-Vedanta Forest Academy, Sivananda appointed Krishnananda professor of Sanskrit and Vedanta. He has continued over the years as the most brilliant teacher and versatile scholar associated with the Academy. Sivananda once said of Krishnananda: "Krishnanandaji is a wonder to me! He has excelled me. He has

excelled Sankara."[36]   Since the death of Sivananda in 1963, Krishnananda has been the secretary-general of the Divine Life Society
and in every way he is the key administrator of the activities and
the functions of the Divine Life Society.   In 1969, he completed his
most significant work, *The Philosophy of Life*, which has a lengthy
but descriptive subtitle, *A Critical Exposition of the Fundamental
Principles in Eastern and Western Philosophy in Light of the Doctrines of Swami Sivananda*.   More than any other work, this sets
forth the philosophical position of the Sivananda movement.

I shall mention here three other *sannyāsin*-disciples who were
with Sivananda in Rishikesh during the late forties and fifties and
who founded "sister" institutions elsewhere.   Svami Vishnu Devananda (Kuttan Nzir) entered the Sivananda Ashram in 1947, and
Sivananda initiated him into *sannyāsa* one year later.   In 1957,
Sivananda sent Vishnu Devananda, an expert in haṭha yoga, to
North America, where he established the Sivananda Ashram Yoga
Camp, north of Montreal.   Since 1957, Vishnu Devananda's organization has spread throughout North America, with sixteen branch
institutions in the major cities of Canada and the United States and
seven branches in England and Europe.

Svami Satchidananda (Ramaswamy Kalyanasunderam) took initiation into *sannyāsa* shortly after he entered the Sivananda Ashram in
1949.   Three years later Sivananda commissioned Satchidananda to go
to Sri Lanka to begin a branch of the Sivanandan organization there,
and in 1965 Satchidananda left Sri Lanka for New York, where he
established the Integral Yoga Institute.   His organization today has
nine branches in the United States and three in Europe.

Although Svami Chinmayananda of Bombay later took initiation into *sannyāsa* from another guru, he was one of the young
ascetics around Sivananda in the late forties.   He established a
large organization with headquarters near Bombay and centers
throughout the world.

The point that I wish to make is that Svami Sivananda drew to
him many dynamic and talented young men who were later to become gurus in their own right, creating, in a limited sense, new
sampradāyas.   These men were typical of those who had taken
sannyāsa by Sivananda, and other biosketches might serve as well
to illustrate those early years.   One woman, who joined the ashram
in 1955, is said to have been closer to Sivananda in his later years
than any other disciple.

Dr. Chellamma, MBBS, DO (later known as Svami Sivananda-Hridayananda) was born on April 18, 1914, in a village near Travancore, which is now part of Kerala. In the biographical account that serves as the introduction to her book, *Sivananda: My God* (1957), her parents are described simply as "orthodox and pious," with no mention of *varṇa* or *jāti*. According to "ashram gossip" (which must be understood as "gossip" as opposed to "fact"), Chellamma is from a *śūdra* caste. Even the name Chellamma tells us nothing, as it translates "dear mother," which was, perhaps, her nickname. Her life story, which was given to my wife in 1978, is both interesting and instructive. Chellamma, typical of Indian women, was married at the age of fifteen and eventually gave birth to two daughters and a son.[37] Her husband was an ophthalmist. Although Chellamma had not been given a formal education, she was exceedingly bright and was able to pass "senior Cambridge examinations privately." About 1935, she entered Lady Harding School in Delhi, and after completing her Intermediate degree, she graduated with a MBBS in 1942. Later that year, she was appointed assistant surgeon at the Government Ophthalmic Hospital in Madras City. In 1951 she entered private practice as an ophthalmist.

About 1954, after her two daughters had married, she became dissatisfied with her roles as wife, mother, and doctor. She first read the writings of Vivekananda, and then, by accident, read Sivananda's *Spiritual Lessons*, which radically changed her life. Chellamma writes of this experience: "There was a magnetic divine attraction in every one of the sentences. There was that thrillingly divine photograph of Sri Swamiji in that book. Oh, the divine ecstasy I then experienced, and the familiarity of that dear divine face—it seemed almost as though I had already known him intimately—the moment is still fresh in my mind. That same evening I had the vision of Sri Swamiji Mah araj in my meditation."[38]

In April 1955, she visited the ashram in Rishikesh and met Svami Sivananda, with whom she literally fell in love—her book *Sivananda: My God* contains the "love letters" of a *bhakta,* who desperately struggled with the decision of what she should do. Traditional loyalties bound Chellamma to her husband and to her son, but her love for Sivananda was too great. She returned to Madras briefly and then, against her husband's wishes, left for the ashram once more. Again, she decided to return home, but suddenly her train was cancelled. This "divine message" told her that she should remain at the ashram with Sivananda. Against her husband's protests Sivananda initiated her into *sannyāsa* on Guru Purnima Day, 1956. He gave her the name Svami Sivananda-Hridayananda. In the following year she became the eye surgeon at the Sivananda General Hospital. According to ashram sources, she became Svami Sivananda's "living shadow" and certainly one of his closest disciples. She remained constantly beside her guru in the days of illness and pain shortly before his death.

These, then, were the ascetic-disciples who represented the inner core gathered about Svami Sivananda at Rishikesh. They were young, bright, talented and charismatic individuals, excellent examples of the "modern"*sādhu*. Sivananda initiated into ascetic orders almost anyone who requested it, especially older men who, in the tradition of the four stages of life, sought the spiritual path at the end of an active career in the work-a-day world. Toward the end of the fifties the number of resident ascetics at the Sivananda Ashram must have been nearly 200, with another 100 who provided the services necessary for the functioning of the ashram. But these figures are based upon an educated guess of the residential capacity of the ashram at that time.

I now turn to a description of the laity who are, so to speak, the outer rings that encircle and support the center. In the forties and fifties lay disciples, who for many reasons could not commit themselves to a life within the ashram, created branches of the Divine Life Society in almost every large urban center throughout India. But smaller societies or study groups of a few committed disciples sprang up in village areas. Today, for example, in the state of Orissa, which has a predominantly rural population, there are sixty-five Divine Life societies that have been extremely active in promoting the ideals and goals of the Sivananda movement. In 1950 the lay movement was given considerable impetus by the All-India-Ceylon Tour that Sivananda made of the perimeter of the Indian subcontinent. Sivananda and his troupe of *sannyāsins* visited every major urban area in India and Ceylon, and he spoke to all types of organizations and all types of people. Svami Venkatesananda edited a work entitled *Sivananda's Lectures—All India Tour* (1950) that includes transcriptions of all of Sivananda's lectures and discussions which had been taped.[39] He also incorporates numerous photographs with the text that substantiate the claim that

Sivananda spoke to thousands of people everywhere he appeared. If we listen to Sivananda for a moment, we hear the Hindu apologetic being preached to the English-speaking audiences of India.

At Madras City he stressed the basic unity of all faiths:

The Upanishads proclaim the Unity of Existence. This once central theme runs through the utterances of all the Seers of the Upanishads: Truth is One though sages have described of it variously. That One pervades everything here. In fact, that alone exists, naught else. The visible world is false, illusory, a product of Maya. When the senses are withdrawn from the objects, when the mind is stilled and the intellect transcended, the inner eye or intuition is opened and man sees everything as God. God alone exists. . . . Similarly, Lord Jesus, Lord Buddha, Lord Krishna, Lord Zoroaster, Confucius—all of them have delivered the same message of Love and Unity, only in different words to suit their audiences. Every Sage's message leads man to the final Goal, which is God-realization.[40]

Appearing before thousands of soldiers at a north Indian Army camp, Sivananda utilized "the scientific simile," punning on the words "atom" and "atman" : "Renunciation is the Atomic Bomb which instantly reduces the citadel of Desire and ignorance to ashes. You must equip yourself with this atomic or Atmic Bomb. Atman-Jnana is the Atmic Bomb. Become desireless, then you will know the formula for the manufacture of this Atmic Bomb."[41] Sivananda said later that : "The All-India Tour (1950) resulted in a continuous stream of visitors flowing into the ashram."[42] But who were the lay disciples who became followers of Svami Sivananda? First and foremost, they had to agree to the following statement of membership:

Anyone devoted to the ideals of truth, non-violence and purity can become a member of The Divine Life Society, which is a non-sectarian institution, embodying in its wide perspective the common fundamental principles of all the religions of the world and of spiritual life in general. The Society accords equal place of honour to all faiths and religious traditions, and its members recognize no distinction or disruptive sentiment on account of each other's different traditional background, or religious affiliation. . . . Through the pages of the various Books and Journals of the Society, what is endeavoured is to reveal the secret of spiritual action, namely that it lies in the Knowledge of the true Self and in the effacement and transcendence of the ego. . . everyone's goal is to strive to manifest this Divinity within by controlling the internal and external nature by "Being Good and Doing Good". The Society is dedicated to humanitarian, cultural and spiritual service. Anyone with the above ideals is welcome to become a member of The Divine Life Society.[43]

This statement of membership conforms with the principles and ideals enunciated in the Hindu apologetic. The lay member of the Divine Life Society, therefore, would be considered a modernist, most likely a Hindu; he or she would be well educated, predominantly English-speaking, although English might be a "second language," and would share the presuppositions inherent in the statement of membership. But this is far too general.

If we were to examine records of membership, lists of donors, etc., we might conclude that many members of the Divine Life Society were middle to upper-class, well-educated professionals (doctors, lawyers, judges, military officers), businessmen and bureaucrats at the managerial level, with a scattering of local politicians and university professors, and a few wealthy individuals, such as maharajas, and a few Western intellectuals and spiritual seekers —this last category was significantly enlarged with the mission that was directed toward the West after 1957. But complete records and lists are difficult to obtain and read like a Who's Who of lesser known Indians. If an Indian anthropologist were to look at these lists of names, he might be able to determine the caste of certain individuals. My guess is, however, that the majority are from *brāhmin* castes with a representative grouping from other (mostly higher) levels in the social structure. It is interesting that Svami Hridayananda, one of Sivananda's closests disciples, is, according to ashram gossip, a *śūdra*. And, as we have seen, Sivananda repeatedly broke caste rules and structures whenever he felt that the situation justified it. I do know that at all major festivals held at the Sivananda Ashram in 1977-78, individuals of all caste groupings moved freely with each other and a sweeper-girl offered flowers before the silver-plated sandals of Sivananda like anyone else. Also, for the celebration of Mahatma Gandhi's birthday, the *sannyāsins* resident at the ashram serve food to lower-caste individuals who sit on the cushions normally reserved for the president and other officers of the Divine Life Society. Therefore, the Divine Life Society is made up of individuals whom we would call "moderns" and who support and practice the principles and ideals as set forth in the Hindu apologetic, and as restated in the statement of membership in the Divine Life Society.

Conclusion: The Sampradāya, Modernity and Sociocultural Change

In my description of Svami Sivananda and the Divine Life Society movement I have frequently used the word "modern" without stating exactly what I mean by it, and in what ways the Sivananda movement could be classified as "modern." Many Western interpreters of Hindu society have considered monastic institutions, and hence *sampradāyas* "other-worldly" oriented and therefore not only traditional institutions, but ones that are working counter to anything that might be called "modern." But this conclusion depends on what we mean by "modern" and more importantly, on what the term means within the Hindu context, which is a point that many Western scholars simply ignore.

From the standpoint of contemporary scholarship what, in fact, do we, as historians of religion, mean by the term "modern" within the Indian context? J.N. Farquhar, in his *Modern Religious Movements in India* (1915), which remains even today a model of the type of thinkers and movements that we might look at, defines the object of his study as "the fresh religious movements which have appeared in India since the effective introduction of Western influence."[44] Later on he states "History has shown decisively that it was the British Government and Protestant Missions working together that produced the Awakening of India."[45] Quite clearly Farquhar equates modernity in India with the introduction of Westernization, especially in its British Christian forms. Those Indian groups that Farquhar identifies as "modern" are the movements, such as the Brahmo Samaj, that favor "vigorous reform" and that denounce caste discriminations, reject Hindu "idolatry" and other such "debased" Hindu practices and customs as *satī*. Those movements, however, that seek "full defence of the old religions," such as the Ramakrishna movement, are "traditionalist" and "revivalist." He interprets "revivalist" to mean a returning to earlier, most often vedic, norms and values that, for the revivalist, not only place Hinduism alongside of Christianity as a universal religion, but that hold it aloft as a superior religious tradition, which in its purest form represents the essence of true spirituality. The more that the revivalist thinker or movement asserts the superiority of Hindu tradition, the more that thinker or movement, according to Farquhar, becomes identified with what he calls "the old faith," as distinguished from the new faith characteristic of the reformist movements.

Farquhar's classification, then, provides us with a scale of sociocultural change that ranges from reformist movements, such as the Brahmo Samaj, that are correlated with modernity at one end, to revivalist movements, such as the Ramakrishna movement, that are correlated with tradition on the other. In the middle places movements such as the Arya Samaj that in part sought to reform Hindu tradition and that in part sought to "defend the ancient faith" without becoming fully identified with either position. According to Farquhar's reasoning, the Sivananda movement would be placed next to or alongside of the Ramakrishna movement and therefore would be characterized as revivalist, traditionalist, and resistant to sociocultural change. Nothing, I would argue, could be further from the truth. Farquhar fails to see the important role that many so-called revivalist movements have played in creating Hindu modernity.

Although recent scholarship might well reject Farquhar's simplistic equation of the introduction of Westernization with modernity in India, we, in the West, continue to define what we mean by Hindu modernity in Western terms and concepts that do not take into account the complexity of Indian patterns and forms of social, cultural, and religious development. Susan Seymour presents this problem and argues for a solution that stresses the adaptiveness of Indian institutions:

Until recent years Western theories of sociocultural change have been tied to a bipolar model of tradition and modernity that viewed these concepts as dichotomously related. As a consequence, attention had tended to focus upon structural differences and implied incompatibilities between the old and the new rather than upon processes of adaptation, thus producing an analytic gap between tradition and modernity. Attention has tended to focus either upon "the modern", excluding its traditional features, or upon "the traditional", overlooking its modern potentialities. More recent observations and analysis of developing nations, however, have pointed to *continuities* between the old and the new, thus diminishing the presumed antithesis between more traditional and more modern ways of doing things. This recognition has led more recently to a dialectical view of change where tradition and modernity are no longer assumed to be in opposition to one another, but rather where traditional and modern elements are believed to be in dynamic interaction.[46]

If we accept Seymour's analysis of the "dialectical view of change," in which traditional and modern elements interact with each other, we see that traditional institutions such as monasticism and asceticism, which many Western observers have labeled "other-worldly," "escapist," or "world-negating" institutions, have provided structures that have been instrumental in the process of change. Indeed, as I have argued elsewhere, the monastic heads, the gurus of Hindu tradition, have often become the principal agents of social, cultural, and religious change.[47] Of course, this fact had been pointed out earlier by G.S. Ghurye in his excellent study, *Indian Sadhus* (1953) and by Agehananda Bharati in his essay, "The Hindu Renaissance and its Apologetic Patterns" (1970).[48]

Working within the Hindu context rather than imposing Western concepts on it from without, Bharati identifies five major groups of individuals who have contributed significantly to the Hindu renaissance, which he notes is: "a revival that began to materialize during the early days of the British Raj and reached its consummation around the time of Indian Independence."[49] Using Neil Smelser's definition, Bharati defines a revival as "an enthusiastic redefinition of religious methods, but not a challenge to basic religious values."[50] Since Bharati's purpose is to examine "the idiom of the Hindu Renaissance as the linguistic medium of the modern Indian apologetic," he uses "modern' to connote that part of the apologetic which harnesses technological simile and parable to vindicate or exemplify ancient truths; 'traditional' would stand for statements which refer to an actual or legendary Indian past by way of extolling or moralizing."[51] Modern is, then, an evaluation of a kind of Hindu thinking that adopts the language of Western science and technology as a model of communication and persuasion without renouncing traditional religious values.

Although Bharati does not state it explicitly, he is well aware of the interaction between traditional and modern values in the thought of Hindus such as Svami Dayananda, Svami Vivekananda, Sri Aurobindo, Svami Sivananda, former president of India S. Radhakrishnan, and the late professor V. Raghavan, to name several of those whom he holds to be representative of the process of change from traditional to modern ways of thinking and acting. But of those individuals who have adopted modern elements into their thought without renouncing basic or traditional religious values, the monastics or the *sādhus* are the most influential groups: "When the *sādhus* are viewed as a total category, they certainly represent the most powerful bloc of agents of the Hindu Renaissance."[52]

Yet, Bharati quickly notes that the Hindu attitude to the *sādhus*, as a composite of many diverse elements, is one of ambivalence:

The modern Hindu disavows the "old-fashioned", non-English speaking, peregrinating or *āśram*-bound sadhu who does not contribute to modern life. Yet, all "modernites" overtly or covertly admire and venerate the "scientific", "modern" man who wears monastic robes: Swami Vivekananda is an undisputed culture-hero not simply of all modern Bengali Hindus. . . . Modern Hindus derive their knowledge of Hinduism from Vivekananda, directly or indirectly . . . it was Vivekananda and his latter day imitators, including the late Sivananda Sarasvati, who really created the diction and the style of the apologetic.[53]

The identification of this ambivalent attitude is important for our discussion of Hindu modernity. We now are able to define Hindu modernity and its agents in a way that gives us a much more adequate picture of the complexity of the Indian religious situation than that given by Farquhar. We can redraw our scale of sociocultural change, placing those individuals and movements who support and promote the Hindu apologetic at the end that correlates with modernity and those individuals and movements who adhere to "the old-fashioned" values at the end that correlates with tradition. But, let us also acknowledge that those two positions are in dynamic tension and interaction with each other and that they are not bipolar opposites. To be a modern Hindu, then, is not only to engage in the rhetoric of the apologetic, but to carry out its pronouncements in religious action, and of those groups directing sociocultural change, the modernist *sādhus* are "at the helm of things."[54]

The mistake that Bharati makes, however, is placing the agents of the Hindu renaissance into seemingly separate categories: the *sādhus* or gurus first, followed by the politicians; the lay devotees; the pundits; and the chroniclers. But, as I have argued earlier, the structure of Hindu monasticism is related to the *sampradāya* as its integrating concept and as its institutional form. The *sampradāya*, with the guru at the center, incorporates the other agents of modernity except those pundits who refuse to acknowledge the "English speaking sadhus." The lay devotees follow the direction of their gurus, and as I have illustrated in another article, politicians continue to play significant supportive roles in the life of certain *sampradāyas*.[55] The *sampradāya*, then, is that which provides, in Seymour's words, "continuities between the old and the new. . . (leading) to a dialectical view of change . . . where traditional and modern elements are believed to be in dynamic interaction."

The study of the Sivananda movement as a "new" *sampradāya* enables us to understand one factor in the complex pattern of social, cultural, and religious change that is taking place in India today. But the Sivananda movement is only one of many such movements; let me repeat the words of Khushwant Singh: "The number of saintly men and women are beyond enumeration. Every district has its quota of *living* saints to whom people turn for advice on spiritual and worldly matters."

Notes

1. Aubrey Menen, *The New Mystics* (London: Thames and Hudson, 1974); Khushwant Singh, *Gurus, Godmen, and Good People* (Bombay: Orient Longman, 1975); Sujan 'Singh Uban, *The Gurus of India* (London: Fine Books, 1977). See also Swami Agehananda Bharati, "The Hindu Renaissance and Its Apologetic Patterns," *Journal of Asian Studies* 29/2 (1970): 267-88.
2. Singh, *Gurus, Godmen, and Good People*, p. xii.
3. Wilfred Cantwell Smith, *The Meaning and End of Religion* (New York: Mentor Books, 1964), p. 143.

4. David M. Miller and Dorothy C. Wertz, *Hindu Monastic Life: The Monks and Monasteries of Bhubaneswar* (Montreal: McGill-Queen's University Press, 1976), p. 4.

5. G.S. Ghurye, *Indian Sadhus* (Bombay: Popular Prakashan, 1964). See also David Miller, "The Guru as the Centre of Sacredness," *Studies in Religion* 6/5 (Summer 1976-77) : 527-33.

6. David Miller, "Religious Institutions and Political Elites in Bhubaneswar," in Susan Seymour, ed., *The Transformation of a Sacred Town: Bhubaneswar, India* (Boulder, CO: Westview Press, 1980), pp. 83-95.

7. Miller, "The Guru as the Centre of Sacredness." See also Susan Seymour, "Some Conclusions: Sources of Change and Continuity," in Seymour, ed., *The Transformation of a Sacred Town*, pp. 257-73.

8. Swami Sivananda, *Autobiography of Swami Sivananda* (Rishikesh: The Divine Life Society Press, 1958), pp. vii-viii.

9. Swami Venkatesananda, *Gurudev Sivananda* (Rishikesh: The Divine Life Society Press, 1960), pp. xxix-xl.

10. Sivananda, *Autobiography*, pp. 47-48.

11. Ibid., p. 4.

12. Venkatesananda, *Gurudev Sivananda*, pp. 3-6.

13. Ibid., p. 17.

14. Ibid., p. 26.

15. Ibid., p. 27.

16. Sivananda, *Autobiography*, p. 11.

17. Ibid.

18. Ibid.

19. Venkatesananda, *Gurudev Sivananda*, p. 81.

20. Sivananda, *Autobiography*, p. 16.

21. Ibid., p. 21.

22. Venkatesananda, *Gurudev Sivananda*, p. 101.

23. Sivananda, *Autobiography*, p. 24.

24. Ghurye, *Indian Sadhus*, p. 82.

25. Venkatesananda, *Gurudev Sivananda*, pp. 123-24.

26. Sivananda, *Autobiography*, p. 34.

27. Ibid., p. 42.

28. Bharati, "The Hindu Renaissance and Its Apologetic Patterns," pp. 272-73.

29. Sivananda, *Autobiography*, pp. 49-50.

30. Most publications of the Divine Life Society Press have, as an appendix, a statement of "The Aims and Objectives of the The Divine Life Society," which are:

I. To Disseminate Spiritual Knowledge
   a. By publication of books, pamphlets and magazines ...
   b. By propagating the Name of the Lord and by holding and arranging spiritual discourses and conferences ...
   c. By establishing training centres or societies for the practice of Yoga, for moral and spiritual Sadhanas ...
   d. By doing all such acts and things as may be necessary and conducive to the moral, spiritual and cultural uplift of mankind ...

    II. To Establish and Run Educational Institutions

   III. To Help Deserving Orphans and Destitutes

   IV. To Establish and Run Medical Organizations

   V. To Take Such Other Steps from Time to Time as may be necessary for effecting a quick and effective moral and spiritual regeneration in the world . . .

(Sri Swami Chidananda, *Light Fountain* [Rishikesh: The Divine Life Society Press, 1972], pp. 222-23.)

31. Ibid.

32. Venkatesananda, *Gurudev Sivananda*, p. 369.

33. The Divine Life Society, *World Parliament of Religions, Commemoration Volume* (Rishikesh: Divine Life Society Press, 1956), p. 64.

34. Venkatesananda, *Gurudev Sivananda*, p. 380.

35. Ibid., p. 250.

36. Swami Sivananda, "I Marvel at Krishnanandaji," in *Glorious Fifty Years of Wisdom and Service* (Rishikesh: Divine Life Society, 1972), p. 10.

37. Lily Cohen-Miller, interview with Swami Sivananda-Hridayananda, September 1977. Although Swami Hridayananda told Lily about her son, no mention of a "son" appears in the introduction to her *Sivananda: My God* (Rishikesh: The Divine Life Society Press, 1957).

38. Sivananda-Hridayananda, interview.

39. Svami Sivananda, *Sivananda's Lectures: All India Tour (1950)*, ed. Svami Venkatesananda (Rishikesh: The Divine Life Society Press, 1951).

40. Ibid., p. 200.

41. Ibid., p. 424.

42. Venkatesananda, *Gurudev Sivananda*, p. 253.

43. The Divine Life Society, *Statement of Membership*.

44. J.N. Farquhar, *Modern Religious Movements in India* (New York: Macmillan, 1915), p. 1.

45. Ibid., p. 8.

46. Seymour, "Some Conclusions: Sources of Change and Continuity," p. 266. The wording from the manuscript in preparation was changed slightly in the published text, which was not available to me at the time of typing my paper.

47. Miller, "The Guru as the Centre of Sacredness."

48. Ghurye, *Indian Sadhus*; Bharati, "The Hindu Renaissance and Its Apologetic Patterns."

49. Bharati, "The Hindu Renaissance and Its Apologetic Patterns."

50. Ibid.

51. Ibid.

52. Ibid., p. 278.

53. Ibid.

54. Ibid., p. 277.

55. Miller, "Religious Institutions and Political Elites in Bhubaneswar."

5

THE AHMADIYAH MOVEMENT: ISLAMIC RELIGIOUS REFORM IN MODERN INDIA

Spencer Lavan

If one must focus a lens on only a couple of modern Islamic movements with a major impact on the Indian subcontinent, the Ahmadiyah movement is both an appropriate and an inappropriate choice.[1] It is inappropriate if one is citing as a positive measure of impact progressive social ideology and missionary religious zeal to improve the status and spread of the Islamic message in India. The Ahmadiyah is an appropriate choice, however, because important aspects of its theology have been deemed heretical by Sunni Islam. Following riots against the Ahmadiyah community, whose international headquarters are now in Pakistan, a 1974 law declared them a non-Muslim minority. One outcome of this legislation was to compel Ahmadis who wished to hold major government and military positions to renounce their membership in the movement and declare their allegiance to Sunni Islam.

At the root of the controversy is a question as old as Islam itself: "Who is a true Muslim?" Shortly after the Prophet Muhammad died in A.D. 632, after he had established a religious state in the territory between Medina and Mecca, several "false prophets" arose, claiming the allegiance of the Bedouin who had been converted to Islam. During the first generation after the Prophet, the Shi'ah, or partisans of 'Ali, claimed that the legitimate succession (khilāfat) should have gone to 'Ali, the Prophet's son-in-law. The

Shi'ah theology in large measure rests on the argument that Islamic leadership should have remained in the family rather than going to the first three *khalīfahs*, Abu Bakr, 'Umar, and 'Uthman, who were chosen as leaders by election. A bloody struggle between the Sunni and Shi'ah factions led to the deaths of 'Ali and his two sons barely thirty years after the death of Muhammad. During the latter part of the seventh century A.D., a group known as the Kharajites ("those who went out") raised the theological issue of works as a necessary corollary to faith. Some of this group took their position to such an extreme that they declared that anyone not accepting their particular views was not a Muslim and should be put to death. The prevailing Sunni position was that a person professing faith, or witnessing that "there is no God but Allah," and doing so with true sincerity of heart need show no other proof that he or she is a true Muslim.

Many of the early Sufis in their rejection of law, tradition, and institutional practice in favor of personal mystic experience fell into disfavor with the Sunni establishment. Well known is the case of al-Hallaj, the Sufi who in a moment of transcendental ecstasy shouted, "I am the Truth." He was put to death for the heresy of declaring he was God's equal. The views of Mirza Ghulam Ahmad and the Ahmadiyah movement he founded for Islamic renewal differ considerably from those of the Shi'ah, Kharajite, or Sufi variations just cited, with differences in theology and operational method. Even in the Indian context, where Muslims were a distinctive minority in a predominantly Hindu culture, Ahmadi views were sufficiently controversial to lead to the disruptions which caused the 1974 legal condemnation of the movement in Pakistan.

The Islamic Messianic Tradition

In order to understand the Ahmadiyah point of view in its Islamic context or to ask questions about the controversial nature of the movement's claims and aims, it is first important to observe the emergence of this religious sect within Islam. That its founder claimed to be a promised messiah, or a *mahdī*, to Muslims was neither original nor unusual. The concept of a *mahdī*, a rightly guided leader who would come at the end of time, had existed within both the Sunni and Shi'ah traditions from the early centuries of Islam. For the Shi'ah, the concept of *imām* had a specific theological connotation, referring to the descendants of the Holy Prophet's son-in-law, 'Ali. The Shi'ah believed them to be the rightful heirs to the leadership of the Islamic community. For the different Shi'ah subsects, the *mahdī* was the *imām* who, in the tradition of that sect, had mysteriously disappeared. The faithful believed that this *imām* would return at an appropriate moment in history to lead the Shi'ah to everlasting glory, especially in their political struggles against Sunni Islam.

By contrast, the Sunni view held the *imām* to be leader of a worshipping community. Sunnis believe in a *mahdī* as God's representative in the person of Jesus who will come at the end of time to lead the believers in a bloody battle against the unbelievers *(kafirs)*. During the medieval period, many religious saints declared themselves to be the *mahdī*, proclaiming religious or political reform. The appearance of a *mahdī* frequently occurred at the end of an Islamic century, a period associated with the apocalypse. Perhaps the most well-known *mahdī* was the one who proclaimed himself in the Sudan in the early 1880s (at the end of the fourteenth Islamic century). This *mahdī* claimed divine inspiration, organizing Muslims in a military *jihād* (holy war, or struggle for God), against the English and Egyptians.

As further background to understanding the role of the Ahmadiyah movement for Islamic reform in modern India, two key Quranic terms require discussion: *nabī* and *rasūl*. These terms describe Muhammad's role as "prophet" and "messenger" of God. While Quranic revelation makes clear the fact that Muhammad was the final prophet or "seal," the possibility was left open for continuing revelation, as expressed in such Islamic concepts as *wahy* (revelation), *ilhām* (inspiration), and *mujaddid* (renewer of the faith). Sufi mystics often used these terms to describe their own religious experiences. In India, attempts at religious renewal by men describing themselves as *mujaddid* had occurred frequently in the seventeenth and eighteenth centuries.

The discussion of these Islamic theological terms is a prerequisite for understanding the religious leadership of Mirza Ghulam Ahmad and the origins of the Ahmadiyah movement. At the same time, the Indian social and political mid-nineteenth century context is crucial. As one can see how, the Brahmo Samaj and Ramakrishna Mission Hindu reform movements arose in a Bengali environment following the advent of the British East India Company, English education and the Christian missions, one must understand the advent of the Arya Samaj and Ahmadiyah movements on Punjabi soil as a reflection of the tensions among the religiously divided population of that province and ethnic area. In the Gurdaspur district north of Amritsar, the district in which the Ahmadiyah movement began, a population of close to one million was divided—49% Muslim, 40% Hindu, 10% Sikh. Although only 4,000 Christians inhabited the district, their impact and support from the missionary movement with its schools and hospitals was obviously significant in far greater proportions than the numbers would indicate. This population mix held true throughout Punjab, an area of India in which serious religious conflict had been a way of life for several centuries.

With the arrival of Muslims from the West in the eleventh century A.D., persecution of the Hindus and mass conversions of low-caste people to Islam had left one legacy of conflict. During the Mughal period, the Sikhs emerged, regularly persecuted by the Muslims. The Sikhs grew in militancy, leaving yet another religious struggle unresolved. In the eighteenth century the decline of Mughal fortunes allowed the Sikhs under Rangit Singh to hold a major portion of Punjab territory against both Muslims and Hindus. With the arrival of the British in the 1840s, a Western presence, foreign in spirit and policy to all three of the indigenous groups, took political control.

The Ahmadiyah Movement: Its Origins and Teachings

It would be fair to say that the two Bengali Hindu reform movements, the Brahmo Samaj and Ramakrishna Mission, developed from a need to respond to spiritual crisis and not nearly so much to a political context, while the two Punjabi movements, the Arya Samaj and the Ahmadiyah, needed deeply controversial soil in which to flourish. All Muslim movements taking shape in India after 1857 need also to be seen in light of the British suppression of the "uprising" or "mutiny" which took place that year. Although the events did not center in Punjab, there lay behind them the hope that the old Mughal empire might be restored to replace encroaching British rule. Because of the major Muslim role in the mutiny events, the Muslim community as a whole became alienated from their British rulers.

While post-1857 is considered a negative period in Indian Muslim history, several developments and individuals stand out as part of a pattern for Islamic renewal. Outstanding among Muslim leaders of the late nineteenth century was Sayyid Ahmad Khan, who broke fresh ground in the fields of education and religious thought by asserting the importance of *ijtihād* (reinterpretation) in religious matters to meet the needs of the times. He believed that the *'ulamā'* in India were neglecting their duty by refusing to recognize the possibility of a *mujtahīd* or *mujaddid,* not in the millennial sense of the Sudanese *mahdi*, but as a renewer bringing an awareness of Islamic needs for a modern world.

Sayyid Ahmad had remained loyal to the British during the mutiny and believed that the British would rule India for many years. He, therefore, urged Muslims to take advantage of what British culture and education had to offer. In 1875, he founded the Anglo-Oriental College at Aligarh in the United Provinces. Through publications emananting from there, the Aligarh movement emerged to call attention to the problems Indian Muslims faced as a minority people in India.[2] Fearing the negative possibilities should parliamentary democracy come to the subcontinent with Hindus outnumbering Muslims four to one, Sayyid Ahmad urged Muslims not to join the Indian National Congress at its inception in 1885. Because Sayyid Ahmad Khan represents Sunni or mainstream liberal thought emerging in the Muslim community several decades before Mirza Ghulam Ahmad's very different reform movement, his views are an important background stage in providing an understanding of Ghulam Ahmad and his movement for Islamic renewal.

Sayyid Ahmad Khan remained loyal to the British and saw the advantages of Muslims using what they had to offer. There were times when he disagreed with the British, however, and found it necessary to explain Muslim interests to the government. This he did through the Muhammadan Anglo-Oriental Defense Association founded in Aligarh in 1893. Among the objectives of the association were the representation of Muslim views to the government and English people, discouraging popular and political agitation among Muslims and working to increase the stability of the British government in India as well as to preserve peace among the populace.

Mirza Ghulam Ahmad, founder of the Ahmadiyah movement, stands in sharp contrast to the liberal, well-educated and politically astute Sayyid Ahmad Khan. There are also similarities between the two men and the movements they developed. During the same period there developed also a number of more traditional and conservative Muslim educational and cultural renewal movements.[3]

Who was Mirza Ghulam Ahmad? He was born in the village of Qadian, Gurdaspur district of northern Punjab. The descendant of a Mughal who had come to India with Babur's armies in the sixteenth century, Ghulam Ahmad was the son of a middle-class family of landowners. The village of Qadian itself received its name because Ahmad's original ancestor settled there and served as village *qadi* or judge. Early in the nineteenth century, the Sikhs under Ranjit Singh took over the family lands, thereby depriving Ahmad's family of its income for a period of more than thirty years. When the British established control of Punjab in the 1840s, Mirza Ghulam Ahmad's father professed his loyalty and became the kind of landowner on whom the British came to rely as they developed their provincial administration. It was in this context then that Ghulam Ahmad received his education in *Qur'ān* and *Hadīth* during the 1840s and '50s from several tutors, both at Qadian and the neighboring town of Batala.

Although Mirza Ghulam Ahmad claimed to have received direct revelations from God during his life as a religious leader and though he frequently used terms also used by Sufis, it is clear from a number of sources that Ahmad was never a Sufi nor was he trained by Sufis. He began his career as a law clerk at Sialkot in an effort to help his father with several pending law-suits involving family lands. After work, he would read the *Qur'ān* and pray. While at Sialkot, Ahmad had his first contact with Christian missionaries, his first acquaintance with the Bible, and his first awareness of the possibilities for missionizing Islam. This is not to suggest that the Ahmadiyah mission was entirely modeled after a Christian one. The germ of the idea must have started with his contact among the Christians; however, it was also shaped by the work of the Hindu Brahmo Samaj and Arya Samaj missionary efforts in Punjab.

There is no doubt that Mirza Ghulam Ahmad was an intelligent man who developed his own organizational methods in addition to drawing on those around him that he judged effective. At Sialkot, for example, he entered, into debate with Christians, and also became familiar with Sayyid Ahmad Khan's commentary on Genesis. A few years later, Ghulam Ahmad outrightly repudiated Sayyid Ahmad's *tafsir* or commentary on the *Qur'ān*, not only because of its naturalistic approach but because of its apologetic attitude, "as if there were anything in Islam that could not hold its own in the face of modern knowledge and science."4

The emergence of Ahmad's defensive attitude towards promoting Islam in Punjab coincided with his return home in 1876 to manage family estates following the death of his father. It also coincided with the appearance in 1877 of Svami Dayanand Saraswati and the latter's initial successful promotion of the militantly self-conscious Hinduism of the Arya Samaj in Punjab. Ahmad felt the need to proclaim the truths of Islam and to challenge opponents, whether Hindu or Christian, to debate the truths of the scriptures and traditions. For the next thirty years, that is, until his death in Lahore in 1908, Ahmad continued to write voraciously in Urdu, Persian, and Arabic, while organizing in 1889 the Ahmadiyah movement, whose journals and newspapers would aid in propagating Islam in Africa, England, and America, as well as in India.

Ghulam Ahmad's theological position emerged over the next two decades, along with his religious reform movement. In 1880 he began publication of the four-volume work, *Proofs of the Ahmadiyah*, a project which took four years to complete. The purpose of the work was the rejuvenation of Islam by a rational, logical, and systematic exposition. The text in Urdu which claimed to be the basis for a dialogue with non-Muslims was in fact just the opposite. Ahmad attempted in these volumes to establish the proofs of Islam as contained without doubt or error in the *Qur'ān*, claiming that such arguments would involve disproving and over-throwing "the wrong beliefs of the Arya Samaj" and the Brahmo Samaj.5

The Arya Samaj6 and Svami Dayanand had through the Svami's book, *The Light of Truth*, already provoked controversy. The work had set forth for Hindus the principles of a "true" vedic faith and had then attempted to repudiate vociferously the teachings of Islam, Christianity, and Sikhism. In particular, the provocations of the Arya Samaj with its *śuddhi* or reconversion movement helped Ahmad to develop a renewed perspective on the Islamic concept of *jihād*. For Sunni Islam, *jihād* had traditionally implied actual armed struggle to defend Islamic territory from attack or incursion by non-Muslim forces. But Ahmad developed the concept in a new way. He meant to use it as a way of getting Islam to reassert itself both in Punjab and throughout India, not only against the growing militancy of the Arya Samaj but also against the emerging self-consciousness of Punjabi Sikhs and also against evangelical Christianity. The use of the term *jihād* even in this new sense proved highly controversial, and Ahmad found himself regularly professing his loyalty to the British government, for whom the word *jihād* was very much a danger signal.

But Ahmad's theology focused on Islamic renewal for its own sake and in the context of his own personality as well. In some places he appears to have referred to himself and his role by the term *nabī* or prophet, a term reserved in Islam for Muhammad only. His followers frequently interpret this as *mujaddid*, "one who has come to renew the faith." By insisting on this latter interpretation, the Ahmadiyah movement has withstood some persecution from within the Islamic community for accepting the unthinkable—a prophet after Muhammad.

The concept *mahdī* was very much in the air at the end of the thirteenth Islamic century (1884). Ghulam Ahmad declared early in his career that Allah had revealed that the epithets *mahdī* and *Masih maw'ūd* (Promised Messiah) applied to him. What was the meaning and significance of such a declaration? To Ahmad it was the fulfilment of the divine promise made to all Muslims "that at the commencement of every century the Most High God will raise a man who will revive and resuscitate His religion."[7]

Ahmad wrote repreatedly about the general decay of Islam in his time and about the need for a messiah. On the basis of scripture he argued that just as Jesus had appeared 1400 years after Moses the Lawgiver, so the Promised Messiah must appear now, "invested with the spirit and power of Jesus son of Mary in the 14th century after the appearance of the Holy Prophet of Islam."

While traditional Islamic belief accepted by Sunnis assumed the *mahdī* and the Messiah of the future to be two separate persons, each of whom would aid Muslims in the bloody battle against the *kafirs,* Ahmad established himself as a peaceful Messiah and *mahdī,* minimizing the traditional "bloody" role of the latter. Ghulam Ahmad's claims seem to have impressed a sufficient number of Punjabi Muslims that by 1889 he was prepared to accept *bay'ah* or an oath of allegiance, as a prelude towards the formation of the Ahmadiyah movement itself. *Bay'ah* required a commitment to ten points, nine of which were traditionally Islamic (five were the five "pillars" of Islamic faith—witnessing to God, prayer, fasting almsgiving, and pilgrimage) while the tenth was a lifetime commitment beyond even the blood relationship to be made by the disciple to Ahmad as Promised Messiah.[8]

The commitment to the pilgrimage to Mecca is particularly worth noting. Ahmad himself never made the pilgrimage although his son and second successor did several times. The reasons given for why the dynamic founder of such a significant Islamic reform movement never made the pilgrimage included poor health and organizational concerns. Of course, in the 1890s such a journey would require several months in the coming and going.

Ahmad and the Death of Jesus

One of the critical points of Ahmad's argument that he was the Promised Messiah for Islam focused around the idea that he was a person like Jesus, although not the same being as Jesus. This assertion required that he disprove both the Muslim view on the presence of Jesus in heaven in his full physical condition and the Christian doctrine of the Resurrection. From many sources, Ahmad assembled evidence that Jesus did not die on the cross, but rather was rescued and cured of his wounds by a secret ointment. According to Ahmad, Jesus had then escaped from Palestine, journeyed across Asia to Kashmir, where he completed his ministry to the lost tribes of Israel, and died at the age of 120.

Although Ahmad developed this understanding of his own messianic role early, he did not spell it out until the publication of *Masih Hindustan Men (Jesus in India)* in 1899.[9] This later work united all Ahmad's arguments against both Muslim and Christian views on the subject of Jesus. At the same time, in explaining his own role as *mahdi*, he combined his arguments about Jesus with those concerned with the fact that he was not a *ghazi mahdi* (bloody warrior messiah) which so many of the *'ulama'* were expecting in the last days. Such an idea, he argued, was totally rejected in both *Qur'ān* and *Hadīth,* and had no place in the thinking or religious life of his age.[10]

Demonstrating that by heavenly signs he had been sent to redeem Islam, Ahmad called upon those morally fit to join with him against those "who hold false hopes of a bloody Messiah or *mahdī.*"[11] The final and perhaps most important proof repudiating traditional Muslim positions on Jesus in favor of Ahmad as the new Promised Messiah was Ahmad's "discovery" of the actual grave site, "a Jewish grave," located on Khan Yar Street in Srinagar, Kashmir.[12]

Without this initial discussion of Ghulam Ahmad's self-definition and variations on traditional Islamic theology, the uniqueness of his Ahmadiyah movement in the context of modern Islamic movements whether in or out of South Asia cannot be fully understood. His own conception of his role and function as Promised Messiah and *mahdī* returns ultimately to his understanding of *jihād.* If the *mahdī* was a spiritual prophet for the present age, and not a *ghazī* or a bloody *mahdī,* then *jihād* against the ruling government could have no place. Ahmad thus publicly attacked the *mahdī* of the Sudan while initiating his own style of *jihād* as a *tablīgh* or missionary program.

The Success of Ahmadiyah During Ahmad's Career

By the 1890s Ahmad's claims and the growth of his following brought him considerable public notice in north India. His views not only brought him opposition from the established Muslim community, but his own claims brought Ahmad into confrontation with Hindus, Christians, and the Sikh community as well. Early in 1891, a *mullah,* 'Abd al-Haq Ghaznavi of Amritsar, challenged Ahmad to a *mubāhala* on the question of the death of Jesus, whom the *mullah* believed "to be sitting in the heavens in his physical body." The practice of *mubāhala* relates to an Arabic term meaning "to curse." The *mubāhala* itself was a debate taken so seriously by all parties that each participant would call down the curses of God upon his opponent. Such a practice had been previously known when Muslims and non-Muslims came into conflict. With Ahmad it was used for the first time when he debated Muslim opponents.

Ahmad appeared to be such a threat that three other north Indian *mullahs* signed a *fatwā* saying that such a debate was permissible among Muslims. Ahmad had no choice but to defend his position against attack. In doing so he was able to present himself publicly. His charismatic personality, his dynamic public presentation, and his message of renewal all succeeded in drawing crowds to his ministry. It is reported that as many as 5,000 persons were in attendance during a major debate held at the Jama Masjid in Delhi.[13]

Ahmadiyah literature describing Ahmad's ministry during the decade of the 1890s likens him to the persecuted Jesus of the Gospels. He seems clearly to have wanted to appeal to those who were already being won over by Christian street preachers. He seems to have learned something about missions from the protestants present throughout Punjab as well as from the outreach of the Bengali Brahmo Samaj and the newly organized Arya Samaj of Svami Dayanand.

Ahmad gained particular notoriety in a debate held in 1893 against an Indian Christian who had been converted from Islam. The acrimonious controversy continued over a twelve-day period, during which time Ahmad predicted the untimely death of his Christian opponent. While the prophecy did not come true, the flurry of excitement it caused and the number of tracts published by Christians against Mirza Ghulam Ahmad began to proliferate. Ahmad took his opponents to court to stop the publication of various critical tracts.

Mirza Ghulam Ahmad's ability to stir up interest in Islam by his controversial tactics, his ardent defense of the faith and his role as a renewer for the faith was the dynamic force behind his success. The primary Indian Islamic movements which attempted to respond to the post-mutiny crisis had been academic in orientation. Sayyid Ahmad Khan's college at Aligarh and the new seminaries at De'oband and Lucknow all spoke more to intellectual needs of a new Muslim learned class than to the emotional needs of the people. Mirza Ghulam Ahmad's direct confrontation, particularly with the neoconservative and militant Hindu Arya Samaj which too had taken root in Punjab, made Ahmad an exciting figure, especially among the educated middle-class in cities such as Sialkot, Ludhiana, and Amritsar.

The conflict and controversy in which Ahmad engaged with the Hindu Aryas, while not new (Hindu/Muslim controversy and violence had existed since the advent of Islam in India), took a new form in the context of the British presence. One might agree with some historians that it was the deliberate purpose of the post-mutiny British rule in India to "divide and conquer" by keeping Muslims and Hindus at odds with one another. Or, one might assume that the British really tried to keep the peace, but in their failure to understand what really motivated the various communities, bungled the task through their various administrators and their obvious exploitation of Indian resources. Whichever overview one takes, the facts are still clear that Ahmad in his context as a Muslim reformer saw the Arya Samaj Hindus as a real threat to his own reform movement.

While it was not an Ahmadi who murdered Arya Lekh Ram on March 6, 1897, the murderer was a Muslim who was instigated by the curse which Ahmad placed on the Arya's life. The controversy between the Aryas and Ahmadis which built over a fifteen-year period has its origins in the publication of *Satya Prakash,* or *The Light of Truth,* the magnum opus of Svami Dayanand, founder of the Arya Samaj movement. The book and the subsequent organization which took firm hold in Punjab both were intended to raise Hindu self-consciousness, to reconvert by *śuddhi* Hindus who had become Christian or Muslim, and to reform Hinduism by abolishing the caste system and permitting widow remarriage.

Lekh Ram was an especially militant Arya who in his writings and speeches advocated the use of Hindi rather than the predominant Urdu, cow protection, and opposition to Ahmadiyah Islam. His knowledge of Persian and Arabic gave him a strong position in arguing against Islam while his 1892 tract, "Jehad or the Basis of Muhammadi Religion," was especially offensive to all Muslims. The acrimony between Lekh Ram and Ghulam Ahmad was reported throughout the Punjab, with Hindu and Muslim newspapers of all viewpoints joining in with editorials and biased coverage. The controversy reached such a point in 1893 that Ghulam Ahmad predicted that unless the Arya recanted his insults against Islam, God would strike Lekh Ram down within six years. On March 6, 1897, a young Muslim, not an Ahmadi, murdered Lekh Ram in Lahore.[14]

While one would expect that the Muslim community would

have appreciated Ahmad for his active campaign against the militant Hindus, in reality he received nothing but abuse from Muslims. The capture of the assassin of Lekh Ram toned down the controversy between Punjabi Hindus and Muslims as it related to the two new sects. Government and police kept a close eye on both communities, to the extent that in 1898 Ahmad was taken to court along with a Muslim opponent, Muhammad Husayn of Batala. Both were put under restraint by the justice to cease publication of inflammatory literature.

It is not difficult to see how charged the atmosphere among the Muslims, Hindu, Christian missions, and government was at the turn of the century. Several factors need to be taken into account so as not to judge Ahmad's behavior or claims as totally outrageous from a contemporary Western point of view. As already indicated, Muslims in the area were responsive to a charismatic preacher of Islamic renewal, even one who made claims to be a *nabi*, a *mahdi*, and a Promised Messiah. While Ahmad's message spoke clearly to popular religious needs, he was also a direct threat to the established Muslim community and religious leadership, especially on the point of his use of the word *nabi* to describe himself in some contexts.

In addition, however, Hindus, especially the younger educated ones, were responsive to the message of renewal offered by Svami Dayanand and his followers, such as Lekh Ram. The Aryas raised issues such as the use of Hindi versus Urdu, the protection of cows against Muslims who ate beef. An undercurrent of discrimination felt by Muslims in their struggle to gain positions in a government bureaucracy dominated by the new Hindu educated class also played a role in the developing tensions into which the Ahmadiyah message fed. One needs also to take into account the defensive attitude of much of the Christian missionary movement, which in some of its publications regularly attacked Ghulam Ahmad as a charlatan and imposter. In order to seek protection for himself and his followers, Mirza Ghulam Ahmad continually professed his loyalty to the British government, one factor which did not make him popular among most proto-nationalist forces.

How Ahmadiyah Worked

The growth of printing and publications in vernacular languages

during the latter decades of the nineteenth century throughout India
was a critical new tool for the communication of ideas and varying
philosophies. Only a few months before the notoriety of the Lekh
Ram incident, Ahmad had initiated publication of *al-Hakam*, a
weekly newspaper from Qadian. The paper was edited by Shaykh
Yakub 'Ali, a man with previous newspaper experience in Amritsar.
By 1902, *Badr,* another more irregularly published journal, was
undertaken. Far more significant was the initiation, also in 1902,
of *Review of Religions*, a journal which, because it was published
both in Urdu and English, made the movement known far better in
the Anglophone world. Established under a separate corporation,
the *Anjumān Ishā'at-i-Islam*, the journal was first edited by
Khawajah Kamal-ud-Din and Muhammud 'Ali, two of the most
educated and capable members of the movement. Both men were
involved in the 1913 split in which they led a small group off from
Qadian to establish a more moderate branch of Ahmadiyah. The
original English circulation of *Review* was 760 copies per month, a
figure which decreased substantially during the 1920s and 30s—
after the split.[15]

Considering the times and the context in which it was written
and published, the early *Review of Religions* was quite remarkable.
Although it devoted much space to the claims of Ahmad and the
organization of Ahmadiyah, it also contained many articles dealing
with other religious movements. One series appeared on Baha'i,
another criticizing various Western translations of the *Qur'ān*, while
others raised theological arguments against Christianity. As well,
the *Review* contained useful information about the progress of the
movement and about the many conflicts and controversies in which
it was engaged. For example, one issue contained the entire text
of *al-Wasīyah*, or the Will of Mirza Ghulam Ahmad, by far the
most important organizational document for Ahmadiyah during the
lifetime of the founder. It set out specific requirements for Ahmadis
to follow and marked a turning point towards Ahmadi exclusiveness
towards other Muslims who did not accept the claims of Ahmad as
Promised Messiah.

That Mirza Ghulam Ahmad seemed to be appealing largely to
a literate, middle-class group of followers and not as a revolutionary trying to mobilize the poor against social oppression is evident
from a list of 313 original "companions" of the Mirza. The list
included 60 men addressed as *miān* (respected one), 49 as *maulvī*

(mawlawī, or *mullah*, a religious teacher), 42 *munshī* (writer or scribe), 22 *shaykh*, 19 *sayyīd* (descendant of the Holy Prophet), 11 *qadī* (religious judge), and 9 *mirza* (one of royal origin). In addition, persons with such honorific titles as *hajī*, *hafīz*, doctor, *muftī*, and *khawājah* were included in the list.

It may well have been the appeal to such a literate group which inevitably led to the "split" in the movement some five years after Ahmad's death in 1908. At the same time there is sufficient evidence from many other religious reform movements such as the Brahmo Samaj and Arya Samaj that varying interpretations of both the teachings of the founder and the nature of his leadership have brought about other splits. In the Ahmadiyah case, the question arose after Ahmad's death as to whom the leadership *(khilāfat)* should fall. Nur-un-Din, a close friend of Ahmad and a physician by profession was chosen successor in 1908. Had he not fallen from his horse within a few years and died shortly after from injuries, the leadership of Nur-ud-Din might have been more sustained in face of issues raised by the co-editors of *Review of Religions*, Kamal-ud-Din and Muhammad 'Ali. These two were both practicing attorneys before their attraction to Mirza Ghulam Ahmad drew them to Qadian to work for the movement. The two appear to have been less impressed with authoritarian leadership or charismatic preaching as an end in itself. They sought Islamic reform which would encourage people to think for themselves, and which would renew Islam in a way more in keeping with Sunni traditions as well as within the context of the modern world.

Increasingly in his later years, Ghulam Ahmad isolated his movement into a sect. Ahmadis were discouraged from marrying outside the movement. Ahmadis were not to pray behind a non-Ahmadi *imām* because the activities of the worship itself were at some variance with those of Sunni practice.

Khawajah Kamal-ud-Din, in 1912, seems to have been the first Ahmadi to go to Europe, in part to carry out family business, but also to investigate founding a mosque. At the same he and his co-editor began to make changes in the *Review* to make it a publication for a more general Islamic readership not specifically espousing the cause of the Promised Messiah. An examination of *Review* articles between 1908 and 1913 indicates a more intellectual and conciliatory tone to the journal, with the exception of articles against the Arya Samaj. One article published during this period was the text of a paper given by Muhammad 'Ali in the ecumenical setting of the Convention of Religions held at Calcutta in April 1909. In this paper, Muhammad 'Ali explained how Ghulam Ahmad had been an effective religious reformer, one whose religious experiences and mission should have a universal appeal.

With the death of Khalifah Nur-ud-Din in 1914, there began a struggle for succession between the more liberal faction under Muhammad 'Ali and Khawajah Kamal-ud-Din, and the more conservative majority led by Ghulam Ahmad's son, Bashir-ud-Din Mahmud Ahmad. Something resembling the Sunni-Shi'ah struggle seems to have been taking place. Love, respect, and admiration for the Promised Messiah led masses of Ahmadis to feel that succession to the leadership (the *khilāfat*) should pass to Mirza Ghulam Ahmad's son. The editors of *Review of Religions* and some of their associates centered in Lahore felt increasingly that Bashir-ud-Din was too young, and that his leadership would emphasize the cult of his father rather than the renewal of Islam in a form acceptable to Sunnis. The selection prior to Ghulam Ahmad's death of a *Sadr Anjumān*, or inner circle, made it even more evident to the Lahori group that leadership in Ahmadiyah would perpetuate in a manner that would not meet the needs they felt Ahmadiyah should serve.

A clash of personalities and philosophy was inevitable. Where polemics and controversy had solidified Ahmadiyah during the first thirty years of its life against Hindus, Sikhs, and Christians as well as against some Sunnis, polemics and controversy now caused a severe split in the movement for Islamic renewal. There was right and wrong on both sides as the Lahore delegation withdrew to form their own branch of the movement under the leadership of Muhammad 'Ali. The final blow causing the separation came over the interpretation of *al-Wasiyah*, the public will of Ghulam Ahmad. Muhammad 'Ali believed that it was the Promised Messiah's purpose in creating a *Sadr Anjumān*, thereby to appoint an *amīr*, or manager of the Ahmadiyah organization, whose role would be separate from that of the *khalīfah*, to whom new converts would make their *bay'āh* or allegiance. Bashir-ud-Din Mahmud Ahmad perceived that Muhammad 'Ali was purely opposed to him and after some negotiation the new *khalīfah* accepted the fact that Muhammad 'Ali would not offer allegiance to him. Numbers in the split should not be exaggerated, for only about 50 of about 2,000 present at the time the new *khalīfah* was chosen decided to withdraw. The fact that the 50 were from the more educated and intellectual segment of Ahmadiyah had more of an effect on the movement.[17]

A resolution of the Sadr Anjumān committee quickly established that in all matters pertaining to the Ahmadiyah community "the orders of Hazrat Mirza Bashir-ud-Din Mahmud Ahmad . . . shall be final and conclusive." It was clear from this that the khalīfah of what was now to be referred to as the Qadiani branch of Ahmadiyah would hold ultimate power, so that questions of organization would not be allowed to slow down the growth process of the movement. This growth was to include a new thrust of tablīgh, or missionary work, to such places as Ceylon, Mauritius, and Madagascar. A Committee for the Propagation of Islam, established shortly afterwards, set as its goals the establishment of Ahmadiyah primary schools in several districts of Punjab, the founding of a training school for Muslim missionaries at Qadian, and the translation of the Qur'ān fully annotated both in Urdu and English.

By 1921, membership in the movement exceeded 28,000 with substantial number of Ahmadis in Gurdaspur, Sialkot, Hoshiarpur, and Gujrat districts of Punjab. Census figures for 1921 indicate only 471 Ahmadis in Lahore, a figure if taken as accurate points to the small numbers affiliated with the Lahori branch.

At Qadian, the second khalīfah, Mirza Bashir-ud-Din Mahmud Ahmad, established a cabinet form of leadership in the Anjumān. A chief secretary served as chair while seven others (nazīrs) had responsibility for treasury, community discipline, external and government affairs, education, missionary work, publications, and hospitality departments. Support of the organization was made through annual assessments of $6\frac{1}{4}$ per cent of income, although many Ahmadis contributed up to 10 per cent. Since many members also supported auxiliary causes, those persons may have contributed even one-third of all their income to related Ahmadi organizations. An Advisory Council to the khalīfah, established in 1922, was made up of 500-600 persons chosen from the regional structure of the Sadr Anjumān. Since the khalīfah was always present at the deliberations of this body, however, it was virtually a rubber stamp. Clearly he was a virtual autocrat over the movement.[18]

Into its fourth decade, then, the Ahmadiyah movement had solidified itself behind its third leader, following the traditional

Islamic *khalifah* pattern; it had adapted to organizational patterns derived from missionary organizations from Europe; it had utilized modern publishing techniques to propagate its point of view and to add to the growing polemics and controversy with other Muslims, Hindus, Sikhs, and the nationalist movement it sharply opposed.

The Ahmadiyah and Politics

Such a clearly delineated sectarian position as that taken by the Ahmadiyah movement in propagating the teachings of Mirza Ghulam Ahmad for the renewal of Islam kept it in perpetual difficulty with those who opposed it on theological or political grounds. The Qadiani branch of the movement knew that it had to protect itself against the potential violence of opponents, and therefore continued to emphasize the loyalty of the movement and its leaders to the government.

As early as 1914 the Lahoris, through their own newspaper, had joined the cause of Muslim journalist Zafar 'Ali Khan. Khan had raised the cause of the Turks and, by implication, the Germans in World War I, to a fevered pitch in the north Indian Muslim community. The support of the Turks and the plight of the Muslims in Balkan countries were indeed legitimate issues for Indian Muslims to be concerned with, but it was clearly a threat from the point of view of the British government. While the Lahoris continued to espouse the cause of the Turks and that of the interned brothers Muhammad and Shaukat 'Ali (founders of the Khilafat Movement which they organized in a pan-Islamic framework), the Qadianis took an opposing position. Calling on all Muslims to be loyal while emphasizing that the war in Europe had no direct effect on Islam per se, the Qadian paper cited the fact that the Prophet had taught obedience to one's ruler, as had the Promised Messiah, Mirza Ghulam Ahmad. The arguments were not theological alone. The Qadiani newspaper also suggested that Turkish reasons for entering the war were political and not motivated by an Islamic injunction.

On the matter of "Home Rule," the Ahmadis were strongly opposed. The Ahmadi press compared the current condition of Indians to that of children unprepared for the responsibilities of adulthood. Without the presence of the British, they argued, India

would not know its present prosperity. It was an effort to make
clear to the government the differences in attitude between the
Lahoris and Qadianis. At the same time, the Ahmadi *khalīfah*
organized the first of many delegations, this one to meet with Sir
Edwin Montague, the visiting secretary of state for India in 1917.
Ahmadi publications made it perfectly clear what the community's
position was:

> The Ahmadiyya Community is a purely religious body and has
> nothing to do with politics. This is why so far it kept aloof from
> all political movements in India. But on the present occasion
> when a majority of the educated people of India are clamoring
> for Home Rule, in the grant of which the Ahmadiyya Community
> sees the ruin of its own interests, the head of the Ahmadiyya
> Community . . . thought it his duty to express the views of the
> Ahmadiyya Community.[19]

The crux of Ahmadi concern about home rule was expressed as
a fear for themselves as a minority within the Muslim minority.
The British government was the only body capable of protecting
the community against "religious bigots."Although they professed
to be non-political in their concerns, three often paragraphs submit-
ted by the community to the visiting Montague-Chelmsford delegation reflect certain political concerns. These included the abolition
of special privileges for Europeans in India, that Europeans tried
for offenses against Indians should be tried only by juries made up
half of Indians or else there could be no justice, and that mines,
railroads, and other utilities should be freed of foreign capital and
worked by government or Indian capital.

The point that needs to be clarified here is the changing role of
the Ahmadiyah community in regard to public issues. On the one
hand, they emphasized their loyalty to the British government; on
the other hand, they began to make self-conscious criticisms of the
government when and where improvements were necessary.

Because the Ahmadiyah movement at Qadian stood strongly
opposed both to the rising star of Mohandas Gandhi and his
satyāgraha movement, and to the growing Muslim agitation connected with the *khilāfat* movement, it has received little or no attention by historians covering the critical events of the twenties.
Ahmadi concerns continued to remain much more closely related
to Islam and its own need to promote the faith.

The publication of the infamous pamphlet *Rangila Rasul* (*The Gay Prophet*) by a member of the Arya Samaj in 1927 led to disturbances in Lahore following the decision of Justice Dalip Singh not to imprison the publisher of the defamatory tract. Ahmadis seem both to have been involved in circulating anti-Hindu posters leading to some riots and also to have pressed the government to prohibit publication of tracts dishonoring "prophets, avatars and founders of all religions."[20] To the extent that the movement received attention in the press, it was over what seem to be issues more petty than those raised by nationalist groups. Mahmud Ahmad's 1930 book, *The Indian Problem*, written as a response to the unpopular Simon Commission Report and the decision to hold a Round Table Conference in London, stated that while independence for India might some day be possible, it was presently "opposed to the divine scheme of things." By this he meant that communal tensions, especially between Hindus and Muslims, were so rife as to warrant the presence of the outside colonialist force. The student of modern religious movements in India might wish to ask whether Mahmud Ahmad himself was not something of a communalist when he attacked the "Hindu mentality" which, he insisted, had always displayed a hatred for Muslims.

It seems probable that Mahmud Ahmad, while not a militant "communalist," recalled the early experiences of his father, in defending the faith against the Arya Samaj, the Sikhs, and the Christian missionaries, which had led him to distrust all Hindus in a situation where Muslims would find themselves in a numerical minority.

Political Issues of the Thirties and Seventies

The increasing self-awareness of the Ahmadiyah movement and its participation in critical political events reached a peak during the Kashmir crisis of the 1931-1934, and during subsequent intercommunal strife in Punjab in 1936, 1954, and 1974. Kashmir, fourth largest in population among the princely states, had been a creation of the British. Ruled by Ranjit Singh from Lahore after 1819, it was turned over to a Hindu maharajah, Gulab Singh, following the treaty of Amritsar in 1846. Despite an overwhelmingly Muslim population, the state had been ruled by Sikhs and a hereditary Hindu dynasty for more than a century.

Why were the Ahmadis concerned with Kashmir? One cornerstone of Mirza Ghulam Ahmad's theology had been his teaching about the death of Jesus and his own succession as *mahdi* and Promised Messiah. Kashmir was the burial place of Jesus, according to Ahmad's studies. It was, therefore, appropriate for the Ahmadiyah movement, whose own center at Qadian was not far from Jammu and Kashmir, to become involved in internal politics at a time when the maharajah and his police were enforcing oppressive practices against Muslims.

As the Ahmadiyah movement was stepping in, so was the *Majlis-i-Ahrar-i-Islam-i-Hind,* an organization of Islamic Freedom Fighters which had emerged as a caucus among Muslims attending the 1930 session of the Indian National Congress at Lahore. Among its founders were several articulate Muslims who had worked for the *khilāfat* movement during the twenties and who were strongly anti-Ahmadi. Withdrawing from the Congress over the Nehru Report, which called for joint rather than separate electorates in a democratic India, the Ahrar turned its attention to communal activities and particularly opposed the pro-British attitude of a Kashmir committee in which the Ahmadis were playing a major role.

While the political issues and factions both inside and outside the Muslim community in Kashmir are too complex to detail here, what is important to note is that the Ahrar organized militant bands, or *jathabandis,* to cause disruptions in Kashmir. By October 1931, some 3,600 Ahraris had been interned in the princely state. The Ahmadiyah movement had during this period been part of a committee supporting Shaykh 'Abdullah, a graduate of Aligarh College and a twenty-five-year-old school teacher who had recently been dismissed from his position for overt political activities. The work of the Shaykh and the Ahmadis led to the formation of a commission to recommend ways of alleviating the grievances in Kashmir, but at the same time the movement came under close scrutiny by the government.21

Of particular note in all these activities in Kashmir was a split that occurred in 1933, exacerbated by hostility towards Ahmadis by non-Ahmadis. The creation of a new committee to support Kashmiri Muslims headed by the two notable Muslims, Sir Muhammad Iqbal and Zafar 'Ali Khan, deliberately excluded Ahmadis, and represents the beginning of forty years of persecution and uncertainty leading to the legal declaration of the Ahmadiyah movement as a non-Muslim minority in Pakistan in 1974.

Partition and Pakistan

The controversies of the 1930s did not stop the progress or expansion of the Ahmadiyah movement. With the establishment of the Tahrik-i-Jadid, or new organization for missions in 1934, the conscious expansion of Islam to other parts of the world was strengthened. The new *tablīgh*, or missionary movement, came partly as a response to continued years of Christian missions in India. It also came from the increasing awareness of the negative perception of Islam which Muslim travelers—Ahmadi and non-Ahmadi—experienced in Europe.

With the decline of the Sufi movement in the eighteenth century, conversion to Islam had all but ceased. The Ahmadiyah missions did not function without difficulty. As early as 1909 conflicts were reported in Hong Kong where Sunnis refused to al'ow an Ahmadi to be buried in a Muslim graveyard. Most impressive has been the Ahmadiyah missionary program in Africa. In Nigeria, the first missionary was 'Abd-ur-Rahman Nayyar, an early follower of the Promised Messiah, who arrived in 1921 during a period of great religious unrest. By 1929, Ahmadiyah had spread to Ghana and Sierra Leona. In the former a hospital on the model of Christian mission hospitals was established. In the post-World War II period a most effective mission has been established in the Ivory Coast as the first Francophone mission.[22]

As the time for Indian independence with the inevitability of partition arose, the Ahmadiyah position on independence was ambiguous. While the *khalīfah*, Bashir-ud-Din Mahmud Ahmad, had written in the thirties that independence might some day be appropriate for India, Ahmadi literature in the 1945-47 period indicates uneasiness at the prospect of being a minority within a Muslim majority in a new Pakistan, just as Muslims in general feared the prospect of being a minority in a Hindu sea in India. A secular state in India was no more positive an idea than was the anticipated difficulty in Pakistan, where schism within Islam might not be tolerated.

While the movement opted for Pakistan and established a new

international headquarters at Rabwah near Chiniot in West Punjab, a small band retained control of the Ahmadi holy places at Qadian, which fell only a few miles on the Indian side of the new border. Not long after the establishment of the new center at Rabwah, controversies arose over the sectarian teachings and practices of the movement. Among the charges leveled at the movement was the one that suggested Qadian had fallen in India because of the views of Muhammad Zafar Ullah Khan, a leading Ahmadi and later foreign minister of Pakistan while on the boundary commission.

A series of militant attacks on the Ahmadis were fomented in 1953 by members of the same Ahrar movement which had caused difficulties in 1936. One noted Ahrar leader who had been prosecuted by the British in 1936 for his role in the anti-Ahmadi riots came out of retirement to begin a new campaign against his old enemies. While Pakistani government suspicions became aroused when he began to describe Zafar Ullah and Ahmadis as "traitors," the government did little to prevent violence. The Ahraris focused their campaign on three slogans: (1) propagation of the assertion of the "seal of the prophet" against Ghulam Ahmad's claims to prophecy; (2) the declaration of Ahmadis as a non-Muslim minority; (3) the removal of Chaudhri Zafar Ullah Khan from public office.[23]

Although he was the butt of much public opposition, Zafar Ullah Khan continued to speak out publicly for both Islam and his community. One speech in Urdu entitled "Islam is a Living Religion" was followed by the destruction of Ahmadi property and business in Karachi. At this point the governor of Punjab was put under such pressure by fourteen Muslim groups, whose leadership included the noted Maulana Sayyid 'Abdul 'Ala Maudoodi, that an inquiry under Justice Muhammad Munir was called into session. The case ran from July 1, 1953, to January 1954, and involved thousands of pages of evidence.

It is in the sections of the report dealing with the nature of the Islamic state, its foundations and essentials, that the judgment turned in favor of the Ahmadiyah movement. Pointing first to the difficulties involved in creating a modern political state on a rigid religious basis, Justice Munir quoted the words of Muhammad Iqbal when Iqbal first proposed the creation of a Muslim state for northwest India. The poet had asserted then that Hindus should not fear that the creation of autonomous Muslim states should mean the introduction of religious rule in those states. "The principle that each group is entitled to free development on its own lines is not inspired by any feeling of narrow communalism."[24]

Quoting also from Muhammad 'Ali Jinnah, first president of Pakistan, Justice Munir stressed Jinnah's statements about all Pakistanis having equal rights as citizens regardless of religion, caste, or creed. The state was intended to serve all and religion would be a purely personal matter. Clearly the representatives of the 'ulamā' now opposed to the Ahmadis did not accept Jinnah's definition of the state. Expounding the Sunni theory of reason and revelation in Islam, Justice Munir went on to defend the rights of Ahmadis while the 'ulamā', one after another, failed to clarify satisfactorily why the Ahmadis were not legitimate Muslims. Each mullah, according to his own standards, defined Islam in such a way as to exclude other mullahs also testifying against the Ahmadis. The Munir decision was a remarkable step in favor of religious democracy in Pakistan. Unfortunately for the Ahmadiyan movement, the decision did little to lessen tensions between Sunnis and themselves. The general populace was always ready to be sent into battle against the Qadianis as heretics.

Although the Ahmadiyah movement existed in relative peace for two decades after the incidents of 1953, under the leadership of khalīfah Mirza Nasir Ahmad, grandson of the Promised Messiah, an incident at Rabwah in June 1974, sparked new riots against Ahmadis and led to President Zulfiqar Ali Bhutto making political decisions against the movement. After secret hearings in the legislative assembly, a bill was passed in October 1974, declaring Ahmadis to be a non-Muslim minority. The effect of the legislation was to require Ahmadis in governmental and military leadership roles to delare they were Sunnis and not Ahmadis. This was a difficult decision of conscience for many Ahmadis, who chose to resign their posts rather than capitulate.

The contribution of the Ahmadiyah movement to Islamic renewal in India has been a significant if controversial one. As is evident from the studies of movements and figures in this volume, religious renewal in modern India, as in so many other contexts, has depended first on charismatic leadership and then on talented disciples to create organization. If one can point to particular significance for the Ahmadiyah movement, it is in the facts just cited, that the movement, with its peculiarities of theology, worship, and organization forced the newly created nation of Pakistan to redefine the oldest issue in Islam: "Who is a true Muslim?" In the events swirling round at the time of the publication of this essay, that question is still on the minds of Muslims and non-Muslims the world over.

Notes

1. This essay is drawn from three previously published works on the subject: Spencer Lavan, *The Ahmadiyah Movement: A History and Perspective* (New Delhi: Manohar Book Service, 1974); Spencer Lavan, *Ahmadiyah Movement: Past and Present* (Amritsar: Guru Nanak Dev University, 1976), published as a student's edition for the north Indian history curriculum; and "Sources for Ahmadiyah History, A Muslim Reform Tradition in the Punjab," in *Sources of Punjab History*, eds. Eric Gustafson and Kenneth Jones, (New Delhi: Manohar Book Service, 1975). Chapters of the original monograph have appeared in *The Muslim World*, *Journal of Religious Studies* (Patiala), *The Punjab Past and Present*, and *Essays in Honour of Ganda Singh*, eds. Harbans Singh and N. Gerald Barrier (Patiala: Punjabi University, 1976).

2. While the literature on Sayyid Ahmad Khan and the Aligarh movement is substantial, the recent work of David Lelyveld, *Aligarh's First Generation* (Princeton: Princeton University Press, 1978), stands out as the newly definitive resource on the subject. This book contains a complete bibliography.

3. The college at Aligarh and the Ahmadiyah movement are not the only Muslim responses to events in late nineteenth-century India. For a general summary of other schools and movements, see Aziz Ahmad, *Islamic Modernism in India and Pakistan, 1857-1946* (Oxford: Oxford University Press, 1967).

4. Abdur Rahman Dard, *Life of Ahmad*, part 1 (Lahore: Sultan Brothers, 1949), p. 40. This biography was written by a thoroughly devoted follower of the movement but when compared against other sources provides an important background of events in Ahmad's life despite the bias of the author.

5. Beg, Mirza Masum, trans., *Mirza Ghulam Ahmad, Barahin-i-Ahmadiya* (Lahore: Ahmadiyah Anjuman Isha'at-i-Islam, 1955), p. 1. The original Urdu texts are also available.

6. For a definitive discussion of the Arya Samaj movement, see the essay by Kenneth Jones in this volume.

7. Mirza Ghulam Ahmad, *Faith-i-Islam*, trans. Mirza Masum Beg, in *The Light* 72, no. 10 (March 4, 1958) : 6.

8. The full text of the *bay'āh*, or oath, is included in Dard's discussion of the context of the original *bay'āh* ceremonies, in *Life of Ahmad*, pp. 102-6.

9. Mirza Ghulam Ahmad, *Masīh Hindustān Mēn* [*Jesus in India*] (Quadian, 1912); written in 1899. This is the decisive text for Ahmad's claims to be the successor to Jesus as *mahdī*.

10. Idid., p. 7.

11. Ibid., p. 11.

12. Ibid., p. 12. The point about the Jewish grave is mentioned on p. 1. H.A. Walter, the earliest Western scholar to prepare a monograph on the movement, attempted unsuccessfully to locate the grave of Jesus in Srinagar. He denies the veracity of Ahmad's "proofs."

13. In particular, Ahmad locked horns with members of the Ahl-i-Hadith, whose journal, *Isha'at-i-Sunnah*, regularly ridiculed him. For details, see Lavan, *The Ahmadiyah Movement: A History and Prespective*, pp. 50-57.

14. For the details of the Lekh Ram murder and controversy with the Arya Samaj, see Lavan, *Ahmadiyah Movement*, pp. 74-87. Information for these events was drawn from Dard, *Life of Ahmad*, Kenneth Jones, *Arya Dharm* (Berkeley: University of California Press, 1976), and numerous issues of the Selections from the Vernacular Press of the Punjab.

15. See Lavan, *Ahmadiyah Movement*, pp. 92-98 for more details.

16. Dard, *Life of Ahmad*, p. 417.

17. Lavan, *Ahmadiyah Movement*, pp. 98-113, and Gustafson and Jones, *Sources of Punjab History*, for details on the pamphlet warfare bibliography.

18. Lavan, *Ahmadiyah Movement*, pp. 114-17.

19. Quoted from *Review of Religions* 16 (October-November 1917).

20. Lavan, *Ahmadiyah Movement*, pp. 136-41, from Government of India, File 132/27 on the "Rangila Rasul" case.

21. See Lavan, *Ahmadiyah Movement*, chapter 7, for details of the Ahmadis in Kashmir.

22. May Yacoub, "The Ahmadiyah : Urban Adaptations in the Ivory Coast" (Ph.D. dissertation, Boston University, May 1979).

23. *Report of the Court of Inquiry Constituted Under Punjab Act II of 1954 to Enquire into the Punjab Disturbances of 1953* (Lahore: Government Printing Office, 1954), p. 75.

24. Ibid., p. 201.

6

THE SPIRIT OF THE JAMIA MILLIA ISLAMIA AS EXEMPLIFIED IN THE WRITINGS OF S. ABID HUSAIN

Sheila McDonough

The Jamia Millia Islamia (Indian National University) was founded in 1920 in response to the appeal from Gandhi and Muhammad Ali asking the Muslim students of the Aligarh College to leave their British-supported institution.[1] From that time until the independence of India, the supporters of the Jamia Millia Islamia retained a distinctive point of view as Muslims, namely, loyalty to Gandhi personally and commitment to citizenship within India. After independence, this attitude was retained, and the members of the Jamia Millia Islamia community have continued to express their views in journals and books in English and Urdu.

There are three phases of the Jamia Millia life that are particularly significant. First, in the period 1919-24, the persons working there represented the attitudes of those Muslims who expected to fight together with Gandhi and the Congress for the independence of India. We shall look at the religious assumptions that led Muslim leaders like the Ali brothers to expect success for their point of view. We shall also ask why Gandhi worked with this group.

The second phase, from 1924 to 1948, was very different. The majority of the Muslims abandoned their interest in, and their financial support for, the Jamia Millia. Muhammad Ali and other Muslim leaders changed their attitudes to the Congress. The members of the small community left at the Jamia Millia Islamia were in certain respects isolated, yet they did not abandon their vision, nor cease to work for it. On the contrary, they endured, in the absence of support from their coreligionists, the many heart-breaks of the communal tensions and riots of the years preceding independence. Thus, they demonstrated considerable stamina and strength of purpose.

In the third phase, after independence, the vitality of this group of Muslims remained strong, and many new activities developed. One interesting matter for those of us interested in religious studies to consider is tenacity of purpose in the face of apparently over-whelming odds. The members of the Jamia Millia Islamia community have exhibited this characteristic. We also see here devout Muslims who remained all their lives loyal to Gandhi. This raises some interesting questions as to the possibilities of mutual inspiration across the boundaries of religious traditions.

Let us look first at some of the issues that characterized the first phase of the life of the Jamia Millia community. The appeal issued to the students of Aligarh to abandon their secure institution and to set out on the adventure of studying at an insecure national university brought forth a response by many Aligarh students. They were filled with enthusiasm for a new existence in which, as Muslim students of a free India, they would hope to control their own destinies, and to work to build a better human community in their native land. Students and faculty shared together the optimism and exhilaration characteristic of moments of experienced liberation and new direction.

Gandhi had invited the poet Iqbal to become the first principal of the Jamia Millia Islamia, but when he declined Muhammad Ali accepted the position.[2] The point of view that animated this first generation of members of the Jamia Millia community was thus an amalgam of the perspectives of Muhammad Ali and Gandhi. Both men had discovered the immediate significance of tradi-tional perspectives in the context of a world in which the power of the "foreign other" had been felt as repressive and debilitating. Gandhi had begun the process of his self-discovery through his refusal to accept meekly his expulsion from a railway car in South Africa.[3] Muhammad Ali had been refused a job at his university Aligarh because the British authority there considered him too dynamic and threatening a personality.[4]

Both men had written manifestos at roughly the same time.

Gandhi's was written in 1909;[5] Muhammad Ali began writing and publishing his journal *Comrade* in 1911.[6] The similarity in dates suggests that those two were in some sense focusing a mood of discontent and groping for direction that was general among their contemporaries. Certainly in both cases the response was enthusiastic.

Gandhi and Muhammad Ali were agreed that the demonic force at work was British domination. In his speeches during the 1919-25 period, Gandhi used symbolism from Hinduism and Islam interchangeably. That is, in speaking to a Hindu audience, he spoke of the necessity to destroy Ravanna Raj and create Ram Raj.[7] In speaking to a Muslim audience, he spoke of fighting the demonic system, Satan, in order to do the work of God.[8] The religious reality for him was the readiness of the individual to perceive the British system as demonic, and to act vigorously to create the system Gandhi envisaged. Whether that latter was called Ram Raj or Muslim theocracy or kingdom of God on earth was not important. The content of the system was the significant reality. For Gandhi, it had to be a society shaped by non-violence and freed from Western values.

Gandhi's warm support for Muhammad Ali is related to his deep affection for persons who would fight and struggle for what they perceived as religious. The worst sin, in Gandhi's eyes, was cowardice, because that had been his own almost overwhelming temptation when he had faced his personal crisis. The readiness of Muslims to act courageously had impressed him greatly in South African days,[9] and helped shape his attitude to Muhammad Ali. He expected the Jamia Millia to produce non-violent fighters for India.

Muhammad Ali similarly exhorted his hearers to vigorous self-confidence. But he did not use Muslim and Hindu symbols interchangeably. On the contrary, he had been one of the founders of the Muslim League, and had supported separate electorates. He was consistent in always seeing Islam as the true answer to the human need for divine guidance. The God acting in history was for him the God who had revealed His will most perfectly through the revelation given to Muhammad. No other system was comparable to this. In his case, the casting off of British influence meant a reaffirmation of inherent Muslim capacity for self-rule.

The message the students of the new Jamia Millia Islamia

received was primarily that of Muhammad Ali. He produced a syllabus for the new institution.[10] The syllabus was intended to agree with the directions laid down for the other national colleges with reference to training for service to the nation, and spinning. But the teaching about religion was based on Muhammad Ali's vision. He had himself been influenced by Shibli Numani's course on the *Qur'an*.[11] He had also been greatly stirred by Iqbal's poetry. The syllabus therefore emphasized the *Qur'an* and Iqbal and Islamic history. The history was presented as an ongoing attempt to realize an ideal. The intent was to urge the present generation to fulfil that ideal in their own country.

Muhammad Ali used the phrase "Federation of Faiths" to describe his ideal for independent India. It meant cultural autonomy for each religious group, as well as cooperation on common problems. Muhammad Ali respected Gandhi as a person, but he did not envisage any kind of theological basis for the recognition of religious values in different traditions. His belief was that the "power behind the universe" would support Muslims once they became dynamic again. He viewed history as salvation history in which the divine plan was to be implemented by Muslims. As citizens of India, Muslims should cooperate with Hindus, but there was no theoretical basis for taking each other's religions seriously.

The anti-British energy in this phase of the nationalist movement seems mainly to have been generated by the Muslims through the Khilafat movement. The affairs of the Khilafat Conference and the non-cooperation movement are inextricably mixed together in this period. The money for the Jamia Millia came from the Khilafat Conference. The Muslims of India had responded vigorously to the appeals of Muhammad Ali and other Khilafat leaders to raise money, and to stir themselves to demand that the British be just to Turkey and the caliph.

In their minds a strong independent Turkish caliph seems to have represented a guarantee of Muslim power and significance in the world. This was a new idea for Indian Muslims. Sayyid Ahmad Khan and the earlier generation of Indian Muslims had denied that the Turkish caliph had any authority over Indian Muslims.[12] As a symbol, the caliph seems to have represented to Muhammad Ali proof of Muslim strength over the British. The change of mood from Sayyid Ahmad Khan to Muhammad Ali is related to greater pessimism about the British.

Gandhi, in working actively with the Khilafat movement, was stepping out in a direction not taken by most of his Hindu fellow countrymen. When Gandhi appealed to the students of Benares Hindu University to leave their university as the Aligarh students had done, and to set up a national educational institution, he was met with refusal from Malaviya, the head of the university.[13] Some students and faculty members did leave, and established the Kashi Vidyapith, but it is noteworthy that Malaviya, who was a significant spokesman for the Hindu community, would not support this activity.

Gandhi's role in the Khilafat movement seems to have had two important facets. In speaking to Hindus, he wanted to stir them up to become as actively anti-British and world-transforming as the Muslims, and to see positive value in cooperating with their Muslim fellow citizens. For example, he commented, on observing Muslim reaction to a young man's death, that Hindus might learn from Muslim courage in the face of death. "I took heart from the fortitude of the Muslim brethren standing about. I observed no weeping and wailing near the body. The scene appealed to me greatly. I thought of the weeping and wailing usual among Hindus. I wished that we were delivered from that horror. I also told myself that we could do a great many things if we discarded this fear of death. I have often felt that the followers of Hinduism, who should least fear death, fear it most. . . . We learn right from our childhood that the soul is immortal and the body transitory, and that every act will have its consequences. Why then do we fear death?"

In this respect, Gandhi's response to the Muslim dynamism of the Khilafat movement was a genuine part of his own conviction that true religiousness should be fearless and world-transforming.

On the other hand, he was also concerned to limit and restrict Muslim readiness to act and to resort to violence if necessary. In the early discussions at the Khilafat meetings, the Muslim leaders were urging boycott of British goods. Gandhi opposed boycott at this stage as having violent overtones. He invented the term non-cooperation out of his struggle to articulate a perspective that would be less ready to leap into action with possibly violent consequences. He succeeded in keeping the brakes on Muhammad Ali and the others, and the term non-cooperation was subsequently adopted by the Congress.

Left to themselves, the Muslim leaders of the Khilafat movement probably would have initiated both boycott and violence. Although they agreed as a matter of practical policy not to use violence, they made it very clear in 1919 that as Muslims they could never accept non-violence as a religious absolute. The *Qur'an* teaches that self-defense in a cause that the leaders of the community deem just is right and necessary. The Muslim supporters of Gandhi did not deviate from that position. One should note that Motilal Nehru also refused to accept absolute non-violence as norm.

There seems to have been a very real affection and mutual respect between Gandhi and Muhammad Ali. Gandhi describes his Muslim friend at work. "I could see how the Ali brothers had been able to win the affection of their community. Their sweet speech, their constant readiness for work, their loving nature and sympathy for all, their religious zeal—who would not be charmed by such qualities. Their very presence fills our Muslim brethren with happiness. They are, as it were, the eyes of the Muslims and now, by their love, they are winning over the Hindus as well."[15] Four years later, when tensions between the two religious groups had greatly increased, a lot of bad feeling was generated by press reports that Muhammad Ali had said that Gandhi was less than the meanest Muslim. It is worth noting that Gandhi himself tried to set the record straight on this, and indicated that he both understood Muhammad Ali's position and respected it. What Muhammad Ali did say was that Islam was a superior religion to any other, but that Gandhi's character was superior to that of any he knew. "But to consider one's creed as superior to that of every non-Muslim is the duty of a Mussalman. By stating this I refuted the charge of Gandhi-worship levelled against me... and not to hurt the feelings of my Hindu brethren or to revile Mahatma Gandhi. If anyone can have reason to complain, it is my own co-religionists, none of whom I considered to be worthy of being ranked with Mahatma Gandhi in excellence of character."[16]

These comments indicate that Muhammad Ali saw no difficulty in affirming Islam as the ultimate value, while at the same time acknowledging excellence of character whenever he met it . This is the attitude that was to be inculcated into the original Muslim students of the Jamia Millia. Their curriculum was to stress Islamic history as an ongoing attempt to realize the original vision brought by the *Qur'an*, but they were to see India as their homeland, and as the place where their vision was to take shape. This did not seem an unreasonable expectation to either Muhammnd Ali, or to Gandhi.

Muhammad Ali was not prepared to acknowledge final truth in any religion other than Islam, but he was ready in practice to acknowledge virtue. His vision of a Federation of Faiths supposed mutual respect as a basis for everyday cooperation. He was not opposed to science and technology as Gandhi was. Gandhi stated in his manifesto of 1910 that all the mechanical works of the demonic West were to be discarded, and simple living was to serve as a basis for the good life. Muhammad Ali, on the contrary, though emphasizing the past glories of Islam, saw his people as potentially great scientists and experts in technology. He was not opposed to modern industry; rather, he wanted Muslims to achieve skills to make such industry their own. The students in the Jamia Millia were spinning as an interim measure, but their final goal was not the same as Gandhi's.

All these hopes were shattered by two events. The first was Gandhi's suspension of the non-cooperation movement after the violence in Chauri Chara. Some hostile later Muslim opinion attributed his act to his fear that Muslims were getting too powerful in India. Although there is no reason to credit Gandhi with such a deliberate motive, the reality of the situation was that his Muslim allies were thoroughly disheartened, not least because their acceptance of his leadership was tentative in any case. It is difficult to know how clearly he saw this issue; he certainly knew that Muhammad Ali and the others were not adherents of absolute non-violence as a basic commitment. Since it was not a religious value for them, Gandhi's suspending a movement into which they had put enormous energy, time, and money could only appear as the folly of an unreliable ally. One could admire Gandhi's character, but to have him call off the revolution meant accepting him as an authority on religious truth, and this most of the Muslims would not do.

The second disaster was the abolition of the caliphate by the Turkish revolution. This seems to have come as a terrible blow to Muhammad Ali. The other leading Khilafat organizer, Maulana Azad, reacted to this shock by going over to the Congress. But Muhammad Ali tried to keep the pan-Islam idea alive. The money for the Jamia Millia had come from the Khilafat Conference.

There would be no more money from that source. There seemed no reason to keep the institution going. Many left and went back to Aligarh. Other national institutions were closing down, since there seemed little hope of independence in the near future.

The second phase of the Jamia Millia Islamia's life begins at this point. Gandhi's response to the failure of the non-cooperation movement was to turn his attention to constructive work. One of the works to be done, in his view, was education so that the next time a nationalist movement got going, leaders would be ready who could work on a disciplined, non-violent way for social change. He wanted the Jamia Millia Islamia kept alive in order to produce new Muslim leaders of this kind. Most of the Muslim leaders, including the Ali brothers, were not sympathetic to this plea, not least because the kind of leader Gandhi wanted was not in any case their ideal.

However, a few Muslims agreed to try to keep the institution going. Hakim Ajmal Khan and Dr. Ansari accepted the responsibility for guiding the remnant left at the Jamia Millia, and for raising money for its support. The institution was moved to Delhi. The most active injection of help came when three young Muslims studying in Germany responded to an appeal from Dr. Ansari and returned to take over the administration. These three were Zakir Husain, Muhammad Mujeeb, and S. Abid Husain. All three were brilliant young students who had been doing doctoral work in Europe. Their commitment to the Jamia Millia Islamia kept the institution alive.

Gandhi's idea was that teachers in such national institutions should vow to devote their lives to the work. The staff of the Jamia Millia agreed to take the vow and did so. They worked for very low wages for more than twenty years.

Zakir Husain and others accepted Gandhi's guidance as their leader in working for an institution that should continue to be entirely free of British control. In so doing, they went further than Muhammad Ali was ready to go. Muhammad Ali and others seemed willing to consider working again with the British, but this Zakir Husain and his group would not do.[17] They committed themselves entirely to Gandhi's constructive program, and were ready as any other workers in the program were to suffer any consequences that might come. The aspect of the program they gave themselves to was national education; the suffering they endured was financial loss for themselves and their families.

They thus exhibited the kind of heroism Gandhi expected of truly religious persons, yet they continued to do so as Muslims. They did not accept absolute non-violence as a creed, nor vegetarianism, nor antitechnology. Religiously, they remained committed to Islam, but they accepted Gandhi as the best guide to an independent India. They also continued to acknowledge the importance of the vision of Iqbal for Indian Muslims. The poet visited the Jamia Millia.[18]

A publishing house, the *Maktaba i Jamia*, was founded in order to publish materials related to the point of view of the members of the Jamia community. S. Abid Husain was particularly active writing and translating. He was professor of philosophy and literature, and later the principal of the Jamia Millia College. He served as editor of the Jamia magazine. He was particularly active as a translator of English and German works into Urdu. **His** translations included De Boer's *History of Philosophy in Islam,* Kant's *Critique of Pure Reason, Selected Dialogues of Plato*, Goethe's *Faust* and *Wilhelm Meister*, Nehru's *Glimpses of World History* and *Discovery of India*, Shaw's *St. Joan* and Spranger's *Psychology of Youth.*

Since students from the national institutions that remained active, namely the Jamia Millia Islamia, the Kashi Vidaypith, and the Gujrat Vidyapith, had not much hope of being accepted by the British-controlled universities, the educational activities tended to be confined to primary school. Zakir Husain was greatly interested in the new ideas about primary education coming from Germany and the United States, and he encouraged the teachers to experiment with new techniques. Efforts were made to develop the project method of developing creativity in the child.

The members of the Jamia Millia community kept out of politics during this period. They saw their function as being concerned exclusively with education. In this, they differed from their fellow teachers in the other national institutions. Most of the latter were actively involved with the salt march and other *Satyagraha* campaigns, in *harijan* uplift, and in spinning and selling *khaddi*. The Jamia Millia community was Gandhian in its own way, but not in the way of the other supports of the Mahatma.

In 1937, when the British had granted autonomy to seven provinces in India, Gandhi called a conference near the village at

Sevagram where he had been living. He wanted to stir his hearers
to initiate a new system of education to be implemented by the new
autonomous Indian provincial governments. Ever since his early
days in South Africa, Gandhi had considered that changes in educational methods should be an integral part of the revolutionary
changes in social life which he envisaged. On the two communities, Phoenix and Tolstoy Farm, which he created in South Africa,
innovative efforts were made in working with the children. A
corollary of Gandhi's own discarding of Western dress, foods, etc.,
was his conviction that Western educational practices must also
be discarded and new methods discovered. His idea was to stress
manual labor and the development of ideals of social service. For
religious development, children were to learn hymns and prayers
from all religions.

Gandhi, from all accounts, seems to have had good personal
rapport with young children. When he lived at Sabarmati Ashram,
he used to take the children on walks near the jail so that they
would get used to the idea that jail was a natural place for people
like him and them.

To begin the conference at Sevagram, Gandhi asked his hearers
to develop a system of education which would stress manual labor
and social service, and which would be self-supporting. The
teachers were to be paid by the money raised from the sale of
work done by the children. The three Muslim leaders from the
Jamia Millia, Zakir Husain, Muhammad Mujeeb, and S. Abid
Husain were present at that meeting. Zakir Husain replied to
Gandhi's request by a speech in which he said that although
training by manual work was a good educational technique, the idea
of schools being self-supporting was not good. "But there is a
danger in overemphasizing the self-supporting aspect of education.
Teachers may become slave-drivers. . . .We shall be laying the
foundations of hidden slavery in our country."[19]

Gandhi's supporter Mahadev Desai saw these comments as
destructive of Gandhi's intent, and replied:

The idea of self-supporting education cannot be divorced from
the ideological background of non-violence, and unless we bear
in mind that the new scheme is intended to bring into being a
new age from which class and communal hatred is eliminated
and exploitation is eschewed, we cannot make a success of it. We

should, therefore, approach the task with firm faith in non-violence and in the belief that the new scheme is evolved by a mind that has conceived non-violence as the panacea for all ills.[20]

Yet, in spite of this retort, which clearly suggests that the attitudes of the Muslims from the Jamia Millia were not acceptable to those for whom commitment to non-violence was an absolute requirement, Gandhi himself nominated Zakir Husain to be president of the Conference. Subsequently, Zakir Husain became the chairman of the committee to draft a syllabus for the new scheme, which was to be called Basic National Education. The scheme was implemented, and the Jamia Millia became involved in training teachers to serve in the new Basic Education schools. A member of the Jamia staff, Saeed Ansari, went to New York to study education under John Dewey. He became principal of the teacher training college at the Jamia Millia. In attempting to understand the religious aspects of the Basic Education issue, the exchange noted above among Gandhi, Zakir Husain, and Mahadev Desai is illuminating. Mahadev Desai, one of Gandhi's closest co-workers, stated clearly that absolute non-violence was a primary commitment for the serious rebuilding of human personality which he understood Gandhi to be articulating for India. Zakir Husain, equally clearly, did not accept this. Why then did Gandhi put Zakir Husain in charge of this scheme, and why did Zakir Husain accept the responsibility?

The answer with respect to Gandhi seems not unlike the answer as to why he committed himself to work with Muhammad Ali on the Khilafat issue many years earlier. Both these instances of Gandhi's initiative toward working with Muslims were not shared by, nor presumably much understood by, many of his own close followers. This aspect of the Gandhian vision was the one least acceptable to his own disciples. It is certainly that part of his teaching that has been least implemented. There have been organizations to carry out all his other main concerns, such as *harijan* uplift, spinning, etc., but not one for Hindu-Muslim unity.

The human quality under consideration might best be termed generosity of spirit. As a virtue, it was shared by Zakir Husain and the other Jamia Millia Muslims. When Zakir Husain, as president of India, later paid a courtesy visit to a Hindu holy man, he infuriated many of his co-religionists. When seeking to explain why Zakir

Husain did this, his friend and co-workers from the Jamia Millia, Muhammad Mujeeb, said that it was a symbolic act of courtesy intended to make up in some small measure for the virulent discourtesy of many Muslims towards Hindu religious life. "He went to the Shankarachara and Muni Shuhil Kumar as an act of atonement for the narrowmindedness of his community."[21] Mujeeb has also suggested that when Gandhi and Zakir met together to discuss basic education, each exhibited toward the other gentleness and respect. Neither tried to argue for a dominating position.

> I always accompanied Dr. Zakir Husain when he went for the meetings of the Hindustani Talimi Sangh at Sevagram. The meeting was generally followed by an interview with Gandhiji, at which Dr. Zakir Husain presented a report of the discussions. There was something very sweet about the interview. Dr. Zakir Husain looked incredibly modest, and his manner was that of a young man talking to an elder of whose benevolence and trust he was completely sure. Gandhiji, on his side, radiated confidence in the person to whom he had entrusted the fulfilment of an idea that was dear to his heart. No one would have suspected that there were differences of any kind. These differences existed but neither Gandhiji nor Dr. Zakir Husain was inclined to be dogmatic.[22]

The quality of a relationship of this kind is not easily described, not least because it implies a readiness to transcend fixed positions in the context of meeting to deal with actual problems. On both sides, readiness to meet, to hear, and to cooperate were present because of the many years of mutual support that had already existed. Gandhi had exhibited his trust in the Jamia Millia community by sending one of his sons to be educated there.

These years in which the members of the Jamia Millia community were attempting to implement the scheme for Basic Education were years in which the antagonisms between the Hindu and Muslim communities were steadily worsening. The Muslim League, angered by Congress' refusal to allow what they felt to be appropriate Muslim representation in the new provincial government in UP, was consolidating its separatist position. Jinnah was abandoning his long fight for cooperation between Hindu and Muslim.

In this context, Muslim suspicion of Basic Education was very great. The scheme was thought to be a Hindu attempt to destroy Islam. Any attempt to use Hindu symbols was seen as a threat. Zakir Husain argued for the scheme with the All-India Muslim Educational Conference. There was great distrust, but the majority of members did agree to support acceptance of basic principles of the scheme—education through the mother tongue, extending over a period of at least seven years, and organized around useful manual work.

The members of the Jamia Millia community carried on their educational efforts as war broke out and political tensions within India increased. They made a significant attempt in 1946 to state their hope for reconciliation. On the occasion of the Jubilee of the college, a function was arranged to which leaders of both the Congress and the Muslim League were invited. Miss Fatima Jinnah had visited the display at the college and apparently gave a good report to her brother. Jinnah came and attended the meeting, along with Maulana Azad, Liaquat Ali Khan, and Mr. Nehru. Zakir Husain, speaking on behalf of his community, begged the political leaders to realize that the healthy and sane education of children was not possible in an atmosphere poisoned by hate and distrust. "We are obliged by the demands of our own vocation to cultivate reverence for children. . . . For God's sake, put your heads together and extinguish the fire."23

The Jubilee celebrations had involved welcoming two hundred guests to a function prepared where running water and electricity were not available, and danger was always present. Later, as the country was tormented by appalling communal riots, the Jamia Millia served as a center to welcome refugees and to attempt to restore order and goodwill.

Finally, after independence, the Jamia Millia Islamia became a university, and received its charter. Zakir Husain became, first, vice-chancellor of Aligarh University, then governor of Bihar, then vice-president of India, and finally, president of India. Muhammad Mujeeb became vice-chancellor of the Jamia Millia University. S. Abid Husain retired from the Jamia Millia in 1956 after thirty years of service. He then worked for three years as director of the Aligarh Department of Education. From 1960 to 1967, he worked as literary adviser to All-India Radio. In 1967, he and his friends decided to establish the "Islam and the Modern Age Society." Until his death in 1978, he worked for his society, editing the English journal *Islam and the Modern Age,* and the Urdu journal.

We have chosen to focus on S. Abid Husain's writings as illustrative of the spirit of the Jamia Millia community because he was the one member of the community who was most committed to writing, editing, and publishing. His editing of the journals in the later periods of his life gives further indication of the direction of thought which he represented. There is a distinctive point of view in all his works, which, while undoubtedly individual, also emerges out of the long process of the experiences of common work, struggle, discussion, and unceasing mutual support which has characterized the group with which he spent most of his life.

The point of view which emerges in the journals is an invitation to conversation about religion in the context of the twentieth century. Much of S. Abid Husain's energy went into organizing seminars on topics which seemed urgent to him. His intention was to get people talking with the expectation that consensus and an enriched sense of direction might eventually emerge. His perspective was not doctrinaire. It was rather like that of the founders of the ecumenical movement in the Christian case, namely, an expectation that when persons seriously meet each other, their misconceptions may disappear and new grounds of agreement may emerge.

We noted that the supporters of the Jamia Millia Islamia in its second phase were more ready than Muhammad Ali was to accept Gandhi's authority. Although Muhammad Ali had acknowledged Gandhi's character, S. Abid Husain and his friends had a more profound respect for the religious seriousness of the Mahatma. Although they never accepted all his teachings, including his concern with non-violence, yet they took him seriously as a religious person. It may be that when attraction occurs between persons from different religious traditions, one is shaped by the tradition one comes from in terms of what one tends to see as positive in the other. For example, a Buddhist responding to Gandhi might have more readily been attracted by the non-violence. As Muslims, S. Abid Husain and his friends were moved by what they saw as a prophetic type of mind in Gandhi. S. Abid Husain has told us of the experience that shaped his own decision. As a young student at Oxford in 1921, he had read Tagore's article, "The Call of Truth," and Gandhi's reply to it. The effect was a revelatory one. Thirty years later he tells us how he had reacted to Gandhi's words.

This was a new voice which made my whole body and soul vibrate. It seemed to go direct to the heart without the mediation of senses or intellect. Three ideas came to my mind—as if in a flash—rather dim at the moment but grown clearer now after one-third of a century. First, that the fundamental truth of life, as experienced by Gandhiji and Tagore was the same. The difference lay in the intellectual moulds in which they tried to mould it. Tagore's was the mystic mind . . . Gandhiji's was the prophetic mind which marches slowly but surely to its goal, fighting and conquering each resisting moment with the weapon of moral action. Secondly Gandhi had come "not to separate but to unite".`. . . Thirdly, that is moving away from Gandhiji in order to come nearer to Tagore, we young men were deceiving ourselves and trying to escape from life. There was no real contradiction in their teaching. If we loved our country, the human race and the pursuit of truth, we had to dream with Tagore and realize our dream in action with Gandhiji.[24]

Prophetic meant in this context a mind concerned with the alleviation of suffering through constructive action. The article of Gandhiji's that had so moved the young S. Abid Husain discussed the helplessness of the Indian poor. The basic attraction of Gandhi for these young Muslims lay in his focusing their attention on real problems, and challenging them to commit themselves to action on behalf of the masses.

An eyewitness has also told us of the reaction at Aligarh in 1920 to Muhammad Ali's impassioned plea to the young Muslims to make sacrifices for their country, and to give up their secure positions. "There was almost an uproar in the hall and rival groups of students were involved in a virtual battle of booing and hooting from both sides. . . . When Rasheed Ahmed Siddiqui . . . looked at his companion, Zakir Husain, he found him sitting almost dumbfounded, tears streaming down his cheeks. As Rasheed dragged Zakir out of the Melee that had followed, he was flabbergasted when . . . he got the reply 'Good-bye Rasheed Saheb! Life has well begun, pray now for its proper end!' "[25]

In both these cases, we have examples of the kind of decision making in response to challenge that Erikson would probably call the point of integration of character. The subsequent lives bear eloquent witness to the reality of these early decisions. Neither of these two Muslims ever swerved from the path they had set out for themselves. They rather spent the rest of their lives explaining in action and word what they had perceived to be true and necessary for their people.

The decision-making crisis in these two cases, unlike that of Muhammad Ali, or of the conservative Muslim leader Maulana Mawdudi, did not come from an insight into Islam as salvation history. They were Muslims, and were shaped in their responses by their expectations as Muslims. But what challenged them was the imperative to give up the security so precious to the educated Indian youth, and to go out into the wilderness of seeking to do something real for the actual conditions of poverty and injustice in the country. They received imperatives to become serious as moral persons.

When S. Abid Husain writes about Islam, he says it is a religion of hope and faith.[26] Elsewhere he has written that men of faith are urgently necessary.[27] Men of faith are found in all traditions. They are characterized by a readiness to recogize virtue wherever they find it, and a willingness to attempt to reconcile human beings, and to work for peace. A good Muslim should be a peacemaker. "Collective welfare is the key to the attitude taken up by the Qur'an towards politics, social as well as other aspects of cultural life."[28]

S. Abid Husain's perspective is not one from which a lucid salvation history is discerned. In his own crisis experience, he did not get a vision of a divine plan working itself out. He rather received an insight which told him that good persons have essentially similar goals, and that conflicts should be resolved. Hence his position makes him opposed to all those who see themselves as instruments of divine purpose in terms of historical processes. His view of the history of Islam as well as the history of Hinduism is that, in both cases, the record is full of imperfections. He writes, "The so-called Muslim states which appeared after the dissolution of the Abbasi Khilafat in the middle of the thirteenth century, were either dynastic states of Muslim rulers or natural states of Muslim peoples and had very little of the political or cultural aspects of Islam in them."[29] On Hindu history, he comments, "So the founders of the Puranic Hindu religion, who had understanding of the conditions of their time and an insight into the Indian mind, instead of making the Hindu religion a closed and rigid system, made it so elastic as to accommodate all the religious trends of that age."[30]

He uses such phrases as "so-called Islam" and "the very soul of religion" and "the salt of religion." His criterion of judgment in all such instances is the person of faith. Such persons may exist in any religious tradition and they will be characterized by inner discipline, freedom from vain attachment to worldly matters, and readiness to abandon their own security in order to find ways to help alleviate the sufferings of others. When Zakir Husain refers to these qualities, he makes reference to the two great poems of Iqbal, *The Secrets of the Self* and the *Mysteries of Selflessness*.[31] For S. Abid Husain, Zakir Husain and their colleagues at the Jamia Millia Islamia, both Iqbal and Gandhi are men of faith in whom the salt of religion is discerned. The Muslims of the Jamia Millia Islamia stayed with India when many of their co-religionists did not, because they agreed with Gandhi that a type of secularism was possible for India that would not be repressive for Muslims.

In the disastrous period after the collapse of the Khilafat and non-cooperation movements, it had been suggested that the Jamia Millia Islamia should remove the word Islamia from its name if it was to stay in India. Gandhi insisted that he would no longer support the institution if they removed the word Islamia. This was one indication of his concern that Muslims should feel entirely at home in the secular and free India he was working for. Secular in this Indian context means a political system in which religious communities are free to develop their own religious and cultural lives. It does not mean a system in which the state is opposed to religion, or actively seeks to replace religion with another set of values. Under this kind of Indian secularism, there would be religious education.

We have noted that "true spirit of religion" is one of S. Abid Husain's expressions. Another one is "the Indian spirit." He has written a lot about the history and culture of India, and the role Muslims have played in India's past and should play in India's future. He argues that the climate and the experiences of invasions by many peoples over the long course of India's history have resulted in a distinctive set of attitudes which represent the Indian spirit. This is a spirit receptive to contemplation, tolerant, ready to coexist with many different cultural groups, and open.

The attitude to problem solving in terms of Indian Muslims is manifested in the approaches put forward in the journals edited by

S. Abid Husain in the last part of his life. The English journal
Islam and the Modern Age, which began publication in May 1970,
gives a good indication of the concerns of its editor.

He sees world history as a process of moving away from tribal
cultures, toward the development of larger social and political
units in which reason serves to create bonds of relationship. Islam
he sees as the last of the great revealed religions. From this
perspective, Islamic society is most healthy when it exhibits confidence in human reason, and opens itself to communication with
others.

S. Abid Husain's method of problem solving is to encourage
discussion and the free exchange of ideas. His philosophical
position is somewhat Platonic, both in his certainty that final truth
is more than the forms through which it is presented, and also through
his interest in debate and exchange as a way of stimulating human
capacity to improve the world. In the various issues of *Islam and
the Modern Age,* one finds S. Abid Husain's presence most often as
the person behind the scenes organizing a conference, and usually
reporting through the journal on all the points of view presented.
One can discern from the topics dealt with at the various seminars
the concerns judged to be most urgent by S. Abid Husain and his
friends. In the eight years following the establishment of *Islam
and the Modern Age Society* the following problems were considered: religion and the modern age;[32] religion and peace;[33] Christian-
Muslim dialogue;[34] religion, morality and law;[35] and the reconstruction of religious thinking in Islam.[36] In every case, contributions
came from persons from different countries and different traditions.

Further, in various issues of the journal, topics are dealt with in
a thematic manner. The issues of Muslim law are considered
several times.[37] The role of women in Islamic countries is also
discussed.[38] S. Abid Husain had himself written a play about
Purdah when he was young. The discussions about women include
information about the actual changes taking place in various
Muslim countries. The journal also discusses the Sikh religion.[39]
Various articles deal with aspects of the tension between revelation and reason.[40] Hindu-Muslim relationships are analyzed.[41] A
number of articles on aspects of Indian Muslim history in India are
included, as well as analysis of other Muslim societies, such as
Pakistan and Turkey.[42] In these latter cases, the focus is on the
nature of secularism and the problems that have arisen.

In relation to the industrialized societies, the attitude as stated in S. Abid Husain's introduction to the first issue of the journal is that materialism and rationalism have become too dominant, so that human values as such are given less priority than they should receive.[43] S. Abid Husain's own method as a commentator on the various seminars he reports on is to paraphrase the various positions put forward, and then himself to suggest possible weaknesses in the arguments. The effect of this is not to discourage his readers, but to suggest that none of these issues are readily solvable. His confidence lies more in developing mutual sympathy and respect between the persons who are ready to talk than it is in any particular final solution.

His article on "The Power of Faith" perhaps best exemplifies his attitude to religion. He writes: "The fountain-head of faith is the mystic vision which came to some great seers at various times in various parts of the world. . . . This mystic experience invests the great seer with a charisma which enables him to attract countless human beings towards him to kindle in their hearts the light of faith and infuse into their lives the spirit of truth, love and compassion."[44] He uses Guru Nank and Gandhi as instances of persons who had this kind of influence on mankind.

One of the most grim of S. Abid Husain's articles is the one he contributed to the volume honoring his friend Zakir Husain's seventy-first birthday. After the fifty years or so of close working together and mutual support through difficult and bitter times, the commemorative offering of S. Abid Husain to Zakir Husain reflects certain realities close to the hearts of both of them. The harshest reality is the contrast between the actual India of the time—1966— and the ideal they had struggled all their lives to implement. He does not hesitate to blame religion for much of the trouble.

But the most intense and vigorous form of group egoism is religious communalism. It is a strange and highly explosive mixture of religious prejudice and political self-interest that exists to a greater or lesser extent in the minds of many of our country men in a latent form, and at the slightest provocation bursts into flames of anger and hatred. . . . As the movements of religious communalism believe that they have Divine Sanction for their policies, they have developed a strong sense of self-righteousness and lost all capacity for self-criticism. . . . Each religious communalist movement is confronted with its ugly and revolting face reflected in that of its rivals, but fails to recognize it as its own true image. . . . Once we start distorting the Moral Law to suit the interest of our community we shall be soon doing it to suit our own personal interest.[45]

Religion in S. Abid Husain's view might be said to have two faces. On the one hand, the cumulative tradition contains within it writings, scripture, poetry, biographies, and so forth that can serve to stimulate the kind of integrated moral persons whom he admires, and whom he considers the salt of the earth. On the other hand, religious persons who see themselves as the instrument of a salvation history, and therefore justified in their mistreatment of other persons, are dangerous. In the article presented to Zakir Husain, he comments on the danger of unthinking adherence to creeds and formulas, as opposed to the involving of oneself in attempts to solve real human problems. This clinging to words instead of actions he sees as one of the worst diseases of India.

"Of the various obstacles in the way of our drooping, decaying faith thriving afresh and bearing fruit in the impelling urge to action, is our traditional reverence for and reliance upon the almighty Word. . . . It was a passing phase in our history when Gandhi infected many of us with his spirit of 'do or die' that incidentally brought us our freedom. After he left us we lost no time in reverting to our age-old wisdom of the 'self-realisation through the Word.' "[46]

Notes

1. *The Collected Works of Mahatma Gandhi* (New Delhi: Publications Division, Ministry of Information and Broadcasting, Government of India, 1965), 18 : 378, 379.
2. Ibid., 19 : 34, and Gandhi's Correspondence, SN 7361, CN 340, Gandhi Memorial Library, New Delhi.
3. M.K. Gandhi, *An Autobiography, The Story of My Experiments with Truth* (New York: Beacon Press, 1957), p. 112.
4. S.M. Ikram, *Modern Muslim India and the Birth of Pakistan* (Lahore: Ashraf, 1965), p. 159.
5. *Collected Works of Mahatma Gandhi*, 10 : 6-64.
6. Rais Ahmed Jafri Nadvi, ed., *Selections from Muhammad Ali's Comrade* (Lahore: Muhammad Ali Academy, 1965), p. 11.

7. *Collected Works of Mahatma Gandhi*, 18 : vii.
8. Ibid., 18 : 387.
9. S. Abid Husain, *Gandhiji and Communal Unity* (Bombay: Orient Longmans, 1969), p. 56.
10. Muhammad Ali, *Scheme of Studies of National Muslim Educational Institutions in India* (Bombay: Bombay Chronicle Press, n.d.).
11. Afzal Iqbal, ed., *My Life a Fragment* (Lahore: Ashraf, 1942), p. 23.
12. Ikram, *Modern Muslim India*, p. 63.
13. *Collected Works of Mahatma Gandhi*, 19 : 71, 347.
14. Ibid., 16 : 514.
15. Ibid., 16 : 513.
16. Ibid., 23 : 56.
17. Gandhi's Correspondence, SN 14925, Microfilm, Gandhi Memorial Library, New Delhi.
18. Madhooli, *Jamia Ki Kaahani* (New Delhi: Maktaba-i Jamia, n. d.).
19. M. Mujeeb, *Dr. Zakir Husain* (New Delhi: National Book Trust, 1972), pp. 104, 105.
20. Ibid., p. 105.
21. Ibid., p. 239.
22. Ibid., pp. 120, 121.
23. Ibid., p. 138.
24. S. Abid Husain, *The Way of Gandhi and Nehru*, pp. xvi, xvii.
25. Anees Chishti, *President Zakir Husain a Study* (New Delhi: Rachna Prakashan), p. 18, quoting Rasheed Ahmad Siddiqui 'Murshid,' *Mazamen-e-Rasheed*, Anjuman Taraqi Urdu, 1946, p. 221.
26. S. Abid Husain, *The National Culture of India* (New Delhi: Asia Publishing House, 1956), p. 76.
27. *Islam and the Modern Age* 4, no. 4 : 36-42.
28. S. Abid Husain, *The Way of Gandhi and Nehru*, p. 81.
29. Ibid., p. 83.
30. Ibid., p. 65.
31. Zakir Husain, *Education Reconstruction in India* (New Delhi: Publications Division, Ministry of Information and Broadcasting, Government of India, 1969), p. 3.
32. *Islam and the Modern Age* 1, no. 2 (August 1970).
33. Ibid., 2, no. 1 (February 1971).
34. Ibid., 3, no. 4 (November 1972).
35. Ibid., 5, no. 1 (February 1974).
36. Ibid., 8, no. 4 (November 1977).
37. Ibid., 5, no. 3 (August 1974). See also vol. 7, no. 2 (May 1976).
38. Ibid., 6, no. 4 (November 1975). See also vol. 7, no. 1 (February 1976).
39. Ibid., 7, no 3 (August 1976) : 53-64.
40. Ibid., 3, no. 3 (August 1972), See also vol. 4, no. 2 (May 1973).
41. Ibid., 7, no. 2 (May 1976) : 64-82.
42. Ibid., 2, no. 3 (August 1971) : 67-88. See also vol. 2, no. 4 (November 1971).
43. Ibid., 1, no. 1 (May 1970) : 1-9.

44. Ibid., 4, no. 4 (November 1973) : 37.
45. *Dr. Zakir Husain Presentation Volume* (New Delhi: Maktaba Jamia, 1968), pp. 289-91.
46. Ibid., p. 299.

THE PARSI COMMUNITY

John R. Hinnells

The word "Parsi" means Persians and refers to those Persians who migrated to India from Iran in the tenth century CE to escape from Islamic oppression in their Iranian homeland. At the 1981 census they totalled 71,630 in India, making them India's smallest racial-cum-religious minority. Typically they are city dwellers (96% are classified as urban dwellers). The main numerical centre nowadays is Bombay, although nearly 12,000 live in Gujarat and there are communities with temples in various cities such as Delhi, Calcutta, Madras, and Bangalore. There are also approximately 3,000 in Pakistan (mainly Karachi) and a small community in Sri Lanka.

The Origin of the Parsis

Theirs is probably the oldest of the world's prophetic religions since the prophet, Zoroaster (or Zarathuštra), is generally dated by western academics at approximately 1,200 BCE. Many Parsi writers would date their prophet much earlier, at 6,000 BCE if not earlier.[1] He lived in the northeast of Iran on the Asian steppes and inherited much of the Indo-Iranian tradition so that Zoroastrianism and Hinduism have something of a common parentage. This results in a number of similarities between the two, such as the place of fire in ancient texts (the *Vedas* and

Avesta) and certain purity laws and attitudes toward the priests. The common ancestry has been emphasized by a number of Parsi writers in recent times. It is not, therefore, a point of merely antiquarian interest.

Zoroaster was a priest who was convinced he had seen God (Ahura Mazdā) in visions, on the basis of which he taught that good and evil were opposed realities and that each person had the freedom and the obligation to choose between the two forces. On the basis of their choice, either to support the path of righteousness (*asa*, of Vedic *rta*) or to choose the Lie (*druj*), men (and women—there is no difference between the fate of the sexes) would be judged after death. Thereafter, they passed to heaven or hell for reward or punishment. Zoroaster saw the world as a battleground between the good Ahura Mazdā (Wise Lord) and the evil Angra Mainyu (Destructive Spirit). But he looked forward to the day of renovation when mankind would be resurrected, the evil ejected from existence, and Mazdā's rule established on earth.

The prophet's teachings are preserved in hymn form in an otherwise unknown language, Gathic Avestan, but one with evident links with Vedic Sanskrit. The 17 *Gāthās* are preserved in the liturgy, and text, of the *yasna* and have been described as, in part, meditations on this ancient Indo-Iranian ritual.[2] The whole of the extant Zoroastrian holy book, the *Avesta*, is of a liturgical nature. It assumed written form at a relatively late date, sometime in the fifth century CE, but the teachings and the ritual practices date back to a much earlier period, some to the pre-Zoroastrian era, and some to the early centuries BCE. For traditional Zoroastrians the whole is the word of the prophet.

We know virtually nothing of Zoroastrian history from the time of the prophet until the foundation of the first Iranian empire, that of the Achaemenids in the fifth century BCE. Thereafter, it was the state religion of three successive Iranian empires, the Achaemenids, the Parthians and the Sasanians until the Muslim Arab invasion of Iran in the seventh century CE. Each of these empires ruled over an area stretching from India to what is now known as Turkey. Zoroastrianism was, therefore, the world's most powerful religion for a millennium.

Within a relatively short time of the Muslim invasion Zoroastrianism became the religion of a persecuted and socially deprived minority in Iran. Conditions became so bad that in the ninth century a small group of faithful Zoroastrians decided that, rather than leave their cherished religion, they must depart from their homeland and seek a new land of religious freedom. The story of their long and hazardous journey is related in the *Qissa-i Sanjan*, "The Tale of Sanjan."[3] This was not written down until 1600, so we cannot be confident of the historical reliability of the details, but it does show how Parsis viewed their settlement in India. The *Qissa* tells how the exiles were guided in their travels by a wise astrologer priest; how their lives were threatened by a terrible storm at sea until they were blown safely ashore in India as an answer to prayer. In short, their arrival in India is seen as being due to the will of God. The *Qissa* relates how the local Hindu prince gave them permission to settle on certain conditions: that they speak the local language, observe the local marriage customs, and carry no weapons. On receiving the necessary assurances and in view of the Parsi account of their religion in sixteen *shlokas*, which stressed the similarities of Zoroastrianism and Hinduism (for example the reverence for the cow), they were not only permitted to settle but were also given a plot of land and permission to build a temple. From the Parsi point of view, Hindu rulers have made only minimal demands upon them, none of these have required them to make substantial change to their religion which they have been allowed to practice in peace.

Parsi History in India

For the first 400 years of their history in India, the Parsis appear to have lived in peace and obscurity. When the Muslim armies invaded Gujarat in the thirteenth and fourteenth centuries, the Parsis fought valiantly, but in vain, alongside the Hindus. Their fears that Muslim rule in India would be as oppressive as it had been in Iran proved unfounded. A much greater impact on the Parsi community was effected by the arrival of European traders in the seventeenth century, especially the British who took over Bombay in 1662. Their intention was to use the islands of Bombay as a trading base, free from the political troubles of the mainland. To do this, they offered

conditions which would attract migrants to help develop what
was largely an uninhabited and unhealthy, marsh land. Two
attractive features for minority groups were freedom of religion
and equality in law. Over the following decades, Parsis migrated to Bombay in greater proportion to their numbers than did
any other community. As a result, at the dawn of the nineteenth century, they owned much of the land and had established themselves in leading positions in key areas, for example,
the dockyard. When private traders entered India after 1813
(previously the monopoly had laid with the East India Company), the port of Bombay boomed and the Parsis flourished as
middle men in trade. As industries such as textiles developed
in the nineteenth century, Parsis were at the forefront. By the
1850s the main centre of the Parsi community was no longer in
the traditional villages and cities of Gujarat, such as Navsari
and Surat, but in the cosmopolitan metropolis of Bombay.
Wealth brought power and Parsis distinguished themselves for
the charitable manner in which they dispensed these acquisi-
tions. Sir Jamsetji Jijibhoy (1785-1859) was the personification
of the Parsi dream of his generation. Orphaned at an early age,
he started as a *batliwala* (collector of empty bottles) but made
a fortune, mainly through the China trade. With his wealth, he
built schools, hospitals, dug wells, and supported the poor and
needy not only of the Parsi community but of all races. He was
knighted, made a baronet, and given the Freedom of the City of
London for his charity—the first Indian to be so honored. His
influence with the Governor of Bombay, though rarely made
public, was significant. He, and others like him, gave status
and respectability to the whole community.[4]

After the "Indian Mutiny" (or "War of Independence") in
1857, the nature of British rule in India changed. Government
now lay not with the East India Company but with Parliament
in London, especially in the person of the Secretary of State for
India, and with the Crown in the person of the Viceroy. Wealth
and local influence were no longer sufficient to affect official
policy. Now it was necessary to exert influence with the British
in England, notably at the parliament in London. What was
needed now was an education, preferably in law, which would
enable Indians to argue with the British in their own terms. The
Parsis were pioneers in adapting to the changed political

situation, largely because the wealth of the earlier generation had been used to build schools which a substantial proportion of the community attended. In 1860, for example, although Parsis represented only 6% of the Bombay population, they occupied 40% of the places in the city's educational institutions. While the moderates dominated the new Indian National Congress, that is until 1907, Parsis were leading figures, for example: Dadabhoy Naoroji (1825-1917) who was four times President of the Indian National Congress and the first Indian to be elected Member of Parliament (M.P.) in the Westminster Parliament, Pherozeshah Mehta (1845-1915), "The uncrowned King of Bombay", and Sir Dinshah Wacha (1844-1936), who acted as Secretary to the INC for some twenty years. Parsis were also leaders in the growing industries of the time, for instance: J.N. Tata (1839-1904) in steel, Sir Sorabji Ponchkanawalla (1881-1937), who founded the Indian Central Bank, Sir Dinshah Petit (1823-1901), who owned a number of textile mills. They were also leaders in a number of social movements, for example, S.S. Bengalee (1831-93) and B.M. Malbari (1853-1912) in the campaigns for women's rights. In the honors, such as knighthoods bestowed on them in the causes they espoused, in the political offices achieved, in the professions they pursued, and in the economic fields they opened up, the Parsis saw themselves, and were seen by others, as being like the British. At the turn of the century, Bombay Parsi fashions in dress, recreation (sport and the theatre), dining, even in personal mannerisms (such as the style of moustache, haircut, etc.), and vocabulary they were typically westernized.[5]

From the Surat conference of the INC (Indian National Congress) in 1907, Parsi fortunes began to decline. Squeezed out of the INC by the Hindu militants, they turned politically to the National Liberal Federation, whose western branch in Bombay they came to dominate through such men as Sir Pheroze Sethna (1866-1938) and Sir Cowasji Jehangir (1853-1934). But this never became an effective political body. As the mighty battalions of the Hindus and Muslims faced up to each other, the minorities in general, and the Parsis in particular (being the smallest of the minorities), were eclipsed. Whereas the British had taken note of Parsi opinion in the nineteenth century, they now ignored it. The wealth and power the Parsis had achieved was, of course, out of all proportion to their numbers and the other communities were now catching up in acquiring their portion. But as militants gained prominence in various quarters, the Parsis began to fear for their own future, recalling what their fate had been in their homeland when religious "enthusiasts" had assumed power. Many, therefore, began to consider leaving India, some to go to Britain, some to Iran where the new Pahlavi dynasty began to show a protecting interest in the ancient religion. The great majority, however, remained in India.[6]

- The period 1857-1947 saw a dramatic dispersion of the community. Although only a relatively small number dispersed for the fear of life in India, quite a number migrated for trade and education. Some travelled in India, notably to help develop the commercial and shipping centre of Karachi, others to Calcutta, Madras, Bangalore, and Delhi. Others went overseas. Parsis were pioneers in the development of the China trade and communities gradually grew in Canton, Shanghai, and Hong Kong. After the 1940s and the Communist take over in China, it was Hong Kong which became the home for Parsis in this region. Others settled in Singapore. In the nineteenth century a number of Parsis, along with other groups of Indians, migrated to East Africa, notably Aden, Kenya, Uganda, and Tanzania (to use the modern names). In the 1960s, Asians felt compelled to leave many African countries. A few Parsis returned to India, some went to the American continent, but most settled in Britain.[7]

Individual Parsis have visited Britain from the early eighteenth century, but the Religious Association was not founded until 1873. Three Parsis have become Members of Parliament at Westminster, all representing London constituencies. In addition to Nauroji, who has already been mentioned, there was Sir Muncherji Bhownagree (1851-1933) and Shapurji Saklatvalla (1874-1936). The main period of growth in the British Zoroastrian community, however, has been in the post-Independence period. A number of doctors came in the late 1940s, attracted by the new National Health Service, but most came in the 1960s when Britain was attractive for Indian migrants.[8] Also in the 1960s and 1970s, Zoroastrians migrated to the United States and Canada. Precise numbers are not available, but it is estimated that there are approximately 4,000. After the fall of the Shah in 1979, they have been joined by a number of Iranian Zoroastrians. Another continent which has become home for Zoroastrians in recent times has been Australia, particularly Sydney. Smaller groups, generally numbering a few hundred, are to be found in the Gulf States and France. Zoroastrianism is, therefore, now to be found in more countries than at any time in its vast history.[9]

The dispersion, however, has serious consequences for the parent community in India. Because of a low birth rate (discussed below), Parsi numbers are declining dramatically in India, at the rate of 20% in the decade 1971-81 to be precise. Outmigration is further depleting those numbers. Parsis are not the only Indian group to migrate overseas. What is different for them, however, is that they are the only ones whose numbers in India are shrinking. There is another problem specific to them. Many Indians who migrate come from particular villages and a substantial proportion are manual workers or small traders. This is not so with Parsis. A recent survey has shown, for example, that 92% of the Zoroastrians in New York have a university or college degree. Only 5% of the total Zoroastrian diaspora are manual workers, whereas 18% are in the professions (notably medicine), 15% engineers, 14% business executives, and 14% are administrators. Among the Parsis, it is the educated, enterprising, ambitious, and young people who are migrating. That inevitably has a consequence not only for the numbers but also for the social 'mix' left in India.[10]

In view of these patterns of migration and the fears with which most Parsis viewed Independence, how has the community in India fared in the last 40 years? There have been some difficulties. The nationalization programme took control of Air India and a number of banks out of Parsi hands. Prohibition took away the main source of income of 50% of Parsis in Gujarat. Many of these people turned to their lands for alternative income, but this income, too, was reduced by land tenancy legislation in 1950. But, there is no sense of these policies being anti-Parsi and the community's experience at the hands of government has generally been good. A number have achieved high office. A Parsi has, for example, held the post of head of each of the branches of the Armed Services (Air

Marshall Aspi Engineer for the Air Force, 1960-64; Field
Marshall Sam Maneckshaw for the Army, 1973; Admiral Jal
Cursetji for the Navy, 1976-79). India's largest commercial
concern, Tata Industries, is Parsi owned, as is South Asia's largest private concern, Godrej Brothers. Parsis have made substantial contributions in diverse fields such as Atomic Energy
(Homi Babha, 1909-69); Education (two Vice Chancellors of
Bombay University, Sir Rustom Masani, 1876-1966 and Dr.
[Mrs.] Bengalee, Vice Chancellor at the time of writing); and
the Arts (Zubin Mehta who was appointed Music Director of
the New York Philharmonic Orchestra in 1978). Politics continues to be a field in which Parsis are distinguished. Individuals
have held the office of Governors of Provinces (Sir Homi Mody,
Uttar Pradesh, 1949) and Ambassador in Washington (Palki-
walla in 1977). One of the co-founders of the Swatantra party,
Minoo Masani (b. 1904), was a Parsi. But perhaps, the most
influential was Feroze Gandhi. He entered Parliament in 1952
where he became known as a campaigner against corruption.
Prior to that, in 1942, he married Indira Nehru—who went on to
become one of India's most powerful political figures. Since
in Parsi terms descent is reckoned through the father, that
means, in the view of many in the community, that technically
Sanjay and Rajiv Gandhi are Parsis. Since Rajiv Gandhi has
taken part publicly in explicitly Hindu acts, for example his
mother's funeral, that may not be his own self-perception.
Nevertheless, Parsis are fond of recalling how he resembles his
father and believe that he, like others, illustrates beyond doubt
the conviction that Parsis have not faced prejudice in Independent India.

Parsi Religious Practice

This brief overview of Parsi history has highlighted the vast
changes which have occurred in the community's fortunes over
the years. Zoroastrianism emerged from its origins on the
Asian steppes in the stone age to become, for over a millennium,
the world's most powerful religion, thence to the religion of a
persecuted minority in its homeland, to an obscure religion of
minority in exile, and finally to the religion of a powerful,

respected, but small community in a different culture. The rest of this chapter is concerned with how those social and political changes have affected the practices and teachings of Zoroastrianism. It must be stressed that it is concerned specifically with Zoroastrians in India, or the Parsis. An account of Zoroastrianism in Iran would be rather different.

Typically, Parsis spend little time in theological study. Few know much of the religion's formal teachings. To most Parsis, their religion is tied up with their identity. It is something which is done, not speculated about. The natural place to begin a study of their Zoroastrianism is, therefore, with the practices, specifically the life-cycle rites and the daily observances of the lay person. A preliminary word on the fundamental concept of purity and pollution, which underlines various practices, is important.

Purity and Pollution

Purity, it has been said, is not next to godliness in Zoroastrianism, but part of it. According to the traditional teaching, death, in all its forms, is the weapon by which evil seeks to destroy the good creation of God. The greatest victory of evil, and consequently the major focus for its presence, is the death of a human being. Fundamentally, the essence of impurity is the presence of evil. Anything which is conducive to death (for example decaying matter), or is considered dead, is impure. Whatever leaves the body is considered dead. Thus blood, cut hair, semen, urine are all impure when separated from the body. It is a human religious duty to preserve the natural purity of the creation, for God created it in a perfect and holy, i.e. pure, state. Zoroastrianism has, reasonably, been described as the world's first ecological religion. Since the human body is also part of God's good creation, it is an essential duty to preserve bodily purity.

Because God is wholly pure, it is vital for worship to be conducted in total purity, that is, in terms of moral, spiritual, and physical purity. A priest is basically a man whose life is dedicated to the pure, the holy life. Obviously, this necessarily involves ethics and spiritual concerns. It also requires the strict preservation of the purity laws so that he may act in the sanctuary, and in other rites, on behalf of community members whose daily lives make it difficult for them to preserve the necessary state of purity.

Women also stand at the forefront of the battle against impurity. Since blood which has left the body is impure, the monthly cycle of menstruation means that women are in a regular state of impurity and, at such time they should avoid contact with anything that is holy, for example a priest, the fire or a temple. In Zoroastrian belief, evil instinctively attacks and seeks to destroy life. Because a woman's body is the ultimate focus for the creation of life on earth, she is particularly subject to the assault of evil. Her monthly cycle of impurity is, therefore, in no way seen as a moral, or religious, failing on her part. Rather she is the innocent victim and temporary abode of evil and impurity. Most religions have a range of purity laws associated with menstruation, child birth, etc. What distinguishes Zoroastrianism is the logic with which it elucidates those laws. Apart from these additional laws relating to purity, the religious obligations and practices of men and women are the same. The same purity laws also mean that a woman cannot be a priest.[12]

Initiation

Initiation should take place before the age of puberty, but not in infancy, since it is considered important that the young person should choose to enter into the responsibilities of the religion. Zoroastrians believe that people have freedom to choose between good and evil. How they use that free will will be what determines their fate after death. A person's good thoughts, words, and deeds will be weighed in the balances. If the good predominates, the person goes to heaven, if the evil predominates, they go to hell. Such a belief presupposes that an individual is responsible for his or her thoughts, words, and deeds. Since a baby cannot distinguish right from wrong, it cannot be responsible for its acts and hence cannot sin. As the child grows up, it learns to distinguish and that is the point at which initiation should occur. There is no sense of cleansing from sin, or of initiation ensuring salvation, rather it is entry into the army of God to fight against evil and into the Parsi community.

A 1906 test case in the Bombay High Court formalized in law what had been normal Parsi practice, namely that only the offspring of a Parsi male can be initiated. In modern practice, the

child of any intermarriage is generally excluded. The most
common explanation preferred by Parsis for this is to say that
religion is part of a person's conditioning from birth and that it
is emotionally and psychologically harmful to change religion.
People should be religious in the tradition into which they were
born. Parsis do not, therefore, typically see any exclusive claim
to religious truth. A supporting practical argument is that
because the Parsis are such a tiny minority, if they were to seek,
or even accept, converts, they would antagonize the dominant
communities. As evidence of this, they point out that they have
fared well in India because they have not been seen as a threat by
the host society. They oppose intermarriage because they fear
that it will inevitably erode the distinctive characteristics of the
community. It is not that they necessarily see themselves
as superior, but rather that they wish to preserve their
identity.

The rite of initiation the *naujote* (commonly explained as
meaning "new birth") begins in private with a ritual bath. Once
cleansed in body by bathing and in spirit through prayer, then
the child is dressed in clean white "pyjama" trousers, a shawl
draped round the upper portion of the body, and wears a small
cap, for the head is always covered during worship. The child
is led into the room where the *naujote* is to be performed. A
senior female member of the family performs a traditional
Indian greeting ceremony. The child then sits before the officiating priest (there are usually several present) and, in the presence
of the fire which, as the representative of God, is present at all
ceremonies. After introductory prayers, basically affirming
belief in Zoroastrian teaching, the child is invested with the
sacred emblems of the religion, the sacred shirt and cord, the
sudre and *kusti*.

The *sudre* is a white, cotton, vest-like garment worn next to
the skin at all times. It is invested with heavy symbolism,
having, for example, a small pocket at the 'V' of the neck which
is said to be the spiritual purse in which the individual should
store up good thoughts, words, and deeds. But to many Parsis,
the *sudre* is more than a mere symbol, it is a spiritually powerful and protective force for the believer. The *kusti* is a long
cord woven (traditionally by the wives of priests) from lambs-
wool. Historically, it is related to the sacred cord of the

brahmin, but for Zoroastrians, it is the badge of all believers and not just of the priests. After the investiture with the *sudre* and *kusti*, the child is then blessed by the officiating priest with prayers for a long and active life in the religion. The child is thus initiated into the responsibilities of the religion and the fellowship of the community.[13]

The Daily Prayers

As the *naujote* is the same for boys and for girls, so the daily practice of prayer is the same for each. At five set times during the day, before bathing, worship, and at the start of many enterprises or journeys, the cord is untied from around the waist (it is not tied round the shoulders as it is by the *brahmin*) and then, facing the light with the *kusti* in hand, the worshipper recites prayers in which he affirms his devotion to God and rejects evil. As the name of God is mentioned, the Zoroastrian bows the head and touches the *sudre* with his or her forehead. As evil is mentioned, the ends of the *kusti* are flicked contemptuously and dismissively. The *kusti* is passed back and forth around the waist with knots before and behind. As the knots are tied, a resolve is expressed to practice good thoughts, words, and deeds. The prayers may be said anywhere, though naturally a pure place should be sought, be that a temple, in the home, or before one of the creations of God (for example, the waters). It is a practice common to all believers, to young and old, to rich and poor, to lay person and priest, in India and overseas.

Temple Worship

Theoretically, there are only two formal liturgical duties for a Zoroastrian, the daily prayers as described above and the observance of the seasonal festivals, the *gāhāmbārs*. The latter observance has declined considerably in India, partly due to restrictions on large festival meals. It is more widely observed in Pakistan and is important in Iran. Zoroastrianism was originally a religion of the open air, so that people commonly worshipped not in human constructions of temples but before the divine creation of the sky and sun or the waters. Temple were a relatively late entry into the religion, probably in the fifth or fourth centuries BCE, as a result of western influence. In Zoroastrian Iran, they became popular as foci of royal piety and munificence. In India, there was for centuries only one permanently burning fire, which is now housed at the quiet seaside village and centre of Parsi pilgrimage, Udwada. Worship before the fire was mainly conducted in the home. But as Parsis became increasingly wealthy in the nineteenth century, they had the resources to build temples. They also had a new religious need. Because they employed servants, who were rarely Parsis, the purity of the home could no longer be preserved in the proper manner for the ritual fire. Temples were, therefore, constructed as centres of purity.

There are two types of fire temple which are distinguished from each other by the grade of fire which burns within them. An *Ātas Bahrām* houses the highest grade of fire, the royal *Bahrām* or "victorious" fire. This takes a year to consecrate and, once installed, is treated as royalty. There are eight such "cathedral fire temples" (as they are sometimes referred to) in India, four in Bombay, two in Surat, one each in Navsari and Udwada. The "ordinary" fire temple (*dar-i Mihr* or "Court of Mithra", also known as an *agiari*, Gujarati for "house of fire") has a less complex consecration. There are approximately 160 such temples scattered throughout India. At first, fire temples were simply centres of purity to which a priest would take a fire. In recent times, however, it has become the rule to keep permanently burning fires in temples. The fire is not only the "symbol of He who is pure undefiled light," but is also considered to be the very presence of God and sometimes referred to as the Son of God.

A Parsi temple is a complex of rooms or buildings. Near the gateway is a place for washing and reciting the *sudre-kusti* prayers. In outer rooms are pictures of the revered figures of the religion from the prophet to the benevolent donors to the temple. These pictures are commonly garlanded and worshippers usually pause before them and touch them to draw, as it were, their spiritual energy to themselves. Before entering the prayer room, worshippers flick off their shoes so that outside impurity is not taken into the centre of worship. The fire is kept in a sanctuary which is marked off on one side of the room with floor to ceiling walls through which there is a door for the priest to enter and windows for the worshippers to venerate the divine presence. There is no formal time for prayer in the temple, but many like to attend at one of the five set times when the fire is fed.

Parsi worship before the fire is an intensely personal activity. As worshippers enter the prayer room they normally stand in the doorway of the sanctuary, kneel and bow the head on the step before the fire, leave a piece of sandalwood as an offering to God, and then take a pinch of ash from the fire, left by the priest in a ladle in the doorway of the sanctuary. This they apply to the forehead, thus receiving its energy and strength. Then, standing (or sitting on a bench if old or infirm), the worshipper will offer prayers in the sacred language of Avestan. Afterwards, vernacular prayers may be offered in petition or thanksgiving for a boon. Essentially, therefore, the visit to the temple is an act of pilgrimage in order to see the living form of God, to stand in the divine presence, and to receive strength from it.[14]

Marriage

Marriage is not merely desirable but doctrinally a duty for Zoroastrians. Because God and his creation are characterized by life and bounty, it is a religious obligation to extend his kingdom through marriage and the raising of a family. This is an obligation laid on all, including priests. Indeed, until the last century a priest was not allowed to perform certain major   ceremonies   unless   he   was   married.   It   is   only with the influence of Theosophy, and a tendency towards asceticism, coupled with a numerical decline in the priesthood, that this tradition has been eased. Until the mid-nineteenth century child marriage was practised in common with the rest of Indian society, but it has no part in the ancient religion and was quickly dropped once the pressures for social reform began.[15]

In the twentieth century, Parsi women have experienced a degree of "liberation" unequalled in Indian society. In 1982, the literacy rate for Parsi women in Bombay was practically the same as for men (97% and 99% respectively). The numbers completing high school or college education were similar (men 45%, women 42%) and a substantial proportion completed a university course (men 21%, women 16%). The consequence is that a high proportion of women are in gainful occupation,

(29% compared with 9% of the general female population in Greater Bombay). Because of these achievements, a high proportion of Parsi women either delay marriage (the average age of Parsi women at marriage was 25)[16] or many do not marry. Thus in 1982, the index of non-marriage of Parsi women was 21%, compared with 3% for the rest of Bombay's female population. Educational and career opportunities have thus dramatically reduced marriages among Bombay Parsis. The resulting declining birth rate is the major reason why numbers are dropping so rapidly, by as much as 20% in the decade 1971-81 down to 71,630. The 1982 survey showed only 1% separated or divorced.

Arranged marriages have been common among the Parsis, but, increasingly in the twentieth century, prospective brides and grooms have been consulted. Love marriages are common. It is difficult to give precise figures because the process is not always clearly defined. It would be rare for Parsi youth to go directly against known parental wishes and virtually unheard of for parents not to discuss marriage prospects with the children. The role of a marriage broker in the old sense has practically disappeared, though as the youth find it increasingly difficult to find a bride in the shrinking community (especially in the more widely dispersed communities outside Bombay, and particularly outside India), the Bombay Parsi Panchayat has begun moves for a marriage bureau. In such a small community, marriage within the wider family is not uncommon. Ten per cent of women were found in the 1982 survey to have married men they were related to by blood, for the most part their cousins. Out-marriage is reported to be a growing phenomenon, but the 1982 survey found only 1% had done so. The situation is different among those who have migrated overseas, where over 10% of the young are already married out. It seems certain that an increasing number will do so in the second and third generations.

The marriage ceremony can be said to commence with betrothal. Because a Zoroastrian's word is considered his bond, the betrothal is thought to be binding. The date of the marriage is fixed by choosing an auspicious day; eclipses, for example, are avoided. The betrothal is known as a naming ceremony (*Nam padvin*), "naming" this person as the boy or girl they will marry. With the wedding itself, there used to be four days of ceremonies, but these are now often performed in one. The bride wears a sari, normally white, and the boy traditional Gujarati dress (*dagli* and white trousers with a hat, *pugri*). The ceremony takes place in either the morning or evening. After a purificatory bath at home, the couple will go to the *baug* or place of the wedding (though the ceremony can be in a temple or the home) in a car bedecked with flowers. They are grand occasions with several hundred guests, in earlier times even more. The couple is greeted on their arrival on the wedding dais by a senior female relative as with the *naujote*. The boy takes his place first. Present with them on the dais are witnesses and senior female relatives. It is customary for these to be married people and it is abnormal for those who have recently been bereaved to participate in this way. The family priest from each side shares in the performance of the ceremony. Traditionally, the wedding commences with the couple sitting facing each other, but with a sheet between them hiding them from each other's view. This is a practice going back to the time when a couple did not see each other before marriage. A ball of wool is passed seven times round the couple, symbolically binding them together. The sheet is then dropped and, by tradition, whichever partner is first to shower the other with rice is thought to be the dominant partner. The couple then sit side by side facing the priest for the strictly religious part of the ceremony the public affirmations of betrothal, admonitions, and blessing by the priests.[17]

Funerals

The ceremonies associated with death have two main concerns: the restriction of the powerful pollution present and the care for the soul. If the approach of death is foreseen, it is traditional to move the dying to a separate part of the house kept specifically for the purpose. The priest is called and prayers are recited affirming the faith and seeking forgiveness for sins. When death has occurred, a fire is brought into the room and the prayers begin. The body is laid on the ground, the corpse bearers summoned, and a member of the family washes the body before it is clothed in a clean, but used, *sudre* and *kusti* (a new one would be wasteful, and waste is sinful in Zoroastrianism). The *sachkar* ceremony is then performed when a circle is drawn round the corpse into which only corpse bearers should enter, for within that area the presence of evil is potent. The corpse is removed to the funeral grounds as soon as possible. Commonly in the twentieth century, this is immediately after death. At the funeral grounds, rooms are set apart which are designed for the various ceremonies in a way few households can manage in crowded city life. The funeral procession is led by *nasārsālārs*, the corpse bearers, who carry the body to its final resting place. They and the mourners walk in pairs, with a white cloth tied between them, binding them together in mutual support in the face of death. A dog, man's ally in the Zoroastrian tradition, is present now, as at several points in the ceremony, because of its ability to "see" death and to guard man. The cropse is laid on a slab and the bereaved take their last leave before the *nasārsālārs* carry it into the "Tower of Silence", or *daxma*, where it is exposed to the vultures.

The *daxma* is generally about thirty feet high. It is round and encircled by high walls so that no one can see inside. There is but one entrance up a flight of steps to a door set high in the wall, through which only the *nasārsālārs* enter. Inside, there are usually three concentric circles of *pavis*, or rectangular spaces into which the corpse is placed (outer one for males, center one for females, inner one for children). The corpse is stripped and the *nasārsālārs* leave. It is estimated that the vultures devour the corpse in approximately twenty minutes, during which time the mourners pray nearby. After the bones have been bleached and powdered by the sun, they are cast into a central pit. The mourning ceremonies last for four days. On the afternoon of the third day, the *Uthamna* ceremony is held at which charities are announced in memory of the deceased. Charities, rather than gravestones, are considered the proper Zoroastrian way to commemorate someone. It is also when an adopted son is named, if necessary, for a son is required to perform the various ceremonies at different stages through the year, and annually thereafter, in memory of the deceased.

The Towers of Silence are a noted feature of Zoroastrian practice, which the journalists have too often sensationalized. In theological terms, the *daxmas* are necessary in order to contain the impurity of evil. Because earth, fire, and water are sacred creations of God, burial, cremation, and disposal at sea

involve defiling the holy. God created nothing unnecessarily
and the purpose of the vulture is to consume that which would
otherwise cause unequalled pollution. In practical terms, Parsis
argue, this method of disposal is swift, economic with land,
hygienic, and, in short, that it is ecologically sensible. As one
of the few Westerners now permitted to visit the funeral grounds
in Bombay perhaps I may be permitted a personal comment.
Prior to my first visit I shared the typical Westerner's apprehension but found them deeply moving centers, characterized by an
air of naturalness and calm. The common Parsi horror of
burial and consumption by worms is, on reflection, understandable.[18]

Worship

The practices described above are part of the daily life of the
ordinary Parsi Zoroastrian. There are numerous other rituals:
the "higher" or "inner" ceremonies of the temple, such as the
yasna, which incorporates the *haoma*, of Indo-Iranian origin, and
the *nīrangdīn*, in which the bull's urine is consecrated for use in
purificatory ceremonies and which also dates back to ancient
times; the great nine-day purification ceremony, the *barasnom*;
the initiation ceremonies of a priest; the consecration rites for
temples and *daxmas*. But important though these undoubtedly
are in the history of the religion, they are not part of the daily
life of the ordinary Parsi today: There are other practices which
are part of many people's lives—the birth ceremonies (surprisingly rather few in view of the importance of Zoroastrian
attitudes to new life) and the *jasan*, a ceremony which with small
modifications can be used in memory of the dead, in celebration
of family or community occasions, or as an act of petition. The
devotional life of Parsis is so rich that it is impossible to provide
a reasonable account of it within the confines of a chapter.
What is more helpful is to consider the fundamental Parsi
assumption as to the nature of prayer and worship. The protestant attitude to prayer can, simplistically but reasonably, be
described as dialogue with God, relating to God one's hopes
and fears, expressing gratitude or penitence; listening for his
response. These can be part of the ordinary Parsi's practice,
but they are not the essence of the traditional understanding.
As described above, the necessary pre-requisite for worship is

purity. The words of worship are the words of the sacred liturgy, the *Avesta*. It is important that the original Avestan words are used. In part this is because they are considered the words of the prophet Zoroaster who had direct experience of God, an experience the worshipper hopes to share. The words of prayer are considered dead while written down, but living forces of spiritual power when uttered, in purity and devotion, in the rites. The priest is a man whose life is dedicated to making real and present the spiritual powers referred to in the prayers. Thus in the *yasna,* as in other rites, there are present the representatives of the seven creations (man, fire, water, cattle, plants, waters, metals) overseen and protected by the seven divine forces, the *Amesa Spentas*. As the priest recites the prayers, the divine forces named in them are thought to be actually, not merely symbolically, present. His gaze consecrates the objects so that they have a sanctity they did not have previously. The words, the actions, the objects all contribute to an actualization of holy power. Non-Zoroastrians are excluded from temples and many ceremonies (not initiations and weddings) because the fact that they do not observe the purity laws would inevitably disrupt the aura, the spiritual powerfield, of the religious activity. In worship, therefore, there may (or may not) be an idea of dialogue with God. More fundamentally, it is the individual Zoroastrian's immediate experience of the divine forces.

Parsi Religious Doctrine

Zoroastrianism is, on the whole, characterized by substantial continuity and the Parsis have typically been remarkably faithful to their heritage, despite living within easy reach of the "eclectic" atmosphere of India. They have, nevertheless, not remained unmoved by the changing spirits of time and place. There are some evident signs of acculturation such as the adoption of the sari by the women, the use of Gujarati, the adaptation of numerous "folk customs", and the garlanding and reverence paid to pictures of religious heroes. If a religion is to be "relevant" and "meaningful" to the lives of its young practitioners, it is natural that, in part at least, it will be presented in contemporary terms. Most religious groups tend to be more tolerant of doctrinal differences than of variations in ritual

practice. This is particularly true among Parsis, where the practices are seen as expressions of ethnic identity in a way that
patterns of belief are not. From the perspective of an outside
historian, one can see three main periods of influence which
have affected the way in which Zoroastrian ideas have been
presented in India.

The First Millennium

This millennium lasted from the time following their arrival
in India when the Parsis lived in relative isolation from other
communities. There were some adaptations, for example dress
and language, and the gradual acquisition of some patterns of
Indian thought, notably the perception of themselves as a distinct caste. It may be that the concept of four classes of society
was part of the Zoroastrian tradition inherited from Indo-Iranian
times, but life in India does seem to have reinforced the sense of
Parsi-Zoroastrian distinctiveness, for example, in attitudes to
intermarriage and eating and drinking with non-Zoroastrians.
It was the sense if identity which preserved the tiny community
in a new culture and amid a sea of change.

The Period of British Rule

This can be subdivided into three periods. From the Parsi
perspective, the period effectively begins with the British acquisition of Bombay in 1662. From then until the early nineteenth
century Parsis, on the whole (a few individuals apart), remained
socially and culturally distinct. At this stage, there appears to
have been relatively little change for Parsis in Gujarat from the
earlier period.

It was with acquisition of wealth and power in the nineteenth
century that the change occurred. The social dimension of
westernization among the Parsis was commented on above. A
comparable development can be observed in religious teaching,
not so much in the traditional centers in Gujarat but certainly in
cosmopolitan Bombay. In the 1830s and 40s the Scottish missionary John Wilson attacked the religion of the Parsis with vigor.
His onslaught on what he labelled Zoroastrian "dualism" (with
reference to the teaching on good and evil) and "polytheism"
(because of the reverence for the *Amesa Spentas*, the divinely
created forces not unlike Christian archangels, though less

mythologically described), his denial of the authority of the *Avesta* and of the status of Zoroaster converted few, but produced shock waves through the community, The reaction was to develop a Religious Education system which would equip members to rebut such allegations. In the 1860s, the German Protestant and Professor of Sanskrit at the Deccan College, Poona, Martin Haug, produced an exposition of Zoroastrianism which seemed to many Parsis to harmonize the religion and modern western knowledge. It incorporated a range of fundamentally Protestant assumptions, for example the rejection of later "medieval" teachings as corruptions of the pure teaching of the prophet; the rejection of elaborate priestly rituals and an emphasis on the religion of the heart; and the importance of prayers in the vernacular and not in a "dead" language, so that one could understand the meaning of the words.

Much Parsi religious literature of the late nineteenth century was concerned to purify Zoroastrianism from the "corruption" of what were seen as Hindu accretions and superstitions. The Reformists were often alluded to within the community as "the Protestant party" because of the influences seen to affect them. Two leading Parsi teachers were K.R. Cama (1831-1909) and the high priest in Karachi, Dastur M.N. Dhalla (1875-1956). Cama was a business man who spent time during a European business trip to study old Iranian languages and history at western universities and then devoted much of his life to teaching his fellow Zoroastrians in Bombay. Dhalla studied at Columbia University, New York, from 1904-1908, under the active Protestant professor of Iranian languages, A.V.W. Jackson. Dhalla was a prolific writer who sought to give a perspective on Zoroastrian history and doctrine which was consistent with western scholarly research, but which also preserved for his community the religious insights of Zoroastrianism. Both men led lives of simplicity and devotion which inspired many of their contemporaries. Though both were controversial, each played a vital role in passing on the religion to the next generation in the major urban centres of Zoroastrianism of that time, Bombay and Karachi.[19]

The third subdivision of the British era is from the start of the twentieth century to Independence. This was a period of conflicting loyalties. Politically, most Parsis remained pro-British, and among these Zoroastrians, the cultural and religious influences remained, on the whole western, specifically Protestant. As the Independence struggle developed, however, a number joined the nationalist cause and among them the influences were inevitably different. Communism was one factor, and so was Hinduism, especially as interpreted by Gandhi. A more potent force at this time was, however, the occult. The process of westernization had gone so far so quickly that a reaction inevitably started. Theosophy provided the rationale for many Parsis to preserve such cherished traditions as prayers in Avestan and the rituals which formed part of the daily life for most people. Yet this did so through a teaching with a western ancestry that gave it respectability among the western educated.[20] Some of the leading intellectuals and reformers toward the end of their life began to display an interest in Theosophical interpretations of Zoroastrianism (notably K.R. Cama). In the early twentieth century, however, with the move of Theosophical headquarters to Madras and the new leadership of Annie Besant, Theosophy was identified by Parsis with nationalism and Hinduism. In the 1920s, what might loosely be termed a Zoroastrianized theosophical movement began, *Ilm- i Khshnoom*. It was started by Behramshah Shroff. who claimed to have visited a secret race of Zoroastrian giants in Iran who taught him their mystical inner paths of spiritual knowledge, one opaque to outsiders, especially to western academics. The teachings are not dissimilar from Theosophy: rebirth, asceticism, vegetarianism, a belief in the individual aura, and the occult power of traditional prayers and ceremonies.[21] But instead of attributing religious insight to Tibetan Masters, it traced its origins to the Zoroastrian homeland which grew in attractiveness to many Parsis in the twentieth century as their fate in an Independent India seemed threatened by religious conflict and as Iran's new rulers, the Pahlavi dynasty promised and provided Zoroastrians with religious freedom. The last half century of British rule, therefore, saw a cauldron of competing, sometimes conflicting, pressures and allegiances. The religious literature of the period reflects that diversity of influences.[22]

Independent India

The religious teachings of Parsis in Independent India

continue to reflect a diversity of influences. The most obvious external influence is no longer the Protestant tradition, so evident in the days of British rule. From an outsider's perspective (a Parsi may argue differently), it seems that Hinduism is exerting a greater doctrinal influence, especially the *Gītā* and some of the great teachers of the last century such as Ramakrishna and Aurobindo, and such teachings as rebirth, yoga, spiritual unfoldment and superconsciousness.[23] At a popular level, a number of modern holy men have attracted a Parsi following, in particular the Babas. The occult teaching of Khshnoom continues to be popular. Indeed, my impression is that it is gaining, rather than losing, influence.

There are two new influences in the 1970s and 1980s. One is the impact of a charismatic teacher, Khojesti Mistree, whe runs an educational body, Zoroastrian Studies. He studied Zoroastrianism at Oxford and London and seeks to provide both an intellectual and a spiritual programme. His work has been particularly influential among the young and well educated Parsis of Bombay. It has also been controversial, not least among some of the established religious authorities and also because some fear that he is introducing "dualism," specifically the idea that evil in the world is due to an independent force, Ahriman, and thereby questioning God's omnipotence. Western academics have generally considered this to be a doctrine characteristic of the early religion. But it is felt by many Parsis that such a categorization of Zoroastrianism results in a downgrading of the status of their faith, somewhat in the way that Wilson dismissed it as a dualism. Whatever scholars may say, virtually no Parsis in India or the West, apart from those influenced by Mistree, nowadays accept this doctrine of evil and are offended when it is attributed to Zoroaster.[24]

The second influence at work in the 1970s and 1980s is the impact of the overseas, or diaspora, communities, above all those settled in the United States. The pattern of modern Parsi migration overseas is different from that of many other Indian communities. Typically, it is the well-educated and professionally successful who have migrated. In the United States and Canada, Zoroastrians are conscious of a need to provide an account of the tradition which will help their young maintain their heritage in the western world. In part, this involves

providing an intellectual explanation which will be found meaningful in the New World. Consequently, the diaspora communities commonly give greater importance to religious education
than is general in India, where the young acquire the tradition by
life in the community rather than through formal classes. The
practices and doctrines found among Parsis in India are not seen
as relevant by those who have assumed a western identity, especially the young, those brought up in the West, and by the Zoroastrians who have migrated from Iran. There is, therefore, a
growing tension between sections of the diaspora communities
and sections of the Indian community. Because the western
groups are educated and highly literate, they are already producing a body of religious literature, some of which is finding its
way back to India and influencing sections of the community
there. Interaction between "the old country" and the diaspora
is a two-way process.[25]

It is not necessarily the case that the diaspora is introducing
"new" teachings and practices (though that may also be the
case), but more that Zoroastrians overseas are choosing to
emphasize different aspects of their own history and doctrine.
So, for example, the writings of M.N. Dhalla are widely quoted
among groups in the United States and Canada becauseh is
teaching is found helpful to them.[26] The solutions he found to
his own religious struggles to integrate western knowledge and
Zoroastrian devotion inspire fewer people in India than they do
in the New World. Diaspora religion may prove influential in
the long term not simply because it introduces new elements,
but also because it may affect which aspects of the tradition are
preserved or emphasized. Another danger many are conscious
of is the proliferation of different forms of Zoroastrianism.
Diversity is possible in religions with millions of practitioners,
such as Hinduism, Christianity, Buddhism, and Islam. But
Zoroastrianism, being the religion of such a tiny minority, cannot bear the divisions others enjoy.

Conclusion

The world's oldest prophetic religion is now practised in
more countries around the globe than at any time in its history.

But with numbers diminishing, the consequence is that, in many, if not in all, centers, the numbers are being reduced to such a low level that what might be called "the necessary self support system" are becoming non-functional (for example the difficulties in finding suitable marriage partners, the supply of priests, the maintenance of temples and so on). There is, perhaps, a minimal size at which community can perpetuate itself. One danger facing Zoroastrianism is that it has almost reached that minimal level. The combination of a variety of factors, for example the diminution of dispersal, the consequences of economic and social success, pressures of acculturation in various countries, the dramatic decline in numbers in the largest centre of Zoroastrianism (namely India), and a sense of uncertainty for the future in Iran, means that Zoroastrianism is, today (1987), under greater threat than ever before. It would be foolhardy to write off a religion with such a long, noble, and distinguished history, but the dangers are enormous, not least in India. It is here that numbers are dropping most dramatically and the pressures of acculturation, though perhaps less obvious than in America, are no less real. Few, if any countries, would have provided Zoroastrians with such security for so long a period. The fact that Parsis have never experienced the equivalent of European anti-Semitism says a great deal about Indian society. Whether that security, identity, and success will last for another millennium is a question many Parsis are asking.

Notes

1. For western views see, for example, M. Boyce, *A History of Zoroastrianism*, Leiden, 1975 and 1982, vol. I, chapter 7, amended vol. II, pp. 1-3; G. Gnoli, *Zoroaster's Time and Homeland*, Naples, 1980, ch. 5. For Parsi views see, for example, J.C. Katrak, *The Age of Zarathushtra*. Bombay, 1968; H.D.K. Mirza, *Outlines of Parsi History*, Bombay, 1974, pp. 361-66.

2. Boyce, *Zoroastrians: their religious beliefs and practices*, London, 1979, ch. 2.

3. S.H. Hodivala, *Studies in Parsi History*, Bombay, 1920, chs. 1-4; R.B. Paymaster, *Early History of the Parsees in India*, Bombay, 1954, ch. 1; P. Axelrod, "Myth and identity in the Indian Zoroastrian community," *Journal of Mithraic Studies*, III, 1980, pp. 150-165. A short selection of passages from the *Qissa* and the *Shlokas* is in Boyce, *Sources for the Study of Zoroastrianism*, Manchester, 1984, pp. 120-23.

4. D.F. Karaka, *History of the Parsis*, London, 1884, 2 vols.; J.R. Hinnells, "Anglo Parsi commercial relations in Bombay prior to 1847," *Journal of the K.R. Cama Oriental Institute*, (hereafter *JCOI*), Bombay, 46, 1978, pp. 5-19.

5. Hinnells, "Parsis and British Education in Bombay, 1820-1880," *JCOI*, 46, 1978, pp. 42-64; C. Dobbin, *Urban Leadership in Western India*, Oxford, 1972; C. Monk, "The Parsis and the emergence of the Indian National Congress," *JCOI*, 52, 1985, pp. 115-243; D. Mellon, "The Parliamentary Life of Dadabhai Naoroji," *JCOI*, 52, 1985, pp. 1-114. On Westrenised Parsi social interests see H.D. Darukhanawala, *Parsis and Sports*, Bombay, 1935.

6. E. Kulke, *The Parisees in India*, Munich and Bombay, 1974, pp 190-216.

7. Hinnells, *An Ancient Religion in Modern Exile : Contemporary Zoroastrianism*, Oxford (in preparation).

8. Hinnells, "Parsis in Britain," *JCOI*, 46, 1978, pp. 65-84; Hinnells, "Zoroastrian migration to Britain : Its history and impact." *World Zoroastrian*, London, 1986, pp. 3-24.

9. J. Pavry, "Brief Summary of Zoroastrians Abroad," in *The Zoroastrian Challenge in N rth America*, Proceedings of the Fourth North American Congress, Montreal, 1982, pp. 88-94.

10. Hinnells as quoted in n. 7.

11. P. Nanavutty, *The Parsis*, Delhi, 2nd ed. 1980.

12. M. Boyce, *A Persian Stronghold of Zoroastrianism*, Oxford, 1977, ch. 5; K. Mistree, *Zoroastrianism : An ethnic perspective* (hereafter simply Mistree), Bombay, 1982, ch. 12.

13. J.J. Modi, *Religious Ceremonies and Customs of the Parsees*, Bombay, 1937 (hereafter simply Modi), ch. 7; B.K. Karanjia, *More of an Indian*, Bombay, 1970 (a vivid novel on the theme of Parsi intermarriage); Mistree, ch. 14; Hinnells, "Parsi attitudes to 'other religions' " in H. Coward (ed), *Indian Attitudes to "Other" Religions*, New York, 1987.

14. B.B. Patel, *Parsi Religious Buildings*, Bombay, 1906 (Gujarati); Modi, ch. 9; F.M. Kotwal, "Some observations on the history of the Parsi; *Dar-i Mihrs*," *Bulletin of the School of Oriental and African Studies*, 1974, 37, pp. 664-69; Kotwal and J V. Boyd, "Worship in a Zoroastrian Fire Temple," *Indo-Iranian Journal*, 1983, 26, pp. 293-318; Mistree, ch. 18.

15. Modi ch. 2; Mistrec ch. 15.

16. The figures vary in different surveys. The 1961 census of India separate volume on *The Parsis of Greater Bombay*, (p. 12) gave 26.55 as the average age of Parsi women at marriage.

17. M. Karkal, *Survery of Parsi Population of Greater Bombay-1982*, Bombay, 1984.

18. Modi ch. 3; Mistree, ch. 11.

19. J.J. Modi, *K R. Cama*, Bombay, n.d. (approximately 1940); N.N. Dhalla, *Saga of a Soul, an Autobiography*, (E.T. by B.S.H.J. Rustomji), Karachi, 1975. For an account of Parsi religious developments at the turn of the century see Hinnells, "Social change and religious transformation among Bombay Parsis in the early twentieth century'" in *Traditions in Contact and Change*, P. Slater and D. Wiebe, eds., Ontario, 1983, pp. 105-26.

20. K.J.B. Vadia, *Fifty Years of Theosophy in Bombay*, Madras, 1931. For an account of contemporary movements in India see J.N. Farquhar, *Modern*

Religious Movements in India, 1914. A recent Parsı theosophical writer is Dastur K.S Dabu, see for example his *Handbook Information on Zoroastrianism*, Bombay, 1969.

21. N.F. Mama, Bombay, *A Mazdaznan Mystic*, 1944; P.S. Masani, *Zoroastrianism Ancient and Modern* Bombay, 1917; P.N. Tavaria, *A Manual of 'Khshnoom'*, Bombay, 1971; M. Master Moos, *Life of Ustad Saheb Behramshah Nowroji Shroff*, Bombay, 1981; K.N. Dastoor, *Zarathushtra the Yazata*, Bombay, 1984.

22. H. Langstaff, *The Impact of Western Education and Political Changes upon the Religious Teachings of Indian Parsis in the twentieth century*, Ph.D. Thesis, Manchester, 1983 (unpublished).

23. For example, J.K. Wadia, *The Inner Man*, Calcutta, 1968; F.A. Bode, *Sharing the Joy of Learning*, Bombay, 1978, chs. 4-6.

24. Mistree ch. 4. Two examples of publications opposed to his interpretations are the newsletters of the Zoroastrian Associations in Montreal (*Gavashni*) and the Zoroastrian Center, California, (*the Zoroastrian*).

25. The publication best reflecting this process is the Bombay based monthly magazine, *Parsiana*.

26. For example the newsletters of British Columbia, Ontario and *The Zoroastrian*.

8

THE SINGH SABHAS AND THE EVOLUTION OF MODERN SIKHISM. 1875-1925

N. Gerald Barrier

Following the annexation of the Punjab in 1849, many contemporary observers felt that Sikhism would disappear within a short time and become one of the many sects within Hinduism. The maintenance of outward symbols, the 5 Ks associated with Guru Gobind Singh and most recently with the Sikh regiments of Ranjit Singh, appeared to be lax. Sikhs and Hindus shared numerous customs and social practices. The traditional Sikh religious leaders, however, showed little interest in articulating a separate and identifiable set of doctrines. While one European scholar declared that "Sikhism is a waning religion, that will soon belong to History," another warned that like a boa constrictor, Hinduism might soon crush and absorb the Sikh faith.[1]

The reversal of this apparent decline marked a decisive turning point in the evolution of Sikhism. By the early 1900s, Sikhs had undergone a dramatic revitalization in doctrine, institutions, and spirit. Much of this transformation was due to a new and expanding set of organizations loosely referred to as the Singh Sabhas. The accepted view is that the Singh Sabha membership halted the decline of Sikhism, reasserted traditional Sikh values, and put the religion and its followers back on the path that originated with the ten Gurus. Another increasingly persuasive interpretation is that the Singh Sabhas played a more complex role and, instead of asserting a lost orthodoxy, put together

elements from diverse and often conflicting traditions so as to
enhance the distinct nature of the religion. This resulted in a
new and different Sikh identity, complete with ideology and
practices commonly associated with Sikhism today.[2]

Understanding the changes among Sikhs in the decades
following the formation of the first Singh Sabha in 1875 involves,
first of all, the historical context within which the Sikh resurgence occurred. As Punjab Sikhs attempted to grapple with the
challenges accompanying Western rule, they did so in light of
teachings associated with the Gurus and *Adi Granth*, as well as
recent religious experience. That in turn led not to the steady
spread of agreed upon doctrines and practices but rather to
heated in-fighting among Sikhs and appreciable conflict with other
Punjabis also experiencing cultural revitalization, most notably
the Arya Samaj. Despite these difficulties, a common set of ideas
and institutions began to emerge between 1902 and 1920, which
were systematically promulgated by a new central organization,
the Chief Khalsa Diwan. The sudden appearance of the
Gurdwara reform campaigns after 1920 brought into prominence
a new group of Sikh activists, the Akalis, whose heroic deeds
enshrined them as the legitimate leaders of the community. The
Akalis and those Sikhs now controlling the shrines and major
resources of the community opposed many of the Singh Sabha
leaders politically. However, public consciousness that under-
lay the success of the Akali and their vision of Sikh religion and
history was due in large part to the work of the Singh Sabha
movement.

Punjab Sikhs and the Challenges of Colonial Rule

Sikh traditions and beliefs in 19th Century Punjab reflected
religious changes occurring over four hundred years. The formative phase of Sikhism stretched between the birth of the first
Guru, Nanak, in 1469 and the death of the tenth and final Guru,
Gobind Singh, in 1708. Guru Nanak emphasized the need for
man to meditate on the *Nam* or name of God, while at the same
time combining worship and deep reverence with active participation in daily life, which included raising a family and serving

others. His teachings were transmitted and elaborated by nine successors, who invested the Sikhs with a sacred scripture, the *Adi Granth*, compiled by Guru Arjan, a tradition of love and sacrifice, and numerous sacred shrines and holy places associated with important events in the evolving tradition. In 1699, Guru Gobind Singh transformed the Sikhs into a disciplined body or order called the *Khalsa*, whose members received a new name, Singh, and symbols (the 5 Ks: uncut hair, comb, tangle, sword, and breeches). The authority and function of the Guru became vested in the *Khalsa* and the *Adi Granth*.[3]

The subsequent rise of the Sikh *misals* and the control of the Punjab by Ranjit Singh (early 1700s-1839) were accompanied by the spread of Sikh political and social dominance in Northwestern India. Although this turbulent period of change requires more research, the general outline of what was happening to Sikhs and their religion seems clear. First, a loose band of teachers, local saints, and wisemen, often associated with a particular area or shrine, came to be seen as a major source of inspiration and authority among Sikhs. These *bhais*, *gyanis*, and local dignitaries cooperated with the heads of the families descending from the Gurus, such as the Sodhis and Bedis, to conduct worship, maintain some sense of continuity with the past, and provide spiritual and moral leadership. Although a handful of literary works were produced, most notably the *janamsakhis* or traditional biographies of the Gurus, Sikh culture tended to be transmitted orally.[4]

Simultaneous with the spread of the Sikh tradition in the rural areas and particularly among the Jats, the religious doctrines found in the Gurus' teachings were given various interpretations and reflected local custom and social practices. Sikhs could be *sahajdhari*, clean-shaven devotees of Guru Nanak who respected the *Granth* and worshipped regularly in the gurdwaras, or *kesdharis*, those who maintained the symbols associated with Guru Gobind Singh and had undergone baptism. Worship of local gods and saints was common, and in terms of daily ritual and important events, many Sikhs accepted the role of Brahmins and lived a life-style quite similar to that of other Punjabis. Marriage networks and social relations mirrored traditional custom that involved accepted linkages between families and respect for caste. Some attempted, after the late 1700s, to

legitimize a particular view of how Sikhs should live by pulling
to gether *rahitnamas* or guides to ritual and practice. This was
accompanied by the emergence of sects such as the Nirankaris
who opposed caste and tried to define and adopt distinctly Sikh
practices. On the whole, however, there was no generally
accepted set of traditions, religious beliefs, and social norms
among Punjabi Sikhs. Instead, there was a diffuse and often
competing group of intertwined traditions perpetuated by local
custom and religious teachers.[5]

The transfer of western institutions and ideology after 1949
contributed to the transformation of the world in which Sikhs
and other Punjabis lived. The region had always been an invasion zone characterized by a variety of cultures and interactions,
with layers of religious belief and an amalgam of life-style and
values. The British, however, differed from past rulers in that
their presence affected major changes in Punjab society and culture which continue to the present. The most obvious innovations arose from the administrative structures and the political
orientation underlying them. Within two decades, the colonial
power introduced a new bureaucratic system, complete with
western-style executive and judicial branches. These opened up
new channels of power and competition, accompanied by emphasis
on western education and attainment of skills necessary for new
occupations in law, administration, and education. The introduction of municipal and district councils created other
arenas of competition, with seats filled initially through patronage and then increasingly by election. The British used these
institutions, and less tangible means of influence such as the
granting of honors and seating at darbars, to develop support
groups that would assist in ruling the province.[6]

After a brief period of disquiet following the end of the two
Sikh wars, the Punjab government came to see Sikhs as an
important element in their colonial strategy. Sikhs were a main-
stay of the army, provided stability in the villages of central
Punjab through traditional leaders and social networks, and
helped fill the coffers of the revenue department by industrious
agricultural activity. Assuming the centrality of religion for the
Sikh population, particular care was taken to provide for the
adequate administration of shrines, most notably the Golden
Temple in Amritsar, and at the same time to control these central

Sikh institutions. British officers headed management com-
mittes, named key officials, and in general, provided grants and
facilities to insure continued Sikh sympathy for the raj.[7]

British rule also was accompanied by the rapid spread of
Christian missionary activities, thus introducing yet another
element in the mosaic of Punjab religious patterns. Prior to the
mutiny of 1857, the government openly sympathized with the
evangelical programs of the missionaries. Although the official
linkage diminished thereafter, tacit support for the proselytizing
efforts continued through educational grants and special advantages. Besides posing a threat by aggressively converting
Punjabis, the missionaries transplanted more effective methods of
communicating their message. The printing press, tract literature, and western world models for organization and propaganda
were new elements that over time were adapted by Punjabis not
only to attack the Christians but to assault each other.[8]

One of the most significant consequences of British penetration, however, involved a shift in the way Punjabis viewed their
surroundings and traditions. Western social, religious, economic,
and political values fostered a new intellectual climate in the
Punjab. Individuals and sects were challenged to re-evaluate their
history, current circumstance, and strategy for survival in terms
of foreign categories and agendas. In the area of religion, for
example, how missionaries and teachers approached matters
such as critical analysis of texts, theological concepts, and the
relationship between science and belief, shaped the debate not
only between Punjabis and Christians but within local communities. Also related was the diffusion of a new print culture in the
urban areas. The spread of literacy, accompanied by new
methods of communication such as journalism, the postal service,
and improved systems of transportation, facilitated the rapid
transmission of ideas. By 1883, there were over a hundred printing presses in the Punjab and over five thousand books and tracts
printed annually. Journalism followed suit, with newspapers
and journals appearing in several towns.[9] The printed material
stimulated and, at the same time, provided new channels for self-
examination and debate. These intellectual pursuits brought
together European rationalism and Indian traditions and mixed
western literary styles with local motifs and symbols.[10]

The resulting cultural upheaval in principal Punjab towns,

such as Lahore and Amritsar, affected the Sikhs from the 1860s onward. Despite their early education in gurdwara schools or through instruction by learned gyanis and local teachers, an emerging Sikh intelligentsia began to study western subjects and joined in associations that discussed religious and social issues. In Lahore, for example, Sikhs were members of G.W. Leitner's orientalist Anjuman-i-Punjab, where they became skilled at literary criticism and debate over historical issues. One especially prominent Sikh, Gurmukh Singh, helped foster Sikh concern over Punjabi literature and eventually taught the subject at the Lahore Oriental College.[11] The introduction of the Arya Samaj in 1875 seemed to open new vistas for reforming society and modernizing Indian religions. A few Sikhs were drawn to the energetic Arya emphasis on personal growth and simplified rituals. For a decade they gave limited support to it before severing bonds in response to Hindu aspersions on the life and teaching of the Gurus.[12]

The atmosphere of questioning theology and current social and religious practices led at least some Sikhs to address the mixture of traditions and sub-traditions prevalent within the community. Differences between the Gurus' teachings and contemporary patterns were obvious, as was the perceived need to revitalize Sikhism before it lost further vitality. Attempts to reform and refine elements of Sikhism already had been made. In the early 19th Century, for example, the Nirankari sect, descended from the followers of Baba Dyal Singh (1783-1854), opposed the worship of Hindu icons and preached a simple message of devotion and "purified" rituals.[13] Similarly, the Namdhari or Kuka sect, founded by Bhai Balak Singh (1799-1862), were instructed to avoid marriage expenses and dowries, to reject meat, wine, and tobacco, and to lead moral lives. Under Balak Singh's successor, Ram Singh (1816-1884), the Kukas became more militant and openly rejected British authority. Attempting to overturn the custom of worshipping at local shrines and intent on protecting the cow, the Kukas soon ran afoul of the government. After several dramatic encounters, the organization was dispersed and their leader deported.[14]

The Kuka outbreaks in the late 1860s and the continued missionary success in converting both Sikh students and ruling chiefs set the stage for the creation of a new association in 1873, the Amritsar Singh Sabha. Unintended by its founders, that Sabha and its successors were to inaugurate a new phase in the history of Sikhism that resolved many pressing issues of Sikh identity and conflicting customs.

Evolution of the Singh Sabha Movement

On October 1, 1873, Sikhs from Amritsar and surrounding districts formed the Amritsar Singh Sabha. The mission of the Sabha included propagation of the true Sikh religion, publishing periodicals and encouraging the use of Punjabi, editing and circulating historical and religious books, developing support from well-wishers (particularly the British government), and education.[15] Five years later, a second Singh Sabha was formed in Lahore and by 1900 there were approximately a hundred similar associations in the Punjab and neighboring areas.[16] The spread of the sabhas was uneven, decentralized, and frequently the product of personal interests or ideological disagreement. The Ferozepur Singh Sabha, for example, emphasized scholarly research, female education, and improvement of home 'life because of the influence of Bhai Takht Singh, a regional leader for almost four decades. To the north in Tarn Taran, Bhai Mohan Singh Vaid's concern with health, the sanctity of shrines, and defense of Sikhism through tract literature set the tone and program of the Tarn Taran group In Bhasaur, Babu Teja Singh's effort to prune Sikh doctrine and ritual from any suggestion of Hindu influence led to a string of dramatic meetings, resolutions, and social experiments.[17]

Two major constellations existed in the Singh Sabh universe. The founding Amritsar Sabha was led by a group of traditional leaders that included gyanis, bhais, and aristocrats.[18] These men, such as Thakur Singh Sandhawalia, Khem Singh Bedi and his son, Gurbaksh Singh, and Kanwar Bikram Singh, had suffered some financial loss because of British conquest and felt increasingly under attack from the west and from missionaries. They used an established network of followers and resources to spread western education, love for Punjabi, preservation of historical documents, and generally tried to strengthen Sikhism in response to new cultural challenges.

As 'Sanatan Sikhs,' however, the Amritsar following recognized the diversity of traditions within the contemporary Sikh community and championed the view that custom provided answers as to who were Sikhs and what they should believe. Anyone accepting the teachings of Guru Nanak, from their viewpoint, was a Sikh, despite any decisions about maintaining the 5 Ks, worship of regional saints, or social practice. A major theme in their discourse, for example, was the danger posed to Sikhism by inattention to custom and pollution through indiscriminate marriage alliances. Descendants of the Gurus were held in high repute. At time they were provided with cushions in worship services and treated as though they possessed extraordinary knowledge. Existing divisions among Sikhs were recognized. Udasis, followers of Guru Nanak who often dressed as Hindu mendicants and controlled central Sikh Shrines, were to be respected. *Sahajdhari* Sikhs also were seen as being "slow learners" within the Sikh tradition, who someday might undergo formal baptism and with it, the discipline, the *rahit* maintained by the bearded *kesdharis*. Those who accepted the outward symbols and conduct associated with Guru Gobind Singh were applauded, but were not seen as superior to other Sikhs.[19]

Sikhs associated with the Lahore Singh Sabha had a very different perspective on the nature of Sikhism. The members of the Lahore association came from different classes and castes, including aristocrats, lawyers, teachers, publicists, businessmen, and minor officials.[20] They were joined primarily not by economic or occupational interests but rather by a shared experience in anglo-vernacular education and participation in intellectual debate in Lahore, the center of the new school system and an emerging print culture. Aware of western criticism and the vulnerability of a Sikh faith that contained contradictions and few, if any, demarcated boundaries, they sought to present and defend a set of coherent principles and actions that would be adopted by most Sikhs.

Their vision of a rejuvenated Sikh tradition came to be known as "Tat Khalsa," that is, a "true" Sikhism stripped of popular custom and clearly separate from Hinduism. As in the case of the Arya Samaj, which reinterpreted the Vedic period so as to legitimize its program, the advocates of Tat Khalsa championed a return to a real or imagined golden age of the Gurus in which Sikhs had a clear and definable identity. The Lahore Singh Sabha attacked caste and other social customs that tended to undercut Sikh brotherhood. Similarly, Sikhs were called upon to quit worshipping "living gurus" such as pirs, local saints, and the families connected with the Ten Gurus. A return to original Sikh values meant also a renewal of attention to the *Adi Granth* as the source of theology and authority, the promulgation of rituals devoid of Brahminical and Hindu influence, and a cleansing of sacred space such as gurdwaras and shrines. Portraits or statues of Hindu gods were to be removed from places of worship, as were depictions of the Gurus that suggested Hindu connections. Historical research and discussion of theology were encouraged, but only if they supported the principal tenets of Tat Khalsa Sikhs.[21]

The Lahore and Amritsar Singh Sabhas occasionally attempted conciliation, but because of the divergence of their views and a series of heated confrontations, much of Sikh public life in the last three decades of the century was dominated by internecine squabbles. Sikhs fought in the press, in meetings, and in the courts. An attack might appear in a local paper or tract and then stir controversy and even a civil suit. In 1887, for example, a leading Tat Khalsa publicist, Ditt Singh, lampooned the major Amritsar leaders in a lightly disguised play, *Svapan Natak*. Offensive passages, such as referring to a descendant of Guru Nanak as a pretentious "guru of Satan," resulted in a slander case that left wounds which festered for years.[22] Any topic or issue could become a battleground. One favorite tactic was to tar opponents with the brush of "sedition" so that official patronage would be withdrawn. The Amritsar Singh Sabha was the target of such a tactic in the 1880s when the efforts of the deposed son of Ranjit Singh, Maharajah Dhuleep Singh, to return to the Punjab created an explosive situation. The location of the first Sikh institute of higher education, Khalsa College, generated similar excitement, as did the proposal in 1897 to light the Golden Temple with electricity.[23]

The most hotly contested argument within the Singh Sabha movement was whether Sikhs were "Hindu." Sanatanists saw Sikhism as an offshoot of a broadly defined "Hinduism." The Vedas and Hindu epics were judged to be important in understanding man's predicament and relationship with God, although the Gurus' teachings, especially the *Adi Granth*, were to be given more respect. Examples from the *Granth* and accompanying literature were used to "prove" that the Gurus had no intention of separating Sikhs from their Hindu roots or from revered Hindu gods and scriptures. Distinct social and ritual boundaries had not been prescribed by the Gurus but were subsequent additions to the tradition. Therefore, they did not have to be honored.[24] Arya Samajists supported these views, criticizing the assumptions of the Lahore-based group and ridiculing their scholarship. The tract warfare over the issue was heated and prolonged.[25]

"Han Hindu Nahin" (We are not Hindu) became the battle cry of the Tat Khalsa Sikhs.[26] They published at least a hundred tracts and books on the subject. Quotes from the scriptures and historical analyses were used to combat what was seen as the most dangerous threat to Sikh survival. The Tat Khalsa raised the flag of "Sikhism in danger" and fought their opponents at every turn.

The divisions among Sikh associations were not limited to ideology. Most of the sabhas had their own agendas and personal projects and conflicts surfaced frequently regarding where conferences would be held or the degree of respect to be shown to particular individuals. In addition, the race for control of institutions and honor was complicated by the regional orientation of Sikh leaders. Competition between Sikhs from the Malwa and Majha region was frequent and bitter.[27]

Despite the time and resources devoted to such controversies, the Singh Sabhas did manage to develop a broad network of new institutions and projects. By 1900, orphanages, a system of Sikh schools, institutions for training preachers and granthis, and other self-strengthening efforts garnered broad support from Sikhs in the Punjab and especially from migrant communities abroad.[28] In the process, the Tat Khalsa interpretation of Sikh history and religion increasingly came to be viewed as legitimate by both Sikhs and the government. How this was accomplished deserves separate consideration.

Ascendancy of the Tat Khalsa in Sikh Affairs

The Sikhs identifying with the Tat Khalsa tradition defined

Sikhism in terms of a theology separate from Hinduism, purified rituals, and distinct norms of behavior. Social and cultural boundaries had to be demarcated successfully in three separate, but sometimes tangled, spheres. First, the Tat Khalsa message had to reach the Sikh population and be recognized as legitimate. This meant confrontation with Sikh opponents, who had conflicting views and could draw upon time-honored networks of patronage and support. The Tat Khalsa and Sanatan Sikhs were engaged in a struggle to determine who would control community resources and attain a place of authority. Secondly, the Sikh activists had to defend themselves and their institutions against external attack, particularly that of the Arya Samajists who allied occasionally with sympathetic Sikhs. Finally, the program centering around the Labore Singh Sabha had to be accepted and supported by the primary patrons in the Punjab political system, the British rulers. The government was somewhat ambivalent toward encouraging the resurgence of Sikhism, but no matter what its strategy, official perceptions and policies tended to be sympathetic to the maintenance of symbols and separation from Hinduism.[29]   The Tat Khalsa had to convert that attitude into active support such as grants and recognition of Sikh claims in legislative and political arenas.

The success of the Lahore group in meeting these challenges was due in large part to the zeal, sacrifice, and oratorical ability of its leadership. Many exceptional individuals rallied to the Tat Khalsa cause and, in doing so, have been recognized as heroes by their contemporaries and by subsequent historians. Two driving forces in Lahore, Gurmukh Singh and Ditt Singh, became almost legendary for their public service. Writing books and publishing papers, they organized meetings, roamed across the Punjab encouraging friends and repelling attacks, and simultaneously laid the groundwork for the creation of new organizations.[30]   Singh Sabhas generally had one or more such individuals who provided continuity, money, and spirit. For example, Bhai Takht Singh of Ferozepur who became known as the *zinda shahid*, the "living martyr," committed his life to female education. At one point, he left home on a world-wide tour and refused to return until he had collected sufficient funds to maintain his school for girls at Ferozepur. Takht Singh succeeded after six hard and often desperate months of travel.[31]

The powerful presence and single-mindedness of Babu Teja Singh Overseer was unmatched. The founder of the Bhasaur Singh Sabha and later the Panch Khalsa Diwan, Teja Singh had the courage and willingness to give and receive abuse, which became part of the folklore of the Singh Sabha movement.[32] The list could go on to include dozens of talented individuals who, although disagreeing on specific points, were held together by a commitment to a resurrection of Sikhism in the Tat Khalsa image.

Without such devoted Sikhs, the Singh Sabha message would have not taken root. At the same time, however, these individuals also were adroit at controlling the centers of powers and the networks of communication that affected daily Sikh life. Whether aristocrat, businessman, or official, they shared common experiences and acquired new skills vital to their mission. The spread of modern means of communication permitted coordination and continuity over time and space. The postal service, for example, facilitated regular contact. The diaries and correspondence of prominent Tat Khalsa advocates, such as Mohan Singh Vaid, Taht Singh, and Teja Singh Bhasaur, suggest the importance of the mails in planning.[33] The expansion of the railroad meant that leaders could meet personally in private gatherings or public sessions. Such innovations also furnished the backdrop for many of the new experiments and organized publicity efforts of the Tat Khalsa.

The Tat Khalsa created and then dominated the rapidly evolving communication facilities linking Sikhs throughout the world. Secretaries of the Singh Sabhas circulated annual reports and resolutions through the mail and the central body in Lahore helped publish local proceedings. The correspondent system was complemented by the circulation of preaching teams and jathas, groups of Sikhs (often with a granthi and singers) who travelled widely to encourage baptism, adoption of outward symbols, and an end to manmat ("un-Sikh") practices (such as the worship of local saints).[34] The Tat Khalsa missionary efforts followed the railroad lines. As soon as the railway expanded, preachers visited the dispersed Sikhs and tried to influence their actions.[35] Festivals and meetings also became routinized. Sabhas sponsored annual diwans, multi-day occasions that brought together local Sikhs as well as zealots from outside. The larger regional and provincial conferences could attract as many as several thousand Sikhs. Moreover, the regular celebration of the various *gurpurabs* (birth and death anniversaries of the Gurus) and related events in Sikh history were popularized. Such activities provided the chance for discussion, worship, raising funds, and, in general, consolidating the Tat Khalsa position.[36]

.Schools, too, were an essential element in the Singh Sabha program. Not only did Khalsa educational institutions equip Sikhs to compete successfully in the new occupations, but they also served to strengthen Sikh identity. Mixing western subjects with the study of Punjabi and religious traditions, teachers were able· to influence generations of upwardly mobile students. Founded in 1894, the Khalsa College at Amritsar became a Tat Khalsa bastion.[37]

Although Sanatanists wrote tracts and published newspapers, both of those important ingredients of modern communication tended to be controlled by Sikhs of the Tat Khalsa persuasion. As in the case of the Christian, Arya Samaj, and Muslim missionary efforts, Sikhs produced an increasing number of small tracts and religious books. Founded in 1894, the Khalsa Tract Society published didactic and polemical pamphlets regularly. Individiuals often specialized in that means of disseminating ideas, such as Ditt Singh and Mohan Singh Vaid who wrote over two hundred books and tracts.[38] One variety of tract contained religious scripture and sermons, often with emphasis on an issue such as the non-Hindu nature of Sikhism. Another related set of pamphlets described incidents or told stories that illustrated the victory of Tat Khalsa arguments. A third popular type called for support of associations or a project. Appeals or *benati* were accepted elements in Sikh life and could generate substantial contributions. Finally, the polemic provided entertainment and contributed to literary exchanges that can only be described as tract warfare.[39]

While production of tracts was impressive, the evolving Sikh communication system revolved around an assortment of journals and papers. Many were short-lived, but the newspapers that began to appear with regularity from the 1880s onward reached more and more Sikhs. The *Khalsa Akhbar*, founded in 1883 and surviving until 1904, served as a base for the Tat Khalsa. Many other papers championed specific causes or aimed at particulár audiences such as the *Punjabi Bhain* (Feroze-pur, on domestic life and female education) and periodicals for one segment of the community, the Ramgarhias.[40]

Approximately fifty Sikh newspapers and journals were published prior to 1900. Most served several related functions. First, the publications circulated news on events and activities of institutions and individuals. In addition, newspapers offered an accepted channel for *benati*, appeal for aid. Increasingly Sikhs were called on to provide money for schools, societies, and special events. The papers also served as scorecards, routinely publishing accounts and lists of donors. Besides providing accountability for funds spent, these reports celebrated public service and good deeds, key fund-raising elements in a society where pride and honor were valued highly. The accounts also kept record of how well particular Tat Khalsa activities were progressing, such as the number of Sikhs who had stopped smoking or quit cutting their hair.[41] Finally, journalism helped mobilize specific groups or the community as a whole on issues and, in general, disseminated a consistent image of past events and current dangers facing Sikhism.

This diverse network for disseminating information and generating support strengthened the Tat Khalsa position among Sikhs. Dozens of meetings and large conferences were held each year and, by 1900, over eighty Singh Sabhas sympathetic to Ditt Singh and his colleagues were active throughout India. Tracts and newspapers applauded victory after victory, ranging from the scattered conversion of Muslim and apostate Sikhs to drama-tic incidents such as occurred in Bakapur on June 13-14, 1903. At a large diwan, Tat Khalsa leaders from all over the Punjab assembled and gave baptism to 35 Muslims and *sahaidhari* Sikhs. Many of the converts became prominent in Sikh education, religious debate, and the gurdwara reform movement.[42] Special committees produced "authentic" versions of historical material, commentaries on the *Granth*, and even went so far as to judge the validity of books and tracts published by others.[43] The mounting pressure for reforms and an end to Hindu practices led to public meetings, petitions for official holidays celebrating the birthdays of Guru Nanak and Guru Gobind Singh, and successful missionary activities in towns and villages. Even foreign collaborators supported the Lahore Singh Sabha's contentions about the uniqueness of Sikh tradition. The most notable example was Max Arthur Macauliffe, a former British civil servant who retired and devoted his life to translating and interpreting early Sikh documents. His multi-volume work, *The Sikh Religion, Its Gurus, Sacred Writing and Authors* (Oxford University Press, 1909) was prepared in close association with Singh Sabha scholars such a Kahan Singh Nabha, and remains one of the most substantial English-language statements of the Tat Khalsa view of their Sikh heritage.[44]

Despite the intensity and volume of such activities, the Lahore Singh Sabha and its affiliates had not managed to supplant the entrenched group of Sanatan Sikhs who controlled shrines and claimed to be the legitimate leaders of the community. The fights were long, bitter, and usually inconclusive. The struggle over location of Khalsa College, for example, was won by the Amritsar Singh Sabha although the better educated Lahore Sikhs came to dominate the faculty and curriculum.[45] Intelligent and articulate defenders of the Sanatan views organized their own newspapers and joined in exchange of tracts. Most notable was Avtar Singh Vahiria, the author of influential guides to Sikh history and practice. He argued in voluminous and well documented books that Sikhism was an outgrowth of Hinduism and should maintain its roots within that religion. The Tat Khalsa innovations were recent additions, he claimed, and artificially separating the two faiths meant confusion in ritual, inappropriate rites, and unnecessary schisms.[46] The vehemence of the attacks on the Lahore leaders accelerated by the late 1890s also suggests their growing power and influence. Battles continued, but in terms of numbers and the ability to control the centre of Sikh news and communication, the Tat Khalsa were beginning to shape the wide range of Singh Sabha activities.

Also accelerating were confrontations with the Arya Samaj. Both the Singh Sabhas and the Samaj launched a campaign of *shuddhi* (purification and conversion ceremonies) after 1890. Aryas openly converted Sikhs and cut their hair in public. The Sikh *shuddhi* sabha in Lahore countered by having Muslims and low-caste Sikhs undergo purification, receive baptism, and then have social relations with Singh Sabha members.[47] The controversy raged, as did the tract warfare. The titles of typical tracts of the period suggest the tone and content of the works : "a

mouth-breaking reply," "the exposure of haugtiness," "a crush-
ing blow," "a real photo of the stupidity of Dayanand," and
"as the face, so the slap, or a face-breaking reply."[48] Colloquial
Hindi and Punjabi are storehouses of insult and derogatory
terms and opponents used them freely to attack sacred scriptures,
leaders, and positions. As tensions mounted, the momentum
clearly was on the side of the Lahore Sikhs. They managed to
sharpen the lines between Sikhs and Hindus and, in doing so,
provoked such open attacks on Sikhism that the Arya tracts
probably injured the position of their pro-Hindu allies.

Tat Khalsa success with the government was also mixed,
although there too the Lahore Singh Sabha tended to have high
visibility and garnered support regularly. The British had reinforced the legitimacy of the kesdhari Sikhs through military
recruitment policy. Only Sikhs with the 5 Ks could join the
army and part of their initiation was baptism and a pledge to
maintain "orthodox" practices. Western officers encouraged
the celebration of Sikh holidays and, in general, tried to insure
the happiness and loyalty of their men.[49] The Punjab government was quite aware of the growing tension among Sikhs
and tried whenever possible to steer clear of controversy.
However, patronage continued to be given to key institutions
such as Khalsa College and schools affiliated with local Singh
Sabhas. In a few instances, district officers also sympathized
with the Tat Khalsa campaigns to end misuse of gurdwara funds
by Udasi managers and to remove offensive symbols and arti-
facts from the vicinity of shrines.[50] Similarly, the provincial
and central governments cooperated in providing limited funds
for the publication efforts of Macauliffe and his Sikh friends.
Assisting the Singh Sabha publishing project was viewed by the
British as a necessary corrective to a former act, arranging for
Trumpp's translation of the Adi Granth in the 1870s. Trumpp
had claimed that Sikhs were Hindus and made numerous scur-
rilous remarks about the Gurus and their teachings. Macauliffe's
volumes were seen as restoring the Sikh honor and tradition
damaged by the earlier work.[51]

By the end of the 19th Century, Sikhs stood once again at a
critical juncture. Acceptance of the Tat Khalsa message was
spreading but as yet had not been institutionalized completely.
Sikhs remained disunited. Numerous institutions had been

created, but funding and administration often were haphazard and lacked coordination. A surge of energy and resources was evident, but so were persistent patterns of division, competition, and conflict. The Singh Sabhas had raised the cry of "Sikhism in danger" and highlighted the many problems facing the community, but solutions still had to be worked out. Without unification and focus, as editorials in Sikh newspapers noted. Sikhism still remained vulnerable to both external and internal threats.[52]

The Chief Khalsa Diwan's Contribution to the Sikh Revival, 1903-1919

In November of 1901, a meeting of prominent Sikhs discussed the need for a central body to coordinate and lead the Singh Sabha movement. Many of the earlier generation of leaders had died or passed on their mantles, thus making it easier to bind old wounds and deal with problems plaguing the Sikhs. Officially inaugurated a year later, the Chief Khalsa Diwan began with a handful of affiliated Sabhas and by 1919, had over a hundred member institutions. During that period, the organization was involved in a spectrum of old and new projects and became acknowledged as the major voice for Sikhs.[53]

The CKD had a formal constitution, amended frequently, and a complex set of committees and procedures. Its aims included promoting the welfare of the Khalsa Panth, spreading *gurbani* or the teachings of the Gurus, disseminating information on tradition and current issues, and safeguarding the political rights of Sikhs. Behind the organization, however, was input from the most active sabhas, whose leaders, such as Vir Singh, Mohan Singh Vaid, Takht Singh, and Teja Singh Bhasaur, participated actively at one time or another. Sundar Singh Majithia, a Sikh aristocrat long identified with the Lahore Singh Sabha, served as secretary and also helped guide Khalsa College.[54]

CKD decisions involved both a system of consultation with member associations and a pattern of private decision-making by twenty or so aristocrats and members of western professions. Often questions would be circulated in journals and tracts and then decisions publicized on a specific issue, such as whether it was appropriate to open the *Adi Granth* in public meetings.[55] More controversial decisions tended to be reached in private or sometimes avoided totally if circumstances warranted. The Finance Committee tended to dominate both the public and private proceedings, insisting on full accountability for all CKD operations.

The goals and strategies of the Diwan changed in light of immediate or long-term problems. On the whole, its main function was the coordination of Sikh public activities and the building of a common base on which many, if not all, Sikhs might agree. This was illustrated by an editorial that portrayed Singh Sabhas as stones filled with bits and pieces of material, lacking strength. Only if the elements were fused could Sikhs move forward and be strong like iron. The CKD role was to try and assist cooperation, to pull together and focus efforts.[56]

This task involved insuring the fiscal stability of Sikh enterprises with a growing system of checks and balances. Once accounts and reports were issued regularly, however, the Diwan turned to the more complex task of developing human resources. It elaborated the existing practice of sending out teams and preachers, training personnel in preaching, singing, and publicity. Outreach was also enhanced by more attention to scheduling local and regional meetings, with the result that attendance rose dramatically. Some conferences and diwans had as many as 4,000-8,000 Sikhs in attendance.[57]

Concern with panthic resources helped generate new initiatives in studying historical documents and publishing "authentic" material. Committees reviewed books and issued corrections, questioning references to mythology and any link with "non-Sikh" custom. While encouraging debate, the CKD urged that the duty of Sikhs "in days of transition" was the preparation of "standard books and references" based solely on the teachings of the *Guru Granth Sahib.*[58]

Appreciating the importance of influencing communications among Sikhs, the CKD regularized the flow of information by improving links between organizations and publishing more literature. Two newspapers—the *Khalsa Samachar* in Gurmukhi and the *Khalsa Advocate* in English—became its spokesmen and assisted in spreading news and heightening public awareness. The influence of these and related journals was significant.

individuals read material aloud in villages and copies circulated widely among students, the army, and emigrant groups throughout the world. Moreover, the Khalsa Tract Society expanded its operation and soon was joined by several other societies committed to influencing Sikhs in areas such as theology, ritual, and social observance.[59]

The CKD mission of unifying Sikhs and putting self-strengthening projects on a sound footing necessitated creating more institutions. Besides providing aid to old Singh Sabhas and helping form new ones, the Diwan built hospitals and orphanages and launched a drive to expand Sikh educational institutions. Some schools fed into the regular educational system, ending with high school or college degrees. Others such as the updeshak (preacher-training) school at Gharjakh and the girls school at Ferozepur prepared Sikhs for other tasks. The Sikh Educational Conference, first held in 1908, became an annual affair that brought together thousands of Sikhs who discussed educational issues, the spread of Punjabi and related matters. The meetings moved from place to place, thus focusing attention on local activities. The resolutions and speeches usually dealt with history, religion, and current affairs. Besides raising money, the Conference became a symbolic gathering of Sikhs who shared common viewpoints and goals.[60]

The CKD also tried to expand the breadth of the community and at the same time overcome factionalism and conflict. Diwan leaders sponsored the formation of the Khalsa Biradari in 1908, an organization committed to modifying Sikh attitudes toward untouchability. Low caste Sikhs such as Mazbhis, Rahtias and Ramdasis had been particular targets for Christian and Arya Samaj conversion attempts. Disturbed by this potential loss in numbers, as well as by the inherent conflict between current social attitudes and the message of equality among all Sikhs, the CKD and the Biradari had some success in improving social conditions and opening gurdwaras to Sikhs who were considered by some to be polluted. A price was paid, however, because this evoked a sharp reaction that included boycotts of CKD activities and public confrontations.[61]

Painfully aware that because of "our self-murdering policy," Sikhs were their own worst enemies (Khalsa Samachar, August 16, 1905), the CKD sought to end disputes and resolve internal conflicts. Conciliation teams assisted when groups or associations fought openly. In 1917, for example, even the Educational Conference became an inflammable issue when the site was moved from Montgomery to Lahore.[62] Differences of opinion, rivalries, and affronts to "honor" consumed much of the Diwan's time and energy.

The CKD used its publicity and influence to institutionalize the acceptance of Sikhism as a separate religion with its own rituals, traditions, and sense of identity. Generally pursuing policies that would further demarcate boundaries and remove lingering Hindu influence, the Diwan's efforts helped facilitate the removal of idols from the Golden Temple in 1905 and sparked similar criticism of Hindu accretions in other local shrines. Another CKD victory, the 1907 passage of the Anand Marriage Bill legitimizing a distinct Sikh marriage ceremony devoid of Hindu trappings, marked a highpoint in the campaign to spread Sikh holidays, rituals, and daily practices.[63]

Although the Tat Khalsa tradition became increasingly dominant in all Sikh institutions except for the gurdwaras, which generally remained in the hands of Sanatan Sikhs or Udasi managers, the CKD did not consistently argue that the only "true Sikhs" were kesdhari or amritdhari (baptized) and that other such as sahajdharis were in fact Hindu. Given the diversity still existing among Sikhs, the Diwan took the position that those who worshipped in gurdwaras and accepted that Sikhism was a separate religion should be considered part of the larger Sikh community. Fully aware of the persistent minority status of Sikhs (approximately 10-13% of the Punjab population) and also sensitive to the devotion of many of the sahajdharis, the Diwan tried to accommodate and be tolerant of diversity as far as possible. This came out continually in newspaper stories about promient sahajdhari Sikhs, such as Harkishen Lal, as well as in discussions of procedures within the Diwan itself.[64] Although only kesdhari Sikhs could serve on CKD committees, special arrangements were made for regular consultation with other groups. Moreover, the Diwan resolved that sahajdharis could play a full role in gurdwara affairs and read the Guru Granth Sahib in services.[65] To clear up misunderstandings, the official paper of the CKD, the Khalsa Advocate, noted that even shorn Sikhs were on the path of religious searching and should be kept within the panth and made part of Sikhism (July 15, 1904).   The CKD leaders did have a long-term goal of seeing all Sikhs maintain common rituals and symbols, but toleration and openness were necessary. Community interest required such an approach. In the past, *sahajdharis*, such as Sewa Ram Singh and Teja Singh, M.A., had eventually been baptized and contributed greatly to Sikhism.[66]   Others could do the same in the future.

Accommodation and tolerance did little to reconcile Sikhs who insisted that they were Hindu.   Some attacked the CKD in the press or openly sided with Hindus, such as Gurbaksh Singh Bedi, son of Khem Singh Bedi, the heart of the earlier Amritsar Singh Sabha. Gurbaksh Singh served as the president of the Punjab Hindu Conference in 1910.   On the basis of the public record, however, it appears that most Sikhs tentatively approved of the Diwan's posture.   A few individuals and organizations did adopt a narrow and increasingly literal interpretation of Sikh tradition. Teja Singh Bhasaur denounced his former colleagues, for example, set up a rival Panch Khalsa Parliament, and tried to rewrite Sikh tradition. Although ostracized and later imprisoned for publishing an edition of the *Adi Granth* with one section, the *ragmala*, excised, Teja Singh persevered in his claim that only *amritdharis* who followed his lead were Sikhs.[67]

For a decade, the Chief Khalsa Diwan consolidated its position and had remarkable success at fostering Sikh identity and strengthening institutions. From approximately 1912 onward, however, the organization came under attack from different quarters. The expansion of the elective principle in municipal committees and the Punjab legislative council placed fresh emphasis upon numbers and, from the Sikh perspective, underlined their permanent minority statuts. The Diwan had a policy of working closely with the government because continued British assistance was seen as vital to the future of Sikhism. This seemed to be effective, as for example in 1907 when the British responded positively to the orchestrated Sikh agitation supporting the Anand Marriage Bill. Similarly, the Diwan was able to have more Sikh holidays placed on the official calendar, Punjabi became legitimized in educational and bureaucratic circles, and turbans accepted in the Indian Medical Service and in the London Inns of law.[68]   However, growing militancy among Sikh students and British uncertainty about Sikh loyalty created a rift with the colonial power that led to expanded British control over Khalsa College and decisions that limited the influence of Singh Sabha members in Golden Temple management.[69]

The atmosphere of confrontation changed to renewed friendship in 1913 and 1914, when the CKD helped negotiate at least a temporary settlement to the crisis generated by British damage to the Rikabganj gurdwara in New Delhi. The Singh Sabhas' open denunciation of terrorism and, particularly, the activities of returned Sikhs belonging to the banned Gadhar party (a U.S. revolutionary group) strengthened ties with the British. The First World War also brought Sikhs and the government closer together, at least in the early years. The CKD spearheaded broad-based Sikh support for the war effort and aided in accelerated recruiting for the army.[70]

Although the Diwan continued to be seen by many Sikhs as an authority in political and religious matters, its prominence and close association with the British increased the vulnerability of CKD leaders. The militants who had urged direct action against the government over alleged sacrilege at Rikabganj produced a stream of tracts, against the Diwan's moderate policies and were aided by two new papers, the *Panth Sewak* and the *Khalsa Akhbar*.[71] By 1917, Sikh concern over recruiting axcesses and other wartime injustices led the CKD to launch a publicity counter-attack. More frequently, however, the charge was made that the Diwan had abrogated its responsibilities and engaged in "unpanthic" activities.[72]

The keystone of CKD political strategy, influencing British patronage through constitutional agitation and personal contacts, sped up the demise of its central place in Sikh affairs Open elections had not worked for the Sikhs. With only an occasional representative elected to the legislature, frustration over future threats to the Sikh minority became apparent even in *Khalsa Samachar* editorials. The CKD attempted to assert Sikh rights because of their war effort and loyal support for the government. but as a significant transfer of power loomed ahead after the war, the campaign to have one-third seats reserved for Sikhs foundered. The British were being pressured from all directions and could not meet Sikh expectations.[73] The CKD's close association with the administration of Lieutenant Michael O'Dwyer also proved disastrous. His excessive responses to disturbances in the spring of 1919 led to the notorious massacre at Jallianwala Bagh in Amritsar. The shootings also destroyed much of the CKD's prestige. Still clinging to a policy of toleration and dependence on British support, the Diwan criticized officials but in less than stringent terms and far too late from the perspective of most Punjabis.[74]

The gurdwara reform agitation grew out of the ashes of Jallianwala Bagh. Distrust of the British was rampant and Sikhs felt the time was right to wrest control of their sacred shrines from the hands of the managers, who generally sided with the government and pro-Hindu interests. Earlier the CKD had attempted to control the gurdwaras through negotiation, legal maneuvers, and public pressure. Now, losing ground rapidly, its leading members attempted to play a role in a new militant organization, the Central Sikh League, but there, too, they lost out to more zealous Sikhs bent on confrontation.[75] Since the Diwan opposed the tactic of direct action and possible law-breaking to protect Sikh interests, they came to be seen as hapless and ineffective religious leaders, out of step with contemporary needs of the community. In a short span of time, the organization that had been at the heart of the Sikh resurgence came to be pictured by its successors, the Akalis, as a threat to Sikhism.[76]

The Gurdwara Campaigns and the Future of Sikhism

The rapid eclipse of the CKD and its allies brought to an end four decades of intense soul-searching and intellectual growth. The Tat Khalsa Sikhs had championed Sikhism as a separate religion with distinct rituals and other boundaries. Under the leadership of the Diwan, that view became prevalent among Singh Sabhas and influenced the development of modern Sikh institutions. At the same time, the intellectual excitement and marked degree of literary activity constituted a high point in Sikh cultural history. Because of the zeal of the movement and the evaluation of its communication network, Sikhs became more conscious of both their historical roots and emerging threats. That consciousness has continued until the present, as have the diwans, the conferences, the new festivals and holidays, tracts, and journalistic endeavors that remain important in Sikh public life.

The Chief Khalsa Diwan influenced the direction and tone of much that was written and done. Although firmly committed to the strengthening of a separate Sikh identity, the Diwan supported an open exchange of ideas, a process of accommodation, negotiation and compromise wherever possible, so that differences could be resolved and disunity averted. This accounts for the organization sometimes avoiding controversial issues and tending to be unspecific and vague when debating doctrines. There were limits to toleration, particularly in areas such as editing the scriptures or questioning beliefs about the Gurus that were considered sacrosanct. But on the whole, the Diwan avoided drawing lines finely or excluding those who wanted to be counted as members of the panth. Such an approach meant that many doctrinal issues were not resolved. The Diwan, for example, worked hard to develop a consensus on a set of rituals and practices applicable to Sikhs, but prior to 1920, no definitive *rahitnama* was published. Similarly, the relationship between *kesdhari* and *sahajdhari* remained cloudy, although there was a general sense of each Sikh being able to contribute in his or her own way.

Similarly, in the external political arena, the CKD pursued a strategy combining active defense of Punjabi and other Sikh priorities with an ongoing effort to create linkages and collaboration judged necessary to ensure the Sikh minority's continued access to resources. Sikh identity, from the Diwan's perspective, did not mean disrespect for others views or creating permanent divisions possibly injurious at a future time. When the trust and mutual assistance that had characterized Sikh-British relations broke down quickly in light of the 1919 disturbances and the new reforms, however, the Diwan could not adapt quickly. Some leaders such as Sundar Singh Majithia remained active in Punjab politics and tried to help Sikh interests through alliances with other Punjabis and occasionally, with the British. As an organization, however, the CKD tended to avoid politics and instead emphasized education and the spiritual dimensions of Sikhism.[77]

Acting as a catalyst, the Diwan and the Singh Sabhas had

helped create the institutions, the identity, and the fervor associated with a revived Sikhism. With their task completed, they virtually disappeared from the scene. During the next decades, except for interest in the Educational Conference and Sikh schools, the Diwan became inactive in public debate. Without such a forum for focusing debate and exchange of ideas, the intellectual life of Sikhs suffered. There were significant developments in literature, such as the writing of Vir Singh, and in scholarship, such as Kahan Singh's monumental *Gurushabad Ratnakar Mahan Kosh* (Encyclopaedia of Sikh religion, history and literature, 1930), but, on the whole, the questioning and the stimulation of the Singh Sabha period languished. Only after partition and the creation of new centers of scholarly and religious discourse has there been an attempt to recapture the vitality and literary renaissance associated with the Singh Sabhas.[78]

The Akalis dominated Sikh life during the 1920s, capturing the attention and support of Sikhs everywhere with their heroic deeds and roaring challenges.[79] In a sense, they completed the work of the Singh Sabhas by controlling the centers of Sikh power and orthodoxy, the shrines. The operation of the 1925 Gurdwara Act ensured the ascendancy of the Akali Dal and Shiromani Gurdwara Parbandhak Committee and permanent Tat Khalsa control of Sikh institutions. After the Akalis, there was little doubt as to who were Sikhs, what they wore, and how they worshipped. Without the earlier work of the Singh Sabhas, however, the Akalis successful confrontation with the British would have been impossible. The spread of Sikh consciousness and the existence of a significant communication network helped the Akalis spread their message quickly and effectively. The Singh Sabha's message of sacrifice and martyrdom paved the way for the Akalis to assume leadership of the community.

Although the Akalis became seen as the legitimate leaders of the Sikhs, their attempts to win new political rights met with the same frustrations experienced earlier. The world in which they operated placed more emphasis on population percentages and transfer of power to majority groups or broad-based alliances. Driven by Akali zeal and growing fear of Muslim politicians, Sikhs tended to identify more quickly with militant action and intolerance for opponents, especially those within the community

who counselled toleration or compromise. Legislative debate
and court cases became pivotal events in determining who was a
Sikh. Distrusting Hindus and, afraid either of Arya or Muslim
dominance, the *kesdharis* insisted that virtually all aspects of
community life be led by "orthodox" Sikhs, that is, those who
maintained the 5 Ks and ostensibly followed set forms of
action.[80] Despite their posturing, however, issues such as authority within the panth and who could legitimately speak for all
Sikhs still remained unresolved and, to some extent, have not
been settled today. The awkward relationship between custom
and a set of accepted practices, *rahit*, continues as a source of
contention within the Sikh community in India and abroad.[81]

While the definition of Sikh tradition was worked out in
many respects by the Singh Sabhas and finally institutionalized
by the Akalis, somewhere in the process, the creative interaction
between intellectuals and politicians that characterized the Sikh
renaissance became dormant. Sikhism today again stands at a
crossroads. Disunity and conflict are evident, as is a renewed
sense of challenge and eminent danger. Perhaps a re-evaluation
of the recent past and a careful assessment of the successes and
failures of the Singh Sabha movement can provide guidance for
Sikhs as they struggle with the implications of Sikhism as an
evolving world religion.

Notes

1. Views represented in Punjab administration reports, the observations on
   Sikhs by John Malcolm, Major Leech, Captain Murray, Dalhousie, and
   especially the assessment of Max Macauliffee, "The Sikh Religion Under
   Banda and Its Present Condition," *Calcutta Review*, CXLV, 1881, pp. 167-8.
   Also reflected in Ernest Trumpp's introduction to his translation of the
   Adi Granth (1877).
2. The most recent assessment is Harjot Singh Oberoi, "A World Recons-
   tructed: Religion, Ritual and Community among the Sikhs, 1850-1909"
   (unpub. diss., Australian National University, 1987). A similar interpreta-
   tion is summarized in Barrier, *The Sikhs and Their Literature* (Delhi:
   Manohar, 1969).
3. Useful introductions to the period of the Gurus can be found in W. H.
   McLeod, *Guru Nanak and the Sikh Religion* (London: Oxford University
   Press, 1968); W. Owen Cole, Piara Singh Sambhi, *The Sikhs: Their
   Religious Beliefs and Practices* (Delhi: Vikas, 1978).
4. McLeod raises questions and suggests fresh directions for research in *The
   Evolution of the Sikh Community* (London: Oxford University Press, 1976).

A review of traditional leadership is found in Oberoi's "World Reconstructed" and his "Bhais, Babas and Gyanis: Traditional Intellectuals in Nineteenth Century Punjab," *Studies in History*, II (1980), 32-62. The *rahitnama* literature, guides to correct Sikh practice and ritual, is reviewed in McLeod, "The Problem of the Punjabi Rahit Namas," in S.N. Mukherjee, ed., *India, History and Thought* (Calcutta: Subarnarekha, 1982), pp. 103-26.

5. Customs are documented in Denzil Ibbetson, Edward MacLagan and H. A. Rose, *A Glossary of the Tribes and Castes of the Punjab and North-West Frontier Province* (Lahore: Superintendent, Government Printing, 1919); articles in *Punjab Notes and Queries*. Evaluated in Oberoi, "World Reconstructed," pp. 49-92.

6. On early British administration and social change, see Ian Kerr, "The Punjab Province and the Lahore District, 1849-72" (unpub. diss., University of Minnesota, 1975); Andrew Major, "Return to Empire: The Sikhs and British in the Punjab, 1939-72" (unpub. diss., Australian National University, 1981). Political consequences and strategies are reviewed in Barrier, "Sikh Politics in British Punjab Prior to the Gurdwara Reform Movement," in Joseph O'Connell, ed., *Recent Studies in Sikh History and Politics* (Toronto: University of Toronto South Asia Monograph, 1988); Barrier, "The Punjab Government and Communal Politics," *Journal of Asian Studies*, 27 (1967-8), pp. 523-39.

7. On administration of the Golden Temple, see Ian Kerr, "British Relationships with the Golden Temple," *The Indian Economic and Social History Review*, 21 (1984), pp. 139-51.

8. The evolution of 19th Century tract literature is reviewed in Kenneth Jones and Eric Gustafson, eds., *Sources on Punjab History* (Delhi: Manohar, 1975); Barrier, *The Punjab in Nineteenth Century Tracts* (East Lansing: Asian Studies Center, Michigan State University, 1969). On early trends, see Kenneth Jones, *Arya Dharm* (Berkeley: University of Calfornia Press, 1975).

9. Press trends and data are found in Barrier and Paul Wallace. *The Punjab Press, 1880-1905* (East Lansing: Asian Studies Center, Michigan State University, 1970); Emmett Davis, *Press and Politics in British Western Punjab, 1836-1947* (Delhi: Academic, 1983).

10. Theoretical issues and implications of the introduction of a print culture in Punjab is presented in Oberoi, "World Reconstructed." Parallel developments in other regions are discussed in essays, Yogendra Malik, ed., *South Asian Intellectuals and Social Change* (Delhi: Heritage, 1972).

11. On the Anjuman, see Jeffrey Perrill, "Anjuman-i-Panjab as a Common Interest Association and Symbol of Social Change in Nineteenth Century Punjab, *"Punjab Past and Present*, 16 (1982), 343-70. Gurmukh Singh's background is reviewed in Oberoi, "World Reconstructed," pp. 203-205. Also see Gurmukh Singh's *My Attempted Excommunication from the Sikh Temple and the Khalsa Community at Faridkot in 1897* (privately pub., Lahore, 1898). I am indebted to Harjot Singh Oberoi for a copy of the document.

12. Sikh-Arya relations are treated in Jones, *Arya Dharm;* Barrier, *Sikhs and Their Literature.*

13. This is discussed fully in John Webster, *The Nirankari Sikhs* (New Delhi: Macmillan India, 1979).

14. On the Namdharis, consult the following: Oberoi, "World Reconstruction," pp. 93-141; W.H. McLeod, "The Kukas, a Millenarian Sect of the Punjab," in G. S. Wood, P. S. O'Connor, eds.. *W. P. Morrell: A Tribute* (Dunedin: University of Otago, 1973), pp. 85-103. Documents in Nahar Singh, ed. *Gooroo Ram Singh and the Kuka Sikhs,* 3 vols (New Delhi: author pub., 1965-71).

15. Background on the Lahore Singh Sabha can be found in the Oberoi dissertation and especially "Bhais"; also details in Harbans Singh, *Heritage of the Sikhs.* Other recent surveys of the Singh Sabha movement include Richard Fox, *Lions of the Punjab* (Berkeley: University of California Press, 1986) and Rajiv A. Kapur, *Sikh Separatism* (London: Allen and Unwin, 1986).

16. The definitive work on the early Singh Sabhas, on which this study relies heavily, is Oberoi, "Reconstruction." The relevant tract and institutional literature, plus interpretation, is reviewed in Barrier, *Sikhs.*

17. The following contain useful biographical information: Attar Singh, *Jinda Shahid Nun Moran Lai Vichar Te Tajviz* (Amritsar: Wazir Hind Press, 1916); Munsha Singh Dukhi, *Jivan Bhai Mohan Singh Vaid* (Amritsar: author pub., c. 1939); *Aduti Jivan Britant Panth Rattan Batu Teja Singh Overseer* (Bhasaur: Bhasaur Singh Sabha, n.d.); Harbans Singh, "The Bakapur Diwan and Babu Teja Singh of Bhasaur," *Punjab Past and Present,* 9 (1975), pp. 322-32.

18. Oberoi, "Bhais."

19. This is most clearly enunciated in the following works by Avtar Singh Vahiria : *Sikh Dharma Tat Darshan* (Amritsar : Wazir Hind Press, 1899); *Khalsa Dharma Shastra* (Anandpur : Ram Narain Singh, 1914, and subsequent editions). Sanatan positions on numerous issues discussed in Oberoi, "World Reconstructed."

20. Background on individuals and the general milieu are found in Oberoi, "World Reconstructed," pp. 197-215. Also, summary in Harbans Singh, *Heritage of the Sikhs,* pp. 234-239.

21. Op. cit. Also for a discussion of differing views in Oberoi, "A Historiographical and Bibliographical Reconstruction of the Singh Sabha in the Nineteenth Century," *Journal of Sikh Studies,* 10 (1984), pp. 108-130. This comes out most clearly in the tracts of Ditt Singh. Also discussed in Barrier, "Vernacular Publishing and Sikh Public Life in the Punjab, 1880-1910", in Kenneth Jones and Barrier, eds., *Vernacular Publishing in Nineteenth Century India,* (Delhi : Manohar, AIIS, 1988).

22. Amar Singh, *Gyani Ditt Singh* (Amritsar : Kirpal Singh, 1962), pp. 66-68; Oberoi, "World Reconstructed," pp. 287-88. The personalities and conflicts are contained in Bhagat Lakshman Singh's autobiography, edited by Ganda Singh, *Bhagat Lakshman Singh Autobiography* (Calcutta : Sikh Cultural Centre, 1965).

23. Episodes are detailed in Gurmukh Singh, *My Excommunication;* Ganda Singh, *A History of Khalsa College* (Amritsar : Khalsa College, 1949); Harbans Singh, *Heritage of the Sikhs.*

24. Tracts are cited in footnote 19. Also, see Narain Singh, *Sikh Hindu Hain* (Amritsar : Matbakanuni Press, 1899).

25. Tract warfare is reviewed in several essays in Gustafson and Jones, *Sources;* Barrier, "Vernacular Publishing."

26. Written by Kahan Singh Nabha, first Punjabi edition, 1899. A recent translation with background is Jarnail Singh, ed., *Sikhs, We are not Hindu* (Toronto : Sikh Social and Educational Society, 1985). Also, background in W.H. McLeod, *Sikhism* (New York : Barnes and Noble, 1984), pp. 133-6.

27. References to such conflicts are interspersed in the tract and newspaper accounts of the period. An especially important review is in *Khalsa Samachar*, Aug. 19, 1913, pp. 5-6. Also see Chief Khalsa Diwan proceedings, Aug. 19, 1917. Originals of CKD documents are in the Diwan headquarters, Amritsar, but copies are available with the author.

28. For a lengthy analysis of links between Punjab and migrant Sikhs, see Barrier, "Sikh Immigrants and Their Homeland : The Transmission of Information. Resources and Values in the Early Twentieth Century," in Barrier and Verne Dusenbery, eds., *The Sikh Diaspora* (Ann Arbor : University of Michigan South Asia Series, 1988).

29. British policies are reviewed in Barrier, "Sikh Politics"; Fox, *Lions of the Punjab;* Kapur, *Sikh Separatism.* Also useful is a confidential CID memo on Sikh politics and British strategy, D. Petrie, "Secret C.I.D. Memorandum on Some Recent Developments in Sikh Politics," *Punjab Past and Present*, 4 (1970), 301-379.

30. References are in footnote 17, and the treatment of publications are in Barrier, "Vernacular Publishing"; Punjab Politics and the Press, 1880-1910," in Margaret Case and Barrier, eds. *Aspects of India* (Delhi : Manohar, AIIS, 1986), pp. 118-33; *Sikhs and Their Literature.*

31. Publications of the Ferozepur Sikh Kanya Mahavidyala, and interviews in December, 1969, with Nahar Singh, M.A., a close associate of Takht Singh and his family.

32. Life and works discussed in Harbans Singh, "Bakapur."

33. Lai Singh, *Kalmi Tasvir;* Dukhi, *Mohan Singh Vaid.*

34 Frequent missionary reports in *Khalsa Akhbar*, 1896-1901.

35. For example, missionary activities in Hazara, *Khalsa Samachar*, Feb. 6, 1913, p. 6.

36. The use of such institutions and the spreading network of contacts discussed in Oberoi, "World Reconstructed"; Barrier, "Sikh Immigrants."

37. Ganda Singh, *History of Khalsa College*. Also C.I.D. analysis in Petrie's overview.

38. Major tracts catalogued in Barrier, *Sikhs and Their Literature;* Eileen Dimes and Ganesh Saur, *Catalogue of Punjabi Printed Books Added to the India Office Library 1902-1964* (London : Foreign and Commonwealth Office, 1975). Background in Barrier, "Vernacular Publishing."

39. Based upon extensive study of the major Sikh tracts of the period. The

network and particularly its ability to generate funds from abroad is discussed in Barrier, "Vernacular Publishing."

40. Information on Sikh papers is found in Barrier and Paul Wallace, *The Punjab Press, 1880-1905* (East Lansing : Michigan State University South Asia Series, 1970); Barrier, *Sikhs and Their Literature*.

41. Virtually every issue of the *Khalsa Akhbar*, edited by Ditt Singh, had stories on contributions and instances of Tat Khalsa success.

42. Harbans Singh, "Bakapur." Oberoi's various essays and dissertation contain example of similar activities.

43. Dukhi, *Mohan Singh Vaid*, pp. 16-18; Harbans Singh and Jagjit Singh, "Singh Sabha Lahir," in Ganda Singh, ed., *Punjab 1849-1960* (Ludhiana: Punjabi Sahit Academy, 1962), pp. 127-8, 139. Discussion of the difficulties in preparing the Faridkot commentary and reaching agreement on other matters can be found in Oberoi, "World Reconstructed."

44. Background in Barrier, "Trumpp and Macauliffe : West Students of Sikh History and Religion," in Fauja Singh, ed., *Sikh Historiography* (Delhi : Oriental, 1978), pp. 155-185.

45. The controversy is discussed in *Bhagat Lakshman Singh Autobiography*, pp. 89-93; Ganda Singh, *History of Khalsa College*. Also, press clippings and manuscripts of Bhagat Lakshman Singh with Dr. Ganda Singh, who has shared his substantial collection and wisdom with me for over two decades.

46. His ideology and writings are discussed in Barrier, "Vernacular Publishing"; Oberoi, "World Reconstructed," pp. 176-84, 278-90.

47. Accounts in *Shuddhi Pattar, 1986-7.*

48. Background is in Barrier, *The Sikh and Their Literature*; Kenneth Jones, "Ham Hindu Nahin," *Journal of Asian Studies*.

49. See, for example, R.W. Falcon, *Handbook on the Sikhs for the Use of Regimental Officers* (Allahabad : Pioneer Press, 1896); A.H. Bingley, *Sikhs* (British recruiting manual, rep. Patiala, 1970, Department of Languages). Background in monographs by Fox and Kapur.

50. Teja Singh, *The Gurdwara Reform Mavement and the Sikh Awakening* (Jullundur : Desh Sewak Book Agency, 1922), pp. 85-119.

51. Correspondence in Government of India Home Public file 192A, Aug. 1902; Feb. 1908, 99-102A; March 1907, 23A; Home-Books, June 1907, 121-2A. Background in Barrier, "Trumpp and Macauliffe."

52. Notes, letters and editorials in *Khalsa Samachar* and *Khalsa Akhbar*, Oct.-Dec. 1901.

53. Background on Chief Khalsa Diwan in Surjit Singh Narang, "Chief Khalsa Diwan," in Paul Wallace, ed. *Political Dynamics of Punjab* (Amritsar : Guru Nanak Dev University, 1981), pp. 67-81; Surjit Singh Narang, "Chief Khalsa Diwan," *Journal of Sikh Studies*, 12 (1981), pp. 97-108; surveys in Kapur and Fox volumes. Detailed treatment of CKD and politics is found in Barrier, "Sikh Politics." The primary documents for the period are reports of two newspapers, *Khalsa Samachar (KS) and Khalsa Advocate (KA)*, along with CKD proceedings.

54. Surjit Singh Narang essays, and a biographical material in Mihar Singh

Ravel, *Sir Sundar Singh Majithia* (Amritsar: no pub., 1942).

55. CKD Aug. 5, 1915.

56. KS, March 15, 1905, pp. 5-6.

57. Reports in KS, Feb.-April, July-Nov., 1906. Background and details are in Barrier, "Sikh Immigrants."

58. KA, Feb. 22. 1905, p. 3.

59. Role of the press is discussed in Barrier, "Punjab Politics" and "Sikh Immigrants." Examples of reports and appeals include material in KS, Jan. 2, 1913 and the special reports and *Masik Pattar* frequently published by the CKD. By 1911, the KTS had issued over 400 tracts numbering at least a million copies. The Sikh Handbill Society issued a flood of small pamphlets, and other agencies, such as Sikh Book Club and the Panch Khalsa Agency, issued dozens of tracts a year. On the general milieu, see Dukhi, *Mohan Singh Vaid*.

60. Education efforts are reviewed in Narotam Singh, "Chief Khalsa Diwan in the Field of Education," *Journal of Sikh Studies*, 8 (1981), 118-129. Also useful is a dissertation by Gurdarshan Singh Dhillon, "Character and Impact of the Singh Sabha Movement on the History of the Punjab" (unpub. diss. Punjabi University, 1972).

61. The Khalsa Biradari published annual reports. One interesting note on the outcaste situation is in KS (Oct. 12, 1904, 4-5), which stated that if outcastes were given amrit, 50,000 new Sikhs would be added. The Sanatan reaction is discussed in the Petrie CID note, and in the accounts in the KS and KA, 1909-1911.

62. Editorials, reports in KS, Feb.-March 1917. Also CKD minutes.

63. Anand marriage agitation and related issues are examined in Oberoi, "World Reconstructed." Also, background material is found in K.S. Talwar, "The Anand Marriage Act," *Punjab Past and Present*, 2 (1968), 400-410. Extensive tract literature on the subject is listed in Barrier, *Sikhs and Their Literature*.

64. KS, April 29, 1908, p. 2.

65. CKD minutes, 1902-6. See also CKD Oct. 1, 1916; KA comments, July 15, 1904, p. 3.

66. Background on Teja Singh missionary efforts is in KS, 1908-1911. Lala Sewa Ram had been important in the Khalsa Yougmen Association and took amrit in 1904, KS, March 23, 1904, pp. 2-3. He played a key role in the Rikabganj negotiations and later CKD affairs.

67. Discussed in Harbans Singh, "Bakapur." A typical tract conveying Teja Singh's perspective in *Khalsa Rahit Parkash* (Bhasaur: Panch Khalsa Diwan, 1908). Analysis of Ideas in Barrier, "Vernacular Publishing."

68. KS, Nov. 25, 1910, p. 5; KS, Sept. 21, 1904, p. 7; resolutions, CKD, 1904-8. Discussed in Government of India Home Public proceedings, 1903-5.

69. KA, Dec. 16, 1910, pp. 3-4.

70. On the Rikabganj agitation, Harjot Singh Oberoi, "From Gurdwara Rikabganj to the Viceregal Palace," *Punjab Past and Present*, 14 (1980), 182-98. War effort is reviewed in M S. Leigh, *The Punjab and the War* (Lahore: Punjab Government. 1922); Barrier, "Ruling India: Coercion and

Propaganda in British India During the First World War," in De Witt Ellionwood, ed. *India and World War One* (Delhi : Manohar, 1978), pp. 74-108.

71. Published in Urdu, the Lahore-based *Khalsa Akhbar* emerged as a strong opponent to the CKD during the Rikabganj agitation. Edited by Chanda Singh, the *Panth Sewak* launched a series of attacks on moderate Sikhs and was warned repeatedly by the British for allegations and pro-nationalist activities. Background in annual reports on the Punjab press, CID.

72. Many CKD discussions in 1917-19 focused on these challenges, which included attacks on supports such as Bhai Takht Singh who was charged with mismanaging his girls school in Ferozepur, CKD, Feb. 11, 1917. Attacks and replies appear frequently in the two major CKD newspapers.

73. CKD, June 3, Oct. 14, 1917. Background on constitutional developments in Gurdarshan Singh, "Sikh Politics in the Punjab," *Punjab Past and Present*, 3 (1970), pp. 67-78; Mohinder Singh, *the Akali Movement* (New Delhi : Macmillan India, 1978). Recent analysis in Kapur, *Sikh Separatism*.

74. Discussion in KS, Sept. 16, 1920, p. 3; CKD, Aug. 1, Oct. 31, 1920. Also press commentary in early summer, 1919.

75. The Sikh League and related activities discussed in a series of articles by Sukhmani Bal in the proceedings of the Punjab History Conference, 1981-3.

76. Kapur, *Sikh Separatism*, pp. 86-100. Akali reaction to the CKD reports on the period, especially V.W. Smith's memo, "The Akali Dal and the Shiromani Gurdwara Parbhandak Committee, 1921-1922," Government of India Home Political file 459/II, 1922.

77. Background on Sikh politics during the 1920s can be found in books by Fox, Kapur, and Mohinder Singh. Two new studies analyze the role of communal politics and the legislative arena : Prem Raman Uprety, *Religion and Politics in Punjab in the 1920s* (New Delhi : Sterling, 1980) and Garfraz Khawaja, *Sikhs of the Punjab* (Karachi : Modern Book Depot, 1985).

78. Based on a forthcoming study of 20th Century Sikh Literature by N.G. Barrier, to be published in late 1988.

79. Secondary sources include those cited in footnote 77. On the Akali literature and British reactions, Barrier, *Banned* (Columbia, Mo.: University of Missouri Press, 1974, pp. 91, 195-202; "The British and Controversial Publications in Punjab," *Punjab Past and Present*, 8 (1974), pp. 32-60.

80. Competition in elections and controversies over the definition of "Sikh" in the legislature reflected such an orientation. This is discussed in the studies by Kapur, Khawaja, and Uprety

81. The "official" *rahitnama* was only published in the late 1940s, and various editions still circulate. The issue of authority and the implications for contemporary Sikh politics assessed in Robin Jeffrey, *What's Happening to India?* (New York : Holmes & Meier, 1986).

9

CHRISTIANITY IN INDIA

Eric J. Sharpe

On December 23, 1972, Prime Minister Indira Gandhi spoke in New Delhi at the nineteenth centenary celebrations of St. Thomas, the Apostle of India. She said, among other things, that from the earliest times Christianity had been accepted as "part of the Indian mosaic," that as a group, Christians had made significant contributions to India's "composite religious heritage," and although at times Christianity had been "erroneously associated with foreign rule in some minds," since then "Christian leaders have largely identified themselves with nationalist aspirations," and deserve their place in the new India.[1]

Each of these points was significant. There have been Christian communities in India for a great many centuries; Christians have played their part—albeit a somewhat limited part—in the development of the religious life of India. Christianity was for many years associated in the Indian nationalist mind with foreign rule, as a *mleccha dharma*; and Christian leaders, beginning in the 1920s, have sought and found a place within the national movement. Christian history in India is nevertheless a highly complex pattern of impulses, missions, churches, personalities and problems, the overall story of which is certainly beyond the reach of any one writer to tell fully, and many parts of which have never been chronicled.[2]

The earliest beginnings of Christianity in India are shrouded in uncertainty. Syrian Christian tradition states that the Apostle

Thomas, one of Jesus' original twelve disciples, came to the
vicinity of Cochin in AD 52, and founded churches on both sides
of India's south coast, finally suffering martyrdom twenty years
later, in AD 72. But supporting evidence from outside India is
almost entirely absent, and what there is, is contradictory or at
least ambiguous.[3] Similar problems are attached to practically
the whole of India's earliest Christian history. Geographical references are fragmentary and uncertain, not to say confused. It is
clear, however, that there was a Christian Church in India
perhaps (on hard historical evidence) as early as the end of the
second century, when Pantaenus of Alexandria visited "the land
of the Indians." This is not to say that the Thomas Christians'
own traditions are unreliable: merely that they are difficult to
support from outside evidence. The intricacies of history aside,
today's "Thomas" or "Syrian" Christians in India have a tradition at least as old as that of the greater part of northern Europe.
These communities however have never shown any great desire
to expand beyond their own natural frontiers. Of their essential
"Indianness" there has never been the slighest question.

The second, Roman Catholic, phase of India's Christian
history began in the 1250s, with the arrival of the first missionaries of the Franciscan and Dominican orders.[4] These however
were not successful, and half a century later had disappeared
almost without trace. After 1500, following the Portuguese
occupation of parts of western India, there was fresh influx of
missionaries, this time in strength. Vasco da Gama landed near
Calicut in 1498, and although the Portuguese came chiefly for
trading purposes, they were also concerned to extend Christianity
in their dominions. In 1500 there arrived eight Franciscan
Friars and eight "secular" priests—the first of many thousands of
such missionaries. The best known of these included Francis
Xavier, who landed at Goa in 1542 and worked in India for ten
years; and Roberto de Nobili, who arrived in Madura in 1606,
adopted a wholly Indian style of life as a *sannyāsin*, learning
Sanskrit and being granted at least some access to the *Vedas*.
De Nobili enjoyed some success in converting high-caste Hindus,
but his work was too controversial to survive his retirement in
1645 and his death in the following year.[5]

In 1961 C.B. Firth wrote that de Nobili's cultural experiment,
so controversial in his own day, "... is the only thorough-

going attempt to Indianize Christianity that has yet been made."[6]
Sixty years after de Nobili's death there began the third phase of
Christian history in India, with the arrival in July 1706 of the first
Protestant missionaries, Ziegenbalg and Plütschau, German by
birth, but sent to India on the initiative of the King of Denmark
and under the auspices of the (British) Society for the Propagation of the Gospel in Foreign Parts.[7] This minute mission was
set up in Tranquebar, one of Denmark's two trading posts in
India, and the first Tamil converts were baptized in September
1707. Generally it is true to say that Protestants at first were in
no position to "indianize" Christianity beyond the fairly obvious
point of using Indian languages wherever possible. Their concern
was rather to rescue "brands from the burning"--to press for
individual conversions against an approaching Day of Judgment—
than to operate within any larger cultural framework. But the
situation in the first half of the eighteenth century was by no
means that of the turn of the twentieth. The Tranquebar
mission was tiny, and although it had some outstanding
workers, chief among them C.F. Schwartz (in India from 1750 to
to 1798) who produced the first Tamil-English and English-Tamil
dictionaries and the first Tamil translation of the Bible, its field
of influence was not large.

The London-based East India Company, founded in 1600,
gained political as well as commercial control over large areas
of India in the middle years of the eighteenth century, and
remained in control for a hundred years. Although many of the
Company's servants were doubtless Christians of a sort, official
policy was firmly against Christian missions, on the grounds
that to interfere with the religious beliefs and practices of the
people of India would endanger the trade which was the
Company's sole official concern, and for which they were publicly
accountable. This policy, which was maintained until 1813, led
to some interesting consequences: on the one hand, to extensive
support for Hindu and Muslim institutions, and on the other, to
the shutting out of Christian missionaries from the Company's
territories. On the first count, most important was the company's
financing of publishing ventures, including the first English
translation of the Bhagavadgītā (1785) and Max Müller's edition
of the Sanskrit text of the Rig Veda (1849-1862). On the second,
it meant that when the English Baptist missionary William Carey

arrived in India—in effect, to inaugurate the most concentrated
phase of Protestant Christian activity—in 1793 he was ultimately
forced to work in Denmark's other little trading post, at
Serampore.[8] However, Carey a few years later was granted a
measure of official Company recognition by being appointed to
teach Bengali (and later Sanskrit and Marathi) at the College of
Fort William. His chief work was in the field of Bible translation, and by the time of his death in 1834 he and his team of
co-workers had translated the whole of the Bible into six Indian
languages, the New Testament into twenty-three and smaller
portions into ten other languages.[9] Some of these translations
were highly defective. However, this activity, together with the
printing presses Carey established, was of considerable importance for the future of Indian literature generally.

Following successive revisions of the East India Company's
charter in 1813 and 1833 the door was thrown open to Christian
missionaries, though initially on a fairly small scale.[10] In 1830
the first missionary sent by the Church of Scotland, Alexander
Duff, arrived in Calcutta, and threw himself into educational
work, on the belief (quite mistaken, as it turned out) that "Every
branch of sound general knowledge which you inculcate, becomes the destroyer of some corresponding part in the Hindu
system."[11] This "general knowledge" was to be communicated in
English, and on that point official policy agreed: in 1835 a
protracted controversy on the issue of English *versus* vernacular
higher education in India was resolved in favour of the
"Anglicists." This decision was of momentous importance for
India's future, and assured one of the directions in which Indian
Christianity was later to develop, in and around colleges and
universities, most notable in the three great centres of Calcutta,
Bombay and Madras.

Actual conversions to Christianity from among college
students were never common, once the initial period had passed,
and by the end of the century had dried up almost completely.
Most of the students were from the highest Hindu castes, and for
these, the acceptance of Christian baptism meant social ostracism
and isolation from the Hindu community. By the 1850s, Protestant Christian opinion in India had settled down into an
attitude of total opposition to caste, a more lenient attitude
being taken by the Roman Catholics and by a small number of

German missionaries (Lutherans of the Leipzig Society) in South India.[12] Controversy on this point was bitter for many years. Most Protestants, however, were adamant: to become a Christian one must renounce caste, finally and publicly, whatever the social consequences. They argued that caste as an institution amounted to legalized inequality under Hindu religious sanction. The outcome was that although many individual Hindus in India might well be impressed, as Rammohun Roy had been impressed, by the moral character of the teachings of Jesus, the vast majority remained detached from, and critical of, institutional Christianity. Those who did become Christians in a formal sense increasingly were those who had least to lose from caste exclusion.

The Great Rebellion (Sepoy Mutiny) of 1857-8 had relatively little immediate effect on the situation of Christianity in India, though once over, it caused a great deal of soul-searching in the missionary community. The 1858 Madras missionary conference outlined the measures that needed to be brought to bear on the Government to prevent further outbreaks:

> All we require is simple Christian Consistency in all their proceedings which have a bearing on religion; the introduction of the Bible into all Government schools, to be read daily by those of the pupils who do not object to it; and, especially, the entire cessation of all patronage and countenance of idolatry and caste.[13]

J.W. Kaye urged in 1859 that " . . . what we have now to do is to possess ourselves in faith, and with faith to have patience; doing nothing rashly, nothing precipitately, less our own folly should mar the good work, and retard the ripening of the harvest."[14]

In 1858 the East India Company was dissolved, and Queen Victoria became India's new sovereign. Although Christian in principle, from the first the new Government proclaimed a policy of religious impartiality, in which not even Christianity would enjoy official "most favoured religion" status. Queen Victoria's proclamation of 1858 contained the words: "Firmly relying Ourselves on the truth of Christianity, and acknowledging with gratitude the solace of religion, we disclaim the Right and

the Desire to impose Our convictions on any of Our subjects."[15]
From this time Christianity in India was neither favoured nor
actively opposed, while missionaries and Indian Christians alike
generally lived in a world far removed from that of India's
British administration, with which they had a few direct contacts
of any kind. This point is worth bearing in mind. Among
European Christians working in India during the heyday of the
Raj, the only ones to have appreciable contact with the seat of
political power were Anglican chaplains to the European community. The remainder would have enjoyed no such contact in
Britain, nor did they generally do so in India: similarly with
other Europeans and Americans. Held at bay by the unwritten
conventions of the British caste system, the average missionary
neither sought nor possessed political muscle of any kind.

During the second half of the nineteenth century, Christianity
in India operated on two widely separated levels: directly at the
bottom of society, and for the most part indirectly through the
educational enterprise at the top. On the latter count, in the post-
Rebellion years English-language higher education in India expanded rapidly, often (though by no means always) in institutions administered by missionary organizations, which included
some Christian teaching as part of their general curriculum.
Measured by actual conversions to Christianity, their impact was
slight. They did on the other hand do a good deal to familiarize
the upper strata of Indian society with Western ideas and values,
social, political and religious. By 1900 the flow of converts from
this source, never much more than a trickle, had dried up almost
entirely.

Sizeable numerical accessions to Christianity did however take
place during these same years as a result of "mass movements"
in rural areas.[16] This has been a controversial subject in the
history of Christianity in India. Doubtless the motives of those
accepting baptism were mixed, though arguably the dominant one
was a desire for social betterment and for protection on both
"natural" and "supernatural" levels. Most of the initial waves
of converts were ill-educated and ill-prepared, and in any case
the decision was a collective rather than a personal one. In the
short term, these mass movements improved missionary statistics
in a remarkable way, the size of the Christian community in India
increasing from about a million in 1858 to almost 3 million in

1901 and almost 4 million ten years later. In the long term, on the other hand, the mass movements created serious problems, stretching the resources of churches and missionary agencies almost to the breaking point. The supply of competent priests, ministers, pastors and catechists became a matter of pressing concern and many Christian village communities had to survive almost without regular pastoral care. Although most Protestant churches maintained their attitude of hostility to caste, there was little in these circumstances to prevent the new Christian communities from coming to resemble sub-castes in all but name.[17] At a later stage it was also possible for the opponents of Christianity to accuse the missions of aiming at indiscriminate conversions by unfair means, ultimately for political purposes.

In May 1866 Keshub Chandra Sen lectured in Calcutta on "Jesus Christ: Europe and Asia."[18] The tone of his lecture was remarkable. Like Rammohun Roy earlier, he expressed the warmest appreciation of the moral character of Jesus, and held up his character as an antidote to racial contempt and violence. As Christians, he said, Europeans "...ought to be baptized into true Christian meekness; their rough nature will be thereby humanized, and their proneness to indulge in violence and ferocity will be effectually curbed."[19] But previously he had said that to Asiatics, " . . . Christ is doubly interesting, and his religion is entitled to our peculiar regard as an altogether Oriental affair."[20] This claim was to be heard very frequently in subsequent years: that Jesus Christ was of the East rather than the West, and that Europeans had never been able to understand him. India, on the other hand, could, accepting him on her own terms as a moral teacher and even as an *avātara*—one among many. Attempts were also made before the end of the century to "prove" that Jesus had either been trained in India, or had died in India, or perhaps both.

The rise of the national movement in the last quarter of the nineteenth century affected Indian Christianity in some ways, and not in others. It had practically no effect on the village communities. But at the other end of the social scale, the emerging alliance between Indian nationalism and renascent Hinduism created serious problems for Indian Christians. Hindu movements like the Ārya Samaj and hybrids like the Theosophical Society (both founded in 1875) were generally anti-Christian. Anti-British

feeling in India, especially after the Ilbert Bill controversy in the
1880s, could and did spill over into anti-Christian sentiment.
Before 1914, few Indian Christians became deeply involved in the
national movement. One who did, was Bhawani Charan Banerjea,
later known as Brahmabandhav Upadhyay. A former member of
the Brahmo Samāj, Brahmabandhav became a Christian in 1891.
Arrested on a charge of sedition in 1907, he died of tetanus in prison a few days later.[21] Christian missionaries were generally critical of the violent side of the national movement, though some—
most notably Charles Freer Andrews, later to become a close
associate of both Tagore and Gandhi—were deeply in sympathy
with its aspirations. In these same years, 1900-1914, there was a
powerful missionary movement, led by the Scotsman J.N.
Farquhar, to emphasize the scholarly and sympathetic study of
Hinduism and Indian culture generally.[22] Another influential
Scottish educational missionary was A.G. Hogg (in India from
1903 to 1939), who, as well as being Radhakrishnan's first teacher
of philosophy, helped to create a new class of Christian intellectual in India from his chair at the Madras Christian College.[23]
More and more Indians assumed positions of leadership. On
Christmas Day 1905 there was founded the Indian National
Missionary Society (*Bharat Christya Sevak Samaj*) under Indian
direction. It was never a very great success, but did give rise to
many later initiatives, including that of the Christian *āshram*. The
first Indian to be appointed Principal of a Christian college in
India, S.K. Rudra, took up his duties at St. Stephen's College,
Delhi, in 1907; the first Indian to become an Anglican bishop in
India, V.S. Azariah, was consecrated in 1912.

   After 1910 the political temperature of India cooled somewhat,
though more as a result of government measures than because
genuine agreement had been reached. Christian missionary
apologetics were best represented at this time by J.N. Farquhar's
book *The Crown of Hinduism* (1913), which argued that Christ
(not Christianity) came to "fulfil"—to bring to completion in a
semi-evolutionary sense—all the highest spiritual and practical
aspirations of Hindu religion and culture.[24]

   The outbreak of war in 1914 showed India that she could not
be immune from world politics; many Indians fought in the war,
and in the years between 1914 and 1918 the internal political and
religious struggle was partially suspended. However, the war

itself did much to discredit the West, and Western religion, in Indian eyes—added to which, Muslim Turkey's alliance with Germany against Britain affected Muslim opinion in India. When the war came to an end, Indian leaders hoped for an improved political situation, partly as a reward for war service faithfully performed. This was not to be. Pre-war security measures were continued, and on April 13, 1919 the Amritsar massacre took place. The officer responsible, Brigadier-General Dyer, was severely censured, but later in the year won the support of the House of Lords and the conservative wing of the British press, and British opinion. Gandhi denounced the British government as "satanic," and India was thrown into a period of fresh turmoil, in which politics took the upper hand of religious reflection.

The events of 1919 left a no less deep mark on the Christian community in India than on Indian society generally. Certainly few Indian Christians were prepared to go as far as Gandhi had gone in his condemnation of the British government: but from that time on there appeared a new phenomenon on the Indian scene, that of the committed Christian nationalist. A new journal, the *Christian Patriot*, was started. Articles devoted to the national cause began to appear in the more liberal missionary journals, written by Indian Christians like K.T. Paul and P. Chenchiah. Their angle of approach remained constant for the next dozen years: that *in the forms in which it had been presented to India*, Protestant Christianity (Catholics played less part in this debate) had been a denationalizing factor, and needed to be reformed and reshaped in accordance with Indian thought and Hindu spirituality. Some missionaries, most notably C.F. Andrews and Stanley Jones, concurred enthusiastically, while others did not. K.T. Paul wrote in the *International Review of Missions* on "How Missions Denationalize Hindus," arguing that for Christianity to find its place in the emergent India, far more room than hitherto would have to be found for Indian forms of cultural expression.[25] Eight years later Chenchiah stated what many Indian Christians by then believed, that

Christ comes to India deeply interwoven in the fabric of Western civilization. Christ and Western civilization, clearly distinguishable in their natures and frequently fundamentally and radically opposed to each other, are cemented together by history and brought to India as a unified indivisible whole.[26]

Whether the two could be disentangled was a more complex question.

The "Christian Patriot" group notwithstanding, the most widely known Indian Christian internationally, the Sikh convert Sadhu Sundar Singh, deliberately held himself aloof from politics.[27] In 1920 and 1922 Sundar Singh went on ambitious preaching tours to the West, being everywhere hailed as living proof that Christianity had at long last found a place at a deep level of Indian spirituality. He was best known as a preacher; he was also a visionary, and later in his life was for this reason drawn away orthodox Christianity and toward the Sweden-borgians.[28] Much of what was written about him (and he generated a vast literature) in the 1920s was of little lasting consequence. But to the West he appeared in the light of a living Christian mystic, a near-martyr, a gifted preacher and a saintly personality. His last years were saddened by a protracted controversy over his bona fides, and by ill health.[29] In April 1929 he set off on a last missionary tour to "Tibet," and was never seen or heard of again. He left a romantic image, but was too individualistic to leave a succession; nevertheless his contribution remains to this day unique.

Of more lasting importance was the "Christian Ashram" movement, which began and flourished, though on a fairly small scale, in these same years. Inspired by the tradition of St. Francis of Assisi (who was in many ways "rediscovered" in the late 19th and early 20th centuries), by Tolstoy, by Social Christianity in Europe and North America, and above all by the example of Gandhi, during the 1920s and 1930s numerous Christian Ashrams were set up in India. Their prototype was the Christukula Ashram in Tirupattur, begun in 1921 by two medical doctors, Savarirayan Jesudason and Ernest Forrester-Paton.[30] In 1922 Jack Winslow, together with five other Europeans and five Indians, began the Christa Seva Sangha in Ahmednagar, on Franciscan principles of fellowship and service.[31] Many more were to follow. None was however large. It must be allowed, on the other hand, that they had some success in overcoming earlier objections to the "foreignness" of

Christianity in India.

Those who became convinced after 1919 that Christianity was
in all essentials the religion of a foreign power were not easily
persuaded to change their minds. Still Christianity in India was
greatly dependent on overseas support. The growing political
crisis did nothing to improve matters. Politically-minded
Christians were on the whole few, a mixed company of radical
Indian Christians and liberal missionaries, having very few
contacts with the seat of political power. In 1925 an
American missionary, Stanley Jones, stated the Indian case in
his widely-read book *The Christ of the Indian Road*.[32] Two years
later a diametrically opposite point of view was taken by another
American, Katherine Mayo, in her notorious book *Mother India*.[33]
Miss Mayo was not a missionary, and was widely suspected of
having written her book for political purposes. But she, like
Jones, was an American, and in the economic climate of the
time, American support was becoming increasingly important.

Another significant American-based organization was the
Young Men's Christian Association (YMCA), whose position as
a Christian agency in India had long been advantageous. The
YMCA was administered, not from London, but from New
York.[34] It was not a church, being rather a non-denominational
para-church organization. It had always been prepared to
advance Indians to positions of leadership, and often individual
YMCA men had taken a pro-nationalist position. In 1920 J.N.
Farquhar (himself a YMCA Secretary) had written that

> The Association is . . . at this moment the one form of Chris-
> tian organization which is trusted and welcomed everywhere.
> At the height of this menacing crisis, it can be friendly with
> all the groups, can play the peacemaker between the races,
> and do the work of the servant of India.[35]

During the troubled years that followed, the YMCA was often
able to fill this role, through its student centres, conferences and
particularly its publishing programme. However, it was becoming progressively secularized throughout the period, moving
from worship and evangelism to sport and "character-building."
In YMCA circles "secular dialogue" was practised long before
the term became fashionable.[36]

It was quite natural, given the circumstances of the time, that in the inter-war years Christianity in India should have settled down into the role of a socio-ethical agency in which (apart from Sundar Singh) the practices of spirituality were little regarded. Little original theology was being written, and much of what was, followed Western patterns rather closely—for instance in the work of A.J. Appasamy, in which, though the material was to a large extent Indian, the treatment owed far more to Hartford and Marburg than to Benares. Appasamy's best book was perhaps his *Christianity as Bhakti Marga* (1927); worthy of mention is also his selection of Hindu scriptures for Christian use, published in 1930 by the YMCA as *Temple Bells*. Here the argument was that if Christ is to be regarded as the "fulfiller" of Hinduism as he was of the Jewish tradition, then logically at least parts of Hindu scripture might replace the Old Testament in the Indian Church. This move, however, won little favour among Indian Christians generally.

In 1938 the International Missionary Council held an important conference on the new campus of the Madras Christian College, Tambaram. In preparation, various volumes were produced, one of which was—and still remains—perhaps the most stimulating symposium of Indian Christian writing ever assembled. *Rethinking Christianity in India* contained essays by seven Indian Christians, Job, Chenchiah, Chakkarai, Devasahayam, Jesudason, Asirvatham and Sudarisanam. It was not uncontroversial. In various ways it maintained the tone of the *Christian Patriot* of earlier years, while moving somewhat further in a Hindu direction: "Christ cannot oppose Hinduism nor does He," Chenchiah affirmed. And further: "Christianity is not going to drive a wedge in national solidarity. Nor is the Eastern Christian likely to be a good child and accept the theology and the Church offered to him by his monitors. . . . Let it be clearly understood that we accept nothing as obligatory save Christ. . . ."[37]

Disunity among Christians has always been a problem in India, as indeed it has in most parts of the world. In the 19th century this began to be tackled by the setting up of local missionary conferences (which Indian Christians generally were not expected to attend) and by the "comity" principle of allocating different areas to different missionary organizations. This clearly did not go far enough. The founding in 1905 of the National Missionary Society, under Indian leadership, was the most important step. Thereafter there followed more and more intricate schemes of union among Protestant Churches, in both north and south India, stimulated equally by the situations in India and in Europe. Although by 1938 the south Indian scheme was well advanced, Chenchiah was not impressed:

> It appears to a convert indescribably funny [he wrote] that anybody should entertain the idea that by knocking together the Church of England, the Church of Scotland, Swedish and Lutheran and American churches, an Indian Church would be produced.[38]

The scheme did, however, reach fruition almost simultaneously with independence in 1947. The Church of south India, comprising fourteen dioceses and about a million members spread over four major language areas, came into being in the month following Independence, on September 27, 1947.[39]

It had taken twenty-eight years of hard work to bring the Church of South India into being. In North Atlantic terms, the experiment was a bold one. It was not able to be fully comprehensive, however. Most notably it did not involve the Roman Catholics or the Lutherans. And although of importance for the future of Christianity in India on the organizational level, it in the end made a somewhat greater impact on Christianity in the West, as a prototype of what might be achieved in the ecumenical age. A similar scheme was brought to fruition in North India some years later, in 1970.

Back in 1926, W.E.S. Holland had criticized the Christian Church in India for its disappointing foreignness, summing up that "The foreign garb such a system wears is by no means its most disastrous consequence. The deadly thing is that a church so exotic in character and expression can have little of creative life or expansive energy."[40] In post-Independence India every effort had to be made to overcome that foreignness. On the Protestant side, what this chiefly involved was a concentration on socio-ethical issues. The new India was to be a secular state, in which the seeking of converts was always frowned upon, and often expressly forbidden. Analyzing Christian social thought in post-Independence India, Bengt R. Hoffman drew attention to two focal points, "to expose improper motivations for Indian nationhood, and to strive for unity in the midst of plurality."[41] Missionaries on the old pattern were no longer welcome in India (and still less so in Pakistan). Secular workers in a secular state, on the other hand, were. A new generation of Indian Christian theologians emerged within the Protestant community, chief among them P.D. Devanandan and M.M. Thomas, following a largely socio-ethical line and making extensive use of sociological inquiry in the pursuit of its aims. The Christian Institute for the Study of Religion and Society in Bangalore, and its journal *Religion and Society* assumed a position of leadership in this regard. From the early 1960s on, a stream of valuable publications emerged from this source.

Following the Second Vatican Council in mid-1960s, the Roman Catholic Church in India, which for a century had lived its own life largely separate from Hindu society on the one hand, and from other Christian bodies on the other, was liberated from many of its earlier restrictions. The Council having affirmed the principle of dialogue, numerous Catholics threw themselves into the practice and the theory of inter-religious *rapprochement*, most notably on the level of spirituality.[42] Many names might be mentioned in this connection; special places were however occupied by Christian contemplatives, H. le Saux (who took the Hindu name of Swami Abhishiktananda) and Dom Bede Griffiths. On a different level, important contributions were also made by Raimundo Panikkar and Klaus Klostermaier, and by many contributors to the *Journal of Dharma* (first published in 1975). On the level of worship, many experiments were made to Hinduize the Church's liturgy by the introduction of elements from the temple and *bhakti* traditions. At first these met with a mixed reception, but some have gradually gained wider acceptance.

From an emphasis on inter-religious dialogue and shared spirituality in the late 1960s, in the 1970s one wing of Catholic opinion in India moved in the direction of social activism, in the style of Latin American "liberation theology." Father Joseph Vadakkan in Kerala asked: "What is the responsibility of a priest of Christ...? Will it be sufficient if he prays in street corners? Or should he fight for a Government which will feed

the hungry and clothe the naked?   This is the issue before me
now."[43]   Some Protestant leaders were asking the same question
under similar influences, one going so far as to state categorically
that in the modern world, Christianity has no other function
than to place economic power in the hands of the economically
powerless

Since the 1970s, the situation of Christianity in India has been
inextricably bound up with developments in an increasingly
complex world order, and has reflected in one way or another
what has been taking place elsewhere in the world. In 1982 S.J.
Samartha wrote:

> We are in the process of reshaping an ancient, powerful and
> intricate civilization into new cultural and social patterns, in
> response not just to impersonal technological forces but also
> to the clear, vocal and aggressive demands of oppressed
> people for a reasonably satisfying human life here and now.
> Basically it is a cultural struggle in which currently the
> economic component is crucial. New political institutions to
> bring about effective change are desperately needed, as well as
> spiritual resources to undergird the struggle to redeem it from
> self-righteouness and direct it toward a hopeful future.[44]

In 1980 there were some 27 million Christians in India out of a
total population of almost 700 million.[45]   This amounts to no
more than 3.9% of the population.   But Christianity is arguably,
for better or worse, the most international of religions. Christianity in India has never been free from outside pressures, social,
economic and political as well as religious in the narrower
individual sense. Increasingly it has chosen an Indian way, to
the extent to which it has been free to choose. But its freedom
has been bounded by circumstances over which it has never been
able to exercise more than a limited control. But that Christians
in India have sincerely and successfully sought to serve India,
often anonymously and with little or no public acknowledge-
ment, is beyond all doubt.

Statistics[46]

Year	Christians	Percentage of Population
1881	1,862,634	0.73%
1891	2,234,380	0.79%
1901	2,923,241	0.99%
1911	3,876,203	1.24%
1921	4,754,000	1.50%
1931	6,296,763	1.79%
1951	8,392,038	2.35%
1961	10,728,086	2.44%
1971	14,223,382	2.596%

Notes

1. Text circulated by Bharat Sevak Samaj, New Delhi, January 1, 1973.
2. The historical literature is vast. Of recent works, see especially S.C. Neill, *A History of Christianity in India* I-II (Cambridge University Press, 1984-5), which however only covers the period down to 1858. A multi-volume history is also under preparation by the Church History Association of India. A useful one-volume summary is C.B. Firth, *An Introduction to Indian Church History* (Madras: Christian Literature Society, 1961).
3. L.W. Brown, *The Indian Christians of St. Thomas* (Cambridge University Press, 1956).
4. The Capuchin Mission Unit, *India and its Missions* (New York: Macmillan, 1923), pp. 81ff.
5. V. Cronin, *A Pearl to India* (London: Hart-Davis, 1959).
6. Firth, *op. cit.*, p. 126.
7. On the Tranquebar Mission, see Neill, *op. cit.*, II, pp. 28ff.
8. *Ibid.*, pp. 187ff. Cf. E.G. Hinson, "William Carey and Ecumenical Pragmatism," in *Journal of Ecumenical Studies* (1980), pp. 73ff.
9. Firth, *op. cit.*, p. 147.
10. On the 1800-1914 period, see K.S. Latourette, *A History of the Expansion of Christianity*, Vol. 6 (New York: Harper and Row, 1944), pp. 65-214.
11. A. Duff, *Missionary Addresses* (Edinburgh: Johnstone and Hunter, 1850), p. 19.
12. On the caste question generally, see D.B. Forrester, *Cast and Christianity: Attitudes and Policies on Caste of Anglo-Saxon Protestant Missions in India* (London: Curzon Press, 1980). Cf. also E.J. Sharpe, "Church Membership and the Church in India," in J. Kant and R. Murray (eds.), *Church Membership and Intercommunion* (London: Darton, Longman and Todd, 1973), pp. 155-179.

13. M. Winslow *et al.* (eds.), *Proceedings of the South India Missionary Conference . . . 1858* (Madras, 1858), p. xi. Cf. A. Duff, *The Indian Rebellion: its Causes and Results* (London: Nisbet, 1858).

14. J.W. Kaye, *Christianity in India: An Historical Narrative* (London: Smith, Elder, 1859), p. 500f. Cf. J.B. Mozley, "Indian Conversion," in *Essays, Historical and Theological* II (London: Rivingtons, 1884), pp. 312 ff.

15. Neill, *op. cit.*, II, p. 428f.

16. J.W. Pickett, *Christian Mass Movements in India* (Cincinnati: Abingdon, 1933).

17. Cf. C.G. Delhi, *Church and Shrine: Intermingling Patterns of Culture in the Life of some Christian Groups in South India* (Uppsala, 1965).

18. K.C. Sen, *The Brahmo Somaj: Four Lectures* (London: W.H. Allen, 1870), pp. 3-36.

19. *Ibid.*, p. 31.

20. *Ibid.*, p. 26.

21. K. Baago, *Pioneers of Indigenous Christianity* (Bangalore: CISRS, 1969), pp. 26ff.

22. E.J. Sharpe. *Not to Destroy but to Fulfil: The Contribution of J.N. Farquhar to Protestant Missionary Thought in India before 1914* (Uppsala, 1965).

23. Idem, *The Theology of A.G. Hogg* (Bangalore: CISRS, 1971).

24. Sharpe, *Not to Destroy . . .*, pp. 329 ff.

25. K.T. Paul, "How Missions Denationalize Hindus," in *international Review of Missions* (1919), pp. 510-521.

26. P. Chenchiah, "Present Tendencies in Indian Religions," in M. Stauffer (ed.), *An Indian Approach to India* (New York: Missionary Education Movement, 1927), p. 60f.

27. A.J. Appasamy, *Sundar Singh : A Biography* (Madras: Christian Literature Society, 1966) is the most recent book-length study.

28. E.J. Sharpe, "Sadhu Sundar Singh and the New Church," in *Studia Swedenborgiana* (January 1984), pp. 5-28.

29. E.J. Sharpe, "Sadhu Sundar Singh and His Critics," in *Religion* (Spring 1976), pp. 48-66.

30. S. Jesudason and E. Forrester-Paton, *The Christukula Ashram* (Madras: National Missionary Society Press, 1940).

31. J.C. Winslow, *Christa Seva Sangha* (London : SPG 1930).

32. E.S. Jones, *The Christ of the Indian Road* (London: Hodder and Stoughton, 1926). First published in England in September, by the following April it had been reprinted fifteen times.

33. Katherine Mayo published three volumes on the subject of public health and child marriage in India, *Mother India* (London: Jonathan Cape, 1927), followed in 1929 by *Slaves of the Gods* and in 1931 by *Volume Two*. The circumstances surrounding their appearance have never been fully investigated. Opposing views are represented by e.g. C.S. Ranga Iyer, *Father India* (London: Selwyn and Blount, 1927) and Lajpat Rai, *Unhappy India* (Calcutta: Banna, 1928).

34. K.S. Latourette, *World Service: A History of the World Service of the American Y.M.C.A.* (New York: YMCA, 1957).

238 ERIC J. SHARPE

35. Letter: J.N. Farquhar to F.J. Nichols, October 11, 1920 (YMCA Historical Library, New York).
36. *International Survey of the YMCA and YWCA* (New York: YMCA, 1932), p. 416.
37. E.J. Sharpe, *Faith Meets Faith* (London: SCM Press, 1977) p. 120f.
38. D.M. Devasahayam and Sudarisanam (eds.), *Rethinking Christianity in India* (Madras: Hogarth Press, 1938), p. 188.
39. For the full story of union negotiations, see B. Sundkler, *Church of South India*: The Movement towards Union 1900-1947 (London: Edinburgh House Press, 1954).
40. W.E.S. Holland, *The Indian Outlook* (London: Church Missionary Society, 1926), p. 218.
41. B.G. Hoffman, *Christian Social Thought in India* (Bangalore: CISRS, 1967), p. 116.
42. For details, see E.J. Sharpe, *Faith Meets Faith* (London: SCM Press, 1977), pp. 118ff., 132ff.
43. J. Vadakkan, *A Priest's Encounter with Revolution* (Bangalore: CISRS, 1974), p. 158.
44. S.J. Samartha, "Indian Realities and the Wholeness of Christ," in *Missiology* (July 1982), p. 304. Cf. M.M. Thomas, "Toward an Indigenous Christian Theology," in G.H. Anderson (ed.), *Asian Voices in Christian Theology* (Maryknoll: Orbis, 1976), pp. 11-35.
45. Statistics from D. Barrett (ed.), *World Christian Encyclopedia* (New York: Oxford University Press, 1982), p. 370.
46. Statistics from G.A. Oddie (ed.), *Religion in South Asia* (New Delhi: Manohar, 1977), pp. 190ff.

10

POLITICIZED HINDUISM:
THE IDEOLOGY AND PROGRAM OF
THE HINDU MAHASABHA

Kenneth W. Jones

The nineteenth century in South Asia was preeminently a period of cultural adjustment, producing new forms of group consciousness which in turn generated political movements during the twentieth century. Hindu tradition was not exempt from this development. It was reinterpreted primarily in key provinces such as Bengal, Maharashtra, and Punjab according to the regional culture and colonial experience. These differing regional expressions of Hindu culture and religion were blended together in the twentieth century, becoming a single overall Hindu consciousness which generated a Hindu nationalist movement. This Hindu nationalism conflicted with the secular nationalism of the Indian National Congress and the Islamic nationalism of the Muslim League. The organizational base of Hindu nationalism lay in the Akhand Bharat Hindu Mahasabha which acted both to express Hindu consciousness and to mold it, and in the process redefined the concepts of Hindu and Hinduism. Unlike the nationalist movements of the League and the Congress, the Mahasabha failed to generate sufficient support to gain its political goals; however, this movement persists today, providing a religious right wing in the Indian political spectrum.

The historical context in which Hindus lived was delineated by a past of defeat and subjugation. Hindus of north India were ruled by Islamic invaders beginning in the early thirteenth century, and the Deccan, the south central area, passed under Islamic domination roughly a century later. The Hindus, as with other groups in south Asia, were conquered by the British in the eighteenth and nineteenth centuries. As a result of centuries of foreign domination the Hindu community, in spite of its majority status, took on many of the attitudes that are typical of suppressed minorities. Their sense of fear and helplessness was strengthened by the challenges of two proselytizing and converting religions, Islam and Christianity. Hinduism did not convert and had no method of competing with conversion religions. Thus, Hindu leaders faced a future threatened with numerical decline and even extinction through conversion to other faiths. This threat was most acute among the untouchables, who comprised the lowest levels of the Hindu social structure. Many untouchables had converted to Islam and during the nineteenth century others began to join the ranks of the Christian community. Protection of the Hindu community from such conversions would have required a fundamental change in the social position of the untouchables, a change that could not be achieved without extreme difficulty. The concern for numbers grew rapidly following the introduction of an all-India census in 1871. The census became a decennial tally sheet which registered the progress of decline of each religious community and also helped to change the very concept of Hindu from a religion to that of a community.[1] This issue of numbers was particularly crucial in Punjab and Bengal, both provinces that saw the rise of Muslim majorities by the beginning of the twentieth century. For Hindus, particularly the educated elite, the nineteenth and twentieth centuries provided great opportunities—economic, cultural, and social—but within a historical context that bred a sense of fear and helplessness.

Origins of the Mahasabha

Throughout the nineteenth century religious societies, Hindu sabhas, appeared in various cities and towns. Often these organizations lasted for only short periods of time. They had a variety of goals ranging from radical reform to a defense of orthodoxy and tradition. Occasionally groups emerged with a mixture of goals and succeeded in attracting support from diverse elements of the Hindu community.[2] These organizations flourished as Hindu society and culture strove to adjust to the new world of British colonialism. One association, which lasted for over a decade and provided a model for the later Hindu Mahasabha, was the Bharat Dharm Mahamandal. It was founded in 1887 by Pandit Din Dayalu and a group of orthodox leaders from Punjab and the United Provinces. The Mahamandal held its first meeting in Hardwar and thereafter held annual meetings much in the style of the Indian National Congress.[3] The annual sessions were convened with great pomp, elaborate religious rituals, and the passing of resolutions which expressed the opinions of Hindu orthodoxy. Pandit M.M. Malaviya and the Maharaja of Dharbanga both supported the Mahamandal, as they would later support the Mahasabha. This organization faded from view in the early years of the twentieth century and did not provide a direct link to the Mahasabha.

During the years 1906-10 events such as the Minto-Morley Reforms, the founding of the Muslim League, unrest in Bengal and Punjab, and the coming census of 1911 greatly heightened Hindu anxieties.[4] As a result Hindu leaders moved to create organizations which would speak for and act to protect their communal interests. In 1906 Pandit Ram Bhaj Datta founded the Hindu Sahayak Sabha in Lahore, an all-Hindu organization, which drew supporters from the Arya Samaj and the Sanatan Dharm Sabha both from Punjab and Uttar Pradesh.[5] Although the Hindu Sahayak Sabha was primarily religious and cultural in its goals, Pandit Datta himself began to call for a new type of politics which would be overtly Hindu. In the following year, 1907, a United Bengal Conference met and raised two fundamental issues: first, the decline in relative numbers of the Hindu community and, secondly, the treatment of untouchables.[6] Also in January 1907, the Punjab Hindu Sabha came into existence, starting a chain of development that led directly to the Mahasabha. In addition to the all-India issues which concerned Hindus, the Punjab Hindu community, a minority faced with a majority of Muslims, became frightened by the Punjab Land Alienation Act and government reaction to the unrest of 1905-7.[7] Many Hindu leaders came to believe that a de facto alliance existed between the Muslim community and the British colonial government, and that it was aimed at restricting the power of the Hindu majority. One of the major factors in convincing Hindus that such an alliance was a fact came with the granting of separate electorates, seats reserved for Muslims only, in the constitutional reforms of 1909.

During 1908 a drift away from the Indian National Congress and toward the need for an overt Hindu politics gathered momentum.[8] Early in 1909 the publication of "Self-Abnegation in Politics" by the Arya Samajist, Lala Lal Chand, delineated this dissatisfaction with the secular nationalism of the Congress and also expressed the general anxieties of the Hindu community. Lal Chand called for the creation of a Hindu political movement to defend the community from its enemies, particularly from an Anglo-Muslim alliance, which he felt sought to dominate the Hindu majority. At nearly the same time a series of letters appeared in the *Bengalee* under the title, "A Dying Race." In these letters Lt. Col. U.N. Mukerji projected past census trends to demonstrate not only that the Hindu community was declining in relationship to all other religious groups but that in a predicted number of years they would disappear altogether.[9] Both Lal Chand and Mukerji gave detailed substance to Hindu fears and anxieties, thus stimulating the move toward the creation of an organization to protect and defend Hindus and Hinduism. As a result the Punjab Hindu Conference held its first annual meeting in Lahore, October 21-22, 1909.

Planned and prepared by leaders of the Punjab Hindu Sabha, this conference called for Hindu-centered political action and heavily criticized the Indian National Congress for failing to defend the interests of the Hindu community.[10] Among the numerous issues raised was the "feasibility of an All-India Conference."[11] Similar concerns appeared in 1910 when a gathering of Hindu leaders at Allahabad took the initial steps of organizing an all-India Hindu Sabha. Goals and rules of such a sabha were agreed upon and officers elected, but internal divisions and factional strife made it impossible actually to set this movement in motion.[12] Although the Punjab Hindu Conference found it difficult to move from symbolic to concrete action, the idea of all-India organization grew in popularity.[13]

The fifth Punjab Hindu Conference, which met in Ambala on December 7-8, passed a resolution to create just such an institution. "This Conference is strongly of the opinion that in order to deliberate upon measures for safeguarding the interests of the Hindu community throughout India and elsewhere it is highly desirable that a General Conference of the Hindus of India be held at Hardwar on the occasion of the Kumbh in 1915."[14] The resolution then went on to name twenty-six Hindu leaders who would plan the new organization and its initial meeting. Little happened during 1914, but with the opening of 1915 Lala Sukhbir Singh, the general secretary of the yet-to-be-organized sabha, sent a circular letter to all those who were supposed to assist in the preparations. Planning meetings were held on February 13, 1915, in Hardwar, February 17 in Lucknow, and a final one on February 27 in Delhi.[15]

The first All-India Hindu Conference met in Hardwar at the time of the 1915 Kumbh Mela. The Maharaja Munindra Chandra Nandi of Kasimbazar acted as president of the conference. A Subjects Committee passed a series of rules for the new organization and defined its goals as follows:

a. to promote greater union and solidarity amongst all sections of Hindu community and to unite them as closely as parts of one organic whole;
b. to promote education among members of the Hindu community;
c. to ameliorate and improve the condition of all classes of the Hindu community;
d. to protect and promote Hindu interests whenever and wherever it may be necessary;
e. to promote good feelings between the Hindus and other communities in India and to act in a friendly way with them, and in loyal co-operation with the Government;
f. generally to take steps for promoting religious, moral, educational, social and political interests of the community.[16]

This new organization was named the Sarvadeshak Hindu Sabha, or the All-India Hindu Society, and was ushered in with great enthusiasm.[17]

The All-India Hindu Sabha held annual meetings in Hardwar during 1916 and 1917 and in Delhi in 1918.[18] The office of the sabha was located in Hardwar and remained there during these years, but in spite of its ongoing existence the sabha had a poor record of achievement. Underlying divisions within the Hindu community made concrete action extremely difficult. Only symbolic action, which expressed general concerns, found wide acceptance when stated in resolutions or public speeches. Perhaps the best example of this dilemma lay in the area of untouchability. Although the sabha might deplore the weakness of Hindu society represented by its untouchables and consequently call for an end to discrimination against them, any attempt to improve the position of untouchables would generate sufficient controversy to make such a a program impossible. Thus the sabha took positions that were widely acceptable to the Hindu community and would not heighten its internal divisions.[19]

The Delhi session of the Hindu Sabha held on December 26-28, 1918, was presided over by Raja Rampal Singh and illustrates the type of issues it could successfully support. This conference passed resolutions against cow-slaughter and separate electorates, asked for an inquiry into the Bakra-Id riots in Kartarpur, and asked for a restoration of all Sanskrit manuscripts in the hands of the now defeated Germans.[20] Sir Rampal Singh in his presidential address laid the groundwork for each of the resolutions and also touched on several crucial themes which would reappear in later gatherings. Hindu unity, the lack of it, and threats against it proved a perennial topic. In this instance Sir Rampal Singh was particularly concerned with the threat posed by Sikhs who did not see themselves as Hindus but as members of a separate religion.[21] He linked fear of Hindu disunity to the issue of numerical decline as well as to the question of untouchability, and all of these raised the possibility of eventual extinction. Yet Sir Rampal could only approach them with an unwillingness to be specific. "The less said about the depressed classes the better. It is for the Hindu Sabha to take up all these matters in hand and to do all that is possible to save the Hindus as Hindus from extinction."[22] Since the appearance of Lt. Col. Mukerji's *A Dying Race* the fear of possible destruction of the Hindu community through differential growth rates and conversion remained embedded in the minds of many Hindu leaders.

An ambiguity similar to the conflict between symbolic and concrete action existed in the sabha's relationship to the British and to Indian nationalism. Initially the sabha was extremely loyal in its statements, but with the rise of nationalistic sentiment in 1918, it too supported "responsible government," moving parallel to the Indian National Congress.[23] They did, however, find it extremely difficult to define their relation to Indian nationalism, for they did not want to be labeled as antinational, nor did they want to abandon all justification for their existence as a separate group. This equivocation can be clearly seen as Sir Rampal tried to express their relationship to the British and to the Congress. "For sometime past a movement towards nationalism has been gaining strength in this country and the best and enlightened minds amongst our community have adopted the so-called non-sectarian attitude of being Indian first and Hindu, Mohammedan or anything else afterwards. Nobody can cavil at the high standard of patriotism that vibrates through their hearts. But there is still a higher patriotism towards which humanity is now moving and it is nothing more, nothing less than what the Hindu Rishis of old, of revered memory preached and practised."[24] These points of ambiguity remained and would reappear in future decades and helped to create an ideological confusion among many of the Mahasabha supporters until clarified in the 1930s.

The ebb and flow of nationalist enthusiasm proved to be a major factor in the history of Hindu efforts at organization and activism, as did the counterwaves of communal competition and conflict. During the years 1919 and 1920 the Sarvadeshak Hindu Sabha did not meet. Most of its leaders were deeply involved in Gandhi's first non-cooperation campaign and the events which led up to it. When the All-India Hindu Sabha surfaced again in 1921, it was a changed organization on the edge of a new world of increased religious conflict which followed the decline of all-India nationalism that marked the mid-1920s.

The Akhil Bharat Hindu Mahasabha

Once again Hardwar was the scene of a Hindu Sabha conference, this time under the presidency of Manichandra Nandi, the Maharaja of Kasimbazar. As in the original meeting of 1915, this session of April 1921, marked a further step in the organizational structure of an All-India movement. The name was changed to Akhil Bharat Hindu Mahasabha and the Constitution altered to bring the sabha into line with the non-cooperation movement. The words "in loyal co-operation with the Government" were replaced by "with a view to evolve a United and self-governing Indian nation."[25]   The new Constitution also formally added "low castes" to its definition of members.   In order to align with the Gandhian struggle the Mahasabha "resolved to non-co-operate with the British bureaucracy till cow-slaughter was stopped and left the settlement of the programme of non-co-operation for a future extra- ordinary session" to be convened in Delhi in November.[26]   But these plans were never completed since events caused an upheaval among Hindus and produced a rethinking of their priorities.   In August 1921, news of the Moplah uprising reached north India. Stories of forced conversions, looting, rape, and kidnapping by the Muslims of Malabar gave substance to the worst Hindu nightmares. B.S. Moonje went south to see for himself and returned to report that the reality was worse than the news stories.[27]   As long as the non-cooperation movement continued, it held stage center in com- parison to the Moplah affair, but when Gandhi suddenly cancelled non-cooperation in February 1922, communal conflict rapidly replaced the nationalist struggle as the major focus for Hindu leaders.

News from southwest India continued to reach the north, as missionaries were sent to Malabar to bring back into the fold of Hinduism those lost through forcible conversion of Islam.   In September 1922, a new atrocity story augmented Hindu fears when a riot erupted in Multan on the occasion of Muharram. "Rioting broke out after and stones were reported thrown at Muslim tazias and Hindus bore the brunt of the riot.   Their homes were looted and burned, temples were desecrated, women ravished and five of their community were killed and three hundred injured."[28] Pandit Malaviya, who was already in Punjab, rushed to the city and returned with tales of horror to an already frightened and angry community.   He also criticized Hindus for failing to defend themselves, a major theme in future communal conflicts.   Shortly afterward a similar riot broke out in Saharanpur.   When the Mahasabha met for its annual session in Gaya, Bihar, it was in an atmosphere of religious conflict, an atmosphere of fear and anger. "Malabar and Multan" became a slogan which stood for Muslim violence and Hindu lack of defense.[29]   As a result the Mahasabha moved toward a greater militancy.   Malaviya exemplified this new attitude when he called for Hindu religious leaders to "unhesi- tatingly" readmit all Hindus lost to Islam through force and coercion.   He urged the establishment of an all-India relief fund to help other victims of communal violence, called upon Hindus to work for communal unity and self-preservation, and promised to organize a grand meeting of the Mahasabha at Benares.[30]

Before the Mahasabha could meet again an event took place which strengthened religious conflict in north India and propelled the Mahasabha toward a more militant policy. At its annual meeting in Agra on December 31, 1922, the All-India Kshatriya Mahasabha voted to readmit the Malkana Rajputs to Hindu society.[31] The Malkanas were a community of Rajput converts scattered throughout the area where three provinces met, Rajasthan, Madhya Pradesh, and Uttar Pradesh. They had requested readmission and it was accepted by an organization of Hindu Rajputs. This opened an acute stage of competition between Hindus and Muslims. Four hundred fifty thousand Malkanas petitioned to be readmitted to Hinduism. When this news was carried in a Hindu journal during the first part of January 1923, Muslims reacted quickly with protest meetings and then the sending of missionaries to the villages near Agra, Mathura, and Bharatpur.[32] Hindu leaders responded by calling a conference of different Hindu organizations for February 13, 1923, in Agra. This gathering resulted in the establishment of the Bharatiya Hindu Shuddhi Sabha, with Svami Shraddhanand as its president. The Shuddhi Sabha quickly moved to conduct missionary campaigns among the Malkanas and any other group of Muslim converts who appeared willing to return to the fold of Hinduism.[33] *Śuddhi* became a major issue among Hindu leaders, a method of defense against the fears of communal extinction through conversion.

The Benares session of the Mahasabha promised by M.M. Malaviya was held in August 1923. In order to make this a grand success he published an appeal which stressed the "lamentable condition of the Hindus" and their apparent inability to defend themselves. Svami Sharddhanand, while on speaking tours in support of *śuddhi,* urged attendance at the Banares session and also linked *śuddhi* to the need for *sangathan,* or unity among all Hindus.[34] These two terms came to symbolize the hopes as well as many of the fears of the Hindu community, and were major themes of the Mahasabha from the Benaras session onward. When this conference opened, it did so with 1,500 delegates from various regions of India and a wide variety of sects within Hinduism, including Sanatanis, Aryas, Sikhs, Jains, Buddhists, and Parsis.

In addition to the delegates thousands of visitors joined the assembly.[35]
Numerous resolutions were passed on subjects that had become
an annual ritual for the sabha, but serious attention focused on
the issue of *śuddhi*, as the Mahasabha stated its public support
for the reconversion efforts of the Bharatiya Shuddhi Sabha. "The
Mahasabha declares it to be perfectly legitimate and proper to
retake such Malkana Hindus into the fold of Hinduism as have
all along observed Hindu customs and kept their marriage ties pure,
whether they are Rajputs, Brahmins, Vaishyas, Jats, Gujars, or
members of any other castes. It expresses its satisfaction at the
reclamation of the Malkanas already taken back into their 'biradaries' and expresses a hope that their 'biradaries' would gladly
welcome them back into their fold."[36] *Śuddhi* as a defense of
the Hindu community against conversion was matched by the
call for a Hindu Volunteer's Corps, which would provide social
services and also act to protect the community from attacks by
other religious groups. In addition the Mahasabha declared the
the necessity of organizing provincial and local sabhas throughout
the country, creating a concrete expression of the persistent dream
of an organized and unified Hindu community.[37]

Following the Benares conference, religious competition grew
steadily with opposing missionary organizations, conversion and
reconversion, and sudden outbreaks of violence. In February
1924, the Mahasabha gathered in Nasik under the presidency of
His Holiness Jagatguru Shankaracharya, a man of great standing
in the orthodox community. Past positions were reaffirmed, particularly *śuddhi*, which was made much more widely acceptable by
its support from an unquestionably orthodox leader. The Shankaracharya proclaimed that "If in these hard times, Hindus do not
take seriously in hand this holy work of 'Conversion' and prevent
their brethren from embracing alien faiths through mistaken views,
I say here as I stand that within ten decades you shall find no
Hindu on the surface of this earth."[38]

Militancy and anxiety, which ran parallel among Hindu leaders,
received a new stimulus with the Kohat riots of September 9, 1924.
The entire Hindu population of this city was expelled and once
again there was a flood of atrocity stories, of Hindu sufferings at
the hands of Muslim mobs. Leaders of the Punjab Hindu Sabha,
headed by Bhai Parmanand, rushed to Kohat, as did Pandit
Malaviya.[39] The Hindu Mahasabha raised a relief fund as once

more Hindu fears were realized. Kohat, like Multan, Malabar, and Saharanpur stirred Hindu leaders to believe that religious violence was inevitable. The rising level of religious tensions posed a difficult problem for those Hindu leaders, such as Lajpat Rai, who had strongly supported the Congress and who believed in an Indian nationalism beyond the limits of any religious community. In a speech Lajpat Rai declared that "we are prepared to subordinate our communal life to national life. For united national existence, we would do anything, but we shall not submit to threats or to coercion." He ended with a plea for Hindu-Muslim unity, but clearly such unity appeared less and less likely as conflict and competition continued.[40]

In the latter part of 1924, political issues began once more to demand the attention of the Mahasabha. It convened a special conference in December 1924, to discuss the issue of communal electorates. Hindu opinion had already been shocked at the Bengal Pact, negotiated by C.R. Das, which gave Muslims 60 per cent of the seats in the Bengal government services.[41] With the move into 1925 and toward the scheduled 1926 elections the issue of politics gained steadily in importance. The annual conference of the Mahasabha was held in Calcutta in April under the presidency of Lala Lajpat Rai. He had not openly identified with the Mahasabha, although he was one of the leaders of the Punjab Hindu Conference. As a strong Arya Samajist, he had an involvement in and loyalty to the Hindu community; yet this loyalty clashed repeatedly with his own sense of Indian nationalism. Communal conflict brought him to the role of president of the Mahasabha, but could only move him so far. Trying to bridge this gulf between religious and secular nationalism Lajpat Rai demonstrated his deep ambiguity.

The Hindus have so far followed a National policy and, I think, they must stick to that. They will be stultifying themselves if they replace their nationalism by communalism. Yet we cannot ignore the fact that there are some communities in India who want to take undue advantage of our nationalism and are pushing forward their communalism to such an extent as is injurious to the interests of the whole nation and certainly disastrous to those of the Hindu community. Such communalism we are bound to oppose as, in our judgement, it can only lead to permanent

slavery, permanent disunity and a state of perpetual dependence.[42]

Caught between two fundamental loyalties, Lajpat maintained a
position that supported Mahasabha activities as long as the organization did not enter into the political arena.

In a speech to the Punjab Provincial Hindu Conference he
outlined his goals for the Mahasabha:

(1) The need of and justification for the Hindu Sangathan;
(2) The need of restoring the ancient spirit of *Varana-Ashrama*
    system with change dictated by modern conditions of life;
(3) Opening the life of *Dwijas* to the Non-Brahmans;
(4) The immediate removal of untouchability and the uplift of
    the Sudras;
(5) Immediate improvement in the conditions of Hindu women
    and provisions for their education;
(6) Taking necessary steps to prevent the divisions of the Hindu
    community into different political compartments.[43]

His vision of the Mahasabha was basically non-political and
limited to internal changes in Hindu social organization. In spite
of his mixed feelings concerning the Mahasabha, he proved an
effective leader during his year as president, touring widely in
colonial India and Burma. He also moved the Mahasabha office
to Delhi where it could act more effectively and where it has
remained ever since.[44]

The forces of communal conflict and national politics provided
the basic setting for the 1926 Mahasabha session, held in Delhi
from March 13-15. Prior to and during these meetings a struggle
developed between Lajpat Rai and Bhai Parmanand over the
question of whether the Mahasabha should enter the coming
elections with its own candidates or not. Both men had a number
of supporters and neither could dominate the meetings. Parmanand
wanted the Mahasabha to nominate its own men and to become in
effect a new political party. Lajpat Rai and a number of Congress
Hindu leaders were unwilling to break with the Congress movement.
A compromise resulted which satisfied most delegates although
not Bhai Parmanand. It was agreed that the Mahasabha would
not nominate its own candidates, but would fight the elections only
where they saw Hindu interests clearly affected.[45] The remainder

of the conference passed the standard resolutions on *śuddhi*, *sangathan*, the need for Hindi as a national language, and the protection of minority rights. Under the leadership of Raja Narendra Nath the Mahasabha took a somewhat stronger position on the issue of untouchability, asking that untouchables be given all public rights to schools, roads, wells, meetings, and temples.[46] In his speech to the assembled delegates Raja Narendra Nath focused on the concern behind the untouchable issue when he remarked that "it is very strange that one belonging to [the] depressed classes has only to embrace Christianity or Islam and his untouchability in relation to Hindus disappears at once. A more illogical position it is difficult to conceive."[47] The greater the focus on Hindu solidarity and the threat of conversion, the more important it became to decry the plight of Hindu untouchables.

Events continued to push the Mahasabha toward a more militant posture when the Arya Samajist and popular leader of the Hindu community, Svami Shraddhanand, was assassinated by a Muslim on December 23, 1926. The trial and later execution of the assassin, Abdul Rashid, produced a bitter tension between Hindus and Muslims, especially in Delhi and the surrounding territories. At a special session of the Mahasabha held in Gauhati a few days after the murder, the assembly pledged itself to raise a fund in honor of their slain hero. During the opening months of 1927 the Mahasabha working committee organized an All-India Svami Shraddhanand Memorial Fund. Trustees were appointed, money collected, and it was decided to spend a quarter of the amount for *sangathan* work and use the rest for a memorial.[48] Shraddhanand's death entered the growing list of atrocity tales supporting Hindu militancy.

The B.S. Moonje Era 1927-33

In April the annual session met in the city of Patna with its president B.S. Moonje, the most militant Mahasabha leader so far in its history. With the ascendance of Dr. Moonje to power within the Mahasabha, power he would hold until 1933, several of the more moderate leaders associated with the movement, such as Lala Lajpat Rai and Pandit M.M. Malaviya, faded from the center of activity and decision.[49] According to Dr. Moonje's priorities there was no point to Congress politics or vain talk of self-government when the Hindu community could not even protect itself from humiliation. "If I cannot guarantee safety and immunity from molestation to my women folk and temples from those of my Moslem brethren who are only armed with lathies, how can I aspire to wrest Swaraj from and maintain it against the cupidity of those armed with machine guns."[50] Yet Moonje had taken over the Mahasabha at a time when communal conflict had begun to wane as another wave of nationalist enthusiasm was on the rise.

The Simon Commission, appointed in 1927 to investigate the present political situation with an eye to future constitutional changes, reached India on February 3, 1928. Opposition to it led by the Indian National Congress produced boycotts and demonstrations throughout British India. The Mahasabha joined in this boycott with the exception of the Punjab Provincial Sabha. It alone cooperated with the commission in the hope that any future legislation would benefit the Hindu community.[51] As in 1926 the Mahasabha chose not to oppose the Congress and all-Indian nationalism but to remain a Hindu pressure group within the broader spectrum of Indian politics. During 1929 and into 1930 the Mahasabha was overshadowed by growing nationalist agitation, which finally culminated in the Salt Satyagraha led by M.K. Gandhi. Congress opposition to the British government, and especially its refusal to attend the first Round Table Conference, aided a cherished goal of the Mahasabha, namely, to be consulted in whatever constitutional change was planned for the future. As a result B.S. Moonje, the working president of the Mahasabha, left for England to attend the first Round Table Conference held from November 12, 1930, to January 19, 1931.[52] This goal seemed to slip from the Mahasabha's grasp as the Congress agreed to join the next round of negotiations with Gandhi as their sole representative. As on other occasions the British seemed to take notice of the Mahasabha when Congress was in opposition and unwilling to negotiate. Once the Congress returned, the Mahasabha would be forgotten.

The Mahasabha held its annual meeting for 1931 at Akola in August.[53] Once again they turned their attention to the decennial census concentrating on the question of categories within the census reports. They hoped that all Hindus could be listed as such regardless of their religious subdivision. This and other long-standing subjects occupied the meetings, but a new and disturbing issue arose in the same month when the Communal Award was announced from London. The original award designated seats in both the central and provincial assemblies as being solely for one religious community or other interest group. Thus it and the modified Poona Pact, which resulted from Gandhi's fast against separate electorates for untouchables, proved totally unacceptable to the Mahasabha. It would remain an example of the anti-Hindu stance of the Congress, the Muslim League, and the British. In the 1932 meeting of the Mahasabha held in New Delhi the Communal Award was strongly condemned in a resolution stating "that in case the Communal Award is not suitably modified within reasonable time the Hindu Mahasabha calls upon the Hindus to take all steps necessary both in legislatures and outside for frustrating the objects of the Anglo-Muslim Alliance on which it is based and directs the Working Committee to prepare a programme of work to give effect to it."[54] It would remain a major issue for the Mahasabha through the creation of independent India.

The 1932 conference saw the Mahasabha turn to another subject that would culminate in a non-violent struggle at the end of the decade, the suppression of Hindu rights in the various Muslim princely states. N.C. Kelkar, president of the New Delhi session, laid the ground for this issue. "That in view of complaints having been received regarding grievances of the Hindu citizens of the Moslem states of Hyderabad (Nizam), Bhopal, Bahawalpur and Rampur in respect of retirement to public services in the States, observances of religious practices, facilities for education and imposition of alien languages."[55] Along with the issue of the Muslim states this session took special notice of "the efforts of Dr. Hedgewar for starting a strong organization of Hindus named Rashtriya Swayam Sewak Sangh" and urged that branches of it be founded in all provinces.[56] Once again the Mahasabha was at the beginning of a period of communal tension as the non-cooperation campaign began slowly to crumble. By 1934 it was over, leaving a vacuum on the political scene and a diminished sense of nationalism.

The Maturing of an Ideology: Parmanand and Savarkar, 1933-42

By the end of the 1930s the dominance of two leaders, Bhai

Parmanand and V.D. Savarkar, brought an end to the ideological ambiguity of the Mahasabha, for it became a movement of explicit Hindu nationalism opposed both to the Indian National Congress and the Muslim League. The 1933 conference of the Hindu Mahasabha met in Ajmer from October 13-15 under the presidency of Bhai Pramanand. B.S. Moonje was once again in England, an absence that was filled by Parmanand, who came to dominate the Mahasabha from 1933 until he stepped aside for V.D. Savarkar in 1937. Bhai Parmanand was a Punjabi, an Arya Samajist, and a militant supporter of the Mahasabha. According to his vision the Mahasabha should become the one true political party in India, for it was the only hope for the salvation of the Hindu community. "The communal construction . . . has made such a change in our politics that for the Hindus no alternative course is left but to seek the shelter of the Hindu Mahasabha and work out their salvation through Hindu Sangathan."

Parmanand recognized, however, that the Hindus lacked the necessary awareness of their situation, a fact which limited the effectiveness of the Mahasabha. "I confess the Hindu Mahasabha is not yet a fully developed organization. The Mahasabha is so because the Hindus as a community lack that national conscious- ness which must be there to make it a living and strong organization." It thus became the goal of the Mahasabha to stimulate and dis- seminate this sense of Hindu nationalism. "Our first task, there- fore, is to create that consciousness, and, more particularly, to direct our energy to the task of creating that consciousness in provinces where it is wholly lacking." And finally, for Parmanand, the methods he would use to create Hindu nationalism were openly political and showed a willingness to act without regard for any possible cooperation with the Indian National Congress. "I think the most important weapon which could be of service to us in this work is the capturing of the Legislative Assembly and Councils. The Hindu Sabhas at various headquarters in provinces should see that only those candidates are returned to represent the Hindus who are pledged to fight thec ommunal constitution. This ought to be the first item of our programme and it should receive our imme- diate attention."[57] Bhai Parmanand had returned to his theme of 1926 when he called for overt Mahasabha politics. He now ended this debate over political action. The Mahasabha stood politically separate from the Congress and began to move directly toward the expression of a Hindu nationalism. Such an ideological position had been inherent in the Mahasabha since the writings of Lala Lal Chand in 1909, but only now came into open expression as part of the Mahasabha program. The existing issues from cow protection to untouchability remained, but politics came to take precedence.

Parmanand moved quickly to further develop the organizational structure and activities of the Mahasabha. He started construction of the Hindu Mahasabha Bhawan on Reading Road in New Delhi, the present headquarters of the movement, and announced the establishment of a Servants of the Hindus' Society. In order to provide financial support for this society Parmanand donated one hundred shares of stock in a sugar mill, which brought in Rs. 4,000 annually. He also started two weekly newspapers, the *Hindu* in Hindi, and *Hindu Outlook* in English, and both lasted into the 1950s.[58] As was customary for the Mahasabha presidents, he toured widely throughout British India, holding numerous meetings which focused primarily on political issues, particularly the Communal Award.[59]

Paralleling the Mahasabha's openly political stance was a search for allies, as Hindu ties to the Buddhist world were given much greater emphasis. In 1933 the Mahasabha passed a resolution stating that it "recognises the fundamental unity of ancient Aryan Culture of India and of countries outside of India such as China, Japan, Siam, Ceylon, etc., and requests the organisers of the Hindu Educational Institutions to found chairs for the study of Japanese, Chinese and Siamese language and literature and the respective Governments of China, Japan, etc. to found similar chairs for the study of Sanskrit."[60] This statement was followed up in 1935 by inviting the Buddhist leader, Bikshu Uttama of Burma, to preside over the annual session at Kanpur. *Sangathan* then was extended to the world beyond India even as internally the Mahasabha continued to work for unity among members of the Hindu community.

In 1936 the Mahasabha took an absolute position on the issue of untouchability when it declared that "the Hindu Maha Sabha further affirms its faith that untouchability must not be regarded as a part of Hindu religion or social system. The Mahasabha recommends to the Hindus the abolition of all distinctions in the Hindu society based on birth or caste in the spheres of public, social and political life in which such distinctions ought to have no application and are out of place in the present age."[61] Hindu nationalism demanded a unified Hindu community which in turn meant support for egalitarian ideas, no matter how foreign such ideas were to traditional values. In this instance the demands of Hindu nationalism moved the Mahasabha into a position of radical social reform, for to defend the Hindu community meant that it was necessary to change it fundamentally.

The movement toward an overt Hindu nationalism continued. In 1936 the Mahasabha declared that "they [non-Hindus] must be made to understand that Hindusthan is primarily for the Hindus and that the Hindus live for the preservation and development of the Aryan Culture and the Hindu Dharma which are bound to prove beneficial to all humanity."[62] India should be a Hindu country and as such the expression of Hindu culture. In turn that depended on a common indigenous language.

The culture of a nation is vitally connected with its language. The stamp of a foreign culture on a nation can be detected from the press of a foreign language on the mother-tongue. Every independent nation guards and preserves its national language for this reason. Hindusthan, therefore, should insist on making Hindi the lingua indica of the country. We should realise the fact that every foreign word admitted into our language spells the death of the original Hindi synonym of it. . . . We should emphasise the purity of the Hindi language just as we insist on the purity of the Hindu culture.[63]

One nation, one religion, one language, and one culture, Hindu nationalism envisioned a unitary nation and not a pluralistic society.

The concept of *śuddhi* also was carried to its logical extreme. Although *śuddhi* had begun as an attempt to win back the newly converted, it was later extended to those who had, like the Malkana Rajputs, once been Hindus. Now *śuddhi* would be open to the conversion of anyone regardless of his heritage. "The Hindu Mahasabha should be considered as the representative body not only of the Hindus by birth or the Hindus in Hindusthan, but also representative of the Hindus abroad and particularly of those who by voluntary choice have enlisted themselves as Hindus and whom we should consider Hindus by adoption."[64] *Śuddhi* had evolved into a true conversion ritual which could, in theory, bring all humanity into the fold of Hinduism.

Accompanying this expanding concern of Hindus everywhere was an increasing focus on the plight of Hindus in the Muslim states of South Asia. At the 1936 meeting the Mahasabha went on record by stating that it "strongly protests against the policy of the Governments of Bhopal, Hyderabad (Deccan), Bahawalpore, Malerkotla, Loharu, Alwar, Khetri (Jaipur) and Pataudi States in depriving Hindu subjects of their fundamental religious and civil rights."[65] The Mahasabha appointed a committee to visit various Muslim states and report on the situation in regard to Hindu rights. "The Committee appointed as aforesaid will make their report with a special reference to the question of music in Hyderabad State, obstruction for Shuddhi work and safety of Hindu women in Bhopal State, compulsion for Muslim dress in Bahawalpur State, and the grievances regarding Hindi and other colloquial languages in the States."[66] Such a committee duly reported and detailed Hindu suffering in those areas. An appeal was made tho the Nizam of Hyderabad's government and when B.S. Moonje, Bhai Parmanand, and others attempted to follow this appeal with a personal visit, they were refused permission to enter the state by the government of Hyderabad.[67] This issue continued to grow in intensity, but did not explode until a new leader took over the reins of the Mahasabha.

V.D. Savarkar, a Mahrattha Brahman, revolutionary and advocate of Hindu nationalism, joined the Mahasabha in May 1937, immediately on his release from confinement at Ratnagiri. Bhai Parmanand stepped aside to have Savarkar chosen president of the 1937 Mahasabha meeting held in Ahmedabad that December."[68] Parmanand continued his own involvement in the Mahasabha, looking on Savarkar as a personal guru. The new president, who would serve in that office until 1943, brought with him a complete ideology of Hindu nationalism.[69] In his speeches and writings Savarkar delineated the basic concepts of an integral nationalism which did not contradict Parmanand's statements, but which were much more fully developed and stated in a Sanskritic terminology. In his presidial address Savarkar outlined these fundamental concepts.

One in national glory and one in national disasters, one in national despairs and one in national hope the Hindus are welded together during aeons of a common life and common habitat. Above all the Hindus are bound together by the dearest, most sacred and most enduring bonds of a common Fatherland and a common Holyland and these two being identified with one and the same country our Bharatbhumai, our India, the National Oneness and homogenity of the Hindu have been doubly sure. If the United States with the warring crowds of Negroes, Germans and Anglo-Saxons, with a common past not exceeding four or five centuries put together can be called a nation—then the Hindus must be entitled to be recognized as a nation par excellence.[70]

Savarkar, in laying claim to cultural unity among Hindus, faced the difficult task of defining them, and in so doing provided a definition of the term Hindu that was accepted by all members of the Mahasabha. "Every one who regards and claims this Bharat-Bhoomi from the Indus to the Seas as his father land and Holyland is a Hindu." In clarifying this idea Savarkar went on to say that "It is not enough that a person should profess any religion of Indian origin, i.e., recognize Hindusthan as *Punyabhū*, his Holyland, but must also recognise it as his *Pitribhū* too, his fatherland as well." This definition lay at the base of *Hindutva*, Hinduness, and Hindu *Rashtravad*, the Hindu nation.[71]

Having clarified the concept of Hindu nationalism, Savarkar redefined the nature of the Mahasabha, emphasizing its political rather than religious or social nature. "The Mahasabha is not in the main a Hindu-Dharma Sabha, but it is preeminently a Hindu-Rahstra-Sabha and is a Pan-Hindu organization shaping the destiny of the Hindu Nation in all its social, political and cultural aspects."[72] For Savarkar the Hindu Mahasabha was primarily a political organization with the goal of creating an independent nation which would be the home of the Hindu people. "The real meaning of Swarajya then, is not merely geographical independence of the bit or earth called India. To the Hindus independence of Hindusthan can only be worth having if that ensures their Hindutva—their religious, racial and cultural identity."[73] Hindus and only Hindus were the true sons of India according to Savarkar, and no Indian nation state could be other than a Hindu state.

After all the Hindus are the bedrock on which an Indian

independent state could be built. Whatever may happen some centuries hence, the solid fact of to-day cannot be ignored that religion wields a mighty influence on the minds of men in Hindusthan and in the case of Mahommedans especially their religious zeal more often than not borders on fanaticism! Love towards India as their Motherland is but a handmaid to their love for their holyland outside of India. Their faces are ever turned towards Mecca and Medina. But to the Hindus Hindusthan being their fatherland as well as their Holyland, the love they bear to Hindusthan is undivided and absolute.[74]

Savarkar's dream of a Hindu nation became the policy of the Mahasabha, breaking any and all ties with either the Indian National Congress or the secular nationalism which it expressed. The Mahasabha now stood for an overt and mature Hindu national-ism opposed to the Congress. Like the Muslim League it too demanded a religiously defined state. For both rested on the political ideals of a religiously-defined people and both pressed for a religiously-defined state, which remained the only way to develop and protect the genius of such a people.

Having delineated the nature of Hindu nationalism, Savarkar called for an electoral policy based on "One man, one vote." He rejected all separate electorates or system of electoral weighting which might hinder the Hindu community from gaining power through its majority status. The Mahasabha also called upon the government to implement the federation scheme as projected in the Government of India Act of 1935. They saw in this a chance to strengthen the princely states and to gain some power for Hindu interests.[75] In addition the conference condemned several Hindu states for suppressing their Hindu subjects, and praised several Muslim states for acting to end discrimination against untouchables.[76] Savarkar mentioned as well "those of our co-religionists and country-men abroad who have been building a greater Hindusthan without the noise of drums and trumpets in Africa, America, Mauritius and such other parts of the world and also to those who as in the Island of Bali are still holding out as remnants of the ancient world empire of our Hindu Race."[77] Thus, Savarkar laid claim to a world basis for Hinduism both contemporary and ancient.

With the arrival of 1938 the Mahasabha became increasingly entangled with the issue of Hindus within various Muslim states,

although the state of Hyderabad drew more attention than any
other. Tension within Hyderabad state grew steadily and finally
exploded into rioting in April. Various Hindu groups were involved,
particularly the Hyderabad Arya Samajists. They were joined by
Aryas from other areas and then members of the Mahasabha. The
ensuing unrest propelled refugees into Maharashtra, drawing the
provincial Mahasabha of that state to the center of the struggle.
Meetings were held throughout Maharashtra in protest and a
delegation was sent to investigate, returning with dramatic tales of
anti-Hindu activities by the police and Muslim gangs.[78] These
reports caused a local Maharashtran leader of the Mahasabha,
Senapati Bapat, to launch a civil disobedience struggle in Hyderabad.
In September Savarkar went south to help in this campaign. Meanwhile Senapati Bapat attempted to enter Hyderabad state, was
arrested, and externed to Poona. He vowed to return again and
did so in November. During this period funds were being raised
both to support acts of civil disobedience and to provide aid for
those refugees who had fled the state.[79] The struggle continued
during the fall and winter in a rather uncoordinated fashion, both
among the Arya Samajists and the Mahasabha members. In
December the Aryas held an All-India Arya Congress at Sholapur
and the Mahasabha met in its annual session at Nagpur. Both
groups passed resolutions to launch major civil disobedience drives
during the coming year if the rights of Hindus were not respected
and protected by the Hyderabad government.[80] On January 11,
1939, these resolutions were forwarded to the prime minister of
the Nizam's government, but produced no acceptable response.

The idea of entering an open struggle with an Islamic state
apparently appealed to Savarkar and to his concept of what needed
to be done in reshaping the Hindu community. At the Nagpur
session he declared his desire to "Hinduise all Politics and Milita-
rise Hindudom," to establish a "Hindu National Front," and to unite
the entire community.[81] At this session the Mahasabha also
created the structure of the "Nizam Civil Resistance Movement"
with three centers at Poona, Nagpur, and Akola, each headed by
a dictator under the overall direction of Savarkar, the supreme
dictator.[82] The twenty-first of each month became Civil Resistance
Day. If featured *hartals* and meetings to sustain popular support
for the campaign.[83] For Savarkar and other Mahasabha leaders
this struggle provided an opportunity to exercise power for the

first time in the Mahasabha's history. All the values of militant Hinduism and of communal unity were demonstrated publicly against a government which stood in their minds for centuries of Islamic dominance.

The Hyderabad *satyāgraha* campaign reached its height in June and July when the Nizam's government ended it by announcing on July 17, 1939, a set of political reforms which would guarantee the civil, cultural, and religious rights of the Hindu community. This was followed on August 17, the Nizam's birthday, with the release of all political prisoners. In response both the Arya Samaj and the Hindu Mahasabha called off their respective civil resistance campaings. The movement drew to a close and left a changed Mahasabha. Under Savarkar's leadership it had engaged in and won its first open conflict with political authority. In future years the Mahasabha was much quicker to use non-violence and direct action than it had ever been in the years preceding the Hyderabad struggle. Yet the Mahasabha, with its completed ideology of Hindu nationalism and its newfound aggressiveness, was overwhelmed by events once more when on September 3, 1939, India was propelled into World War II.

The Mahasabha chose to support the British government's war effort at a working committee meeting held on September 10, 1939, in Bombay, and also to decry those who would attempt to exploit the war as an opportunity for political bargaining. It did, however, define its position in a series of meetings which culminated in the annual session held on December 27 at Calcutta. The Mahasabha demanded complete political independence for India, to be granted at the end of the war. Savarkar outlined a three-pronged program "to remove untouchability, to compel all universities, colleges and schools to make military training compulsory to students and to prepare the Hindu Electorate to the utmost measure possible to vote only for those Hindu Sangathanists who openly pledged to safeguard Hindu interests."[84]

The war years seemed to promise to the Mahasabha a chance of much greater importance, especially within any constitutional negotiations that might take place. The Congress chose the war and so was swept from the political scene, leaving the British, the League, and the Mahasabha, or so it seemed. In response to the departure of Congress, the Mahasabha celebrated Hindu Nation Day on April 14. The Mahasabha was free of Congress competition and its newly-gained importance produced three interviews granted to V.D. Savarkar by the viceroy during July 1940.[85] Once again the Mahasabha reiterated the position that it and it alone could speak for the Hindu community. But by December, when the annual session met in Madura, it appeared that they were less successful than they had hoped. The meetings between the viceroy and Savarkar and the correspondence which followed them proved that the viceroy's responses were "evasive, unsatisfactory and disappointing."[86] Once again British interest in the Mahasabha proved both limited and transitory, emerging only when negotiations with the Congress seemed temporarily suspended.

Within the Mahasabha a shift of leadership took place. V.D. Savarkar was reelected president, but his health had been slowly deteriorating and he could not carry the burdens of that office by himself. Consequently, a working president, Dr. Shyama Prasad Mookerji, was also chosen. Dr. Mookerji had joined the Mahasabha in 1938 as the result of communal tensions in Bengal and the dominance of that province by the government of Fazul ul Huq. This partnership between Savarkar and Mookerji remained throughout 1941-43, as Savarkar continued to serve at least formally as president and Dr. Mookerji as working president. Finally, in December 1944, Dr. Mookerji was chosen president of the Mahasabha and Savarkar retired both in fact and in name.[87] He would not, however, leave the movement until his death and there is no question that he remained the foremost Hindu nationalist in the opinion of all those who supported the Mahasabha.

The years 1940-41, besides witnessing the beginnings of a shift in leadership, also saw the rise of that decenial anxiety, the coming census and Mahasabha reactions to it. Letters, articles, and editorials appeared in the pages of the *Hindu Outlook* which discussed the tactics to be used by Hindus in filling out the 1941 census. Writing about this in June 1940, Parmanand noted that "No country in the world ascribes to the census the peculiar type of political significance which is done in India."[88] All aspects of the census were discussed by numerous contributors, covering such subjects as the untouchables, tribals, how to fill out the forms, and a recent deputation by the Mahasabha to the superintendent of the census.[89] Fear generated by the upcoming census reports had grown steadily from the latter two decades of the nineteenth century. They were heightened by the increasing tie between political power and the numerical status of a given religious community plus worry over possible conversion of Hindus to other faiths. In the year or two preceding each census these anxieties would peak, only to subside and return again ten years later.[90] The growing strife between Hindus and Muslims during these war years acted to heighten and exaggerate this pattern.

During 1942 communal tensions in Bihar were acute, a situation that set the stage for a dispute between the Mahasabha and the provincial government. The Mahasabha had decided to hold its annual session in Bihar, finally choosing the town of Bhagalpur. It was located on the sacred Ganges and in an area of religious strife, both factors which appealed to the Mahasabha. These same factors made the Bihar government extremely reluctant to see the Mahasabha meet in their jurisdiction. Thus, they banned the proposed conference under the Defense of India Rules, after considerable negotiations with the Mahasabha. Meeting on October 9, the working committee formally protested this ban and resolved to hold the annual meeting as scheduled.[91] Planning for the expected struggle went on through October, November, and into December. Savarkar arrived in Calcutta during November and shortly afterward dictators were then appointed to lead civil disobedience if necessary. The first of the Mahasabha officials were seized on December 17. Savarkar, plus numerous other leading Mahasabha members, were arrested on December 25 when they arrived at the Gaya station.[92] Meetings were held both inside and outside of the jail, and afterward the Mahasabha could claim to have held its annual session in spite of the Bihar government. The Bhagalpur struggle, along with the civil disobedience campaign in Hyderabad, a local campaign in Delhi during 1938-39, the Shiv Mandir struggle, and another conflict at the 1943 session in Amritsar, all demonstrated the growing militancy on the part of the Mahasabha.[93] Each of these conflicts provided the Mahasabha with an opportunity to demonstrate its strength and willingness to defend Hindu rights in a period of steadily increasing communal conflict.

Politics and Partition, 1942-47

Paralleling this religious conflict was a period of political stalemate typified by outbreaks of violence, civil disobedience, and, above all else, an intermittent process of negotiations with the British. Throughout this period the Mahasabha sought to win a place in these negotiations. It reiterated its position that the Congress could not speak for the Hindu community, fought against the demand for a Pakistan, or anything that resembled a separate country carved out of India, and called for a one-man, one-vote electoral system.[94] Dr. Mookerji did manage to meet with the viceroy in September 1942, where he demanded immediate independence and the formation of a national government. A similar position was taken by a special committee of the Mahasabha, which then sent its demands to President Roosevelt and Chiang Kai-Sheik.[95] During 1943-44 the Mahasabha claimed to be gaining strength and in April, 1944, held its first All-India State Mahasabha Conference at Shimoga with the aging Savarkar in the chair.[96] This was the first meeting specifically of Mahasabha delegates from princely India. Yet the Mahasabha was unable to play any effective role in the political negotiations leading to independence and any possibility that they might ended with the elections of 1946. The results of these elections demonstrated that only two parties, the Muslim League and the Indian National Congress, had any significant mass support.[97] Partition and independence arrived with the Hindu Mahasabha at the fringe of politics, drawn into a new world which it could not mold to its own ideology and to which it must adjust.

The Mahasabha and Independent India

The creation of independent India provided new opportunities and new challenges to the Mahasabha. Meeting November 30-December 1, 1947, in New Delhi, under the presidency of Dharmveer Bhopatkar, the working committee appointed a special group "to re-orient the policy of the Mahasabha so as to make it more effective as an organ of progressive opinion in the field of social, economic and political uplift of the Indian masses, and parties and organizations with similar objectives." The committee was asked to submit a report by February 1948.[98] The special committee never reported because the assassination of Mahatma Gandhi on January 30, 1948, produced a wave of anti-Mahasabha feeling which overwhelmed the organization. Its leaders and workers were arrested, the organization banned, and in the minds of many citizens it was blamed for the death of Gandhi. The working committee did manage to meet on February 14 to suspend all of its political activities and instead "concentrate on real sangathan work, the relief and rehabilitation of refugees and the solution to our diverse social, cultural and religious problems for the creation of a powerful and well organised Hindu society in independent India."[99] Little was done during the first half of 1948, and on May 27 public attention focused on the opening of the Gandhi murder trial. Shri Bhopatkar acted as defense counsel and succeeded largely in clearing the Mahasabha of responsibility for the assassination. In August the working committee reversed itself and called for the resumption of political activity.[100] This action, however, brought to the fore the deep division of opinion as to how the Mahasabha should proceed.

Dr. Shyama Prasad Mookerji argued that the Hindu Mahasabha needed to change drastically its approach to politics on the grounds that after independence the older methods would not work. He maintained, and has done so since independence, that the Mahasabha should abandon politics and that a new organization with a new name should enter politics to challenge the Congress. This new political party should open its doors to all religious communities, using the broadest possible definition of the term Hindu.[101] With the resumption of politics and the refusal to accept his policy, Dr. Mookerji decided in December 1948, to resign from the working committee and from his position as vice-president of the Mahasabha. This internal debate of political strategy continued into 1951, but in the end the Mahasabha stayed with its longstanding political program and S.P. Mookerji turned to founding the Jan Sangh as an expression of his own ideology.[102] During 1950 and 1951 the Mahasabha became increasingly involved with preparations for the first general elections in the newly independent India. Electoral politics became the new method for restructuring India and thus Hindu society.

The Hindu Mahasabha entered three general elections in search of political victory, but that proved an unattainable goal.

In all areas, the number of seats, per cent of seats, and per cent of votes, the Mahasabha steadily lost support. They found themselves competing unsuccessfully not only against the Congress, but also against the other two openly Hindu parties, the Jan Sangh and the

Mahasabha Results in the
Lok Sabha Elections 1952-62[103]

Election	Number of Candidates	Number of Seats	Per cent of Seats	Per cent of Votes
1952	31	4	0.8	0.95
1957	19	1	0.2	0.86
1962	32	1	0.2	0.44

Ram Rajya Parishad.[104]   After the 1962 election the Mahasabha no longer could be considered a politically active organization. In 1961 the Indian government passed a law banning "communalist" political parties. It did not affect the 1962 elections, but did affect those which followed. Yet the Mahasabha still continues to produce its election manifestos, but the dream of winning at the polls had to be abandoned for the forseeable future.

By the late 1960s the Mahasabha had failed to gain significant political power, yet it remained the spokesman for a religious nationalism opposed to an critical of the existing political system. To the Mahasabha the community, and thus the state, transcended all, man lived for the state and not the state for the individual. "Democracy or any 'cracy' is good only if it strengthens the country and the nation, and if the verdict of the majority is reflected in the government. If on account of democracy, the country disintegrates, people fight against each other and the spirit of nationalism gets weakened, we must ponder and assess the value of such democracy."[105] Democracy has one major weakness in that it stresses individualism rather than responsibility, especially toward the state. "Every citizen must produce for the State and the nation. A citizen must feel that he lives for the State, not for his own self alone." This society should be founded on Hindu socialism and thus would be a moral and spiritual society, with justice and equality for all, and as such would be superior to all other forms of socialism. "Hinduism has all the sympathy for the 'have nots' as expressed by Karl Marx, but it has something more than that. It assesses everything from the viewpoint of Spiritualism.

While Marxian theory is based on pure materialism, Hindutva demands economic uplift and social equality through class-coordination, while Marxism advocates equality through class-conflict." The ancient concept of *varṇāśramadharma* was transformed into a coordinated society with justice for all citizens.

In order to achieve this socio-political dream the Mahasabha called for the establishment of a "collective dictatorship" as a "better alternative to the present Corrupt Democracy for a fixed period of say 10 years to create a psychological oneness and dutifulness." The country would be headed by a five-man junta or *panchayat*, drawing its authority from the president and based on the present Constitution, not unlike the recent Emergency declared by Indira Gandhi. In the Mahasabha state economics would be organized (although there would be no state competition with private trade), Hinduism would be the official religion, cow-slaughter would be banned, and India would follow a foreign policy based on "national interest," with a particular concern for Indians living abroad. There is as well running through all Mahasabha programs an emphasis on national strength and a strongly anti-Pakistan bias.

The Mahasabha made a special appeal to the middle class as the bulwork of the nation and called for the protection of this class. "The middle class intelligentsia has always played an important role in Indian politics, particularly in its recent political history. All the leaders and workers of all political parties today and in recent past belong to this middle class. This is mainly because they have selfless character and spirit of service." Accompanying this special subject was another, namely, opposition to family planning. It was linked both to the long-standing concern for numbers and the rejection of recently passed laws regulating Hindu family life:

No Family Planning By Hindus
Till Communal Laws Are Repealed

Hindu codes enacted by the Congress Government have cut at the very root of Hindu conception of life and society on which the culture and heritage of this land are based. New Hindu Marriage Law legally forbids Hindus alone to have more than one wife, while the Muslims are free to take four wives, though

Muslim countries, even Pakistan, has prohibited the same. Last 1961 census has disclosed that Muslims have increased by 5.32% more than the Hindus of India.

The fears expressed by U.N. Mookerji and Lala Lal Chand still dominate much of the Mahasabha ideology, while the dreams of Parmanand and Savarkar remain embedded in the goals of this organization.

In summing up the goals of the Mahasabha, N.N. Banerjee stated that "the main object of this organization is to establish Hindu Rashtra in Bharat by all legal means. At certain period of the history, the Mahasabha had to fight the mischievous activities of the Muslim League, which opposed its ideal. But the ideal of the Hindu Mahasabha still remains to be achieved. Mahasabha must continue to exist and work till the false concept of secularism introduced by the Congress and its allies are removed from the minds of the Hindus of India, i.e., till the Hindus are Hinduised." At the most fundamental level this ideology rests on a definition of Hindus as a people and not a religion. "The Mahasabha holds that the Hindus are a nation and not a community in Bharat and that they have a right to have a homeland for their own religion, culture and philosophy. We repeat that we want to establish a State in Bharat which will be based on principles of Hinduism." Hinduism for the Mahasabha became, like Islam for the Muslim League and Judaism for the Zionist, the defining factor for a people who in turn look for the establishment of their own state.

The basis of the Hindu Mahasabha and of their tactics rested on the conceptualization of the Hindus as a religiously-defined community. It was recognized as such by themselves, by governmental policy, the census reports, and various constitutional reforms. This vision of Hinduism was held mainly by educated, upper caste Hindus of the cities and towns. Mahasabha leadership was heavily brahminical. Support for the movement came largely but not exclusively from members of the traditional elites—landlords, merchants, and aristocrats. As a result many commentators saw the Mahasabha as a reactionary and revivalistic movement bent on defending orthodoxy and traditional elites. Yet such an assessment is simplistic and ignores the nature of the Mahasabha. Its fundamental goal lay with the defense of the Hindu community and that goal superseded all other aims. Thus, in the case of untouchability, the Mahasabha took a position which demanded radical social change in the Hindu social order, since such change was necessary to defend the community. They also developed a rather un-Hindu concern for egalitarianism when considering the rights and duties of citizens in their ideal nation state. Concern for the community then predominated over defense of tradition or the status quo. The degree of radicalism and militancy stemmed from the perceived threats against the Hindu community. With the creation of independent India and Pakistan such threats have diminished and consequently so has the support of the Mahasabha. The organization still functions and continues to express its ideology of Hindu nationalism. Should the Hindus of South Asia face another period of conflict and insecurity they might turn to the ideas of the Akhil Bharat Hindu Mahasabha.

Notes

1. For a discussion of this subject see the author's article, "Religious Identity and the Indian Census," in *The Census of British India: New Perspectives*, ed. N.G. Barrier (Delhi: Manohar, 1980).

2. An example of one early Hindu society can be found in Pandit Bihari Lal, *Tajawiz Kameli Dharm Sabha* (Lahore: Koh-i-Nur Press, 1873).

3. Pandit Harihar Swarup Sharma, an untitled, unfinished and unpublished Hindi biography of Pandit Din Dayalu Sharma by his eldest son. A printed version of this manuscript is now in the posssesion of the author (hereafter cited as Sharma, *Biography*), p. 84.

4. Kenneth W. Jones, *Arya Dharm: Hindu Consciousness in 19th-Century Punjab* (Berkeley: University of California Press, 1976), pp. 261-94.

5. Ibid., p. 208.

6. Indra Prakash, *A Review of the History and Work of the Hindu Mahasabha and Hindu Sangathan Movement* (Delhi. Akhil Bharatiya Hindu Mahasabha, 1938), pp. 12-13.

7. Ibid., pp. ii-iii.

8. Jones, *Arya Dharm*, p. 282.

9. Upendra Nath Mukerji, *A Dying Race* (Calcutta: Mukerjee and Bose, 1909). The original letter appeared in the *Bengalee* between June 1, 1909, and June 22, in a series of twenty-two letters.

10. Jones, *Arya Dharm*, pp. 289-90.

11. Ibid., p. 287.

12. Indra Prakash, *A Review*, the 1952 edition, p. 17.

13. Jones, *Arya Dharm*, pp. 298-99.

14. Svami Shraddhanand, *Hindu Sangathan, Savior of the Dying Race* (Delhi:

Arjun Press, 1924), p. 107.

15. Ibid., p. 108.
16. Ibid.
17. Ibid., p. 110.
18. Indra Prakash, *A Review*, 1952 edition, p. 15.
19. G.R. Thursby, *Hindu Muslim Relations in British India: A Study of Contro- versy, Conflict and Communal Movements in Northern India, 1923-28* (Leiden: E.J. Brill, 1975), pp. i, 60.
20. Shraddhanand, *Hindu Sangathan*, p. 114.
21. Indra Prakash, *A Review*, 1938 edition, p. 68.
22. Ibid., p. 96;also see p. 85.
23. Ibid., p. 163.
24. Ibid., p. 85.
25. Shraddhanand, *Hindu Sangathan*, p. 116.
26. Ibid., pp. 117-18.
27. Indra Prakash, *A Review*, 1938 edition, pp. 22-23.
28. Thursby, *Hindu-Muslim Relations*, p. 161.
29. Ibid., p. 162.
30. Ibid.
31. Indra Prakash, *A Review*, 1952 edition, p. 27.
32. Shraddhanand, *Hindu Sangathan*, p. 122.
33. Thursby, *Hindu-Muslim Relations*, pp. 35, 83, 150-53.
34. Ibid., p. 163.
35. Indra Prakash, *A Review*, 1938 edition, p. 31.
36. Ibid., p. 169.
37. Ibid., pp. 32, 168.
38. Ibid., p. 90.
39. Ibid., pp. 34-39, and also see pages 228-30.
40. Lajpat Rai, *Writings and Speeches, Volume II, 1920-28*, ed. V.C. Josh (Delhi: University Publishers, 1966), pp. 220-21.
41. Ibid., pp. 32-33; also see Thursby, *Hindu-Muslim Relations*, p. 172.
42. Indra Prakash, *A Review*, 1938 edition, p. 93.
43. Lajpat Rai, *Writings and Speeches*, 2:257.
44. Indra Prakash, *A Review*, 1938 edition, pp. 41-43.
45. See Indra Prakash, *A Review*, 1938 edition, pp. 43-45, and Thursby, *Hindu- Muslim Relations*, p. 172.
46. Prakash, *A Review*, 1938 edition, pp. 126, 171.
47. Ibid., p. 97.
48. Indra Prakash, *A Review*, 1952 edition, pp. 58-61.
49. Indra Prakash, *A Review*, 1938 edition, pp. 59-61, and Thursby, *Hindu- Muslim Relations*, p. 172.
50. Indra Prakash, *A Review*, 1938 edition, p. 105.
51. Ibid., pp. 63-64.
52. Ibid., p. 65.
53. There was no annual session of the Mahasabha during 1930.
54. Indra Prakash, *A Review*, 1938 edition, p. 198.
55. Ibid., p. 199.

56. Ibid.
57. Quotes above from ibid., pp. 134-35.
58. Indra Prakash, *A Review*, 1952 edition, p. 85.
59. Indra Prakash, *A Review*, 1938 edition, p. 69.
60. Ibid , pp. 206-7.
61. Ibid., pp. 72-73.
62. Ibid., p. 142.
63. Ibid., p. 144; from the speech by Shri Shankaracharya at the Lahore Session, October 1936.
64. Ibid., p. 145.
65. Ibid., p. 216.
66. Ibid., p. 217.
67. Indra Prakash, *A Review*, 1952 edition, p. 117.
68. Ibid., pp. 100-102.
69. B.R. Purohit, *Hindu Revivalism and Indian Nationalism* (Sagar, Madhya Pradesh: Sathi Prakashan, 1965), p. 134.
70. V.D. Savarkar, *Hindu Rashtra Darshan (A Collection of the Presidential Speeches delivered from the Hindu Mahasabha Platform)* (Bombay: Laxman Ganesh Khare, 1949), p. 10.
71. Savarkar's writings have been published over a number of years; however, they are available in a multivolume collection, *Samagra Savarkar Wangmaya* (Poona: Maharashtra Prantick Hindu Sabha). His English works are in volumes 5 and 6, published respectively in 1963 and 1964.
72. Indra Prakash, *A Review*, 1938 edition, p. 147.
73. Ibid., p. 152.
74. Ibid., p. 151.
75. Indra Prakash, *A Review*, 1952 edition, p. 104.
76. Indra Prakash, *A Review*, 1938 edition, pp. 219-21.
77. Savarkar, *Hindu Rashtra Darshan*, p. 3.
78. Indra Prakash, *A Review*, 1952 edition, p. 118.
79. Ibid., p. 120.
80. Ibid., p. 125.
81. Quotes are from ibid., p. 110.
82. Quotes are from ibid., p. 124.
83. Ibid., p. 138.
84. Ibid., pp. 143-44 and 146.
85. Ibid., pp. 150-51.
86. Ibid., p. 157.
87. Ibid., p. 198.
88. *Hindu Outlook*, June 1, 1940, p. 5.
89. *Hindu Outlook*, August 17, 1940, p. 14; September 14, 1940, p. 11; October 12, 1940, p. 16; November 23, 1940, pp. 1, 4; November 30, 1940, pp. 12, 16; December 7, 1940, pp. 2, 12, 14, 15, 16.
90. See the author's article, "Religious Identity and the Indian Census," in *The Census of British India: New Perspectives*, ed. N.G. Barrier (Delhi: Manohar, 1980).
91. Indra Prakash, *A Review*, 1952 edition, p. 169.

92. Ibid., pp. 170-71.
93. The Amritsar conflict arose when uniformed members of the Mahabir Dal joined in the procession at this annual meeting. The police objected and a riot resulted. See ibid., p. 189.
94. The working committee of the Mahasabha rejected the Cripps proposals since they contained provisions that allowed provinces to opt out of the proposed government and form their own political groups. See ibid., p. 176.
95. Ibid., pp. 180-81.
96. Ibid., p. 195.
97. Ibid., p. iii; also see pp. 212, 243.
98. Ibid., p. 250. S.P. Mookerji was no longer president, having stepped out in 1946 due to ill health. See ibid , p. 231.
99. Ibid., p. 251.
100. Ibid., p. 256.
101. Balraj Madhok, *Portrait of a Martyr*, *Biography of Dr. Shyama Prasad Mookerji* (Bombay: Jaico, 1969), pp. 93-94.
102. Ibid., pp. 94-110.
103. Robert Hargrave, *India: Government and Politics in a Developing Nation* (New York: Harcourt Brace and World, 1970), pp. 159-60.
104. Ibid., p. 151.
105. Nitya Narayan Banerjee, *Presidential Address, Akhil Bharat Hindu Mahasabha* (New Delhi: Akhil Bharat Hindu Mahasabha, 1968). Quotes below from pages 2 through 28.

PART II

RELIGIOUS THINKERS

11

RAMMOHUN ROY

James N. Pankratz

More has been written about Rammohun Roy than about any other Indian who lived during the first half of the nineteenth century. His contributions to Indian culture are so substantial that many of his contemporaries,[1] whose contributions are significant but much more limited, have been largely neglected in the study of nineteenth-century India.

Rammohun set precedents in many of his activities. He was one of the first Indians to establish his own press and publish pamphlets and books as well as regular newspapers.[2] He was the first, and always the most prominent Indian, to become involved in the campaign for the abolition of *satī* (the concremation of widows).[3] He was, in the early years of the nineteenth century, the most articulate Indian to protest against British administrative injustices.[4] He was one of the most active proponents of a broadly based educational system which would incorporate both Indian and European knowledge.[5] He was a leader in the translation and distribution of traditional religious texts,[6] the focus of numerous religious controversies, and a spokesman for the defense of Indian religious thought against the criticisms of Christian missionaries.[7]

And yet, although Rammohun set many precedents which were later followed by political, social, and religious reformers, many of his contemporaries criticized and opposed him vehemently. They accused him alternately of being a Christian or an atheist.[8] They accused him of attempting to destroy the Hindu tradition, and some accused him of attempting to undermine all religious traditions.

These controversies have attracted the attention of many historians of nineteenth-century India. Rammohun's religious thought has been summarized in numerous books, articles, and public addresses.[9] But there has been very little systematic analysis of his religious thought. During his own lifetime his translations of religious texts and his participation in theological debates generated substantial discussion; but that discussion was more polemical than analytical. Since his death in England in 1833 most discussions of his life and religious thought have been descriptive and adulatory. Only in recent years have a few analyses of his religious thought appeared.[10]

This lack of analysis is unfortunate, since it has obscured several significant issues in the development of religion in modern India.[11] Certainly it has made it very difficult to evaluate the role of Rammohun in the development of modern Indian religious thought. For example, even though it has been common to call him the "father" of modern India, it is not at all clear just who his "children" are. During centenary celebrations of his death in 1933 and bicentenary celebrations of his birth in 1972 it was common to assert that most Indians are spiritual descendants of Rammohun.[12] But this claim is belied, insists R.C. Majumdar, by "the illuminated gates of two thousand Durga Puja pandals in Calcutta whose loudspeakers and *Dhak* or trumpets proclaim in deafening noise, year after year, the failure of Rammohun to make the slightest impression from his point of view on 99.9 per cent of the vast Hindu Samaj either in the 19th or 20th century."[13]

The broad outlines of Rammohun's religious activities are well known. He opposed polytheism and image worship, arguing for an iconoclastic, ethical monotheism. He defended the Hindu tradition against criticisms of Christian and challenged the theological adequacy of trinitarian Christianity. Near the end of his life he established the Brahmo Samaj as a place of worship for those who shared his religious convictions. On closer analysis of these activities, however, several themes emerge which are not only central to his religious thought, but also significant in the modern development of Hindu religious thought.

Early in his public life Rammohun wrote a Persian pamphlet, *Tuhfatul Muwahhidin*,[14] in which he criticised established religious traditions and castigated religious leaders. He concluded his introduction to that work by asserting that "falsehood is common to all religions without distinction."[15] He argued that religious leaders benefited from the fragmentation of religious groups and from the elaboration of religious ceremonies, and therefore they emphasized the importance of customs which distinguished traditions from each other, rather than reason which united them. In fact, reason was denigrated. As Rammohun put it, "When enquiries are made about the mysteries of these things which are so wonderful that *reason* hesitates to believe in their truth, the leaders of religion, sometimes explain for the satisfaction of their followers, that in affairs of religion and faith, reason and its arguments have nothing to do; and that the affairs of religion depend upon faith and Divine Help."[16]

But when the critical power of reason served their purpose, they used it gladly. The adherents of one religion would mock the claims of others, and would delight in showing how unreasonable others were. They disclaimed the sensational miraculous accounts of other religions, they presented elaborate theological refutations of the doctrines of other religions, and they pointed out the inadequacies of the social systems sanctioned by other religions. Each group pronounced judgment on the adherents of other groups and on those who belonged to no specific religious groups.[17]

They did all this without apparently recognizing the inconsistency of their position. For while the adherents of one religion disclaimed the miracles of other groups and mocked the gullibility of those who believed them, they advanced their own accounts of the miracles performed by the power of their gods and their leaders; while they demanded consistency and credibility in the theology of their opponents, they argued that their own theological position should be accepted on other grounds; while they criticized the social implications of other religions, they were unwilling to acknowledge the social injustices which their own religion fostered; and while they pronounced doom on those who rejected their special teachings, they refused to admit that everyone, regardless of religion, enjoyed the goodness and suffered from the discomfort of life equally.[18]

Implicit in Rammohun's criticisms of religious leaders in the *Tuhfatul* were two criteria which he applied throughout his writings. He maintained that the canons of reason demanded universality and freedom from contradiction of all religious statements. In the

Tuhfatul he argued that all religious traditions failed to meet these criteria. In his later writings he was less skeptical and he used these criteria as hermeneutical tools in his attempt to refine and reconcile the doctrines of Hindus and Christians.

In 1818 he used these criteria in a debate about Vaiṣṇava theology with Gosvami.[19] In the course of the debate Gosvami suggested that Kṛṣṇa was the embodiment *ākāra* of *brahman*, but that he was visible only to his disciples. Rammohun replied that this amounted to a plea for special perception for Vaiṣṇavas, and because this contradicted the criterion of universality, it was an unreasonable and unacceptable position. Such a position was dangerous because it made it possible for others to make similar unverifiable claims. If the standards of perception and interpretation were different for various individuals and groups, it would be impossible to authenticate or disprove the various claims one encountered. In religious discussion it would be impossible to distinguish between genuine and spurious statements unless the universal standard of reason was applied uniformly.

Rammohun used similar arguments in his debates with Christians. When he published his summary of the life of Jesus he omitted any references to miracles.[20] Some Christians objected to this omission. Rammohun replied that he was prepared to accept the biblical accounts of miracles as well as the miraculous stories in scriptures of other religious traditions. That was the only consistent position to take once he had accepted the miraculous accounts of one tradition. But by accepting miracles universally, he noted, he was undermining the primary use of these accounts, which was to establish the superiority of a god or a religion.

Rammohun maintained his confidence in reason throughout his writings, but in later years he seemed more aware of the limits of reason. It was reasonable, he wrote, to look at the world and say that it must have a Creator and Governor; but reason alone could not determine the specific characteristics of this Being.[21] This additional information was revealed through the *śāstras*. Reason could not discover this information; but reason could make the *śāstras* intelligible and could reject apparent revelation which was contradictory and not universally valid. Reason was not the only means by which things might come to be known, but it was the final authority on the validity of what was known.

This emphasis on reason as a fundamental constituent of

religious debate was not new in the Hindu tradition. Indian philosophers and theologians have distinguished themselves for centuries
by the rigor and subtlety of their thought. Rammohun's theological
writings reflect a continuity with this tradition of religious debate.

What distinguished Rammohun's thought from his predecessors,
and even from many who have written since his time, was his
insistence that religious traditions must be evaluated by external
rather than internal criteria. He suggested that there is an Archi-
medean point outside all traditions, and that point is reason. The
grounds for validating knowledge are universal, and no claims of
esoteric knowledge outside the normal categories of validation can
be admitted. This undermines the possibility of one tradition being
used as normative for others.

This approach to interreligious discussion provided Rammohun
with the means of defending the Hindu tradition against its Christian
critics and even of challenging the adequacy of trinitarian Chiristian
theology. It was a crucial stage in the Indian response to Europe,
for it undermined the assumption that the Christian tradition should
be normative in interreligious debate. It established a neutral norm,
reason, by which this debate should be evaluated.

Rammohun's Hindu contemporaries appear to have had little
interest in his debates with Christians, and many of them rejected his
rationalistic interpretations of Hinduism.[22] Even succeeding generations of Brahmos were more inclined to devotionalism than rationalism. Yet his contribution to the modern articulation of the
Hindu tradition is great. He defined the essence of the tradition in
terms of the philosophical religious texts rather than the sectarian
literature. In so doing he provided a hermeneutical tool for a
discriminating understanding of the Hindu tradition and a rigorous
response to the Christian tradition.[23] This approach has had a
noticeable effect on the way in which Hindu religious thought has
been reinterpreted during the nineteenth and twentieth centuries.
Even the Ramakrishna movement, a movement which owes its
inspiration to a man who valued religious experience more than
rational reflection, has articulated its understanding of the Hindu
tradition largely in terms of the central religio-philosophical literature, the Upaniṣads and *Brahma Sūtra*, rather than in terms of
sectarian literature or ritual experience.

A second major theme in Rammohun's work emerged out of the
controversies surrounding his personal life. He frequently found

it necessary to justify his own participation in theological discussions. He had to do so generally as well as specifically; that is, he had to explain why a person in his position, a *grhastha* (householder) had the right to be involved in theological debates, as well as why he in particular had this right. In discussing these issues Rammohun articulated his understanding of the role of the *grhastha* in religious life. He also had to defend his practice of engaging in theological debate in public, through pamphlets and newspaper articles. In responding to these questions he set several significant precedents which have greatly affected the context of religious discussion in modern India.

In a debate with Rammohun in 1820, Kavitaker challenged Rammohun's right to be involved in public theological debate.[24] He noted that Rammohun had stated that the purpose of his religious quest was to understand *brahman* more fully. This, insisted Kavitaker, was inappropriate for a householder actively involved in social life. Only those who had completed their social obligations were qualified to devote their time to a fuller understanding of *brahman*.

Rammohun responded by citing numerous examples of people who had become renowned for their knowledge of *brahman*, but who were nevertheless actively involved in the obligations of a householder's life.[25] He also noted, in several of his publications, that the *śastras* praised the qualities of the householder who had realized *brahman*;[26] for this realization could only be accomplished through rigorous control of natural instincts, disciplined meditation on the meaning of self, and careful study of the Vedas.

Sometimes, however, Rammohun's critics raised more specific objections to his participation in theological debate. Kavitaker suggested that Rammohun's disregard for and criticism of rituals and customs was based on Rammohun's unwillingness to adhere to their strict requirements.[27] A writer in the *Samāchār Darpan* suggested that Rammohun's distribution of *śastras* was an indication of his pride and of his arrogant assumption that he could determine what was true religion and what was not.[28] Other writers accused him of indulging in excessive physical pleasures,[29] of eating with foreigners,[30] and of having unjustly amassed his personal wealth.[31] All of his opponents argued that these faults disqualified him from participation in theological discussion. Their conclusion seemed to be reinforced by the fact that although he participated in and patronized several forms of worship during his lifetime, he did not become a spiritual leader in any of them. His life did not have the qualities expected of those who spoke with authority on religious issues.

This was compounded by his frequent criticisms of religious authorities. Already in the *Tuhfatul* Rammohun had accused religious leaders of self-interest. As he put it, "Most of the leaders of different religions, for the sake of perpetuating their names and gaining honour, having invented several dogmas of faith, have declared them in the form of truth by pretending some supernatural acts or by the force of their tongue, or some other measure suitable to the circumstances of their contemporaries, and thereby have made a multitude of people adhere to them so that those poor people, having lost sight of conscience, bind themselves to submit to their leaders."[32] In his later writings he noted that religious leaders emphasized the importance of rituals and image worship because these forms of worship required their services and were a "source of their worldly advantage."[33]

True authority, wrote Rammohun, did not depend upon adherence to dietary regulations, avoidance of foreigners, position, birth, or personal claims to revelation.[34] The basis for authority was knowledge and morality. Institutional religious leaders had legitimate authority only to the extent that they were moral and knowledgeable. *Grhasthas* like himself gained recognition and authority on the same basis, and could, if they met these criteria, be active participants in theological discussions.

It is possible to argue about whether Rammohun's life provided evidence that he complied with the standards of morality and knowledge which he expected of others, but that would be to miss the central issue in this debate. The effect of Rammohun's activities and his arguments about the *grhastha* life was to challenge the context in which theological discussion took place. He stated that such discussion should take place publicly and that it could involve people from all walks of life. The issues involved in such discussions were not only for debate by scholastic groups and religious leaders. Just as Rammohun was interested in a theology which was universally valid, so he wanted that theology to be debated as widely and openly as possible. As a consequence, the individual, like Rammohun, advocating his personal interpretation of an exegetical or theological position, had as much potential authority

as the recognized spokesman for a religious community. The interpretation of the representative of the corporate community had no
more prior claim to validity than the interpretation of any
individual.

Rammohun's opponents not only argued that his involvement in
theological debates was inappropriate because of his *grahstha* life,
they also argued that the open and public context in which he
engaged in these discussions was inappropriate. In fact, Kavitaker
said that the publication of Rammohun's books was undermining
dharma and causing uncounted evils and natural calamities.[35] He
said that if Rammohun was genuinely concerned about the good of
the people he would recognize that most people were not competent
to benefit from reading and hearing the translations of the Upaniṣads
which Rammohun was publishing. It was better for people to read
the simpler *śāstras*, the Purāṇas, before they read the Upaniṣads.
If they read the Upaniṣads without the proper predisposition they
would likely become confused and irreligious.[36]

Rammohun disagreed. He argued that most people were capable
of understanding that the world was created and governed by a
Supreme Being who could not be adequately understood through
the stories in the Purāṇas and who could not be properly worshipped
through the use of images. Therefore, when he established the
Brahmo Samaj in 1828 he inaugurated a form of worship consistent
with these assumptions. The worship was congregational. The
service consisted of readings from the Upaniṣads, *Brahma Sūtra*
and Vedas, exposition of these readings, prayer, and singing. In
the worship service there were no prohibitions against the attendance of any caste, religion, or nationality.[37]

The objections to Rammohun's translations of the Upaniṣads
and to the worship of the Brahmo Samaj were based on a fundamental disagreement over man's natural capacity to understand
religious truth. Hindu social and religious life is based on the
premise that there are significant natural differences between
individuals. This is expressed in the concept of *adhikāra-bheda*,
which denotes the difference in capacity or competence between
people. The *adhikāra*, competence, of one person may be significantly different from the *adhikāra* of the next.

Part of the elaboration of this concept of the uniqueness of
individual inclinations has been the traditional distinction between
the three (sometimes four[38]) ends of man: *kāma* (pleasure),

artha(wealth), and *dharma* (order). It is considered natural that
men may wish to pursue pleasure, wealth, or order. Some will
pursue one more than the others, while other men may pursue all
of these ends simultaneously or serially. It is assumed that the end
which is pursued will be determined by the individual's inclination
and capacity.

Another way in which this concept has been elaborated is
through the discussion of the three basic qualities (*guṇas*) of human
beings; *sattva* (goodness), *rajas* (passion), and *tamas* (ignorance).
Again, it is assumed that each individual will have some unique
combination of these qualities. These categories are broad but
not restrictive. They acknowledge what might be called the
different psychological dispositions of men and describe appropriate
life-styles for those in each category.

This concept of *adhikāra-bheda* is also at the basis of the social
structure. The general *varṇa* structure of Indian society can be
understood as a very basic sketch of several fundamentally
different groups of people. These classifications are not intended
to limit resourcefulness, but they are intended to point to general
characteristics of people in the different roles in society.

This recognition of variety is equally important in religious
matters. Radhakrishnan suggests that Indian religion and philosophy acknowledge the inherent variety in human inclinations by
the very terminology which they use. He points particularly to
the word *darśana*, which is customarily translated as "philosophy."
The word means a view or a viewpoint, a perception; it suggests
that all philosophy is essentially a particular view or vision of
reality held by one person or one school of thought. That view is
based on the particular capacities and experiences which that
"viewer" has had. This means, says Radhakrishnan, that "the
Hindu philosophy of religion starts from and returns to an experimental basis. Only this basis is as wide as human nature itself."[39]
As Aurobindo puts it in *The Foundations of Indian Culture*, "Indian
religion has always felt that since the minds, the temperaments,
the intellectual affinities of men are limited in their variety, a
perfect liberty of thought and of worship must be allowed to the
individual in his approach to the infinite."[40]

Rammohun shared the assumption that people had a great
variety of dispositions and capacities. But he stated repeatedly
that these capacities were being underestimated. In his judgment,

all but a very small minority could understand the basic teachings of the Upaniṣads. He did not expect everyone to benefit fully from the teachings of the Upaniṣads, but he argued that the effect produced in each person would be proportionately successful "according to his state of mental preparation."[41] Certainly he did not agree that people would be confused or made irreligious by hearing the Upaniṣads read and exegeted in theological debate or worship.

Rammohun's discussions of *adhikāra* and the *gṛhastha* life were challenges to the assumption that religious truth was esoteric. This assumption is widespread in the Hindu tradition. One expression of it is the prohibition against permitting certain members of society to hear the Vedas being recited. Another manifestation of this assumption is the distinction made between what can be taught to the initiated (*dīkṣita*) and to the uninitiated (*adīkṣita*). Rammohun's introduction of congregational worship, his public distribution of vernacular translations of Upaniṣads, and his defense of *gṛhastha* participation in theological discussion were among the first signs of an egalitarian emphasis in religous and social reform movements in modern India.

A third major theme which emerges from the life of Rammohun was identified very aptly by Kissory Chand Mitra when he referred to Rammohun as a "religious Benthamite."[42] By this Mitra seemed to mean that Rammohun evaluated religious beliefs and practices largely by whether they seemed to improve human life. There is ample evidence of this in Rammohun's works.

Even in the *Tuhfatul,* where Rammohun was most cynical about religious beliefs, he acknowledged that there was some utility to religion. Two essential religious beliefs, he said, were a belief in a soul and a belief in an afterlife during which the soul was rewarded or punished according to the deeds done in this world.[43] He acknowledged that the truth of these beliefs could not be demonstrated, but yet it was reasonable to perpetuate them. It was reasonable, he said, because these beliefs helped to restrain people from participation in immoral or illegal acts. Religion, in its essence, functioned to maintain social order.

His concern for the social implications of religious doctrine contributed significantly to his interest in the teachings of Jesus. As he wrote in his introduction to *The Precepts of Jesus,* "This simple code of religion and morality is so admirably calculated to elevate

men's ideas to high and liberal notions of God . . . and is so well
fitted to regulate the conduct of the human race in the discharge of
their various duties to themselves, and to society, that I cannot but
hope the best effects from its promulgation in the present form."[44]

It was also largely his concern for the social well-being of his
countrymen which made him so relentless in his attack on polytheism and image worship. He was convinced that polytheism and
image worship resulted in the destruction of "every humane and
social feeling."[45] In the introduction to his *Translation of an
Abridgement of the Vedant*[46] he charged that the "rites introduced
by the peculiar practice of Hindoo idolatry" destroy the "texture
of society." He acknowledged that significant religious change
needed to occur for the sake of his countrymen's "political advantage and social comfort." His campaign against *sati* was a good
example of his own determination to bring about such change.

Rammohun also opposed polytheism and image worship because
he was convinced that they led to immorality. Stories of Kṛṣṇa,
he wrote, encouraged the belief that uncleanness, nudity, debau-
chery, and murder were sanctioned by the example of Kṛṣṇa.
The worship of Kālī was even more offensive, since it included
human sacrifice.[47]

There seems to be ample evidence to support a growing number
of scholars who have recently interpreted Rammohun primarily as
a religious utilitarian whose central concern was the well-being of
society. Susobhan Sarkar remarks that Rammohun's reason for
"reviving public interest in the Vedanta was prompted by his desire
to promote the comfort of the people and to unite the different
groups into which society had split up. He considered the forms
of direct worship as a liberation from priestly tyranny and a means
of realization of human brotherhood."[48] Rammohun's social
concern signalled a change from an emphasis on "mystery and
metaphysics to ethics and philanthropy."[49] This change of
emphasis which Rammohun's work expresses so clearly is characteristic of a substantial amount of nineteenth-century Indian thought.
Theology and metaphysics became tools of ethics and social
change.

Rammohun's contributions to modern Indian religious thought
are diverse. Some of them, such as his emphasis on the Upaniṣads
and *Brahma Sūtra*, and his iconoclasm, are a continuing legacy
maintained by the Brahmo Samaj. Others have been more diffuse

in their impact; that is, it is difficult to determine what influence Rammohun's position has had on subsequent thinkers. Whether those continuities can be traced or not, several significant features of his religious thought can be noted in summary.

First, Rammohun's rationalistic theism provided him with a hermeneutic by which to evaluate critically his own tradition and Christianity. In the early years of the nineteenth century this was a useful means of refining the Hindu tradition and challenging the Christian. He could be a student of "comparative religion" without making one tradition normative for others.[50] Second, Rammohun's arguments in support of the *grhastha* involvement in religious discussion, and his personal campaign of publication and debate, contributed to the individualization of religious authority. To some extent he was assisted by technology. Printing technology has made it possible for more individuals to read scriptures outside the influence of religious leaders. Privately nurtured interpretations soon began to question the accepted wisdom of traditional authorities. Rammohun not only took advantage of the possibility of doing this, he also argued strongly in favor of greater individualization of authority. Third, Rammohun's utilitarian approach to religious thought and social practice challenged the established priority of salvation (*mokṣa*) over social order (*dharma*). Rammohun wrote very little about salvation but a great deal about the social order.[51] Fourth, Rammohun shifted the focus of ethical discussion from asceticism to humanitarianism. He argued that the many regulations of food and drink were burdens which obscured people's ability to see and respond to the needs of other people.

Although Rammohun never systematically developed these aspects of his thought into a unified philosophy, it is worth noting that these features of his thought provide adequate premises for articulating a philosophy of a secular state.

Notes

1. For example, Dwarkanath Tagore (1764-1846) was a dominant influence in early Indo-British commercial relationships. Radhakanta Deb (1784-1867) was instrumental in the development of numerous educational and publishing projects. Mritunjay Vidyalankar (1762-1819) was an instructor at the College of Fort William and later a pandit attached to the Supreme Court.

2. Rammohun's press was known as the Unitarian Press, established in 1823. He used it to publish his pamphlets. His newspapers, the Bengali *Sambād Kaumudī* and the Persian *Mirat-ul-Akhbar*, began in 1821 and 1822 respectively and were not published at his own press. For more information about his publishing activities see Sophia Dobson Collet, *The Life and Letters of Raja Rammohun Roy*, 3rd ed. (Calcutta: Sadharan Brahmo Samaj, 1962), pp. 157-205 *passim*.

3. Collet, *Life and Letters*, pp. 251-66, 346, 537.

4. Rammohun's most famous protests were against the Press Ordinance of March 14, 1823 (see Collet, *Life and Letters*, pp, 423-54), and the Jury Act which became effective in 1827 (see Collet, *Life and Letters*, pp. 266-69).

5. His precise involvement in the establishment of educational institutions such as the Hindu College has been questioned in recent years. See Ramesh Chandra Majumdar, *On Rammohun Roy* (Calcutta: The Asiatic Society, 1972), pp. 20-39. But his commitment to a broadly based educational system is not in dispute.

6. He was aware that he was establishing a precedent by doing this. He remarks on this in "A Defense of Hindoo Theism" (1817), in *The English Works of Raja Rammohun Roy*, eds. Kalidas Nag and Debajyoti Burman (Calcutta: Sadharan Brahmo Samaj, 1946), 2 : 85. Hereafter this collection of his English writings is referred to as *Works*.

7. A list of Rammohun's publications is included in Collet, *Life and Letters*, pp. 525-41. More recently a list of Rammohun's religious publications has been included in Ajit Kumar Ray, *The Religious Ideas of Rammohun Roy* (New Delhi: Kanak Publications, 1976), pp. 99-103.

8. Two terms are used interchangeably here. *Nāstik* refers to one who does not believe, an atheist. *Pāsaṇḍa* refers to a heretic or to one who falsely assumes the character of a Hindu.

9. The most extensive summaries appear throughout the biography written by Collet; in Amitabha Mukherjee, *Reform and Regeneration in Bengal, 1774-1823* (Calcutta: Rabindra Bharati University, 1968), pp. 125-202; and in several Bengali biographies, most notably Nagendranath Chattopadhyay, *Mahātmā Rājā Rāmmohun Rāyer Jiban Charit*, 5th ed. (Allahabad: Indian Press Ltd., 1928).

10. The most noteworthy analyses are those by Ajit Kumar Ray, *The Religious Ideas of Rammohun Roy*; by Sisir Kumar Das, in Niharranjan Ray, ed., *Rammohun Roy: A Bi-Centenary Tribute* (New Delhi: National Book Trust, 1974), pp. 71-91; and by several authors in V.C. Joshi, ed., *Rammohun Roy and the Process of Modernization in India* (New Delhi: Vikas Publishing House, 1975).

11. One such issue is the development of religion in eighteenth-century India. For a brief description of how eighteenth-century religious thought is usually dismissed, see James N. Pankratz, "The Religious Thought of Rammohun Roy" (Ph.D. diss., McMaster University, 1975), pp. 7-10.

12. This claim was made often during the 1972 bicentenary celebrations, most dramatically in a speech read on behalf of Indira Gandhi in Calcutta in June at the National Library.

13. Majumdar, p. 40.
14. Published in English as *Tuhfatul Muwahhuddin or a Gift to Deists*, trans. Moulavi Obaidullah el Obaide (Calcutta: Sadharan Brahmo Samaj, 1949).
15. *Tuhfatul*, n.p.
16. Ibid., p. 11.
17. Ibid., pp. 11-12, 16-17.
18. Ibid., pp. 6-7.
19. Rāmmohun Rāy, *Rāmmohun Granthābalī*, eds. Brajendranath Bandyopadhay and Sajanikanta Das (Calcutta: Bangiya Sahitya Parishat, n.d.), 2 : 41-64. Hereafter cited as *Granthābalī*.
20. "The Precepts of Jesus: The Guide to Peace and Happiness" (1820) in *Works*, 5 : 1-54.
21. This is essentially his point in his "Translation of an Abridgement of the Vedant" (1816), in *Works*, 2 : 57-72.
22. In fact, his involvement in theological debates with Christians seemed to convince many of his contemporaries that he was probably inclined toward Christianity and thus a traitor to his Hindu tradition.
23. His response to Christians is contained in various publications now collected in *Works*, vols. 4-6. Christian criticisms were mostly directed against the sectarian rather than the philosophical literature, and Rammohun's approach diverted the criticisms substantially.
24. This debate may be found at *Granthābalī*, 2 : 67-93.
25. Among the many examples Rammohun cited were Janaka, an ancient philosopher-king of Mithilā; Yājñavalkya, a famous sage and teacher; and Vasiṣṭha, the sage of the *Ṛg Veda*, Epics, and Purāṇas.
26. See especially "Translation of the Ishopanishad" (1816) in *Works*, 2 : 43-44; and "Brahmaniṣṭha Grhasther Lakshman" (1826), in *Granthābalī*, 4 : 29-33.
27. *Granthābalī*, 2 : 75.
28. Brajendranath Bandyopadhyay, ed., *Sangbād Patre Sekāler Kathā*, 2nd ed. (Calcutta: Bangiya Sahitya Parishat, (1949), 1 : 327.
29. Gaurikanta Bhattacharya, *Jñanānjan*, 2nd ed. (Calcutta, 1838), pp. 4, 14-17.
30. Collet, *Life and Letters*, p. 125, records how careful Rammohun was not to give evidence for this accusation.
31. Kavitaker raises this issue at *Granthābalī*, 2 : 72-73.
32. *Tuhfatul*, p. 1.
33. *Works*, 2 : 88.
34. Ibid., 2 : 114, 159.
35. *Granthābalī*, 2 : 71-72.
36. Ibid., p. 78.
37. For a description of the establishment of the Brahmo Samaj see Collet, *Life and Letters*, pp. 209-50. The Trust Deed outlining the purposes of the Brahmo Samaj is reprinted in ibid., pp. 468-77.
38. The fourth end *mokṣa* (liberation), is sometimes regarded as one of this group and at other times is considered a separate goal which involves turning away from the other three.

39. S. Radhakrishnan, *The Hindu View of Life* (London: Unwin Books, 1960), p. 16.
40. Sri Aurobindo, *The Foundations of Indian Culture* (Pondicherry: Sri Aurobindo Ashram, 1959), p. 138.
41. *Works*, 2 : 132.
42. Kissory Chand Mitra, "Rammohun Roy," *Calcutta Review*, 4 (July-December, 1845) : 388.
43. *Tuhfatul*, p. 5.
44. *Works*, 5 : 4.
45. Ibid., 2 : 52.
46. Ibid., 2 : 60.
47. Ibid., 2 : 92.
48. Susobhan Sarkar, *Bengal Renaissance and Other Essays* (New Delhi: People's Publishing House, 1970), p. 11.
49. Iqbal Singh, *Rammohun Roy* (Bombay: Asia Publishing House, 1958), p. 78.
50. Many authors have credited him with being the "first student of comparative religion."
51. His most clear, although very short, statement about salvation/liberation is in *Works*, 2 : 197-98.

12

SVAMI DAYANANDA SARASVATI

Arvind Sharma

Modern India, that is to say, the India of the nineteenth and the twentieth centuries, produced several remarkable thinkers to whose originality the other chapters of this book bear witness. But when we speak of Svami Dayananda Sarasvati,[1] we are talking of a case in which both the man and his message were not merely original but perhaps unique. He was unique as a man in the sense that while all the other thinkers of the period under discussion had an effective knowledge of the English language, Svami Dayananda was innocent of it. "When Keshub expressed his regret that Dayananda did not know English, since if he had he could have become his companion on his next visit to Britain, Dayananda retorted that it was a greater pity that the leader of the Brahmo Samaj knew no Sanskrit and spoke in a language most Indians could not understand."[2] And his message was unique in the sense that while the other thinkers of his time were moving away, in one way or another, from the dogma of infallible revelation, Svami Dayananda declared that "the Vedas were not only true, but they contained all truth, including the ideas of modern science."[3]

This essay, therefore, naturally falls in several parts. The first part will deal with the man, especially with his changing ideological patterns and the directions of that change. This will naturally lead us finally to identify his more mature thought, chronologically and hopefully logically as well. In the rest of the essay his views on Vedic revelation, attitudes to other religions, reconversion to Hinduism and social and political issues will be considered.

Changing Ideological Patterns

To being with, the main events of the life of Svami Dayananda (1824-83) may be narrated, though necessarily with a certain economy.

Dayananda was born into a Brahman family in a princely state of Gujarat, a section of western India relatively untouched by British cultural influence. His well-to-do father instructed him in Sanskrit and Shaivism from the age of five, but Dayananda revolted against idol-worship at fourteen, and to avoid being married ran away from home at nineteen to become a sannyasi (religious mendicant) of the *Sarasvati* order. He spent the next fifteen years as a wandering ascetic, living in jungles, in Himalayan retreats, and at places of pilgrimage throughout northern India. A tough, blind old teacher completed his education by literally beating into him a reverence for the four Vedas and a disdain for all later scriptures.

For the rest of his life Dayananda lectured in all parts of India on the exclusive authority of the Vedas. Time after time he challenged all comers to religious debates, but few could withstand his forceful forensic attack, idol-worship is not sanctioned by the Vedas, he pointed out, nor is untouchability, nor child marriage, nor the subjection of women to unequal status with men. The study of the Vedas should be open to all, not just to brahmans, and a man's caste should be in accordance with his merits. Such revolutionary teachings evoked the wrath of the orthodox and numerous attempts were made on Dayananda's life. His great physical strength saved him from swordsmen, thugs, and cobras, but the last of many attempts to poison him succeeded. Like John the Baptist, he accused a princely ruler of loose living, and the women in question instigated his death by having ground glass put in his milk.[4]

An ideological-analytical approach, as opposed to a merely biographical-factual one as presented above, enables one to distinguish six more or less clearly marked phases in Dayananda's life. The first one may be dated from 1824-45 and represents the period of his stay with his family, during the course of which he formed an intense desire to seek his personal salvation—a decision to which the loss of his sister and favourite uncle must have made its contribution.[5]

The second phase must be dated from 1845-60, when the young man, now turned Svami, roamed the sacred regions of north India,[6] and especially the Himalayas, in search of salvation through yoga, during the course of which he temporarily took to using hemp as well.[7]

The third phase, which may be dated from 1860-67, is represented by his discipleship of Virajananda,[8] which was a turning point in his career as it turned him from a private spiritual aspirant into a public religious crusader.

The fourth phase is represented by the period from 1867-72 which witnessed Dayananda's first efforts in the direction of reforming Hinduism. It was also a formative period in the growth of his new ideology. The climactic event during this phase was provided by the famous debate over the Vedic sanction of idolatry at Banaras.

Thi fifth period, from 1872-75, is extremely significant, as it saw Svami Dayananda come in contact with the Hindu elite of Calcutta. This did not affect the content of his teachings,[9] but did much to change his style. As a matter of fact Keshub Chandra Sen gave "the Svami two useful concrete pieces of advice, which he readily accepted," namely, that the Svami cover his body fully rather than appear in a loincloth, and that he lecture in Hindi rather than Sanskrit. It was also at Calcutta that the Svami discovered the importance of public lectures and publication.[10] His public lectures were enthusiastically received and the *Satyārtha Prakāśa*, his well-known work, appeared in 1875.[11]

The last phase of the Svami Dayananda's life is covered by the period 1875-83, which saw the formation of the Arya Samaj and its success, especially in the Punjab. It ends with his death in the course of his efforts to enlist the rulers of Rajputana on his side. During this period he also produced a revised edition of the *Satyārtha Prakāśa*, among other works.

We will now concern ourselves with a few examples of the changing patterns of his values. It may be particularly useful to choose those areas in which his thoughts changed significantly over the years. It may further be useful to choose aspects of mature thought in some important areas associated with Svami Dayananda which give the impression of being set from the very beginning, though they really underwent a process of gradual crystallization.

The last chapter of the *Satyārtha Prakāśa* (last edition)[12] contains a statement of Svami Dayananda's beliefs and disbeliefs. It might be illuminating to subject some of these to the analytical process outlined above.

> (1) "I hold that the four Vedas (the divine revealed knowledge and religious truth comprising the Samhita or Mantras) as infallible and as authority by their very nature."[13]

Up until 1870 Svami Dayananda seems to have held the view that the Brahmanas could be considered as Veda along with the Samhita portions.[14] As a matter of fact the process of the gradual narrowing of the focus on the Samhita and especially on the *Rg-veda-samhitā* alone had been detected long ago by B.P. Pal, as the historian R.C. Majumdar pointed out[15] when he observed:

> The absolutely authoritative character of the Vedas, and Vedas alone, formed the fundamental creed of Dayananda. At first he included within the Vedas both Brahmanas and Upanishads, but when it was pointed out that the Upanishads themselves repudiated the authority of the Vedas as the highest or the only revelation, Dayananda modified his views. Ultimately the Samhita portion of the Vedas, and particularly the *Rigveda Samhita*, was alone held to be the real Vedic revelation, at least for all practical purposes.[16]

We may next take a case which exemplifies change in theological orientation over the years.

> (2) "There are three things beginningless: namely, God, souls and *Prakriti* or the material cause of the universe."[17]

This is a fairly standard position in non-advaitic Vedānta but in the first edition of the *Satyārtha Prakāśa* Svami Dayananda had propounded what is a strikingly Christian idea: the concept of creation *ex nihilo*![18] The Lord was regarded as being close to a creator in the Christian sense in 1875. But this meant that the universe was not beginningless and endless—and this is indeed what Svami Dayananda believed. The theological transformation involved here has been discussed in detail by J.T.F. Jordens.[19]

(3) "Moksha or salvation is the emancipation of the soul from all woes and suffering . . . and resumption of earthly life after the expiration of a fixed period of enjoying salvation."[20]

In 1875, however, Svami Dayananda had declared *mokṣa* to be an eternal state.[21] But by the time of the second edition of the *Satyārtha Prakāśa*, Swami Dayananda had departed from this position and come round to the view expressed above. The logic underlying it seemed to relate to the logic of karma. J.T F. Jordens points out:

The second edition omits all these special powers of the *sannyasi*: he remains bound by works. It clearly states that the *jiva's* knowledge, even in *moksha*, can never become unlimited, and goes as far as declaring that "the relation between the *jiva* and *karma* is an eternal one." The essence of Dayananda's argumentation is as follows: *moksha* is achieved by the application of certain means, these being right actions. Whatever change is affected by the application of means can be undone by the application of means of the same order. *Moksha*, a change of condition effected by human action, can be undone by human action. Man's activity itself is an eternal quality, but its effects, even its major effects, bondage and liberation, are necessarily of limited duration: *moksha*, therefore, must be limited in time.[22]

Sometimes, even when the ideas themselves did not change, the logic underlying them was extended or refined over time. In 1875 Svami Dayananda was perhaps already moving in the direction that the Sūdras had a right to study the Vedas, but the argument had to be somewhat circuitous. He began by maintaining that "the Shūdras who in a properly structured society are those lacking the necessary intelligence, are excluded"[23] from the study of the Vedas. It could, however, be understood that this did not "refer to the Shūdras *of the time*, because the society has not yet been properly structured."[24] Technically, therefore, the Sūdras were to be excluded, but actually it may not be so. Subsequently, however, Svami Dayananda became forthright in the advocacy of the right of the Sūdras to study the Vedas and liberated himself from the vestigial traces of the orthodox tradition by arguing that could God be "so biased as to forbid the study of the Vedas to them and prescribe it for the twice-born?"[25] He also brings his familiarity with the Vedic corpus to bear on the point and quotes Vedic verses indicating that Vedas could be studied by the Sūdras. The verse quoted is *Yajur-Veda* 26.2.[26]

Thus it is clear that the thought of Svami Dayananda was molded by the experiences he had, the men he met, and the situations he encountered. His mental firmament, like that of any dynamic thinker, was in motion even while giving the appearance of being unchanging. If, however, there was any orientation to this cosmic movement of his thought, it is to be found in the polar role the concept of Vedic revelation came to play in it. After a somewhat diachronic study of his ideas, it is to a synchronic study of this concept of his to which we must now turn.

Scriptural Authority

When the Arya Samaj was founded by Svami Dayananda to propagate his ideas, one of these was represented by the motto: "Go back to the Vedas."[27] What then was Svami Dayananda's attitude towards the Vedas as representative of scriptural authority within Hinduism?[28]

The "Veda is precisely the sign, perhaps the only one," of Hindu *orthodoxy*,[29] as distinguished from Hinduism, so that one need not be surprised if Svami Dayananda offers the traditional salutation to the Vedas. But while "even in the most orthodox domains, to reverence the Vedas ha[d] come to be a simple 'raising of the hat,' in passing, to an idol by which one no longer intends to be encumbered later on,"[30] it became, in the case of Dayananda, a direct "source of inspiration."[31] Dayananda preached in "favour of returning to an unqualified adherence to the Veda, and claimed that explicit principles of pure monotheism and of social and moral reform could be found in the hymns."[32] A key aspect, therefore, of Dayananda's attitude towards spiritual authority in his wholehearted acceptance of the Vedas, which he regarded vitally and not merely formally as the "ultimate source of religious authority."[33] This attitude may be contrasted with that of Ramarkrishna who "did not fear to teach that 'the truth is not in the Vedas, one should act according to the Tantras',"[34] although elsewhere he "is more moderate, or let us say, indifferent."[35] And although Vivekananda's attitude was perhaps "more deferential"[36] even he is known to have remarked that "in India . . . if I take certain passages of the Vedas, and I juggle with the text and give it the most impossible meaning . . . all the imbeciles will follow me in a crowd."[37] These remarks may be contrasted with the forthright statement by Dayananda in his statement of Beliefs and Disbeliefs (svamantavyāmantavya) on the acceptance of Vedic authority quoted earlier.

The intensity of belief in the Vedas Dayananda seems to share with the Mīmāṁsā and Vedānta schools of Hindu philosophy,[38] although the form of his belief seems to be more in the tradition of the Nyāya school, for he bases the authoritativeness of the Vedas not on the doctrine of their eternal self-existence,[39] but on the Nyāya belief that "the Vedas were uttered by Īsvara himself."[40]

However, although Svami Dayananda agrees with most of Hinduism in paying homage to the Vedas and surpasses much of it in his commitment to them,[41] he departs radically from tradition in his definition of the corpus of literature which may legitimately be regarded as the Veda.[42] Thus, although "In accepting the Vedas as the only authority Dayananda was practically on a line with Raja Rammohan Roy,"[43] he differed with him both in the definition of the corpus of the Veda and in its interpretation. Rammohun Roy turned to the Upaniṣads for inspiration, but though at first Dayananda "included within the Vedas both Brahmanas and Upanishads . . . when it was pointed out that the Upanishads themselves repudiated the authority of the Vedas as the highest or the only revelation, Dayananda modified his views."[44]

Dayananda also held to "the four Brahmanas of the four Vedas, the six Angas and Upangas, the four Up-Vedas, and the

1127 *Shakhas* of the *Vedas* as books composed by *Brahma* and other *Rishis*, as commentaries on the *Vedas*, and having authority of a dependent character. In other words, they are authoritative insofar as they are in accord with the *Vedas*, whatever passages in these works are opposed to the *Vedas*, I hold them as unauthoritative".[45] This rather "narrow" conception of the scriptural base of Hinduism is generally believed to have limited the appeal of his movement.[46] D.S. Sarma writes:

> It is regrettable that, while insisting on the authority of the Veda, Swami Dayananda has not sufficiently emphasized the improtance of the Upanishads, which explain and amplify what is really valuable in the Samhita, and that he has not recognized the authoritativeness of a scripture like the *Gita*, which is the essence of all the Upanishads, because he was apparently repelled by the Puranic pictures of Krishna *given* in the *Vishnu Purana* and the *Bhagavata*. He could have strengthened his hand a thousand-fold if he had included the *Gita* in his canon and rightly interpreted its dynamic gospel of action so congenial to his own temper and outlook. As it is, Dayananda arbitrarily limited the extent of the Hindu religious canon and thus to a certain extent stultified himself, as the leaders of the Brahmo Samaj stultified themselves by their blatant rationalism and the right of private individual judgment at every step in going through the Hindu scriptures. But probably the very limitation of his canon added to the powerfulness of his message and served his immediate purpose of purifying Hinduism and bringing all Hindus under one banner and enabling them to ward off the attacks of alien religions in India. For there is no doubt that the Arya Samaj, which Dayananda founded, is the church militant in the bosom of Hinduism.[47]

The significance of these developments may now be assessed. The attitude of Svami Dayananda may be described as "dogmatic" in that he accepted the doctrine of the infallibility of the vedic authority in Hindu philosophical speculation.[48] According to B.C. Pal, in this Dayananda was following the example set by Christianity and Islam,[49] although Dayananda criticized severely the claims of Christianity and Islam to be regarded as revealed religions.[50] Dayananda was in turn criticized severely by Mahatma Gandhi for the severity of his criticisms.[51] Mahatma Gandhi's criticisms seem to stem at least in part from the fact that Dayananda's position seems to repudiate Hindu tolerance of other religions. One may note here, however, "the view of Jaimini and Kumārila (acceptable to all authorities such as Śaṅkara and Rāmānuja) that the Vedic faith is exclusive" which "shows that Hinduism is as exclusive as the Semitic faiths and brooks no rivals".[52] Thus Dayananda's dogmatic exclusiveness could as well be related to a strand within the Hindu tradition itself. It may be pointed out, however, that although Dayananda gave his own interpretation of the Vedas, "theoretically every member of the Arya Samaj is free to form his own conclusions," though "in practice, the *Samhita* of the Rigveda, as *interpreted by Dayananda* . . . formed the bedrock on which stood the entire structure of Arya Samaj".[53] If, as will be shown later, Dayananda (1) meant only the Saṁhitā portions of the Vedas by the term Veda;[54] and (2) also believed in the doctrine of *karma* and rebirth[55] then (3) if in the Vedas and earlier Brahmana literature the doctrine of transmigration is nowhere clearly mentioned,[56] one is faced with something of a problem.[57] Another consequence of this concept of the Vedas was that Dayananda came to recommend certain social usages which had gone out of vogue. Thus *Ṛg-Veda* X.40.2 refers to *Niyoga* or levirate.[58] Dayananda allows it,[59] although it had gone out of vogue.[60] Dayananda has been criticized for trying to revive an "immoral" practice.[61]

Dayananda's emphasis on the Saṁhitā raises not only the theological and sociological issues; his concept of scriptural authority also raises epistemological issues. In Hindu thought the means of valid knowledge (*pramāṇas*) constitute one list and the sources of *dharma* (*dharma-mūla*) (see Manusmṛti II.6, etc.) a separate list, although in both the cases vedic authority is regarded as supreme. Dayananda, working on the basis of the supremacy of Vedic authority, it would appear, combines these two lists under the name of *parīkṣās* or tests of knowledge into one and remarks: "There are five kinds of tests of knowledge. The first is the attributes, works and nature of God, and the teachings of the *Veda*. The second is eight kinds of evidence such as direct cognition, etc. The third is 'Laws of Nature'.

The fourth is conduct and practice of *aptas*; the fifth is purity and conviction of one's own conscience. Every man should sift truth from error with the help of these five tests, and accept truth and reject error."[62]

Dayananda's attitude toward the scriptures of Hinduism differed from that of many other leaders of the Hindu renaissance not only on the question of what these scriptures were but also the manner in which they were to be interpreted. Thus, while Raja Rammohun Roy " 'accepted the authority, of the Vedas as interpreted by the exegetics of ancient Hinduism', Dayananda altogether rejected the commentaries of Sāyaṇa and Mahīdhara and did not consider any other commentary as binding on anyone. Dayananda therefore gave his own interpretation,"[63] which, strikingly, though at variance with both the traditional and the modern approaches to the Vedas, tries to read in the Vedas the results of modern science. Thus, Dayananda's approach is not "scientific" in the scholarly sense but is science-oriented in the sense that he uses his scholarship to show the presence of science in the Vedas. Such an interpretation of the Vedas is of profound significance in the context of his attitude towards scriptural authority. This significance may be summarized thus:

> The word *Veda* means "knowledge". It is God's knowledge, and therefore pure and perfect. This transcendent and heavenly knowledge embraces the fundamental principles of all the sciences. These principles God revealed in two ways: (1) in the form of the four Vedas . . . and (2) in the form of the world of nature, which was created according to the principles laid down in the Vedas. . . . The Vedas, then, being regarded as "the Scripture of true knowledge", the perfect counterpart of God's knowledge so far as basic principles are concerned, and the "pattern" according to which Creation proceeded, it follows that the fundamental principle of Vedic exegesis will be the interpretation of the Vedas in such a way as to find in them the results of scientific investigation.[64]

The significance of this position, in the light of the traditional Hindu attitude towards scriptural authority, is nothing less than revolutionary. The traditional Hindu position on scriptural

authority, especially as developed in the school of Advaita
Vadānta, has been that scriptural authority is supreme *only* in the
suprasensuous realm. It is not supreme in the realm of experience represented by the senses, the mind, etc., for *pramāṇas* such
as perception and inference suffice to provide us with valid knowledge of this realm of experience. It is in matters relating to
dharma, or the determination of right and wrong, and *brahman*,
or the nature of ultimate reality, that scriptural authority is
supreme. Hence Śaṅkara's well-known statement that even if a
thousand scriptures were to tell us that fire is cold they will have
to be disregarded because the scripture here is making a statement outside its proper jurisdiction.[65]. Whether fire is hot or
cold is to be determined properly by *pratyakṣa* and not by *śabda*.
Such an attitude towards scriptural authority disjoins religion and
science and may in fact be one of the factors why the conflict
between religion and science was felt less keenly within Hinduism
than in certain other religions. Svami Dayananda, however,
reverses this position by bringing the results of scientific investigation within the scope of scriptural inquiry.

Svami Dayananda thus gave his own interpretation to the
Vedas, defined as consisting of the *Saṁhitā* portion only.[66] If
the sincerity of Dayananda's motives has occasionally been doub-
ted[67] his methods and results have far more often been criticized[68]
with varying degrees of intensity.[69] In view of this generally
adverse reception to his interpretation, for which Max Muller
uses the expression "incredible"[70] and which Renou describes as
"extremely aberrant"[71] but not without realizing its cultural
significance, it is remarkable that Sri Aurobindo should remark:

There is then nothing fantastical in Dayananda's idea that the
Veda contains truths of science as well as truths of religion.
I will even add my own conviction that the Veda contains
other truths of a science which the modern world does not at
all possess, and, in that case, Dayananda has rather under-
stated than overstated the depth and range of the Vedic
wisdom. Immediately the character of the Veda is fixed in the
sense Dayananda gave to it, the merely ritual, mythological,
polytheistic interpetation of Sayanancarya collapses, and the
merely mateological and materialistic European interpretation collapses. We have, instead, a real scripture, one of the

world's sacred books and the divine word of a lofty and noble religion.[72]

One circumstance renders Aurobindo's endorsement remarkable. While Dayananda was innocent of English and Western culture, Aurobindo "was sent by his father to England when he was only seven . . . and returned to India only in his twenty-first year, after completing his education in London and Cambridge. He became a scholar in Greek and Latin and got record marks in these languages in the Indian Civil Service Examination. He also learned French, German and Italian and could read Dante and Goethe in the original."[73] Inasmuch as the modern Western interpretation of the Vedas draws on comparative linguistics, that Aurobindo, notwithstanding his wide acquaintance with classical and modern languages should not have opted for the Western method (or for that matter, the traditional Indian) but for one "who stands absolutely alone as an interpreter of the Veda"[74] is remarkable. It should be noted, however, that Dayananda himself regarded his beliefs to be "in conformity with the beliefs of all the sages from Brahma down to Jaimini."[75] Now back once more to Aurobindo. Is it a mere coincidence that Dayananda incorporated science in the interpretation of the Vedas and his admirer in this respect, Aurobindo, incorporated evolution into the interpretation of Hinduism? Be that as it may, Aurobindo "shares a return to the Vedic hymns with Dayananda Sarasvati, whom he admired for his attempt 'to re-establish the Veda as a living religious scripture', though rejecting the detail of Dayananda's interpretation."[76] To take an extreme example of such detail, Dayananda interpreted Ṛg–Veda 1.2.7, usually regarded as an invocation to Mitra and Varuṇa to mean that "water is generated by the combination of hydrogen and oxygen."[77]

The attitude of Svami Dayananda towards scriptural authority also differs in another crucial respect from that of his forebears and peers. It was shown earlier how he establishes their correspondence with nature. It was also shown how he regards the Vedas as the sole revelation of God. Accordingly, Svami Dayananda argued that the Vedas were "the fountainhead of science and religion for all mankind."[78] Thus, the "principle that all the sciences have their revealed source in the Vedas is enlarged by the further principle that all religions have their original and inspired source in the same early literature."[79]

Attitudes toward other Religions

At this point the attitude of Dayananda toward other religions and his attitude toward scriptural authority intersect. Before one proceeds further, however, the attitude of Dayananda toward other religions calls for a clarification. Dayananda is believed to have been hostile toward religions other than Hinduism[80]—perhaps more so than any other leader of the Hindu renaissance—but his position needs to be analyzed with greater care than seems to have been bestowed on it.[81] He clearly states in his autobiography that "My sole object is to believe in what is true and help others to believe in it. I neither accept the demerits of different faiths whether Indian or alien, nor reject what is good in them."[82] It is noteworthy that Dayananda "attacks what he calls 'untrue elements' in Islam or Christianity the same way as he does in regard to Hinduism. He shows no leniency to the latter on account of its being his own, or that of his forefathers' religion."[83] It is well known that Svami Vivekananda attended the Parliament of World Religions at Chicago in 1893; it is not as well known that Svami Dayananda "went so far as to invite a conference of the representatives of all religions on the occasion of the Delhi Durbar in 1877. Keshub Chandra Sen, Sir Syed Ahmed, and Munshi Alakhdari were among those who responded to the invitation. Dayananda's proposal was premature, but his idea that the exponents of various faiths should put their heads together to evolve a formula of united activity was unique in those days."[84] In the introduction to *Satyārtha Prakāśa* he writes: "At present there are learned men in all religions. If they give up prejudices, accept all those broad principles on which all religions are unanimous, reject differences and behave affectionately towards each other, much good will be done to the world. The differences of learned people aggravate the differences among the common masses with the result that miseries increase and happiness is lost."[85] It is also noteworthy that he concludes his statement of beliefs and disbeliefs with the following comment:

> In short, I accept universal maxims: for example, speaking of truth is commended by all, and speaking of falsehood is condemned by all. I accept all such principles. I do not approve of the wrangling of the various religions, against one another for they have, by propagating their creeds, misled the people and turned them into one another's enemy. My purpose and aim is to help in putting an end to this mutual wrangling, to preach universal truth, to bring all men under one religion so that they may, by ceasing to hate each other and firmly loving each other, live in peace and work for their common welfare. May this view through the grace and help of the Almighty God, and with the support of all virtuous and pious men, soon spread in the whole world so that all may easily acquire righteousness, wealth, gratification of legitimate desires and attain salvation, and thereby elevate themselves and live in happiness. This alone is my chief aim [86]

These are noble sentiments. However, to argue on their basis that Dayananda had moved from his position that "all truth is found in the Vedas"[87] to the position that "truth, wherever it is found, is of the Veda,[88] is perhaps unwarranted. For the one religion under which all were to live in harmony seems to have had for him both a moral and a revelatory component. Men of all religions could act together on the moral plane but if they were to belong to one true religion it had to be the Vedic revelation.[89] In order to accomplish this latter goal it was the duty of the Arya Samaj "(a) to recall India to the forsaken Vedic paths and (b) to preach the Vedic gospel throughout the whole world."[90]

Reconversion to Hinduism

Before the gospel could be preached to the world, however, it had to be preached in India. But this presented a problem. Hinduism, especially in the nineteenth century, was regarded as a non-missionary religion.[91] It existed, however, in the midst of religions which were actively missionary, especially Islam and Christianity. This meant that these two religions, to the extent that their missionary activities were successful, continued to gain adherents at the expense of the Hindu community. This state of affairs did not go down well with Svami Dayananda,[92] as the logic of his position unfolded itself. First, if the Vedic message had to be broadcast in the world one had to begin with India. Second, if the Vedic religion was meant to purify Hinduism, should it not also be used to purify those Hindus who had ceased to be Hindus, that is, had become Muslims or Christians but could now be purified and re-admitted into the Hindu fold? Thus the themes of conversion of the world to Vedic Hinduism and the reconversion of the Indian Muslims and Christians to Vedic Hinduism converged—indeed, the latter in a sense geographically if not necessarily logically preceded the other. It was in the Punjab that Svami Dayananda reconverted some Christians and according to J.T.F. Jordens "this was the only area where Dayananda showed an active interest in *shuddhi*, although he occasionally reiterated his stand that *shuddhi* was a proper and necessary procedure."[93] Although Svami Dayananda did not pursue the idea with particular zeal, it was to become a major element in the activities of the Arya Samaj, which he founded, in subsequent years.[94]

The repercussions of the Śuddhi movement were far-reaching; on the one hand it infused a missionary expert in Hinduism[95] but by the same token, it contributed to the increase in communal tension,[96] especially in the Punjab.[97]

Social and Political Issues

Svami Dayananda's views on social and political issues may now be briefly considered. Dayananda emphasized the value of education, especially with a Vedic orientation for all, irrespective of caste and sex. As for English he "advocated its study for one hour a day and the rest of the time was to be devoted to the study of the Vedas."[98] The Arya Samaj subsequently developed internal differences on the role of Western education.[99] Svami Dayananda also favoured cow protection and is believed to have been the "*first* who pleaded for the protection of the cow on a *utilitarian* principle."[100] Here again we find an element in his teaching which can only be partly traced to the Vedic hymns,[101] but "he rightly claimed that they had nothing to say on image-worship, caste, polygamy, child marriage and the seclusion of widows"[102] and agitated for reform in these areas. It has been noted that while initially Dayananda advocated education for all, Sūdras were to be excluded from Vedic education,[103] and he consequently modified his views to include not only the Sūdras but also *ati-Sūdras*, those below the Śudras,[104] which is more in line with the Vedic hymns. Thus the germ for the movement for the amelioration of the depressed classes had been laid, as had been the case with re-conversion or Śuddhi. Indeed, "out of the *shuddhi* movement there logically developed about the beginning of the twentieth century a campaign to recruit low castes and untouchables, with a ceremony evolved to invest the new recruits with the sacred thread"[105] thus making them equal with the high caste Hindus.

The political ideas of Dayananda have received less recognition than his social views. He did not approve of foreign rule over India, and asked foreigners "not to live here as rulers,"[106] a sentiment which Gandhi was to echo in almost identical words. Towards the end of his life, he was urging the local rulers of India, especially in Rajputana, to form some kind of a confederation.[107] The Arya Samaj promoted nationalism along with Hindu revivalism. It is no accident that among the later Arya Samajists, Svami Shraddhananda was killed by a Muslim[108] and Lala Lajpat Rai died probably as a result of being bludgeoned by a British officer.[109] Svami Dayananda had advocated indigenous rule (*svadeshi raj*) as opposed to foreign rule (*videshi raj*) and harked back to the universal and presumably golden rule of the Vedic age.[110]

All the various constituents of Dayananda's approach may now be pulled together. This task has been admirably performed by H.D. Griswold in a rather extended but comprehensive passage. He writes:

Let us first notice the problem of the regeneration of India, religious, political, and scientific, as it presented itself to the mind of the founder of the Arya Samaj. He found himself confronted by a variety of faiths both indigenous and foreign. Of religions of foreign origins there were Islam, introduced in the tenth century and Christianity, a comparatively recent importation from the West. The Indigenous

religion of India, namely, Hinduism, presented itself as a
vast congeries of faiths, ranging all the way from the strict
advaita doctrine of Sankaracharya to the crudest and grossest
superstitions embodied in the Tantras, the whole being held
together in a kind of external unity by the vast hierarchical
organization of caste. Such was the religious environment of
Svami Dayanand. There was also a political environment furnished by the vast and impressive administration of the British
Government in India, and a scientific environment consisting
of the spectacle on all sides of railways, canals, telegraph
wires, steam-engines, etc. Thus, as Svami Dayanand wandered
up and down over India, he studied not only the past but also
the present, not only the thought of India as embodied in
Veda and *Upanisad*, *Sutra* and *Epic*, but also the thought of
Europe as embodied especially in the inventions of modern
science, everywhere manifest in India.

The problem which confronted him was how to reform
Indian religion, how to effect a synthesis of the old and the
new, of the East and the West, in such a way as to guarantee
the intellectual and spiritual supremacy of the Indian people,
do full justice to the attainments of other nations, and provide
a universalistic programme of religion. The solution of this
problem was found by Svami Dayananda in the doctrine of
the Vedas as the revealed Word of God.[111]

It is precisely because of this centrality accorded to Vedic
revelation that even though the movement launched by
Dayananda shares several features in common with the reform
movements of the nineteenth and twentieth centuries, it is considered the "leading instance of revivalism"[112] rather than of
reformation, despite the fact that Dayananda shares the dynamism of the other leading lights of modern Hinduism.[113]

Notes

1. This is a transliterated form of the name which will be favored throughout
   the essay. For the sake of brevity he may be referred to as Svami
   Dayananda or only as Dayananda. For more on his name see James
   Hastings, ed., *Encyclopedia of Religion and Ethics* (New York : Charles
   Scribner's Sons, 1909) 2:57; on his initiation see J.N. Farquhar, *Modern
   Religious Movements in India* (New York: Macmillan, 1915), p. 105.

2. J.T.F. Jordens, *Dayānanda Sarasvatī, His Life and Ideas* (Delhi: Oxford University Press, 1978), p. 82. But also see p. 56.

3. Ainslee, T. Embree, ed., *The Hindu Tradition* (New York: Vintage Books, 1972), p. 300.

4. William Theodore de Bary, ed., *Sources of Indian Tradition* (New York: Columbia University Press, 1958, 2:76). For an autobiographical account see K.C. Yadav, ed., *Autobiography of Dayanand Sarasvati* (Delhi: Manohar, 1976); for a hagiographical account of his life see Har Bilas Sarada, *Life of Dayananda Sarasvati* (Ajmer, 1946); for a modern critical account see Jordens, *Dayānanda Sarasvatī*.

5. An important incident of his life during this period is his inconoclastic experience in the Siva temple, though its exact significance has been variously interpreted (see Yadav, ed., *Autobiography of Dayanand Sarasvati*, pp. 14-16; Jordens, *Dayānanda Sarasvatī*, p. 5; Sisirkumar Mitra, *Resurgent India* [New Delhi : Allied Publishers, 1965], p. 168ff).

6. He also visited Kumbha Melā at Hardwar; see Yadav, ed., *Autobiography of Dayanand Sarasvati*, pp. 27-28; Jordens, *Dayānand Sarasvati*, pp. 23-24.

7. See Yadav, *Autobiography of Dayanand Sarasvati*, pp. 39-40; Jordens, *Dayānanda Sarasvatī*, pp. 29-30.

8. Yadav prefers the form Vrijananda, *Autobiography of Dayanand Sarasvati*, p. 43.

9. See Sisirkumar Mitra, *Resurgent India*, pp. 169-70.

10. See A.L. Basham, ed., *A Cultural History of India* (Oxford: Clarendon Press, 1975), p. 371.

11. The year 1875 stands out as particularly significant in Svami Dayananda's life. At least three major events cluster around it: the foundation of the Arya Samaj, the publication of the *Satyārtha Prakāśa*, and the writing of *Ṛg-Veda-Bhaṣya-Bhūmikā*.

12. Dayananda Sarasvati, *Satyᵎrthaprakāśaḥ* (New Delhi: Saradesika Arya Pratinidhi Sabha, 2030 Vikram), pp. 589-95 (in Hindi).

13. As translated in Yadav, ed., *Autobiography of Dayanand Sarasvati*, p. 57.

14. Jordens, *Dayānanda Sarasvatī*, pp. 55-56.

15. R.C. Majumdar, ed., *British Paramountcy and Indian Renaissance*, part 2 (Bombay: Bharatiya Vidya Bhavan, 1965), p. 157, n. 29.

16. *Ibid.*, p. 112.

17. Yadav, ed., *Autobiography of Dayanand Sarasvati*, p. 58.

18. Jordens, *Dayananda Sarasvati*, pp. 251-56.

19. *Ibid.*, also see pp. 251-256.

20. Yadav, ed., *Autobiography of Dayānand Sarasvatī*, p. 59.

21. Jordens, *Dayānanda Sarasvatī*, pp. 109-10.

22. *Ibid.*, p. 256.

23. *Ibid.*, p. 104.

24. *Ibid.*, p. 311, emphasis added.

25. *Ibid.*, p. 262. This last aɪgument is interesting as it could only flow from theistic genesis of the Vedas as proposed by Svami Dayananda in opposition to its atheistic non-genesis in Purvamimāmsa.

26. Dayananda Sarasvati, *Satyᵘrthaprakāśaḥ*, p. 64.

27. R.C. Majumdar, R.C. Raychaudhuri, and Kalikinkar Datta, *An Advanced*

History of India (New York: Macmillan, 1950), p. 883.

28. For a valuable account of scriptural authority in advaita, see K. Satchidananda Murty, *Revelation and Reason in Advaita Vedanta* (New York: Columbia University Press, 1959).

29. Louis Renou, *The Destiny of the Veda in India*, ed., Deva Raj Chanana (Delhi: Motilal Banarasidass, 1965), p. 2. The expression in the original "Indian orthodoxy," (?), has been altered to Hindu orthodoxy; see Satischandra Chatterjee and Dhirendramohan Datta, *An Introduction to Indian Philosophy* (University of Calcutta, 1968), pp. 6-7.

30. Renou, *The Destiny of the Veda in India*, p. 2. For a somewhat different metaphorical statement see *Gandhi Marg* 19, no. 2/3 (April 1975); 216-20.

31. Louis Renou, *Religions of Ancient India*, (New York: Schocken Books, 1968), p. 45.

32. *Ibid.*, p. 108.

33. Thomas J. Hopkins, *The Hindu Religious Tradition* (Belmont, CA: Dickenson, 1971), p. 135.

34. Renou, *The Destiny of the Veda in India*, p. 3.

35. *Ibid.*, p. 61.

36. *Ibid.*, p. 3.

37. *Ibid.*, p. 61.

38. T.M.P. Mahadevan, *Outlines of Hinduism* (Bombay: Chetana Ltd., 1971), p. 130.

39. Eliot Deutsch and J.A.B. van Buitenen, *A Source Book of Advaita Vedānta* (Honolulu: University of Hawaii, 1971), pp. 5-8.

40. Surendranath Dasgupta, *A History of Indian Philosophy* (Cambridge University Press, 1957), 1:355; Dayananda Sarasvati, *Satyārthaprakāśah*, p. 188ff.

41. J.L. Brockington, *The Sacred Thread* (Edinburgh: Edinburgh University Press, 1981). 179.

42. Majumdar, ed., *British Paramountcy*, p. 113.

43. *Ibid.*

44. *Ibid.*, p. 112; see Dayananda Sarasvati, *Satyārthaprakāśah*, pp. 190-91.

45. Yadav, ed., *Autobiography of Dayanand Sarasvati*, p. 57.

46. See D. Mackenzie Brown, "The Philosophy of Bal Gangadhar Tilak," *the Journal of Asian Studies* 12, no. 2 (February 1958), p. 202.

47. Sarma, *Hinduism Through the Ages*, p. 95.

48. See Chatterjee and Datta, *An Introduction to Indian Philosophy*, pp. 7-9; but also see Murty, *Revelation and Reason in Advaita Vedanta*, pp. 212-13.

49. See Majumdar, ed., *British Paramountcy*, p. 113.

50. Sarasvati, *Satyārthaprakāśah*, pp. 463-588; also see de Bary, ed., *Sources of Indian Tradition*, 2:79-81.

51. *Hindu Dharma* (Ahmedabad: Navajivan, 1958), p. 14; but also see Sarma, *infra*, p. 96.

52. Murty, *Revelation and Reason in Advaita Vedanta*, p. 219; see also p. 271.

53. Majumdar, ed., *British Paramountcy*, p. 113.

54. Spear, ed., *The Oxford History of India*, p. 44.

55. Farquhar, *Modern Religious Movements in India*, p. 14.

56. de Bary ed., *Source of Indian Tradition*, (2:36).

57. But see Moni Chakravarti, "Metempsychosis in the Samhitā and Brahmanas of the Rg-Veda," *Annals of the Bhandarkar Oriental Institute* 42, parts 1-4 (1961), pp. 155-62.

58. See P.V. Kane, *History of Dharmaśāstra*, vol. 5, part 2 (Poona: Bhandarkar Oriental Research Institute, 1962), p. 1268.

59. Dayananda Sarasvati, *Satyārthaprakāśaḥ*, pp. 99-108.

60. See A.L. Basham, *The Wonder That was India* (New York: Taplinger, 1967), p. 176.

61. See Farquhar, *Modern Religious Movements in India*, pp. 121-22; see also Dayananda Sarasvati, *Satyārthaprakāśah*, pp. 99-108, in defense of the practice).

62. Yadav, ed., *Autobiography of Dayanandā Sarasvati*, p. 62.

63. J.L. Brockington, *op. cit.*, p. 179.

64. Hastings, ed., *Encyclopedia of Religion and Ethics*, 2:59. As E.D. Maclagan remarks: "The bases of the Aryan faith are the revelation of God in the Vedas and the revelation of God in nature and the first practical element in this belief is 'the interpretation of the Vedas in conformity with the proved results of natural science' *(Census of India*, 1891, xix, 175). In other words, there is involved the assumption that the Vedas as 'the books of true knowledge' must contain 'the basic principles of all the sciences,' and accordingly that every scientific discovery and invention of modern times must be found expressed, germinally at least, in the Vedas. The science of the West, then, is but the realization of the scientific programme anticipated by the seers of the East, over one hundred billion years ago" *(ibid.)*. Also see Yadav, ed., *Autobiography of Dayanand Sarasvati*, p. 62, item 39.

65. Also see T.M.P. Mahadevan, *Outlines of Hinduism*, p. 13: "There is a popular saying to the effect that not even a thousand scriptural texts will be capable of converting a pot into a piece of cloth."

66. Majumdar, ed., *British Paramountcy*, p. 113.

67. Farquhar, *Modern Religious Movements in India*, pp. 118-20.

68. *Ibid.*, 116.

69. Hastings, ed., *Encyclopedia of Religion and Ethics*, p. 59; Majumdar, ed., *British Paramountcy*, pp. 113-14, etc.

70. Hastings, ed., *Encyclopedia of Religion and Ethics*, p. 59.

71. *The Destiny of the Veda in India*, p. 4; but not without realizing its cultural significance, *ibid.*; *Religions of Ancient India* (New York: Schocken Books, 1968), pp. 44-45.

72. Quoted with enthusiastic approval in Haridas Bhattacharyya, ed., *infra*, p. 634.

73. Sarma, *Hinduism Through the Ages*, p. 204.

74. Farquhar, *Modern Religious Movements in India*, p. 116.

75. de Bary, ed., *Sources of Indian Tradition*, 2:83.

76. Brockington, p. 184.

77. Majumdar, ed., *British Paramountcy*, p. 113.

78. Hastings, ed., *Encyclopedia of Religion and Ethics*, 2:59.

79. *Ibid.*

80. Farquhar, *Modern Religious Movements in India*, p. 112.

81. Yadav, ed., *Autobiography of Dayanand Sarasvati*, pp. 7-10. Majumdar, Raychaudhuri, Datta, *An Advanced History of India*, p. 884ff.

82. Yadav, ed., *Autobiography of Dayanand Sarasvati*, p. 7.

83. *Ibid.*, pp. 7-18. Also see Dayananda Sarasvati, *Saty·rthaprakāśaḥ.*, p. 3

84. Haridas Bhattacharyya, ed., *The Cultural Heritage of India* (Calcutta: Ramakrishna Mission Institute of Culture, 1937), p. 635; Yadav, ed., *Autobiography of Dayanand Sarasvati*, p. 7, n. 23.

85. Yadav, ed., *Autobiography of Dayanand Sarasvati*, p. 8.

86. *Ibid.*, p. 64. It may be noted that the illustration of universal maxim which he provides is a moral one. Those who seek the universal at a mystical rather than at an ethical level point out that "moral virtues cannot provide the common core of religions" because "though they may be common they are not the core. From the religion point of view ethics is always derivative" (Huston Smith, in the introduction to Frithjof Schuon, *The Transcendent Unity of Religions*, [New York: Harper and Row, 1973] p. xxiiii).

87. Farquhar, *Modern Religions Movements in India*, p. 113.

88. Bhattacharyya, ed., *The Cultural Heritage of India*, p. 635.

89. de Bary, ed., *Sources of Indian Tradition*, 2:83.

90. Hastings, ed., *Encyclopedia of Religion and Ethics*, 2:59.

91. F. Max Muller, *Chips from a German Workshop* (London: Longmans, Green and Co., 1880) Vol. IV, p. 254.

92. His experience in the Punjab was crucial here, see J.F. Seunarine, *Reconversion to Hinduism Through Suddhi* (Madras: The Christian Literature Society, 1977), p. 12.

93. Jordens, *Dayānanda Sarasvatī*, pp. 170-71. But also see Seunarine, *Reconversion to Hinduism Through Suddhi*; Radhey Shyam Pareek, *Contribution of Arya Samaj in the Making of Modern India* (Jaipur: Sarvadeshik Arya Pratinidhi Sabha, 1973), pp. 130-131.

94. See J.T.F. Jordens, *Swāmī Shraddhānanda: His Life and Causes* (Delhi: Oxford University Press, 1981), p. 131ff.

95. Majumdar, ed., *British Paramountcy*, p. 114; G.R. Thursby, "Aspects of Hindu-Muslim Relations in British India: A Study of Arya Samaj Activities, Government of India Policies and Communal Conflict in the Period 1923-1928" (Duke University, 1972). Unpublished Dissertation.

96. Majumdar, ed., *British Paramountcy*, p. 111.

97. For a more detailed treatment see Kenneth W. Jones, *Arya Dharm: Hindu Consciousness in 19th-Century Punjab* (Berkeley: University of California Press, 1976).

98. Radhey Shyam Pareek, *op. cit.*, p. 181.

99. *Ibid.*, Chapter V. Also see Brockington, *The Sacred Thread*, p. 180.

100. Bawa Chhajju Singh, *Life and Teachings of Swami Dayanand Saraswati* (New Delhi: Jan Gyan Prakashan, 1971), p. 151.

101. R.C. Majumdar, ed., *The Vedic Age* (Bombay: Bharatiya Vidya Bhavan, 1965), p. 399, 464, 530.

102. Brockington, *The Sacred Thread*, p. 179.

103. Jordens, *Dayānanda Sarasvatī*, p. 96, 115.

104. *Ibid.*, p. 262, 285.

105. Brockington, *The Sacred Thread*, p. 180; also see Jordens, *Swāmī Shraddhānanda* Chapter VI.

106. Pareek, *Contributions of Arya Samaj*, p. 221.

107. Jordens, *Dayānanda Sarasvati*, Chapter X.

108. Jordens, *Swāmī Shraddhānanda*, p. 166.

109. Jawaharlal Nehru, *An Autobiography* (London: The Bodley Head, 1958), pp. 174-75.

110. Jordens, *Dayānanda Sarasvati*, p. 265.

111. Hastings, ed., *Encyclopedia of Religion and Ethics*, p. 58.

112. Philip H. Ashby, *Modern Trends in Hinduism* (New York: Columbia University Press. 1974), p. 33.

113. Louis Renou, ed., *Hinduism* (New York: Washington Square Press, Inc., 1963), pp. 32-33.

13

SVAMI VIVEKANANDA

George M. Williams

The image of the warrior-monk (*kṣatriya-sannyāsin*) marching into the citadels of Western materialism and triumphantly demonstrating the powers of Indian spirituality is so strongly believed (almost as a cardinal tenet of Indian patriotism) and so carefully managed by his followers that one may not be easily able to find the historical Svami Vivekananda. The archetype of Vivekananda as the Hindu spiritual hero is so pervasive, and notions about the Hindu spiritual stages so predetermined, that Vivekananda the human being has been lost to the legend. A simple search for the patterns of this man's ultimate concerns leads immediately into a labyrinth of methodological considerations, and their solutions predict success or failure.[1]

"That which concerned Svami Vivekananda ultimately" will require two lines of development. These penetrate through dual consideration of the hero legend created by well-meaning followers, and of the camouflaging effect created by Vivekananda himself as he changed his patterns of ultimate concern during his lifetime.[2]

The contention of this study is that the practice of fitting Svami Vivekananda into a Hindu hero archetype has been costly for those who wish to know about the human quest for meaning and purpose in the life of the individual. The more the historical Vivekananda has been lost to the archetype of the spiritual hero, the more his life story fits into predetermined stages thought to be ideal exemplars of cultural goals. The less his own quest for ultimacy follows a human course, the less he is an example of human doubt and struggle.

Some might suggest that it is a sacreligious act to question a spiritual hero legend. However, the gain from demythologizing the Vivekananda legend will offset any loss.

The following table summarizes the four stages in Vivekananda's spiritual development posited in the official accounts[3] and most other studies.[4]

Archetype of the Spiritual Hero

I.   Wondrous Child:
     —Visions
     —meditations
II. Exceptional College Student:
     —master of Western thought
     —independent thinker
III. Carefully trained by Sri Ramakrishna
IV. Warrior-monk:
     —conquers West
     —awakens India

Different historical periods appeared as the data was allowed to cluster according to the question asked in a previous study ("What pattern of ultimate concern was held and when?").[5] This study draws from that earlier study but finds that the first two periods (childhood and college) were more important than previously seen. The following table makes explicit these periods in Vivekananda's life.

Historical Periods of Doubt and Faith

I.   Childhood: 1863-78
II. College: 1878/9-86
     —Brahmo Samaj
     —Freemason
     —skeptic

III.   Ramakrishna's disciple: 1886-89
IV.   Renewed search: 1889-90
V.   Break with Ramakrishna *gurubhāis*: 1890
    —reestablishing contact from America: 1894
    —return and founding of Order: 1897-1902.

Each of the historical periods will be presented and, in spite of the evidential difficulties, the pattern of ultimate concern held during each period will be posited.

I. Childhood (1863-78)

While there is rich lore about the future Svami Vivekananda's childhood, it lacks the historical substance to support conclusions about a pattern of ultimacy during this period. Even so, the accounts of his early childhood suggest a far more traditional upbringing than one would suspect by beginning with his college days. Two themes in these childhood stories will be examined: predictions that he would become a *sannyāsin*, and stories of his early spiritual powers.

Future Sannyāsin. Born minutes before dawn on January 12, 1863, on the festival day of Makrasamkrānti, the future Vivekananda was given the name Vireshwar in honor of and in gratitude to Śiva. The birth had maternal and cultural significance from the points of view of Hindu astrology and folk piety. The childhood legends seem to indicate that his mother and relatives believed that this child was a gift from Śiva, that he had a special destiny, and that he would become a *sannyāsin*.[7] Stories about his special attraction to and concern for *sādhus* and *sannyasis* abound.[8] When he was about eight, Biley (Vireshwar Datta's childhood nickname) proclaimed: "I must become a Sannyasin, a palmist predicted it."[9] Many books on Vivekananda go to the expense of including a photostat of his palm print.[10] When all these are linked with the possible influence of his grandfather, who renounced married life in his late twenties,[11] one must appreciate the centrality of the *sannyāsa* issue for the legend. Even though there remains none of the documentation which would raise these stories to historicity, or refute them as invention, one cannot miss the central role which the issue of marriage versus its renunciation for religious reasons had during Narendranath Datta's late teens and early twenties (Vireshwar, "Biley," received the adult name of Narendranath

according to the Hindu custom). Another example, one that
totally depends on the astrological prediction, was his future guru's
use of the seven stars, linking these with the seven *ṛṣis*, and identifying Narendra as Nara reborn.[12]

Early Spiritual Powers. The childhood legend abounds with
stories very familiar to Indian expectations. Biley was a naughty
boy (like Lord Kṛṣṇa),[13] meditated through the visit of a snake at
five or six ("I knew nothing of the snake or anything else, I was
feeling inexpressible bliss"),[14] demonstrated kingly attributes,[15] had
no caste consciousness,[16] and confounded his teachers.[17] His
vision of and merger into the Absolute when he was fourteen (1877),
is cited to prove his special gifts and his readiness for the perfect
guru who could harness these *siddhis* for their proper goal.[18]

While the issue of development of spiritual powers (*siddhis*) will
become important after Narendra meets Sri Ramakrishna, there is
too much documentary evidence to suggest that Narendra had no
background of siddhic experiences to draw upon when he first met
Ramakrishna in 1881. The point will be developed later.[19]

Paternal Influence. If the legends have any historicity, the world
of Vireshwar Datta was molded by his mother's deep and traditional piety, peopled by *sādhus* and *sannyāsis*, and enriched by spiritual and psychic experience. Its experiential content, that of a
Hinduized childhood, would suggest a traditional Hindu piety.

This maternal influence was challenged in 1877 when the family
moved to Raipur for two years. There he seems to have been
first influenced by his father's rational, progressive ideas. The
curious stories of the boy "flying into a rage" during the discussions
between his father and other progressive civil and religious leaders
bear the unmistakable marks of his first identity crisis, which
would fully explode in 1880.[20] But by the time the family returned to Calcutta in 1879, his father's encouragement motivated him
to begin study towards a law degree, to join the most radical branch
of the Brahmo Samaj, to attend the Freemasons, and to consider
further study in England, as well as marriage.

Had the maternal world been operative when he joined the
Hindu reform movement, he would have lost caste (been "out-
casted"), as happened to most other college students who joined.[21]
Yet his mother's traditional influence would account for his attraction to the more devotional aspects of the Hindu tradition. This
attraction and repulsion would contribute to a nervous breakdown.

II. College and Legal Studies (1878/9-86)

In 1878/9, when he was sixteen, Narendranath Datta passed the entrance exam and began studies at Presidency College. There were two pivotal crises within the college period. One occurred in 1884 when his father died; the existential crisis which resulted eventuated in his break with the Brahmo Samaj. His despair led him into a period of skepticism and then to Ramakrishna. But by focusing on this crisis, as have all previous studies, including my own, the developments are interpreted as follows: the Brahmo period was a mere prelude to his encounter with Ramakrishna; it allowed him to discover that Brahmos could not "see God."[22] This interpretation is immediately weakened when an earlier crisis is recognized and given proper perspective.

The precise dates are sketchy, but after about a year at Presidency College in Calcutta, Narendra had a nervous breakdown. No one disputes this occurrence; it just did not seem worthy of exploration. Since complete access to all the extant Vivekananda documents has been denied scholars, even the desire to explore such a seemingly important event could only end in frustration.[23] But several facts do emerge. The breakdown and the following recuperation at Buddha Gaya occurred sometime in 1880. *Before* this period Narendra had attended Presidency College and was a member of the most social reform-minded faction of the Brahmo Samaj movement. *After* his return to Calcutta in 1881 he changed colleges to the Scottish Church College and switched his affiliation within the Brahmo Samaj to the Adi Brahmo Samaj, which was more conciliatory toward the Hindu community, more devotional in religious expression, more gradual in the area of social reform, and more strongly led by one religious leader, Keshab Chandra Sen.

Could this be only circumstantial? Is it probable that the nervous breakdown had nothing to do with the religious changes which such affiliations suggest? Perhaps enough of the evidence is not available to decide these questions fully, but an examination of each group and Narendra's activities within them will suggest important tendencies which continued beyond this period.

David Kopf's study of the Brahmo Samaj revealed three radical ideas[24] that reflected notions which were becoming important to liberal religions in other parts of the world at that point in time. First was their notion of rational faith versus what they saw as the

enslavement of meaningless superstitions. Second was their belief
in social reform, including the emancipation of workers, peasants,
and women. Third was their belief in a universal theistic progress
of religion, positing the perfectability of mankind and believing that
this could be achieved by joining social reform to radical religion.[25]
Spencer Lavan's study on the influence of American Unitarianism
on the Brahmo movement emphasized twin pillars of reasoned faith
and social or humanitarian reform.[26] This reform of every aspect
of Indian society and religion had been going on for sixty years
when Narendra joined in 1878/9, yet 1878 was crucial to the movement. Pressures from within, between those for rapid change and
those who wished to accommodate the Hindu community, irreparably
burst apart the movement. Pressures from outside the Brahmo
movement would push individuals back into caste structures or hurl
them out into a non-spiritual, skeptical, materialistic world. As a
movement, this rupturing meant ever decreasing power and influence
to accomplish its reforms. But individuals now occupied themselves
with changing affiliations within the varying factions or by returning
to an orthodox Vaiṣṇava, Śaiva, or Śakta piety. Few had a stable
religious identity.[27]

Narendra's joining with the most radical faction of the Brahmo
movement linked him to the use of reason against superstition,
magic, and miracle.[28] The Sadharan Brahmo Samaj was led by
Shivanath Shastri and Vijay Krishna Goswami (who will later be
won back to Shaktism by Sri Ramakrishna). They fought to break
with caste Hinduism, to raise the status of women and the masses,
and to allow the individual through hard work to become self-reliant
and self-sufficient.[29] While the Brahmos wished to reform Hinduism
of its multiform varieties of idolatry and superstition, Hindus actively
opposed them, sometimes physically and economically.[30] But the
most effective weapon was to "out-caste" anyone taking the Brahmo
oath.

Shivanath Sastri's writings show two emphases which Narendra
would later adopt from its Sadharan Brahmo formulation. The first
involved the belief that universal religion was practical.[31] It entailed
service to mankind. Rammohun Roy's famous dictum was cited,
"The true way of serving God is to do good to man."[32] Like other
Brahmos both before and after him, Sastri blamed India's "pessimistic view of life" upon the teachings of Vedanta.[33] The Brahmo
Samaj or "the Theistic Church of India was to raise Hinduism and

Hindu society from this sombre and gloomy view of life and this tainting touch of Vedantism by teaching that human society is a Divine dispensation, and all its relationships are sacred and spiritual."[34]   Sankara and his doctrine of *māyā* had "drawn away into the life of mendicancy hundreds of spiritually disposed persons, and has thereby robbed society of their personal influence and example.[35]

The second emphasis has already appeared in these quotations: the sacredness of all social relationships—even marriage. The Brahmo emphasis upon the liberal spiritual life as one within both society and-marriage was stressed especially by Sastri.[36]   This was a general theme of the Brahmos, of course, but it had special meaning in 1878 when Brahmos were splitting organizationally over the role and equality of women in their quest for universal religion.

Sastri had another interesting idea: to preach "universal theism" not only to the educated but also to the uneducated masses.[37] This idea would be adopted by the future Vivekananda.

If the rule of full membership in the Sadharan Brahmo Samaj was enforced for Narendra, he would have only been an associate member, awaiting his eighteenth birthday for the final oath and full membership.   That would not have been done until January 1881. In the meantime he had suffered a nervous breakdown and the recuperation in Buddha Gaya.   Since the Buddha was an important figure in the Brahmo faith because of his compassion for and service to mankind, his place of enlightenment would not have been a strange choice for a Brahmo.

Upon Narendra's return to Calcutta a change occurred. He became active in the Adi Brahmo Samaj, Keshab Chandra Sen's Church of the New Dispensation.   While Keshab had begun with a repudiation of Hindu superstitions and priestcraft with universal reason as the guide, by 1876 he was becoming increasingly anti-rational and was being drawn toward ecstatic religious devotion. Keshab's visits to Sri Ramakrishna during 1882-84 leap from the pages of Mahendranath Gupta's account of the priest of Kālī.[38] As the Sadharan Brahmo Samaj became more concerned about changing society, Keshab and his group turned toward "non-progressive, asocial, personal, spiritual realisation."[39] Keshab's later writings showed an increasing tendency to turn inward through prayer and devotion.[40]

From 1881 until Keshab's death in 1884, Narendra was active

in the Adi Brahmo Samaj's Band of Hope.[41] He took part in the theatrical performances which sought an awakening of Indian spirituality. One of these, in which Keshab played the part of Pavhari Baba, introduced him to a yogi of great powers (*siddhis*) to whom he would go seven years hence.[42] His brother would later remember his evaluation of Keshab's influence on his life: "But for Ramakrishna, I would have been a Brahmo missionary."[43]

One other factor cannot be evaded. Keshab experienced an opposition between spirituality and sexuality during this last phase of his life. His opponents in the radical factions of the Brahmo Samaj accused him of degrading women.[44] It was true that he found their presence at Brahmo worship objectionable, but he eventually yielded and allowed them to be segregated to the left side of the assembly. But he could not shake a perception that sensual contact with women, and even the possible thought of it, was inherently evil. The only way to avoid pollution in sexual contact with one's wife was to practice "mental" renunciation. Keshab shared this view with Sri Ramakrishna, who expressed this conception explicitly and even required those who had not "touched women" to go beyond this to renunciation "in actuality."[45] Narendra's brother indicated that Narendra believed in celibacy when he was a Brahmo—a strange belief for a Sadharan Brahmo but not for a follower of Keshab in his ascetic period.[46] Keshab's gradualism toward full equality for women rested on the subtleties of this renunciation of the senses, not on any explicit idea of women's inferiority. The radical brand of Brahmos were tampering with changes which went to the heart of several Indian religious systems' conclusions about sense contact in general and sexual contact specifically—only one who renounced the world both "mentally and in actually" could achieve *mukti*, liberation. Keshab was perhaps leading Narendra back toward the renunciation of his grandfather and the prediction of the palmist.

The second crisis during his college period would eventuate in his abandoning the reform of Hinduism as a Brahmo. In fact, after his period of skepticism (1884-85) and the period of training with a Kālī priest (1885-89), he would become a revivalist of true Hinduism rather than a reformer.

Prior to his father's death in 1884, Narendra had joined the Freemason's Lodge in Calcutta at his father's urging. Freemasonry in India concerned itself with equality, social reform, philanthropy, and a "common denominator approach to religious unity."[47] It was another force in the drive toward breaking the caste system, communalism, and dietary laws. Narendra's father arranged an appointment for his son as a law clerk with Nimai Charain Bose. He also pushed his son toward marriage plans, which only his untimely death prevented. He suggested that Narendra might use his wife's dowry to go to England for further law studies.

Keshab died a month before Narendra's father. The double deaths seemed to have had a profound effect on Narendra's life. From wealth and power his family plunged into poverty and weakness. He would become involved in a family lawsuit for the next three years to try and retain the house for his mother against other members of the joint family. How far he had moved from the Sadharan Brahmo ideal of the married man working in the world for the good of mankind can be observed in his struggle to keep from getting married. A marriage into a good family and with sizable dowry would have ended his financial cares.[48] He obtained employment from Pandit Iswar Chandra Vidyasagar, the grand old Hindu atheist, but that lasted only a month.[49] It is doubtful that Narendra represented the kind of rational, reform-minded model for boys that Vidyasagar wanted in his school. Throughout 1884 and the beginning of 1885, Narendra struggled with unemployment and the existential, and for him spiritual, crisis of unmerited suffering. He moved into skepticism and despair. But simultaneous with these later events (1881-85), Narendra had begun going to Sri Ramakrishna and would eventually become his disciple.

III. Ramakrishna's Disciple (1885-89)

From the first meeting in November 1881, between Narendranath Datta and Sri Ramakrishna, *pūjāri* of the Dakshineswar Temple outside Calcutta, until the final submission of Kālī in June 1885, a complex series of events were to transpire, ending Narendra's revulsion of idol worship.

As Keshab Chandra Sen began to move back to inward-directed spirituality, he found Ramakrishna, a traditional Śakta priest who shared many of the ideals of the New Dispensation Church. As Keshab turned against Unitarian social action, especially the urgency with which the American field worker, Rev. Charles Dall, the British Unitarian social activists, Mary Carpenter and Annette Akroyd, and the radical Samajis pressed the issue about equality for women, Keshab began to mention Ramakrishna in his magazine in 1879.[50]

In 1881 Narendra heard a classroom example in which Ramakrishna was mentioned by Professor Hastie.[51] Hastie tried to explain a trance that Wordsworth alluded to in his poetry, stating that Ramakrishna of Dakshineswar went into deep trance states. Narendra and the others in the class did not know about trance states, according to official histories.[52] And if that is the case, based on a memory of Svami Vivekananda many years after this event, it would cast doubt on the legend about childhood experiences of meditation and the altered state experience in the oxcart on the way to Raipur.[53] Whichever the case, the first meeting with Sri Ramakrishna was at Surendra Nath Mitra's house in November 1881, where Narendra had sung.[54] There are substantial difficulties with the evidence to reconstruct the first three meetings.[55] The first meeting appears to have been embarrassing for Narendra. Ramakrishna immediately identified him as Nara, the sage incarnation of Nārāyana, thus punning his name. Ramakrishna told of a past vision of the seven ṛṣis identifying Narendra with Nara: now "born on earth to remove the miseries of mankind."[56] Possibly to assuage his embarrassment, the legend has Narendra asking this Kālī priest if he had seen God. To Narendra's amazement, he reported later, Ramakrishna answered, "Yes, I see Him just as I see you, only in a much intenser sense. God can be realized; one can see and talk to him as I am doing to you."[57] (The likelihood that he asked the question in this way is almost nil. As a Brahmo, God was Spirit, so the question could not have been asked this way. Both the hand of the legend-makers and that of Vivekananda's later retelling are seen here).

Almost a month passed. Then on December 27/28, 1881, Narendra went to see Ramakrishna at Dakshineswar. There he was invited to sit on Ramakrishna's small bed. Immediately Ramakrishna put his foot[58] on Narendra's chest. Narendra began to lose sensory awareness of his body.[59] He was deeply frightened by the experience. There appears to have been little in his background upon which he could have drawn to explain the occurrence.[60] Narendra did not initiate the next contact. Ramakrishna had to come to the Simla Brahmo temple on January 1, 1882, to see him at the annual festival of the Brahmo Samaj. Keshab

Chandra Sen was also there.[61]

The pattern for much of the next four years has emerged. Narendra is more sought after than seeking Sri Ramakrishna. Yet Ramakrishna's ability to induce altered states of consciousness both in himself and in others both attracted and repelled. The evidence is clear from both Narendra's subjective accounts (and they do vary widely as he valued the experiences differently at different times in his life) and from other observers within the Ramakrishna circle, that Sri Ramakrishna was able to induce in Narendra altered states of consciousness with his touch.[62] Narendra experienced varying degrees of loss of body consciousness, loss of an ordinary sense of time, loss of or changes in personal identity, a sense of euphoria, and a range of experiences which in the last quarter of the twentieth century are now beginning to be easily recognized as a pattern. But this was hardly the case in the 1880s. These experiences defied explanation—and that was especially true in terms of nineteenth-century Western thought.

After the third visit, during which Ramakrishna again used his touch to induce a hypnotic state in Narendra, Ramakrishna complained regularly that Narendra must not love him, as he continually stayed away and ignored his invitations to Dakshineswar.

During August 1883, Narendra began to visit Ramakrishna more regularly.[63] But that was short-lived. There is no documentary evidence that Narendra visited Dakshineswar between August 1883, and March 2, 1884. On January 8, 1884, Keshab Chandra Sen had died. Narendra's father died before March 2, probably in February. It was then that Narendra returned to Ramakrishna.[64] But he informed Ramakrishna that he was now studying the "views of atheists."[65]

The encounters were few during 1884, usually in Calcutta and when Narendra was singing on holy days at the Samaj.[66] Narendra was running the lawsuit against those members of the joint family who tried to take his father's house, and he was preparing for law exams. But when Narendra came, Ramakrishna would touch him and Ramakrishna would go into an altered state, *samādhi*. Once this occurred with Ramakrishna sitting on Narendra's back while he lay on the floor on his stomach.[67]

But a year after his father's death, Narendra began to alter a stance which he would later identify as the key to his resistance to Ramakrishna: he would worship Kālī and finally break the letter

of his Brahmo oath, although the spirit may have been broken
years before. There is no evidence that he worshipped as a Brahmo
after March 1885.[68]

Several days before March 1, 1885, Narendra had an altered
state experience in Calcutta without Ramakrishna's inducement.[69]
This brought him to Dakshineswar and an abortive attempt to
meditate on Kālī.[70] "Why, I have meditated on Kālī for three or
four days, but nothing has come of it."[71]

After this initial turning to Kālī, Narendra seemed to go into a
period of skepticism for three months. But even then Ramakrishna
used his touch to alter Narendra's moods.[72] On June 13, in
absolute despair, Narendra's *pūjā* to Kālī resulted in an experience
of her as living presence.[73] He like Vijay Krishna Goswami, had
been won away from the Brahmo Samaj.[74] Sri Ramakrishna had
continually used his powers (*siddhis*) and influence to modify the
religious path of both Vijay Goswami and Narendra. Both were
led to do *pūjā* before Kālī's image. Image worship was one of the
most important things for Brahmos to avoid; it was a meaningful
outward expression of their faith in God without form. Its practice
was to condone the total system of inequality and superstitions
which the Brahmos had taken an oath to reform. It seems impossible to avoid the conclusion that Sri Ramakrishna had converted
Narendranath Datta and Vijay Krishna Goswami from their faith
and practice as Brahmos and returned them to identities which
were consonant with the Hindu tradition.

Ramakrishna had led Narendra to an experience of Kālī as the
Supreme Mother of the Universe. Ramakrishna also had
Narendra study the Vedanta to see that his Brahmo prejudices
were wrong about it as well. Ramakrishna taught that the
Absolute of Vedanta, *brahman*, and the goddess of form of Śaktism,
Kālī, were the same. Therefore Narendra had to lay aside his
Brahmo repudiation of Vedanta and Sankara and realize Vedanta's
truth. Devotional expressions, even before images and even persons (*guru-pūjā*), was proper. Ramakrishna taught Narendra that
special persons (Iśvarakoti) had extraordinary powers (*siddhis*) and
were able to know the divine directly (*nirvikalpa samādhi*). The
goal of life was God-realization through renunciation of "women
and money."

The long struggle between Sri Ramakrishna and Narendra
culminated in Kālī *pūjā* in June 1885. One year later, Ramakrishna

would die of throat cancer. In this brief period the full impact of his spiritual achievements produced their results upon Narendranath Datta. Even though he did not/ receive initiation from Ramakrishna, he received a kind of commission in two parts: "Teach my boys"; "Keep them together." He sought to accomplish this by forming a monastic gathering at a Baranagore house (euphemistically called a Math). With a non-traditional self-initiation they began wearing ochre robes.[75]

Ramakrishna's death left Narendra with an unenviable task. First there was the problem of his own doubts about realizing God, and even God's existence. He had had extraordinary experiences—most induced by Ramakrishna—but without a living guru these experiences did not yield certainty. His personal mixture of *jñāna* and *bhakti* were fragile at best and at their worst they erupted in fits of skepticism which greatly disturbed his fellow monks (*gurubhāis*). Kālī *pūjā* and Ramakrishna *pūjā* were less meaningful to him than study of the scriptures. But the scriptures seemed to be a patchwork of dualistic, modified monistic, and monistic concerns. If Vedanta, and monistic Vedanta at that, was the highest form of expression about God-realization, then how could it be acquitted of the charge that its doctrine of *māyā* promoted social apathy. How could service to others and the social concerns of the reformers of "New India" movements be found in traditional Indian sources? What was to be the "mission" of this band of disciples of Ramakrishna?

This period of search, within the confines of Ramakrishna's last words ("Keep my boys together" and "Teach them"), spanned 1886-89. It was relatively successful as it included the practice of various spiritual disciplines. But personal liberation (*mukti*) seemed to act as a centrifugal force spinning disciples away from the Baranagore Math and sending them on solitary quests for God-realization. (Another explanation of why they left the Math so often is that only then were they free to pursue their own *mukti* without Narendra's searing doubts.)

IV. Neo-Hinduism: Search for Universal Foundation (1889-90)

All the worship and discipline of the Baranagore period began to become distasteful to "Svami Narendra."[76] By August 1889, he is convinced that a reinterpretation of the Vedas would provide a scriptural base for a socially concerned Vedanta. This reformed

Vedanta would be free from caste distinctions and injustices. Thus it would be that universally true religion all religious liberals were seeking, and it would be based on the Vedas.

Pundit Mitra of Varanasi and "Svami Narendra" corresponded during August 1889 over his new scriptural discoveries. "Narendra" believed, like any good student, that in the proper question there was already contained the answer. He only had to ask his brilliantly constructed questions, and the answers to liberate Vedanta from its besmirched reputation would be provided by none less than Pundit Mitra, Sanskrit scholar of Varanasi.

These questions involved some of Ramakrishna's central realizations. Ramakrishna taught that Vedanta was the highest expression of universal religion (sanātana dharma). Sankara's interpretation of Vedanta was recognized as the most authoritative. But Sankara's doctrine of the world as illusory (māyāvāda) had been bitterly attacked by Brahmo thinkers. If the future Svami Vivekananda was to prove Sri Ramakrishna's realizations about Vedanta, then he would have to find some way to answer this criticism. But there was an even more troubling one: Sankara seemed to teach that persons could be denied study of the Vedas on the basis of their birth (jāti). This would lend credence to the Brahmo charge that caste discrimination was integral to Vedanta and its scripture.

What excited Svami "Narendra" was the discovery that Sankara based his "birth doctrine" on less authoritative scriptures (smṛti).[77] His questions to Pundit Mitra were planned to elicit answers which would have judged Sankara's interpretations on caste as erroneous. Pundit Mitra's letters are not available for study,[78] but the young questioner would remark:

"Why has no foundation for the authority of the Vedas been adduced in the Vedanta-Sutras?"[79]

"The Vedanta requires of us faith, for conclusiveness cannot be reached by mere argumentation. Then why has the slightest flaw, detected in the position of the schools of Sankhya and Nyaya, been overwhelmed with a fusillade of dialectics?"[80]

"Why should the Shudra not study the Upanishad?"[81]

Pundit Mitra's kind responses instructed him to "give up arguing and disputing"—the solution of overcoming doubt in the adequacy of a belief system by giving up doubt.[82] He had not succeeded in gaining recognition for his ideas for reinterpreting Vedanta by asserting the primacy of *śruti* over *smṛti*, especially on the caste issue. He would have to return to these notions after his worldwide recognition as Svami Vivekananda.

The months of correspondence had come to naught. All hope of finding a universally acceptable scriptural foundation for Sri Ramakrishna's realizations (and linking them to liberal social concerns) had to be abandoned.

Search for a New Guru. It is difficult to determine whether Svami "Narendra" searched for support from a traditional *siddha* and yogi, Pavhari Baba, or for someone who would give him the religious certainty he lacked.

There is evidence for both views. At the end of this period, Svami "Narendra" would state: "I am Ramakrishna's slave, having laid my body at his feet 'with Til and Tulasi leaves'. . . . Now his behest to me was that I should devote myself to the service of the order of all-renouncing devotees founded by Him, and in this I have to persevere, come what may, being ready to take heaven, hell. . . . His command was that his all-renouncing devotees should group themselves together, and I am entrusted with seeing to this."[83] Even though this period of search is over, an anguished tone is evident. "Having to persevere" is a phrase which demonstrates this well. Note also that the service is to the order of *bhaktas*, a telling confession of his perception at this time of Ramakrishna's commission to him.

But just what his visit to this renowned yogi was to accomplish is something of a puzzle. The question about Ramakrishna's use of *siddhis* in Narendra's training may have motivated a quest for answers. Since he was soon to seek initiation from Pavhari Baba, the problem of an unorthodox ordination could be considered as well. Yet Svami "Narendra" seemed to be working on a new solution: India's spirituality could be proven by the extraordinary accomplishments of its gurus, *siddhis*, and *sādhus*. He saw "all Gurus are one and are fragments and radiations of God, the Universal Guru." If asceticism brought godliness and power, as Ramakrishna taught, then this "air eating" Baba might induce in him permanently what Ramakrishna had only provided in an impermanent taste.

Svami "Narendra" received instruction in *rāja* yoga and practiced austerities in a lemon grove. He had found a *sādhu* who could remain, "it was rumoured," in a state of *samādhi* for months. In a land (Bengal) that hardly knew of yoga he had found a master *rāja* yogi. When Svami "Narendra" sought initiation, he ran into the same problem he met with Ramakrishna. Pavhari Baba was a solitary monk, working out his own salvation; he was slow to take on the *karma* of disciples. Eventually Narendra lamented that he would get "no help from this ritualist." But even when he stated that Ramakrishna "must be an Avatara," he stayed in Ghazipur waiting for initiation from Pavhari Baba.[84] Only circumstances forced him to leave Ghazipur. His "great agitation of mind" led him to describe himself as "a man driven mad with mental agonies."[85]

His return to Baranagore Math was brief. As soon as he took care of some of their financial difficulties, he left with the intention of never returning. He had sought certainty in the scriptures but found contradictions. But he had developed a way of excising caste discrimination of Vedanta (at the expense of Sankara). Pavhari Baba's *rāja* yoga had become so important that he would begin with its exposition to his first formal classes in America three years hence.

V. Neo-Hindu Missionary (1890-1902)

This period of Narendranath Datta's life involves three phases; the break with his *gurubhāis* (1890-93), the reestablishing of contact from America with these *śaktas* of Ramakrishna (1893-97), and the return to India and founding the Ramakrishna Order (1897-1902).

The Break with His Former Gurubhāis (1890-93). It appears evident that the future Svami Vivekananda (at this point in time he had adopted the name Svami Sachchitananda) could not lead his *gurubhāis* from their *bhakti* with its worship of Kālī and Ramakrishna or from *jñāna* with its direct approach to God-realization in *brahmajñā* into combining either of these with radical social concern. Ramakrishna had taught that *bhakti* was the best form of religion of the *kaliyuga* and his former *gurubhāis* were not willing to follow Sachchitananda's call to social reform.[86]

In July 1890, Sachchitananda left the Baranagore Math with a promise that he was leaving them for good. He believed that he would be able to find laborers in India, ten in every town he visited. This was to be the "work of Kālī."[87] For almost two years he sought out the *rājas* of India, for "a prince has the power of doing good."[88] He believed that India's condition was not the fault of its religion but that it had abandoned its religious identity. He believed that Vedanta was the key to raise the masses. His social program included education of women and the masses, improving agriculture, and ending child marriage. But he discovered that these were not concerns of the privileged, powerful, or religious.

By May 1892, the idea of going to the West, to the World Parliament of Religions, was beginning to take shape. But first he would have to discard one of Ramakrishna's key dogmas—the renunciation of "gold." He could not go to the West without handling money. The Kanyakumari vision of his "mission to the West" went through many changes, each a testimony to the agony of deciding what was perceived as an eternal question, even when doubt and uncertainty prevailed.[89] He needed funds for India, needed to defend Hinduism in the West from attacks of conservative Christian missionaries, and would swap spirituality for science and technology.

On May 21, 1893, the newly named Svami Vivekananda (he received his name from a suggestion of the Maharajah of Khetri) sailed for the U.K. Arriving several months too early, he quickly exhausted his funds. Americans aided him, even getting him credentials for the conference, although he represented no religious organization. He told the organizers he was a member of the oldest order of *sannyāsis* in India founded by Sankara.[90] The Parliament of Religions made him a celebrity. Within two months of his first speech *The Statesman* (Calcutta) carried the first news of the "Brahmin Sanyasin."[91] But it was the *Indian Mirror* which championed the svami. On December 20, 1893, it reported that he "was one of the actors on the stage which was erected at the house of the late Babu Keshub Chunder Sen to represent a religious drama, composed, we believe, at the advice, and under the guidance of Babu Keshub."[92] But Calcutta heard on November 30 that this svami was "a nephew of our late friend, Tarak Nath Dutt, of Simla, who was an *Adhyeta* of the Adi Brahmo Samaj. Narendra Nath was for sometime a Brahmo, and with his sweet voice led the orchestra of a certain Brahmo Samaj, of this city. He was for a time one of the actors in the Nava Brindaban Theatre, when our Minister was in the flesh."[93] The article added "that he is not a Hindu of the old Orthodox School; he is a representative of the Neo-Hindus."[94]

Svami Vivekananda left the Parliament of Religions a celebrity. He conceived a plan to earn enough money to continue his mission in India. First he joined a lecture bureau, but quit in July 1894. His next moves were not for hire: he lectured at the Greenacre Conference sponsored by Christian Scientists, moved about as a soiree ornament in Boston and New York, entertaining the wealthy and curious. Finally he settled into giving regular classes in Brooklyn. From February until June 1895, the classes on *rāja* yoga were transcribed by Miss S.E. Waldo, and were transformed into the book by that name. It is important that his first formal teachings to his American followers involved "psychic control"— such meditative methods as *mantrayāna, prāṇāyāna, pratyāhārā, dhāranā,* and *dhyāna.*[95] Patanjali's yoga aphorisms were translated and studied to explain the mastery of spiritual powers, which were still a matter to be fully integrated in his own understanding. Next, he turned to what was to become the hallmark of his teachings, *karma* yoga.[96] J.J. Goodwin took down the lectures which began in December 1895, and ended in book form on February 24, 1896. Other lectures were compiled into books on *Bhakti Yoga* and *Jñāna Yoga.*

Reestablishing Contact. His work in America, England, and Madras was commenced before he was able to bring his former *gurubhāis* to his spiritual conception and program. His first extant letter to a former *gurubhāi* was on March 19, 1894.[97] In it he told of his plans to raise up the masses in India, working in America to get money, giving spirituality in return, depending "on no one in Hindustan." "If any of you help me in my plans, all right, or Gurudeva will show me the way out." Shortly thereafter (August 1894) he wrote a scathing letter suggesting that these *gurubhāis* were failing him at the moment and had failed the masses for centuries.

If you want any good to come, just throw your ceremonials overboard and worship the Living God, the Man-God—every being that wears a human form—God in His universal as well as individual aspect. The universal aspect of God means this world, and worshipping it means serving it—this indeed is work, not indulging in ceremonials. . . . If now you can show this in practice, if you can make three or four hundred disciples in India within a year, then only I may have some hope.[98] (This second set of illusions are in the published text of the letter; the original has long ago deteriorated, and the photostats are not available for study by scholars.)

He called upon his former *gurubhāis* to renounce their personal goal of *mukti.* "It is only by doing good to others that one attains to one's own good, and it is by leading others to Bhakti and Mukti that one attains them oneself."[99] He gradually drew some into famine relief work, goading them into practical service. But these were monks who had renounced the world to seek their own salvation through methods such as *sādhanas, tapas, japas, puja, dhyāna*—all designed to remove the *karma* already acquired from past activity. Now Vivekananda called them back into action—organized activity at that! In an April 1896, letter he reorganized the Math: "If you consider it wise to be guided by my ideas and if you follow these rules, then I shall supply on [sic] all necessary funds."[100] The letters which evidence the struggle are discussed elsewhere.[101] All these letters have been carefully edited, but even then the anger displayed by Svami Vivekananda toward his former brothers was not completely excised. His Madrasi disciples began publishing his speeches in the *Brahmacharyin.*[102] The popular press in India was constantly publicizing his remarks, often for their political content.[103] When he left America and England in December 1896, he left Vedanta societies in New York and London and some totally committed disciples.

Return to India and Founding the Ramakrishna Mission. The triumphal return of Svami Vivekananda to India has been explored extensively. But what must be noted is the gradual and subtle crisis which beset Vivekananda 'upon his return. He had been turned into a living archetype by the Indian press, the spiritual warrior who had shown the superiority of Hinduism to the world. Yet his reason for defending the glories of Hinduism lay in the fact that something eternal was there to be awakened. That awakening had not yet been effected. But as he attempted to rally Indians to their "mission"[104] he encountered opposition and hostility. Even the most generous assessment of the months between his return to India and the departure again to the West can find no *satya yuga.* The Ramakrishna Math and Mission were founded in 1897, training of disciples was begun, and plans were laid. But Vivekananda would not live to see the awakening. It was the message of the

Eternal Religion that was his final triumph. His return to America served to give that work a firm foundation. But the second trip was more of a psychological than an organizational necessity. Vivekananda's pattern of ultimate concern during this period brought together many of the elements which had troubled him in earlier periods. Vedanta was fully exonerated from the Brahmo charge that its doctrine of *māyāvāda* prevented humanitarian concern. Vedanta was conceived not as the true religion but as the eternal truth behind all religion.

The Message of the Religion Eternal: Sanātana Dharma. Svami Vivekananda's Vedanta proceeded from the epistemological question: What is that by realizing which everything is realized? This question set the goal of the belief system and directed it toward a special kind of knowledge. It affirmed that the goal is that unity in which everything is realized. This special knowledge is *aparokṣānubhūti* (transcendental meditation) which seeks "to find unity in the midst of diversity. . . . In reality, the metaphysical and the physical universe are one, and the name of this One is Brahman; and the perception of separateness is an error—they called it Maya, Avidya, or nescience. This is the end of knowledge."[105]

Thus, true knowledge or truth is oneness, unity. The test of truth is oneness.[106] The principle by which truth is judged, which Svami Vivekananda has designated "reason,"[107] is unity. "Unity is the goal of Religion and Science."[108] Unity or "Absolute Truth is God alone."[109] Truth is to be judged by truth and by nothing else."[110]

The svami's quest for meaning has as its goal nothing less than absolute truth.[111] To be absolute is to be unaffected by change. The absolute cannot be part of an order limited by space, time and causation (*deśa kāla nimitta*). Yet all that confronted the senses is necessarily within the phenomenal realm, even the written Vedas. So one cannot begin with the scriptures as the foundation for the realization of changeless knowledge. The scriptures had first been accepted "on faith" in order that they might be used to prove the existence of the Absolute. This could never grant certainty. Therefore, the traditional starting point had to be discarded.

Svami Vivekananda found that the foundation of every level of knowledge is personal experience. True knowledge must never be accepted "on faith" in an outside authority. If it is universally true, it must be capable of verification by each seeker after truth when he has reached that level of understanding.

The discoveries of *ṛṣis* and *avatāras*, which are repeatable when one reaches that stage of spirituality, have shown that the founda-tions of knowledge (*pramāṇas*) in the sensate world are not untrue but actually lower levels of truth which point beyond themselves to the direct experience of the Absolute (*aparokṣānubhūti*). Because of this structure of true knowledge all relative knowledge must be judged by the highest principle. That principle is unity. Accord-ing to the process of generalization, which was seen by Svami Vivekananda as the scientific way of acquiring knowledge, all lower apprehensions of truth depend upon each higher synthesis, until, at last, the highest generalization is reached—the unity or oneness of all the universe.

Svami Vivekananda identified the changeless, infinite, eternal unity as the most meaningful concern of life.[112] But even as the sources of knowledge were found to yield impermanent knowledge, so also the process of perception was found to leave a radical break between the impression of an object upon the mind and the knowledge of the object-in-itself. That which was external to the individual (*jīva*) was found to be unknowable in its essence. The *jīva* merely reacted to what came from beyond its mind (*manas*) and was limited to its created visions—its own illusory universe.

Not only was the *jīva's* knowledge of objects incomplete and ever changing, it also suffered from the impossibility of true knowledge of itself. The mind of the individual was limited by space, time, and causation, and because of this the mind differen-tiates that which is really one as a multiplicity by name and form (*nāma-rupa*). The *jīva* cannot know the true perceiver because the *jīva* has relative existence on the sensate plane where true percep-tion does not occur. The real is beyond the mind. It is beyond differentiation.

This analysis led the svami through the sources of knowledge to the process of perception. Each analysis has pointed beyond itself.

The unique aspect of the svami's teachings about the cosmos is not that the cosmos lacks ultimate reality.[113] While he says this, it is commonplace among *advaitans*. Nor does his usage of the notions of *māyā* and *avidyā* suggest originality. Through these notions, he was able to demonstrate, like those before him, that the world which we see is *vivārta* (appearance). What is unique

is the svami's combination of two theories of causation and their
corollary views of the universe. He combined *pariṇāma* from
sāṁkhya with *vivarta* from Advaita Vedanta and made them refer
to two complementary but distinct realms of reality. Accordingly,
pariṇāma referred to a real transformation of the cause into a
multiplicity of effects. But this was viewing the universe from
beneath, within *māyā* and bound by *deśa kāla nimitta*. According
to *vivarta* the relative view is transcended and the apparent multiplicity of objects can no longer be found. For beyond the bonds
of time, space, and causation there is only *brahman*.

When viewing the pattern of ultimacy from the vantage point
of the solution, one is struck by its nearly perfect relationships.[114]
Even if it be granted that Svami Vivekananda was slightly ambiguous in his formulations about *saguṇa* and *nirguṇa brahman*, still,
the solution was eventually brought to the doctrine of *neti neti*, the
absolute negation of formulations about the Absolute in categories
limited by space, time, and causation. Thus, each component of
the pattern of ultimacy points to *advaita* (non-duality) or to *eka*
(oneness). The epistemology of *sanātana dharma* was based upon
the principle of unity which was found by the *ṛṣis* and *avatāras* to
be the highest principle of knowledge. By it the relative value of
sensate knowledge could be determined, and from it the structure
of knowledge could be deduced. Thus, only data which proved
unity are real data; all else (data which suggest multiplicity) must
be understood in the light of the principle of unity. The process of
perception found that behind a radical split between the individual
perceivers and the perceived was the one perceiver, the *ātman*.
His analysis of the cosmos determined that the multiplicity of
objects of perception was only apparent and that behind this
illusion was the source of all objects, *brahman*. Finally, *ātman* and
brahman were realized as one, and that beyond all qualities of
space, time and causation is the perfect existence, consciousness,
and bliss of the inexpressible. The solution in the quest for
ultimate meaning finally leaps beyond all categories of rational
and sensate processes to the experience of the Absolute in *nirvikalpa*
samādhi (changeless absorption in the One).

Except for placing the *sanātana dharma* on the epistemological
foundation of personal experience judged by the principle of unity
instead of the Vedas, Svami Vivekananda's formulation offers
little that has not already appeared in Indian thought. What is

novel is the application of the *sanātana dharma* to the social problems in *deśa kāla nimitta* to provide direction and purpose on the plane of *vivārta*.

In practical Vedanta (note an old Brahmo emphasis) Svami Vivekananda applied changeless principles to the problems of a changing age. The problem for Vedanta can be summarized: the only Real is *brahman*, realized only in *nirvakalpa samādhi*, the changeless state of consciousness of oneness.[115] Limited existence is suffering, brought about by ignorance (*avidyā*). Ultimately it is illusion (*māyā*). Liberation from the bonds of suffering (*mukti*) is knowledge (*jñāna*) of one's true nature as the Unmanifested, who alone is beyond all activity. Since Vedanta teaches that *mukti* is not in the world, why should not the seeker of *brahman* turn from all activity in the world to a life of contemplation (*dhyāna*) of the Real?[116] But if this is done, what benefit will Vedanta be for the suffering masses of India and the world? (A question which is meaningful for a Brahmo but not a strict advaitan!)

This philosophical dilemma posed by the apparent opposition of *jñāna* and *karma* could be solved in two steps. First, Vedanta had shown that relative truths are levels or stages (*avasthās*) in realizing the one truth. These stages of interpreting the Vedanta—dvaita (dualism), *visiṣṭādvaita* (qualified monism) and *advaita* (monism)— are complementary, fulfilling each other as one "stepping stone to the other until the goal, the Advaita, the Tat Tvam Asi, is reached." From the strict viewpoint of *advaita*, which is the highest stage of truth, there can be no duality. There is no doer or deed; there is no desire or attraction. There is only *brahman*. However, this viewpoint is eschatological. While in the world of multiplicity, the *jīva* must act. Even thought is activity. Thus Svami Vivekananda concluded: "The highest Advaitism cannot be brought down to practical life. Advaitism made practical works from the plane of Vishishtadvaitism."[117] At this level activity is real and plans can be made for the good of all beings. Thus, since activity is inevitable in the world of multiplicity, the real problem concerns the binding effect of activity (*saṁsāra*). The *Bhagavadgītā* has properly shown that the *jīva* is only bound to the results of its actions (*karma*) if it is attached to them through egotism (*ahaṁkāra*) or desire.[118] By renouncing the fruits of its action, the *jīva* will be freed of the binding effects of *karma*. With regard to self (*jīva*) the actions can be given in the service of the Self (*ātman*), the totality of all beings. The discipline of activity without selfish motives can also, therefore, lead to the attainment of liberation from *deśa kāla nimitta*. But more important, in this age of suffering (the *kaliyuga*), *karma yoga* is the means by which Vedanta serves practically in the world.

Practical Vedanta could both harmonize and revolutionize all of life in the world. It could produce "the new order of society"[119] and "can change the whole tendency of the world"[120] by putting the forces which have become destructive in check. This plan could be accomplished through education and service. "Our work is to ground knowledge of the real Self within the masses."[121] Ignorance of the real Self within has brought weakness, suffering and evil.[122] Education about the potentiality within man will reverse the process of deterioration and begin the process of expansion toward men's true nature. The process of growth gradually develops the powers within until "Brahminhood" is reached.[123] "Liberty is the first condition of growth."[124]

Trained in the fiery mantras of the Upaniṣads and in the principles of practical Vedanta, the masses will be awakened to their own strength. The radical reform of society, based upon the harmony of science and Vedanta, will have begun. Each man, woman, and child will grow according to their own nature; none will need to rule them. "They will solve their own problems O tyrants, attempting to think that you can do anything for any one! Hands off! The Divine will look after all. Who are you to assume that you know everything?"[125]

The twin principles *vairāgya* (renunciation) and *jīvanseva* (service to mankind)[126] provide the basis for all activity in the world.[127] They teach mankind to discover "their divinity, and how to make it manifest in every moment of life."[128] "I believe that the Satya Yuga (Golden Age) will come when there will be ône caste, one Veda, and peace and harmony. This idea of the Satya Yuga is what would revivify India. Believe it."[129] He believed that practical Vedanta's principle of unity would create this new India. He saw the masses being liberated from dualistic customs and superstitions.[130] *Advaita* had never been allowed to come to the people. Now it would come to them so that the impersonal idea would gradually take "away all trade from the priests, churches, and temples."[131] True knowledge of the Self would gradually raise all to "Brahminhood."[132]

Able to assimilate the entire spiritual pilgrimage of makind, Vedanta would be able to provide a rationale for being religious in the modern world. In its spiritual bankruptcy, the West would turn to Vedanta and be saved by "the religion of the Upaniṣads." It would change "the whole tendency of the world," bringing in the *satya yuga*.[133]

VI. Facing Death (1902)

Throughout the last two years of his life, Vivekananda's medical problems with diabetes began to slow down the "cyclonic Hindu."[134] In this time he began to gravitate toward meditation and devotion.[135] Kālī *pūjā*, the very type of religious expression he pressured his *gurubhāis* to drop, became increasingly meaningful the last six months of his life. He left no written expression of this devotion to Kālī during this last period of his life.

He died on July 4, 1902, with great serenity and dignity. It is said that he predicted his death a week in advance. It is in the calm with which he faced death that one sees no evidence of his wrenching, lifelong doubts. But these very doubts moved him through an extraordinary religious pilgrimage.

Notes

1. These methodological considerations have been discussed in deail in an earlier study, George Williams, *Quest for Meaning of Svāmī Vivekānanda* (Chico: New Horizons Press, 1974), pp. 1-9.
2. Ibid., pp. 7-9. The camouflage effect of Svami Vivekananda's different versions or valuings of the same event is overcome through careful examination of contemporaneous and later documentation and through understanding the significance of periods of belief.
3. Official accounts of the life and teachings of Svami Vivekananda designate three types of literature coming from the Ramakrishna movement. First, there are the direct sayings and writings of Svami Vivekananda. These have been collected and carefully edited by the Ramakrishna Order and published in *The Complete Works of Swami Vivekananda*, 8 vols., 6 eds. (Calcutta: Advaita Ashrama, 1964); hereafter *CW*; and in innumerable monographs, usually selecting sayings topically. Second, there is the "direct disciple" literature collected by the Order. This includes *The Life of Swami Vivekananda by His Eastern and Western Disciples*, 4th ed., currently undergoing another revision (Calcutta: Advaita Ashrama, 1965; hereafter *LVK*). *Reminiscences of Swami Vivekananda by His Eastern and Western Admirers*, 2 eds. (Calcutta: Advaita Ashrama, 1964; hereafter

RSV); and Sister Nivedita's *The Complete Works of Sister Nivedita*, 4 vols., 2 eds. (Calcutta: Sister Nivedita Girls School, 1972). Third, there are the class of works by svamis and laymen of the Ramakrishna movement. Jean Herbert's *Swami Vivekananda: Bibliographie* (Paris: Advien Maisonneuve, 1938), lists some of this third class as well as some of the first. Studies by Svamis Abhedananda and Nikhilananda are representative, while lay followers would be typified by Majumdar, Rolland, Isherwood, and Yale. Secondary articles are to be found in such journals as *Prabuddha Bharata* and *Vedanta Kesari*.

Marie Louise Burke's *Swami Vivekananda in America: New Discoveries*, 2 eds. (Calcutta: Advaita Ashrama, 1958), and *Swami Vivekananda: His Second Visit to the West. New Discoveries* (Calcutta: Advaita Ashrama, 1973) report even damaging data before interpreting it in a light positive to the movement.

4. Even historians like R.C. Majumdar, *Svami Vivekananda: A Historical Review* (Calcutta: General Printers & Publishers, 1965), and V.S. Naravane, *Modern Indian Thought* (New York: Asia Publishing House, 1964) follow this schema.

5. Williams, *Quest for Meaning*, p. 6.

6. *LVK*, p. 9.

7. Ibid., pp. 12, 14.

8. Ibid., pp. 10-11.

9. Ibid.; p. 16.

10. *Vivekananda: A Biography in Pictures* (Calcutta: Advaita Ashrama, 1973), p. 12.

11. *LVK*, pp. 4-6. Charan Dutta became a monk at twenty-five, leaving his wife and baby son.

12. Ibid., p. 46.

13. Ibid., pp. 9ff., and *The Story of Vivekananda: Illustrated* (Calcutta: Advaita Ashrama, 1970), a children's book in English for young Indians, pp. 8-11.

14. *LVK*, pp. 13-14.

15. Ibid., pp. 13, 19.

16. Ibid., pp. 18, 14.

17. Ibid., pp. 13, 15-16, 21, 23.

18. Ibid., p. 18; "Had Naren's powers not been checked by this accident, he would have shattered the world." This remark is attributed to Sri Ramakrishna.

19. Cf. section 3 (Ramakrishna's Disciple).

20. *LVK*, p. 22: "So Ambitious was he in this respect that if his mental powers were not given recognition, he would fly into a rage, not sparing even his father's friends and nothing short of an apology would quiet him."

21. David Kopf, *The Brahmo Samaj and the Shaping of the Modern Indian Mind* (Princeton, NJ: Princeton University Press, 1979), p. 103.

22. The significance given to Narendranath Datta's asking religious leaders if they had "seen God" is central to the legend. By struggling with this

aspect of the biography, we have all missed the significance of the nervous breakdown.

23. The existence of the photostats at the Belur Math Library is a well-kept secret. Scholars are encouraged by this author to ask to see them.

24. Kopf, *The Brahmo Samaj*, pp. 3-14.

25. Ibid.

26. Spencer Lavan, *Unitarians and India: A Study in Encounter and Response* (Boston: Beacon Press, 1977).

27. Kopf, *The Brahmo Samaj*.

28. Ibid., p. 18.

29. Ibid., pp. 26-31, 39-41, 92-94.

30. Ibid., pp. 98ff.

31. Shivanath Sastri, *The Brahmo Samaj: Religious Principles and Brief History*, abridged ed. (Calcutta: Sadharan Brahmo Samaj, 1958), Chapter 3.

32. Ibid., p. 26.

33. Shivanath Sastri, *The Mission of the Brahmo Samaj or the Theistic Church of India*, 2nd. ed. (Calcutta: Kuntaline Press, 1910), p. 57.

34. Ibid., p. 51.

35. Ibid., p. 50.

36. Sastri, *The Brahmo Samaj*, chapter 3.

37. Sastri, *The Mission of the Brahmo Samaj*, pp. 97ff.

38. *The Gospel of Sri Ramakrishna*, recorded by Mahendranath Gupta and translated from Bengali into English by Svami Nikhilananda (New York: Ramakrishna-Vivekananda Center, 1969); hereafter *GRK*.

39. Kopf, *The Brahmo Samaj*, p. 26.

40. Keshab Chandra Sen, *Spiritual Progress: Sayings and Writings* (Calcutta: Navavidhan Publication Committee, c. 1934), pp. 6, 7, 25.

41. Bhupendranath Datta, *Svami Vivekananda: Patriot-Prophet* (Calcutta: Nababharat, 1954), p. 259.

42. *GRK*, p. 198.

43. Datta, *Svami Vivekananda*, p. 154.

44. Kopf. *The Brahmo Samaj*, p. 124.

45. *GRK*, pp. 82, 112, 113, 157, 166, 247, 438-39, 583-84, 670, 748, 817, 819.

46. Datta, *Svami Vivekananda* , p. 102, and *GRK*, p. 127.

47. Robert F. Gould, *A Concise History of Freemasonry* (London: Gala & Polden, 1903), esp. p. 398.

48. Datta, *Svami Vivekananda*, p. 109.

49. *LVK*, p. 90. Cf. Kopf, *The Brahmo Samaj*, pp. 47ff., concerning Vidyasagar.

50. Kopf, *The Brahmo Samaj*, p. 32.

51. *LVK*, p. 26.

52. Ibid. See also citations in n. 3 above.

53. R.C. Majumdar, ed., *Swami Vivekananda Centenary Memorial Volume* (Calcutta: Swami Vivekananda Centenary Committee, 1963), p. 47; hereafter *SVCMV*.

54. Ibid., p. 48.

55. Williams, *Quest for Meaning*, p. 26.

56. *LVK*, p. 46.
57. Ibid., p. 47.
58. *GRK*, p. 841; *LVK*, p. 65; *SVCMV*, p. 48. Three of the four versions of this event say "hand" instead of "foot": *GRK*, pp. 231, 717, 770.
59. *GRK*, pp. 231, 717, 770.
60. Scientific research in a sufficient number of fields to produce significant interpretive breakthroughs began to take place in the late 1970s. Altered (or alternative) States of Consciousness (ASC) is now a recognized field of research engaged in from neurophysiology, biofeedback research, drug research, transpersonal psychology, etc. Danile Goleman and Richard J. Davidson, eds,, summarize what has transpired to date in *Consciousness: Brain, States of Awareness, and Mysticism* (New York: Harper & Row, 1979). Two more edited works which survey the field are recommended to those wishing to survey the research (1) Charles T. Tart, ed., *Altered States of Consciousness* (Garden City, NY: Doubleday, 1969), and (2) Norman E. Zinberg, ed., *Alternate States of Consciousness: Multiple Perspectives on the Study of Consciousness* (New York: Free Press, 1977).
61. *GRK*, pp. 1019-20.
62. Ibid., pp. 231, 717, 770, 841; *LVK*, pp. 65, 93-94; Williams, *Quest for Meaning*, pp. 25-26.
63. *GRK*. p. 279.
64. Ibid., p. 394.
65. Ibid., p. 397.
66. Ibid., pp, 462, 508, 562.
67. Ibid., p. 569.
68. Ibid., p. 727.
69. Ibid., p. 711.
70. Ibid., p. 987; Williams, *Quest for Meaning*, p. 21, nn. 77, 78.
71. *GRK*, p. 734.
72. Ibid., p. 735.
73. Ibid., p. 724ff.
74. Ibid,, pp. 538ff., 581.
75. Williams, *Quest for Meaning*, p. 22, and *LVK*, pp. 158-59, 168.
76. Svami "Narendra" is a construct to indicate that he now had self-ordination but had not yet come to the name he would be known by later. Since the redactor's hands is present once again in the extant data, all his letters are signed as if he were already using "Vivekananda" at this time. How he perceived himself by name would be important information.
77. *CW*, 6:208-9.
78. Unfortunately the Order only saved Vivekananda's part of the correspondence.
79. *CW*, 6:211.
80. Ibid., p. 212.
81. Ibid., p. 209.
82. Ibid., p. 214.
83. Ibid., p. 239.
84. Ibid., pp. 231-32; and Williams, *Quest for Meaning*, pp. 47-51.

85. *CW*, 6:239; and *LVK*, p. 200.

86. Williams, *Quest for Meaning*, pp. 54ff.

87. Ibid., p. 55.

88. *RSV*, pp. 38-39.

89. *LVK*, pp. 251-55.

90. This is demonstrated in the biographical entries of the histories of the parliament: Walter R. Hougton, ed., *Neely's History of the Parliament of Religions and Religious Congresses at the World's Columbian Exposition* (Chicago: F.T. Neely, 1893), p. 64; John Henry Barrows, ed., *The World's Parliament of Religions*, 2 vols. (Chicago: Parliament Publishing Company, 1893); J.W. Hanson, eds., *The World's Congress of Religions* (Chicago: International Publishing Company, 1894), pp. 366ff. Marie Louise Burke, *Swami Vivekananda in America* (pp. 69-70) details some of the times he identified himself as a *brahmin* monk.

91. S.B. Basu and S.B. Ghosh, eds., *Vivekananda in Indian Newspapers, 1893-1902* (Calcutta: Dineshchandra Basu Bhattacharyya and Co., 1969) p. 8.

92. Ibid.

93. Ibid., p. 9.

94. Ibid.

95. *CW*, 1:119-313.

96. Ibid., pp. 25-118.

97. Ibid., 6:250.

98. Ibid., 6:263.

99. Ibid.

100. Ibid., 8:489-94.

101. Williams, *Quest for Meaning*, p. 120, n. 36.

102. Swami Satprakashananda, *Swami Vivekananda's Contribution to the Present Age* (St. Louis: Vedanta Society of St. Louis, 1978), p. 128.

103. Basu and Ghosh, eds., *Vivekananda in Indian Newspapers*.

104. Vivekananda's use of the term "mission" reflects a borrowing from his Brahmo Samaj background.

105. *CW*, 5:519-20.

106. Ibid., 2:304.

107. Vivekananda has used the English word "reason" in two ways: (1) as the activity of the mind, *anumana* (*CW*, 7:91: inspiration is higher than reason) and (2) as the criterion of truth (*CW*, 2:335-36: reason is the universal authority: "I believe in reason and follow reason having seen enough of the evils of authority, for I was born in a country where they have gone to the extreme of authority"; 5:315: "The Vedas, i.e., only those portions of them which agree with reason, are to be accepted as authority"; 5:411: "Personally I take as much of the Vedas as agrees with reason").

108. *RVK*, p. 396.

109. *CW*, 7:120.

110. Ibid., p. 101.

111. For more than adequate documentation of this summary see Williams, *Quest for Meaning*, pp. 63-67.

112. Ibid., pp. 67-73.
113. Ibid., pp. 74-79.
114. Ibid., pp. 80-85.
115. Ibid., pp. 85-104.
116. *CW*, 7:181.
117. Ibid., 6:122.
118. Ibid.,   1:446-80;   4:102-10;   5:239-42;   246-49;   6:83-84;   7:273-75
     (note svami is being challenged on his particular usage of *karma* yoga);
     88:-9, 484.
119. Ibid., 3:161.
120. Ibid., pp. 158-59.
121. Ibid., 2:358.
122. Ibid., p. 355.
123. Ibid., 3:293.
124. Ibid., 3:246.
125. Ibid.
126. Ibid., 2:285; 5:228.
127. Ibid., 5:382; 7:133.
128. Ibid., 7:498.
129. Ibid., 5:31.
130. Ibid., 3:225, 263-65, 279.
131. Ibid., 2:320, 303: "You know in your inmost heart that many of your
     limited ideas, this humbling of yourself and praying and weeping to
     imaginary beings are superstitious."
132. Ibid., 3:293.
133. Ibid., pp. 159, 197-98, 293-304; 5:31; 7:95.
134. Burke, *Swami Vivekananda in America*.
135. *CW*, 7:129f; 5:391f; 7:139f, 252f., 230, 264; 8:517; 6:515f.

14

ULTIMACY AS UNIFIER IN GANDHI

Boyd H. Wilson

Mohandas K. Gandhi has been variously depicted as a politician, a social reformer, and a religious leader. Although these are divergent fields, they are not necessarily mutually exclusive. On the one hand, Gandhi's activities can be characterized by a diversity of goals. But on the other hand, there is a consistency, even a certain myopia, to his activities. It will be seen that Gandhi's diversities are unified under the aegis of his ultimate concern.

When Erik Erikson tried to understand and explain Gandhi in his book entitled *Gandhi's Truth*, he did so by applying Freudian analysis to Gandhi's early life. This was an attempt to explain why Gandhi did what he did. Such an investigation into Gandhi's childhood and development is not necessary in the present study because the questions at hand are "What did Gandhi do?" and "How did he do it?" Even Gandhi's development as a thinker is not germane to the study. D.K. Bedekar maintains that to understand Gandhi, one must realize that by 1920 Gandhi had established the "form" of his thought and action. After this, there was no substantial change or development.[1] Whereas this conclusion is basically sound, the date is a bit late. All the strands of Gandhi's thoughts and actions can be found in incipient form in his tract entitled *Hind Swaraj*, which was written while Gandhi was in South Africa, and published in 1908.

In his autobiography, Gandhi marks as the turning point in his life an encounter in a South African train station in which he was

forced out of a first-class berth because he was "colored." It was
then that he decided to champion the causes of the minorities and
"little people" in the world. Subsequent to this encounter, he
began developing the programs and methods that characterized his
lifelong endeavors. Although he continued clarifying and honing
his ideas, there were never any significant changes or drastic jumps
in development. Gandhi was conscious of criticisms of inconsistency, and in 1932 disclaimed any attempt at consistency in his
writings and his work, but this was unnecessary.[2]   There is a consistency. There are many edited works which collate and assimilate Gandhi's writings on any particular subject. In these works,
no effort is made to distinguish between early writings and later
writings, and when so juxtaposed, it is not possible to discern any
marked change or development in his later writings. Therefore,
for an understanding of Gandhi on the level sought here, it is not
necessary to delve into his early life, nor look for development and
change in his writings. It is possible to treat the writings of his
active period (1900-1948) as a homologous whole, and this is the
method applied here.

Yet, simply treating the writings of Gandhi as a homologous
whole does not guarantee a unified picture of Gandhi. Gandhi is
often characterized as being quite diversified in his activities, as
pursuing various goals in different arenas. One writer, in an introduction to a study guide on Gandhi, writes,

From one angle of view, he [Gandhi] appears as a virtual saint,
seeking to bring moral regeneration to India, to her British
masters, and even to a troubled world at large. Seen in another
light, he seems a shrewd politician, drawing out the latent force
of India's millions, guiding and directing it in channels of non-
violent direct action toward the goal of Indian freedom from
British rule. . . . Finally, in still another dimension of his protean
career, Gandhi stands out as a social reformer, attempting to free
India from scars of poverty, caste and class antagonism, untouchability, and conflict between the adherents of Hinduism and
Islam.[3]

So characterized, Gandhi is seen as a person with multiple levels of
goals and interests which are only tangentially related. He is a
religious man—a "saint"; he is a politician; he is a social reformer;

and (a category overlooked by the writer quoted above) he is an economic theorist. This is Gandhi in diversity, and it is one way of understanding him. Gandhi can be described as a man operating under several different categories and performing in as many different arenas. This is how he will first be studied here: Gandhi in the four arenas of religion, politics, social reform, and economics.

Gandhi considers himself a "Hindu." In his autobiography, Gandhi tells of his encounters with other religions, his questioning of Hinduism, and his conclusion that Hinduism is his religion. He later concluded that "Hinduism with its message of Ahimsa is to me the most glorious religion in the world."[4] He is careful to delineate what he means by Hinduism: he rejects the Hinduism of untouchability, superstitions, and sacrifices. His Hinduism is the Hinduism of the *Gītā*, the Upaniṣads, and Patañjali, which teaches *ahiṃsā*, the oneness of creation, and the pure worship of the formless imperishable God.[5] Gandhi says that he is a Hindu because he believes in the Vedas, *varnāśrama dharma*, in cow protection, in idol worship, in the *śāstras*, and in the oneness of God.[6] To Gandhi, the essence of Hinduism is *ahiṃsā*, non-violence; without *ahiṃsā*, there would be no Hinduism.[7] For Gandhi, *ahiṃsā* is more than the negative aspect of harmlessness and non-violence; it includes the positive state of love and of doing good even to the evildoer.[8]

The goal of Gandhi's religion is truth, *satya*.[9] To him, only truth is eternal; everything else is momentary.[10] At one point, Gandhi describes his goal in terms of God: "What I want to achieve—what I have been striving and pinning to achieve these thirty years—is self-realization, to see God face to face, to attain *Moksha*. I live and move and have my being in pursuit of this goal."[11] But later, he says he does not regard God as a person; for him, truth is God.[12] His goal, then, is to find truth, which he equates with God: "I am but a humble seeker after Truth and bent on finding it. I count no sacrifice too great for the sake of seeing God face to face."[13] So, when Gandhi says he is trying to achieve self-realization, when he says he seeks to see God face to face, when he says he wants to attain *mokṣa*, all these are different expressions of the same religious goal: truth. The means of attaining this goal, for Gandhi, is *ahiṃsa*.[14]

But in the political arena, Gandhi has a quite different stated goal: *svarāj*. Although *svarāj* literally means "self-rule," Gandhi used it more as a synonym for freedom. *Svarāj* for him includes freedom of speech, freedom of association, and freedom of the press.[15] This freedom in his *svarāj* includes freedom of opinion, even, as he says, if they are distasteful opinions.[16] Freedom of opinion extends to freedom of religion as well. Gandhi did not envision a nation that supported and recommended one religion over the others. This would have gone contrary to his view of freedom. He felt that any imposition in the personal life of the citizens on the part of the government was not *svarāj*. *Svarāj* implies not only the freedom of the nation to rule itself, but also the freedom of each individual to rule himself. Gandhi sees this as a process that can work two ways: either the government gains freedom and filters this freedom down to the individuals, or the individuals in the nation gain *svarāj*, or freedom for themselves, and institute it in the ascending levels of government.[17]

Gandhi's *svarāj* is not an isolationist policy; he does not want foreigners in control of India, but neither does he recommend their expulsion. Foreigners are welcomed by Gandhi to merge with the nation of India and enjoy their own *svarāj*.[18] *Svarāj* for India means the throwing off of foreign control of sources of revenue and expenditures.[19] Gandhi saw this economic drain of foreign industry and commerce to be one of the greatest hindrances to *svarāj*. Until India becomes economically free, it could never become politically free. *Svarāj*, then, is an all-encompassing concept for Gandhi; it includes political freedom, economic freedom, social freedom, and personal freedom. He was content to let the ambiguity of the concept of *svarāj* continue because he thought this would encourage the growth of the concept. He says: "To give it one definite meaning is to narrow the outlook and to limit what is at present happily limitless. Let the content of Swaraj grow with the growth of national consciousness and aspirations."[20]

Gandhi's *svarāj* can be interpreted as a movement of national consciousness and national pride. He considered the civilization that had evolved in India to be unexcelled in the world.[21] If the foreign influence, the English control, were thrown off without an infusion of national consciousness, Gandhi feared there would be a retention of English customs and laws. This was not the *svarāj* he wanted: in this case India would "be called not Hindustan but Englistan."[22] Gandhi's *svarāj* includes a reinstitution of Indian customs, Indian laws, and Indian values. This reinstitution starts with the abolition of English as the national language. Gandhi thought that the national language of India should be Hindi, with the option of writing it in Persian or Nagari characters.[23] This return to the native language would instill in the people a sense of nationhood based on Indian roots. Often when Gandhi spoke of *svarāj* as a return to the pristine values of early India, he used the term *rāmarājya* (or *rāmarāj*). This recalls the days when India was ruled by a beneficent and moral monarch. By *rāmarājya*, Gandhi means the sovereignty of the people based on pure moral authority.[24] This government based on morality implies that both the ruler and the ruled are pure. Gandhi believed that India's heritage and history proved that it was suitable for such a rule.

In the political arena, then, Gandhi's goal is *svarāj*, or self-rule, and freedom of the people and the government. The means to this goal include the development of national consciousness and national pride, the institution of Hindi as the national language, and the removal of foreign control. But to complete the means to his political goal of *svarāj*, Gandhi moves into the social and economic arenas. Gandhi sees social and economic reforms as necessary preparations for *svarāj*.

In the social arena, Gandhi has three items on his agenda: Hindu-Muslim unity, the removal of untouchability, and equal distribution of wealth, or *sarvodaya*. Gandhi feels that there can be no social harmony until there is a settlement with the Muslims. He sees the religious differences of these two groups as segmenting and alienating the Indian people. He does not ask that either the Hindus or the Muslims change; what he wants is for them to accept each other as equals and respect each other's religions. He stalwartly maintains that until the differences are overcome and communal unity is established, *svarāj* would be only an idle dream.[25] *Svarāj* depends on the idea of nationhood and nationhood depends on the unity of society. As long as the Muslims and the Hindus are divided, there can be no Indian nation.

Besides the division caused by the Hindu-Muslim rift, Gandhi sees another problem in society hindering social harmony. This division, though, is solely in the Hindu camp: the problem of untouchability. On this question, Gandhi's problem is not with the institution of caste, or *varṇa*. He considers the four castes to be fundamental, natural, and essential. The caste system is not

based on inequality or inferiority, but on ability.[26] Gandhi sees
the law of *varṇa*, or caste, as descriptive rather than prescriptive;
that is, a person fulfils the duties in society that he is best equipped
to do, based on his natural tendencies and limitations.[27] Usually,
though, the law of *varṇa* prescribes that a person will, if capable,
follow the heritage and traditional calling of his forefathers.[28]
Gandhi thinks that the law of caste, as originally formulated,
promotes national well-being, because it insures the presence of
qualified personnel in all occupations.[29] Gandhi's argument, then,
is not with the institution of caste, but with the aberration of that
institution found in the practice of untouchability.

Gandhi considers untouchability to be a "heinous crime against
humanity."[30] He does not consider it to be a part of Hinduism;
he finds no justification for it in the *śāstras*.[31] Although it is
supported by the so-called orthodox party, Gandhi sees it as a
device of Satan to destroy religion.[32] He refers to untouchables
in his writings with the word *harijan*, which means "man of God."
He reasons that if God is, as all religions claim, the friend of the
friendless, the help of the helpless, and the protector of the weak,
then no one is more worthy of being called *harijan*, man of God,
than the untouchables.[33] This appellation also imbues the untouchables with a feeling of dignity and worth. First the untouchables
must respect themselves, and then others will respect them and
accept them as part of the human family. Until this acceptance
is accomplished, Gandhi says there will be no social harmony, no
social unity, and no hope for nationhood. Like the rift between
Muslims and Hindus, the division between caste Hindus and
untouchables stands in the way of *svaraj*.

A third division that Gandhi sees in society is the gap between
the rich and the poor, the "haves" and the "have-nots." His
solution to this division is termed *sarvodaya*, the welfare of all.
In this program, Gandhi asks those who have money and property
to behave as trustees, holding their wealth on behalf of the poor.[34]
Gandh's goal in *sarvodaya* is equal distribution of wealth. He wants
to reduce the gulf between the rich and the indigent. He does not
ask those with money to give up all their wealth and drop to the
same level as the poor, but asks merely that those who have more
money than is necessary to live on a comfortable level hold this
excess wealth as a trust for the needy.[35] The implication of equal
distribution to Gandhi is that everyone will be able to supply for

themselves all the natural wants of food, clothing, and shelter.[36] This program of *sarvodaya* would, then, truly be for the welfare of all, because everyone benefits from this equal distribution. The poor would be raised above the mere subsistence level, and the wealthy would learn to love the poor and regard them as brothers and sisters. This would result in a harmonious society.

Sarvodaya can also serve as a solution to the other problems of social disharmony: the Hindu-Muslim problem and the question of untouchability. The key to *sarvodaya*, according to Gandhi, is looking upon every person as an equal. The humblest and lowest Indian is regarded as equal with the rulers of India. The program of *sarvodaya* makes no distinctions between Muslim or Hindu, caste or outcaste. All are regarded as equal and held together with the bond of love.[37] This is the answer to the problem of social disharmony: to consider the welfare of all in every action. The Hindus and the Muslims will reconcile their differences in light of the good it will bring society. The untouchables will be accepted as fellow human beings in society when it is seen that this is for the general welfare of all of society. And the wealthy will look upon the needy as their trusts. All this, according to Gandhi, will be done in the spirit of *sarvodaya*.

In the social arena, then, Gandhi's goal is social harmony and communal unity. The means to his goal are the settlement of the Hindu-Muslim dispute, the removal of untouchability, and the equal distribution of wealth. But Gandhi's social goal of harmony and unity has been shown to be penultimate to his goal of *svarāj*. Each means to the goal, and the goal itself, in the social arena become means to Gandhi's political goal of *svarāj*. The significance of this observation will be noted below.

In the economic arena, Gandhi sees the solution to India's poverty to lie in his program of *svadeśi*. *Svadeśi* literally means "one's own country," and Gandhi applies this principle to all orbs of life. Gandhi claims that

> Swadeshi is that spirit in us which restricts us to the use and service of our immediate surroundings to the exclusion of the more remote. Thus, as for religion, in order to satisfy the requirements of the definition, I must restrict myself to my ancestral religion. . . . In the domain of politics I should make use of the indigenous institutions and serve them by curing them

of their proved defects. In that of economics I should use only
things that are produced by my immediate neighbours and serve
those industries by making them efficient and complete where
they might be found wanting.[38]

Svadeśi in general, then, means the enlistment of things from one's
immediate surroundings to meet all human needs. In the area of
economics, it means using goods manufactured in India to the exclusion
of foreign goods. But this principle extends only as far as protecting the native industries. It does not mean the boycotting of all
foreign goods, but only those which compete with a native industry
and put Indian laborers out of work. Gandhi is against the importation only of those foreign goods which hurt the Indian economy.[39]
At one point, Gandhi says that he derives his principle of svadeśi
from the Gītā's teaching of svadharma. The Gītā says it is better
to die performing one's own duty (svadharma) because another's
duty (paradharma) is fraught with danger. Gandhi says, "What
the Gita says with regard to swadharma equally applies to Swadeshi
also, for Swadeshi is swadharma applied to one's immediate
environment."[40]

Gandhi thinks that the establishment of svadeśi in economics is
the foremost reform necessary in India. He sees the immediate
problem as not how to run the government, but how to feed and
clothe the people. Svadeśi is for Gandhi the automatic solution to
India's grinding poverty.[41] The first economic market that he
attacks is the cloth industry. Gandhi finds this industry to be the
single largest drain on the Indian economy: Indian cotton is shipped
to England, woven into cloth, and then sold back to the Indians.
India loses on both ends of the deal. Gandhi's solution to this
drain is symbolized by the charkha—the hand-spinning wheel.
Gandhi says, "That winter of despair can be turned into the
'sunshine of hope' only through the life-giving wheel, the charkha."[42]
His idea is to shut off this foreign market by having each household
spin the cotton from its own region into khadi (home-woven cloth)
to meet its own needs. This provides a means of industry as well
as income and worth to each individual. People without other
employment can spin and weave in their own homes; people with
jobs can spin in their spare time; people with seasonal jobs (agriculture, etc.) can spin in the off-season.[43] This activity is gain for
those without jobs and it is sacrifice and service for those with jobs.

Everyone benefits from hand-spinning.[44]   Hand-spinning is for
Gandhi the essence and spirit of *svadeśi*.[45] It uses local materials,
local labor, and the local market.

Gandhi sees *svadeśi* leading to economic freedom.   But he sees
it leading to something else as well: *sarvodaya*.   *Svadeśi* also means
equal distribution of wealth to Gandhi.[46]   The follower of *svadeśi*,
particularly one who spins as a sacrifice, not a necessity, is serving
his immediate neighbors.   There is no room for selfishness in
svadeśi, or distinction between high and low.[47]   *Svadeśi* is for the
benefit of all Indians, and all Indians can participate.   When the
poorest person in society can produce *khadi* just as can the highest
person in society, there is an equalization of society.   The lower
person gains self-respect and a sense of worth; the higher person
gains understanding and empathy, as well as a sense of service
toward fellow humans.   This is the spirit of *sarvodaya*.

Furthermore, *svadeśi* leads to *svarāj*.[48]   Economic independence
is the first step toward political independence.   Gandhi feels that
once India is able to throw off its dependence on England for its
economic well-being, *svarāj* will follow as a matter of course.
Svadeśi exemplifies the spirit of sacrifice and the spirit of nationalism that is necessary for Gandhi's *svarāj*.

In the economic arena, then, Gandhi's goal is economic independence.   His means for achieving this goal is *svadeśi*—the use of
native materials, native labor, and native markets.   Gandhi's main
example of this *svadeśi* is the *charkha*.   Home-spinning and home-
weaving are very important steps toward his goal of economic
freedom.   Yet, again, it was seen that this goal is not an end in
itself: the goal of economic freedom and the means of *svadeśi* serve
as means for other goals.   *Svadeśi* is a means for the social goal of
sarvodaya. *Svadeśi* and economic independence also serve as means
for the political goal of *svarāj*.

When Gandhi is viewed in diversity, as he has just been depicted,
he appears to have one ultimate goal and three other goals that
are, at various times, either penultimate or temporarily elevated to
the level of ultimacy.   His ultimate goal is stated in his religious
quest for God, *mokṣa*, or truth.   This goal does not appear to
impinge on or intersect any of his other goals.   But Gandhi's other
three goals appear to be interrelated.   His political goal of *svarāj*
is dependent on his social goal of social harmony and unity, and
his economic goal of *svadeśi* and economic independence.   In

logical order, his economic goals seem to come first. Gandhi's social goals are dependent for their realization, at least partially, on his economic goals, and his political goals are, in turn, dependent on his social goals. So, viewed in this way, Gandhi could be said temporarily to elevate first his economic goals of economic independence and *svadeśi* to the level of ultimacy, because they are the cornerstone of his programs. Once these goals are achieved, however, his social goals would be temporarily elevated to the level of ultimacy. Again, though, once achieved these goals are subordinated to his political goal of *svarāj*, the capstone of his program.

Although there is, then, a certain organic unity to Gandhi's penultimate goals, apparently none of them are related to his ultimate religious goal. All his subordinate goals are temporarily elevated to a level of ultimacy, but it seems that none of them contribute to his stated ultimate goal of seeing God, reaching *mokṣa*, or finding truth. It is this apparent discrepancy that leads to the characterization of Gandhi as a man with a diversity of goals, and a man operating in several distinct and separate arenas. In the problem, though, also lies the solution. Gandhi's ultimate concern —his stated religious goal—can be found to be the unification of all his other goals. There is a relationship between all of his goals, even his religious goal, and it lies in his view of truth.

The truth that Gandhi speaks of, that he seeks, is not mere factual truth, or accuracy and veracity of statements. Nor is it logical truth reached by deduction from accepted premises. For Gandhi, "Truth is the sovereign principle which includes numerous other principles. This truth is not only truthfulness in word, but truthfulness in thought also and not only the relative truth of our conception but the absolute Truth, the Eternal principle, that is God."[49] Truth, for Gandhi, is a metaphysical principle; it is *the* metaphysical principle. Nothing really exists except truth: "The word *satya* [truth] is derived from *sat*, which means 'being'. Nothing is or exists in reality except Truth. That is why *sat* or Truth is perhaps the most important name of God. In fact it is more correct to say that Truth is God, than to say God is Truth . . . *sat* or *satya* is the only correct and fully significant name for God."[50] Whenever Gandhi speaks of seeking God, he is reiterating his desire to find this eternal principle that he calls truth.

For Gandhi, truth is the metaphysical principle of the world: "the world rests on the bedrock of *satya* or truth."[51] The main manifestation of truth in this world is *ahiṃsā*. Gandhi believes that truth and *ahiṃsā* are two sides of the same coin. Truth is known in the world through non-violence.[52] For all practical purposes, then, *satya* and *ahiṃsā* are synonymous to Gandhi. This is significant to note because both these concepts play an important role in the description and attainment of all Gandhi's various goals. It will be seen that truth is the overarching goal lying behind all of his other goals, and *ahiṃsā* is the overarching means lying behind all of his other means. This is the unity of Gandhi.

Gandhi tenaciously maintains that all activities, all endeavors, must be founded on truth, or they will amount to nothing.[53] Since truth is the foundation of the world, if one's endeavors are not built on truth, there is no foundation at all. Not only should all activities be founded on truth, though, they must also be in the pursuit of truth. Gandhi claims that all of his activities, whether social, political, humanitarian, or ethical, are directed toward the goal of finding truth.[54] For this reason, Gandhi subtitled his autobiography *The Story of My Experiments with Truth*. As he understands it, truth was the hub around which the rest of his life revolved. Gandhi said his search for truth, or God, naturally sent him into the political arena. He states, "Man's ultimate aim is the realization of God, and all of his activities, political, social and religious, have to be guided by the ultimate aim of the vision of God. The immediate service of all human beings becomes a necessary part of the endeavor simply because the only way to find God is to see Him in His creation and be one with it. This can only be done by service to all. And this cannot be done except through one's own country."[55] In this statement, Gandhi proclaims that his ultimate concern is the unification of his diverse activities in the various arenas. The full implication of this will now be investigated in each of the four arenas previously depicted as the segmentation of Gandhi.

Gandhi's religion—his "Hinduism"—is informed by his concept of truth. As noted above, he considers Hinduism to be the most glorious religion of mankind because it brings with it the message of *ahiṃsā*, which is the manifestation of truth on earth. He does, however, also concede that non-violence is the common element, the truth factor as it were, of all religions.[56] But for Gandhi, Hinduism best embodies the truth of *ahiṃsā*; it is the religion of humanity and includes the best of all religions.[57]

Although Gandhi calls himself a Hindu, he readily avows that "Truth is my religion and Ahimsa is the only way of its realization."[58] He is the most comfortable with Hinduism because he considers truth to be the essence of Hinduism. He argues this point by citing texts from the *Sāma Veda*, the *Muṇḍaka Upaniṣad*, the *Taittirīya Upaniṣad*, the *Mahābhārata*, the *Rāmāyaṇa*, the *Bhagavadgītā*, the *Bhāgavata Purāṇa*, the *Laws of Manu*, and the *Hitopadeśa*, which teach truth as the central feature of Hinduism.[59] Yet Gandhi does not derive his understanding of truth from the *śāstras* of Hinduism alone; the texts themselves are subject to the judgment of truth. Gandhi does not accept something simply because it is cited in the Vedas or the *śāstras*. He measures the teachings in scriptures against truth. He maintains, "In Hinduism we have gotten an admirable foot-rule to measure every Shastra and every rule of conduct, and that is Truth. Whatever falls from Truth should be rejected."[60] On this basis, Gandhi rejects untouchability, even though some argue its validity from scripture. He also rejects animal sacrifice. Gandhi says that he cares not that the Vedas teach animal sacrifices; it is enough for him that such sacrifice is not consistent with truth and *ahiṃsā*.[61] Gandhi says that anyone who has not attained the perfection of truth and non-violence does not know the *śāstras*, so quoting them becomes an academic question.[62] In Gandhi's Hinduism, then, the principles of truth and non-violence are primary and absolute, whereas belief in and study of the scriptures, the Vedas, *śrutis* and *smṛtis* are secondary and relative.[63] His ultimate goal, then, surely is the focus of his activities in the religious arena: truth and non-violence are the hub of his religion.

This is not a great surprise, because Gandhi's ultimate concern clearly impinges on the religious arena. But Gandhi's political goal is also informed by his quest for truth. As noted above, Gandhi envisions the search for truth as necessarily concomitant with the service of humanity.[64] It is this service that draws him into the political arena. Gandhi says, "I could not be leading a religious life unless I identified myself with the whole of mankind, and that I could not do unless I took part in politics."[65] Gandhi's religion is the quest for truth, and he sees its realization in politics, in the service of mankind. He claims that politics which are not committed to the search for truth are like a corpse, fit only for burial.[66] Gandhi says that all of his activities, in every realm including the

political, are derived from his religion, his search for truth. There
is no distinction between actions that are religious and actions that
are political; they have the same basis.[67] Gandhi says one need
not choose between politics and religion because to do so would
imply that there was a difference between the two. He says, "I do
not conceive religion as one of the many activities of mankind. . . .
There is no such thing for me therefore as leaving politics for religion. For me every, the tiniest activity is governed by what I consider to be my religion."[68] Gandhi's activity in the political arena,
then, is not distinct from his ultimate concern: it is part of his
search. In 1924, Gandhi told his followers, "I have plunged into
politics simply in search of truth."[69] So politics, rather than being
a separate goal, is seen as a means to Gandhi's ultimate goal of
finding truth.

Conversely, though, Gandhi's truth is also depicted as the
means to the political goal of *svarāj*. This is consistent with
Gandhi's theory of means and ends: they are interchangeable.
Truth is both the end and the means; *ahiṃsā*, likewise, is both the
end and the means. Gandhi says that if every Indian lives according to truth, "swaraj will come of its own accord."[70] Living a
life of non-violence, which Gandhi frequently calls the doctrine of
law of love, will produce the same result. He says, "If India
adopted the doctrine of love as an active part of her religion and
introduced it in her politics, Swaraj would descend upon India
from heaven."[71] Truth and its manifestation, *ahiṃsā*, are necessary
means for achieving *svarāj*. *Svarāj* gained by any other means would
be *asatya*, a word which Gandhi employs because it implies both
"untrue" and "unreal". *Svarāj* based on untruth is unreal
svarāj.

Gandhi uses the term *rāmarājya* to delineate his goal of *svarāj*:
it means, as noted above, a rule based on moral authority. This
moral authority is truth or *ahiṃsā*. Gandh explains that *rāmarājya*
means "the Kingdom of God on earth," referring not to the Hindu
god, Rāma, but the god of all religions: truth.[72] The rule of God
is the rule of *ahiṃsā*; when all live by that rule, there will be
rāmarājya.[73] Gandhi used the term *rāmarājya* to emphasize what
sort of rule he sought in his *svarāj*, his self-rule. The issue was
not, then, who made the rules, but rather the basis of the rule.
The only legitimate basis for Gandhi was truth. That is why
England was not qualified; she ruled with violence and force.

This made the English rule *asatya*—untrue and unreal. An Indian home rule based on violence and force would be the same. Gandhi's political goal of *svarāj* was informed by his ultimate goal of finding truth. One place to find it and one place to exercise it was the political arena.

Gandhi also brings his ultimate concern to bear on his pursuits in the social arena. Just as he was drawn into politics in order to find truth in the service of mankind, so he was compelled to enter the field of social reform. His religion demanded that he identify with the lowest on the social scale and endeavor to elevate these forgotten representatives of humanity. Gandhi said in this regard, "The bearing of this religion on social life is, or has to be, seen in one's daily social contact. To be true to such religion one has to lose oneself in continuous and continuing service of all life. Realization of Truth is impossible without a complete merging of oneself in, and identification with, this limitless ocean of life. Hence, for me, there is no escape from social service, there is no happiness on earth beyond or apart from it."[74] Gandhi's social activities, then, are also part of his search for truth. Truth in society is the institution of love, *ahiṃsā*, on all levels of society. Gandhi interprets the removal of untouchability as a facet of *ahiṃsā*. He states, "Removal of untouchability means love for, and service of, the whole world, and thus merges with *ahimsa*."[75] Gandhi rejects the classification of "untouchable" not because it is not taught in the scriptures, but because it is not consistent with *ahiṃsā*, and therefore is *asatya* . Untouchability is more than a social ill, then, it is a religious problem. Its solution is found through religious means: truth and *ahiṃsā*.

This holds true for Gandhi's analysis of the Hindu-Muslim problem as well. The hatred between the Hindus and Muslims is wrong, not only because it disrupts the social harmony, but because it is founded on untruth. Such hatred does not follow the law of love ; it does not view all people as brothers and sisters. It is, therefore, according to Gandhi, *asatya*. Again, a social ill relieved by the religious means of truth and *ahiṃsā*.

If social service begins, as Gandhi says, with the identification with all humankind, then *sarvodaya* is surely its pinnacle. Gandhi's program of *sarvodaya* demands that everyone consider the needs of others to be as important as one's personal needs. When everyone achieves this, there will be *sarvodaya*—the welfare of all humankind. The basis, the bedrock, of this program is love, or *ahiṃsā*. It is *ahiṃsā* that causes the rich person to hold money as a trust for the poor person; it is *ahiṃsā* that causes a man to think of his brother before himself. This, for Gandhi, is truth. In all his social concerns, Hindu-Muslim unity, removal of untouchability, and equal distribution of wealh, it is truth demonstrated by *ahiṃsā* which is Gandhi's impetus. His goal of social harmony and communal unity is not an end in itself; nor is it simply another step toward *svarāj*. This goal is another manifestation of Gandhi's ultimate concern: the search for truth.

Gandhi's ultimate concern draws him into the economic arena as well. It is his religion, he says, to observe *svadeśi* and *khadi* (homespun cloth).[76] Truth and love demand that he serves his immediate neighbors, his fellow Indians, first. This is done, on the economic scale, by establishing *svadeśi* and economic independence.[77] It is not love, it is not *ahiṃsā*, to support a foreign country's economy at the expense of one's native brothers. This is particularly true when the foreign country is not founded on truth. Gandhi saw the presence of England as an exercise in exploitation. This exploitation was based on greed, and did not take into consideration the economic burden it placed on the Indians. This policy was not, then, based on *ahiṃsā*, and therefore it was *asatya*. Gandhi did not approve of England's economic policy, but he did not bear, nor recommend, hatred for the English. That would be contrary to truth. Gandhi says, "A true votary of Swadeshi will never harbour ill-will towards the foreigner; he will not be moved by antagonism towards anybody on earth. Swadeshism is not a cult of hatred. It is a doctrine of selfless service that has its roots in the purest Ahimsa, i.e., love."[78] To follow truth in economics, Gandhi saw the necessity of *svadeśi*. *Svadeśi*, when properly established, is based on love. It is not *svadeśi* when an Indian merchant exploits a fellow Indian. This is no better than the English. It is *savdeśi* when an Indian merchant serves a fellow Indian in love, providing the best possible merchandise at the best possible price. It is *svadeśi* when an Indian patronizes his local Indian merchant in order to help the local economy, even if the local products cost more than imported ones. This is love; this is *ahiṃsā*. Sacrifice on the part of the merchant and the patron for the good of India is *svadeśi* performed in the spirit of truth and love.

Sacrifice based on love lies behind Gandhi's program of the *charkha* as well. He calls on those who do not need to spin, those who can afford to buy cloth, to consider spinning as *yajña*, a sacrifice.[79] Spinning then becomes a religious endeavor in the spirit of the *yajña* taught in the *Gītā*, it becomes a demonstration of *ahiṃsā*. This understanding is fueled by Gandhi's ultimate concern: truth manifest in love.

Gandhi desires *svadeśi* and economic independence in order to prepare the proper environment for *svarāj*. But this is not the only reason. The support of other countries at the expense of India is for him *asatya*; it is untrue and unreal. The economy, as well as everything else, must be based on truth. This truth for Gandhi is *svarāj*. *Svarāj* must be based on truth, starting on the level of economics.

So all of Gandhi's apparent separate and distinct goals—his religious, political, social, and economic goals—can be seen to be unified under the aegis of his ultimate concern, his search for truth. All these goals are unified, too, by his means to his ultimate concern: *satyagraha*. Gandhi says, "Satyagraha is literally holding on to Truth and it means, therefore, Truth-force. Truth is soul or spirit. It is, therefore, known as soul-force. It excludes the use of violence."[80] As Gandhi describes *satyāgraha*, there is no end that cannot be achieved by *satyāgraha*.[81] This means is functional in realizing goals in any arena because it is founded on truth. Thus, it is capable of overturning untrue laws and institutions. Untruth in any area cannot stand up against the power of truth as applied in *satyāgraha*. Gandhi explains, "The world rests upon the bedrock of *satya* or truth. *Asatya* meaning untruth also means that which *is*. If untruth does not so much as exist, its victory is out of the question. And truth being that which *is* can never be destroyed. This is the doctrine of satyagraha in a nutshell."[82] There is the reason that *satyāgraha* can be effective in any arena. It is based on truth, reality, and can defeat untruth or unreality. The truth that *satyāgraha* is based upon is the major manifestation of truth on earth, the truth of *ahiṃsā*. The most important facet of *satyāgraha* for Gandhi is its unrelenting demand for adherence to *ahiṃsā*.[83]

Naturally, *satyāgraha* is the means to Gandhi's religious goal. But it is the central means in the attainment of all his other goals as well. In his first work on *svarāj*, *Hind Swaraj*, Gandhi avows that the way to self-rule is through soul-force or love-force, i.e., satyāgraha.[84]   A home rule gained by any other means would not be true home rule to Gandhi.[85]   In the social arena, Gandhi sees the spirit of satyāgraha to be the solution to the Hindu-Muslim split.[86]   It is also the principle that guarantees the success of sarvodaya.[87]   In his economics, Gandhi believes that the charkha is the symbol of satyāgraha, and it is the most effective weapon of the satyāgrahi (a follower of satyāgraha).[88]   The entire svadeśi movement is a satyāgraha campaign in the eyes of Gandhi, and its success lies in the strict adherence to non-violence.[89]   Gandhi can implement the same means to achieve his various goals because he sees all these goals not as separate, but parts of the same whole. This whole is his search for truth, his ultimate concern.   Satyāgraha is a means for discovering and establishing truth.   Gandhi utilizes it in all arenas because the search for truth is his one overarching goal.

It has been seen, then, that Gandhi can be viewed as a man with one goal that could be called "religious" and three goals that could be termed "this-worldly."   From this perspective, he appears to be one who is willing to suspend his ultimate goal, the goal of seeing God or finding truth, and temporarily elevate his penultimate goals to the level of ultimacy.   In this context, he has an economic goal, svadeśi, that feeds into his social goals of social harmony and sarvodaya, which, in turn, contribute to the realization of his political goal of svarāj.   This is the depiction of Gandhi in diversity.

But such a depiction underplays the extent of his ultimate concern.   Gandhi's ultimate concern is all-embracing and shades all his other goals.   His ultimate goal is a search for truth, which he finds demonstrated in ahimsā.   This goal extends to the fields of politics, social activism, and economic reform.   It is capable of doing this because Gandhi sees truth as the foundation of the world, the metaphysical basis of all reality.   Therefore it is necessary for him to search for truth in all fields.   Such a view of the world, then, unifies all his concerns.   Truth is the focus for Gandhi.   Gandhi's ultimate concern unifies all his other concerns, and his major means satyāgraha, is further testimony to the unification.   All Gandhi's goals are pursued through this one means that spring from his search for truth.   Thus it can be said that for Gandhi, ultimacy is the unifier.

Notes

1. D.K. Bedekar, *Towards Understanding Gandhi* (Bombay: Popular Praka-shan, 1975), pp. 8-9.
2. M.K. Gandhi, *The Way to Communal Harmony*, ed. U.R. Rao (Ahmedabad: Navajivan Press, 1963), p. ii.
3. Martin Dening Lewis, ed., *Gandhi—Maker of Modern India?* (Boston: D.C. Heath, 1965), p. vii.
4. Gandhi, *The Way*, p. 47.
5. Ibid., p. 48.
6. Charles F. Andrews, *Mahatma Gandhi's Ideas* (New York: Macmillan, 1930), p. 35.
7. Gandhi, *The Way*, p. 48.
8. M.K. Gandhi, *Young India 1919-1922* (New York: B.W. Huebsch, 1924), p. 247.
9. Krishna Kripalani, ed., *All Men are Brothers* (Lausanne: UNESCO, 1958), p. 59. This is a collection of Gandhi's writings.
10. Shriman Narayan, ed., *The Selected Works of Mahatma Gandhi* (Ahmeda-bad: Navajivan, 1968), 6 : 96-97.
11. M.K. Gandhi, *Autobiography: Or the Story of My Experiments With Truth* (Ahmedabad: Navajivan, 1927), p. xix.
12. Nirmal K. Bose, ed., *Selections From Gandhi* (Ahmedabad: Navajivan, 1948), p. 6.
13. S. Abid Husain, *The Way of Gandhi and Nehru* (Bombay: Asia Publishing House, 1959), p. 35.
14. Narayan, ed., *Selected Works*, p. 156. Cf. ibid., pp. 157, 166.
15. Gandhi, *Young India 1919-1922*, p. 947.
16. Ibid., p. 307.
17. M.K. Gandhi, *Hind Swaraj or Indian Home Rule* (1908; reprint ed., Ahmedabad: Navajivan, 1938), p. 93.
18. Ibid., pp. 62-63.
19. Gandhi, *Young India 1919-1922*, p. 653.
20. M.K. Gandhi, *Young India 1927-1928* (Madras; Ganesan, 1935), p. 25.
21. Gandhi, *Hind Swaraj*, p. 85.
22. Ibid., p. 25.
23. Ibid., p. 146; cf. p. 141f.
24. M.K. Gandhi, *Sarvodaya*, ed. Bharatan Kumarappa (Ahmedabad: Nava-jivan, 1954), p. 75.
25. Gandhi, *The Way*, p. 184. Cf. ibid., pp. 136, 137.
26. Gandhi, *Young India 1919-1922*, p. 480.
27. Gandhi, *Sarvodaya*, p. 57.
28. Gandhi, *Young India 1927-1928*, p. 462.
29. Gandhi, *Young India 1919-1922*, p. 397.
30. Ibid., p. 482.
31. Gandhi, *Young India 1927-1928*, pp. 414-15.
32. Ibid., pp. 156-57. Cf. Gandhi, *Young India 1919-1922*, p. 470.
33. M.K. Gandhi, *The Removal of Untouchability*, ed. Bharatan Kumarappa (Ahmedabad: Navajivan, 1954), pp. 14-15.

34. Kripalani, ed., *All Men are Brothers*, p. 137.

35. Ibid., p. 132.

36. Ibid., p. 131.

37. Gandhi, *Sarvodaya*, p. 5.

38. V.B. Kher, ed., *Economic and Industrial Life and Relations* (Ahmedabad: Navajivan, 1959), 2 : 69. This is a collection of Gandhi's writings.

39. Gandhi, *Sarvodaya*, p. 25.

40. Bharatan Kumarappa, ed., *Khadi: Why and How* (Ahmedabad: Navajivan, 1955), p. 43. This is a collection of Gandhi's writings.

41. Gandhi, *Young India 1919-1922*, p. 484.

42. Kumarappa, ed., *Khadi: Why and How*, p. 5.

43. Ibid., p. 3.

44. Ibid., p. 5.

45. Gandhi, *Young India 1919-1922*, p. 510. Cf. Kumarappa, ed.; *Khadi: Why and How*, pp. 43, 40.

46. Gandhi, *Young India 1919-1922*, p. 488.

47. Kumarappa, ed., *Khadi: Why and How*, pp. 42, 43, 13.

48. Gandhi, *Hind Swaraj*, p. 152.

49. Gandhi, *Autobiography*, p. xiii.

50. M.K. Gandhi, *From Yeravada Mandir* (Ahmedabad: Navajivan, 1932), p. 2.

51. M.K. Gandhi, *Satyagraha in South Africa* (Ahmedabad: Navajivan, 1968), p. 389.

52. Gandhi, *Young India 1927-1928*, p. 154. See Narayan, ed., *Selected Works*, p. 166.

53. Gandhi, *Sarvodaya*, p. 8; *From Yeravada Mandir*, pp. 2-3.

54. Gandhi, *Autobiography*, p. xix. Cf. Husain, *Gandhi and Nehru*, p. 35.

55. Kripalani, ed., *All Men are Brothers*, p. 63.

56. Gandhi, *The Way*, p. 47.

57. V.B. Kher, ed., *In Search of the Supreme* (Ahmedabad: Navajivan, 1961) 2:265. This is a collection of Gandhi's writings.

58. Gandhi, *The Way*, p. 44.

59. Bhabani Bhattacharya, *Gandhi the Writer* (New Delhi: National Book Trust, 1969), p. 46.

60. Kher, ed., *In Search of the Supreme*, 1:114.

61. Gandhi, *Sarvodaya*, p. 48; *From Yeravada Mandir*, pp. 53-54.

62. Husain, *Gandhi and Nehru*, p. 20.

63. Ibid.

64. Kripalani, ed., *All Men are Brothers*, p. 59.

65. Ibid., p. 69.

66. Kher, ed., *Economic and Industrial Life and Relations*, 2:71.

67. Kher, ed., *In Search of the Supreme*, 2:179. Cf. Kripalani, ed., *All Men are Brothers*, pp. 68-69.

68. Kripalani, ed., *All Men are Brothers*, p. 64.

69. G. Ramachandra and T.K. Mahadevan, eds., *Quest for Gandhi* (Bombay: Bharatiya Vidya Bhavan, 1970), p. 255.

70. Narayan, ed., *Selected Works*, 4: 79-80.

71. Gandhi, *Hind Swaraj*, p. xxviii. This is an introduction to the second edition, and includes materials from *Young India*, January 1921.

72. Kher, ed., *In Search of the Supreme*, 1:221. Cf. Kher, ed., *Economic and Industrial Life and Relations*, 1:18.

73. Husain, *Gandhi and Nehru*, p. 39.

74. Kher, ed., *In Search of the Supreme*, 2:266.

75. Gandhi, *From Yeravada Mandir*, p. 29.

76. Gandhi, *Young India 1919-1922*, p. 280.

77. Kripalani, ed., *All Men are Brothers*, p. 120.

78. Kumarappa, ed., *Khadi: Why and How*, pp. 44f.

79. Gandhi, *Sarvodaya*, p. 137.

80. Bharatan Kumarappa, ed., *Satyagraha* (Ahmedabad: Navajivan, 1951), p. 7. This is a collection of Gandhi's writings.

81. Ibid., p. 323.

82. Gandhi, *Satyagraha in South Africa*, p. 389.

83. Gandhi, *Satyagraha*, pp. 201-2.

84. Gandhi, *Hind Swaraj*, pp. 168f. Cf. Gandhi, *The Way*, p. 259.

85. Gandhi, *Hind Swaraj*, p. 130.

86. Gandhi, *The Way*, p. 25.

87. Kripalani, ed., *All Men are Brothers*, p. 132.

88. Kumarappa, ed., *Khadi: Why and How*, p. 13.

89. Gandhi, *Young India 1919-1922*, p. 486. Cf. Kumarappa, ed., *Khadi: Why and How*, p. 43.

15

RABINDRANATH TAGORE :
RELIGION AS A CONSTANT STRUGGLE
FOR BALANCE IN THE RELIGION OF MAN

Donald R. Tuck

Introduction

Religion, like so many other cultural expressions, seems simple on the surface levels, but becomes increasingly complex in itself, and even more so in its various interrelationships with other aspects of culture. For the scholar, its pattern of ultimate concern cannot be drawn merely in hierarchical pyramidic form. It is more like the complex molecular structures of a living organism within which each part can be studied as something in itself, but which is a whole greater than any of its parts, and ultimately inexpressible. This pattern of interhuman relationships functions to give balance and harmony to human life, so that people know who they are as personalities, and what their duties and responsibilities are within a society of transactional beings.

Such an understanding of religion is necessary at the beginning of our study of Rabindranath Tagore (1861-1941). Tagore's religion of man contains both expressions of personality and social interrelations. Religion is a balanced whole which radiates good in society. Tagore's life experiences transformed his analytical ideas into human transactions in which he learned to differentiate inharmonious extremes from the harmonious whole. Extremities cause suffering because they overload and imbalance a positive and affirmative relationship of religious beings with this world of human persons and nature. Tagore does not confine religion only to the horizontal relationships between man and men. He was an artist of life who recognized a vertical dimension, which linked man to an ultimate spiritual being. The horizontal and vertical dimensions did not exhaust the complexity of religious relationships, however.

Other dimensions complicate the model, but added together the dimensions do not exhaust religion, because beyond the manifestations of religion is a harmonious whole, which is in essence indescribable but ultimately most satisfying. Manifested religion is a part of the whole. It may be received in part by the human consciousness, logically understood by the mind, described by means of the senses or experienced by a complex mixing of human characteristics, but the whole is beyond these partial manifestations. If the manifestations are complex and frustrate religious man's attempts to adequately understand, describe and experience them as parts, the religious whole elusively stands beyond the manifestations. The religious artist (Tagore uses this illustration extensively), who attempts to materialize the parts in view of catching a glimpse of the whole, finds his best efforts and talents frustrated. At best, the results of his artistic struggles have manifested the whole as a complexity of ever deepening perspectives; the more apparent perspectives manifest simpler characteristics of the whole, and the deeper perspectives become more complex and more interrelated. Tagore selectively drew out of the reservoir of historical Indian wisdom and experience materials which could be used to describe the indescribable ultimate at various levels understandable to human persons for whom the quest for religious satisfaction was ever deepening, interrelational, and qualitative. Religious man, Tagore says, progresses from surface perspectives to deeper perspectives until he experiences the whole from which perspective he can see all parts in relationship to the whole.

This paper will attempt to analyze and describe aspects of the religious dimension of Tagore's *The Religion of Man*, the Hibbert Lectures of 1930. It will examine the influences which Bengal Vaiṣṇava thought exerted upon Tagore's exposition of religion. He delivered these lectures in English to the Oxford community. In these lectures he demonstrates how deeply he has drawn from the Vaiṣṇava traditions.

To understand *The Religion of Man*, we will first examine certain continuities and changes which occurred in Tagore's conceptions of religion from 1913 until 1930. In 1930 Tagore delivered the Hibbert Lectures at Oxford. These lectures had been cancelled several times on account of Tagore's health, so they reflect the thought of many years. We will examine *The Religion of Man* and study that period of Tagore's life from those lectures back to a former visit to England, where his own translations of poetry originally written in Bengali were translated by him and published as *Gitanjali*, which became the literary basis for his being awarded the Nobel Prize for literature in 1913.

Context for *The Religion of Man*

Tagore was an elite Bengali. Until 1912, when he translated and transformed some of his earlier published verses into English on a trip to England, the English-speaking world outside India was unaware of his art and literary production. By that time the Bengalis had known that one of their already famous families had produced a writer of diverse literary genre: verse, drama in verse, musical drama, songs, comic plays, novels, short stories, essays and letters by a traveling intellectual who penetratingly described Europeans outside India.[1] Europeans, who came to know him as "The Poet" after the Nobel Prize was awarded to him, would soon know him as a multigenre artist about whom many wanted to know more, and who would no longer be an Indian writer, but one who belonged to the developing and spatially expanding collected human consciousness in the twentieth century.

By 1912, Tagore was a mature writer and fifty-one years old. The next thirty years of his life were spent in producing a greater volume of publications, developing their quality and experimenting with new forms and non-European symbolisms. The mere quantity of his published writings (estimated to cover over one hundred thousand pages in print) staggers the bibliographer and exhausts the abilities of those who attempt to grapple with content analysis and hermeneutical understanding.[2]

Bibliographical data will quantify these statements. A certain amount of interpretation has been exercised on this data because Tagore's genre do not fit English categories and several genre were published in one volume. The conclusions sought are that Tagore was both creative and productive, and that an understanding of his religion is at once complex, developmental, and interculturally active. From 1912 till 19 41 (some were published posthumously), Tagore continued to write in Bengali while a variety of translators struggled to bring his former writings to people outside Bengal and to try to keep up with this fertile and creative man. During these later years, Tagore's expanded and extensive publications included 28 volumes of verse, 6 musical dramas, 3 collections of songs, 2 comedies, 7 novels, 5 short story works, 15 collections of essays, another autobiographical work, 13 books of letters and several other categories, e.g., a book of epigrams, 3 dance dramas, 4 collections of lectures and addresses, 3 travel-diary works, as well as his continuing effort at revisions of earlier works into creative combinations of the aforementioned genre.

After 1912, the English reading world had translations of his verse, drama, songs, novels, short stories, essays, autobiography, letters, epigrams, lectures, and travel descriptions. Although the translations varied in quality and were often transformations of his Bengali originals, enough of his writings were available to give readers an idea of his genius and to show that he was more than a poet. Selections of his works were published by special interest groups ranging from faith-motivated devotees to discrediting negative critics.

Continuities in Tagore's Religion

The concepts of Tagore's religion are complex, even when they may be written in and translated into seemingly simplified English. He never felt completely at home in the English language, and his ideas, as has been noted by Tagore specialists, have suffered in translation. His writing career, until his trip to England (1912) when he experimented with English translations of poems from several publications, was in the Bengali language and filled with historical, ideological, and sociological references to the subcontinent of South Asia. Our hermeneutic will grapple with that complexity as it was transformed by Tagore from the Bengali into the English language.

Freedom from Sectarian Orthodoxy

In a letter dated February 25, 1916, and addressed as "Dear Madam," Tagore summarized his own understanding and personal approach to religion.[3] In it Tagore stressed that he neither belonged to any exclusive religious sect nor subscribed to any confining creed. Those familiar with his *magnus corpus* and the development of his religious consciousness, realize that he had experimented with a vast amount of the historical, sectarian Hindu religions, i.e., Vaiṣṇava, Śaiva, and Śākta variations, and he had studied various reforms both within the subcontinent and caused by movements coming from outside it. (For example, *The Religion of Man* contains allusions and references to Buddhist, Zoroastrian, Muslim, and Christian religions).

In his attempt to communicate to readers beyond India's borders and whose religious presuppositions were different from his own, Tagore tried to show that his own interpretations of religion were a constant struggle in which he attempted to be freed from the enforced conformity both of Indian and Western theologians. In theology religious people are required to believe and are dominated by a set of ideals formulated into a normative creed, which itself arises from a canon of accepted scriptures and is perpetuated by an organized body of worshippers. In particular, he had in mind such examples as British Christianity in India or Sunni Islam which formulated their norms from the results of their triumphal mission activities.[4] Tagore's critique of ideologies which claim exclusive, and thus divisive authority and which demanded unified conformity to a normative interpretation of truth is often sharp and Tagore relegated such claims to the level of lower comprehension of what is commonly called "religion." We will not attempt to critique all of Tagore's facile and generalizing statements about religions from which he drew illustrative material, but we will attempt to grapple with statements which help us sympathetically understand what he calls the religion of man.[5]

Scholarly Credentials

Speaking to the Oxford University community Tagore asserted that he was neither a scholar nor a philosopher.[6] These disclaimers must be analyzed and evaluated before we attempt to grapple with Tagore's religious continuities and changes.

I mention these references especially because of their contextual significance. The first comes within the chapter on the prophet Zarathustra in which Tagore emphasized the element of personal leadership in religion. Tagore used the voice of the prophet to air religious ideas to which he ascribed.   He believed that truth is not reached through analytical processes alone,[7] and that it cannot be confined to a single people.[8] Zarathustra's message of truth was based on both intellectual and intuitive knowledge and experience; the message was for all humankind, not for Persians exclusively.

Having discussed a few major ideas of Zoroastrian-"Persian" religion and sampling some of the songs (gāthās) and writings of the prophet, Tagore stated that the detailed facts of religious history were not his area of expertise and that he was a singer rather than a textual scholar of Avestan, Pahlavi, and Persian languages.

Tagore did not have an earned university degree.   His temperament and early distaste for mediocre and repetitive education led him instead to a qualitative, guided education under the tutelage of his extended family. His writings give evidence that he had been acquainted with both primary and secondary sources in a variety of historical religions. He did not, however, devote his life to the writing of commentaries, historical criticisms, nor philosophical treatises on sectarian texts. That Tagore should have felt inferior in scholarly circles for these reasons is more an indication of the scholarly norms of the times rather than an indication of his own ability to exegete and interpret textual meanings for religious thought and human-cultural situations.

The second reference to his disclaimer of university credentials is in the chapter which he called "The Vision." Here Tagore emphasized the inner realization of truth--the realm of personal religious experience—which can give balance to the outer intellectually guided social manifestations. Tagore is objecting to an overly rational approach to religion which was prevalent in the 1920s and 1930s, and he is attempting to bring balance among the varied manifestations of what he sees as ultimately real. The religion of man which Tagore exposed to inquiring minds of Europe and America was not a conglomeration of vague conceptions; rather, those who understood the philosophical and scholarly traditions from which Tagore came realized that many of his notions were based on major perceptions (*mahavakya*) of Sanskritic literature (The Great Tradition) and also reflected religious debates carried on in vernacular and specialized religious languages of the Little Traditions.[9] (More will be said later in reference to some of these ideas, i.e., Lord of My Life, *jīvan-devatā*, and the technical vocabulary of Vaiṣṇavas of Bengal.)

Our analysis of Tagore will examine him for what he was—a literateur of religion —and will not critique him for what he was not, a specialist in Indian philosophical argumentations or a philological scholar.

Tagore's importance for the study of religion is based on his translated writings and his influences upon Indian civilization rather than the academic degrees which he received belatedly and for "honorable cause" from both Indian and Western universities.

Vaiṣṇava Sources for Tagore's Religion

The sources for Tagore's religious thought and expressions are varied, for he drank from many wells. One of the many contributing satisfactions for his constant thirst was the rich traditions of Bengal Vaiṣṇavas.

By Vaiṣṇavism we mean that form of religion which, by the practice of *bhakti*, faithfully regards Viṣṇu as the ultimate god, and believes that such religious practices and symbolizations directed to him remove devotees from the rounds of rebirth (*saṃsāra*) to be free and to enjoy the bliss of Viṣṇu as a foretaste in this life *(jīvan mukti)* and more fully after the destruction of one's physical form in the presence of Lord Viṣṇu himself, in *vaikuṇṭha* (transcendental *vṛindāvan* or *vraja*).[10]

Bhakti comes from the root √*bhaj* which means "to serve" or "to adore." Historically *bhakti* came to mean faith in Viṣṇu as one's personal god, and especially love *(prema)* for him, which included the dedication of the devotee's whole life to Viṣṇu's service and which resulted in the attainment of divine realization *(mukti)* by disciplined personal attitudes and actions of devotion to Viṣṇu.[11]

Bengal Vaiṣṇavism was a revitalization movement with the ultimacy of Viṣṇu brought about by the Bengali leader-saint, Caitanya-dāsa (1486-1534). Among other emphases, Caitanya directed the Vaiṣṇava *bhakti* religion to the *(avatāra)* incarnation of Kṛṣṇa in the *Bhagavadgītā*, and especially Kṛṣṇa's manifestations as ultimate Lord among devotees in the Mathurā-Vṛndāvan area as discussed in the *Bhāgavata-Purāṇa*. Caitanya also drew upon Vaiṣṇava developments like those poetically dramatized in the *Gīta Govinda*, and which identified the favored cowherdess of Kṛṣṇa's love-play *(līlā)* as Rādhā. The resulting Kṛṣṇa-Rādhā religious patterns came to be called Gauṛiya (or Bengal) Vaiṣṇavism, which was associated with Caitanya's emphasis upon corporate singing and dancing *(samkīrtana)* as efficacious witness to one's devotion to Kṛṣṇa and the transformation of devotees into the servants *(dāsya)* of Lord Kṛṣṇa. The ecstatic and emotional Vaiṣṇavism of Caitanya was transmitted to his earliest disciples, called the six Gosvāmins, whose knowledge of Sanskritic and Tantric traditions brought intellectual acumen to the intuitive experience,[12] and who propagated the religion as far west as Vṛndāvan, Uttar Pradesh.

Caitanya himself spread Kṛṣṇa-Rādhā religion not only throughout Bengal, but into neighboring Orissa, where he took up residence in Puri during the latter period of his life. Thus, Bengal Vaiṣṇavism is a religious system of beliefs, practices, and symbolizations not confined to Bengal, but radiating out of three epicenters, i.e., Navadvīpa, Bengal; Vṛndāvan, Uttar Pradesh; and Puri, Orissa.

It is the thesis of this paper that Tagore knew Bengal Vaiṣṇava religious norms and that they influenced his writings to a great extent, especially during the period under review (1913-30), and that *The Religion of Man* reflects the impact Bengal Vaiṣṇavism had upon him.

The American lectures, *Sādhanā* (published in 1913), the short story "Bostami" written in 1913, songs in *Gitīmalya* (1914) and *Gitali*, the character Lilanandaswami in the novel *Chaturanga* (1915), letters written to W.W. Pearson (March 10, 1918) and to C.F. Andrews (October 18, 1920), love poems in the novel *Sesher Kavita* (published in 1929), and the poems of *Mahua* (1929) exemplify the impact of Vaiṣṇava religious thought, practices, and symbolism upon Tagore from 1913 until 1930.

Vaiṣṇavism in *The Religion of Man*

Tagore views religion as containing both intellectual and intuitive knowledge. He calls it a poet's religion and attempts to balance objective and subjective attitudes in his exposition. Though Bengal Vaiṣṇavism is a major influence he does not approach religion systematically or textually. His understanding is sympathetic, but he tries to avoid being dogmatic. Neither does Tagore attempt to be apologetic for a specific group. His restraint (*epoché*) from writing as a devotee's faith-oriented position is substantial, although he lacks certain criteria that are accepted by the scholarly world of South Asian religious academics.

Although Tagore knew some of the literature of the structure and anti-structure of Indian religious traditions, his own religion was a creative construction of thought, practice, and symbolizations which drew upon Sanskritic as well as regional and local Hindu traditions. Tagore's writings had similarities to these but also differences. He criticized both structure and anti-structure and then set up his own collective ideas which ran contrary to many of these contemporary restatements of religious motifs and structures. Bengal Vaiṣṇavism included elements of the Great Tradition as well as Little Traditions. As a proponent of *bhakti* as the superior means of religious satisfaction Bengal Vaiṣṇavism is a good illustration of anti-structure. Tagore drew nourishment from these wells, but added enough condiments to enhance the taste. Consequently, the analysis of the "religion of man" leads us to other analytical categories which help us understand Tagore's developed structures of behavior and thought. The result is a symbiosis rather than an enforced synthesis; intellectual conflict is avoided by the means of a more satisfying and holistic harmony.

Vaiṣṇava "Religion of Man"

Tagore was an unusual Bengali in that he had traveled extensively and lectured on various religious topics. His travels had taken him to England, the United States, Japan, several cultural areas of Europe, China, Argentina, Southeast Asia, and Canada by the time of the Hibbert Lectures in 1930. Elements drawn from many religious traditions affected his lectures, but it is the Vaiṣṇava influences which will be examined in the following sections.

The ideas propounded by Tagore in Bengali suffer when they are translated into English. Tagore experienced this himself, when he tried to communicate some of his earlier poems via the English

language, and subsequently, translators have travailed to bring forth
his ideas into the medium of the English-speaking world. The
Hibbert Lectures are an appropriate example of these problems
because Tagore wrote them in English.

In a letter in response to Alice Rothenstein's invitation to join
them in France, Tagore touches upon the problem of translation:
"I have to prove, so long as I am in the west, that Indians . . . in
the language of their conducts observe the same accents and idioms
as you do. In fact, we have to translate ourselves—otherwise you
do not understand us, or what is far worse, misunderstand. . . .
But the translation has to observe a different grammar and be
correct."[13]

One of Tagore's harshest critiques of an English author's misunderstandings of himself was aimed at E.J.A. Thompson's
Rabindranath Tagore: Poet and Dramatist. In a letter written to
William Rothenstein in 1927 from Visva-Bharati, Tagore voiced his
bitter protest against Thompson's book by saying:

> It is one of the most *absurd* books that I have ever read dealing
> with a poet's life and writings . . . he has a very imperfect
> knowledge of Bengali language which necessarily prevents him
> from realising the atmosphere of our words and therefore
> the colour and music and life of them. He cannot make distinc-
> tion between that which is essential and non-essential and he
> jumbles together details without any consideration for their signi-
> ficance. For those who know Bengali his presentation of the
> subject is too often ludicrously disproportionate. He has been
> a schoolmaster in an Indian school and that comes out in his
> pages too often in his *pompous spirit of self-confidence* even in a
> realm where he ought to have been conscious of his limitations.
> The book is full of prejudices which have no foundation in facts.
> . . . Then again, being a Christian missionary, his training makes
> him *incapable of understanding* some of the ideas that run all
> through my writings—like that of *jivan-devata*, the limited aspect
> of divinity which has its unique place in the individual's life in
> contrast to that which belongs to the universe. . . . On the whole,
> author is never afraid to be unjust, and that only shows his want
> of respect.[14]

Aware of the problems involved in interpreting Tagore and

acknowledging our own limitations, we turn to an analysis of *The Religion of Man.*

Tagore's Sources of Authority
(Intellect and Intuition)

Tagore, like the Bengal Vaiṣṇavas, refers to the revealed texts (*śruti*) as authorities in themselves, viz., he rests his ideas on the etymological/denotative or primary meanings of the texts (*mukhyā vṛtti*). Theoretically, he raised the question of the means of valid knowledge (*pramāna*) and assumed that the highest means for revealing ultimate reality is scriptural testimony (*śabda*). In the Hibbert Lectures, Tagore leaned heavily on what he calls Hindu Sanskritic scriptures, and specifically he referred to Vedas, i.e., *Atharva Veda*, the Upaniṣads, i.e., Iśa, and the Epics. In his references to these *śruti* and *smṛti* texts, he does not argue their authority, but assumes them to be valid knowledge (*pramā*), and appeals to their primary meanings.

Missing in these lectures is any reference to the *Brahamasūtra* which would give clues as to which schools of the Vedānta Tagore is aligning his thought and to which he objects, for example, the commentaries of Sankara, Ramanuja, or Madhva. Such references would involve Tagore in the questions asked by traditional Indian religious thinkers, but Tagore is more interested in what he calls "The Vision." In this view, he withdraws from scholarly debate by referring to his growing up in the Tagore extended family and his own personal experience of "freedom from the dominance of any creed that had its sanction in the definite authority of some scripture, or in the teaching of some organized body of worshippers."[15]

Another lack of reference in Tagore's *The Religion of Man* is his failure to mention the Purāṇas. Tagore's relationship with the Bengal Vaiṣṇavas is through his acquaintance with their poets, not by means of the philosophical-religious thinkers who based their ideas on interpretations of the Purāṇas. He refers specifically to the influences of these poets upon his early life, and although he mentions neither the *Bhāgavata Purāṇa* nor the *Viṣṇu Purāṇa*, the contents of these writings are reflected by the poets and affected both Tagore's "vision" and helped shape him as an artist. He

does include, however, a poem by the medieval Vaiṣṇava poet
Chandidāsa in *The Religion of Man*.

Omitted also in *The Religion of Man* is Tagore's intellectual
leap from the Vedas to the modern period, and basic assumptions
which Tagore failed to identify and which were included in the
(*bhakti*) devotional, personalistic religions, as they were revitalized
by Caitanya and established in the religious thought systems of the
Gosvamins, especially Jiva Gosvamin and Rupa Gosvamin. During
the period of Tagore's exposure to English (European and American
readers), Tagore constantly complained that his readers misunderstood him.   He could have assisted their understanding by referring
specifically to these *bhakti* studies.   The Bengal Vaiṣṇavas included
within their ideas of scriptural testimony (*śabda*) the equal authority of the derived post-vedic texts, i.e., *Itihāsa, smṛti,* and *Purāṇas*.
To Jiva Gosvamin, especially, the spiritual sense of the Vedas
was exposed by these sources of *śabda* for the present age (*kaliyuga*).
Vyasa, the classifier of the four Vedas, is regarded as the composer
of the Purāṇas, in which he unveiled the unfathomable and incom-
prehensible mysteries of the Vedas and completed or fulfilled
their sense as well as made the essence of them available to persons
irrespective of caste, sex, or age.   It was Jiva Gosvamin who
established the supremacy of the *Bhāgavata Purāṇa*, which Bengal
Vaiṣṇavas regard as Vyasa's most reliable commentary on the
Brahmasūtra and the other Purāṇas.   To the Bengal Vaiṣṇavas all
cases of conflict arising out of these texts are brought to the hermeneu-
tics of the *Bhāgavata Purāṇa*.

Bhāgavata Purāṇa

How does Tagore's Vaiṣṇavism compare to this?   Perhaps, if
we take as an illustration his initiation (*upanāyana*) rite, and the
Gāyatri mantra in particular, we can catch a glimpse of the poet's
religion.   The Gāyatri is found in the *Ṛg Veda* 111.62.10 and is
not only a part of every *brahmin's* rite of spiritual birth (*dvija*), but
his daily meditation.   Tagore translated its meaning as: "Let
me contemplate the adorable splendour of Him who created the
earth, the air and the starry spheres, and sends the power of
comprehension within our minds."[16]   Tagore's father, the Maharṣi,
arranged the ceremony and personally presided over the rite for

his sons and grandson. Affected by the teachings of the Brahmo Samaj, the Maharṣi had revolted against many orthodox ideas and practices, but he retained this celebration. With golden earrings and shaved head, Rabindranath retreated within the Tagore mansion for three days to meditate upon this rite of the twice-born. It continued to be a source of inspiration throughout his life, long after he had discontinued wearing the sacred thread as a sign of his spiritual rebirth.

This same verse is the opening verse (śloka) of the first book (Skandha) of the Bhāgavata Purāṇa, and has been interpreted variously by Vaiṣṇava teachers. Tagore's translation is mainly denotative and he uses it to differentiate his poet's religion from the orthodox man of piety or from a theologian's interpretation. Tagore's "vision" in The Religion of Man is different from the explanation of Sridhara, the oldest commentator of the Bh.P., who was a non-dualist (advaita), from that of Vira-raghava, a follower of Ramanuja (viśiṣṭādvaita), and from that of Vijaya-dhvaja of the dualistic (dvaita) school of Madhva. Nor does he make any specific reference here to the Bengal Vaiṣṇava's emphasis upon the love between a man and a woman who is the wife of another person (parakīyā preman), viz., the loves of Kṛṣṇa and Rādhā, where Rādhā is interpreted as the paramour of illicit erotics. It is no wonder that his Western audiences understood imperfectly, and that Indian religious thinkers wondered how Tagore's religion of man fit into the traditional systems of Indian thought (darśana). A reference here could have helped the listener-readers' comprehension. His avoidance of dogmatism and criticism is not as thorough as he assumes, and his method of exposition suffers on account of this lack of specificity.

Tagore's Vaiṣṇavism had another source—the Bāul singers of Bengal. In his lecture on "The Man of My Heart," Tagore refers specifically to these singers and quotes some of their lyrics.[17] K.M. Sen's article on the Bāuls is included in the appendices of The Religion of Man. Tagore was one of the first modern writers to collect their songs and show interest in their religious lyrics, which were heavily influenced by Vaiṣṇava thought, practices, and symbols. Tagore describes his affinity to them by saying:

I have mentioned in connection with my personal experience some songs which I had often heard from wandering village

singers, belonging to a popular sect of Bengal, called Bāuls, who
had no images, temples, scriptures or ceremonials, who declare
in their songs the divinity of Man, and express for him an intense
feeling of love. Coming from men who are unsophisticated,
living a simple life in obscurity, it gives us a clue to the inner
meaning of all religions. For it suggests that these religions are
never about a God of cosmic force, but rather the God of human
personality.[18]

Although Tagore was not a classical teacher āchārya, he did
address himself to the sources or means of valid knowledge (pramāṇa) and appealed to śruti and smṛti scriptural sorces (śabda) in
his The Religion of Man as self-authoritative, and employed a
denotative method (mukhyā vṛtti) to his interpretations of those
texts.

But Tagore did not confine his religion to textual evidences
(śabda) as discussed in the preceding paragraphs. He appealed
more often, and particularly in The Religion of Man, to what he has
variously called personal experience, the creative spirit in man, the
surplus, freedom of expression, feeling, personality, inner principle
of religion, or the vision which leads to a "perfect harmony of
relationship, which we realize in this world not through our response
to it in knowing, but in being."[19]

In the epistemology of Indian philosophy, valid knowledge
(pramā) includes discussion of the sources of right knowledge
(pramāṇa) and the validity of knowledge (prāmāṇya). Tagore does
appeal to scriptural authority (śabda), but employs perceptions (pra-
tyaksa) by both the truly learned or great seers (vaidusa) and also
the village singers (avaidusa), inference (anumāna), comparison
(upamāna), postulation (arthāpatti), especially the assumption of a
fact in order to explain what is known from scriptures (śrutārthā-
patti), and tradition (aitihya). All of these sources are regarded by
Tagore as valuable aids to the knowledge of truth. Tagore is not
interested in a philosophy which is divorced from life's problems,
but rather religion which is founded upon human experiences, both
ordinary and spiritual. Religion satisfies more than the mind or
intellect. On a higher level, it is a direct, immediate, and holistic
realization of truth for the solution of human problems. Or in other
words, Tagore's religion is not primarily a discursive knowledge of
the highest concern (a lower level) but it is on its highest level an

intuitive experience which is meaningful for man's life within this world.[20]

Definition of Religion in *The Religion of Man*

Tagore linked religion and philosophy to poetry. Describing an incident in a remote Bengali village, Tagore reflected upon an operatic performance which he had attended. In the dialogue, a pilgrim approached Vṛndāvana but was detained by the watchman because the visitor was smuggling the self into this holy area. The religious sect described in the performance was obsolete during Tagore's day, but the point he was making was that by means of a poetic drama, the village actors were enacting ultimate meaning through the genre of dance, music, and humorous dialogue. Tagore observed, "This illustration will show how naturally, in India, poetry and philosophy have walked hand in hand."[21] The philosophy to which Tagore is referring is that which "guides men to the practical path of their life's fulfilment."[22] Such a correlation is religiously based and the fulfilment toward which Indian philosophy points is a freedom in truth which seeks to be led from the unreal to the real. For Tagore, then, religion is not a separate category unrelated to ethics and aesthetics, but is expressed in social relationships, the arts and humanities.

The Sanskrit word Tagore uses for religion is *dharma*. In its denotative sense *dharma* means the essential quality or virtue of a thing, but in its derivative meaning it implies the principle of relationship that holds man firm. Thus, Tagore explains, "Religion consists in the endeavor of men to cultivate and express those qualities which are inherent in the nature of Man the Eternal, and to have faith in him.[23]

Tagore uses the English word philosophy in at least two ways: philosophy is used pejoratively when it retreats into abstractions or negations, and it is employed synonymously with religious thought when it leads to spiritual fulfilment and realization (*mukti*).

The exclusive method of non-dualism is rejected by Tagore because it is too abstract for the religion of man. He calls this cult of union (yoga) non-religion when its aim is to merge the personal self into an impersonal entity which is without quality or definition. Although Tagore recognizes the philosophical position of non-dualism (*advaita*) as a time-honored tradition in India, he does not take the time to grapple with its arguments. Rather, he refers to the *Iśopaniṣad* for a more harmonious and balanced view.[24]

A philosophy of negation is also rejected by Tagore. He refers to the royal poet Kalidasa. In Ujjaini, Kalidasa sang about the ideal norm of the forest dwelling (*tapovana*). Those who dwelled there were seekers of truth; they "lived in an atmosphere of purity, but not of Puritanism, of the simple life, but not the life of self-mortification."[25] Religion, to Tagore, is not a negative renunciation but rather a complete and comprehensive realization.

The philosophy to which Tagore refers synonymously with religion is that to which the Upaniṣads refer as knowledge (*vidyā*), which is the antonym of *avidyā*, acceptance of error born of un-reason. Religious knowledge (*vidyā*) can be obtained through the intermediaries of love and action. To put this into the history of Indian religion, the way or means (*mārga*) for religious attainment includes knowledge (*jñāna*) and actions (*karma*), but both are mediated through loving devotion (*bhakti*) which gives balance and harmony to life.

Religion to Tagore is "the creative principle of unity, the divine mystery of existence."[26] This unity is not merely a subjective idea, but is an energizing truth. The consciousness of this unity is spiritual and man's efforts to be true to its direct vision of complex interrelationships in the world of appearance is his religion working through various names, forms, and states. Tagore began his lectures by stating that their main subject is "the idea of the humanity of our God or the divinity of Man the Eternal."[27] Ultimately such religion baffles analysis, but Tagore attempts to describe it penultimately. Religion to him is manifested through personality and suggests to the human intellect, imagination, feeling, and experience, an intuitive vision of a unified whole.

Brahman to Tagore and Bengal Vaiṣṇavas: God

What is the clue to the inner meaning of religions? Tagore found this clue in the religion of the God of human personality. This Supreme Person (*parma puruṣaḥ*) is the supreme reality of man, the divine Narāyana, or the Mahātma, the Supreme Spirit.

Tagore quotes the vedic poet who exclaims in a poem addressed to the Sun, "Reveal thy exceeding beauty to me and let me realize that the Person who is there is the One who I am,"[28] and again the poet of the Vedas states, "Nothing is greater than the Person; he is the supreme, he is the ultimate goal."[29] This truth, explains Tagore, is not the exclusive possession and insight of the *rsis* of ancient India, but it is also the experience of persons since that time and even of the village poets of East Bengal. It is in such a perspective of human personality that man finds his religion.

These references lead us to a discussion of Tagore's use of the words *brahma*, *brahman*, and *parabrahman*. As indicated above, Tagore rejects the advaita vedantic interpretations of *parabrahman* as the impersonal It of absolute truth and man's enlightenment to a pure state of consciousness of undivided unity. He states in his conclusion that his religion "can only have its significance in this phenomenal world comprehended by our human self . . . (and we are to accept the testimony of those who) have felt a profound love, which is the intense feeling of union, for a Being who comprehends in himself all things that are human in knowledge, will and action. And he is God, who is not merely a sum total of facts, but the goal that lies immensely beyond all that is comprised in the past and the present."[30]

Such a conclusion has not been drawn without considerable influence from the Indian religious tradition which we are calling Bengal Vaisnavism. As stated above, the Bengal Vaisnavas developed their personalitic religion as a revitalization of the Upanisads, the *Bhagavadgītā*, the Puranas (especially the *Bhagāvata·Purāna*), the thoughtful writings of the Gosvamins (Jiva Gosvamin in particular), and Jiva's student Krishnadasa in his *Caitanya-caritāmrta*.

To the Bengal Vaisnava, ultimate reality has three aspects, which are hierarchically arranged and ascend in order from *brahman*, to *paramatman*, to *bhagavat*. The *bhagavat* is the highest reality, the Supreme Person who is infinitely qualified and infinitely differentiated by perfect attributes. *Brahman* and *paramatman* are included in or are a part of *bhagavat* and, consequently, are to be transcended by means of knowledge and experience to the truth of the whole which is *bhagavat*.

Tagore, like the Bengal Vaisnavas, probes the qualities and differentiations of God/*bhagavat*. What is unsystematically scattered throughout Tagore's lectures can be analyzed and compared with the Bengal Vaiṣṇavas.   Ultimately inseparable (svābhāvikī) but penultimately able to be understood, there are among the infinite numbers of active powers and operative energies of divinity (śaktis), those which have been grouped under three main categories, namely, svarūpa-śakti, jīva-śakti and māyā-śakti.   If Tagore had discussed these categories, his readers would have understood him better.

Bhagavat's svarūpa eternally exists with him, is inseparable from him (it is technically termed pure existence, śuddha-sattva and is called his internal and intimate power (antaranga-śakti).   This power is a complexity of three aspects, viz., (1) sandhinī, the power which upholds his own existence, (2) saṁvit, the śakti by which he knows and make himself known, and (3) hlādinī, that aspect through which he enjoys and make others enjoy his bliss.   It is the hlādinī to which Tagore refers in his lectures, for with this aspect in preponderance, Bhagavat manifests himself in bhakti or loving devotion (called guhyavidyā by the Vaiṣṇavas).   Bhagavat in his pure existence is untouched by māyā,[31] but it is fulfilled through bhakti, loving devotion.   Had Tagore referred more specifically to these elements so important for the Bengal Vaiṣṇavas, his readers would have been able to understand him better.

In his discussion of "Spiritual Union," Tagore describes God as the Supreme Person (parama puruṣaḥ) who is love itself.   That love is not static, but is dependent and relational.   Tagore says, "For the God in Man depends upon men's service and men's love for his own love's fulfilment."[32]   When asked how this love is demonstrated, Tagore refers to Bhagavat's relation to man as Father, Friend, and Beloved.   Rather than continuing a discussion of the divine essence, Tagore turns to the human realization of Bhagavat, for he concludes, "Whatever character our theology may ascribe to him, in reality he is the infinite of man towards whom men move in their collective growth, with whom they seek their union of love as individuals, [and] in whom they find their ideal of father, friend and beloved."[33]

Jīva as the Same Essence as Bhagavat (bheda)

The second aspect of bhagavat as understood by Bengal Vaiṣṇavas is jīva-śakti, the power to manifest himself through human individualization. *Bhagavat* in this aspect is known as *paramātman*. When *paramātman* assumes the smallest indivisible part of his infinitely qualified existence *(anu)* the ultimate becomes man, the *jīvātman*. As a part of *bhagavat*, the *jīva* participates in a limited sense in the infinite qualities of *bhagavat*. *Jīva* is a *śakti* of Bhagavat and as such is a possessor of *śaktis; jīva* is a *śaktimat*. *Jīva-śakti*, then, along with *paramātman*, is the intermediate operative energy of the divine, and links the *jīvātman* with *bhagavat*. Conceived as a part of Bhagavat, who participates in *bhagavat's* qualities, the *jīva* is the same *(bheda)* as Bhagavat.

Jīva as Different Essence Than Bhagavat

Yet the *jīva* to Bengal Vaiṣṇavas is different *(abheda)* from *bhagavat*. To them the *jīva's* qualities are not infinite, and a *jīva* remains distinct from both *bhagavat* and other *jīvas*. This sameness yet difference *(bhedābheda)* is the keynote of Bengal Vaiṣṇavism, and is especially propounded in Jiva Gosvamin's writings.[34] As Dimock observes, the point of such a discussion is that because of the sameness of *bhagavat-jīva*, it is possible for the *jīva* to approach *bhagavat* and to retain a loving relationship with him. Also, because of the difference between *jīva* and *bhagavat*, there remains the need for an eternal worship by the *jīva* which is directed toward *bhagavat*, and which increases the pleasure of both the deity and the worshipper for eternity.[35]

Man in Tagore: Jīva

Although Tagore does not footnote his *The Religion of Man* with reference to the writings on *bhedābheda*, the influence of Bengal Vaiṣṇavism is represented strongly in his thought. It is the diversity of religion, Tagore states, that reveals the unity. We have discussed the *bhagavat*, let us turn to Tagore's ideas about man *(jīva)*.

When Tagore discusses man, he refers to a favorite concept of his, the personality. He defines personality as "a self-conscious principle of transcendental unity within man which comprehends all the details of facts that are individually his in knowledge and

feeling, wish, will and work. In its negative aspect it is limited to
the individual separateness, while in its positive aspect it ever
extends itself in the infinite through the increase of its knowledge,
love and activities."[36] Religion for Tagore is not confined to the
physical or material interests of man, but rather centers in the
personality of man. Man, as a part of *bhagavat*, is endowed with
surplus. This surplus frees him from attachments or limitations
of his physical nature, liberates him from the bondage of the mind
in which man limits himself by individual separateness, and it
relates him to a harmonious whole, which is a "mysterious unity
of interrelationship complex in character, with differences within
the forms and function."[37] The surplus gives man leisure and
detachment and upon the basis of this surplus man becomes a
creator too. He is not only a recipient of *bhagavat's* favor and
gracious creation, but man himself offers gifts to his God/*bhagavat*.

Curiously enough, the text to which Tagore refers in his discussion of the surplus is the *Atharva Veda*. By means of this surplus
man is aware that he is greater than the parts of his own character,
and realizes that he is not imperfect, but only incomplete, so he
must exceed himself and search for ultimate meaning not yet
realized. The surplus is an inner truth in man's personality, which
the Bengal Vaiṣṇavas identified as *bhagavat's jīva-śakti*. Tagore
describes it as "him in whose image we are made."[38] When man
becomes a creator he realizes himself in the perspective of a
dependent relationship to *bhagavat*, and with the experience of his
self-realization, man becomes aware of his religion.

Religion as Self-Realization in Tagore
and Bengal Vaiṣṇavism

Self-realization (*mukti*) is the experience of union in truth for
Tagore in which the *jīvan-devatā*, God, the Lord of Life, and the
jīvan-mukta, liberated man, are mutually dependent. The union
is characterized by freedom, love, and joy in its individual experience and is shared with other *jīvas* by means of disinterested, selfless, and creative works of social welfare. *Mukti* demands a
disciplined life in which the *mukta* progresses normally through the
four stages of life, and which is characterized by a life of simplicity.
Such a union of parts make up Tagore's religion of self-realization.

The Sanskrit term which Tagore uses for self-realization is *mukti*, which he defines as freedom in the unity of truth. This spiritual union has two dimensions: one that is inner, which reconciles the complex parts of human personality into a harmony of self-adjusting interrelationships within his whole personality; and the second dimension is the outer, in which the liberated *jiva* finds his larger and truer self in his interrelationships with the community of *jivas*, humanity. Man's consciousness of this spiritual unity and his efforts to be true to such a vision Tagore calls religion. Such liberated personalities are not historicised as beings out of a past, more religious age, nor are they confined to those whose birth and development have given them the privilege of high caste, for even an unsophisticated village fisherman was known to Tagore as a *jivan mukta*. To such a freed personality is given the name of the "twice born" for they maintain a relationship with the Divine which is of mutual dependence. Finally, Tagore teaches that self-realization is attained by means of disciplined effort. As an illustration of the mutual relationship of the infinite being and the finite self, Tagore refers to the upanisadic parable of two birds sitting on the same bough. One is feeding while the other observes. Both of these birds are in man: the objective one busies himself in this life's matters, while the subjective one looks on with disinterested joy. Both the inner and the outer dimensions of self-realization affect one another and overlap in the human personality. What is imprecise in Tagore's lectures can be clarified when we turn to the writings of the Bengal Vaisnavas.

The Bengal Vaisnavas differentiate a third active power (*sakti*) of *bhagavat*, namely *maya-sakti* (see above for *svarupa* and *jiva saktis*). *Maya-sakti* is outer or external (*bahiranga*) to *bhagavat*, that is, it is not directly connected with the essential self of *bhagavat*, but is known only at the lower levels of existence. *Paramatman* is the cause, sustenance, and dissolution of the created world and exerts control over human beings and the material nature. The *jiva* of the *jiva-sakti* of *bhagavat* shares his qualities, but as *maya-sakti jiva* possesses an organic body which has a limited form. As long as the *jiva* identifies itself with the body, it is under *maya's* control. But when the *jiva* no longer identifies his self with the material form (*prakrti*) and experiences the liberating realization that the *jiva* is in its highest form and essence (a part of the *svarupa-sakti* of *bhagavat*), he is no longer a captive of the inferior physical form of *māyā-śakti*.

The Bengal Vaiṣṇavas differentiated *māyā-śakti* further as *jīva-māyā* and *guṇa-māyā*. *Jīva-māyā* obscures the vision of the individual (*jīva*) *atmān*, so that it does not realize that it possesses pure consciousness (*cit*), a quality it shares with *bhagavat*. *Guṇa-māyā* refers to the binding power of *māyā* which keeps the *jīva* from liberation by overdue involvement with the tripartite material world, viz., the material (*prakṛti*) of the *sattva-guṇa*, *rajas-guṇa* and *tamas-guṇa*. The *jīva* as part of *bhagavat* can transcend both *guṇa-māyā* and *jīva-māyā* and experience by means of *bhakti* the liberating, loving relationship with *bhagavat*, in which the *jīva* is a part of the whole and both dependent upon and interdependent with *bhagavat*.

The inner dimension of self-realization is characterized by Tagore as one of freedom, love, and joy. The *jīva* is free to realize his divine dignity. Such freedom is not just independence but "lies in a perfect harmony of relationships, which we realize in this world not through our response to it in knowing, but in being... through the union of perfect sympathy."[39] This freedom is religious in that it is "the liberation of our individual personality in the universal Person who is human all the same."[40] Without the Bengal Vaiṣṇava technical vocabulary, the reader of *The Religion of Man* could easily misunderstand Tagore.

To Tagore, man's freedom is for expressing the infinite by continually breaking through imposed limitations. Just as physical man overcame physical limitations when he stood upright, developed his eyesight and mind to be able to comprehend a larger view, attained skill and grace by the coordination of his functional parts for actions, so religious man used his divine gift of mind and imagination (Tagore's surplus) to apprehend the Supreme Person by breaking through the limitations and binding power of *māyā*. With the vedic *mantra* inspiring his energies and aspirations, the human devotee progresses from the unreal to the real, and man exercises his freedom by breaking through the isolation of the self. But freedom is more than a negative release from something incomplete; freedom is religious when it is a positive realization which finds its personal fulfilment in the apprehension of and companionship with the Supreme Person.

From the period of his youth until his mature age, it was the love poems of the Vaiṣṇavas that influenced his thinking. Dissatisfied with various religious alternatives in his contemporary milieu,

Tagore, during the period under review, began to examine these love poems for meanings beyond their obvious and surface expressions. Without mentioning him by name it is apparent that the religious movement revitalized by Caitanya and perpetuated by his followers became a major source of his understanding of the religion of man. In his search for religious meanings, Tagore was interested in the religious expressions of villagers in remote Bengal areas. Their dramas reminded him of the events which happened in Vrndāvan, when Krsna played his flute, calling devotees to come and to experience religion as expressed by means of the metaphors of personal love.

Like the Bengal Vaisnavas, he presupposed the position of dualism, in which man finds his spiritual satisfaction via a progressive growth in loving devotion for the Supreme Person, *bhagavat*. Tagore does not always use the technical Vaisnava terms, but in order to avoid confusion his English transformations are forced to use them if we are to understand *The Religion of Man*, *bhakti*, Bengal Vaisnavism, and Tagore.

The word *bhakti* comes from the verbal root √bhaj, which signifies complete servitude. By derivation the essential characteristic of *bhakti* is servitude or submission of body, mind, and words to *bhagavat*. This term was translated by Tagore as loving devotion.

True devotional feeling for the Vaisnavas is developed through two stages: *vaidhī-bhakti* and *rāgānuga-bhakti*. *Vaidhī-bhakti* is that form of devotion which is external and involves ritual activities. The majority of people who read the scriptural texts are instructed as to how to perform devotional actions which will remove the human fears of transgressing the normative injunctions. These activities are formal and require correct mechanical performance. This is the preliminary stage of *bhakti*; it is indispensable for the beginner as a guide for introductory knowledge and practice. The means of *vaidhī-bhakti* have been enumerated by Rupa as sixty-four acts of piety.[41] These positive actions bring the devotee's body, senses, and mind into a devotional state of worship. They also assist the devotee, negatively, by helping him to avoid the offenses to devotion.

The devotee advances, according to the Vaisnavas, beyond the outward forms of rules and actions to the higher stage of *bhakti*, called *rāgānuga*. At this level, the devotee experiences a deep and inseparable love for *bhagavat*, and the emotional part of his

character is stirred. The *bhakta* experiences intimate human sentiments in his relationship with *bhagavat*, and he imitates a variety of
human relationships, i.e., that of a child to his parents (*vātsālya*),
relative to relative, lover to beloved (*mādhurya*), friend to friend
(*sākhya*) or servant to master (*dāsya*). *Rāgānuga* is the advanced
stage of the way to spiritual fulfilment.

When *bhakti* matures for the Bengal Vaiṣṇavas it develops into
the human sentiment of love (*prema*). *Prema* is the highest stage
of devotion and its sequence begins with faith (*śraddhā*) and advances through hierarchical stages until it is fulfilled.

Comparable ideas are found in Tagore's *The Religion of Man*;
in his lectures we see the imaginative mind of a poet seeking
to translate these Indian ideas of love into English for an audience which probably did not know the variations within Bengal
Vaiṣṇavism.

In dualistic and theistic terms, Tagore defines the Supreme
Person as love, and also the relationship between the spiritual
aspirant and *bhagavat*, the Supreme Love, in terms of love. When
man experiences the love of nature's beauty, of an animal, child,
comrade, his beloved or the highest love of *bhagavat*, he tastes
prema. But the love of man for the Supreme Person is greater than
all other loves and is the most perfect relationship. That highest
love is characterized as one of mutual dependence. The lover's
flute is Kṛṣṇa's, and the flute notes urge man to come out of his
existence in separation to one of loving union. Those who answer
the call of the flute meet *bhagavat* in the "hall of union."[42] Present
just beneath the descriptive words of the poet are the Bengal
Vaiṣṇava love actions (*līlā*) in which Kṛṣṇa carried on his love-
drama with the *gopis* (cowherdesses) and *gopas* (cowherds) of
Vṛndāvan. In English Tagore is restrained; he does not use
Vaiṣṇava erotics. Instead his approach is to interpret those sensual
actions on a level of spiritual relationships, and consequently the
English reader misses the deeper meanings. Yet, he states that
love is the perfect commingling of physical, mental and spiritual
associations.[43] Vaiṣṇava erotics would have assisted his translation even if he demanded that his readers become acquainted with
Vaiṣṇava normative literature.

Like the Bengal Vaiṣṇavas, Tagore explains the dualism of the
relationship between the *jīvā* and *bhagavat* as one of mutual dependence. Because of his love for man, *bhagavat* graciously responds

to the *prema* of the worshipping *jīva*. As father, friend, and supreme lover, *bhagavat* depends upon man's service and sacrificial love; that service and love is needed by *bhagavat* to fulfill himself. The *jīva's* love, prompted by his willingness to sacrifice his own pleasures for fulfilling loving devotion to *bhagavat*, is always mutually dependent upon the prompting and response of the Supreme Person.

In following the Bengal Vaiṣṇavas in his exposition of dualism, Tagore rejects what he characterizes as the advaita vedantic (nondualistic) ultimate state of abstract Being. The Infinite, in *The Religion of Man,* at its highest level is expressed in human terms, and this ultimate Person needs the reciprocal love and cooperation of the devotee. In a poem which he translated in the Oxford lectures, Tagore assumes the relationship of a love partner to illustrate this mutual dependence. Most of Tagore's discussion is sexually restrained, but in this poem addressed to *Jīvan devatā,* "The Lord of My Life," Tagore wonders if his failures and wrongs are forgiven and if his days without service and nights of forgetfulness of the Supreme Person have affected their love relationship. Flowers which should have been offered, tunes which should have been played on the lute, and lyrics which ought to have been sung in praise of *Jīvan devatā* have all been neglected. In the last section of the poem, the poet asks:

But have my days come to their end at last,
Lord of My Life, (*Jīvan devatā*),
while my arms round thee grow limp,
my kisses losing their truth?

He answers his own question and implores *bhagavat* to renew this love drama, which is reminiscent of the Vṛndāvan metaphors:

Then break up the meeting of this languid day
Renew the old in me in fresh forms of delight;
and let the wedding come once again
in a new ceremony of life.[44]

It is unnecessary for this discussion to explain the implications of Hindu erotics, and Tagore suggests to our imagination the love battle of the bed chamber. Human love has two interdependent phases, viz., love in sexual union, and the anticipation of union while the lovers are separated. This human love can be elevated to the plane of human-divine relationships, in which the pain of separation always suggests the joy of union. Perhaps Dimock can help us understand Tagore's communication problem: "The essential problem of poetic expression is the communication through image and symbol of those intuitions and perceptions that often lie beyond consciousness and that cannot be expressed by what is often called 'denotative language.'"[45] More explicit reference to Bengal Vaiṣṇava *prema* would have enhanced the level of comprehension in Tagore's audience.

Finally, Tagore denotes the relationship between the *Jīvā* and *bhagavat* as one of love by stating that *prema* is both the means and the end of *bhakti*. We have already introduced *bhakti* as a means to the religious end, *mukti*. Like the Bengal Vaiṣṇavas, Tagore lectures on the superiority of *bhakti* over the other modes of worship, viz., *Jñāna*, yoga, and *karma*. The way of knowledge (*Jñāna*) leads to the realization of *brahman*. Yoga is the disciplined effort which is another means to self-realization, and sacrificial activities (*karma*) induce the devotee from selfish pleasures, desires, intents, and activities to a higher state which is characterized by loving devotion of the Supreme Person. These modes are inferior because they are means. The unmixed or pure (*śuddhā*) *prema bhakti* is the superior mode and the highest expression of the means to ultimate satisfaction.[46]

To the Bengal Vaiṣṇavas, there is a hierarchy of the modes of worship; *bhakti-mārga* is superior to the *jñāna*, yoga, and *karma* ways. When, as a means, *bhakti* is accompanied by the desire for fruits it is *sakāmā*; such *bhakti* progresses to the level of its highest means, when it is accompanied by actions free from inferior desires (*niṣkāma-kārmasahitā*). *Sakāmā bhakti* can be mixed with a desire for activity; this arises out of the *rajas guṇa*. It can also be prompted by the lower passions such as envy or pride when it is mixed with *tamas guṇa*. As the inclination and capacity of the devotee develop, the *bhakta* progresses into the experiential relationship of pure *bhakti* (*śuddhā*) in which resides divine pleasure and *prema*. This is the best mode for attaining the highest good. Thus, of the traditionally accepted ways of religious progress and guidance (*mārga*), *bhakti* is superior to *jñāna*, yoga, and *karma*.[47] The Bengal Vaiṣṇavas consequently do not reject these other modes of worship, but relegate them to preliminary or penultimate status. They are inferior means to the end, yet they are parts which make up the whole. Saints or devotees who follow these mixed paths are encouraged to progress further in their devotion and to become the highest type of devotees of *bhagavat (bhakta siddha)*.

Bhakti, then, is the highest means to the *prema* of *bhagavat*. Jīva Gosvamin had written in his *Bhakti-samdarbha*, "True mokṣa (*apavarga*) consists in a direct vision (*sākṣātkāra*) or attainment (*prāpti*) of the deity in his highest appearance as the Bhagavat, which is realizable by *bhakti* alone."[48]

Tagore, like the Bengal Vaiṣṇavas, regards *bhakti* as the end of religious aspiration and ultimate satisfaction, because the Ultimate is the Supreme Lover. The technical vocabulary is translated into English as: "We must realize not only the reasoning mind, but also the creative imagination, the love and wisdom that belong to the Supreme Person, . . . love for whom comprehends love for all creatures and exceeds in depth and strength all other loves, leading to difficult endeavors and martyrdoms that have no other gain than the fulfilment of this love itself."[49] Within this same dualistic and theistic model for the religion of man, Tagore concludes his lectures by appealing to the reader, "Let us have faith in the testimony of others who have felt a profound love, which is the intense feeling of union, for a Being who comprehends in himself all things that are human in knowledge, will and action. And he is God, who is not merely a sum total of facts, but the goal that lies immensely beyond all that is comprised in the past and the present."

Like the vision of the Bengal Vaiṣṇavas, Tagore's self-realization (*mukti*) is an experience of freedom which leads from the isolation of the self to a unifying relationship with the Supreme Person. This union is characterized by love, in which the *jīvan-mukta* expresses his gratitude for the gift of love by means of service and devotion to *bhagavat*. *Bhagavat*, in turn, depends upon man's cooperation and reciprocal love (*prema*). Such devotional responses continue throughout the lifetime of the devotee and are involved in the maze of physical, mental, and spiritual associations.

Conclusion

Bengal Vaiṣṇavism is one of the many religious traditions from which Tagore drew for his exposition of the religion of man. Many writers in the secondary literature on Tagore have mentioned its influence, but have neglected to substantiate it.

Tagore emphasized both intellectual knowledge and intuitive knowledge as means for understanding and experiencing religion.

He drew heavily upon religious thought patterns connected with the *acintya bhedābheda* school founded by Sri Caitanya and systematized and elaborated by the six Gosvamins of the Vaiṣṇava traditions of Bengal.

When Tagore translated the Ultimate as God in English, he removed from the word a complexity of Vaiṣṇava thought unknown to many of his readers or listeners, and the result of this reduction led some of his listeners to oversimplify and misunderstand him.

Jīva is both of the same essence (*bheda*) and different from (*abheda*) *bhagavat*. The mutually dependent relationship of *bhagavat* and *jīva* is ultimately indescribable (*acintya*). The experience of inner self-realization is characterized by freedom, love, and joy, and the application of these inner characteristics to the outer community of humankind is their creative expression in the social context.

Religion understood as the pattern of ultimate concern demonstrates Tagore's constant struggle for balance, when he attempted to explain it in his Hibbert Lectures in *The Religion of Man*.

Notes

1. N. Sen, "The Foreign Reincarnation of Rabindranath Tagore," *Journal of Asian Studies* 25 (1966) : 275-86.
2. B. Bose, *An Acre of Green Grass* (Calcutta: Orient Longmans, 1948), p. 1.
3. R. Tagore, *Wings of Death* (London: John Murray, 1960), pp. 95f.
4. R. Tagore, *The Religion of Man* (Boston: Beacon Press, 1961), p. 92. Hereafter cited as *RM*.
5. M. Singer, "Text and Context in the Study of Contemporary Hinduism," in *When a Great Tradition Modernizes* (New York: Praeger, 1972), pp. 39-52.
6. *RM*, pp. 89f.
7. *RM*, p. 79.
8. *RM*, p. 82.
9. A.K. Ramanujan, trans., *Speaking of Siva* (Baltimore: Penguin, 1973).
10. T.S. Rukmani, *A Critical Study of the Bhagavata Purana* (Varanasi: Chokhamba Sanskrit Office, 1970), p. 182.
11. Rukmani, *A Critical Study*, p. 174.

12. See especially the developments initiated by Rupa, Jīva, Sanatana, who returned to Vṛndavana to write theological texts for Gauḍiya Vaiṣṇavism. They expounded Caitanya's ideas and emphasized Kṛṣṇa bhakti. Rukmani, *A Critical Study*, p. 96.

13. The letter was written on September 1, 1930, and is cited in M. Lago, *Imperfect Encounter* (Cambridge: Harvard University Press, 1972), p. 330.

14. Lago, *Imperfect Encounter*, pp. 320-22.

15. *RM*, p. 92; see also his disclaimer of being a scholar or philosopher, ibid., p. 90.

16. Ibid., p. 43.

17. Ibid., pp. 109ff.

18. Ibid., pp. 18f.

19. Ibid., p. 172.

20. Religion is *darśana*, a way of apprehending the world, or a *rasavastu*, a life to be enjoyed rather than a theory to be propounded.

21. *RM*, p. 183.

22. Ibid.

23. Ibid., p. 144.

24. Ibid., p. 117.

25. Ibid., p. 167.

26. Ibid., pp. 14f.

27. Ibid., p. 17.

28. Ibid., p. 115.

29. Ibid., p. 116.

30. Ibid., pp. 205f.

31. R.G. Nath, "The Acintya-bhedābheda School," *Cultural Heritage of India* (Calcutta: Ramakrishna Mission, 1953), 3.367. E.C. Dimock, Jr., *The Place of the Hidden Moon* (Chicago: University of Chicago Press, 1966), pp. 124ff.

32. *RM*, p. 72.

33. Ibid., p. 165.

34. Dimock, *The Place of the Hidden Moon*, p. 124; *RM*, pp. 46ff. See also S.K. De, *The Early History of the Vaisnava Faith and Movement in Bengal* (Calcutta: K.L. Mukhopadhyay, 1961), pp. 281ff.

35. See below for a discussion of *māyā-śakti*.

36. *RM*, p. 119.

37. Ibid., pp. 46f.

38. Ibid., p. 126.

39. Ibid., pp. 172f.

40. Ibid., p. 193.

41. De, *The Early History of the Vaisnava Faith and Movement in Bengal*, p. 181.

42. *RM*, p. 106.

43. Ibid., p. 124.

44. Ibid., pp. 47f.

45. Dimock, *The Place of the Hidden Moon*, p. 4.

46. S.C. Chakravarti, *Philosophical Foundation of Bengal Vaisnavism* (NP: Academic Publishers, 1969), pp. 177f.

47. *RM*, p. 119.

48. De, *The Early History of the Vaisnava Faith and Movement in Bengal*, p. 356.

49. *RM*, p. 24.

16

SRI AUROBINDO AND EXPERIENCE: YOGIC AND OTHERWISE

Robert N. Minor

Sri Aurobindo Ghose (1872-1950) has been thought of as one of the most important religious thinkers in modern India. A large body of secondary literature demonstrates the interest in his thought,[1] and centers for the study of his thought and yoga are located throughout the world today.

The evolution of the mature form of Aurobindo's thought, which is of interest to most students and scholars, is traceable from his early days as a student in England to his final days as a yogi in Pondicherry.[2] His system of thought attempted to affirm both a transcendent Unity in the tradition of Vedanta, and the reality of the multiplicity which is the phenomenal world.

Though Aurobindo placed himself within the vedantic tradition, his decision, as to what would be accepted, rejected, or reinterpreted from that tradition was based upon the authority of his own religious experiences. The experiences which were authoritative for his ultimate concern were both yogic and non-yogic, and this paper traces the relationship of these experiences to his religion. At first, in England, only an aesthetic experience of nature was the authority for his religious stance. Upon his return to India, the experiences of others, the yogi-seers of the Upaniṣads, were considered authoritative. These, however, did not deny his own aesthetic appreciation of the phenomenal world. His own yogic experience became fully authoritative only when it too affirmed the reality and worth of this world as well as the reality of the upanisadic Unity behind and within the phenomena. At Pondicherry, in the final period of his life, he wrote as a "realized" yogi,[3] or, better, a yogi in the process of realization, for then his yogic experience, and it alone, was the authority for all truth.

Religion and the Aesthetic Experience of Nature in England

Sri Aurobindo was born on August 15, 1872, in Bengal, India. His father was an English-educated physician who wanted his son to receive a British education. After attending an Irish-Catholic school in India, Aurobindo was sent to England, to Kings College, Cambridge. Though he never qualified for the Indian civil service, the vocational goal of his studies, these years were marked by the receipt of a number of academic awards.

In England Aurobindo wrote a dozen or so poems and a number of prose works which remained incomplete. In *The Harmony of Virtue* he attempted to develop an ethical system without a "religious" basis. In this he rejected what he had experienced as a Christian worldview, beliefs which affirmed a personal Divine Being who acted as a law-giver.[4] Instead, Aurobindo wrote that his ultimate concern was "to restore the harmony to the Universe," the experience of which was open to all. *The Harmony of Virtue* is a Socratic-style dialogue, and the person who is convinced of the truth by Aurobindo's philosopher summarizes: "I see now that to be in harmony with beauty, or, in other words, to take the guiding principle of the universe as the guiding principle of human life, is the final and perfect aim of the human species."[5] In this he believed that he was taking a principle which was found in nature and which all could experience, and applying it to the task of the human ultimate concern. There was no sense of an absolute which transcended Nature. What was ultimately real for Aurobindo was Nature's principle of harmony. Nature's beauty consists in "harmony of effect and proportion in detail."[6]

Every element of Nature contained both an internal harmony and, in taking its place in the universe, exhibited an external harmony with all else in the universe. In another prose work of the period Aurobindo adds that this harmony exists even though at times one might think otherwise: "However she may seem to grow grapes from thistles, [Nature] is really too wise and good to do anything so discordant, and only by her involved and serpentine manner gives an air of caprice and anarchy to what is really apt and harmonious."7

Only the human being falls outside of this harmony, and this because of humanity's wilful choice of what Aurobindo calls "False Reason," which causes it to misunderstand Nature and her ways. The human being should choose now to follow Nature by taking a place in her harmony.

There is no evidence of spiritual or yogic experiences for Aurobindo in England. He later says that there was some sort of "realization" in the year of his departure for England, but he knew nothing of yogic practices at this time. The system of thought was limited to his experience of Nature, but this was an experience of Nature in harmony, articulated as overwhelmingly aesthetic and obviously real. His poetry reflects his experience of the beauty and harmony of Nature. "Songs to Myrtila" is a debate between two fictional Greek aesthetics over the relative beauty of night and day. In "Phaethon" he sighs with the trees a requiem for "Pale-gilded Autumn, aesthete of the years." In "To a Hero-Worshipper" he claims to have studied Nature and found no message, yet like "a russet nightingale/Who pours sweet song, he knows not why," he sees beauty and harmony there. Aurobindo, in spite of even contradictory yogic experience, would always be committed to the world in such a manner. Yogic experience would have to conform before he would completely accept its authority.

One poem highlights Aurobindo's desire to return to India, a desire which he realized in February 1893, and which was accompanied by "spiritual experiences." In "Envoi"8 Aurobindo writes that to stay in England is to experience unfulfilled hopes and dreams:

Depart and live for seasons many and few
If live you may, but stay here to pain
My heart with hopeless passion and renew
Visions of beauty that my lips shall ne'er attain.

His intense desire to return to India is described as a call:

Me from her lotus heaven Saraswati

Has called to regions of eternal snow
And Ganges pacing to the southern sea,
Ganges upon whose shores the flowers of Eden blow.

India, a land in which he was born, but about which he knew
little, seemed to be beckoning to him, and he returned. He later
recalled experiences which he evaluated as indicative of the importance of experiential understanding. Upon stepping on Indian soil,
he experienced "a vast calm which descended upon him . . . (this
calm surrounded him and remained for long months afterwards)."[9]
As he looked back on this event, he believed the "spiritual experience" confirmed his divine call.

Religion and the Experiences of the Upanisadic Seers

Aurobindo spent about thirty years in Baroda in the state
service. Here he first read Sanskrit and Bengali literature, and
translated portions of the *Mahābhārata* and the *Rāmāyana* epics as
well as the *Bhagavadgītā*. This placed him in touch with a tradition he was to identify as his own. He claims to have been adverse
to metaphysical speculation, but he read the sayings of Ramakrishna Paramahamsa, some of the speeches of Svami Vivekananda,
and the Upaniṣads. In Baroda he began his study of the Upaniṣads,
writing *Philosophy of the Upanishads* and *On Translating the Upanishads*, the latter to critique Max Müller.

In the former work he identified his own position as that of the
upanisadic seers. He believed this position reflected a common
Indian spiritual experience as well as the center around which
Indian thought developed. "The idea of transcendental Unity,
Oneness and Stability behind all the flux and variety of phenomenal
life is the basal idea of the Upanishads: this is the pivot of all
Indian metaphysics, the sum and goal of our spiritual experience."[10]
The teachings of the Upaniṣads, understood as consistent, became
his own religion and were affirmed as the religion of India because
they were based upon her spiritual experience. This last element
was the key: spiritual experience.

Aurobindo claimed to have had "spiritual experiences" in the
Baroda period. They are later described as "the realisation of the

vacant Infinite while walking on the ridge of the Takhti-Suleman in Kashmir; the living presence of Kali in a shrine on the banks of the Narmada; the vision of the Godhead surging up from within when in danger of a carriage accident in Baroda in the first year of his stay, etc."11 These may have reinforced his sense of truth of the Upaniṣads, but the importance of the Upaniṣads for him was that they were based upon experiences resulting from the yogic practice of their authors.He could not identify his experiences with theirs at this period, but he was convinced of the truth of their experiences. These reinforced the harmony of existence he sought in his early writing in England, and the reality of the world by means of intuitive realizations which he believed were as real as experiences of everyday life might be to others. He affirmed their experiences as authoritative, though they were not his own, and *The Philosophy of the Upanishads* regularly refers to their knowledge as experiential.

The seers, by means of yoga, realized first the existence of the Unity behind all of the flux, called absolute *brahman*.12 *Brahman* as Absolute is beyond the limitations of speech and conceptualization, like the *nirguṇa brahman* (*brahman* without characteristics) of the tenth-century non-dualist Sankara. The *brahman* that may be known, however, is not *saguṇa brahman* (*brahman* with characteristics) of Sankara, which is also spoken of as a personal deity or lord, *iṣvara*. The *brahman* known is designated by the traditional upanisadic formula *saccidānanda*. This compound speaks of the absolute as *sat*, "pure existence, pure being," as *cit*, "pure consciousness," and *ānanda*, "absolute bliss." The undeveloped hints of Aurobindo's later evolutionary theory of consciousness are found in his statements at Baroda about the origin of the phenomenal universe in the envisaging of himself by *brahman*. It is at this point that "Brahman chooses to regard himself as qualified."13

Aurobindo interprets the doctrine of *māyā* in terms of experience. *Māyā*, for Aurobindo, is not a declaration of the illusoriness of existence in ultimate terms, as it is for Sankara. Instead it is a designation for two apparently contradictory facts which are experienced. First, the universe is experienced as an Absolute Unity, *brahman*, as the essence of the world, in the yogic experience of the upanisadic seers. Second, the universe in its multiplicity is also experienced as real in non-yogic experience. Since Aurobindo will not relegate the duality to a lower level, as does Sankara, because it is also experienced as real, *māyā* is seen as a term which embodies both facts of experience, though apparently contradictory: "Maya is no theory but a fact: no mere result of logic or speculation, but of careful observation and yet unassailable by logic and unsurpassable by speculation."[14]   *Māyā* is not a part of experience, but it is the one postulate which Vedanta demands in order to account for the apparently contradictory experiences of the Unity and the Diversity.[15]

The second realization from yogic experience which Aurobindo finds in the Upaniṣads and which he himself affirms is "that the transcendent absolute Self of things was also the Self of living beings, the Self too of man, that highest of the beings living in the material plane on earth."[16]   *Brahman* is not to be found as separate from the world of existence, but as the essential part of it. The third upanisadic realization amplifies this further: "The Transcendent Self in individual man is as complete because identically the same as the Transcendent Self of the Universe."[17]   As traditionally put, *brahman*, the Absolute, is *ātman*, the "self," or as the Upaniṣads put it, *tat tvam tsi*, "you are that."

Though ignorance clouds the realization of this reality, these are experienced facts of the seers of the Upaniṣads. Aurobindo spends much time discussing the levels of yogic experience revealed in the Upaniṣads. His ultimate concern was not just the exposition of the Upaniṣads, but twofold: first, the experience of the realization of *ātman* as *brahman*, pure, absolute consciousness, and second, the realization by the whole world itself of *brahman* in its outer life, conforming all beings to the nature of the Absolute. The method was available to all, though Aurobindo did not spell out its details. It required the recorded revelation of the Upaniṣads, *śruti*, "that which is heard," to seize the mind and saturate it with the ideas of the supreme. Then it required a sacred teacher, who would teach what the *śruti* implies. Third, it required the practice of yoga, a practice which Aurobindo did not explain at this point. Finally, it required the "Grace of God," to enable one to persevere in the faith.[18] No further information is spelled out. Aurobindo may have only been making a start in study of the scriptures, seeking a like experience of the Absolute. It would not be until 1908 that he would seek out a guru, or teacher, to help him to rise to upanisadic realizations.

Though Aurobindo began a type of yogic practice in 1904, he

did not practice it for "spiritual reasons," but in order to gain strength and endurance for his political work. It was mainly a practice of *prāṇāyāma*, "breathing exercises."[19] This continued for about four years until, frustrated, he turned to a teacher for help. He later said that this early yoga brought "an increased health and outflow of energy, some psycho-physical phenomena, a great outflow of poetic creation, a limited power of subtle sight (luminous patterns and figures, etc.) mostly with the waking eye,"[20] but no deep religious experience. In fact, in 1910 he would emphatically downgrade *prāṇāyāma*.[21]

Thus, in this period he accepted upanisadic thought on the basis of the experiences of others, the vedic seers, not on the authority of his own yoga. Aurobindo would later be convinced that his experiences were like theirs, but only through his own experience would his elaboration of the evolutionary scheme become the central element of his thought. In the period spent in England, Aurobindo had committed himself to the positive affirmation of this world as a place of beauty and harmony. While in Baroda he saw that affirmation as a part of the upanisadic realization. Soon he would seek to make the upanisadic realization his own and be satisfied with his yogic experience only when it would affirm both *brahman* and the world.

A Temporary Nationalism and Yogic Interests

Though Aurobindo had been interested in the politics of Indian independence earlier, attending sessions of the Indian National Congress and writing a few essays for *Indu Prakash*, the independence of India, which was a penultimate issue, was temporarily raised to the level of ultimacy in 1905-6 with the writing of a revolutionary pamphlet entitled *Bhawani Mandir*. Aurobindo had previously identified his own *Weltanschauung* with that of the Vedanta of the upanisadic seers. India, he believed, was the key to the promotion of that Vedanta in the whole world, changing the world in terms of vedantic truth. As David Johnson has shown, worship of the nation was a necessary condition for the realization of the ultimate, and thus it is incorrect to argue, as the Mukherjees did, that Aurobindo was merely using Vedanta for political purposes.[22]

Prior to a decisive yogic experience of 1908, Aurobindo continued his search for the experience of the absolute *brahman*, an
experience which was not his, but which he saw behind the writings
of the upaniṣadic seers: "Our aspiration can be satisfied with
nothing short of the Omnipresent. In littleness there is no bliss. So
we must not run after petty ideals. The Universal alone should
be the one object of our knowledge and pursuit. Then the Vedas
explain the nature of the Universal."[23] This aspiration was articulated as late as August, 1907, in the journal which was primarily
concerned with the extreme "Nationalist" cause, the immediate
independence of India.

Added to this goal was the concept of India as the *śakti*, the
"energy or power" of the Ultimate. Aurobindo joined other Ex-
tremists in using this concept, which was borrowed from traditions
which revered the goddess in India. The goddess was thought of
by her devotees as the active power *(śakti)* of the god and was
often worshipped in her own right. Most commonly she was the
consort of Śiva and schools of thought developed which elaborated
upon worship of the *śakti*. Ramakrishna, the modern religious
figure whom Aurobindo admired, was a devotee of the goddess
Kālī at the Dakshineshwar Temple outside of Calcutta.

The *śakti*, the Mother, was conceived of by Aurobindo as the
energy of the Absolute *brahman*. In *Bhawani Mandir* he wrote:
"When, therefore, you ask who is Bhawani the Mother, She herself
answers you, 'I am the Infinite Energy which streams forth from
the Eternal in the world and the Eternal in yourselves. I am the
Mother of the Universe, the Mother of the Worlds.'"[24] Since the
Absolute was believed to be behind the movement toward independence with the goal of bringing Vedanta to the world through India,
the guru to the nations, India was the greatest incarnation of the
Absolute's energy. India, then, was the Mother, the *śakti*. Therefore, Aurobindo exhorted all to see India as *śakti*: "It is not till
the Motherland reveals herself to the eye of the mind as something
more than a stretch of earth or a mass of individuals, it is not till
she takes shape as a great Divine and Maternal Power in a form of
beauty that can dominate the mind and seize the heart that these
petty fears and hopes vanish in the all-absorbing passion for the
Mother and her service, and the patriotism that works miracles
and saves a doomed nation is born."[25] Because he believed the
movement was the work of the Divine *śakti* himself, for the remainder

of his life Aurobindo affirmed that Indian independence was inevitable: "For this thing is written in the book of God and nothing can prevent it, that Sati shall wed Mahadeva, that the national life of India shall meet and possess its divine and mighty destiny."[26] For Aurobindo, then, nationalism, as the immediate stage in the promotion of the vedantic Absolute in the world, was a religious movement. He called it a "religion" as well, meaning by this that it was an activity whose goal is the realization of the Divine. It was an "active path" (*pravṛtti mārga*) and, therefore,

there is no rationality in asking us to practise religion and morality first and politics afterwards: for politics is itself a large part of religion and morality. We acknowledge that nothing is likely to become a universal and master impulse in India which is not identified with religion. The obvious course is to recognise that politics is religion and infuse it with the spirit of religion; for that is the true patriotism which sees God as the Mother in our country, God as *sakti* in the mass of our countrymen, and religiously devotes itself to their service and their liberation from present suffering and servitude.[27]

Aurobindo recognized the influence of religion in India and was not hesitant to identify his political activities with it, but this was because they in fact *were* a "religion" in his mind, a path to the divine, temporarily of ultimate concern, because the result would be the freedom of India to spread Vedanta to the world.

In the pages of *Bande Mataram*, Aurobindo preached the cause of Indian independence as the way to spiritual liberation. However, as 1907 drew to a close he was becoming more and more frustrated because of the lack of his own vedantic-type realizations. He had no realizations like the upanisadic seers, no assurance of the Unity he affirmed. Politically he looked ahead to the Surat Conference in December 1907. This he hoped would be the final confrontation between the more moderate positions in the Indian independence movement and the "nationalists." In the pages of *Bande Mataram* he called all "nationalists" to attend the conference and to spread the view of immediate Indian independence against the compromises of the "loyalists" (i.e., the "moderates" who were willing to accept a period of British tutelage). Writing immediately before the conference, on December 13, 1907, he exhorted,

If Bengal goes there in force it will, we believe, set flowing such a
tide of Nationalism as neither bureaucrats nor Bombay Loyalists
are prepared to believe possible. . . . We must go as poor men
whose wealth is our love for our Motherland, as missionaries
taking nothing with them but the barest expenses of the way, as
pilgrims traveling to our Mother's temple. We have a great work
to do and cannot afford to be negligent and half-hearted. Be
sure that this year 1907 is a turning-point of our destinies, and do
not imagine that the session of the Surat Congress will be as the
sessions of other years.[28]

The "moderates" outnumbered the "nationalists" at the conference. There was much spirited debate and the outcome was a split
in the Congress. Aurobindo, who chaired the separate meetings of
the "nationalists,"gave the order to break up the Congress because
there was no hope of compromise. The Congress would not take
nationalist sentiment into consideration.

Thus, by the end of 1907 Aurobindo had seen what was an
apparent setback in the progress of nationalism as well as what he
later called "failure" in his attempts to attain a personal experience
which would make his own the experience of the upanisadic seers.
He later recalled, when asked whether he had realizations in this
period, "If it is the flow of experiences, that did come after some
years, but after I had stopped the *prāṇāyāma* for a long time and
was doing nothing and did not know what to do or where to turn
once all my efforts had failed. And it came not as a result of years
of *prāṇāyāma* or concentration, but in a ridiculously easy way, by
the grace either of a temporary Guru [but it was not that, for he
was himself bewildered by it] or by the grace of the eternal
Brahman and afterwards by the grace of *ahakali* and Krishna."[29]
In what he calls a "failure" in his attempts at vedantic experience,
and at the time of the failure of his goals at the Surat Conference,
Aurobindo turned to a "temporary *guru*," a Maharashtrian *bhakta*,
Vishnu Bhasker Lele. The resulting experience, though not recognized as central in some other studies of Aurobindo's religious
experiences,[30] was what Aurobindo would much later call "the
foundation of my Sadhana [yogic discipline],"[31] and the first of
"four great realisations on which his yoga and his spiritual philosophy
are founded."[32]
The experience did not add new content to Aurobindo's ultimate

concern, but it provided the beginnings of the authoritative personal experience which he sought. Aurobindo's later recollections of the experience show his desire to communicate a divine destiny at work and only a minimal reliance upon a human guru,[33] but they speak of the experience as an advaitic, non-dual, experience of *brahman* and negatively "attended at first by an overwhelming feeling and perception of the total unreality of the world."[34]

Lele was a dualist *bhakta* and, therefore, Aurobindo's experiences did not correspond with Lele's hopes: "The Brahman experience came when I was groping for a way, doing no Sadhana at all, making no effort because I didn't know what effort to make, all having failed. Then in three days I got an experience which most Yogis get only at the end of a long Yoga, got it without wanting or trying after it, got it to the surprise of Lele who was trying to get me something quite different."[35]

Thus, the three days spent in seclusion with Lele resulted in the beginnings of yogic experiences which Aurobindo would understand as authoritative over all other experiences and religious claims.

The description of the experience in non-dualist terms in Aurobindo's later assessment is noteworthy, for Aurobindo did not affirm in his later period "the total unreality of the world," or that the world is understood from yogic experience "as a cinematographic play of vacant forms in the impersonal universality of the Absolute Brahman."[36] His concern in his later writings in which these recollections are found was to affirm that the world is not illusion, but that it is the Absolute in evolutionary Becoming. The experience of the unreality of the world is called "an overwhelming feeling and perception" in which "feeling disappeared after his second realisation."[37] Such a perception could not have been accepted, for Aurobindo had already affirmed that the world of multiplicity was real, as was the Unity of the Absolute, and was certain that both must be affirmed. Thus, his own yogic experience was not yet the only authority in his religious thought, for, he tells us, it did not affirm the world, while he continued to do so.[38]

Aurobindo's writings and speeches following this experience show a continuing concern for the elevation of India to independence, so as to be the guru of the nations, spreading the vedantic vision throughout the world. Yet, beginning with his first lecture after the yogic experience, sponsored by the Bombay National Union on January 19, 1908, he placed a greater emphasis on the

application of yoga to nationalism, and especially the concept of
letting the divine work in oneself as its instrument: "If you are
going to be a Nationalist, if you are going to assent to this religion
of Nationalism, you must do it in the religious spirit. You must
remember that you are the instruments of God. . . . Do you hold
your political creed from a higher source? Is it God that is born in
you? Have you realised that you are merely the instruments of
God, that your bodies are not your own? You are merely instruments of God for the work of the Almighty. Have you realised that?
If you have realised that, then you are truly Nationalists; then alone
will you be able to restore this great nation."[39] Likewise Aurobindo places more emphasis upon yogic detachment and a quieting
of the mind, which allows the work of the divine to flow through
one. The difference between his nationalism prior to the experience and following it is the *attitude* of the nationalist as he works
toward independence. His work is in *faith*, not in terms of the
intellect, just as in the fight in Bengal, "the intellect having nothing
to offer but despair became quiescent, and when the intellect ceased
to work, the heart of Bengal was open and ready to receive the
voice of God whenever He should speak."[40] So all should have a
conviction of the heart, an *experience* which authoritatively says
that this is the right thing to do, that the divine is at work in it:

> What is the one thing needful? . . . They have had one and all of
> them consciously or unconsciously one over-mastering idea, one
> idea which nothing can shake, and this was the idea that there is a
> great Power at work to help India, and that we are doing what it
> bids us. Often they do not understand what they are doing.
> They do not always realise who guides or where he will guide
> them; but they have this conviction within, not in the intellect
> but in the heart, that the Power that is guiding them is invincible,
> that it is the Almighty, that it is immortal and irresistible and
> that it will do its work. They have nothing to do. They have
> simply to obey that Power.[41]

Following Aurobindo's first yogic experience, which began to
make the experiences of the Upaniṣads his own, the emphasis
upon the application of elements of the attitude of a yogi to politics
and the emphasis upon the need of nationalists to experience the
divine work became central in his writing and speaking. The

intuition, not the intellect, was central even in the political   sphere.
Thus, the authority for nationalism is yogic experience, the model
for nationalism is yogic technique.[42]   This model and that authority
would guarantee the attainment of Indian guruship, the penultimate concern raised temporarily to the level of ultimacy:

> You see a movement which no obstacle can stop, you see a great
> development which no power can resist, you see the birth of the
> Avatar in the Nation, and if you have received God within you,
> if you have received that power within you, you will see that God
> will change the rest of India in even a much shorter time. . . . It
> will continue its work with the matured force of Divinity until
> the whole world sees and until the whole world understands him,
> until Sri Krishna, who has now hid himself in Gokul, who is now
> among the poor and despised of the earth . . . will declare the
> Godhead, and the whole nation will rise, filled with divine power,
> filled with the inspiration of the Almighty, and no power on
> earth shall resist it, and no danger or difficulty shall stop it in its
> onward course.   Because God is there, and it is his Mission,
> and he has something for us to do.   He had a work for this great
> and ancient nation.[43]

India will bring vedantic truth, that *ātman* is *brahman*, to the world.

Alipur Jail and the Authoritative
Experience

On May 5, 1908, Aurobindo was arrested in connection with a
bombing incident in which his brother may have taken some part.
He spent the next year in jail and in court, until on May 6, 1909, he
was acquitted of the charges against him and released.   While in
jail the second of the "four great realisations" of his integral yoga
took place.   On May 30, 1909, he delivered his famous Uttarpara
speech, in which he revealed publicly what had befallen him while
in the Alipur jail.   With this "realisation" yogic experience became
the exclusive authority for the remainder of his life, and the cause
of Indian independence, which independence he continued to accept
as inevitable, was no longer raised to the level of ultimacy.
His arrest and imprisonment had shaken his faith in the belief

that the divine was working a mission through him. He cried out, "What is this that has happened to me? I believed that I had a mission to work for the people of my country and until that work was done, I should have Thy protection. Why then am I here and on such a charge?"[44] In jail he spent time studying and practicing a yoga related to the *Bhagavadgītā* and meditating on the Upaniṣads. He later also recalled that he heard the voice and felt the presence of Vivekananda.[45]

The content of the experience was presented at Uttarpara in terms of the vedantic vision which Aurobindo had previously affirmed. What before he had only intellectually understood, now he had confirmed in spiritual realization. "I was not only to understand intellectually but to realise what Sri Krishna demanded of Arjuna . . . I realised what the Hindu religion meant."[46] "He made me realise the central truth of the Hindu religion."[47] Yet the experience, unlike that with Lele, also confirmed that which Aurobindo accepted but which the advaitic experience with Lele seemed to reject. In the Alipur jail, the divine message was that the world is real because it is *brahman*. This is called the "central truth of the Hindu religion" which he only now personally realized.

> I looked at the jail that secluded me from men and it was no longer by its high walls that I was imprisoned; no, it was Vasudeva who surrounded me. I walked under the branches of the tree in front of my cell, but it was not the tree, I knew it was Vasudeva, it was Sri Krishna whom I saw standing there and holding over me his shade. I looked at the bars of my cell, the very grating that did duty for a door and again I saw Vasudeva. . . . It was Narayana who was guarding and standing sentry over me. Or I lay on the coarse blankets that were given me for a couch and felt the arms of Sri Krishna around me, the arms of my Friend and Lover. . . . I looked at the prisoners in the jail, the thieves, the murderers, the swindlers, and as I looked at them I saw Vasudeva, it was Narayana whom I found in these darkened souls and misused bodies.[48]

This experience was seen to fulfil what was missing in the experience of Lele, an affirmation of this world and work in it. "I strove long for the realisation of Yoga and at last to some extent I had it [the Lele experience], but in what I most desired I was not satisfied."[49] Now his realisation affirmed that the world is real; the world is Divine. Therefore, work in the world is good, valuable after all.

The experience also raised to a higher point the value of yogic experience in Aurobindo's life and thereby devalued the place of the independence of India. It was not that Indian independence would not continue to play a role for Aurobindo, but in his Uttarpara speech Aurobindo lowered the fight for independence of India to less ultimate level and re-enthroned the spread of the vedantic vision, which was the eternal religion, *sanātana dharma*, essential to all else.

I spoke once before with this force in me and I said then that this movement is not a political movement and that nationalism is not politics but a religion, a creed, a faith. I say it again today, but I put it another way. I say no longer that nationalism is a creed, a religion, a faith; I say that it is the Sanatan Dharma which for us is nationalism. This Hindu nation was born with the Sanatan Dharma, with it it moves and with it it grows. When the Sanatan Dharma declines, then the nation declines, and if the Sanatan Dharma were capable of perishing, with the Sanatan Dharma it would perish. The Sanatan Dharma, that is nationalism. This is the message that I have to speak to you.[50]

The promotion of the vedantic vision, true yoga, the upanisadic realization that the self is *brahman*, will result in the promotion of India, not vice versa. "To magnify the religion means to magnify the country."[51]

To spread the vision, Aurobindo inaugurated two new journals. On June 19, 1909, the *Karmayogin,* an English language weekly, appeared, and on August 23 of the same year its counterpart in Bengali was published. Their specific purpose, he wrote in the first issue of *Karmayogin,* was to promote "spirituality, the force and energy of thought and action arising from communion with or self-surrender to that within us which rules the world."[52] *Brahman,* the vedantic Absolute, is to be experienced, and, unlike those who would on that account devalue the world, the world is to be affirmed in the process. It is as real as *brahman* because it is *brahman.* He held this on the authority of his personal yogic experience.

With this authority in hand, Aurobindo began openly to devalue the formulations of the great thinkers of vedanta in India's past.[53] Aurobindo believed that he was in agreement with the viewpoint of the Upaniṣads. He did not see these texts as a collection of a variety of metaphysical gropings, but as setting forth a consistent position, not necessarily in the logical sense but consistent with the realizations of the yogic experience. The great advaitan, Sankara, attempted to understand this, but his view was only "temporarily satisfying" as an interpretation of the Upaniṣads.[54] Likewise the other interpretations have no ultimate value. *"Advaita, viśiṣṭādvaita, dvaita* are merely various ways of looking at the relations of the One to the Many, and none of them has the right to monopolise the name Vedanta."[55] *Advaita* emphasizes the fact that all are merely manifestations of the one *brahman.* *Viśiṣṭādvaita* emphasizes that the manifestations are real and in the One. *Dvaita* speaks from the point of view of the manifestations and says that they are "persistently recurrent." Aurobindo's system, it is implied, sees these other interpretations in their correct perspective because it is based upon the Upaniṣads—upon the seers' experiences, not the later systematizers' logical constructions. Aurobindo laments as well that modern Indians are not basing their lives and religions on experience as did the upanisadic seers, but on *"aptavakyam,* or authority, the recorded opinions of men who had *viveka,* or traditions and customs founded on an ancient enlightenment."[65] We must get back to the experience: "The recent mould of Hinduism had to be broken and replaced by knowledge and Yoga and not by the European spirit."[57]

As a result, by the beginning of 1910 Aurobindo faced the increasingly tense political situation in Bengal with nationalism as a lower priority. His goal was the promotion of Vedanta in the world which affirmed that reality was both one and many, that the world was the one in manifestation and, therefore, as real as the One, and that the ideal was the experience of the One through practice of yoga so that there would result a change in the world itself.

When Aurobindo heard from a police official that the office of the *Karmayogin* was to be searched and that he was to be arrested again, he recalls hearing "a command from above, in a Voice well known to me, in three words: 'Go to Chandernagore."[58] Thus, with nationalism no longer of ultimate concern, but with his yoga uppermost in his mind, on February 14, 1910, Aurobindo turned his responsibilities over to others and left British India to pursue his yoga in solitude, to spend his complete time with it and to reject all attempts to bring him back into the spotlight of Indian political leadership. His yoga and its "realisations" were all-consuming.

Pondicherry and the Development of Authoritative Yogic Insights

On April 4, 1910, Aurobindo, in response to inner guidance, reached Pondicherry in French India. The letters sent to those who asked him to return to politics indicate his concern for the development of his yoga. In a letter of January 1920, he answered Joseph Baptista, a prominent Indian nationalist leader, "I came to Pondicherry in order to have freedom and tranquillity for a fixed object having nothing to do with present politics... and until it is accomplished, it is not possible for me to resume any kind of public activity."[59] He did not view this as a withdrawal from life, however, but as a temporary retreat so as to return with a greater, more effective participation in it.[60] In a letter to his younger brother he affirmed his commitment to his yogic experiences: "I have been till now and shall be for some time longer withdrawn in the practice of a Yoga destined to be a basis not for withdrawal from life, but for the transformation of human life. It is a Yoga in which vast untried tracts of inner experience and new paths of Sadhana had to be opened up and which, therefore, needed retirement and long time for its completion. But the time is approaching, though it has not yet come, when I shall have to take up a large external work proceeding from the spiritual basis of this Yoga."[61]

In 1914 Mirra Richard met Aurobindo and found herself attracted to his spiritual interests and yoga. As "the Mother," whom Aurobindo came to affirm was the incarnation of the descent of the Supermind itself, she came to stay with him in 1920 until his death. She would be in charge of the Sri Aurobindo Ashram from the official date of its founding on November 14, 1926, until her own death in November 1973.

As a yogi at Pondicherry Aurobindo wrote all of his best known works. Most appeared serially from 1914 to 1921 in a magazine, the *Arya*, devoted to the spread of Aurobindo's vision. In this period Aurobindo's complete evolutionary schema appeared, a schema which he believed he had progressively seen in his yogic experiences.

As at Baroda, the highest reality, he said, was *brahman*, best thought of in terms of the upanisadic formula *saccidananda*. As *sat*, "existence, truth," it is beyond all distinctions. It is "pure existence, eternal, infinite, indefinable, not affected by the succession of Time, not involved in the extension of Space, beyond form, quantity, quality—Self only and absolute."[62] Though this sounds like the Absolute referred to by monists of the Indian tradition, Aurobindo affirms that *brahman* is also not merely static Being, but also Becoming, or better, beyond the very distinction of Being and Becoming. Similarly, *brahman* is beyond the distinction of unity and multiplicity.[63]

As *cit, brahman* is "consciousness-force." It is pure consciousness, a consciousness which sees identity not in terms of subject and object, but an intelligent movement of energy which manifests its knowing. As *ānanda*, it is absolute bliss of delight, being what it is for its own sport, *līlā*.

Yet to speak of the Absolute as beyond the world is to ignore the very movement of consciousness-force in Becoming which brings it its very bliss. The universe is real, a manifestation of *sat*. It is no illusion, as the Indian thinkers Aurobindo calls *mayavadins* claimed. It is a progressive evolution of *cit*, consciousness, an evolution of the previously involuted Absolute from the nescience of Matter to highest consciousness. The order of the involution, the reverse order of which is the evolution, is: (1) the Supreme *Saccidananda* Unmanifest; (2) *Saccidananda* in Manifestation; (3) Supermind (the Absolute in its active aspect); (4) Overmind or *māyā* (that which "sets up each Truth" of Supermind "as separate force and idea"); (5) Intuitive Mind; (6) Illumined Mind; (7) Higher Mind; (8) Mind (the level of the human being currently); (9) Psyche or Soul (Animal Life); (10) the Vital (the Organic level represented by plant forms); (11) Physical (Matter, the extreme involution and most inconscient).[64]

The key to the evolution of this world is Supermind. It is described as "a truth-consciousness, a consciousness always free from the Ignorance which is the foundation of our present natural or evolutionary existence and from which nature in us is trying to

arrive at self-knowledge and world-knowledge and a right consciousness and the right use of our existence in the universe."[65]
It is a consciousness that directly possesses the truth, not merely
images of the truth as does the mind. It is described as a unitary
consciousness and a "knowledge by identity."[66] Unlimited by
mental consciousness, it exists in what Aurobindo calls three poises
or sessions of consciousness. The first, the transcendent, stands
above and beyond the process of evolution unchanged or affected
by it. The second modifies the unity of the first and involves and
evolves the many in its manifestation. The third modifies itself so
as to evolve the individual.[67] Thus, Supermind is above the process,
is the process itself, and is also the essence within, the $\bar{a}tman$.

All of humanity exists currently on the level of Mind, a limited
and only indirectly illuminated consciousness which is characterized
by ignorance because it views reality exclusively from its own
standpoint.[68] It is not a unitary consciousness but a divided and
dividing one which takes the division as exclusively real and, thus,
overasserts itself in the midst of the evolution of Reality with an
egoism which is the source of all that is evil: "A limited consciousness growing out of nescience is the source of error, a personal
attachment to the limitation and the error born of it the source of
falsity, a wrong consciousness governed by the life-ego the source
of evil."[69] Mind is, therefore, the location of the human predicament, but it is also the level of consciousness in which nature is
first able to participate consciously in the evolutionary process, as
well as inhibit the process. "There can be . . . an evolution in the
light and no longer in the darkness, in which the evolving being is
a conscious participant and cooperator, and this is precisely what
must take place here. . . . There is then no longer any necessity for
the slow pace of the ordinary evolution; there can be rapid conversion, quick transformation, what would seem to our normal present
mind, a succession of miracles."[70] Integral Yoga, a combination
of the various paths of Indian religions according to Aurobindo's
formula, is the means by which the human being can participate.
It is "a means of compressing one's evolution into a single life for
a few years or even a few months of bodily existence."[71] For all
life is yoga when seen correctly and nature's evolution is nature's
yoga by which the Divine moves toward the increasing manifest
expression of the Supermind in the world and, thereby, raises the
whole earth-consciousness to that of Supermind.

Since he affirms that this world is real and divine, Aurobindo's yoga does not reject this world but places upon each yogin the duty of raising the world and all its elements together with him to higher stages of consciousness. There is what Aurobindo calls a "Triple Transformation" along the way.[72] In cooperation with the fact that the Supermind both descends from higher levels to raise the lower, and ascends from within the lower levels to evolve higher levels, the transformation of the yogin involves both ascent and descent. The first transformation of the individual is a "psychic change." By the practice of yoga, the whole person is changed into an instrument of the true self. The second is a "spiritual change" in which the newly attained consciousness descends into lower levels of one's life and body to prepare them for the third transformation. This third or "supermental transmutation" is the "ascent into the Supermind and the transforming descent of the supramental Consciousness into our entire being and nature."[73]

The individual result is the "gnostic being" whose whole person would be supramental in nature. The gnostic being would attain integral knowledge, "his cosmic individuality would know the cosmic forces and their movement and their significance as part of himself, and the Truth-Consciousness in him would see the right relation at each step and find the dynamic right expression of that relation."[74] In short, he would "be fully."[75] Action, thought, and intuition would be perfectly harmonized and integrated in the light of knowing reality directly.

Though the ultimate concern of Aurobindo begins with individual change, his goal is perfection of the entire world. The individual would join with others to create an atmosphere in which the environment itself would change spiritually, for all is the Absolute in evolution. Thus, Aurobindo rejects ascetic withdrawal; the body, the mind, and the environment are to be affected by Integral Yoga. Auroville, a city founded by the Mother in February 1968, attempts to put the principles of Aurobindo's vision in practice.

Aurobindo did not understand the above as a system which he derived from philosophical speculation: "There is very little argument in my philosophy—the elaborate metaphysical reasoning full of abstract words with which the metaphysician tries to establish his conclusion is not there. What is there is a harmonising of the different parts of a many-sided knowledge so that all unites logically together. But it is not by force of logical argument that it is done, but by a clear vision of the relations and sequences of knowledge."[76]   The authority for true knowledge is not mental argument, for Mind is not sufficiently conscious to explain Reality.[77] The only authority adequate for integral knowledge is obtained by yoga, a higher knowledge than the lower knowledge of "science, art, philosophy, ethics, psychology."[78]   Yogic experience has been the only authority for Sri Aurobindo at Pondicherry.

Though Aurobindo believed that he was experiencing the supramental levels of consciousness which had been attained by the upanisadic seers, he continued to find the systems of the later systematizers wanting when judged by his own intuitive knowledge. These later thinkers of the schools of Indian thought "started from Reason and tested the results it gave them, holding only those conclusions to be valid which were supported by the supreme authority. . . . Hence the rise of conflicting schools each of which founded itself in theory on the Veda and used its texts as a weapon against the others."[79]   The ultimate result of the use of reason as a method of knowing is negativism and the rise of "the great world-negating religions and philosophies."[80]   In India, Aurobindo said, the two main influences in such negation were the Buddha and Sankara, but Aurobindo argues that the analogies used by Sankara and other *mayavadins* to prove the illusory nature of the world, such as comparing it to a dream, fail.[81]   To see the world in such an illusory fashion is to make the unbelievable claim that there is a stupendous cosmic illusion "*sui generis*, without parallel."[82]   Instead, Aurobindo argues, if the world is in fact the way he has seen it, as a great evolution of the Divine, then, there is no place for negativism.[83]   The disagreements of the later thinkers in deviation from upanisadic experimental truth were caused by their attempts to develop logical constructions in an age of rational knowledge, a time which had left the intuitive age of the Upaniṣads behind.[84]   The result was the absolutizing of one side of vedantic truth,[85] or at best overstating an element of the experience, such as *māyā*.[86]   Aurobindo, however, viewed his own system as one based exclusively upon the intuitive and its "supramental logic," and, thus, as a balanced and integral thought system.

Aurobindo refers to his yogic experience during this period as including the final two of his "four great realisations."[87]   The first of these two is difficult to relate to precise experiences.   He describes it as a realization "of the supreme reality with the static and dynamic Brahman as its two aspects." The second he describes as the realization "of the higher planes of consciousness leading to the Supermind." Feys believes the third realization is reflected in Aurobindo's *Essays on the Gita*, written between 1916 and 1920. He calls it "a protracted period of maturing: the gradual harmonisation of the opposite experiences of Baroda and Alipore."[88] He dates it as the ten-year period from 1909 to 1920, which, unlike the other three, would not, then, be a single experience. He also relates it to a later reference by Aurobindo in 1932 to a period of "ten more years of intense yoga under a supreme inner guidance," to work out his teaching.[89] One wishes that there were more evidences to support such an identification, but what is clear is that during this period Aurobindo was attempting to develop his yogic practice and to attain realizations which would break through the limitations of his past experience. His complete trust was in these yogic experiences and he was certain that they would reveal the path and nature of perfection. Not surprisingly, Aurobindo regularly stressed persistence, faith, and a "positive inner call" as requisites for those who would embark upon his yoga.[90]

The fourth experience is easier to identify, for it refers to November 24, 1926, the date Aurobindo calls his "Day of Siddhi." On that day Aurobindo believed he directly experienced the descent of the Overmind, which is said to have assured him of the certainty of the coming descent of the Supermind to this plane.[91] Aurobindo claims to have seen the levels of consciousness which relate Mind to all that is above: Higher Mind, Intuitive Mind, Illumined Mind, and Overmind.[92] It is not surprising, then, that after this experience chapters 24, 25, 26, and 28 were added to *The Life Divine* when it was revised in 1939-40, chapters which did not appear in the edition printed serially in the Arya from 1914 to 1919.

Aurobindo's experiences, however, continued to inform his worldview even after the last revision of *The Life Divine*. He was soon to see that the Overmind itself should be divided into levels (Formative Maya, Overmind Logos, Intuitive Overmind ?).[93] Charts found among his manuscripts and published after his death indicate further elaboration of the evolutionary schema and experimentation with its terminology.[94] The authority of his yogic experiences would not let his systematizing remain in a completed state and Aurobindo would at times indicate that he had more to see in order to complete his thought, but that in the interim he had to extrapolate from what he had already seen.[95]

At his death in 1950, Aurobindo had not completed his system, but he had presented a system which he believed was integral, a construction on the level of Mind which was informed by the descent of superamental knowing. Because Aurobindo believed in the possibility of returning to lower levels to raise them up by means of the higher consciousness, to "integrate" the lower and the higher, he believed that his system had a validity above all others. It was more complete, he believed, not emphasizing one fact of experience over the other but able to integrate them into a total "integral understanding." He could not accept that this may have been what earlier yogins had done as well, unless they had seen what he had.[96] His yogic experiences were not without content, though the understanding involved was also not limited to the mental. They revealed truth as well as truths, [97] and, thus, his writing was seen as an automatic flow from higher levels of consciousness, the descent of the Supramental into Mind.

Conclusions

Central to Sri Aurobindo's developed and most well-known system of thought and practice in the Pondicherry period is the authority of yogic experience. This, he believed, molded all else, determining the validity of other viewpoints of reality in the Indian tradition as well as informing his developing system as a yogi progressively realizing the Absolute. However, the authority of yogic experience itself moved from the authority of the experiences of others in earlier periods to the exclusive authority of his own yogic experiences.

Even before his knowledge of yoga began, he was committed in England to a strong personal attachment to both the reality of the phenomenal world and a harmony within it. When he returned to India he embraced the metaphysics of the Upaniṣads as he understood them because they were based upon "realisations" of the seers. They affirmed the One *brahman* behind the world as well as the Many, the phenomenal world. In the midst of the Indian independence movement, yogic experience became his own, but the fact that it seemed to negate the reality and importance of the phenomenal world kept Aurobindo from accepting the experience as finally authoritative. His experience of the world's reality was more authoritative than the yogic experience of its vacuity. In the Alipur jail Aurobindo experienced the world as the manifestation of the divine and, therefore, as real as the Unity itself. After this experience, the pursuit of yoga became a driving passion which ended his relationship with the Indian independence movement and turned him more and more to the searching out of the experiential truth which he believed was no longer just that of the upanisadic seers, but actually his own. Yogic experience became the medium by which all else would be understood, for it brought him a higher knowledge, the Supramental.

Thus, yogic experience became authoritative when it affirmed his non-yogic aesthetic experience of the world and brought the world into its scope. This, he says, constituted the difficult work of his years of yoga: "The only real difficulty which took decades of spiritual effort to work out towards completeness was to apply the spiritual knowledge utterly to the world and to the surface psychological and outer life and to effect its transformation both on the higher levels of Nature and on the ordinary mental, vital and physical levels down to the subconscience and the basic Inconscience and up to the supreme Truth-Consciousness or Supermind in which alone the dynamic transformation could be entirely integral and absolute."[98]

Notes

1. For example, see H.K. Kaul, *Sri Aurobindo, A Descriptive Bibliography* (New Delhi: Munshiram Manoharlal, 1971). This work needs considerable updating, of course.
2. For a more extensive delineation of the various stages in Aurobindo's thought see Robert N. Minor, *Sri Aurobindo: The Perfect and the Good* (Calcutta: Minerva Associates, 1978).
3. See Robert A. McDermott, "*The Life Divine,* Sri Aurobindo's Philosophy of Evolution and Transformation," in Robert A. McDermott, ed., *Six Pillars: Introductions to the Major Works of Sri Aurobindo* (Chambersburg, P.A.: Wilson Books, 1974), pp. 164-66. John Collins' essay in the same work, "*Savitri,* Poetic Expression of Spiritual Experience" (pp. 7-33), traces the development of the poem in terms of Aurobindo's spiritual experience.
4. Sri Aurobindo, *Birth Centenary Library* (Pondicherry: Sri Aurobindo Ashram Trust, 1971), 3:23, 30. Hereafter this 30-volume set of Aurobindo's complete works will be abbreviated *BCL.*
5. *BCL,* 3:23.

6. Ibid., p. 33.
7. Ibid., p. 52.
8. Ibid., 5:28.
9. Ibid., 26:50. Aurobindo often spoke of himself in the third person.
10. Ibid., 12:1.
11. Ibid., 26:50.
12. Ibid., 1:6.
13. Ibid., p. 27.
14. Ibid., p. 36.
15. Ibid., p. 23.
16. Ibid., p. 7.
17. Ibid.
18. Ibid., 3:59.
19. Ibid., 26:19-20.
20. Ibid., pp. 78-79.
21. Ibid., 3:345.
22. David L. Johnson, *The Religious Roots of Indian Nationalism: Aurobindo's Early Political Thought* (Calcutta: Firma K.L. Mukhopadhyay, 1974), p. 64, See also pp. 35-40 and Minor, *Sri Aurobindo*, pp. 50-67. Johnson argues against the works of Haridas and Uma Mukherjee who have accused Aurobindo of using religion for political goals. See, for example, their *Sri Aurobindo and the New Thought in Indian Politics* (Calcutta: Firma K.L, Mukhopadhyay, 1964).
23. *BCL*, 1:513.
24. Ibid., p. 70.
25. Ibid., 3:347.
26. Ibid., 1:895; cf. 1:653, 729, 364, 414
27. Ibid., p. 235.
28. Ibid., p. 639.
29. Ibid., 26:77.
30. For example, see Robert A. McDermott, "The Experiential Basis of Sri Aurobindo's Integral Yoga," *Philosophy East and West* 22, no. 1 (January 1972): 15-32.
31. *BCL*, 26:68 (September 1946).
32. Ibid., p. 64 (cir. April 1945).
33. Besides the following quotations, Aurobindo described Lele as "a Bhakta with a limited mind but with some experience and evocative power" *BCL* 26:79, may 1932), He also called Lele "one who was infinitely inferior to me in intellect, education and capacity and by no means spiritually perfect or supreme" (ibid., p. 80, March 1932).
34. Ibid., p. 64 (April 1945).
35. Ibid., pp. 77-78.
36. Ibid., p. 79 (May 1932).
37. Ibid., p. 64 (April 1945).
38. Though this vision does not affirm Aurobindo's later position, or even his discussions at that time, Jan Feys tries to relate the first three "realisations" to the stages of *kṣara brahman, akṣara brahman* and *Puruṣottama* in

his *Essays on the Gita* (*The Yogi and the Mystic: A Study in the Spirituality of Sri Aurobindo and Teilhard De Chardin* [Calcutta: Firma KLM, 1977], pp. 38-49).

39. *BCL*, 1:652-53.
40. Ibid., p. 658.
41. Ibid., p. 660: Cf. p. 664.
42. Johnson, *The Religious Roots,* discusses the use of yogic conceptions in Aurobindo's political activity, pp. 74-97.
43. *BCL*, 1:665.
44. Ibid., 2:3, 7.
45. Ibid., 26:68 (September 1946); ibid, 27:435 (cr. 1913).
46. Ibid., 2:3.
47. Ibid., p. 4; cf. p. 7.
48. Ibid., p. 4; cf. p. 5.
49. Ibid., p. 7.
50. Ibid., p. 10.
51. Ibid., p. 8.
52. Ibid., p. 14.
53. The term Vedanta, meaning "end of the Vedas," is usually taken as a general name designating those religious positions which trace their views back to the Upaniṣads, the last books of the Vedas. The three major systems, which do not necessarily agree on major points, were *advaita vedānta*, the non-dualism for which Sankra (A.D. 788:820) is best known, *viśiṣṭādvaita vedānta*, qualified non-dualism, whose major exponent was Ramanuja (A.D. 1017-1137), and *dvaita*, dualism, whose thirteenth century A.D. proponent was Madhva.

54. *BCL*, 3:344.
55. Ibid., p. 364.
56. Ibid., p. 439.
57. Ibid., p. 437.
58. Ibid., 26:57.
59. Ibid., pp. 429-30.
60. Aurobindo's early letters (*BCL*, 27:423-501) written 1912-20, indicate both his intention to return to the active path within a short period and his belief that he was withdrawing to practice yoga so as to affect the political situation by means of the accumulated power of a yogi on the basis of his yogic practice. In this he was accepting a traditional idea that yogi attained powers to affect others. His fourth goal, he tells Motilal Roy in a letter of January 1913 (?), for example, is "the determining of events, actions, and results of action throughout the world by pure silent willpower" (*BCL*, 27:429). It would seem to be a misunderstanding to accuse Aurobindo of denying the political struggle of India in his temporary withdrawal to be more effective in the long run. For example, see June O'Connor, *The Quest for Political and Spiritual Liberation: A Study in the Thought of Sri Aurobindo Ghose* (Cranbury, NJ: Fairleigh Dickinson Press, 1976), pp. 34-40.
61. *BCL*, 26:435. See also n. 60 above.

62. Ibid., 18:77-78.
63. Ibid., p. 579.
64. For a discussion of these levels see Minor, *Sri Aurobindo*, pp. 108-13, or Beatrice Bruteau, *Worthy Is the World: The Hindu Philosophy of Sri Aurobindo* (Rutherford, NJ: Fairleigh Dickinson Press, 1971), or Robert A. McDermott, "Sri Aurobindo: An Integrated Theory of Individual and Historical Transformatian," *International Philosophical Quarterly 12*, no. 2 (June 1972): 175-76. For a full presentation of Aurobindo's evolutionary theory see Rama Shanker Srivastava, *Sri Aurobindo and the Theories of Evolution* (Varanasi: Chowkhamba Sanskrit Series, 1968), pp. 57-146.
65. *BCL*, 16:41.
66. Ibid., 18:272, 135, 215, 318.
67. Ibid., pp. 145-47.
68. Ibid., 21:599.
69. Ibid., 18:623.
70. Ibid., 16:44.
71. Ibid., 20:2.
72. Ibid., 19:891.
73. Ibid.
74. Ibid., 19:974.
75. Ibid., p. 1023.
76. Ibid., 26:374.
77. Ibid., 18:118, 366, 372.
78. Ibid., 20:492-93.
79. Ibid., 18:69.
80. Ibid., p. 415.
81. Ibid., pp. 419-32.
82. Ibid., p. 432.
83. Ibid., pp. 471-81.
84. Ibid., pp. 67-70.
85. Ibid., 19:635.
86. Ibid., 16:428.
87. Ibid., 26:64.
88. Feys, *The Yogi and the Mystic*, p. 46.
89. *BCL*, 26:78.
90. See Minor, *Sri Aurobindo*, pp. 121-25, and M.P. Pandit, *Sadhana in Sri Aurobindo's Yoga*, 3rd ed. (Pondicherry: Dipti Publications, 1971).
91. For discussions of this event see K.R. Srinivasa Iyengar, *Sri Aurobindo, A Biography and History*, 3rd ed, (Pondicherry: Sri Aurobindo Ashram Trust, 1972), pp. 987-91, and R.R. Diwakar, *Mahayogi Sri Aurobindo: Life, Discipline and Teachings of Sri Aurobindo* (Bombay: Bharatiya Vidya Bhavan, 1972), pp. 193-94, 208.
92. *BCL*, 26:369-70.
93. Ibid., 22:261, 263; cf. p. 32.
94. Ibid., pp. 28-32.
95. For example see *BCL*, 19:1013.
96. Robert N. Minor, "Sri Aurobindo's Integral View of other Religions,"

Religious Studies 15, no. 3 (September 1979), pp. 367-79.

97. Eliot Deutsch ("Sri Aurobindo's Interpretation of Spiritual Experience: A Critique," *International Philosophical Quarterly* 4, no. 4 [December 1964]: pp. 581-94) critiques Aurobindo's certainity concerning his thought system as a commission of the "fallacy of mis-placed certitude." For another interpretation and a defense see Minor, *Sri Aurobindo*, pp. 174-77.

98. *BCL,* 26:86.

17

SARVEPALLI RADHAKRISHNAN AND "HINDUISM" DEFINED AND DEFENDED

Robert N. Minor

A study of the history of religious thought and practice in India reveals a diversity of religious positions, not unlike such studies in other large geographic areas with long histories. There are idealists, theists, monists, dualists, materialists, and others. There are also some which attempt to synthesize other positions into a higher stance, especially, though not exclusively, in India in the modern period, with the growth of a "Hindu" consciousness. The resulting modern definitions of "Hinduism" which have appeared have varied with the thinker who interpreted the tradition, but the two thinkers most responsible for well-known definitions are Svami Vivekananda and Sarvepalli Radhakrishnan.

Sarvepalli Radhakrishnan (1888-1975) defined, defended, and promulgated a system of thought which emphasized the centrality of a non-dual experience of the Absolute and, which, at the end of this life, he called a "religion of the spirit."[1] This, he believed, was not a new revelation but the essence of all "religion," most faithfully presented in what he called "Vedanta," "Hinduism," or, at times, the essence of "Indian thought." The promotion and promulgation of such a system was necessary in order to attain his ultimate concern: the attainment of perfection in the world by individuals, by all creatures, and by the world order, the manifestation of the "Vedantic Absolute." The purpose of this study is to trace the process of definition, defense, and promulgation of

this "religion of the spirit" or "Hinduism" in the writings of Radhakrishnan.   His thought is not divisible into clearly defined periods
which reflect a changing position, but one can note emphases that
develop and lead into his final writings which proclaim that only
the "religion of the spirit" will enable the world to attain perfection,
solving its profoundest problems.

The Early Defense of "Vedanta" as Ethical

Radhakrishnan was born on September 5, 1888, in a small town
northwest of Madras in southeast India.   His early life was spent
in Tirutani and Tirupati, which were pilgrimage centers.   He was
educated in Christian missionary institutions, finishing in 1908 with
B.A. and M.A. degrees in philosophy from Madras Christian
College.

In his later writings he recorded two impressions of his education which bear heavily upon his later work.   The first is that he
felt a continual criticism of "Hinduism" as a religion by his
teachers and Christian missionaries.   He took this criticism to
heart, agreeing that much he saw around him was not accompli-
shing that which he believed a religion ought.   His recollection in
1936 was:

> I was strongly persuaded of the inefficiency of the Hindu religion
> to which I attributed the political downfall of India.   The critic-
> isms leveled against the Hindu religion were of a two-fold
> character.   It is intellectually incoherent and ethically unsound.
> The theoretical foundations as well as the practical fruits of the
> religion were challenged.   I remember the cold sense of reality,
> the depressing feeling of defeat that crept over me, as causal
> relation between anaemic Hindu religion and our political failure
> forced itself on my mind during those years.   What is wrong
> with the Hindu religion?   How can we make it somewhat more
> relevant to the intellectual climate and social environment of
> our time?[2]

A second impression which he was to remember was the impact of
the work of Svami Vivekananda.   Vivekananda's speaking and
writing brought to him the confidence that "the Hindu religion"

was essentially other than that which was portrayed in the criticisms of his teachers. In 1973 he wrote to fellow Indians: "It is that kind of humanistic, man-making religion which gave us courage in the days when we were young, When I was a student in one of the classes, in the matriculation class or so, the letters of Swami Vivekananda used to be circulated in manuscript form among us all. The kind of thrill which we enjoyed, the kind of mesmeric touch that those writings gave us, the kind of reliance on our own culture that was being criticized all around—it is that kind of transformation which his writings effected in the young men in the early years of this century."3

Thus Radhakrishnan remembered both a critique of "the Hindu religion" and a defense of "the Hindu religion." The issues which remained with him throughout his life were already posed and the important category of "Hinduism," which treats the variety of positions and practices of the people of India as one, was given to him. Not only was there a critique of *it*, but there needed to be a defense of *it* as inspired by Svami Vivekananda. *It*, an entity called "Hinduism" or "the Hindu religion," needed defense and a clear definition of the features that were essential to it.

One may not be able adequately to defend what one has not defined, and therefore, his earliest writings, beginning with his master's thesis, *The Ethics of the Vedanta and Its Metaphysical Presuppositions,*4 were a series of publications with an explicit apologetic motive in mind and with a systematic definition of Vedanta which would remain unchanged throughout his life. Though he refined it, *Weltanschauung* with which he early identified himself was the background for his religion until his death.5 The first category which he used to designate this position was "Vedanta."6

Radhakrishnan's ultimate concern was the realization of the Absolute Reality in and by the world and, as a part of that, in and by each individual, a realization which he at times called the attainment of perfection. Both the individual and social goals should be noted, for Radhakrishnan rejected all attempts at a personal realization which ignored the whole phenomenal world. In 1916 he put it: "Thus we see that the function of religion is not merely to pacify the troubled soul but make it enter with faith and hope into the work of God which is to make the earth the visible symbol of God's law."7 In his earliest writings his defense of Vedanta indicated that he believed it could lead to this end. He was a religious thinker or "philosopher," and not merely a historian, while he wrote these articles.[8]   Thus, though he did not always indicate explicitly that he was writing about his own beliefs, he argued in these apologetic pieces that Vedanta is able to solve the ethical problems encountered by other philosophers. In " 'Nature' and 'Convention' in Greek Ethics,"[9] he defined the problem of egoism and altruism in ethics (How can one want to do the good one ought to do?), as he did in "Egoism and Altruism—The Vedanta Solution," but in the latter he indicated that Vedanta alone is able to solve the problem, though Plato in his more vedantic moments suggested the solution. A concluding statement indicates that Radhakrishnan personally affirmed this solution: "The Vedantic explanation is the practical recognition of a positive fact that we are all bound up together as sharers of the same eternal life.   The Vedantic formula, *Tat Tvam Asi, That Art Thou,* affirms the whole truth."[10]   Radhakrishnan had begun to affirm the Vedanta he defended.   Soon this affirmation would completely dominate his writings.

In these early defensive pieces Radhakrishnan wished to show that Vedanta was ethical, that it provided a basis for ethics and morality in this life.   Not surprisingly, then, most of his early articles center around questions of ethics.[11] In doing this he was taking up the vedantic viewpoint as the definition of the nature of the world's perfection and the acceptance of that viewpoint as the means by which the world could attain that perfection, though this latter he would emphasize later.

Now Vedanta needed defense against three charges made against it in order to establish that it is concerned with and is a basis for ethics.   First, it must be shown that Vedanta is not a mystical flight into other-worldly experience, but a rational system of thought deserving the name "philosophy" and the praise of philosophers.   These early articles exalt the importance of reason with little mention of intuitive religious experience.   "The universal law of *karma* has nothing to do with the *real* man, if he has once understood what he is in his *real* nature.   It is not the *'senses'* that make a man what he is, for the brutes also possess them. It is only *reason* that is the peculiar characteristic—the *differentia* of man."[12]   That which makes the human being human is reason and only the use of reason will enable man to be truly free from the bondage of his past and present.[13]   India is praised as the "ancient abode of an intellectual and philosophical race,"[14] and early Indian thinkers are said already to have dealt with the issues of modern philosophy in the Vedas.[15] This argument for the rational basis of Vedanta culminated in Radhakrishnan's *The Reign of Religion in Contemporary Philosophy*, where he summarized and critiqued other contemporary approaches and concluded that Vedanta is the most rational solution to the human predicament.[16]

The reasonableness of Vedanta is an important assertion because reason is the key to the ethical life: "It should be a life of reason. Without reason, man is on a level with a grass that withers and the beasts that perish. Life according to nature is, for man, life according to reason."[17] Conversely, the key to a system of philosophy is its ethical doctrine.[18] It is important, then, to see that Vedanta is reasonable and, therefore, capable of ethics. Radhakrishnan quoted Max Müller with favor: "The Vedanta philosophy has not neglected the important sphere of ethics; but, on the contrary, we find ethics in the beginning, ethics in the middle, and ethics in the end, to say nothing of the fact that minds, so engrossed with divine things as the Vedanta philosophers, are not likely to fall victims to the ordinary temptations of the world, the flesh, and other powers."[19]

Second, Vedanta needed defense against the charge that its doctrine of *karma* taught that people were not responsible for their deeds and, therefore, the concept results in fatalism. "Thus it becomes essential that we should dissipate the fallacy underlying the charge that there can be no 'Ethics of the Vedanta'; for according to the law of Karma man acts of necessity and not of his free will."[20] *Karma* from past lives, he argued, results in certain "fixed tendencies which are termed the 'likes' and 'dislikes'" which form the predispositions of a human being, but the human being's free will enables him to "make the lower sensuous self yield to the higher rational self" by combating these tendencies.[21] Thus he anticipates his well-known comparison of *karma* and freedom with a game of cards: "We can use the material with which we are endowed to promote our ideals. The cards in the game of life are given to us. We do not select them. They are traced to our past Karma, but we can call as we please, lead what suit we will, and as we play, we gain or lose. And there is freedom."[22] The vedantic solution, he argued, gives one real freedom, for its doctrine of the transcendent self enables the human being to resist his passions and regulate them by reason. Without the existence of the transcendent self he saw no hope of victory at all. One would remain mired in his lower propensities.[23]

The third argument in defense of the ethics of Vedanta was against the criticism that Vedanta taught that the world was unreal, illusory. If the world were not real in any sense, there would be no reason to advocate living the good life in the world, for that would be a performance of unreal action. This argument would be reflected again and again in Radhakrishnan's works, though later it would not be as central to his argument.[24] Those who argued that according to vedantic thought the world was unreal criticized Indian teachings as world- and life-negating in an aspiration to flee this world altogether rather than confront its problems.[25] In his defense of the vedantic view of reality, Radhakrishnan established the interpretation of *māyā* which he would maintain throughout his life. *Māyā* in Vedanta does not mean "illusion," he declared, but refers to the fact that the world is not independently real. Only the Absolute is independently real; the world's reality depends on the Absolute. The Upaniṣads, the texts of the Vedanta, taught that "everything in the universe, instead of being dismissed as illusory, is thought to be produced by Brahman. But this principle of Brahman is recognized as immanent in the universe."[26] The world is an expression of the Absolute though only a partial expression of it; it is "real as a part of the Absolute."[27]

Radhakrishnan maintained this position throughout his life, but at this early period he did not believe that Sankara, the famous *advaitan*, agreed. Before writing *The Reign of Religion in Contemporary Philosophy* in 1920, he attributed Sankara with belief in the illusoriness of the world. Not only did he believe Sankara was responsible for importing the conception of *māyā* into Vedanta from "Buddhistic teaching,"[28] but Sankara was listed as one who held that the world is illusory in his article, "The Vedantic Approach to Reality," which would be revised as the thirteenth chapter of *The Reign of Religion*, and which in the revision would have all references to Sankara's advocacy of the illusoriness of the world removed. For example, in the article of 1916 he wrote, "So a severe logician of the type of Sankara who thinks to the very foundations, with his intellectualist bias, reduces the universe to an opposition of self and non-self, God and the world, the infinite and the finite. Certainly both cannot be real, for the two are exclusive of each other. The finite world is dismissed as illusory and the absolute posited as real."[29] The revision in *The Reign of Religion* in 1920 reads: "The universe is reduced to an opposition of self and non-self, God and the world, the infinite and the finite."[30] By the time of the writing of *The Philosophy of Rabindranath Tagore* in 1918,[31] Radhakrishnan declared emphatically that Sankara did not believe that the world is an illusion, a view Radhakrishnan held until his death and argued most strongly in his *Indian Philosophy*.[32]

Vedanta Defined

In this early period Radhakrishnan defined Vedanta. This definition and his identification with it remained constant throughout his life, except that he soon came to call it "Hinduism," "Hindu thought," "Indian thought," and later "religion of his spirit." Its most systematic presentation was published in 1932 in *An Idealist View of Life,* based on the Hibbert Lectures given at the University of Manchester and University College, London, in 1929 and 1930.

Where one discovers the Absolute in his philosophical search depends upon where one begins. If one begins with the world about him or her, the objective side of reality, one perceives the necessity of an underlying unity and this unity is the Absolute which Indians have called *brahman. Brahman* is not definable, though it may be known in intuitive experience, for "Brahman, which symbolizes the absolute reality, means also holy knowledge, intuitive wisdom."[33] Put in traditional terms, however, *brahman* is *saccidānanda. Sat,* "existence, reality," indicates that all that is, is *brahman* and that *brahman* is Being itself: "The Upanisads lead us from the imperfect existences in the world to the Supreme and Absolute Being which is on every side, beneath, above, beyond, whose centre is everywhere, even in the smallest atom, and whose circumference is nowhere, as it spreads beyond all measure. The existence of the world means the primacy of Being."[34] *Cit,* "consciousness, awareness," affirms that when one experiences this Absolute, one realizes that the key to reality is consciousness. "Consciousness and being are not there different from each other. All being is consciousness and all consciousness being. Thought and reality coalesce and a creative merging of subject and object results."[35] The identity of consciousness and being results in

Radhakrishnan defining *cit* as "absolute reality," and "truth,"[36]
and in his early works he calls this position "monistic idealism."[37]
In his later works, such as *An Idealist View of Life*, however, he
defined "idealism" more generally as the belief that there are
forces within the universe which are moving it to an ideal end.[33]
In either case the highest reality, the Absolute, is a state of consciousness, and consciousness as a category is thus a key to the
understanding of the nature of the universe.

Ānanda, "pure delight, freedom, bliss," attempts to suggest the
relationship of Being to that which is, as well as to refer to the joy
of the one who experiences *brahman* in an intuitive experience.
Brahman relates to all else which is produced in a non-reciprocal
manner. It undergirds the universe, but as immutable Being the
relationship is free; *brahman* is in no manner touched by the real,
though temporary, change which is the evolution of the universe.
Brahman is free from the effects of phenomena, though it is the
foundation of all that is. "The real which accounts for the existence of the universe is Being (*sat*), its character which accounts
for the ordered advance is consciousness (*cit*) with freedom and joy
(*ānanda*)."[39]

Yet a danger in such descriptions of the Absolute is inherent in
the fact that they treat *brahman* as an object like other objects and,
therefore, they, if so understood, result in misunderstanding. It is
best to speak of the Absolute only in negative terms, *neti . . . neti*,
"not this . . . not that." "A wise agnosticism is more faithful to
the situation. But the logical mind of man is not willing to admit
defeat. It cannot rest in the idea that the Absolute is incompre-
hensible and that the world hangs on it somehow."[40]

Brahman, however, is not an object to us, but subject. In fact
the Absolute is our very self, or as traditionally put, *ātman* is *brahman, tat tvam asi*, "you are that." Therefore, if in one's philosophical search one begins with the human being, the Absolute is
ātman, the true self, and the reality which is *sat*, the consciousness
which is *cit*, and the pure bliss which is *ānanda*, and characteristics
of one's own deepest Being. "Being, truth and freedom are distinguished in the divine but not divided. The true and ultimate condition of the human being is the divine status. The essence of life is
the movement of the universal being; the essence of emotion is the
play of the self-existent delight in being; the essence of thought is
the inspiration of the all-pervading truth; the essence of activity is

the progressive realization of a universal and self-effecting good."[41] *Brahman* is a state of consciousness which is to be found essentially within, a subject, not an object to us.[42] To realize this in an intuitive experience is to attain a state of consciousness which is above the phenomena but not a denial of the phenomena. Rather than calling it a "pure consciousness" which no longer recognizes the objects about it, it is better to call it a "universal consciousness." The emphasis is upon the understanding and recovery of the all, not indifference to the many. "The true self is the universal self, which is immanent as well as transcendent. . . . There is nothing outside it. It is the real active divine self, which is the life and inspiration of our actual selves. It contains all consciousness of objects implicitly. There is nothing in the universe which is not involved in the infinite self in us. This world self which embraces all is the sole reality containing within itself all the facts of nature and all the histories of experience."[43] This identification of the self and the Absolute in the tradition of such thinkers as Sankara enabled Radhakrishnan to proclaim the divinity of the human being as the basis for his ethical stance, for his appeals to those of other religious positions, and for his proclamation in his political speeches of the centrality of the human being in political affairs. Yet it caused those who affirmed an absolute distinction between the Divine and the human being to be less enthusiastic about his metaphysical stance, a cool response which he never indicated that he understood in the terms of his critics.[44]

For Radhakrishnan the personal Divine Being, the Other of the theists, was identical with the impersonal Absolute which he affirmed. Yet the conception of *Isvara*, the personal "Lord," or "God," is relativized by Radhakrishnan in a manner that the impersonal Absolute is not. *Isvara* refers to the Absolute *in its relationship* to the world, whereas *brahman* is the Absolute in itself. God is the Absolute seen imperfectly from a lower level. "God who is creator, sustainer and judge of this world, is not totally unrelated to the Absolute. God is the Absolute from the human end. When we limit down the Absolute to its relation with the actual possibility, the Absolute appears as supreme Wisdom, Love, and Goodness. The eternal becomes the first and last."[45] Thus Radhakrishnan was able to affirm that the Absolute about which he spoke was the same as that which is called "god" by others, but these others understand it from a lower level: "While the Absolute is pure consciousness and pure freedom and infinite possibility, it appears to be God from the point of view of the one specific possibility which has become actualized."[46] Though this relegation of the idea of "god" to a second place could not satisfy the theists who believed the Absolute was to be located without, Radhakrishnan believed he was doing no injustice to their religious stance because, in fact, this is the fact of religious experience and the result of a search which understands that Absolute reality is behind all symbols. Those who continued to claim otherwise are misguided and deficient in understanding. "The monotheists are quite certain that the gods of the polytheists are symbolic if not mythological presentations of the true God, but they are loth to admit that their own God is at bottom a symbol. All religion is symbolic, and symbolism is excluded from religion only when religion itself perishes. God is a symbol in which religion cognizes the Absolute."[47] The reason some absolutize symbols is that they lack intuitive uuderstanding, they have had "no contact with reality, no insight into truth."[48] *Iśvara* is the name for the creative function of the Divine and is the conception by which the relationship of the Absolute to the world is understood by many.

Radhakrishnan affirmed the clustering together of three of the personal gods worshipped in India as the *trimūrti*, "the one with three forms." These gods which were worshipped in their own right were, according to this relatively late and unpopular conception, aspects of the one divine and not three different gods.[49] Radhakrishnan first used the concept in volume 1 of *Indian Philosophy*, published in 1923. Speaking of the *Mahābhārata*, he wrote, "We have now the trimūrti conception that Brahmā, Viṣṇu, and Śiva are different forms of the One Supreme, fulfilling the different functions of creation, preservation and destruction."[50] Brahmā, who is the cognitive aspect of the Absolute or wisdom, is the creator; Viṣṇu, who represents divine sacrificial love, preserves or redeems; and Śiva, the divine as omnipotent power and infinite goodness, judges in a final conflagration. In the *trimūrti*, then, Radhakrishnan saw the wisdom, love, and justice of the Divine personified.[51] The remainder of the gods on the Indian scene were accepted as symbols by Vedanta for the sake of the people.[52]

Though referred to in his discussion of upanisadic philosophy in Indian Philosophy,[53] Radhakrishnan first made a third stage, aspect or poise of being of the Absolute as part of his own thought in his lectures printed in 1939 as *Eastern Religion and Western Thought*. The Absolute is relationship to the world may also be seen as *hiranyagarbha*, the "world soul." This is the Absolute as the spirit that pervades and empowers the world. "*Hiranyagarbha* or *Brahmā* is the World-soul and is subject to changes of the world. He is *kārya Brhamā* or effect *Brahman* as distinct from *īśvara* who is *kāraṇa Brahman* or causal *Brahman*. *Hiranyagarbha* arises at every world-beginning and is dissolved at every world-ending."[54] The concept of *hiranyagarbha* affirms that, that which is inherent in the world, moving it toward the manifestation of its prefection is the Absolute. It gives the world meaning, denies that it can be said to have an illusory status, and means that ethics relate to the very warp and woof of things. More than this, however, the world is a manifestation of one of the possibilities of the Absolute, for the world itself is divine, though it is incorrect to suggest that the Absolute is only the world, for *brahman* is more than all this and, therefore, also beyond. "For Hindu thinkers, the objective world exists. It is not illusion. It is real not in being ultimate, but in being a form, an expression of the ultimate."[55] It is the world's relationship to *brahman* which is within and without that gives the world the reality it possesses. One must not emphasize exclusively the transcendence of *brahman*. "Thus, everything in the universe, instead of being dismissed as illusory, is thought to be produced by Brahman. But this principle of Brahman is recognized as immanent in the universe. . . . It is not apart from the world—it is the world. The world is the product of Brahman, and, therefore, Brahman. Hence, instead of being an illusion, the world is the sole reality."[56] The world, then, is divine and because it is *brahman*, it is real.

From this early period, Radhakrishnan understood the world to be in a process of evolution, an evolution guided by and an evolution of the Absolute. "The ultimate reality sleeps in the stone, breathes in the plants, feels in the animals and awakes to self-consciousness in man. It progressively manifests itself in and through these particulars."[57] Evolution is not merely physical or biological. The facts destroy distinctions between the material and spiritual for it is an evolution of consciousness, a growth to the realization of the Absolute in the world. "The facts of evolution compel us to assume the reality of a single spirit inspiring the whole course of evolution and working in different ways at different stages."[58]

This was Radhakrishnan's definition of Vedanta, and, therefore, his own theoretical stance toward Reality—a stance which he would maintain throughout his life. The world was not in opposition to the Absolute as he defined it, for the world partook of divinity and was even the divine activity as it progressed towards the revelation of that fact. History, then, is real and purposive. The world is a place for ethical action. Yet behind the world is the Ultimately Real, the Absolute, and this *brahman*, *saccidānɹnda*, is identical with the human self, the Universal Consciousness. Not surprisingly, then, did Radhakrishnan say that the history of the world "can be understood by a study of the underlying spirit of man."[59]

Vedanta as "Hinduism"
And the Essence of "Religion"

Beginning in 1922, Radhakrishnan placed a new perspective on his Vedanta. He identified it not merely as one school of Indian thought but as "Hinduism" and even as the essence of all "religion." Whereas, in 1908, he spoke of the affirmation of the Absolute *brahman* as only the final stage of Indian thought,[60] and whereas his articles spoke mostly of Vedanta, beginning with "The Heart of Hinduism" and "The Hindu Dharma" in 1922, there came about a change in the *designation* of the religious position he had previously defended, even though there was no change in the theoretical *content* of that position. He began to speak of "the faith of the Hindus," "the Hindu religion," "Hinduism,"[61] "Indian thought,"[62] and "the Hindu view" of various religious doctrines.[63]

The content of each of these is defined either as Vedanta or as a correlate of it as previously defined. For example, speaking to a Christian audience in "Hindu Thought and Christian Doctrine," he defined, "some of the fundamentals of the Hindu faith . . . those common ideas which have characterised the different forms of Hinduism in their long history, regarding the problems of God, man and his future."[64] First, God is not comprehensible by the intellect. Yet we think of him as "the unity of wisdom, love and goodness" of the *trimūrti* doctrine. Second, the world is organically related to the divine. "Hindu thought is not afraid of asserting the presence of God in all things." Third, there are no unique revelations but there are people who are *avatars*, who incarnate the divine "in a more striking way and to greater degree." This relativized a traditional Indian teaching of *avatāra*, "descent," in which the divine is believed to come to earth temporarily to restore the good and destroy evil. Fourth, human beings are given freedom to realize their destiny. Fifth, the goal of life is liberation, *mokṣa*, from the bonds of ignorance which hide the truth of the divine.[65]

This new designation of Vedanta appeared most strikingly in the Upton Lectures of 1926 at Manchester College, Oxford, published as *The Hindu View of Life:* "Hinduism is not to be dismissed as a mere flow and strife of opinions, for it represents a steady growth of insight, since every form of Hinduism and every stage of its growth is related to the common background of the Vedanta. . . . The germinal conceptions are contained in the Vedanta standard."[66] Those elements of the tradition which seem not to agree must be understood as representations of "popular theology," less significant, an acquiescence of the "majority of the Hindus," or "outbursts of sectarian fanaticism," "superstition," or "crude beliefs and submerged thoughts which the civilization has not had time to eradicate."[67] Concerning the views of religious thinkers, the essential teaching is the *advaita*, non-dualism, of Sankara as well. In a defense of his *Indian Philosophy* he confessed that "it is difficult to decide whether it is the *advaita* (or non-dualism) of Sankara or the modified position of Ramanuja that is the final teaching of the parent gospel [of the *Upaniṣads*]," yet he reconciled the two positions of these thinkers is terms of a "duality of standpoints" in which Sankara's position is a viewpoint of the "nature of reality" and Ramanuja's understanding represents "the absolute from the human end."[68]

This definition and application of "Hinduism" as a category continued throughout Radhakrishnan's work. "Hinduism" is *advaita*: "To define the real is to turn it into an object and so to degrade it. Its inwardness of spirit resists division in time or space. We cannot even say that it is one; we say that it is non-dual (*advaita*)."[69] This is "Hinduism" though the majority of Hindus may not so understand it. "While the thinking few understand the philosophical subtleties of Sankara's *advaita*, the popular religion of India is theism."[70] The people are incapable of seeing past the symbols which they take as absolute.

In this period Radhakrishnan also identified what he had previously called Vedanta, and now called "Hinduism," with the essence

of "religions" and "religion." This was not the case, for example,
in 1910, when "religion" was defined as belief in a higher power or
powers.[71] In 1926, however, he could say, "The Vedanta is not a
religion, but religion itself in its most universal and deepest significance."[72] This identification of Vedanta, "Hinduism," as the
essence of "religion" resulted in a two-fold understanding of the
"religions": Buddhism, Christianity, Islam, Judaism, etc. On the
one hand he asserted the essential unity of all "religions," a position which he maintained from the early 1920s to the end of his
life. Speaking of Islam in 1923, Radhakrishnan suggested, "If the
Indian Moslem combines his inherited tradition [the "Indian tradition"] with his acquired faith and effects a synthesis of the old and
the new, he will be led to emphasize these neglected aspects of the
truth of Islam which really promoted culture and civilisation and
brought to life a dying world and discard those unimportant details
which happened to be exaggerated out of all proportion on account
of historical accidents."[73] Similarly, Christianity, when understood
in its essentials, has many "affinities" to "Hinduism."[74] With the
growth of New Testament criticism, in fact, early Christianity would
be shown to be Vedanta. "Jesus is the example of a man who has
become God and none can say where his manhood ends and divinity begins. Man and God are akin, 'That art Thou,' *Tat tvam
asi*."[75] Though it was later corrupted, "Christian teaching in its
origin, before it became externalized and organized, was about
awakening from sleep through the light shed by the inner
wisdom."[76]

On the other hand, there was much in other religions which was
misunderstood, overemphasized, or unconsciously added by their
practitioners which is unessential and, therefore, needs pruning
from the main branch. This, of course, included the beliefs and
practices of some in the "Hindu" tradition as well. Some of it
could be easily removed. "Apparently there is not very much
serious difference between Hinduism and Christianity on the question of the nature and means of salvation, if we do not take into
account the doctrine of Atonement. . . . But the sacrifice of Christ
has no significance for man as a propitiation for sin.[77] The essential
element in all religions, when they are carefully and philosophically
compared, is religious experience. The early twenties witnessed a
growing emphasis upon the element of intuitive experience in
Radhakrishnan's writings. It is this experience, he believed, which

must be the test of truth for the "religion," and it is this universal religious experience which is emphasized in "Hinduism". "The Hindu attitude to religion is interesting. While fixed intellectual beliefs mark off one religion from another, Hinduism sets itself no such limits. Intellect is subordinated to intuition, dogma to experience, outer expression to inward realization."[78] Even though the importance of intuitive religious experience received more emphasis than reason, which was emphasized in earlier writings, Radhakrishnan was convinced that the results of intuition are not contrary to reason but actually move beyond it. Intuition and reason ideally complement each other, for the intuitive experience must also be tested in the light of philosophy, or reason, and its application in life: "We can discriminate between the genuine and the spurious in religious experience, not only by means of logic but also through life."[79]

It is difficult to distinguish between those characteristics of the experience which are essential and universal and those which reflect the cumulative tradition of the subject and are mixed with the essential.[80] However, Radhakrishnan affirmed that the following elements were universal: (1) The experience is self-authenticating: "In the experience itself no question is raised whether the object experienced is real or not."[81] (2) It is an experience which involves the whole person.[82] (3) It is, of course, intuitive and not intellectual. "The truths of the ṛṣis are not evolved as the result of logical reasoning or systematic poilosophy but they are the products of spiritual intuition, dṛṣṭi or vision."[83] (4) It is self-satisfying: "The experience itself is felt to be sufficient and complete."[84] (5) It results in the feelings of "inward peace, power and joy."[85] (6) It is fundamentally ineffable: "The unquestionable content of the experience is that about which nothing more can be said."[86] (7) Most important, and most required from Radhakrishnan's viewpoint, the experience is non-dual. It is an experience of the universal Self, ātman, which is brahman. "That the soul is in contact with a mighty spiritual power other than its normal self and yet within and that its contact means the beginning of the creation of a new self is the fact, while the identification of this power with the historic figures of Buddha or Christ, the confusion of the simple realization of the universal self in us with a catastrophic revelation from without, is an interpretation, a personal confession and not necessarily an objective truth."[87]

Even the Buddha, with his doctrine of *anatta* (Skt. *anātman*), non-self, when understood correctly, was not denying the existence of a permanent *ātman*, but only of the permanent reality of the ego. "The Upaniṣads arrive at the ground of all things by stripping the self of veil after veil of contingency. At the end of the process they find the universal self which is none of these finite entities, though the ground of them all. Buddha holds the same view, though he does not state it definitely."[88] Since this experience is essential to all religions, it may be said that there is an essential unity in the "mystic traditions of the different religions" which flows from the universal experience which is emphasized in "Hinduism."[89]

With this experience as the key to religion, i.e., with a vedantic definition of religious experience, Radhakrishnan was able to distinguish the essential from the non-essential in "religions." The absolute, unchanging essence of "religion" was the non-dual experience of the Absolute, but attempts to express that experience were only relatively true. The different systems are only "tentative adjustments, more or less satisfactory to spiritual reality."[90] However, he did not believe that his own expression of the essentials of religious experience in non-dual terms was a result of reflection. Though he stated that "there is no such thing as pure experience, raw and undigested," yet *saccidānanda* and *tat tvam asi* represent the fact of the experience, not its interpretation. "The great text of the Upaniṣad affirms it—*Tat tvam asi* (That art Thou). It is a simple statement of an experienced fact. The Biblical text, 'So God created man in his own image; in the image of God created he him,' asserts that in the soul of man is contained the true revelation of God."[91] Similarly, "The three noteworthy features of spiritual experience are reality, awareness and freedom."[92]

As the experienced fact these elements of experience were always exempt from questioning. "In living religion there is no subjection to any authority except to the compelling one of immediate spiritual perception."[93] Though experience must be tested by reason, such interpretations must not be under bondage to traditions, dogmas, and creeds, and "Hinduism," of all the "religions," understands this best. "The Hindu attitude is based on a definite philosophy of life which assumes that religion is a matter of personal realization. Creeds and dogmas, words and symbols have only an instrumental value. Their function is to aid the growth of spirit by supplying supports for a task that is strictly personal."[94]   The problem is that those who misunderstand and, therefore, take other elements as essential to their "religion," tend to absolutize those elements, believing them to be crucial and, then, considering others outside of their current religious stance when these others do not accept these so-called important elements. This, for Radhakrishnan, is dogmatic, exclusivist "religion."

In the essential agreement of religious experience and the wide intolerence of "religions" in non-essential elements, Radhakrishnan is provided with one of the most often discussed themes of his writing and speaking.   The essential unity of religious experience should result in a tolerance for other "religions" in the midst of the current world crisis and provide the key to a universal world community.

The Religion of the Spirit (Hinduism, Vedanta) As the Solution to the World's Need

As Radhakrishnan's intercourse with the West became regular and stronger, and as World War II loomed on the horizon, he began to speak of Vedanta with a new emphasis. It was clear to him that the world was at a crucial point in history; threats to humanity appeared on all sides. Therefore, he proclaimed that "Hinduism," which he would often call the "religion of the Spirit," was the only solution to the human predicament and as such must be the religion of the future. He was no longer on the defensive as he was in his first writings. He proclaimed a religious position which could bind the world together and prepare it for a great leap forward in its evolution. Though during World War I he believed that the West was materialistic, egoistic, and overly possessive, and that the war "revealed to India the soul of Europe,"[95] his pleas that the world turn to "Hinduism" were unequivocal in the thirties and forties due to the rise of Fascism and the failure of the League of Nations, and in the fifties and sixties in the light of the "Cold War" and the threat of atomic war.

In the late twenties, Radhakrishnan believed the world was at a time of great transition, a time of spectacular growth in its evolution to the manifestation of the divine. In all areas of human knowledge and intercourse there had been much progress, yet it

seemed to him that the growth of the spirit was lagging behind.[96]
"Religions" were suffering because they had not kept up with the
changes of the modern world, and therefore people were beginning
to question the validity of the "religions." Radhakrishnan spoke of
this theme often from the late twenties through the early seventies.

The coming of World War II underlined the crisis of the present
age in the mind of Radhakrishnan. There was a threat of increasing disunity in the world which was caused by growing national
egoism. "War is really devil's work and cannot be deleted from
the pages of history until national isolation and selfishness are
abandoned."[97] Nationalism is "a pernicious creed" which may
have had its purpose in the past world of physical barriers, but
which today stands blocking the path to world unity and world
community.[98] War has exposed to all the problems of government, economic structures, and educational institutions, and shows
that the weakness of the world is an inward disease of spirit. "We
are witnessing today the end of an era, the agony of a whole
civilization, the liquidation of forces in which we have all been
steeped. This world war which is heaping gratuitous and senseless
horrors on the helpless and harmless people is not to be traced to
the malevolence of a few individuals, nor is it to be dismissed as
the conflict of rival imperialisms. It is the proclamation of the
bankruptcy of the present world order which is marked by the
decline of spiritual life and the degradation of moral values."[99]
A world community is needed in order to establish world unity,
turning the tide against the current evils of materialism, egoism,
and the failure of the "religions."[100]

One must note that the questioning of "religions" by twentieth-
century minds was not the questioning of "religion." Though
science had rightly caused the rejection of many traditional beliefs,
this rejection constituted a preparation for a more spiritual faith.
"It is no use repudiating the religious implications of science. I
believe that the growing dissatisfaction with established religion is
the prelude to the rise of a truer, more spiritual, and so more
universal religion."[101] Most of all, this was the repudiation of
"religions" which appealed to dogma and doctrine instead of
experienced fact. "The scientific temper is opposed to the acceptance of dogma. The scientist pursues truth without any bias or
presuppositions. He does not start with the idea that his conclusions
should square with dogmas. Religion as revelation or dogma has

no appeal to the believer in science."[102]

People were not rejecting "religion," but only the formulations and dogmas of traditional "religions." "Those who stand outside organised religions do so because they are persuaded that the vision of God and the impulse of humanity embodied in organised religions are defective."[103] These religions, then, fail to capture the modern mind for three reasons. First, they are not consistent with the discoveries of science. Second, they are incapable or ineffective in solving social problems. "The unscientific character of religious beliefs and the unsocial nature of religious practices are responsible for the increasing indifference to religion."[104] Concerning their relationships to social problems the religions have many times capitulated to the status quo. "The truly religious are those who feel dissatisfied with the way in which religions are compromising with worldly values and who demand a transformation of the social order into conformity with the spiritual pattern."[105] The third reason for the failure of the religions is that they are exclusivist and therefore incapable of uniting a world which desperately wishes to unite. "We have to give to the new society a psychological unity, a spiritual coherence. To sustain a world community, we need unity, if not identity of spiritual outlook and aspiration. Unfortunately religions tend to keep people apart. Humanity is broken up into a number of separate worlds each with its particular religious tradition."[106]

The issue of tolerance in the religions of the world became crucial in Radhakrishnan's writings, for a spiritual solution, he believed, required a united spirituality, a universal faith. "The greatest of the temptations we must overcome is to think that our own religion is the only true religion, our own vision of Reality is the only authentic vision, that we alone have received a revelation and we are the chosen people, the children of light and the rest of the human race live in darkness."[107] The creation of one world was called "the most significant feature of our time," yet: "The barriers of dogmatic religions are sterilising men's efforts to co-ordinate their forces to shape the future."[108] This exclusiveness is the result of greed and selfishness, taking one's own symbol of the Absolute as absolute.[109] In short, it is "idolatry,"[110] and is found where "intellectualism" has won the day in "religions."[111] However, theistic views are most often responsible for filling "men's minds with dogmatism and their hearts with intolerance."[112] The crucial feature of a "religion" which will solve the human predicament, then, is a universality which embraces all viewpoints. Yet this is not merely indifference to the many "religions" but a tolerance which "follows from the conviction' that the Absolute Reality is a mystery of which no more than a fraction has ever yet been penetrated."[113] Thus, it is a tolerance which flows from a certain affirmation about the nature of the Absolute and a tolerance which includes respect and fairness toward those other religions.

A religion is needed, in summary, which is scientific, ethically effective, and universal.[114] Secular humanism will not do either, for it has also failed to meet human needs. "The civilisation built on practical reason, scientific · power, industrial efficiency and national patriotism has disclosed its insufficiency in the aggressive ugliness of modern life, its perpetual unrest, its economic chaos, its lack of inner freedom and its oppressive mechanical burden."[115]

While Radhakrishnan called for the correction of these defects in the religion of the future, he was convinced beyond any doubt that the religion of the hour that fulfilled these requirements was "Vedanta" or "Hinduism," the essence of all religions. Its promulgation will return society to the spiritual foundation which will fill the world's need. "The mystic religion of India which affirms that things spiritual are personal, and that we have to reflect them in our lives, which requires us to withdraw from the world's concerns to find the real, and return to the world of history with renewed energy and certitude, which is at once spiritual and social, is likely to be the religion of the new world, which will draw men to a common centre even across the national frontiers."[116]

This religion is the *philosophia perennis,* sanātana dharma," or "Hinduism," the spirit of India.[117] In a 1946 article, "The Voice of India in the Spiritual Crisis of Our Time," Radhakrishnan summarized his arguments and more fully identified his position with Vedanta. The Real is within; its reality is non-dual; it is *Iśvara* when understood in relationship to the creation; the world is in an evolution to the highest realization of the Absolute. "The end of man is to recognise that the Divine is his real self, to discover and consciously realise it."[118] It is this "eternal religion" which can "help to re-integrate this bruised, battered, broken world and give to it the faith for which it is in search."[119]

In all of this, it must be borne in mind that Radhakrishnan did not believe that he was proclaiming a "religion" among the others even though he identified it with the essence of a certain tradition. He was convinced that he was promoting "religion" in its very essence. He was so certain of this that even though he spoke against extreme nationalism, this position was often identified with India. So much was this true that before the representatives of the United Nations Educational, Scientific, and Cultural Organization, he said, "The fundamental ideas of Indian culture will have a great formulative influence on the world of the future."[120] More specifically he was referring to Vedanta: "The regeneration of the world can come only from an idealist view of life and a return to religion. As Indian religion is not entangled in unscientific dogmas or doubtful history, one need not fear for its future."[121] Though sometimes he spoke of this as the religion of the East, the "religion of the spirit" is most clearly found in India.

The fact that India would influence the religion of the world greatly, however, is not to be understood as a new role for that nation. Her influence had been great in the past in matters of spirit. In *Eastern Religions and Western Thought* he preferred to see mystical, spiritual influences from India as an explanation of the spiritual in the West. "There is thus enough justification for regarding the mystic element in the West as Indian."[122] He believed that Greece, Palestine, and Rome were influenced by the East, and he concluded, "The whole life and teaching of Jesus is so distinctive that it cannot be regarded as a natural development of Jewish and Greek ideas." Thus, even the "heart of Christianity is Eastern."[123]

Similarly, Radhakrishnan believed that Chinese thought was essentially vedantic: "While Confucianism stressed the karma aspect, Taoism the mystical or the jñāna side, Buddhism supplied a philosophy and an ethics which dealt adequately with these two sides of religion."[124] Yet, as he told audiences in China, India's influence on China has been decisive. Taoism actually reflects the influence of the Upaniṣads,[125] and Buddhism entered India to produce the appearance of "a new China."[126]

"Religion of the spirit" was what he began to call this position in 1936, for it was a faith which emphasized the deep spiritual essentials of "religions" and, therefore, the essence of "religion." It was also able to unite the world, providing a scientific, ethical, and universal solution in the current human predicament. Before the World Congress of Faiths held in London in 1936, he affirmed, "It [fellowship of faith] is understanding, insight, full trust in the basic reality which feeds all faiths and its power to lead us to the truth. It believes in the deeper religion of the Spirit which will be adequate for all people, vital enough to strike deep roots, powerful to unify each individual in himself and bind us all together by the realisation of our common condition and common goal."[127] This it could do because it "regards dogmas as more or less tentative views."[128] It is also scientific. "A true understanding of science supports a religion of spirit."[129] Like science it affirms a unity behind and in nature, it is empirical and non-dogmatic, basing itself upon religious experiences,[130] and it is universal, showing no boundaries at continents or between races.[131]

As vice-president and president of India, Radhakrishnan indi-cated that he believed that this "religion of the spirit" could and should be the basis for an adequate political philosophy. "Reli-gion correctly interpreted gives value to the individual" and this correct interpretation requires an emphasis upon the divinity of the human being. This is the basis for a democracy.[132] Similarly, the unity perceived in religious experience is the fact which demands that this democracy also be socialistic: "A universal welfare state where we look upon the whole world as our sacred home."[133] For Radhakrishnan this could be called a "secular" state, not because it was against religion or did not take the reality of the Absolute into consideration, but because it did not support sectarianism. "The ideal of secularism means that we abandon the inhumanity of fanaticism and give up the futile hatred of others. In a secular State there will be the spirit of true religion, and the environment necessary for the development of a gentle and considerate way of life";[134] "Secularism here does not mean irreligion or atheism or even stress of material comforts. It proclaims that it lays stress on the universality of spiritual values which may be attained in a variety of ways."[135]

Accepting this definition of the "secular state" enabled Radha-krishnan to experience no conflict between the espousal of the "religion of the spirit" as he defined it and also the "secularism" of India. India can be "secular" for it does not prefer a dogmatic, sectarian "religion" and yet it can prophetically promote the "religion of the spirit," for that position is on a different level than the "religions." Secularism was non-sectarianism, and Radhakrishnan was convinced that he had transcended sectarian divisions in his own position. When the state "respects all religions," it is merely a practice of the fundamental principle of the Indian genius, of the Indian spirit itself.[136] The Constitution guarantees freedom of "religion" and even the freedom to propagate one's position, but Radhakrishnan understood one limit upon such propagation. Religions may spread their viewpoints "so long as they do not hurt the conscience of other people."[137] He offered no clear definition of this limitation.

Summary

By the time of his retirement in 1967 and his death on April 17, 1975, Radhakrishnan had spoken and written about his "religion of the spirit" to a wide variety of audiences, both Western and Eastern. He was convinced that at the present time in the evolution of the world mankind needed this "religion" in order to progress spiritually as well as materially. He viewed the failures of other "religions" in their refusal or inability to evolve to what he believed was a more spiritual position because these religions were too dogmatic. The "religion of the spirit," however, was identifiable with "the Indian religious tradition," and especially with what he had defined as Vedanta in his earlier writings. There he had already identified Vedanta with a position he believed was held by the non-dualist Sankara. Soon he affirmed that Vedanta was the essence of "Hinduism" or "Indian religion," and, in fact, the essence of all religions. It was not "a religion" but "religion itself." Since it was the essence of all "religions," to promote it was to promote no single "religion" but "religion" in essence. By promoting this "religion of the spirit," by defense, definition, and promulgation of Vedanta, he believed he was participating as best he could in the evolutionary push of the world toward the perfection which is the manifestation of the Absolute, and this throughout his life was his ultimate concern: to bring each individual and the world into perfection as defined by Vedanta.

Notes

This investigation was partially supported by a University of Kansas General Research Fund Allocation.

1. See, for example, "The Spirit in Man," in *Contemporary Indian Philosophy,* eds. S. Radhakrishnan and J.H. Muirhead, 2nd ed. (London: George Allen & Unwin, 1952), p. 483; "Religion and Religions," in *Faiths and Fellowship: Being the Proceedings of the World Congress of Faiths Held in London July 3rd—17th 1936,* ed. A. Douglas Millard (London: J.M. Watkins, 1936), pp. 111, 115; "The Religion of the Spirit and the World's Need: Fragments of a Confession," in *The Philosophy of Sarvepalli Radhakrishnan,* ed. Paul Arthur Schilpp (New York: Tudor, 1952), p. 78; *East and West: Some Reflections* (London: George Allen & Unwin, 1956), p. 121. Radhakrishnan's use of the word "religion" will be evident in this paper. As the "religions" it refers to the categories of the "isms" (e.g., Christianity, Hinduism, Buddhism, Islam), and as "religion" it refers to the essence of "religions" as he defined it. When referring to "religion" or "religions" in this study, the word is being used in these senses when in quotation marks. Otherwise, the word is to be defined as "that which concerns the person or group ultimately."

2. "The Spirit in Man," pp. 475-76. See also "My Search for Truth," in *Radhakrishnan: Selected Writings on Philosophy. Religion, and Culture,* ed. Robert A. McDermott (New York: E.P. Dutton, 1970), pp. 37, 40. This was originally in Vergilius Ferm, ed., *Religion in Transition* (London: George Allen & Unwin, 1937), pp. 11-59. See also "The Religion of the Spirit and the World's Need," p. 9.

3. *Our Heritage* (Delhi: Hind Pocket Books, 1973), p. 97. This is a collection of Radhakrishnan's speeches from the 1960s. The reference was originally a speech given in Calcutta, January 20, 1963, and published in Sarvepalli Radhakrishnan, *President Radhakrishnan's Speeches and Writings, May 1962-May 1964* (New Delhi: Publications Division, Ministry of Information and Broadcasting, 1964), p. 123. See also "My Search for Truth," p. 37. Radhakrishnan believed that Svami Vivekananda and the Svami's guru, Ramakrishna Paramahamsa, were in touch with the essence of "Hinduism." See *President Radhakrishnan's Speeches,* p. 120; "Hinduism and the West," in *Modern India and the West,* ed. L.S.S. O'Malley (London: Oxford University Press, 1941), p. 346; *Fellowship of the Spirit* (Cambridge: Harvard University Press, 1961), p. 21.

4. Radhakrishnan, *The Ethics of the Vedanta and its Metaphysical Presuppositions* (Madras: Guardian Press, 1908).

5. There are a number of important introductions to Radhakrishnan's thought. See especially, P.A. Schilpp, ed., *The Philosophy of Sarvepalli Radhakrishnan;* J.G. Arapura, *Radhakrishnan and Integral Experience* (New York: Asia Publishing House, 1966), and Robert A. McDermott, "Radhakrishnan's Contribution to Comparative Philosophy," *International Philosophical Quarterly* 10, no. 3 (September 1970): 420-40.

6. The term "Vedanta," meaning "end of the Vedas," usually is taken as a general name for those religious positions which trace their views back to the Upaniṣads, the last books of the vedic collection. The three major systems which were developed were *advaita vedānta*, the non-dualism for which Sankara (A.D. 788-820) is best known; *viśiṣṭādvaita vedānta*, "qualified non-dualism," whose major exponent was Ramanuja (A.D. 1017-1137); and *dvaita*, dualism, whose thirteenth-century exponent was Madhva. In this paper the term "Vedanta" is used as Radhakrishnan uses it, to refer to his own systematization and understanding of the Upaniṣads and these systems.

7. "Religion and Life," *International Journal of Ethics* 27, no. 1 (October 1916): 99. Radhakrishnan's use of the term "God" is two-fold: (1) as a popular term for the Absolute generally conceived by non-technical audiences; (2) for the Absolute viewed from the cosmic side (see below). For similar statements which affirm this ultimate concern throughout his life the following are examples: "The Heart of Hinduism," *The Hibbert Journal* 21, no. 1 (October 1922): 9; *An Idealist View of Life*, 2nd ed. (London: Unwin Books, 1937), pp. 165-66; *East and West in Religion* (London: George Allen & Unwin, 1933), p. 104; "The Voice of India in the Spiritual Crisis of Our Time," *The Hibbert Journal* 44, no. 4 (July 1946): 304; "The Religion of the Spirit and the World's Need," pp. 43, 45; *Our Heritage*, p. 37; *Recovery of Faith* (Delhi: Hind Pocket Books, 1967), pp. 13, 14.

8. At times, Radhakrishnan explained that he perceived his task as something other than mere description of the positions he discussed. In a defense of the first volume of his *Indian Philosophy* (London: George Allen & Unwin 1923), he said ("Indian Philosophy: Some Problems," *Mind* [New Series] 25 [April 1926]: 154): "The historian of philosophy must approach his task not as a mere philologist or even as a scholar but as a philosopher who uses his scholarship as an instrument to wrest from words the thoughts that underlie them. . . . A philosopher . . . realises the value of the ancient Indian theories which attempt to grapple with the perennial problems of life and treats them not as fossils but as species which are remarkably persistent."

9. " 'Nature' and 'Convention' in Greek Ethics," *The Calcutta Review* 130 (January 1910) : 9-23.

10. "Egoism and Altruism—The Vedanta Solution," *East and West* (Bombay) 9 (July 1910) : 630.

11. One finds in these early articles such statements as: "The lowest forms of religion are lowest because they have no ethical significance" ("The Relation of Morality to Religion," *The Hindustan Review* [September 1910]: 295); "All the world knows that education has for its aim and object the *ethical* man—the man in whom all the capacities are harmoniously developed" ("Morality and Religion in Education," *The Madras Christian College Magazine* 10[1910-11]: 233). Similarly one need only look at the titles of articles from this period which include other than those mentioned previously: "Karma and Free Will," *The Modern Review* (Calcutta), 3

(May 1908) : 424-28 ;   "The Ethics of the Bhagavadgita and Kant,"
International Journal of Ethics 21, no. 4 (July 1911); 465-75; "The
Ethics of the Vedanta," *International Journal of Ethics* 24, no. 2 (January
1914) - 1688-83.

12. Radhakrishnan, "Karma and Free Will," p. 426.

13. Ibid., pp. 426, 427.

14. Radhakrishnan, "Indian Philosophy: The Vedas and the Six Systems."
The Madras Christian College Magazine 3 (1908): 22.

15. Ibid., p. 23.

16. Radhakrishnan, *The Reign of Religion in Contemporary Philosophy* (London:
Macmillan, 1920). In the preface (p. vii) he states his purpose as follows:
"This book attempts to show that of the two live philosophies of the
present day, pluralistic theism and monistic idealism, the latter is the more
reasonable as affording the spiritual being of man full satisfaction, moral
as well as intellectual."

17. Radhakrishnan, "The Ethics of the Vedanta," pp. 169-70.

18. Ibid., p. 168.

19. Ibid.

20. Radhakrishnan, "Karma and Free Will," pp. 424-25. Cf. "The Ethics of
the Bhagavadgita and Kant," p. 467.

21. Ibid., p. 425. Cf. Radhakrishnan, "The Ethics of the Bhagavadgita and
Kant," pp. 471-74 ; and "The Ethics of the Vedanta," pp. 181-82.

22. Radhakrishnan, *The Hindu View of Life* (London: Unwin Books, 1927),
p. 54. For other statements of this analogy, somewhat more developed,
see his *The Bhagavadgītā With an Introductory Essay, Sanskrit Text,
English Translation and Notes* (London: George Allen & Unwin, 1948),
p. 49 ; and his *An Idealist View of Life*, pp. 221-22.

23. Radhakrishnan, "Karma and Free Will," p. 425. Cf. his "Religion and
Life," *International Journal of Ethics* 27, no. 1 (October 1916) : 99.

24. Its most well-known later form is as a critique of Albert Schweitzer's
claim that Indian thought is world-negating. This is found in Radha-
krishnan's *Eastern Religions and Western Thought* (London: Oxford
University Press, 1940), pp. 64-110, For analyses of their debate see
William F. Goodwin, "Mysticism and Ethics: An Examination of
Radhakrishnan's Reply to Schweitzer's Critique of Indian Thought,"
Ethics 78, no. 1 (October 1956): 25-41; and Milton D. Hunnex.
"Mysticism and Ethics: Radhakrishnan and Schweitzer," *Philosophy
East and West* 8, nos. 3, 4 (October 1958—January 1959): 121-36.

25. Radhakrishnan, "The Ethics of the Vedanta," pp. 179-80.

26. Radhakrishnan. "The Vedanta Philosophy and the Doctrine of Māyā,"
International Journal of Ethics 24, no. 3 (April 1914) : 436.

27. Ibid., p. 440. Māyā refers, then, to the fact that one cannot know the
exact nature of the relationship between the world and the Absolute. See
also, his "The Metaphysics of the Upanisads, II," *The Indian Philosophical
Review* 3, no. 4 (October 1920): 349; "The Doctrine of Maya: Some
Problems," in *Proceedings of the Sixth International Congress of Philosophy*,
ed. Edgar Sheffield Brightman (New York: Longman, Green & Co.,

1927), p. 688 ; *An Idealist View of Life*, p. 272. Yet it does indicate that the universe is not independent of *brahman*. See also Radhakrishnan "The Vedantic Approach to Reality," *The Monist* 26, no. 2 (April 1916):226, his *Eastern Religions and Western Thought*, pp. 27, 85-86; "Reply to Critics," in Schilpp, ed., *Philosophy of Sarvepalli Radhakrishnan*, pp. 800-802. Finally, it results in the fact that we misunderstand the nature of the universe. See "Reply to Critics," pp. 801-802; and *Eastern Religions and Western Thought*, p. 28. For a helpful study see Donald R. Tuck, "The Doctrine of Maya: Radhakrishnan," *Darshana International* 16, no. 4 (October 1976): 51-62.

28. Radhakrishnan, "The Vedanta Philosophy and the Doctrine of Māyā," p. 432.

29. Radhakrishnan, "The Vedantic Approach to Reality," p. 215.

30. Radhakrishnan, *The Reign of Religion in Contemporary Philosophy*, p. 430. Cf. also his "The Vedantic Approach to Reality," p. 216, with *The Reign of Religion*, pp. 430, 1.

31. Radhakrishnan, *The Philosophy of Rabindranath Tagore* (London : Macmillan, 1918).

32. Radhakrishnan, *Indian Philosophy* (London : George Allen & Unwin, 1927), 2: 562-74. Cf. his "Intellect and Intuition in Sankara's Philosophy," *Triveni* 6, no. 1 (July-August 1933): 14; his *Eastern Religions and Western Thought*, pp. 86-88, 91; his "Vedanta—The Advaita School," in *History of Philosophy Eastern and Western*, ed. S. Radhakrishnan (New York: Barnes & Noble, 1952), 1: 276-81; his *Occasional Speeches and Writings: October 1952-January 1956* (New Delhi: Publications Division, Ministry of Information and Broadcasting, Government of India, 1960, pp. 261-62.

33. Radhakrishnan, *An Idealist View of Life*, p. 101.

34. Radhakrishnan, *Recovery of Faith*, p. 79. Cf. his *An Idealist View of Life*, pp. 11, 272.

35. Radhakrishnan, *An Idealist View of Life*, p. 72.

36. See Radhakrishnan, "The Metaphysics of the Upanishads, I," *The Indian Philosophical Review* 3, no. 3 (July 1920): 214; his *Idealist View of Life*, p. 80.

37. Radhakrishnan, *The Reign of Religion in Contemporary Philosophy*, p. vii, and *Indian Philosophy* (London: George Allen & Unwin, 1923), 1: 31-32, 48. In his "Religion and Life," p. 99, he calls it "immanent or objective idealism."

38. Radhakrishnan, *An Idealist View of Life*, p. 10.

39. Radhakrishnan, *Recovery of Faith*, p. 83. Cf. "The Hindu Idea of God," *The Quest* (London: 15, no. 3 (April 1924): 310; his *Religion and Society*, 2nd ed. (London: George Allen & Unwin, 1948), p. 103.

40. Radhakrishnan, *The Hindu View of Life*, p. 50. Cf. "The Vedanta Philosophy and the Doctrine of Māyā," p. 442; "Hindu Thought and Christian Doctrine," *The Madras Christian College Magazine* (Quarterly Series) (January 1924): 18; *The Religion We Need*, Affirmation Series (London: Ernest Benn, 1928), p. 22; *Kalki or The Future of Civilization* (London:

Kegan, Paul, Trench, Trubner & Co., 1929), p. 59; "Progress and Spiritual Values," *Philosophy: The Journal of the British Institute of Philosophy* 12, no. 47 (July 1937) : 273-74. *Eastern Religions and Western Thought,* p. 24; *Occasional Speeches and Writings: October 1952-January 1956,* p. 130; *East and West: Some Reflections,* p. 124.

41. Radhakrishnan, *An Idealist View of Life,* p. 80.

42. Radhakrishnan, "The Metaphysics of the Upanishads, I," pp 217-19.

43. Ibid., pp. 221-22. Cf. Radhakrishnan, "The Vedantic Approach to Reality," pp. 210, 4 ; "The Heart of Hinduism, pp. 8, 9; "Hindu Thought and Christian Doctrine," pp. 26, 32; *The Religion We Need,* pp. 22-23; *An Idealist View of Life,* pp. 78-83, 162-63, 217; *East and West in Religion,* p. 131; "Spiritual Freedom and the New Education," *New Era in Home and School* 17 (September-October 1936): 235; "The Spirit in Man," p. 484; *Eastern Religions and Western Thought,* pp. 32, 300, 125; "The Cultural Problem," in *The Cultural Problem,* Oxford Pamphlets on Indian Affairs, no. 1, ed. A.I.J. Appasamy (Madras: Oxford University Press, 1942), p. 43; "The Voice of India in the Spiritual Crisis of Our Time," pp. 301-4; "The Nature of Man," in *Creators of the Modern Spirit: Towards a Philosophy of Faith,* ed. Barbara Waylen (New York: Macmillan, 1951), p. 65; *Occasional Speeches and Writings: October 1952-January 1956,* pp. 52. 202, 244; *Occasional Speeches and Writings. Third Series: July 1959-May 1962* (New Delhi: Publications Division, Ministry of Information and Broadcasting, Government of India, 1963), pp. 236, 259; *Religion in a Changing World* (London: George Allen and Unwin, 1967), pp. 109, 120; *Our Heritage,* pp. 19, 55, 140; etc.

44. His strongest statement of this position is: "The assertion of the self as something other than the true reality of God is the fall or the original sin (*avidyā*)" (*An Idealist View of Life,* p. 87).

45. Ibid., p. 273. Cf. "The Hindu Idea of God," pp. 291, 309-10; *The Hindu View of Life,* pp. 23-24; 30-34; *Eastern Religion and Western Thought,* pp. 92, 125; "Hinduism and the West," p. 340; "The Voice of India in the Spiritual Crisis of Our Time," p. 303; "Science and Religion," in *Art and Thought: A Volume in Honour of the Late Dr. Ananda K. Coomaraswamy,* ed. K. Bharatha Iyer (London: Luzac & Co., 1947), p. 184; "The Religion of the Spirit and the World's Need," pp. 39-40; *Occasional Speeches and Writings, October 1952-January 1956,* p. 130; *Occasional Speeches and Writings. Third Series,* p. 232; *Religion in a Changing World,* pp. 121-22; *Recovery of Faith,* pp. 85-86; etc.

46. Radhakrishnan, *An Idealist View of Life,* p. 272.

47. Ibid., pp. 85-86. Cf. Radhakrishnan, "Religion and Religions," p. 110; "Hinduism," in *The Legacy of India,* ed. G.T. Garratt (London: Oxford University Press, 1937), pp. 271-72.

48. Radhakrishnan, *Eastern Religions and Western Thought,* p. 29.

49. For a discussion see J. Gonda, "The Hindu Trinity," *Anthropos* 63 (1968): 212-26.

50. Radhakrishnan, *Indian Philosophy* 1:480.

51. Cf. Radhakrishnan, "The Heart of Hinduism," p. 6; "Hindu Thought and

Christian Doctrine," pp. 19-20; *The Hindu View of Life*, p. 21; *An Idealist View of Life*, p. 265; "The Voice of India in the Spiritual Crisis of Our Time," p. 303; "The Religion of the Spirit and the World's Need," p. 40; *Occacional Speeches and Writings: October 1952-January 1956*, pp. 257-58; etc.

52. Radhakrishnan, "The Heart of Hinduism," p. 7.

53. Radhakrishnan, *Indian Philosophy* 1:171-72.

54. Radhakrishnan, *The Principal Upanisads* (New York: Harper & Brothers, 1953), p. 72. Cf. his *Eastern Religions and Western Thought*, p. 127; *The Bhagavadgītā*, p. 228; "Reply to Critics," p. 797; *Occasional Speeches and Writings: October 1952-January 1956*, p. 259.

55. Radhakrishnan, *Eastern Religions and Western Thought*, p. 31. Cf. his "The Vedantic Approach to Reality," p. 224.

56. Radhakrishnan, "The Vedanta Philosophy and the Doctrine of Māyā," pp. 436-37.

57. Radhakrishnan, "The Vedantic Approach to Reality," p. 225.

58. Radhakrishnan, "Evolution and its Implications, "*The New Era* 1 (November 1928): 111. Cf. his "The Metaphysics of the Upanishads, II," pp. 348-49; "The Role of Philosophy in the History of Civilization," in *Proceedings of the Sixth International Congress of Philosophy*, ed. Edgar Sheffield Brightman (New York: Longmans, Green & Co., 1927), p. 547; *An Idealist View of Life*, pp. 86-87, 165-66, etc.; *East and West in Religion*, pp. 124-25; *Eastern Religions and Western Thought*, pp. 91-92: "The Cultural Problem," p. 48; "Science and Religion," p. 183; "The Religion of the Spirit and the World's Need," pp. 31, 44; etc.

59. Radhakrishnan, "Progress and Spiritual Values," p. 261.

60. Radhakrishnan "Indian Philosophy: The Vedas and the Six Systems,' p. 27.

61. E.g., Radhakrishnan, "The Heart of Hinduism," pp. 5, 19; *The Hindu View of Life*, pp. 11-19, 31, 39, etc.; "Islam and Indian Thought." *The Indian Review* 24 (November 1923): 666, 672; "The Spirit in Man," pp. 475-76; "Introduction to the First Edition," in *The Cultural Heritage of India*, 2nd ed. (Calcutta: Ramakrishna Mission Institute of Culture, 1958), p. xxx; *Eastern Religions and Western Thought*, p. 338; "The Cultural Problem," pp. 43-44; "My Search for Truth," pp. 41,45; "Reply to Critics," p. 802; *The Recovery of Faith*, pp. 103-5; etc. Radhakrishnan admitted disagreements among those placed under this designation, but these disagreements, based upon his definition of the essential nature of "Hinduism," were insignificant. See his *Education, Politics and War* (Poona: International Book Service, 1944), p. 30; and *The Hindu View of Life*, pp. 13, 25, 91.

62. For example, in his discussion of "The General Characteristics of Indian Thought" in *Indian Philosophy* 1:24-49, "monistic idealism" is called "the truth of things" (p. 31).

63. See, for example, Radhakrishnan, "The Hindu Dharma," *The International Journal of Ethics* 33, no. 1 (October 1922): 1-22; "The Hindu Idea of God," pp. 289-310; etc.

64. Radhakrishnan, "Hindu Thought and Christian Doctrine," p. 18.

65. Ibid., pp. 18-27. Cf. his *Indian Philosophy* 1:24-49; "Hinduism" in *The Legacy of India*, pp. 261-85; "Introduction to the First Edition," pp. xxiv-xxxvi; "Hinduism and the West," pp. 339-44; etc.

66. Radhakrishnan, *The Hindu View of Life*, p. 18.

67. Ibid., pp. 21, 24, 25, 28, 38, 40. Cf. his "The Spirit in Man," pp. 476-78. Radhakrishnan looked forward to the day when these elements would be eliminated: "It is true that the Hindu religion tolerates some of the forms of worship which are not in accord with the spirit of reason and the demands of conscience in the hope that in the general atmosphere of Hinduism, these forms of worship and practices will fade away" (*Occasional Speeches and Writings. Third Series*, p. 241). Educated Hindus can best further this process: "This work of discriminating between the permanent and the transitory in our tradition can be done only by the educated classes who have sufficient respect for the past and trust in the present" (*Freedom and Culture* [Madras: G.A. Natesan, 1936], p. 56).

68. Radhakrishnan, " 'Indian Philosophy' : Some Problems," pp. 157-58. Cf. his *Indian Philosophy* 2:712, where Ramanuja's view of the Absolute is called "the highest *expression* of the truth." The emphasis is Radhakrishnan's own.

69. Radhakrishnan, "Hinduism and the West," p. 340.

70. Ibid , p. 341.

71. Radhakrishnan, "The Relation of Morality to Religion," p. 293.

72. Radhakrishnan, *The Hindu View of Life*, p. 18. Cf. his *Kalki or the Future of Civilizatian*, p. 68.

73. Radhakrishnan, "Islam and Indian Thought," p. 666.

74. Radhakrishnan, "Hindu Thought and Christian Doctrine," p. 18.

75. Ibid., p. 23.

76. Radhakrishnan, *Religion and Culture* (Delhi: Hind Pocket Books, 1968), p. 14. Cf. his "Hindu Thought and Christian Doctrine," pp. 23-30; *East and West in Religion*, pp. 57-68; *Eastern Religions and Western Thought*, pp. 169, 324, 342; "Reply to Critics," pp. 87-88; *Occasional Speeches and Writings, October 1952-January 1956*, pp. 233-34; *East and West: Some Reflections*, pp. 71-72, 79; etc.

77. Radhakrishnan, "Hindu Thought and Christian Doctrine," p. 28.

78. Radhakrishnan, *The Hindu View of Life*, p. 13, cf. p. 16. Cf. his *An Idealist View of Life*, pp. 70-71; "Intuition and Intellect," in *The Golden Book of Tagore*, ed. Ramananda Chaterjee (Calcutta: Golden Book Committee, 1921), p. 310; *Eastern Religions and Western Thought*, p. 21; "Introduction to the First Edition," p. xxiv: "Hinduism" in *The Legacy of India*, pp. 261-63; "The Cultural Problem," pp. 42-43; *Occasional Speeches and Writings. Second Series, February 1956-February 1957* (New Delhi: Publications Division, Ministry of Information and Broadcasting, Government of India, 1957), pp. 50, 245; etc.

79. Radhakrishnan, *The Hindu View of Life*, p. 15. Cf. his "Review of *The Interpretation of Religion: An Introductory Study of Theological Principles*, by John Baillie," *The Hibbert Journal* 28, no. 4 (July 1930): 740; "Intellect

and Intuition in Sankara's Philosophy," pp. 13-14; "The Spirit in Man," pp. 487, 492; *Eastern Religions and Western Thought*, pp. 24-25; "Reply to Critics," pp. 794, 820; etc.

80. Radhakrishnan *An Idealist View of Life*, p. 72.

81. Ibid., pp. 66-67.

82. Ibid., p. 69.

83. Ibid., p. 70.

84. Ibid., p. 72.

85. Ibid., p. 73.

86. Ibid., p. 75.

87. Ibid., p. 78. Cf. his "The Spirit in Man," pp. 492-97; "Religion and Religions," pp. 109-10: *Eastern Religions and Western Thought*, pp. viii, 61-62; *Education, Politics of War*, p. 30; "The Cultural Problem," pp. 42-43; "Religion and World Unity," *The Hibbert Journal* 49 (1951): 220-23; "Religion and the World Crisis," in *Vedanta for Modern Man*, ed. Christopher Ishwerwood (London: George Allen & Unwin, 1952), p. 339; *Occasional Speeches and Writings. Second Series*, pp. 34-35, 266; *Recovery of Faith*, pp. 133-38; etc.

88. Radhakrishnan, *Indian Philosophy* 1:388. Cf. his " 'Indian Philosophy': Some Problems" p. 158; "The Teaching of the Buddha by Speech and Silence," *The Hibbert Journal* 32, no. 3 (April 1934): 348-49, 353-55; *The Heart of Hindustan* (Madras: G.A. Natesan, 1932), p. 129; *The Dhammapada* (London: Oxford University Press, 1950), pp. 29-32, 44-46; *Occasional Speeches and Writings. Second Series*, pp. 224-26.

89. Radhakrishnan, *Eastern Religions and Western Thought*, p. viii.

90. Radhakrishnan, *East and West in Religion*, p. 19. Cf. p. 26; his *Eastern Religion and Western Thought*, pp. 301, 316-18; "Religion and Religions," pp. 109-11; "The Cultural Problems," p. 45; "Indian Culture," in *Reflections of Our Age: Lectures Delivered at the Opening Session of UNESCO at Sorbonne, Paris* (New York: Columbia University Press, 1949), pp. 127-28; *East and West: Some Reflections*, pp. 246, 124-25; *Occasional Speeches and Writings. Second Series*, p. 266; *Religion and Culture*, p. 62; *Occasional Speeches and Writings. Third Series*, pp. 223, 232-33, 239-50; *Recovery of Faith*, pp. 133-34; "The Indian Approach to the Religious Problem," in *The Indian Mind*, ed. Charles A Moore (Honolulu: East-West Center Press, 1967), p, 180; etc.

91. Radhakrishnan, *An Idealist View of Life*, p. 81,

92. Ibid., p. 80.

93. Radhakrishnan, "Religion and Philosophy," *The Hibbert Journal* 20, no. 1 (October 1921): 38.

94. Radhakrishnan, *Eastern Religion and Western Thought*, pp. 316-17. Cf. his *The Hindu View of Life*, p 16.

95. Radhakrishnan, "A View from India on the War," *Asiatic Review* 6 (May 1915): 371.

96. Radhakrishnan, *Freedom and Culture*, p. 6; *The Religion We Need*, p. 3; *East and West in Religion*, pp. 77-78; *Kalki or The Future of Civilization*, pp. 7, 41-42; *Religion and Society*, pp. 9, 13; "General Statement," p. 47;

Occasional Speeches and Writings. Third Series, p. 211; *Religion in a Changing World*, pp. 7, 28, 138, 155; etc.

97. Radhakrishnan, *Education, Politics and War*, p. 114.

98. Ibid., p. 68. Cf. pp. 111-13; his "Religion and Religions," pp. 104-5; "Silver Jubilee Address," *Annals of the Bhandarkar Oriental Research Institute* 24, parts 1-2 (January-April 1943): 3; "General Statement," p. 50; *Records of the General Conference of the UNESCO: Fifth Session, Florence, 1950* (Paris: UNESCO, 1950), p. 95; "UNESCO and World Revolution," *New Republic* (July 10, 1950): 15; etc.

99. Radhakrishnan, "The Cultural Problem," p. 41; *Education, Politics and War*, pp. 188, 205; *Religion and Society*, pp. 40, 42, 221-23; "The Voice of India in the Spiritual Crisis of Our Time," p. 295. After the war, Radhakrishnan lamented that the spirit of the war lives on: "Moral Values in Literature," in *Indian Writers in Council: Proceedings of the First All-India Writers Conference (Jaipur, 1945)*, ed. K.R. Srinivasa Iyengar (Bombay: International Book House, 1947), pp. 88-89.

100. Radhakrishnan, "Indian Culture," p. 115; "Mahātmā Gandhi," *The Hibbert Journal* 46, no. 3 (1948): 197, etc. Promotion of this world community was what he believed was the main purpose of UNESCO. See "Coethe," in *oeGthe: UNESCO's Homage on the Occasion of the Two Hundredth Anniversary of His Birth* (Paris: UNESCO, 1949), p. 101.

101. Radhakrishnan, *The Religion We Need*, p. 10. Cf. his *Religion in a Changing World*, pp. 9-10.

102. Ibid., pp. 10-11

103. Radhakrishnan, "The Renascence of Religion: A Hindu View," in *The Renascence of Religion: Being the Proceedings of the Third Meeting of the World Congress of Faiths* (London: Arthur Probsthain, 1938), p. 11.

104. Radhakrishnan, "The Voice of India in the Spiritual Crisis of Our Time," p. 296. Cf. his "Science and Religion," pp. 181, 185.

105. Radhakrishnan, "The Renascence of Religions: A Hindu View," p. 14. Cf. his "Religion and Religions," p. 105; *Religion in a Changing World*, pp. 46-47.

106. Radhakrishnan, *Recovery of Faith*, p. 33. Cf. his *Religion in a Changing World*, pp. 51-52.

107. Radhakrishnan, *Occasional Speeches and Writings. Second Series*, p. 269.

108. Radhakrishan, "Religion and World Unity," p. 219.

109. Radhakrishnan, "Education and Spiritual Freedom," *Triveni* (N.S.) 10, no. 3 (September 1937): 10, 19.

110. Radhakrishnan, "Introduction to the First Edition," p. xxxi.

111. Radhakrishnan, *East and West in Religion*, pp. 50, 65; "The Spirit in Man," p. 503.

112. Radhakrishnan, *Occasional Speeches and Writings. Second Series*, p. 223. Cf. his *Idealist View of Life*, p. 94.

113. Radhakrishnan, *Occasional Speeches and Writings. Third Series*, p. 250 Cf. p. 223, and his "UNESCO and World Revolution, p. 15; *Our Heritage*, p. 88.

114. See Radhakrishnan, *Occasional Speeches and Writings: October 1952-*

January 1956, pp. 192, 228; *Occasional Speeches and Writings. Third Series*, p. 216.

115. Radhakrishnan, "Indian Culture," p. 128. Cf. his "The Nature of Man," p. 64.

116. Radhakrishnan, *Religion and Society*, p. 49. Cf. his *Eastern Religions and Western Thought*, pp. 258-59; "Hinduism and the West," p. 349; "Silver Jubilee Address," p. 5.

117. Radhakrishnan, *Religion and Society*, p. 43.

118. Radhakrishnan, "The Voice of India in the Spiritual Crisis of Our Time," p. 304.

119. Ibid. Cf. Radhakrishnan, *Education, Politics and War*, pp. 184, 196; "P.E.N. Dinner Speech," *P.E.N. News*, no. 142 (March 1946): 8-9; etc.

120. Radhakrishnan, "Indian Culture," p. 115.

121. Ibid., p. 130; cf. p. 132.

122. Radhakrishnan, *Eastern Religions and Western Thought*, p. 293. Cf. p. 290; his "P.E.N. Dinner Speech," p. 8.

123. Radhakrishnan, *East and West: Some Reflections*, pp. 79, 80. Cf. his *Fellowship of the Spirit*, p. 32.

124. Radhakrishnan, *India and China: Lectures Delivered in China in May 1944* (Bombay: Hind Kitabs, 1947), p. 16.

125. Ibid., pp. 30-31, 89-97.

126. Ibid., p. 33.

127. Radhakrishnan, "Religion and Religions," p. 115.

128. Ibid., p. 111. Cf. his *Recovery of Religion*, pp. 185-86.

129. Radhakrishnan, *East and West: Some Reflections*, p. 121. Cf. his "The Voice of India in the Spiritual Crisis of Our Time," p. 298; *Our Heritage*, p. 20.

130. Ibid., pp. 122-23.

131. Cf. Radhakrishnan, "The Religion of the Spirit and the World's Need," pp. 25-26, 78.

132. Radhakrishnan, *Occasional Speeches and Writings. Second Series*, pp. 34-35. Cf. "Spiritual Freedom and the New Education," pp. 233-34; *Education, Politics and War*, pp. 8, 14, 31, 39; *Occasional Speeches and Writings: October 1952-January 1956*, pp. 52-53; *Our Heritage*, p. 61; etc.

133. Ibid., p. 38. Cf. p. 264; his *Education, Politics and War*, pp. 14, 42; "Clean Advocate of Great Ideals," in *Nehru Abhinandan Granth: A Birthday Book* (New Delhi: Abhinandan Granth Committee, 1949), p. 95; *Our Heritage*, p. 149.

134. Radhakrishnan, *Occasional Speeches and Writings. October 1952-January 1956*, p. 218.

135. Ibid., p. 392. Cf. pp. 52-56; 199-200; his *Occasional Speeches and Writings. Third Series*, pp. 338, 241; *Recovery of Faith*, p. 184; *Our Heritage*, pp. 36, 93, 149.

136. Radhakrishnan, *Our Heritage*, p. 149; etc. Note that it is probably in this manner that his vision of UNESCO could be called a "secular priesthood," for it could promote the "religion of the spirit" and still promote

no "religion." See his speech in *Records of the General Conference of the UNESCO, Fifth Session, Florence, 1950*, p. 97; "UNESCO and World Revolution," p. 16. As he told UNESCO in 1947 *(Records of the General Conference of the UNESCO, Second Session, Mexico, 1947* [Paris: UNESCO, 1948] I, 59), "unless we are able to re-educate him [man] to a realization of spirit and freedom, this steady flow, this relentless decline into the abyss, cannot possibly be arrested."

137. Radhakrishnan, *President Radhakrishnan's Speeches and Writings*, p. 145.

18

A PLEA FOR A NEW SHRINE:
THE RELIGIOUS VISION OF MUHAMMAD IQBAL

Ronald W. Neufeldt

Introduction

Muhammad Iqbal (1877-1938)[1] has been hailed as both the spiritual father and poet-philosopher of Pakistan. The titles are intended to convey Iqbal's popularity in, and influence on, the Muslim communities of the Indian subcontinent. This popularity and influence resulted from the inspirational power of his poetry, philosophical writings, speeches, and statements in which he denounced the forces of decadence within the Islamic community and the world and called upon fellow Muslims to become masters of a destiny which was rightfully theirs. In particular, he called for cultural autonomy for Muslims in northwest India to allow for the full and free development of the latent possibilities within the Islamic community.[2] His popularity has not, however, been confined to the Indian subcontinent. In 1922 his contributions as a poet were recognized through the conferring of knighthood. His thought, and in particular his poetry, have been the subject of numerous books and articles within the subcontinent and in the West.[3]

The scholarly attention which Iqbal has received underlines the fact that it is not enough simply to place him within a particular tradition and community. He was, of course, born in a particular Islamic community and he wrote for that community and for all of

Islam. How he himself understands the Islamic community, the pillars of faith and Islamic history, and how these should be understood is the subject of much of his writing. However, on both the aesthetic level (the appeal of his poetry) and on the level of ideas (his interpretation of the spirit and values of Islam) he speaks to the wider human community. The concern of this paper is to portray Iqbal's understanding of the message of Islam through asking the question of his ultimate values and goals and the means to achieve these goals, not only in terms of his mature thought but also in terms of his early ideas. Through this portrayal an attempt will be made to show that while there is change in Iqbal's thought, early in his career he enunciates certain themes which later become the focal point of his comprehensive philosophy.[4]

As the title indicates, Iqbal is being treated as a religious thinker, one of many significant religious figures on the Indian subcontinent in the nineteenth and twentieth centuries. The term religious is to be understood in two ways. First, Iqbal was religious in the sense that he self-consciously stood within the Islamic tradition and spoke to that tradition in an attempt to reconstruct it for the present and the future. Iqbal himself saw this tradition as religious, albeit implying a polity and social order. Second, in his attempt at reconstruction, Iqbal offered to the world a vision of values and goals which man should hold as true and strive to achieve.

Iqbal, The Poet of Beauty, Harmony, and Unity

A common perception of Iqbal's early work is that while it forms a starting point for the development of his philosophy, it also contains ideas which are later repudiated by him. For example, the Iqbal scholar Annemarie Schimmel states in her discussion of Iqbal's doctoral thesis:

Iqbal was, at that time, still under the spell of traditional Persian and Urdu poetry and its outlook on life which is close to pantheism and even looses [sic] itself completely in pantheistic flights. Hence his sympathy for Ibn 'Arabī, the leader of the pantheistic monistic current in Islamic mysticism, hence his quotation of Hegel's appraisal of the pantheism of Maulana

Rumi, the Persian mystical poet whom he later on choose [*sic*] as his spiritual guide in the way of theistic mysticism, and many other judgements which are exactly contrary to his mature ideas.[5]

A reading of Iqbal's early works seems to substantiate the exist-ence of such pantheistic monistic elements in his thought. In 1900, for example, Iqbal wrote a short study of Al-Jilini, a fourteenth-century Islamic thinker, entitled *The Doctrine of Absolute Unity As Expounded by Abdul Karim Al-Jilini*. The emphasis in Iqbal's treatment is on unity, to the point of saying nothing exists but God.[6] In discussing Al-Jilini's ideas on the material world as the objecti-fication of Absolute Being, he seems to accept the idea that the Absolute, in its effort to know itself, evolves out of itself diversity through the necessary principle of difference.[7] Similar thoughts are echoed in Iqbal's treatment of the development of Persian thought. Here he comes down decidedly on the side of the Sufi as completing and spiritualizing other systems of thought or religions. Over against the Ismailis who emphasized nature at the expense of the concept of God, and the Asharites who emphasized God at the expense of nature, Iqbal places the God-intoxicated Sufi, who "saves and spiritualizes both aspects of existence, and looks upon the whole Universe as the self-revelation of God—a higher notion which synthesizes the opposite extremes of his predeces-sors."[8] Of schools of Sufi thought Iqbal clearly favors Al Ishraqi, to whom he refers as the synthesizer of the elements of truth found in all aspects of Persian speculation and as a "pantheist insofar as he defines God as the sum total of all sensible and ideal existence."[9]

In his dicussion of the Sufi experience of unity Iqbal moves in the direction of forgetting self, and even of self-annihilation through the principle of love. This unity, he claims, is a higher truth than other schools of Islamic thought and an all-embracing struc-ture transcending the incompleteness of non-Islamic systems. Over against the Semitic formula for salvation, which asks for a trans-formation of the will, and the Vedanta formula, which preaches transformation of understanding, Iqbal places the Sufi, who asks for a transformation of both through a transformation of feeling, which includes both will and understanding. Iqbal speaks here of the "higher category of Love" which avoids the incompleteness of a strict rule of conduct on the one hand, and a cold system of thought on the other, and which asks the individual to "Love all, and forget your own individuality in doing good to others."[10] Thus, Iqbal sees in the Sufi experience of unity a complete structure which synthesizes thought and ethics through love, which includes forgetting or annihilating one's individuality.

In Iqbal's early poetry, besides themes of unity and love, one finds expressed the themes of harmony and beauty brought about by passionate and ceaseless toil. The poetry is filled with expressions of despair, desolation, and pain concerning man's condition of constant roving, toil, striving, seeking, and finally death. Thus, in a sense earthly existence is seen as an arena of torment. Part of the torment results from the longing he feels for sight, light, and meaning, and for the resolution of dualities he perceives in his own life and in his relationships with nature and other men. However, in the context of the cries of despair and longing one finds constant references to the meaningfulness of longing, toiling, and striving. Thus, like the moon, man is born to seek and rove, but unlike the moon he does this in the light of love, the ability to feel miseries, the thirst for consciousness, and the gleam of knowledge.[11] It is through man's ceaseless striving that he becomes creation's gardener, and in making the earth lovely teaches the world the passion of love.[12] Since the world's life hangs on motion, man is to reject loitering, for in repose one finds only death.[13]

Of importance in early poetry are the constant references to love, a theme which is also found in Iqbal's treatment of Persian thought. Significantly, the references to love are usually found in conjunction with references to man's ceaseless toil and striving. Thus man is creation's gardener, the creator of beauty already resident in man because he is "Love's own scroll."[14] It is in the light of love that man is born to seek and rove. Making earth lovely, indeed, finding a new immortal life, is associated with "the long passion of love."[15] It is through the "wine of love" that suspicions are lifted and divisions are healed.[16] Thus love in Iqbal's early poetry is never divorced from activity or striving; rather it is a passion which finds its outlet in ceaseless toil, indeed a passion which becomes the motive power for ceaseless activity. One finds this expressed clearly in the moon's words to the stars:

Swift runs the shadowy steed of time
Lashed by desire's whip into foam,

And there's no loitering on that path
For hidden in repose lurks death:
They that press on win clear—the late,
The laggard, trampled underfoot.
And what the goal of all this haste?—
Its cradle love, beauty its quest.[17]

One sees in Iqbal's early poetry, therefore, expressions of both despair and hope. The despair could be summarized with the cry:

Why chained in the dark, past reach of any ray,
Ill-faring and ill-fated and ill-doing must I stay?[18]

The hope is contained in the expression that all this doing, this passionate activity is for something. On the one hand, there is the creation of beauty. Through activity man becomes creation's gardener, the giver of beauty to nature, the remolder of nature's chaotic work. Beauty is the goal of activity. On the other hand, there is the longing for reconciliation, for union of some sort, and eventually immortality. Iqbal feels himself to be exiled and longs for a single path in his wanderings instead of his wild rovings. He laments over a lost sense of destiny and yearns to overcome the dualities he senses within himself, between man and nature and between man and man. Through this all Iqbal hopes to find an immortal new life. The means to gain these ends is love, or the passionate activity that issues from the cradle of love. For Iqbal, to love means to strive passionately to create beauty and order, to reconcile, to unify, and through this to gain immortality.

Iqbal and the Call for Islamic Self-Assertion

Iqbal's stay in Europe from 1905 to 1908 seems to be a water-shed in the development of his thought, for following his return from Europe he began to enunciate ideas which were absent in his earlier work. Javid Iqbal wrote that his father, in his early years under the influence of poets like Wordsworth and Hafiz and the teachings of Ibn al-Arabi, had become a pantheist and accordingly wrote lyrical poems on themes like Indian nationalism.[19] One might add that he also addressed himself to themes such as beauty, harmony, unity, love, and creative striving. However, as a result of his experiences in Europe and his reflections on the state of Islam in India and abroad, Iqbal began to sound the theme of Islamic self-assertion toward the eventual achievement of Islamic solidarity.

> Iqbal himself signaled this change when he wrote: I have myself been of the view that religious differences should disappear from this country, and now even act on this principle in my private life. But now I think that the preservation of their separate national entities is desirable for both the Hindus and the Muslims. The vision of common nationhood for India is a beautiful ideal, and has a poetic appeal, but looking to the present conditions and unconscious trends of the two communities, appears incapable of fulfilment.[20]

The theme of Islamic self-assertion finds obvious expression in essays, poetry, and reflections written between 1908 and 1915. The thrust of *Islam as a Moral and Political Ideal* is that "every great religious system starts with certain presuppositions concerning the nature of man and the universe."[21] Islam, Iqbal claims, is neither pessimistic nor optimistic, for it recognizes the universe as a reality, that there is sin, pain, sorrow, and struggle in the universe, that the universe can be reformed through the elimination of sin and evil, and that destructive forces can become sources of life through the control of a man who understands and uses them.[22] Accordingly, he argues that Islam's presuppositions are "the possibility of the elimination of sin and pain from the evolutionary process and faith in the natural goodness of man," a faith which is not realized owing to man's fear and ignorance of himself and God.[23] The ethical ideal of Islam then is to remove fear from man and to give him a consciousness of himself as an individual personality with infinite power.[24] Thus Iqbal condemns outright those aspects which result in dependence or a weak spirit rather than in the intensification or assertion of human personality. In general he singles out poverty, slavish obedience, self-renunciation, Christian doctrines of redemption, and belief in an infallible head of the church.[25] In the case of the Indian Muslim he bitterly criticizes contentment, indifference in commercial morality, shrinking from advocating causes, and attempts to please influential Hindus for the sake of personal distinction.[26]

Ideally, the means to achieve the preservation and intensification of human personality would be the force of great personalities. But since these are rare, Iqbal argues for an education which would keep alive the social and historical traditions of Islam.[27] The context in which this should take place, and the principle which would limit the freedom of the individual, is the Islamic community or nation based on an identity of belief rather than race or geographical locality.[28] The goal of such education and Islam's duty is to civilize and elevate life toward the achievement of a society of free and equal individuals. Ironically, Iqbal sees this duty being performed by the British Empire rather than by Indian Muslims, for they suffer from both religious and social caste systems.[29]

Similar sentiments are expressed in *Political Thought in Islam* and *The Muslim Community*. Again, Iqbal points out that Islamic ethics is based on the development of the individual, but in the context of a community itself ruled by law based on revelation and the decisions of lawyers and the Muslim community as a whole.[30] The fulfilment of Islam's duty to elevate life, he states, requires on the one hand the assimilation of Muslim culture to provide a uniform mental outlook and a clearly defined community or corporate individual with a definite purpose and ideal, and on the other hand, strong individuals who assimilate all that is good and reject all that is hostile to Islamic traditions and institutions.[31]

The theme of self-assertion on the part of the individual and the community becomes a central component in Iqbal's reflections on various topics, contained in a notebook entitled *Stray Reflections*. For example, in his discussions of personal immortality Iqbal states that "personality being the dearest possession of man [it should] be looked upon as the ultimate good," and therefore as the standard by which to test our actions.[32] Arguing that personality is an arrangement of forces, he maintains that one can dissolve personality through activities such as humility, contentment, and slavish disobedience, or one can strengthen personality through high ambition, generosity, charity, and just pride in one's traditions to the point where one's personality survives the shock of death.[33]

The complaints about the decay of Islam in *Complaint and Answer* further emphasize Iqbal's concern for the individual and corporate self-assertion of Muslims. Written in the interests of Islamic reform and renewal, the complaint laments the loss of past glories which had been brought about by the belief that God is one, and ends with a call to Muslims to disregard artificial differences and to arise again to the call that God is one.[34] The answer to the complaint begins with God's condemnation of Islam, singling out problems such as impotence, lack of community, new forms of idolatry, division among Muslims, and lack of order or feeling, and ends with the plea to seize the world and beyond with reason as defense and love as weapon.[35]

An important aspect of Iqbal's call to Muslims to arise, indeed, an aspect which lends an urgency to the call, is the frequent juxtaposition of Islam with other traditions. Arguing for a sense of realism he finds Islam to be superior to other traditions in that it is more compatible with that which he sees as true in life. The Islamic description of God as power, for example, is seen as superior to the Christian description of God as love, for in history God reveals himself as power.[36] Such a description also fits well with the law of life—continual struggle.[37] Taking his cue from God as power, man is to be powerful in this struggle, creating environment, civilization, the *mahdī*, and paradise, and taking suffering as a gift to drive him on to the realization of the latent possibilities within.[38] The Islamic community is seen as indispensable to the world as the only real testimony to the unity of God and potentially as the only viable protest against modern forms of idolatry such as patriotism.[39] Admitting that Muhammad, Jesus, and Buddha all preached equality, Iqbal sees Islam as the only force still working in that direction.[40] The Christian view of human depravity is clearly seen as inferior to Islam's more optimistic view of man, for the Christian view leads to the ruinous consequences of priesthood in religion and autocracy in politics.[41] Certainly criticisms of other cultures, civilizations, and traditions are intended in Iqbal's attempt to describe the true nature of Islam:

We know that Islam is something more than a creed, it is also a community, a nation. The membership of Islam as a community is not determined by birth, locality or nationalization; it consists in the identity of belief. . . . Islam in its essence is above all conditions of time and space. . . . But inasmuch as the average man demand a material centre of nationality, the Muslim looks for it in the holy town of Mecca, so that the basis of Muslim nationality combines the real and the ideal, the concrete and the abstract.[42]

Iqbal as Philosopher of Islamic Self-Assertion

It is the theme of Islamic self-assertion directed to the realization of man's true ideals or destiny which receives fuller and more philosophic treatment in Iqbal's lengthy philosophic poems and in his essays on the reconstruction of Islamic thought. It is the principle theme of the two lengthy philosophical poems, *Secrets of the Self*, written in 1915, and *Mysteries of Selflessness*, written in 1918. The focus of the first is individual self-assertion, while the second deals with communal self-assertion. These two poems are in turn illumined by the six lectures on *The Reconstruction of Religious Thought in Islam*, delivered in 1930.

The vision of *Secrets of the Self* is told in the prologue. Iqbal puts forth an invitation to immortality, to the winning of heaven and earth.[43] To this end he asks for the wine of love to enable him to stir mankind to effort and striving, to make men's hearts bleed and burn, and to fill the world with his aspirations.[44] The obstacles which need to be overcome have been identified by Iqbal in previous writings—human fear, melancholy, and servitude.[45] Iqbal cries for growth, development and evolution toward perfection through effort and striving. Thus the secret of life which Iqbal attempts to unveil for his fellow man, and particularly for his fellow Muslim, is:

That the drop may become co-equal with the sea
And the grain of sand grow into a Sahara.[46]

According to Iqbal, the source and expansion of life is the self manifesting itself, asserting itself through the exercise of its power, driven by desire and purpose.[47] It is necessary, therefore, to form ideals, to fuel desire, for this is how life is maintained and developed. Here we meet again a familiar concept of love which Iqbal understands to mean the desire to assimilate and the striving for assimilative action, the aim of which is to draw near to God, to realize in one's own life the attributes of God.[48] The opposite, of course, is the attitude of asking or begging. But even worse for Iqbal is the practice of construing man's contentment with what is and lack of self-assertion as moral culture.[49]

Adversity in the form of nature and man are to be seen as obstacles which can teach man who he is by awakening in him a consciousness of his own potentialities, and which can force man to assert himself to realize those potentialities. Thus Iqbal counsels man to

> Be a diamond, not a dewdrop!
> Be massive in nature, like mountains.[50]

Thus, the Sheikh is said to instruct the *brahmin* to be worthy of his ancient culture by asserting himself, rather than losing himself and his tradition in useless cloud-like speculations. Likewise, the Himalayas are said to tell the Ganges to force the ocean to beg for its waters rather than glorying in the loss of herself in the ocean.[51] This is not to suggest that Iqbal abhors solitude, contemplation, and the pursuit of speculative knowledge. As an end in themselves, they are to be viewed as death, but as instruments for further activity to inspire and move men they are to be accepted and used.[52]

The end result or goal of self-assertion on earth is the creation or development of the vicegerent of God. To this end Iqbal sees men as progressing through three states of education.[53] The first is obedience to Islamic law. Every created entity is seen as having a law within, which, if followed, makes it vital and strong. For man, this law within is the Islamic or religious law. The second stage is self-control. Without such control man is bound to become a receiver of commands and subject to fear. It is to be achieved through the exercise of love and adherence to the pillars of Islam. The third stage is divine vicegerency, Iqbal's version of the perfect man. For the individual this means to rule the elements, to know the mysteries of the whole of life, to execute the commands of Allah, to assimilate the attributes of God, and, to achieve a harmony of mind and body, power and knowledge, thought and action, instinct and reason. For mankind this means the inauguration of a new epoch, the establishment of a kingdom of God on earth characterized as a "democracy of more or less unique individuals presided over by the most unique individual possible on earth."[54] Vicegerency thus applies both to the individual and to the community. Iqbal sees it in man's power to build a new world through action, through conquering and controlling himself and his own fears, and through overcoming the obstacles which stand in the way of his development. Ultimately, the end of self-affirmation, the education of the individual ego, is the achievement of personal immortality by maintaining the personality through love, that is, through adopting those modes of thought and action which maintain and assert the individual personality.[55]

The discussion of the three stages of education makes it clear that *Secrets of the Self* is not a call to anarchical individualism. The education of the individual is to take place within the context of the Islamic community and Islamic law, both of which have their foundation in the assertion that there is no God but Allah. This theme becomes the burden of *The Mysteries of Selflessness*. Indeed, for Iqbal the two, the self-affirming individual and the community, are necessary to teach other for the proper development of both. The individual and community mirror each other and support each other. The community provides security, identity, discipline, and purpose through acting as a link to the past, the present, and the future.[56] The community in turn persists as long as there is one person who remembers its foundation and its reason for being.[57] Further, the health of the community can be seen in the individuals it produces and vice-versa.

When Iqbal speaks of community, he means, of course, the Islamic community based on the *Qur'ān*, the belief in the unity of God, the law, and the apostleship of Muhammad. For him Islamic society is historically and potentially superior to other societies and therefore the only matrix for the development of the individual. The historical perfection of this society is owed to Muhammad, who brought individuals into the circle of one law and reschooled them in the unity of God.[58] The result is a community without despair, grief, and fear, and unity which cuts across boundaries of country, race, color and lineage, boundaries which Iqbal sees as modern forms of idolatry.[59] In this sense Iqbal sees the Islamic community as the seal to all peoples, just as Muhammad was the seal to all prophets.[60]

The identity of the community is to be found in Islam alone rather than in some geographic entity bound by time and space. The mission of the community in turn is to civilize the world towards the achievement of true community.[61] For Iqbal the point on which the world turns and the conclusion of all worldly affairs is "there is no god but Allah." The secret of the community's life, its central focus and objective, is to propagate this cry until all people proclaim the name of God.[62] Thus Iqbal calls the community to cut through mankind's current idolatrous inclinations:

> Having his Book beneath thy arm, stride out
> With greater boldness to the battlefield
> Of works; for human thought, idolatrous
> And idol-fashioning, is all the time
> In quest for some new image; in these days
> It follows once again old Azar's trade,
> And man creates an ever novel God
> Whose joy is shedding blood, whose hallowed name
> Is Colour, Fatherland, Blood-Brotherhood.
> Humanity is slaughtered like a sheep
> Before this worthless idol.[63]

One sees here certain parallels between Iqbal's view of the individual and his view of the community. For both, life is a stage for conflict to enable one to master hidden powers, to enlarge the soul, and to become God's co-creator in remaking the world through mastering the world order and ruling the elements. Like the individual, the community must grow in self-awareness, which means an awareness of one's own history and the possibilities that can be realized in the future. Like the individual, the community is not to be a beggar and is not to live a borrowed life, but is to depend on its own power, its own traditions, and its own history working to actualize the potentials that these hold for mankind. The parallels are clearly underlined by Iqbal when he states:

> No man to Individuality
> Ever attained, save that he knew himself,
> No nation came to nationhood, except
> It spurned to suit the whim of other men.
> Then our prophet's message be appraised,
> And have then done with other lords but God.[64]

The community, therefore, in Iqbal's understanding, becomes the individual writ large, with the same laws applying to it as applied to the development of the individual.

R.A. Nicholson, in his introduction to *The Secrets of the Self*, points out that Iqbal had in mind a new Mecca, a fraternity of free and independent Muslims with the *Ka'bah* as center and united by love for God and devotion to Muhammad.[65] Such a society is to be built through the action or striving of the individual, whose self-affirmation, self-development, and self-expression is motivated by, and finds expression within, Islamic society. Thus, for Iqbal, Islam functions both as context and goal. However, when Iqbal speaks of Islam as the proper context for the development of the individual and society he means Islam as he understands the *Qu'rān* and Muhammad, and as he finds it expressed in the best years of Islamic history, namely, the first thirty years.[66] In effect we return here to the presuppositions of Islam which Iqbal had addressed already in his 1909 essay, *Islam as a Moral and Political Ideal*—the recognition of the universe as a reality, the facts of sin, pain, sorrow, and struggle in the universe, the truth that the universe can be reformed and that obstacles or destructive forces can become sources of life through the control of the man who understands and uses them.[67] The limiting principle for the activity or liberty of such an individual is the community based on a unity of belief and characterized by a democracy that recognizes the equality and uniqueness of its individuals.[68]

For Iqbal these are not simply presuppositions of Islam, but facts of the universe. In his explanation of his own philosophy he states that the fundamental fact of the universe is the individual proceeding from God who is the most unique individual. Further, the universe is an association of individuals who bring about orderliness through their own activity. The universe is therefore incomplete, moving from chaos to cosmos, and man, through aiding in this process, becomes more and more like God. For Iqbal this means to create in oneself the attributes of God rather than to become absorbed or lost in God. True life is therefore a forward assimilative movement which takes place through the assimilation of obstructions in the path of self-realization.[69] Assimilation leads not to loss of individuality but a heightening of the sense of individuality and its worth and a respect for the individuality of others.

While Iqbal's concern in *The Reconstruction of Religious Thought in Islam* is to provide a rational foundation for these facts, a significant theme in these essays is that these facts of the universe coincide with the thrust of the *Qur'ān*, the meaning of the prophethood of Muhammad, the spirit of Islamic culture, and the principle of movement in the structure of Islamic society. Here Iqbal claims that the *Qur'ān* views the universe as a divine creation, capable of extension, change, and evolution. The instrument for this is man, an ascending spirit rising from one state of being to another and, as co-worker with God, shaping his destiny and the destiny of the universe.[70] He understands the Qur'ān to be emphasizing a vitalist theme which speaks of nature's passage through time as a continuous creative flow, the working out of the creative possibilities of God.[71] Emphasizing the Qur'ān's belief in the possibility of improvement in man's control over himself and natural forces, Iqbal interprets the story of the Fall to indicate man's rise from a primitive state of instinctive appetites to the conscious possession of a free self, and the importance of man's painful environment to develop the potentialities within man.[72] The function of prayer enjoined by the Qur'ān is to relate the finite ego to the absolute ego with a view to becoming a participator in the creative life of God.[73] The finality of the prophethood of Muhammad, Iqbal argues, is to teach us that life can't be kept on leading strings, but that to perfect itself it must be thrown back on its own resources.[74] Finally, Iqbal emphasizes the importance of ijtihad as the dynamic element of divinization which serves to reconcile society with the reality of change and development.[75]

Such an understanding of the Qur'ān, Muhammad, and the true spirit of Islamic culture and society necessitates the rejection of those ideas and influences which tend to undermine the dynamic view of life. One finds in the works of this period not only assertions of Islam's superiority to other traditions, but also increasingly bitter denunciations of influences and developments which support a static view of life and teach man acquiescence and the attitude of begging. Such denunciations are applied both to developments within Islam and to developments without.

Within Islam, Iqbal rejects exclusive emphases on the mystical experience, on meditation and withdrawal, preferring rather the prophetic experience which results in creative activity.[76] He condemns as detrimental the influence of Plato and the Sufis which tend to create virtues out of fear, lack of courage, poverty, and the spirit of begging.[77] In particular, he denounces the Muslim of India for having turned from the greatness of the truths of his own tradition and from his own potential as an individual in order to experiment with ideas and attitudes which are foreign to Islam. Thus Iqbal cries that the mosque is consumed by monasticism, the watchword of Islam has been neglected, the Ka'bah is filled with modern idols, spiritual directors are laughing-stocks, and preachers and Sufis have become mere traffickers in religion, forgetting true religion and trading on the honor of Muhammad's name.[78]   These criticisms as well as the beliefs of Iqbal are powerfully expressed in the following statements:

Life, like the arts of Poetry and Painting, is wholly expression. Contemplation without action is death.

At least in one respect sin is better than piety. There is an imaginative element in the former which is lacking in the latter.

Suffering is a gift from the Gods in order to make men see the whole of life.

Power is more divine than truth. God is Power. Be ye, then, like your Father who is in heaven.

The powerful man creates environment; the feeble have to adjust themselves to it.[79]

No less severe are Iqbal's denunciations of developments outside of Islam, particularly those political and intellectual developments which have an influence on developments within Islamic countries. His disenchantment with Europe eventually results in a denunciation of Europe as the greatest hindrance to the ethical advancement of man. He sees Europe as characterized by a perverted ego, devoid of spiritual ideals and bent on exploiting the poor in the context of democratic government.[80]   He blames Europe for creating forms of sovereignty or nationalism, which are essentially idolatry in that they do not recognize God as the only sovereign and which lead of necessity to division and bloodshed.[81] Finally, he decries the promises of Western democratic governments as intoxicants which lead to human slavery:

The legislature! The Reforms!
The Grants and Concessions!
The protection of Human Rights!—
These recipes of the Western Pharmacopaeia
Are sweet to taste, no doubt,

But in effect, they bring
An endless Sleep![82]

Similar criticisms are leveled at Communism. It is not only the
West that has fled from God, keeping its eyes only on this world.
Communism as well is concerned only with the material, with the
body. As Iqbal says through Afghani in *Javid-Nama*, it is a religion
"founded upon equality of the belly."[83]

Hindus as well, or *brahmins*, come under frequent censure in
Iqbal's writings. The use of images is not only useless but idolatrous. Speculations, particularly those of the non-dual variety, are
harmful in that they cause man to lose sight of himself and the
world and develop effete attitudes and beliefs. Thus, it is possible
for a tiger to forget his nature and adopt the nature of sheep
through the acceptance of the following teachings:

Whoso is violent and strong is miserable:
Life's solidity depends on self-denial.
The spirit of the righteous is fed by fodder:
The vegetarian is pleasing unto God,
The sharpness of your teeth brings digrace upon you
And makes the eye of your perception blind.
Paradise is for the weak alone,
Strength is but a means to perdition.
It is wicked to seek greatness and glory.
Penury is sweeter than princedom.[84]

Indeed, Iqbal argues that the Muslim is to find a home in neither
East nor West. In the first place, concepts such as East and West
create artificial boundaries which are essentially idolatrous and
have no place in the Muslim's worldview. In the second place, the
East has fled the world in order to see only God, and the West
has fled from God in its preoccupation with the world.[85] Both
therefore are death to the soul. Thus he calls upon the Muslim to
chart a course which is neither East nor West, delving into the
secrets of his own self and uncovering the true meaning of the
Qur'ān and Muhammad. He understands the *Qur'ān* and
Muhammad to be saying that life is essentially spiritual, that matter
or the universe is simply spirit, seen, however, in terms of space and
time. It is the free creative movement of God working out the

infinite creative possibilities in his own being.   Man, who proceeds
from God, is to work out the creative possibilities in his own being,
thus becoming co-creator in the forward movement of life.
Regeneration, and ultimately, salvation for mankind lies in the
uncompromising adherence to the belief in the oneness of God
and the consequent ceaseless activity to shape one's own destiny
and the destiny of the world in the attempt to be like God.   This,
for Iqbal, is true religion.[86]

Conclusion

In an early poem Iqbal addresses a *brahmin* lamenting the fact
that the *brahmin's* idols have taught man to hate his fellowman
and that Islam's preachers have taught mistrust and strife.   He
then invites the *brahmin* to help him build a new shrine based on
a foundation of love, in order to eliminate suspicions and divisions,
and to move anew the hearts of men, for love is the source of
mankind's salvation.[87]   It is this theme of love which creates
continuity in Iqbal's thought.   It must, of course, be understood
in Iqbal's terms as passionate assimilative activity which results
in constant creative effort and struggle.   The call to love is a
call for creative activity, for remaking life, for molding something
out of the apparent obstacles which stand in one's way rather than
giving in to these obstacles.   Further, the ultimate goal of such
activity is to be beauty, harmony, and unity, the overcoming of
divisions, strife and dualities, and eventually the achievement of
personal immortality.

In spite of this continuity, however, there are significant shifts
in both the content of belief and the emphasis given to ideas as
one moves from Iqbal's early writings to his works following his
return from Europe.   In the early writings, for example, the heavy
emphasis on individual self-assertion is missing.   Indeed, the
exercise of love includes self-annihilation rather than self-assertion.
Later, however, love means to intensify the individual personality,
resulting in a consciousness of the infinite worth and potential of
the individual personality.   Indeed, Iqbal looked not only for the
assertion of the individual, but for an expansion of the individual
personality through the realization of one's potentials.

The call to love itself becomes much more specifically directed to individual Muslims and Muslim communities, particularly the Muslim communities in India. While the favorable juxtaposition of Islam to other traditions is not entirely missing in Iqbal's early works, in his later works it is much more pronounced and detailed. The emphasis is no longer on a general appeal to creative effort and struggle for the sake of unity, harmony, and beauty, but on the triumphant self-assertion of the individual Muslim, who is called to realize the infinite potentialities of the individual personality, and of the Islamic community as a corporate individual based on a common outlook and belief.

Further, the earlier concerns for beauty, harmony, and unity, even to the point of supporting the ideal of a united India, have given way to a concern for the evolution of history and mankind or the elevation of mankind through the gradual realization of the ethical and political ideals of Islam. Just as effort and struggle based on love were to create harmony and beauty out of the chaos of life, so now it is to create the individual personality, aware of its own worth and power, capable of achieving immortality, and a brotherhood which recognizes the absolute supremacy of God's law and the quality and uniqueness of its individuals. For Iqbal, this is the idea of Islam and the purpose of religion.[88] His reflections on his experiences in the modern world in both India and the West led him to the conclusion that such life-giving capacity was not to be found in the teachings of the modern world, but in the Islamic ideals, the Islamic past, and the genius of the Islamic community rightly understood.

Ultimately Iqbal still hopes for and believes in harmony. But it is not a harmony in which the individual is lost sight of, rather it is a harmony of individuals growing ever more unique. Further, as a goal it is pushed off into the distant future in favor of an emphasis on the immediate self-assertion of Islamic individuals and nations through which the world will eventually be recreated into a brotherhood linked by common faith and ideals.

Essentially Iqbal's work is a call to action, whether it be the call to become creation's gardener in his early poetry, or the call of Islamic self-assertion in his later works. It is in this sense that Iqbal should be understood to be offering a reconstruction of Islamic thought. In no sense does he offer a blueprint, an elaborately worked out code of conduct or system of law.[89] Rather, he enunciates his understanding of the facts of the universe, that the lives of the individual and the universe are essentially spiritual and dynamic, and his insights into the nature of the *Qur'ān* Muhammad, and the spirit of Islam, that they are essentially a call to man to be dynamic and creative, to become part of the forward movement of life and thus to become more and more like God. It is this call and these insights which are powerfully expressed in the images of his poetry and prose, images which are intended to be evocative rather than detailed explanations.

Notes

1. As Annemarie Schimmel reports, there is some dispute over the date of his birth. While 1873 is the generally accepted date, 1877 seems to be more acceptable to scholars who have paid some attention to the chronology of Iqbal's life. See A. Schimmel, *Gabriel's Wing* (Leiden: E.J. Brill, 1963), p. 35; and Hafeez Malik, ed., *Iqbal, Poet-Philosopher of Pakistan* (New York: Columbia University Press, 1971), n. 1, p. 391.

2. See Iqbal's presidential addresses to the All-India Muslim League and the All-India Muslim Conference of 1930 and 1932 respectively, contained in S.A. Vahid, ed., *Thoughts and Reflections of Iqbal* (Lahore: Sh. Muhammad Ashraf, 1964), pp. 161-219.

3. For the extent of the scholarly attention which Iqbal has received see the bibliographies in Schimmel, *Gabriel's Wing*, and Malik, ed., *Iqbal, Poet-Philosopher of Pakistan*.

4. For more complete biographical treatments see Iqbal Singh, *The Ardent Pilgrim: An Introduction to the Life and Work of Muhammad Iqbal* (London: Longmans, Green & Co., 1951); Schimmel, *Gabriel's Wing*; and Malik, ed., *Iqbal, Poet-Philosopher of Pakistan,*

5. Schimmel, *Gabriel's Wing*, p. 38.

6. Vahid, *Thoughts and Reflections of Iqbal*, pp. 25-26.

7. Ibid., pp. 24-25.

8. Muhammad Iqbal, *The Development of Metaphysics in Persia* (Lahore: Bazmi-Iqbal, 1964), pp. 61-62.

9. Ibid., pp. 114-15.

10. Ibid., pp. 82-83.

11. See "The Moon" in V.G. Kiernan, trans., *Poems From Iqbal* (London: John Murray, 1955), pp. 6-7.

12. See "Man and Nature" and "Morning Star" in Kiernan, *Poems From Iqbal*, pp. 2-4, 7-8.

13. See "Moon and Stars" in Kiernan, *Poems From Iqbal*, p. 11.

14. See "Man and Nature" in Kiernan, *Poems From Iqbal*, p. 3.

15. See "Morning Star" in Kiernan, *Poems From Iqbal*, p. 8.

16. "A New Altar," in Kiernan, *Poems From Iqbal*, pp. 8-9.

17. "Moon and Stars," in Kiernan, *Poems From Iqbal*, p. 11.

18. "Man and Nature," in Kiernan, *Poems From Iqbal*, p. 3.

19. Javid Iqbal, ed., *Stray Reflections, A Notebook of Allama Iqbal* (Lahore: Sh. Ghulam Ali & Sons, 1961), p. xx.

20. Ibid., p. xxi.

21. Vahid, *Thoughts and Reflections of Iqbal*, p. 32.

22. Ibid., p. 54.

23. Ibid., pp. 34-36.

24. Ibid., pp. 36-37.

25. Ibid., pp. 37-38.

26. Ibid., pp. 41-42.

27. Ibid.

28. Ibid., pp. 50-51.

29. Ibid., p. 5.

30. Ibid., pp. 61-62.

31. Ibid., pp. 379-80.

32. Javid Iqbal, ed., *Stray Reflections*, p. 19.

33. Ibid., pp. 18-20.

34. Iqbal, *Complaint and Answer*, trans. A.J. Arberry (Lahore: Sh. Muhammad Ashraf, 1961), pp. 6-9, 13-15, 33.

35. Ibid., p. 72.

36. Javid Iqbal, *Stray Reflections*, p. 10.

37. Ibid., p. 62.

38. Ibid., pp. 90-94, 102-3, 110.

39. Ibid., pp. 15, 29, 99.

40. Ibid., p. 87.

41. Vahid, *Thoughts and Reflections of Iqbal*, pp. 35-36.

42. Ibid., pp. 50-51.

43. M. Iqbal, *The Secrets of the Self*, trans. R.A. Nicholson (Lahore: Sh. Muhammad Ashraf, 1972), p. 6.

44. Ibid., pp. 9-11.

45. Ibid., p. 12.

46. Ibid., p. 14.

47. Ibid., pp. 19-24.

48. Ibid., p. 117,

49. Ibid., p. 55.

50. Ibid., p. 10.

51. Ibid., pp. 110-15.

52. Ibid., pp. 123-24.

53. For a full discussion of the three stages see M. Iqbal, *Secrets of the Self*, pp. xxv-xxix, 73-94. Annemarie Schimmel makes the point that the education of the ego has two significant components; love as an intuition grasping the whole of reality and as a passionate element enabling growth, and poverty understood as freedom from dependence on everything besides God. See *Gabriel's Wing*, pp. 128-41. Immortality for Iqbal is not something static. Eternal life means to travel on without a stop, to see no end. For a discussion of this see *The New Rose Garden of Mystery* and *The Book of Slaves*, trans. M. Hadi Hussain (Lahore: Sh. Muhammad Ashraf, 1969), p. 33.

54. M. Iqbal, *Secrets of the Self*, pp. xxviii-xxix.
55. Ibid., pp. xxi-xxiii.
56. M. Iqbal, *Mysteries of Selflessness*, trans. A.J. Arberry (London: John Murry, 1965). pp. 5-18.
57. Ibid., p. 35.
58. Ibid., p. 10.
59. Ibid., pp. 12-16.
60. Ibid., p. 21.
61. Ibid., pp. 29-30.
62. Ibid., pp. 54-55.
63. Ibid., p. 55.
64. Ibid., p. 74. For a discussion of these parallels see Schimmel, *Gabriel's Wing*, pp. 146-47.
65. M. Iqbal, *Secrets of the Self*, pp. x-xi.
66. Vahid, *Thoughts and Reflections of Iqbal*, pp. 51-52.
67. Ibid., p. 54.
68. Ibid., pp. 50-52. See also "The Political Thought of Islam" in Vahid, *Thoughts and Reflections*, pp. 58-62.
69. M. Iqbal, *Secrets of the Self*, pp. xvi-xx.
70. M. Iqbal, *The Reconstruction of Religious Thought in Islam* (Lahore: Sh. Muhammad Ashraf, 1971), pp. 8-12.
71. Ibid., pp. 45-49.
72. Ibid., pp. 81-88.
73. Ibid., pp. 89-90.
74. Ibid., p. 126.
75. Ibid., p. 148.
76. Ibid., p. 124. See also M. Iqbal, *Secrets of the Self*, p. 37, and the words of Ahriman in M. Iqbal, *Javid-Nama*, trans. A.J. Arberry (London: George Allen & Unwin Ltd., 1966), p. 48.
77. M. Iqbal, *Secrets of the Self*, pp. 55-57.
78. Ibid., pp. 131-32. See also M. Iqbal, *The Guide*, trans. Tariq and Azia (Lahore: Pan-Islamic Publications, 1965), p. 13. Iqbal condemns two forms of imitation: the uncritical acceptance of tradition and the uncritical borrowing from other cultures and civilizations. See A. Schimmel, *Gabriel's Wing*, p. 143.
79. Vahid, *Thoughts and Reflections of Iqbal*, pp. 78-79.
80. M. Iqbal, *Mysteries af Selflessness*, p. xiii.
81. Ibid., p. 32.
82. Ibid.; see also his *The Guide*, p. 23.
83. M. Iqbal, *Javid-Nama*, p. 57.
84. M. Iqbal, *Secrets of the Self*, pp. 51-52.
85. M. Iqbal, *Javid-Nama*, p. 40.
86. Ibid., pp. 55-56.
87. "A New Altar," in Kiernan, *Poems From Iqbal*, pp. 8-9.
88. Vahid, *Thoughts and Reflections of Iqbal*, p. 378.
89. See Sheila McDonough, "Some Leading Ideas Constitutive of Pakistan's Nationhood," *Islamic Studies* 7, no. 1 (March 1968) : 9-20.

19

SHIBLI NU'MANI : A CONSERVATIVE VISION OF REVITALIZED ISLAM

Sheila McDonough

Shibli Nu'mani (1857-1914) was a complex person whose influence on the Muslim community is not easily measured nor evaluated. A person with great literary gifts, he wrote in Urdu, Persian, and Arabic on a number of diverse subjects. His writings included poetry, history of Persian poetry, philosophy of religion, theology, biographies, and tracts on various political and religious issues of his time. The combination of literary ability with theological interest enabled him to write about religious subjects in a way that assured him a mass audience. Thus, although he was involved in many controversies, and was sometimes unable to fulfil his own projects, he has nevertheless left behind him books which have exercised considerable influence on the Muslims of the Indo-Pakistan subcontinent and elsewhere.

Reportedly a precocious child, he was born into a land-owning family of Azamgargh, UP. His formal education began early with the study of the *Qur'an* and of Persian poetry. Subsequently, he studied Islamic jurisprudence, theology, philosophy, and Arabic and Persian poetry under a number of different teachers at various centers in north India. This itinerant mode of education was characteristic of the Mughal culture of which Shibli was, in his own way, a distinguished representative.

One of the teachers who exercised considerable influe..ce on him was Muhammad Faruq of Ciryakot. The training center for 'ulamā' at Ciryakot dealt more with issues of philosophy and rationalism than was usually the case. Other such training centers tended to view philosophy as subversive of faith. These issues were part of the theological heritage dating back to the first Islamic centuries. Shibli's early training thus prepared him to participate in debates about rationalism in the context of traditional Islamic modes of reasoning. Muhammad Faruq was, however, opposed to any kind of intellectual commerce with Western forms of education. He opposed the educational innovations being established by Sayyid Ahmad Khan and his supporters at the new Anglo-Muhammadan Oriental College at Aligarh, where classes began in 1878.

Shibli, at the age of twenty-six, accepted a position as professor of Persian at Aligarh. Sayyid Ahmad Khan took a close interest in him, and encouraged him to use his personal library. Sayyid Ahmad Khan had himself undertaken, through writing critiques of Western scholarship on Islamic subjects, to disparage Western misrepresentations of Islamic history and thought, and to stimulate respect for the Islamic cultural heritage. The encouragement he gave to the young Shibli is indicative of his interest in helping a new generation of scholars to recover and reinterpret their heritage.

To appreciate the mental processes of a young Muslim intellectual like Shibli in the 1880s, it is important to realise that, as he would discover by means of Sayyid Ahmad Khan's library, the work of Western Orientalists showed contempt for his tradition at almost every turn. An example of the typical Western attitudes to Islam in the nineteenth century is the following excerpt from the *Encyclopaedia Britannica*: "The Christian religion is the religion of a civilised people, and is entirely spiritual; in it everything tends to mortify the senses, nothing to excite them. Islamism is the religion of a people in the infancy of civilisation, and it appeals to the senses alone. . . . In the history of its diffusion, Christianity presents the most striking evidence of its divine origins and the omnipotence of truth. But it is not so with Islamism, which, engendered in fanaticism, was propagated by the sword, and established by terror, by conquest, and by extermination."[1]

One can understand why Muslims like Shibli's teacher would

recommend no contact at all with the Western exponents of such contempt for Islam. Even the Western teachers at Aligarh sometimes displayed such attitudes, notably by emphasizing that the new training they were giving their students in morality and hygiene, etc., was lifting them to a higher level of civilization than their old Islamic habits.[2]

Although we do not know whether or not Shibli knew of this particular encyclopaedia article, we can see that one goal of his major writings was the refutation of attitudes such as those indicated there. He was particularly interested in the training of the 'ulamā' because he saw them as the necessary bearers of the cultural tradition. At their best, he envisaged them as the potential intellectual leaders of a much higher and more moral level of civilization than anything produced in Europe.

Sayyid Ahmad Khan's purpose in establishing a "Muslim Cambridge" for India had been to begin the process by which the hostility from the European side, and the refusal of contact from the Muslim side, could eventually be transcended. His encouragement of Shibli's scholarship was one element in that process. Another was the support he gave to young Englishmen who wanted to discover Islamic culture as it was understood by Muslims. The English scholar who responded most effectively to this challenge was Thomas Arnold, also a young man in his early twenties, who came to Aligarh to teach philosophy. He and Shibli became good friends, worked together in their researches into Islamic history, and stimulated each other's scholarship. On Arnold's side, one fruit of these joint efforts was the book The Preaching of Islam.[3] In this volume, Arnold tried to refute the traditional Western stereotypes about the early Muslim conquests, and to demonstrate that in reality Islam had succeeded because of its own virtues, and also because of internal weaknesses in the Christian and Persian worlds.

Shibli spent sixteen years as a professor at Aligarh. He was very productive during this period. He met and became known to many of the best known Muslims of his era, and became well-known himself. His controlling interest continued to be the developing of modes of Islamic education which would enable Muslims to become self-confident and effective participants in the modern world. He traveled to Turkey, Syria, and Egypt where he visited educational institutions and met leading Muslim educators. He was given an award by the Turkish government for his contributions to Islamic learning. His writings during this time included poetry, articles on historical subjects, a study of the Caliph Ma'mun, and biographies of Abu Hanifah and the Caliph Umar. The government of India awarded him the title *Shams-ul-Ulama*. In addition to his work at Aligarh, he also founded a national school in his native town of Azamgargh.

When Sayyid Ahmad Khan died in 1898, Shibli and Arnold both left Aligarh. Arnold went to Lahore, where he subsequently became a teacher and friend of the young Iqbal. Shibli's departure from Aligarh is an indication of his dissatisfaction with the way Sayyid Ahmad Khan's experiment had turned out. The institution had not served to produce Muslims of the type he had envisaged as leaders of a new Islamic renaissance. As David Lelyveld has persuasively shown in his study of the first generation of Aligarh students, the English professors dominated the institution in the years after 1877, and their values were essentially those of the English public school system.[4] From Shibli's point of view, Aligarh had failed to encourage students to take a sufficiently serious interest in their own cultural heritage.

After leaving Aligarh, Shibli spent some time looking after the school he had established at Azamgargh. He went to Hyderabad in 1901 and stayed till 1905. Then he accepted a position as secretary of the Nadwat-ul-Ulama at Lucknow. This institution had been founded in 1894 to be a center for training 'ulamā'. Shibli had been interested in it from its inception, and now he became actively involved. He sought patrons, raised funds, erected new buildings, hired new instructors, and brought in changes in the syllabus.

His intent was to create a center in which a new generation of religious leaders could think through the problems of restating their traditional values in the light of modern problems. He particularly stressed the development of skill in writing because he hoped that the new religious leaders would be able to convey their thought effectively. He devoted a great deal of time to the intensive training of a few particularly able students. Two of these students, Maulana Abul Kalam Azad, minister of education in the first government of independent India, and Suleyman Nadvi, scholar, respected leader of the 'ulamā', and Shibli's biographer, went on to particularly distinguished careers. Both of them had notable literary abilities.

To reform modes of theological education is never easy. Shibli's efforts at the Nadwat-ul-Ulama excited considerable controversy. He was in a sense going too far too fast. In the years after leaving Aligarh, he had written more poetry and political articles, as well as studies of Ghazali and Rumi, and two volumes, *Ilm ul Kalam*, and *Kalam*, on philosophy of religion and on theology. His critics objected to what they perceived as innovation. Shibli wanted to revive the philosophical sophistication of the early years of the Abbasid Caliphate, and of Gazali, and to train new philosophers of religion who would be able to criticize and to reevaluate the philosophical positions of their age as effectively as the first Islamic philosophers and theologians had done for their times.[5] This meant both to revive traditional Islamic philosophy, something most of the traditionalist 'ulamā' would not do, and also to take European thought seriously.

As a result of the controversies engendered by his efforts, Shibli resigned in 1913. He returned to Azamgargh and founded a center for training writers. His last years were spent working on his life of the Prophet Muhammad, a volume which subsequently became the most popular of all his writings. He died in 1914 and was buried at Azamgargh.

Shibli's life had been a tumultuous one in which he had been struggling to articulate a point of view that was distinctive. Because of his literary abilities, he was able to make his ideas widely known. In particular, the three biographies, namely those of Abu Hanifah, Umar, and the Prophet Muhammad, have been read throughout the community. Shibli's artistry made him an effective biographer; he succeeded well in conveying to his readers a sense of the reality of the persons he was dealing with. In each case, he presented the persons as exemplars of Muslim virtues, and the popularity of the books indicates his success. These three biographies have been translated into English.

Shibli knew that the writing of biographies was one of the ways in which Muslims at the creative periods of their history had conveyed their vision. The first classical biographies of the Prophet were written within two hundred years after his death. The collections of traditions were replete with biographical information about the first believers. The fact that pious lives were exemplary was well understood. The emphasis on the authority of the early community springs from this conviction. Hence, there is every reason for Muslims to wish to understand their forefathers.

We will use these three biographies as the basis for our study of Shibli's concerns. He was self-conscious about his method. In fact, his introductory sections, in particular, read almost like training manuals for future Muslim scholars as to how they are to handle their materials. In the volume on Abu Hanifah, he explains that Muslim scholars in writing biographies of this kind must employ the methods of the historians, of the *Hadith* scholars, and of the *Mujtahids*.[6] He notes that his understanding of method in historical studies derives largely from the great fourteenth-century Muslim philosopher of history, Ibn Khaldun.[7] Thus, although Shibli is advocating that Muslims approach their past differently, he is also maintaining that the various methods involved existed at least in embryo in the Muslim past. He notes in reference to his own work: "I have not recorded a single fact for which there was no authority and have not cited a single authority from any book which I have not myself read, conscious as I was of the fact that second-hand reports can seldom be accurate."[8]

Historical method he understands to mean careful scrutiny of primary sources, sifting of materials for anachronisms and other improbable forms of evidence, and in general moving away from the hagiographical qualities of the medieval biographies. In each of his biographies, he carefully notes the authors and the dates of the earlier biographies. With reference to Abu Hanifah, he points out that more biographies have been written about him than about any other Muslim.

The essence of Shibli's innovative approach can perhaps best be understood through a recognition of the differences he sees between his work and the medieval biographies. It is a difference not unlike in certain respects the diffrences one might note between medieval Christian paintings of heaven, angels, humans, and demons systematically arranged in hierarchical fashion, and the person-centered works of Rembrandt. The focus of attention shifted from the cosmic hierarchy to the potentialities of the human. Shibli says that the medieval biographers did not try to understand the mental processes of the persons in question. He, however, is attempting to recreate for his readers a sense of the realities of these persons, and hence he wants to know how their minds worked. The old biographies will not give such information, but study of the legal decisions and other evidences of the reasoning processes will give some insight into these matters.

From the scholars of *Hadīth*, Shibli takes the method of questioning the chain of transmission of evidence. He notes that this method is superior to that of the Western historians, because these latter never ask what the moral characteristics were of the persons who transmitted alleged facts. Shibli is particularly critical of Western studies of Islamic subjects in this respect because he says that the Western scholars often picked up bits of scandal or gossip without paying serious attention to the sources of the evidence.

Shibli thus indicates that a modern Muslim form of historical writing will hope to do justice to the realities of the Islamic past in a way that Western historical writing could not do. He also says that the linguistic and other skills of Western scholars do not guarantee the accuracy of their writings. If their attitudes are contemptuous, the conclusions will be poisonous, no matter how well-trained the writer. Shibli sums up his views on Western scholarship as follows: "Those who have specifically studied Islamic and religious literature, for example, Palmer and Margoliouth. One could expect much from them but in spite of their knowledge of Arabic and extensive study and research their position is: 'I see everything, but understand nothing.' Margoliouth has read every letter of the six huge volumes of *Musnad* of Iman Ahmad Ibn Hanbal. We can definitely say that in our time not one Muslim can claim comparison with him in this respect, but in the entire history of the world there is not another book containing as much falsehood, accusation, misinterpretation and prejudice as his work on the life of the Prophet."[9]

Shibli also says that some scholars have less knowledge yet do better. "It is surprising that some of them (Gibbon for instance) are so sound in judgement and are such lovers of justice, that they can take out particles of gold even from the heaps of ashes; but they are few in number."[10] Although Shibli sees his historical writings as innovative in the sense that he is asking certain questions of the materials not asked by medieval writers, he is in no way blindly copying Western models of historical scholarship. As indicated in these comments, he considers the vast majority of Western scholars incapable of doing justice to the religious seriousness of the Islamic subjects in question.

In the case of Abu Hanifah, he argues that the biographers must possess the skills of a *mujtahid* as well as those of the historian and *Hadīth* scholar. A *mujtahid* is one qualified to make legal judgments. If, for example, one were to write a biography of a judge, using his legal decisions as a basis for understanding the qualities of his mind, and of his values, one would have to understand the issue involved in making the decisions as well as the judge did. One would have to be able to follow his thought processes.

Since Abu Hanifah has been revered and written about with awe and respect by Muslims of many different times and places, it is clear, in Shibli's view, that the qualities most important in him are the reasoning abilities which made him the founder of one of the major Islamic schools of jurisprudence. In order to understand his mind, one must have the technical qualifications to understand the issues. Also, to understand his piety, one must have the capacity to appreciate his seriousness as a religious person.

Shibli's attempt to make Abu Hanifah a credible person for his modern readers includes some complex argument against some of the traditionalist criticism of the Muslim jurist. These critics have sometimes said that Abu Hanifah was not entirely reliable, since he trusted too much to independent reasoning and did not pay sufficient attention to *Hadīth*. If this criticism were to be taken seriously, it would undercut Abu Hanifah's authority, since it would mean that he did not sufficiently understand the Islamic vision that he was attempting to make practicable through his legal reasoning. Shibli answers this criticism at length using a number of different kinds of evidence. First, did Abu Hanifah transmit *Hadīth*, and if not, why not? If he did not transmit *Hadīth*, does this mean that he was a person ignorant of religious values, and hence not to be trusted?

Behind these questions lies the issue of legitimation for his views. Muslims do not hold that legitimation is transmitted by heredity, nor by any form of sacred anointing. What legitimates is accurate knowledge of the conditions of life at the time of the Prophet. When Shibli wants to demonstrate that Abu Hanifah should be taken seriously, he has to demonstrate that the legalist had access to the best possible knowledge of that early period. The matter is evaluated in the traditional way by studying the list of the persons who are known to have been Abu Hanifah's teachers. We are told that he began life as the owner of a successful silk-weaving factory. But then he felt the urge to acquire religious education.

"In those days the educational curriculum consisted of literature, genealogy, history of Arabia, *Fiqh, Hadīth* and *Kalam. Kalam*
was not then what it is today, as philosophy had not yet influenced
the discussion of Islamic religious questions. Nevertheless, it
provided the widest scope then available for penetration, imaginativeness and originality in discussions relating to religion."[11]

This description is significant not only for the light it throws
on Shibli's perception of how Abu Hanifah's mind was formed, but
also because it suggests Shibli's own criterion for a good religious
education. When he later tried to reform the training of the
'ulamā' in order to induce in them penetration, imaginativeness, and
originality, he did not meet a uniformly enthusiastic response.
Nevertheless, he persisted throughout his writings in insisting that the
best religious education should have these characteristics.

He comments further on Abu Hanifah's training.

As for religious learning, narration of traditions and discussion of
theological questions were so common at Kufah that any man of
ordinary intelligence could work up a fair acquaintance with them
by simply attending learned gatherings. Abu Hanīfah in this way
acquired so much competence in *Kalam* that even leading masters
of it used to fight shy of engaging in debate with him. . . . Although
in course of time he gave up taking part in these debates and
devoted himself wholly to *Fiqh* for the rest of his days, yet he
never completely lost his gusto for *Kalam* and records of his
debates with the Kharijites and others are masterpieces of this
genre.[12]

Shibli is indicating that Abu Hanifah's credentials were good,
because of his participation in these early theological debates.
Further, he suggests that an expert on legal matters who is also
familiar with theology is of more value than one trained in legal
matters alone. This is a criticism of almost all the subsequent legal
thinkers. Shibli's ideal for training experts on Islamic law would
thus include theology and philosophy. This was the point on which
many of the traditionalist *'ulamā'* of his own time disagreed most
vigorously with him. For many centuries, the notion had been
current in the centers for training *'ulamā'* that too much theology,
and certainly philosophy, were bound to produce doubt and wrong
ideas. The very conservative wanted to confine themselves to

legal matters only. Thus Shibli, in stressing the theological aspect
of Abu Hanifah's training, is going against received opinion.

Another way of legitimating the viewpoint of a Muslim scholar
from the early period is to ask whether he was personally acquainted with any of the persons who had known the Prophet, that is the
Companions, or of the next generation, that is the persons who had
known some of the Companions. Shibli says that Abu Hanifah
was particularly careful to choose his teachers from the second
category whenever he could. "He mostly chose for his teachers
Tabi'in who were at only one remove from the Prophet, or people
who had associated with *Tabi'in* and were regarded as models of
learning, honesty and piety."[13]

Shibli further demonstrates the validity of Abu Hanifah's training by describing his visits to Mecca and Medina, and the studies
he did with scholars there. His education is described as a process
of absorbing into himself the wisdom of the second generation of
Muslims through close association with many of the best teachers
of that age. Shibli lists the names and describes the qualities of
many of those teachers. In brief, Abu Hanifah is presented as one
who had integrated into himself the wisdom that was being transmitted to him. He also had the intellectual ability to arrive at new
ways of working out the implications of this wisdom.

Abu Hanifah acquired the status of a *mujtahid* (final authority)
at forty. Students were then coming from every part of the Muslim
world to study legal matters with him. In the latter part of his
life, he came into conflict with the political rulers. The Caliph
Mansur is said to have ordered him to serve as a qādī (judge).
When Abu Hanifah refused, he was imprisoned. He continued to
receive students in prison. Finally, the Caliph had him poisoned.
Shibli presents this conflict with the state as further evidence for
the integrity of Abu Hanifah.

"The *Imam*, while dying had expressed the wish to be buried
in the graveyard at Khaizran, because the ground of that graveyard
had not, in his opinion, been seized by force. Accordingly, his
tomb was built in the eastern part of the graveyard. We have it on
the historian Khatib's authority that for full twenty days people
went on performing funeral prayers for him. There could be no
better proof of the *Imam's* great popularity."[14]

Shibli sees a number of exemplary virtues manifested in the
character of Abu Hanifah. "Soundness of judgment, adroitness,

sagacity, intelligence and penetration are qualities which friend and
foe alike regard as characteristic of Abu Hanifah."[15]

He also says that Abu Hanifah possessed virtues which are not
generally characteristic of the *'ulamā'*:

> The qualities that are specially attributed to *ulama* in our memoirs
> and biographies are keenness of intellect, a retentive memory,
> unworldliness, humility, contentment and piety; not a word is
> said about their possessing qualities like good judgment, discre-
> tion, sagacity and shrewdness, as if these qualities were reserved
> for worldly men. Ibn Khaldun clinches the matter by saying
> bluntly that the *ulama* as a class are not suited to administration
> and management of affairs: and this is true, although in reality
> the *ulama* need to be suited to these tasks more than other people.
> Unlike other religions, Islam lays down laws not merely for the
> spiritual but also for the temporal life. Who for example, among
> the kings and rulers of the world could surpass the early Caliphs
> in stagecraft and administration? Abu Hanifah is undoubtedly
> in a class by himself among the *ulama* in that he was skilled in
> worldly matters in addition to being an expert in religious affairs.
> That is why his school of jurisprudence is better fitted to govern-
> ment and public affairs than any other school. Most of the great
> ruling dynasties in Islamic history were, therefore, followers of
> Abu Hanifah.[16]

Shibli's dissatisfaction with the mental characteristics of the
'ulamā' of his age can be discerned behind these arguments. His
response to the dilemma of his time is to call for a renewed vitality
among Muslims. He assumes that intellectual leadership for such
a renewal must come from the *'ulamā'*. But the *'ulamā'* who have
come through the *madrassa* system of education have had their
imaginations and their practical intelligence stultified by the educational system. Hence, a renewed emphasis must be laid upon the
intellectual vigour and freshness of intellect of the great jurist Abu
Hanifah. He should serve as a model for the new activist *'ulamā'*,
whom Shibli hopes will lead a reinvigorated Islamic civilization.

Shibli further argues that Abu Hanifah avoided making Islamic
law unduly rigid by emphasizing a distinction between *Hadīth* which
would be binding under all circumstances, and *Hadīth* which related
to particular contexts of the Prophet's lifetime, and which were not

binding on subsequent generations. "What essentially distinguishes the Hanafi school from other schools is the fact that all its rules are based upon this distinction, and it is this which gives them a breadth and liberality not found in the rules framed by any other school."[17]

In Shibli's view, the distinguishing mark of Hanafi *Fiqh* (principles of jurisprudence) is that it bases laws upon expediency and beneficiality. The laws of the other experts are often so rigid and unimaginative as to be difficult to enforce. "For example, Shafi and some other *mujtahids* maintain that no one but a reliable man can be a witness to a marriage, that it is impermissible to sell gifts, that the testimony of *Dhimmis* is not admissible in any circumstances. Laws of this kind are simply not workable."[18]

On the matter of the cutting off of the hand of a thief, Shibli points out that in Hanafi law, as opposed to the other Sunni schools, a number of situations are listed in which the punishment should not apply. These are as follows: "A theft committed jointly by a number of persons, a theft committed by a non-adult, theft of a shroud, theft of a wife or husband's goods, theft of the goods of near relation, theft committed by refusing to return a thing taken on loan, when the thief becomes the owner of the thing stolen by subsequent gift or purchase, thefts committed by followers of other religions living under Muslim protection, theft of a copy of the Qur'an, theft of wood or other perishable goods."[19]

Shibli gives numerous other examples of rigidity and lack of practical intelligence in the formulations of the other jurists as contrasted with the practical good sense of Abu Hanifah. One instance makes his point lucidly.

"A famous traditionalist taunts jurists in the following words: 'These people think that when a suit is filed regarding a piece of land it is necessary to state in the complaint its situation, boundaries and legal position, although in the Prophet's time there was no question of furnishing these particulars'. For the traditionalist, this is a matter of reproach, but if he had lived in a civilized country and had something to do with business transactions he would have known that the things he considers reprehensible are essential to civilized living."[20]

The main fallacy of the unimaginative and unrealistic, in Shibli's view, is thus a rigid literalism which fails to grasp the real problems of actual situations. Abu Hanifah, on the other hand, represents an exemplary practical intelligence.

He notes that Abu Hanifah's school gave more rights to women than the other schools. "With Abu Hanifah a woman's evidence is as reliable as a man's. Abu Hanifah considers women as fit to be appointed *Qadis* (judges) whereas the other imams do not. As in these matters, so in marriage, Abu Hanifah concedes to women an independent legal status equal to men's."[21]

The Hanafi school is more liberal in its interpretation of the rights of the woman to divorce. It also grants more rights to non-Muslims. If a Muslim kills a non-Muslim, he must suffer the same penalties as if he had killed a Muslim.

"There are many other laws framed by Abu Hanifah in respect of *dhimmis* in all matters he invested them with rights to those of Muslims. . . . For instance, if a *dhimmi* refused to pay *Jizyah* or committed adultery with a Muslim woman, or spied for infidels or induced a Muslim to abjure Islam or uttered a blasphemy against God or the Prophet, he rendered himself liable to punishment, but would not be considered as a rebel or a traitor and would not forfeit his citizenship rights."[22] The other schools are much harsher in their laws in these matters.

Finally, Shibli points out that he does not consider Abu Hanifah's judgments as infallible, since he was a *mujtahid* and not a prophet. The gist of the argument, however, is that Abu Hanifah knew the sources of Islam well through his many contacts with persons who had known the Companions, and that he had performed an exemplary task by organizing the imperatives of the *Qur'an*, and the practice of the first generations, into a realistic and practical system of religious law.

The second of the great biographies deals with the life of the Caliph Umar. In this case, Shibli is concerned to indicate the characteristics of the greatest administrator of Islamic history, the person who did more than any other to design actual governing procedures so that the huge empire which had been conquered by the Muslim armies might be governed not only well, but also in a way that conformed effectively to the vision conveyed by the *Qur'an*. Shibli praises the virtue of a man whose inner life has been transformed by a vision, and who has been able to translate that vision into effective social realities.

The translator of the English version of Shibli's volumes comments that the life of Umar "took the Muslim world by storm when it was first published."[23] It ran into several editions quickly, and was translated into Turkish and Persian. Shibli completed his work on the volumes in 1898. Shibli's great contribution had been to gather the requisite information available in the primary sources, and then to synthesize that material into a portrait of a human being which would be intelligible and attractive to readers.

Shibli again begins with a list of the earlier writings on the subject. He points out that incidents from Umar's life had sometimes been distorted or used out of context by later writers concerned to use him to validate their own positions. For these reasons, those religious writers on Islamic subjects whom Shibli is hoping to train must learn discretion in the use of primary sources.

For example, later writers often referred to the fact that Umar was alleged to have said that Christians living under Muslim rule should not be allowed to ring bells. Shibli examines the sources for this claim, and comes to the conclusion that the later writers have been misusing Umar in order to justify their own anti-Christian sentiments. Shibli says that the earliest sources say only that Umar had ordered the Christians not to ring their bells while Muslims were praying. Where this kind of discrepancy exists, Shibli insists that the earlier sources are more reliable.

The first phase of Umar's life, as recorded in the biography, is that during which he lived and worked in close association with the Prophet. Umar represents, in certain respects, a sort of St. Paul of Islam. He is portrayed as a strong and important personage of the Mecca of the time, and as one who had vigorously opposed Islam. He had persecuted and abused Muslims, including members of his own family, because he saw them as traitors to their own traditions. There are parallels with Paul's persecution of Stephen. Umar's conversion, in the sixth year of Prophet's Meccan period, represents a significant turning point. The conversion seems to have resulted from a combination of wonder on his part at the firmness of those he was persecuting, plus a sudden confrontation with a verse of the *Qur'an*.

He took hold of his brother-in-law and laid severe hands on him. His sister tried to intervene, but he smote her too till her body was streaming with blood. In this plight she exclaimed "Umar, do as you will, Islam can never get out of our hearts." These words produced a strange effect on his mind. . . . Fatimah brought the fragmentary parchments of the Qur'an from where she had hidden them and placed them before him. He took them up and met the Surah, "All things that are in the heaven or on the earth sing the praises of God and He is Omnipotent and Omniscient." He read the passage with rapt attention and each word seemed to inspire his heart with awe. . . . He instinctively cried out: "Verily, I believe that there is no god but Allah and that Muhammad is his Prophet."[25]

This account of a sudden conversion by means of a verse of scripture reminds one of Augustine and of Luther. Umar resembles those strong persons who, once having made their commitment, never turned back, nor faltered in their devotion. He also is one who used his own intelligence extensively to discover ways of making his received vision intelligible in the light of the actual conditions of his age.

Umar further resembles Paul in the sense that he was the main person responsible for the subsequent elaborations as to what the vision should mean in terms of administrative and legal structures. Unlike Paul, he was concerned with formulating instructions for a society as a whole, rather than just for a church. Both could be said, however, to be bureaucratizers of the original charisma.

Shibli wanted to help his readers understand in concrete detail how the "world-transforming splendour" of the original vision was actually made tangible in concrete historical decisions and judgments. As we have indicated, Shibli's own motivation was to encourage the Muslims of his generation to stir themselves into vigorous thinking as to how the Islamic ideal could be made practicable in the modern world. Umar, therefore, as the one who did most to make those ideas workable in the golden age of the immediate successors of the Prophet, was a vitally important role model for the new 'ulamā' whom Shibli hoped to train.

Umar combined in himself the virtues both of intimate knowledge of the Qur'an, and of the Prophet's ways, and of intelligence and imagination. He thus knew the sources well, and yet was capable of devising new ways to make the ideals meaningful.

In his life of the great caliph, Shibli indicates the role Umar played in the community during the Prophet's lifetime. He was the "right hand" of the Prophet, particularly during times of conflict and stress, such as the battle of Badr. He thus had the highest qualifications as one intimately trusted by the Prophet. After

Muhammad's death, Umar was instrumental in arranging that Abu Bakr become the first caliph. When the latter died after two years at the task, Umar himself was selected as the second caliph. He retained the position until he was assassinated in 644.

The years of Umar's caliphate are of central importance as a time when a great many decisions were taken which have served to shape subsequent Islamic society. At the end of his biography, Shibli includes a list of forty-five important "innovations" made by Umar.[26] These include the establishment of a public treasury, establishment of courts and appointing judges, organization of the war department, putting army reserves on the payroll, survey and assembly of lands, founding of cities, imposition of customs duties, organization of jails, permission given to foreigners to trade in the land, organization of police, establishment of military cantonments, provision for care of fondlings, and establishment of schools. Other innovations included decisions in regard to prayer, divorce, and inheritance legislation.

Shibli attempts to convey to his readers a sense of the realities of Umar's situation as he was struggling with the many problems brought about by the successes of the conquests. During Umar's caliphate, a great deal of new territory, including Iraq, Syria, and Egypt, came under Muslim rule. Of necessity, therefore, Umar had to design a governing apparatus for all these peoples, many of whom were accustomed to the administration of the earlier complex empires, the Sassanaian and the Byzantine. Umar's problem was thus to replace older administrative structures with new ones designed in the light of the priorities established by the new faith of Islam. Shibli presents Umar as a man of genius whose priorities were clear because of the profundity of his personal religious commitment, and who was therefore able to make creative and constructive innovations. For example, since his priorities included both peace and justice as well as Muslim rule, he designed modes of governing the conquered peoples which would not be oppressive or humiliating. He initiated measures to discipline the soldiers. Looting was forbidden, and the troops were not allowed to seize land for themselves. The armies had to live in the new cantonments, but were not permitted to become a source of harassment and oppression in the conquered cities.

The taxation measures were in some instances less oppressive than those of the earlier rulers. The administration of the taxation system was established so as to prevent abuses by the army. It was a remarkable instance of civilian control over the army. Umar was theoretically head of the army, but he did not take part in the military campaigns. He rather devoted his energies to designing the administrative structures. He also tried to create a system in which complaints could be heard and dealt with. He consulted with others, and made himself available to hear complaints. His method of controlling the army included careful supervision of soldiers' pay so that the troops would not be restless, unpaid, and likely to work out their grievances in hostile measures towards civilians. Hence pensions were provided.

Various measures taken after the conquest of Egypt will indicate something of how Umar's priorities worked in practice. The assessment of land for taxation was done in a more equitable manner than had formerly been the case.

> The greatest reform, which was in fact a revolution, which Umar effected in revenue administration, and which resulted in sudden and phenomenal improvement in the prosperity and economic condition of the subject peoples, was the abolition of the oppressive agrarian system that had prevailed in the conquered countries before Islam. When the Romans conquered Syria and Egypt all the arable areas in the two countries were seized by the conquerors and were divided up among army commanders and court officials. . . . When Umar took possession of the country, he abolished the tyrannical system straightaway. . . . Umar by introducing these laws, set up a model of justice and fair-dealing which has no parallel in history, for no conquering people has ever treated the conquered peoples with such generosity, agriculture and the general prosperity of the people made rapid strides.[27]

One can see that Shibli's Muslim readers could easily be moved by this presentation of their caliph as a great exemplar of justice and fair treatment. Shibli is also appealing to their reason by indicating that Islam at its best, as under the rule of Umar, produces a situation in which conflicts between persons can be resolved because the system provides justice for all, and in which general prosperity results from the implementation of wise laws. Umar is thus evidence for the notion that the command of God, if properly and intelligently applied, will lead to a better earth, reconciliation between peoples, and general prosperity.

Shibli also says that Umar took a great interest in religious education. The civilization he was establishing would only be feasible if the Muslims knew their faith well. Hundreds were set to memorizing the text of the *Qur'an*, and salaried teachers appointed. Everyone was asked to learn at least five *surahs* of the *Qur'an* by heart.

Umar also concerned himself with *Hadīth*. Shibli argues that Umar was concerned lest the spreading of the false *Hadīth* confuse the people. The dispersion of knowledge of the *Qur'an* was the central concern. Shibli also says that Umar took a lively interest in legal questions.

> As far as time and leisure permitted, Umar taught the people the law of religion in person. On Friday sermons he expounded the more important teachings and commandments of Islam, while in the addresses delivered on the occasion of pilgrimage, he explained the various rites and ceremonies. . . . Similarly in his famous addresses delivered at various places in the course of his journey to Syria and Palestine he expatiated upon all the important principles and institutions of Islam. These addresses were delivered in the presence of large masses of people, and the publicity thus given to the teachings was not possible otherwise. . . . The Caliph occasionally himself wrote on religious teachings and points of law to the provincial governors and officers.[28]

These instructions dealt with such matters as the proper rituals, evidence and judicial procedure, and the administration of *zakat*. Shibli indicates that Umar bore in mind the principle of consultation, and was careful to consult with others before taking significant legal decisions.

Shibli presents Umar as the founder of *Fiqh*, or the science of legal reasoning. He says that Umar had to make hundreds of decisions on legal matters because the newly appointed judges and governors referred to him on difficult questions. His method of handling problems has exercised great influence on all subsequent Muslim legal thought. Hence, Shibli is at pains to show that Umar relied relatively little on *Hadīth*, and insisted that the authenticity

of *Hadīth* must be carefully checked. As a model of legal reasoning, Umar is noted for his reliance on the *Qur'an* and his own
judgment as to what decisions were in the common interest. Shibli
further notes, in agreement with Shah Waliullah, that Umar had
taken for granted that a decision made by the Prophet was not
necessarily binding on the community as the *Qur'an* was. "Umar
was encouraged to make the distinction by the fact that when he
offered opinions contrary to those of the Holy Prophet on different
occasions the Holy Prophet did not disapprove of his inter-
ference."29 The independence of mind of Umar in disagreeing
with the Prophet and the other companions is thus put forward as
an admirable characteristic in a great legal mind. "For instance,
up to the reign of Abu Bakr, slave-girls who were mothers were
bought and sold freely. Umar stopped the practice entirely."30

This instance perhaps best reflects the virtues that Shibli has
chosen to emphasize in his study of Umar. As an exemplary
Muslim personality, Umar is notable for seeing implications of the
Revelation that had not formerly been perceived, and for improving
the quality of the justice manifested through the structures of the
community. With such an ideal in mind, Shibli's readers could
begin to think that good legal reasoning was not a matter of endless
repetition, but rather of participating in a process of continual
re-evaluation and refinement of the ways in which the society must
attempt to realize its ideals.

In sum, Shibli presents Umar as a person whose conversion was
a profound experience, whose subsequent life bore eloquent testimony to the seriousness of his religious commitment, and whose
great abilities enabled him to give shape to a number of distinctive
Muslim institutions and practices. His greatness, in Shibli's eyes,
lay in his innovative capacity. In other words, a profoundly
religious person will be free of the fallacy of blind repetitiveness of
others' ideas, because the reality of his faith will constrain him to
seek ways of making his vision practicable.

The last of Shibli's biographies became the most popular of all
his writing; this was his life of the Prophet Muhammad. In order
to gain a perspective on what might be the distinctive aspects of
Shibli's life of the Prophet, we will compare it with one of the
earliest and most influential of the biographies of Muhammad, that
written by Ibn Ishaq, who died in the year 151 of the Muslim era.
Ibn Ishaq was thus close to the origins of Islam in point of time.

A comparison of the two volumes suggests that Shibli has, in many ways, repeated the original feat of Ibn Ishaq, namely, to recreate in the minds of his readers a powerful sense of the reality of Muhammad's life, struggles, and victories. The drama of the Prophet's life is presented as the elemental struggle of light against darkness. In both volumes, roughly the first sixty pages are given to setting the stage, describing the milieu, and preparing for the climax of God's decisive intervention in human history. The drama thus is cosmic in scope.

Ibn Ishaq begins with a genealogy from Adam, through many names to Abraham and Ismael, and finally to Muhammad. Hence, all meaningful human history has been preparation for Muhammad. The crisis point of his life is also the crisis for humanity as a whole; his response shapes the possibilities for future existence. Eternity touches time through him. Ibn Ishaq conveys the awesome quality of Muhammad's experience of receiving revelation as follows: "When Muhammad the apostle of God reached the age of forty God sent him in compassion to mankind . . . when God sent him, in the month of Ramadan in which God willed concerning him what He willed of His grace. . . . When it was the night on which God honoured him with his mission and showed mercy on his servants thereby, Gabriel brought him the command of God. 'He came to me,' said the apostle of God, 'while I was asleep . . . and said Read . . . So I read it, and he departed from me. And I woke from my sleep and it was as though these words were written on my heart.' "[31]

The words were Surah 96, verses 1-5, of the *Qur'an* which are considered the first revelation. In this dramatic presentation of Revelation, Ibn Ishaq stresses that the event occurred because of God's decisive intervention. Revelation was a result of divine grace.

Shibli's presentation of the preparation for, and climax of Revelation, is basically similar, but has certain characteristics which reflect the attitudes and concerns of his century. As with his other biographies, he gives many instructions along the way as to how the source materials are to be used. He is also concerned to refute the errors and misconceptions of the various Western studies of the life of Muhammad. But these are secondary concerns. His main effort is to bring alive again the reality of the struggles and triumphs of Muhammad's life and mission.

Throughout his volume, he spends much less time on genealogies than did Ibn Ishaq. The latter not only gives us long lists of all the participants in major events, but also tells us what many of those persons said in response to those events. Almost all that material is omitted from Shibli's study. He tells us that his intention in this volume was to present the simple narrative, and that he hoped to produce further volumes which would deal more thoroughly with the problems raised by the events.

He gives a list of all the major biographies of the Prophet. He introduces his narrative with a description of the geography of Arabia, and the tribes who lived there. Their beliefs and customs are described. He notes that the *Qur'an* itself laid down the principles of research by warning persons to verify what they were told. Hence he is advising his Muslim readers that a lot of unreliable material has been accumulated about the Prophet's life, both because of the inevitable processes of the accumulation of stories over the centuries, and because of the prejudices of Westerners who have attempted to malign Muhammad. He is thus attempting to sift, to verify, and to find the essential core.

Shibli begins his presentation of Muhammad's ancestry with Abraham and Ismael. He maintains that the religion of Abraham was pure monotheism. He devotes several pages to denying the validity of those writings which try to cast doubt on the authenticity of the narratives about Ismael's journey to Arabia, and about the building of the Kaaba by Abraham and Ismael. He lays particular emphasis on the sacrifice of Ismael. He ends his introductory chapter with a discussion of the exemplary quality of Ismael's readiness to sacrifice himself. "The firmness, the resolution and the wonderful self-effacement with which the son offered himself for sacrifice, could not better be rewarded than that the ritual of sacrifice would continue till the day of judgment in commemoration of this offering."[32]

Thus the preparation for Muhammad included earlier lives of heroism and selflessness which are rightly remembered through Muslim ritual. Shibli presents as follows the birth of the Prophet Muhammad:

Many a soul-nourishing spring has passed over the gardens of time, and the heavenly sphere capable of strange deeds, has at times decorated this universe with things that dazzled the eye.

But this is the day, for which the hoary time had waited millions of years. The heavenly planets in great anxiety had been looking forward for this day since eternity. . . . The biographers have but inadequately referred to it in their words thus:

"Tonight fourteen minarets of the palace of Chosroes collapsed, the fire in the temple of Persia was extinguished, and river Sawah dried up."

The truth, however, is that not the palace of Chosroes but the lofty edifices of the pomp of Persia, the grandeur of Rome, and the greatness of China, toppled down; not the fire of Persia but that of the hell of evil, the fire-place of misbelief and the temple of misguidance, was damped. The temples of idolatry became deserted and reduced to dust, the organization of Magism disintegrated, the autumnal leaves of Christianity fell off one by one. The clarion call of *tawhid* rose high, the flowers in the garden began to diffuse all around, and the mirror of the morals of humanity began to shine in the holy light.[33]

This vivid imagery reminds us that Shibli was steeped in Persian poetry, and that he had himself written numerous poems. The popularity of his biography is undoubtedly, in part, a tribute to his eloquence. The above quotation also tells us how Shibli himself envisaged certain aspects of the superiority of his work over against those of the earlier biographers. He is looking at the historical process in a more linear manner. The actual transformation of human social, economic, and legal structures that brought about the rise of Islam is seen by him to constitute the real and serious miracle.

God's mercy from Ibn Ishaq's perspective was manifested chiefly in that Divine Unity was made known, and the certainty of the End proclaimed. Shibli's emphasis is more on the victory of light over darkness, perceived as an intervention in history which makes possible the transformation of conditions of life on earth. The miracle is "the mirror of the morals of humanity." This means a model of the possibilities of human existence. From this perspective, an Islamic society advised by *'ulama'* would be one in which people learned to model themselves and their common life on this ideal.

The structure of Shibli's biography of Muhammad follows that of Ibn Ishaq fairly closely. Less attention is paid to miracles, and genealogies. Sometimes Shibli uses the phrase "according to a popular narration"[34] to refer to some of the alleged miraculous events. He spends some time explicitly refuting the Western emphasis on sexuality and violence in early Islam. He points out that Western writers dwell in an exaggerated manner on minor events, and that sometimes they use unreliable evidence. In other words, if there is anything they can dig up that might smell bad, they pounce on it, and blow it up out of all reasonable proportion.

The three major battles of the Medina period are discussed at length in both works. Ibn Ishaq gives many details as to the actual persons involved. Shibli tends more to a pedagogical manner, namely, what were the causes, events, and results of the military activities in question. Both authors note that military activity was understood to be an unfortunate necessity at best. Ibn Ishaq tells us that when the call to fight came many responded reluctantly "because they had not thought that the Apostle would go to war."[35]

This comment indicates that some of the early believers had not expected war. In his comments on the lessons to be learned from the way, Ibn Ishaq says that God had tried to teach the people the attitude to take to war.

"Then he admonished and instructed them how they ought to conduct their wars and said: 'O believers, when you meet an army, whom you fight in the way of God "Stand firm and remember God often". . . . Let not your affair be outward show and the subject of Gossip, nor concerned with men, and purify your intention towards God and your efforts for the victory of your religion and the help of your prophet.' "[36]

Shibli was well aware that the Western critics of Islam had focused on the idea of holy war as their major criticism of the religious seriousness of Muslims. His reply, couched in language not much different from that of Ibn Ishaq, is that war became a duty to Muslims under certain circumstances. It was a duty, however, which constrained them to a radically different attitude to wars as such, i.e., they should not be aggressive as individuals nor take pride in military prowess. "Islam made the *jihad*, apparently a brutal thing, so pure and sacred that it changed into an act of worship . . . *jihad* was meant to eradicate strife from and establish peace in a country where mischiefs and disorder prevailed and people could not live in peace."[37] Islam, for Shibli, is predominantly a religion of peace. It also, however, requires selfless adherence to duty, even if the duty be war.

Shibli has gained a certain notoriety as "the first Indian Muslim who discovered the value of making religion the basis of political appeal."[38] Certainly his response to the dilemmas of his age was to encourage the 'ulamā' to become the bearers of culture and the moral guides of the people. In his address to the First Congress of Nadwat al-ulama in 1895, he said that the 'ulamā' of India had degenerated under British rule since they had lost their judicial functions and their social responsibilities. They had sunk into apathy and fossilized dogma. Instead, they ought to give the community moral leadership.[29]

Shibli's most effective disciples were those who related themselves to the Dar-al Musannifin (Academy of Authors) which he had established at Azamgargh. S.M. Kram has commented on this group: "The Dar-ul-Musannifin became the leading literary centre of Muslim India, and the Muarif, its publication, became the most influential scholarly journal of the community."[40]

These two indications of Shibli's influence, the encouragement of political activity by the 'ulamā', and the development of Islamic scholarship, show that he was the kind of seminal thinker whose followers might be expected to venture into many different kinds of activities. Through the biographies, in particular, he has reached a wide segment of Muslim opinion in the subcontinent and has helped generate confidence among his co-religionists in the religious and cultural roots of their community.

Notes

1. *Encyclopaedia Britannica*, 1842 ed., 14:39.
2. D. Lelyveld, *Aligarh's First Generation* (Princeton: Princeton University Press, 1978), p. 280.
3. T. Arnold, *The Preaching of Islam* (reprinted., Lahore: Ashraf, 1961).
4. Lelyveld, *Aligarh's First Generation*, pp. 277-99.
5. For a discussion of Shibli's theology See Mehr Afroz Murad, *Intellectual Modernism of Shibli Nu'mani: An Exposition of his Religious and Socio-Political Ideas* (Lahore: Institute of Islamic Culture, 1976).
6. M. Hadi Husain, trans., *Imam Abu Hanifah Life and Work, English translation*

of *Shibli Nu'mani's* '*Sirat-i-Nu'man* (Lahore: Institute of Islamic Culture, 1972), p.x.

7. Sham-ul' Ulema Allamah Shibli Nu'mani, *Umar the Great (The Second Caliph of Islam)*, trans. Maulana Zafar Ali Khan, 3rd ed. (Lahore: Ashraf, 1947), 1:17.

8. M. Hadi Husain, trans , *Imam Abu Hanifah Life and Work*, p. x.

9. Fazlur Rahman, trans., *Allamah Shibli's Sirat al Nabi* (Karachi: Pakistan Historical Society, 1970), p. 95.

10. Ibid., p. 94.

11. M. Hadi Husain, p. 13.

12. Ibid., p. 14.

13. Ibid., p. 35.

14. Ibid., p. 46.

15. Ibid., p. 74.

16. Ibid., p. 75.

17. Ibid., pp. 172, 173.

18. Ibid., p. 178.

19. Ibid., p. 191.

20. Ibid., p. 196.

21. Ibid.

22. Ibid., pp. 212-303.

23. Maulana Zafar Ali Khan, trans., *Umar the Great*, p. iii.

24. Ibid., p. 17.

25. Ibid., pp. 40, 41.

26. Shams-ul' Ulama Allamah Shibli Nu'mani, *Umar the Great (The Second Caliph of Islam)*, trans. Muhammad Saleem, 1st ed. (Lahore:Ashraf, 1957), 2:341-44.

27. Ibid., pp. 56-68.

28. Ibid., pp. 146, 147.

29. Ibid., p. 272.

30. Ibid.

31. A. Guillaume, trans., *The Life of Muhammad, A Translation of Ibn Ishaq's Sirat Rasul Allah* (reprint ed., Lahore: Oxford University Press, 1967), pp. 104-6.

32. Fazlur Rahman, trans., *Allamah Shibli's Sirat al Nabi* (Karachi: Pakistan Historical Society, 1970), p. 149.

33. Ibid., pp. 159, 160.

34. Ibid., p. 249.

35. Guillaume, trans., *The Life of Muhammad*, p. 289.

36. Ibid., p. 235.

37. Rahman, trans., *Allamah Shibli's Sirat al Nabi*, p. 289.

38. S.M. Ikram, *Modern Muslim India and the Birth of Pakistan*, rev. ed. (Lahore:Ashraf, 1965), p. 138.

39. Aziz Ahmed, *Islamic Modernism in India and Pakistan, 1857-1964* (London: Oxford University Press, 1967), pp. 109, 110.

40. Ikram, *Modern Muslim India*, p. 141.